The Negro Leagues
Were Major Leagues

The Negro Leagues Were Major Leagues

*Historians Reappraise
Black Baseball*

Edited by TODD PETERSON

McFarland & Company, Inc., Publishers
Jefferson, North Carolina

This book has undergone peer review.

LIBRARY OF CONGRESS CATALOGUING-IN-PUBLICATION DATA

Names: Peterson, Todd, 1963– editor.
Title: The Negro leagues were major leagues : historians
reappraise black baseball / edited by Todd Peterson.
Description: Jefferson, North Carolina : McFarland & Company, Inc.,
Publishers, 2020. | Includes bibliographical references and index.
Identifiers: LCCN 2019039505 | ISBN 9781476665146 (paperback) ∞
ISBN 9781476636429 (ebook)
Subjects: LCSH: Negro leagues—History. | Negro leagues—Statistics. |
Baseball—United States—Statistics.
Classification: LCC GV875.N35 N44 2020 | DDC 796.357/6408996073—dc23
LC record available at https://lccn.loc.gov/2019039505

BRITISH LIBRARY CATALOGUING DATA ARE AVAILABLE

ISBN (print) 978-1-4766-6514-6
ISBN (ebook) 978-1-4766-3642-9

Front cover: Homestead Grays catcher Josh Gibson

Printed in the United States of America

*McFarland & Company, Inc., Publishers
Box 611, Jefferson, North Carolina 28640
www.mcfarlandpub.com*

Table of Contents

Acknowledgments

In a way, it all began with the statues—during SABR's 2015 Jerry Malloy Negro Leagues Conference in Pittsburgh, the removal by the host city's Major League club of several Negro Leagues monuments that used to grace their ballpark generated much conversation and eventually the genesis of this book. So thanks, I guess, Pirates. Much more credit should go to the organizers of the Malloy Conference, the venerable Larry Lester and Dr. Leslie Heaphy, both of whom I cannot praise enough for their help and support over the years. I would also like to thank the several historians who willingly shared their research and provided input during the preparation of this volume, including Gary Ashwill, Mark Armour, Dan Levitt, John Holway, and Daniel Nathan.

I am eternally grateful to the individual authors of this collection, all of whom responded to my questions and requests with patience and enthusiasm. Kudos as well to Diane Quinn, of Nativity Parish School in Leawood, KS, for much appreciated technical advice, and David Cox, of the Kansas City Public Library, for graciously filling several microfilm requests. Enough credit cannot be given to Jim Overmyer and the other peer reviewers whose feedback proved tremendously helpful. Lastly, I could not have completed this project without the love and support of my wife, Ellen, who made many sacrifices (but no bunts).

As a friend of mine likes to say, there are "a lot of facts," out there, and it is difficult to keep them all straight. However, all the errors found herein are mine.

For most of the events of the past, through lapse of time, have fought their way, past credence, into the country of myth.

—Thucydides

Introduction

How good were the Negro Leagues? While many of the ballplayers who participated in segregated baseball are now rated very highly, the leagues themselves are generally held in lower esteem. The website Baseball-Reference.com classifies the segregated circuits as "Negro Majors" and groups them below the American and National Leagues in their organizational hierarchy, in a section which also includes Japanese baseball and the minor leagues.[1]

The hard-core baseball fan generally has a lesser opinion of black ball as well. A contributor to the online message board Baseball-Fever.com insisted that "the Negro Leagues overall weren't as good as the majors, despite the fact their best players were every bit as good as the best in the majors," while a fellow commenter asserted, "the best estimates are that the overall level of play in Negro Leagues was equivalent to Triple A minor league and I think even that may be a little generous." Yet another online expert noted the wide range of Standard Deviation in black ball statistics and posited that the Negro Leagues were "0.75–0.90 of MLB," and fell somewhere between Nippon Pro Baseball and Double A in terms of quality. In his *Historical Baseball Abstract*, sabermetrics guru Bill James reasoned that "much of the evidence that is needed to evaluate these players is not available, and it would be very difficult to reconstruct it."[2]

Even historians who specialize in writing about the Negro Leagues are somewhat ambivalent. When asked, John Holway, author of the classic *Voices from the Great Negro Leagues*, replied, "I don't think it's possible to say with certainty if the Negro leagues were major league or not." During the preparation of this book, one esteemed black ball writer ventured that the Negro Leagues were of a lesser quality than the majors because their available talent pool was smaller, while another historian pointed out how the Negro Leagues fell short of the Major Leagues in terms of playing conditions, salaries, and record-keeping.[3]

It is this volume's contention, however, that the Negro Leagues (1920–1948) were as good as the American and National Leagues of their time and should be included in MLB's official record, with commensurate membership in the National Baseball Hall of Fame. With that purpose in mind, several preeminent black ball researchers and historians have weighed in on the subject, each in their own inimitable fashion.

The first part of this book, "Equality," demonstrates how the Negro Leagues were equal to the Major Leagues on the playing field. Using the most up-to-date statistics available, the contributors to this volume have carefully examined and analyzed Negro Leaguers' performances in their own circuits, against big league competition, and in Organized Baseball after integration. It should be added, however, that the contributors do not therefore see their subject through rose-tinted glasses. A frank discussion of the anomalies that haunt Negro Leagues box scores leads off the proceedings.

Nor do the authors believe that all Negro Leagues were created equal. The view expressed here holds that while the top black ball circuits—the two Negro National Leagues, Eastern Colored League, Negro American League, for instance—compare favorably to the all-white AL and NL, lesser organizations such as the Negro Southern League (save for 1932), Texas Colored League, and Negro American Association do not.

Which brings to mind the question at the heart of this endeavor: What makes a baseball league "major"? As many experts have pointed out, the level of performance in the white big leagues could be wildly uneven. While Dodgers executive Branch Rickey famously characterized the black loops as "a racket," it is worth noting that they never suffered a catastrophic scandal, such as the one involving the 1919 Black Sox, and Negro Leaguers enjoyed a level of career mobility and free agency that major league players didn't achieve until 30 years after integration.

The idea that black ball teams were bush league in nature is refuted in part by a detailed account of the Homestead Grays' overwhelming success against minor league squads. The myriad ways in which the Negro Leagues outpaced defunct Major Leagues such as the Union Association or Federal League likewise garners close inspection, while black players' salaries relative to white ballplayers, before and after integration, is also explored.

The second half of the book, "Equity," veers away the numbers to focus on the Negro Leaguers' herculean labors to achieve equality, beginning with a comprehensive history of 19th century professional black baseball and a blow-by-blow rundown of the Cuban Giants' games with big league teams. Many of the black ball legends who made integration possible are also given their due: Andrew "Rube" Foster's lifetime struggle to establish a lasting Negro League is eloquently recounted, as is the saga of John Donaldson, the greatest pitcher never to play in the Majors, and Jackie Robinson's battle to smash the color line in the International League.

Equality was not always such a positive thing. One essay illustrates how in some cases the failure of a Negro Leagues team in a particular market predicted the futility of Major League squads to come. Another assertion of this collection is that the discrimination against black ballplayers did not end with the erasure of the color line, but instead persists to this day. To that end, light has been shone on the duplicitous manner in which Major League Baseball stole the legacies and shaped the public memory of the Negro Leagues to its own advantage. The long and protracted struggle to get more Negro Leaguers into the Hall of Fame is related by one of the historians who helped make it happen.

Six appendices accompany the main text. Three of these list the outcomes of every known game between Negro League and Major League-quality squads, as well as the batting, pitching, and fielding statistics of the 748 black ball players who participated in these contests. An additional appendix is devoted to the batting and pitching records of the 127 Negro Leaguers who reached the upper echelons of Organized Baseball; still another chronicles the minor league careers of post-segregation black players; while the final appendix provides the results of more than 80 MLB/NLB throwback games since 1994.

Every one of the 16 Major League franchises that operated between 1901 and 1960 faced a black team at some point in their history. Since 1994, 23 MLB squads have worn the uniforms of former Negro League clubs while playing a regular season ball game. John Holway once observed that Organized Baseball and the Negro Leagues shared a common ancestry and predicted they would eventually "be recognized as one intertwined whole."[4] The purpose of this book is to expedite that process.

Notes

1. Baseball-Reference.com, "Negro Leagues (NLB)," http://www.baseball-reference.com/register/.

2. Jalbright, "Two Sources of Negro League Stats Online," Baseball-Fever.com, September 4, 2013, accessed August 12, 2015, http://www.baseball-fever.com/showthread.php?39148-Negro-Leagues-vs-Major Leagues&s=6086b28ebc6e705636848c4fc10aa990; TerryB, September 28, 2013, comment on Jalbright, "Two Sources of Negro League Stats Online," Baseball-Fever.com, September 4, 2013, accessed August 12, 2015, http://www.baseball-fever.com/showthread.php?39148-Negro-Leagues-vs-Major Leagues &s=6086b28ebc6e705636848c4fc10aa990; Eric, "Negro Leagues: Measuring the Quality of Competition," The Hall of Miller and Eric, May 10, 2017, accessed June 26, 2017, https://homemlb.wordpress.com/2017/05/10/negro-leagues-measuring-the-quality-of-competition/; Eric, "Negro Leaguers and Standard Deviation, Part I," Hall of Miller and Eric, June 14, 2017, accessed June 26, 2017, https://homemlb.wordpress.com/2017/06/14/negro-leaguers-and-standard-deviation-part-i/; Bill James, *The Bill James Historical Baseball Abstract* (New York: Villard, 1986), 310.

3. John Holway, e-mail message to author, September 9, 2015; Jim Overmyer, e-mail message to author, September 9, 2015; Daniel A. Nathan, e-mail message to author, August 26, 2015.

4. John Holway, with Lloyd Johnson and Rachel Borst, editors, *The Complete Book of Baseball's Negro Leagues: The Other Half of Baseball History* (Fern Park, FL: Hastings House, 2001), 11.

PART ONE

Equality

You just knew you were a better player than the major leaguers. Sometimes when we had a day off, we'd go see them, and you just knew you were a better player. Like Chick Galloway of the Athletics and fellows like that. Why hell, Chick Galloway couldn't carry my glove.
—Paul "Jake" Stephens

Baseball Is the
Music of Mathematics

LARRY LESTER

The Challenge: Are the Negro Leagues the Equal of the Major Leagues?

At times, the late Dick Clark, Wayne Stivers and I felt like Sisyphus of Greek mythology, who was subjected to the dreadful punishment and hopeless labor of eternally rolling a rock to the top of a mountain, only to have the stone fall back to ground zero from its own weight. With dedicated persistence and passionate efforts, the Negro Leagues box score discovery project we undertook is nearly complete. Our team of researchers found more than 90 percent of the scheduled games played during the 1920s. Data from the 1930s was sparse, as leagues and teams often folded mid-season while many Americans struggled in the aftermath of the Great Depression. There was a resurgence of sports coverage in the early 1940s. The mindset of fans changed as well as they began to challenge the reason for separate leagues at the same time the country was fighting fascism in World War II.

After the Major League debuts of Jackie Robinson, Larry Doby, and other black players in 1947, coverage by the black and white presses of Negro Leagues games dropped significantly. To date, we are still unable to find many of the box scores from the 1948 World Series between the Homestead Grays and the Birmingham Black Barons. Often there was only one sportswriter on the staff of minority newspapers. Perhaps they felt compelled to report on the progress of Major League integration, as black fans slowly migrated to support their local big league team, featuring their favorite Negro Leagues star.

Major League seasonal and individual records are still being challenged today by SABR statisticians. Who won the American League batting title in 1910, Nap Lajoie or Ty Cobb? Who holds the record for the most consecutive years leading the league in batting averages, Rogers Hornsby or Ty Cobb? In 1961, who really led the American League in RBIs, Roger Maris or Jim Gentile? National Baseball Hall of Fame curator Tom Shieber recalls that during the early 1980s more than half of the daily MLB box scores collected by baseball's "bible," the *Sporting News*, contained discrepancies. Miscalculations, data omissions, and errors in reporting can all lead to crowning the wrong league leader. As a scholar once said, there are three types of lies; Lies, Damned Lies and Statistics. So be it![1]

With help from researchers such as Gary Ashwill and Kevin Johnson, our team gave the unexplored task our best efforts. Listed below are the anomalies in examining the weight of the stone presented to Sisyphus' squad of myself, Clark, and Stivers.

Box Score Anomalies: Irregularities, Inconsistencies and Insanities

Box Score Information:

- Microfilmed box scores are difficult to read because of poor print quality.
- Sometimes game dates are difficult to verify.
- Two newspapers covering the same game report different results.
- Game text will mention players not listed in the box score.
- Game text will differ from the data provided by the box score.
- All nine positions are not listed, or two players are playing the same position.
- Misspelled names are common, especially Latin American names.
- Some names are spelled phonetically.
- Only a nickname is listed.
- No first names listed in the lineup.
- Fewer than nine players listed.

Batting:

- Total team hits do not equal total of individual hits.
- Total team hits do not equal hits given up by the opposing pitcher(s).
- Total team runs do not equal total of individual runs.
- Total team runs do not equal runs given up by the opposing pitcher(s).
- Sometimes At-Bats are not listed.
- Sometimes Runs Scored are not listed.
- Sometimes RBIs are not credited.
- Calculation of walks is a challenging task.
- Sacrifice hits and sacrifice flies are not distinctively identified.
- Sometimes Sacrifices (hits and/or flies) are counted as At-Bats.
- Sometimes extra-base hits are not listed.
- Sometimes fielding errors are not listed.
- Sometimes stolen bases are not listed.
- Caught stealing is never listed in a box score.
- Strikeouts by individual batters are not listed.
- No Hit Batsmen are listed (making it difficult to calculate walks).
- Pinch-hitters and pinch-runners are sometimes omitted.
- No breakdown of defensive innings for multi-positions players.
- Batting orders are not always sequential, with player substitutes at the bottom (this makes it difficult to calculate missing At-Bats, etc.).

Pitching:

- Total team hits do not match total hits given up by pitcher(s).
- Total team runs do not match total runs given up by pitcher(s).
- Number of innings pitched not listed.
- Breakdown of innings pitched by pitcher is not available.
- Breakdown of runs allowed not listed or runs not listed at all.
- Breakdown of earned runs not listed or earned runs not listed at all.
- Breakdown of hits allowed not listed or hits not listed at all.
- Breakdown of strikeouts not listed.

- Breakdown of walks not listed or walks not listed at all.
- Only the winning pitcher is listed.
- Starting pitchers are not identified.
- Some box scores are totally void of pitching statistics.

Overall, we found more than 14,000 box scores that were entered into a Microsoft Access database for analysis. Mathematical formulas were developed to calculate the missing number of at-bats, runs batted in, walks and putouts, etc., for each player. In some cases, strikeouts and walks were underreported, due to the lack of information from the box score and printed narrative. Our Sisyphean efforts revealed that Negro Leagues players were statistically as talented or untalented as their Major League counterparts.

In our comparison of league batting and pitching records from the American League, National League, Eastern-based Negro Leagues, and Midwestern-based Negro Leagues, we found the aggregated totals, from 1920 to 1948, to be uniquely similar:

Table 1.1 League Totals 1920–1948

League	BA	SLG	ERA
Eastern Negro Leagues	.268	.383	4.17
Midwestern Negro Leagues	.272	.383	4.16
National League	.274	.382	3.87
American League	.276	.392	4.16

Let's note that Negro Leagues teams during this period played under the same ground rules as big leaguers, often in Major League facilities like Shibe Park, Comiskey Park, Yankee Stadium, Municipal Stadium, Griffith Stadium, and the Polo Grounds, to name a few, and not corn fields as some dreamers have reported. Teams used black and white minor league and ex–Major League umpires. The players donned Wilson uniforms, threw Wilson W-150CC baseballs, wore gloves made by A.G. Spalding Sporting Goods, and ordered their regulated lumber from Louisville Slugger. The distance between home plate and the pitching mound for all leagues was the same, and ditto for the distances between the four bases. Let us also note that black and white teams played under the same terms of engagement dating all the way back to the Knickerbocker rules of 1845.

Thus, in our humble opinion, it was a level playing field for comparative analysis, and therefore we believe that, from 1920 through 1948, the Negro Leagues were the equal of the Major Leagues.

Notes

1. Shieber was an intern at the *Sporting News* at that time and worked with Larry Wigge, the statistician responsible for auditing and collating box scores from news agencies and official MLB scorers. Tom Shieber, conversation with author and editor, San Diego, CA, June 29, 2019.

The Case for the Negro Leagues

Todd Peterson

The Negro Leagues were equal in quality of play to the Major Leagues of their day. This is fact, not conjecture, and thanks to the wealth of historical and statistical data now available, it can be demonstrated in a number of ways. The term Negro Leagues is used to describe a series of professional baseball organizations composed of African American and Latin American players that operated in the United States from 1920 until 1962. The designation is also applied to the many professional black clubs that operated before the onset of league play or operated outside of their jurisdiction. The leagues themselves existed because, from 1899 until 1946, black players were banned from Organized Baseball because of the color of their skin.[1]

Table 2.1 The Seven Major Negro Leagues

Negro National League (I) 1920–1931
Eastern Colored League 1923–1928
American Negro League 1929
East-West League 1932
Negro Southern League 1932
Negro National League (II) 1933–1948
Negro American League 1937–1962

Source: Clark and Lester, *The Negro Leagues Book*, 1994.

Prior to the establishment of the color line, more than 100 black players participated in baseball's minor leagues. Three African Americans, William White, Moses "Fleetwood" Walker, and his brother, Welday Walker, played an aggregate of 48 Major League games in 1879 and 1884.[2]

African Americans began forming their own teams prior to the Civil War, with the earliest professional outfits emerging out of the Midwest in the 1870s. The first significant Negro League, the Southern League of Colored Baseballists, debuted in 1886, followed a year later by the National Colored Base Ball League, but neither circuit survived its inaugural season.[3]

The odious march to baseball segregation began in October 1867, when the Pennsylvania State Baseball Association denied membership to the Pythian Club of Philadelphia. That December the National Association of Base Ball Players banned all clubs with black players. On September 3, 1869, the Pythians took part in baseball's first interracial game when they were beaten, 44–23, by the Olympics, Philadelphia's oldest team, before an overflow crowd that broke through the ropes ringing the field Two weeks later, the Pythians defeated the City Item club, 27–17, in front of another large gathering. During the next 80 years, top-flight African American squads played more than 7,000 games with white semi-pro, college, minor league, and Major League teams and beat them nearly 65 percent of the time.[4]

Drawing on statistics from these contests, games played in the Negro Leagues, and the events of post-integration baseball, seven indisputable truths emerge:

1. Negro League teams had a winning record against Major League squads.
2. The Negro Leagues compare favorably to the Major Leagues in several statistical categories.
3. Negro League clubs were markedly better than minor league teams.
4. Negro League players flourished after entering Organized Baseball.
5. Black players have dominated the post-segregation era.
6. The black population of the Major Leagues has surpassed that of the Negro Leagues.
7. Major League Baseball has colonized the history and culture of the Negro Leagues.

After all the individual factors have been carefully examined, it becomes clear that the black ball circuits were every bit the equal of the American and National Leagues.

Negro League Teams Had a Winning Record Against Major League Squads

From the first year of the upstart American League in 1900 through the last year of the second Negro National League in 1948, African American clubs posted a record of 315–282–20 (.527) against big league teams. This tally includes contests against intact Major League outfits, as well as games against All-Star aggregations.[5]

The success of the black squads was a constant irritant for the Lords of the Major Leagues. In October 1917, Brooklyn Dodgers owner Charley Ebbets fined star pitcher Rube Marquard for pitching against the Lincoln Giants without permission, noting that, "The Brooklyn team is averse to permitting its team, or any of its players, participating in games with Negroes," because when they lost, "it tends to lower the caliber of ball played in the big leagues in the eyes of the public." Five years later, New York Yankees owner Colonel Tillinghast L'Hommedieu Huston fumed: "Think of several teams of major leaguers losing farcical contests to colored teams! Either they ought to quit playing or at least draw the color line."[6]

In order to prevent such perceived embarrassments, Organized Baseball enacted several prohibitive measures. In January 1910, motivated by the Leland Giants' strong showing against the mighty Chicago Cubs the previous October, baseball's National Commission extended players' contracts for a full year, not just the regular season, and forbade teams under their control from leasing ballparks to barnstormers (i.e., African American teams). However, that fall, the World Champion Philadelphia Athletics were beaten several times by black clubs in Cuba, prompting the Commission to quickly pass a rule forbidding future World Series winners or any of their players from participating in exhibition games. American League President Ban Johnson grumbled, "We want no makeshift club calling themselves the Athletics to go to Cuba to be beaten by colored teams."[7]

In 1916, Organized Baseball enacted a de facto ban against interracial contests by requiring that players get written permission from their owners before they could barnstorm. Several big leaguers were thus prevented from participating, but because games against black teams were too financially lucrative to pass up, others risked being fined and played anyway. As Lincoln Giants shortstop Frank Forbes later noted, "They wouldn't let Negroes in the league, but hell, we were very attractive to them in October."[8]

One of Judge Kenesaw Mountain Landis' goals after being installed as Major League Commissioner in January 1921 was to curb black versus white games. In 1922, the integration obstructionist set a deadline of October 31 as the latest date major leaguers could play post-season contests, with only three World Series participants allowed to appear at any one time. After black teams posted an 8–3–1 record against the Detroit Tigers, Philadelphia Athletics, and St. Louis Browns in October 1923, Landis insisted that big league barnstorming squads could no longer appear as specific Major League clubs or wear their own uniforms, but must advertise themselves as All-Star teams.[9]

Against intact Major League teams, black squads posted a record of 47–59–7 (.447) (see Appendix I). However, from the inception of the Negro National League in 1920 through 1924, African American teams went 29–30–2 (.492) in head-to-head competition. When several undocumented contests are factored in, the Negro Leaguers' overall tally would be better than the big leaguers. A 1913 article in the *San Francisco Call* claimed that the Chicago American Giants once beat the Cincinnati Reds four consecutive times at West Baden, Indiana. Black ball pitcher Jesse Hubbard insisted that the Lincoln Giants won seven straight games from the New York Giants in 1919, while the *New York Age,* a leading African American newspaper, reported that the Lincolns posted "a number of double victories" over the National League Giants in the fall of 1920. The white mainstream press was sometimes reluctant to record black clubs' successes. After the American Giants edged the Major League-stocked Camp Grant team in 1918, the *Chicago Defender* reported, "So stinging was the defeat that the downtown daily papers omitted on purpose the write up in their sports columns."[10]

Table 2.2 NLB vs. MLB Head to Head 1900–1924

	WINS	PCT	RPG
NLB 1900–1919	18	.394	3.75
MLB 1900–1919	29	.606	4.21
NLB 1920–1924	29	.492	4.44
MLB 1920–1924	30	.508	4.62
NLB Total	47	.447	4.12
MLB Total	59	.553	4.43

Sources: Peterson NLB vs. MLB Database; Holway, Johnson, and Borst, *The Complete Book of Baseball's Negro Leagues,* 2001.

When Bill James' Pythagorean Theorem, which calculates the difference between the runs a team scores and allows to determine what its record should have been, is applied to these totals, the Negro Leaguers' winning percentage is .482, leading one to surmise that the big leaguers were somewhat lucky, or were at the least recipients of a few favorable calls. In 1889 the *Washington Post* reported that the Cuban Giants dropped a hard-fought 3–2 contest to the Senators because of "the evident partiality of Umpire Quinn." During a 1935 game in Yankee Stadium against Dizzy Dean's All-Stars, Negro Leagues legend James "Cool Papa"

Bell safely raced home all the way from second base after a deep fly-out to center field, but was called out by the home plate arbiter, who laughingly told him, "I'm not gonna let you do that on major leaguers."[11]

When the overall batting, pitching, and fielding statistics from these games are tabulated, the big leaguers hold a slight edge (Tables 2.3, 2.4, 2.5). However, the gap between the two entities closed during the first five years of Negro Leagues play, and the black squads wound up with a better overall slugging percentage, hit twice as many triples, smashed more home runs, and stole more bases.

Table 2.3 NLB vs. MLB Head to Head
Batting Statistics 1900–1924

	AB	R	H	D	T	HR	BB	SB	BA	OBP	SLG	OPS
NLB 1900–1919	1493	170	365	63	17	9	84	29	.244	.292	.328	.619
MLB 1900–1919	1507	198	386	76	9	8	106	36	.256	.315	.334	.649
NLB 1920–1924	1837	248	471	52	27	21	106	50	.256	.301	.348	.649
MLB 1920–1924	1891	268	492	70	15	17	136	29	.260	.311	.340	.651
NLB Total	3330	418	836	113	44	30	190	79	.251	.297	.339	.636
MLB Total	3398	466	878	146	24	25	242	65	.258	.313	.338	.650

Table 2.4 NLB vs. MLB Head to Head
Pitching Statistics 1900–1924

	GS	CG	IP	WIN	K	SH	HBP	PCT	R/9	ERA	WHIP	K/9
NLB 1900–1919	46	36	396	16	230	3	23	.390	4.50	2.32	1.24	5.23
MLB1900–1919	46	38	394	25	315	5	16	.610	3.88	1.61	1.14	7.17
NLB 1920–1924	55	37	481	25	257	1	3	.472	5.01	3.13	1.31	4.81
MLB1920–1924	55	39	476	28	296	3	11	.508	4.69	3.07	1.21	5.60
NLB Total	101	73	877	41	487	4	26	.436	4.78	2.70	1.28	5.00
MLB Total	101	77	870	53	610	8	27	.564	4.32	2.31	1.18	6.31

Table 2.5 NLB vs. MLB Head to Head
Fielding Statistics 1900–1924

	PO	A	E	FA	DP
NLB 1900–1919	1187	548	107	.942	30
MLB 1900–1919	1183	519	92	.949	14
NLB 1920–1924	1514	589	117	.947	31
MLB 1920–1924	1426	663	103	.953	15
NLB Total	2701	1137	224	.945	61
MLB Total	2609	1182	195	.951	29

Note: Statistics were not available for all 113 contests. The data was based on box scores from 101 games.
Source for Tables 2.3, 2.4, and 2.5: NLB vs. MLB Database.

After Landis' ban on intact Major League clubs playing black squads was enacted, the Negro Leaguers contented themselves with pounding big league All-Star teams. The annual practice of African American outfits playing the premier white players of a particular area was an established tradition in many cities, including New York, Philadelphia, Baltimore, Indianapolis, Chicago, St. Louis, Los Angeles, and San Diego. Between 1902 and 1948, black clubs defeated the best white batters, pitchers, and teams they were *allowed* to play nearly 55 percent of the time (Appendix II). The All-Star squads included in this tally were comprised of five or more players with big league experience (including the starting pitcher) and at least three players who had appeared in the Majors that particular year.

Table 2.6 NLB vs. MLB All-Stars 1902–1948

#Major Leaguers	W	L	T	Pct.	NLRPG	MLRPG
Five	32	22	1	.591	3.93	3.44
Six	34	29	0	.540	4.71	4.52
Seven	38	31	4	.548	4.49	4.02
Eight	32	25	2	.559	4.09	4.00
Nine	91	86	3	.514	4.79	4.43
Total	268	223	13	.545	4.52	4.19

Sources: NLB vs. MLB Database; Holway with Johnson and Borst, *The Complete Book of Baseball's Negro Leagues.*

It should also be noted that the number of big leaguers involved in many of these games was actually higher than the reported total. The major leaguers often resorted to the use of aliases to avoid detection. In October 1933, the Chicago American Giants downed Jimmy Shevlin's All-Pros, 3–0, and the *Chicago Defender* reported that while only three big leaguers, including Leo Durocher, "were laboring under their own names, the entire nine was made up of [National League] players." The *Defender* had noted a few years earlier, "these big league fellows like to grasp the mazuma that rolls in at Schorling Park, but somehow, even with big league ball curtailed, they wish to clutch the green under assumed names."[12]

As for the farfetched notion that the big leaguers were taking it easy or not giving their all, black ball historian Robert Peterson astutely opined, "there are very few professional baseball players who go to the plate without hoping for a base hit or pitch a game without trying to win, even when they are competing against sandlotters." Indeed, in contests against minor league, semi-pro, college and military teams, Major League squads racked up a record of 2674–904–71 (.747) between 1901 and 1950. Only the Negro Leaguers had their number (Table 2.7).[13]

Table 2.7 NLB and MLB vs. Other Classifications 1900–1950

Class	NLB						MLB					
	W	L	T	PCT	RF	RA	W	L	T	PCT	RF	RA
MLB/NLB	315	282	20	.528	4.35	4.12	282	315	20	.472	4.12	4.35
Milb	821	606	40	.575	5.22	4.45	1690	677	49	.714	6.56	3.97
Military	6	4	0	.600	4.30	2.70	151	61	5	.712	7.12	4.02
Semi-Pro	2322	1027	70	.693	6.21	3.76	690	155	17	.817	6.92	3.03
College	38	7	0	.844	8.18	3.64	143	11	0	.929	9.88	2.57
Total	3502	1926	130	.645	5.76	3.80	2956	1219	91	.708	6.43	3.78

Note: Milb—Minor League Baseball.
Sources: Simkus, *Outsider Baseball*, 2014; NLB vs. MLB Database; Peterson NLB vs. MILB Database.

Every important white player of the first half of the 20th century, including Ty Cobb, Babe Ruth, Rogers Hornsby, Joe DiMaggio, and Ted Williams, played against Negro Leagues teams. The black squads defeated the best pitchers the Major Leagues had to offer—Christy

Mathewson, Walter Johnson, Pete Alexander, Lefty Grove, Dizzy Dean, and Bob Feller among them.[14]

The non–big leaguers on these All-Star teams were no slouches either. During the segregation era, many of the so-called bush leaguers who faced the black clubs were Major League–quality players. As Bill James wrote of the period in his *Historical Baseball Abstract*, "A conservative assessment is that some of the players who made their living in the minor leagues were just as good as some of those who played in the Majors…. A more generous assessment would be that some of the best players in the game were in the minor leagues." However, career minor league pitchers were almost never used by All-Star clubs when facing top-flight black squads. The results were disastrous for the big leaguers when they did.[15]

It should also be remembered that not all of the black squads that took on the Major League All-Star outfits were supremely talented. No one would ever confuse the 1920 Pittsburgh Stars, the 1938 Omaha Monarchs, or the 1945 Oakland Giants with a top-notch or even average Negro Leagues team, but as the adage goes, "there's no crying in baseball."

As might be expected from their decisive winning percentage over the course of these contests, the Negro Leaguers significantly outperformed their big league counterparts in almost every hitting, pitching and fielding category except assists and walks (Tables 2.8, 2.9, 2.10). However, as the black teams outslugged major leaguers by more than 30 points, they probably didn't need to be very patient at the plate.

Table 2.8 NLB vs. MLB All-Stars Batting Statistics 1902–1948

	AB	R	H	D	T	HR	BB	SB	BA	OBP	SLG	OPS
NLB 1902–1919	3296	335	764	106	35	27	202	107	.233	.283	.310	.592
MLB 1902–1919	3227	369	738	125	31	23	300	140	.229	.302	.308	.609
NLB 1920–1948	9074	1313	2495	373	129	124	633	265	.275	.326	.385	.711
MLB 1920–1948	9205	1118	2224	347	105	119	790	146	.242	.306	.341	.647
NLB Total	12370	1648	3259	479	164	151	835	372	.263	.314	.365	.679
MLB Total	12432	1487	2962	472	136	142	1090	286	.238	.305	.332	.637

Table 2.9 NLB vs. MLB All-Stars Pitching Statistics 1902–1948

	GS	CG	IP	WIN	K	SH	HBP	PCT	R/9	ERA	WHIP	K/9
NLB 1902–1919	100	81	873	45	582	16	37	.459	3.81	2.10	1.19	6.00
MLB 1902–1919	100	94	895	53	581	8	31	.541	3.37	1.96	1.07	5.84
NLB 1920–1948	276	164	2409	161	1704	30	68	.601	4.18	2.60	1.25	6.37
MLB 1920–1948	276	136	2313	107	1495	14	48	.399	5.11	3.27	1.35	5.82
NLB Total	376	245	3282	206	2286	46	105	.563	4.08	2.47	1.23	6.27
MLB Total	376	230	3208	160	2076	22	79	.437	4.62	2.88	1.27	5.82

Table 2.10 NLB vs. MLB All-Stars Fielding Statistics 1902–1948

	PO	A	E	FA	DP
NLB 1902–1919	2615	1130	234	.941	55
MLB 1902–1919	2450	1265	199	.949	46

	PO	A	E	FA	DP
NLB 1920–1948	7262	2616	435	.958	159
MLB 1920–1948	6971	2878	485	.953	168
NLB Total	9877	3746	669	.953	214
MLB Total	9421	4143	684	.952	214

Note: Box-scores were not available for all NLB vs All-Star games.
Source for Tables 2.8, 2.9, 2.10: NLB vs. MLB Database.

As the losses to Negro Leagues teams continued to mount, Judge Landis came up with new measures to prevent black versus white contests. He managed to cancel a 1922 showdown between the American Giants and Detroit Tigers because the Cubs and White Sox were playing a city series at the same time. In October 1925, he forbade Jack Quinn and Mickey Cochrane from taking the field against the Lincoln Giants, as the Major League post-season had not yet been completed. Because their Philadelphia Athletics team had finished second in the American League, the duo couldn't play because they were eligible for a World Series share. In December 1935, an edict came down from the American League office that players could now participate in exhibition games for only ten days after the close of the "championship season."[16]

By 1932, Landis' machinations had nearly eradicated interracial games from being played in big league cities. Chicago American Giants owner Robert Cole was unable to book any All-Star teams for his park that fall, leading the *Chicago Defender* to wonder sarcastically if the "lily-white" Cubs or White Sox were behind the blockade:

> The Chicago White Sox management is known to have advised its players against such games, even though several of the players are to participate in barnstorming.
> Fonseca, manager of the Sox, is taking no chances, perhaps, on having his club, which was able to beat the Boston Red Sox out of the cellar rights, to hurt their chances to repeat the accomplishment next season.[17]

When the combined results of the games between the Negro Leagues squads and Major League teams of varying composition are tabulated, the black clubs are once again revealed to lead in almost every hitting, pitching, and fielding statistical category (Tables 2.11, 2.12, 2.13). The big leaguers drew more walks and hit 24 more doubles over the course of 477 games. Amazingly, both sides fielded at an identical .951 clip, but the Negro Leaguers turned more double plays. With the near-disappearance of the African American Major League pitcher in the 21st century, it is also interesting to note that the black twirlers decisively outpaced their big league counterparts during these contests in runs allowed, strikeouts, preventing base runners, and shut-outs.

Table 2.11 NLB vs. MLB Batting Statistics 1900–1948

	AB	R	H	D	T	HR	BB	SB	BA	OBP	SLG	OPS
NLB 1900–1919	4789	505	1129	169	52	36	286	136	.236	.285	.315	.601
MLB 1900–1919	4734	567	1124	201	40	31	406	176	.237	.306	.316	.622
NLB 1920–1948	10911	1561	2966	425	156	145	739	315	.272	.321	.379	.701
MLB 1920–1948	11096	1386	2716	417	120	136	926	175	.245	.307	.341	.648
NLB Total	15700	2066	4095	594	208	181	1025	451	.261	.310	.360	.670
MLB Total	15830	1953	3840	618	160	167	1332	351	.243	.307	.333	.640

Table 2.12 NLB vs. MLB Pitching
Statistics 1900–1948

	GS	CG	IP	WIN	K	SH	HBP	PCT	R/9	ERA	WHIP	K/9
NLB 1900–1919	146	117	1269	61	812	19	60	.439	4.02	2.17	1.21	5.76
MLB 1900–1919	146	132	1289	78	895	13	47	.561	3.53	1.85	1.10	6.25
NLB 1920–1948	331	201	2890	186	1961	31	71	.579	4.32	2.67	1.26	6.11
MLB 1920–1948	331	175	2789	135	1791	17	59	.421	5.04	3.24	1.33	5.78
NLB Total	477	318	4159	247	2773	50	131	.537	4.23	2.52	1.24	6.00
MLB Total	477	307	4078	213	2686	30	106	.463	4.56	2.76	1.25	5.93

Table 2.13 NLB vs. MLB Fielding Statistics 1900–1948

	PO	A	E	FA	DP
NLB 1900–1919	3802	1678	341	.941	85
MLB 1900–1919	3633	1784	291	.949	60
NLB 1920–1948	8776	3205	552	.956	190
MLB 1920–1948	8397	3541	588	.953	183
NLB Total	12578	4883	893	.951	275
MLB Total	12030	5325	879	.951	243

Source for Tables 2.11, 2.12, 2.13: NLB vs. MLB Database.

The major leaguers held their own for the first 20 years of the 20th century, but once black squads started playing league ball in 1920, the tide began to turn. As the old saying goes, "practice makes perfect." In 1913, the 14 leading black independent clubs played an average of 21 games. During the 1923 season, the 14 squads of the Negro National and Eastern Colored Leagues participated in about 65 contests each.[18]

The Negro Leagues Compare Favorably to the Major Leagues in Several Statistical Categories

Philadelphia Athletics owner and manager Connie Mack once said that pitching makes up 70 percent of baseball. Historians John Thorn and Pete Palmer asserted in *The Hidden Game Of Baseball* that the figure is more like 44 percent, but allowed that "it is undeniably important." It is not a stretch to say that the truest indicator of a baseball league's quality would be the strength of its pitching. In this regard, it would stand to reason that circuits with *lower* batting, slugging, and on-base percentages are superior to those with higher averages.[19]

For example, it is a relatively safe assumption that the Major Leagues of the 1950s were far superior in quality to the Class C circuits of the same time, and indeed when compared, the bush leaguers' hitting averages are indeed higher across the board than the big leaguers'.

Table 2.14 MLB and Class C Hitting Totals 1950–1959

	BA	OBP	SLG	OPS
Major Leagues	.259	.331	.391	.723
Class C Leagues	.271	.364	.393	.755
% Difference	4.6	10.0	0.5	4.4

Source: Baseball-Reference.com.

Even when a larger sample size and a higher class of league are considered, the hypothesis still holds up. When the hitting averages of the Major Leagues and those of the three highest minor circuits—the International League, American Association, and Pacific Coast League—are considered from 1912, the year these three organizations were elevated to Double A status, through 1945, the last season of segregation, the Majors consistently posted the lower batting totals.

Table 2.15 MLB and Class AAA Hitting Totals 1912–1945*

	BA	OBP	SLG	OPS
Major Leagues	.272	.336	.377	.713
Class AAA	.278	.340	.383	.723
% Difference	2.2	1.2	1.6	1.4

*The three Double A Leagues were reclassified Triple A in 1946.
Sources: Baseball-Reference.com; Snelling, *The Pacific Coast League: A Statistical History*, 1995; Wright, *The American Association Year-by-Year Statistics*, 1997; Wright, *The International League Year-by-Year Statistics*, 1998.

However, when the Major League averages are compared to those of the Negro Leagues, a different truth emerges. Using statistics from 1906, when the first black ball circuit of the 20th century, the International League of Independent Professional Base Ball Clubs, was formed, through the last season of the Negro National League in 1948, the batting totals of the significant black squads are noticeably *lower* than those of the Major Leagues (Tables 2.16, 2.17).

Table 2.16 NLB and MLB Hitting Averages 1906–1948

	NLB				MLB			
Year	BA	OBP	SLG	OPS	BA	OBP	SLG	OPS
1906	.258	.319	.327	.646	.247	.306	.314	.621
1907	.245	.295	.296	.591	.245	.305	.309	.614
1908	.256	.312	.334	.646	.239	.297	.305	.602
1909	.251	.305	.331	.636	.244	.306	.311	.618
1910	.255	.308	.344	.652	.249	.318	.326	.644
1911	.271	.332	.358	.690	.266	.336	.357	.693
1912	.269	.321	.351	.672	.269	.337	.359	.695
1913	.267	.323	.349	.672	.259	.325	.345	.670
1914	.269	.332	.360	.692	.254	.321	.337	.659
1915	.246	.312	.318	.630	.250	.318	.332	.650
1916	.256	.328	.328	.656	.248	.312	.326	.638
1917	.245	.317	.308	.625	.249	.311	.324	.635
1918	.266	.335	.335	.669	.254	.317	.325	.642
1919	.249	.324	.334	.658	.263	.322	.348	.670
1920	.251	.318	.323	.641	.277	.335	.372	.707
1921	.270	.333	.368	.702	.291	.347	.403	.750
1922	.275	.338	.381	.719	.288	.348	.401	.749
1923	.278	.337	.383	.720	.284	.347	.391	.738
1924	.272	.330	.370	.700	.287	.348	.394	.742
1925	.279	.344	.398	.742	.292	.354	.411	.765
1926	.273	.340	.384	.724	.281	.345	.389	.734
1927	.276	.337	.384	.721	.284	.345	.393	.738

	NLB				MLB			
Year	BA	OBP	SLG	OPS	BA	OBP	SLG	OPS
1928	.281	.338	.391	.729	.281	.344	.397	.741
1929	.289	.353	.411	.765	.289	.353	.417	.770
1930	.285	.340	.399	.740	.296	.356	.434	.790
1931	.265	.328	.363	.691	.278	.339	.391	.730
1932	.270	.325	.361	.685	.277	.337	.400	.737
1933	.274	.327	.385	.712	.270	.330	.376	.706
1934	.269	.328	.351	.679	.279	.342	.397	.739
1935	.285	.344	.414	.759	.279	.341	.397	.738
1936	.271	.334	.388	.722	.284	.349	.404	.753
1937	.268	.326	.376	.702	.277	.343	.399	.742
1938	.266	.332	.373	.705	.274	.343	.396	.739
1939	.267	.331	.367	.698	.275	.344	.397	.741
1940	.266	.333	.366	.701	.267	.334	.392	.726
1941	.253	.312	.346	.658	.262	.334	.375	.709
1942	.253	.316	.335	.651	.253	.323	.350	.673
1943	.267	.330	.354	.684	.253	.323	.344	.667
1944	.264	.310	.354	.664	.260	.326	.358	.684
1945	.264	.320	.354	.674	.260	.329	.355	.684
1946	.257	.321	.356	.676	.256	.328	.360	.688
1947	.277	.346	.383	.729	.261	.336	.377	.713
1948	.274	.339	.370	.709	.263	.341	.382	.723

Note: Higher averages are shown in Gray

Table 2.17 NLB and MLB Hitting Totals 1906–1948

	BA	OBP	SLG	OPS
NLB	.266	.327	.360	.687
MLB	.268	.332	.369	.702
% Difference	0.6	1.6	2.7	2.1

Sources for Tables 2.16, 2.17: Negro Leagues Researchers and Authors Group; Baseball-Reference.com; Seam-heads.com Negro Leagues Database; *Center for Negro League Baseball Research*; Overmyer, *Black Ball and the Boardwalk: The Bacharach Giants of Atlantic City*, 2014.

Granted, Negro Leagues squads didn't play each other as often as big league clubs played each other every season, but the difference does not diminish the relevance of their statistics. Between 1920 and 1948, black ball teams averaged 55 league games a season, a sum which does not include innumerable interleague and so-called "exhibition" matches, but which is still more than the benchmark of 48 contests that sabermetricians have established for seasonal sample size.[20]

Once again, the value of league play is apparent as black ball pitchers induced lower batting totals than their Major League contemporaries in nearly every season from 1920 through 1942. Only the loss of manpower caused by player defections to Latin America during the 1930s and 1940s, the outbreak of World War II, and the integration of Organized Baseball in 1946 tilted the field back towards the big leaguers. Most tellingly, the Negro Leaguers' batting average in their own circuits from 1920 to 1948 (.270) is nearly identical to the figure they posted against Major League competition during the same time frame (.271).[21]

Table 2.18 NLB and MLB Hitting Totals 1920–1948

	BA	OBP	SLG	OPS
NLB	.270	.331	.372	.703
MLB	.275	.340	.388	.728
% Difference	1.7	2.7	4.3	3.6

Sources: Negro Leagues Researchers and Authors Group; Baseball-Reference.com; Seamheads.com Negro Leagues Database; *Center for Negro League Baseball Research*; Overmyer, *Black Ball and the Boardwalk*.

The big league quality of the black ball circuits becomes even more apparent when the pitching metrics for base-runners allowed (WHIP) and strikeouts (K/9) are considered. The black hurlers annually allowed far fewer walks and hits than the big leaguers, and struck out many more batters. Although bases on balls were not as meticulously documented by Negro Leagues scorekeepers as their Major League counterparts, the black ball totals are certainly in the ballpark, and the similarly slighted strikeout totals are eye-popping enough as is.

Table 2.19 NLB and MLB Pitching Metrics 1906–1948

	WHIP		K/9	
Year	NLB	MLB	NLB	MLB
1906	1.295	1.196	3.431	3.800
1907	1.151	1.190	3.757	3.600
1908	1.252	1.137	3.685	3.700
1909	1.228	1.184	4.332	3.800
1910	1.230	1.243	4.558	3.900
1911	1.355	1.352	5.111	4.000
1912	1.307	1.355	4.893	4.000
1913	1.309	1.285	4.907	3.900
1914	1.372	1.261	4.696	4.000
1915	1.246	1.248	4.719	3.800
1916	1.343	1.217	4.529	3.800
1917	1.285	1.210	4.395	3.500
1918	1.374	1.239	3.748	2.900
1919	1.327	1.272	4.136	3.100
1920	1.277	1.352	4.345	2.900
1921	1.374	1.435	4.308	2.800
1922	1.363	1.439	4.557	2.800
1923	1.405	1.439	3.779	2.900
1924	1.382	1.439	4.061	2.700
1925	1.444	1.497	3.677	2.800
1926	1.393	1.423	3.466	2.800
1927	1.370	1.428	3.420	2.800
1928	1.397	1.426	3.879	2.900
1929	1.430	1.494	3.686	2.900
1930	1.364	1.521	3.184	3.300
1931	1.358	1.442	4.358	3.200
1932	1.330	1.430	4.172	3.200
1933	1.351	1.384	4.733	3.100
1934	1.341	1.466	4.702	3.500

| | WHIP | | K/9 | |
Year	NLB	MLB	NLB	MLB
1935	1.478	1.457	4.462	3.300
1936	1.509	1.509	4.597	3.400
1937	1.375	1.470	5.154	3.700
1938	1.404	1.474	4.956	3.500
1939	1.392	1.459	4.465	3.500
1940	1.431	1.418	4.769	3.700
1941	1.321	1.416	4.281	3.600
1942	1.327	1.346	4.549	3.400
1943	1.419	1.331	4.563	3.400
1944	1.312	1.354	4.369	3.300
1945	1.341	1.377	4.927	3.300
1946	1.328	1.369	4.767	3.900
1947	1.429	1.415	5.082	3.700
1948	1.438	1.452	5.466	3.700

Note: Higher Whip averages and lower K/9 totals are shown in Gray

Table 2.20 NLB and MLB Pitching Totals 1906–1948

	WHIP	K/9
NLB	1.352	4.249
MLB	1.368	3.390
% Difference	1.2	20.2

Table 2.21 NLB and MLB Pitching Totals 1920–1948

	WHIP	K/9
NLB	1.382	4.222
MLB	1.429	3.241
% Difference	3.4	26.3

Sources for Tables 2.19, 2.20, 2.21: Baseball-Reference.com; Seamheads.com Negro Leagues Database; *Center for Negro League Baseball Research*; Overmyer, *Black Ball and the Boardwalk*.

Included in the big league totals are the results of the ill-fated Federal League, a rival organization to the American and National Leagues that operated during the 1914 and 1915 seasons, and classified as a Major League by the Special Baseball Records Committee. Although the black ball teams of the time had no league of their own, they defeated Fed players and clubs on several occasions and compare favorably to the rebel circuit in several statistical categories.[22]

Table 2.22 NLB and Federal League Hitting and Pitching Totals 1914–1915

	BA	OBP	SLG	OPS	WHIP	K/9
NLB	.256	.322	.338	.659	1.307	4.708
Federal League	.259	.324	.348	.672	1.282	3.922
% Difference	1.2	0.6	2.9	1.9	-2.0	20.0

Sources: Baseball-Reference.com; Seamheads.com Negro Leagues Database.

There is an even more direct comparison between the two entities. Between 1911 and 1929, nine Cuban-born Negro Leaguers crossed over to play in the Major Leagues. Although the sample size is relatively small (1450 NLB at-bats/3000 MLB at-bats; 223 NLB innings pitched/251 MLB innings pitched), the results are revelatory. The Cubans posted lower batting totals, allowed more runs per game, and had a lesser winning percentage while facing Negro Leagues competition (Table 2.23).[23]

Table 2.23 Cuban NLB and MLB Hitting and Pitching Totals 1904–1931

	BA	OBP	SLG	OPS	R/9	PCT
NLB	.250	.304	.310	.613	5.12	.461
MLB	.266	.323	.326	.648	4.66	.565
% Difference	6.4	6.3	5.2	5.7	9.0	22.6

Sources: Clark and Lester, *The Negro Leagues Book*; Baseball-Reference.com; Seamheads.com Negro Leagues Database.

The Negro Leagues did not top the Majors in every statistical category. Black ball pitchers allowed more runs per game, and their fielders committed more errors on average than big league players did. Negro League baserunners did steal many more bases, though (Tables 2.24; 2.25).

Table 2.24 NLB and MLB Run, Stolen Base, and Errors Per Game Averages 1906–1948

	NLB			MLB		
Year	R	SB	E	R	SB	E
1906	4.49	1.38	2.80	3.62	1.22	1.73
1907	3.93	0.97	2.32	3.53	1.13	1.73
1908	4.98	0.93	2.63	3.38	1.09	1.71
1909	4.59	0.61	2.62	3.55	1.23	1.81
1910	4.84	0.74	2.61	3.84	1.31	1.78
1911	5.53	1.29	2.58	4.51	1.38	1.84
1912	4.96	0.89	2.23	4.52	1.38	1.81
1913	4.83	1.22	2.25	4.04	1.32	1.64
1914	5.30	1.58	2.30	3.86	1.22	1.71
1915	4.63	1.08	2.26	3.81	1.10	1.58
1916	4.87	1.17	2.14	3.56	1.10	1.52
1917	4.26	0.90	1.85	3.58	0.97	1.50
1918	4.97	0.68	2.29	3.63	0.99	1.51
1919	4.76	1.01	2.07	3.87	0.93	1.43
1920	4.48	0.89	1.94	4.36	0.70	1.42
1921	5.39	1.10	2.17	4.85	0.60	1.39
1922	5.39	1.01	1.97	4.86	0.59	1.30
1923	5.67	0.79	1.87	4.81	0.64	1.35
1924	5.52	0.76	1.95	4.75	0.61	1.24
1925	5.63	0.94	1.83	5.13	0.57	1.34
1926	5.54	0.94	1.80	4.63	0.52	1.27
1927	5.45	0.74	1.74	4.75	0.58	1.31
1928	5.45	0.80	1.80	4.72	0.52	1.21
1929	5.73	0.88	1.77	5.19	0.54	1.20

	NLB			MLB		
Year	R	SB	E	R	SB	E
1930	5.71	0.72	1.77	5.55	0.44	1.23
1931	5.14	0.59	1.69	4.81	0.44	1.21
1932	5.02	0.80	1.67	4.91	0.40	1.19
1933	5.34	0.65	1.58	4.48	0.35	1.11
1934	5.17	0.65	1.44	4.90	0.37	1.14
1935	5.77	0.74	1.63	4.90	0.36	1.17
1936	5.49	0.67	1.54	5.20	0.39	1.18
1937	5.89	0.62	1.58	4.87	0.41	1.13
1938	5.29	0.70	1.75	4.89	0.37	1.12
1939	5.40	0.76	1.84	4.82	0.39	1.15
1940	5.56	0.62	2.00	4.68	0.39	1.15
1941	5.12	0.64	1.53	4.49	0.35	1.12
1942	4.94	0.53	1.77	4.08	0.39	1.11
1943	5.20	0.66	1.80	3.91	0.41	1.06
1944	4.94	0.89	1.80	4.17	0.37	1.12
1945	4.96	0.77	1.62	4.18	0.40	1.10
1946	5.05	0.76	1.84	4.01	0.36	1.03
1947	5.39	0.71	1.66	4.35	0.31	0.90
1948	5.49	0.62	1.71	4.57	0.33	0.95

Note: Higher averages are shown in Gray.

Table 2.25 NLB and MLB Run, Stolen Base and Errors per Game Totals 1906–1948

	R	SB	E
NLB	5.16	0.85	1.95
MLB	4.40	0.69	1.34
% Difference	15.9	20.8	37.1

Sources for Tables 2.24, 2.25: Negro Leagues Researchers and Authors Group; Baseball-Reference.com; Seamheads.com Negro Leagues Database; *Center for Negro League Baseball Research*; Overmyer, *Black Ball and the Boardwalk: The Bacharach Giants of Atlantic City*, 2014.

However, a closer inspection of the factors behind the numbers again reveals a basic equivalence. For example, the disparity in errors can be attributed mostly to poorer playing conditions. There were few, if any, grounds crews in the Negro Leagues, and baseballs and gloves were used until they fell apart. As for the playing venues, 28-year Negro League veteran "Cool Papa" Bell recalled that black ball teams usually "played out in little playgrounds," where "the ground was hard and rough," and only used Major League parks on "weekends when the home team was out." It should be noted that in 473 head-to-head contests, where the playing conditions were equal, the Negro Leaguers and big leaguers averaged nearly the same number (1.87 NLB to 1.85 MLB) of errors per game (Table 2.13).[24]

Similarly, the difference in scoring between the two entities is probably not due to inferior pitching (NLB batting, slugging, and on-base percentages were generally lower, remember), but more likely because of the Negro Leagues' more vibrant style of play. Cool Papa Bell observed that Major Leaguers followed the tenets of "written baseball" and played for one big inning. Negro Leaguers, on the other hand, relied more on "unwritten baseball":

I think we had a better system than the majors. Whatever it takes to win, we did…. When we played the big leaguers after the regular season, our pitchers would curve the ball on the 3–2. They'd say, "What, are you trying to make us look bad?" We'd bunt and run and they'd say, "Why are you trying to do that in the first inning?" When we were supposed to bunt, they'd come in and we'd hit away. Oh, we played tricky baseball.[25]

Philadelphia Stars centerfielder Gene Benson insisted that Organized Baseball was easier to play because "In the majors you didn't have to worry about being thrown at, you didn't have to worry about anybody cuttin' the ball or sailin' the ball, or thowin' spitballs…. You couldn't dig in on those guys in our league. They would *leave* you there." In the big leagues, Benson maintained, "all you had to do was concentrate on hittin' the ball." Interestingly, black ball pitchers who reached the highest rungs of Organized Baseball allowed more runs per game on average in the Negro Leagues than they did in Triple A or the Majors, despite allowing fewer baserunners and earned runs, while striking out more batters (Table 2.26).[26]

Table 2.26 Negro League Pitching Averages in NLB, AAA, and MLB

	IP	R/9	ERA	WHIP	K/9
NLB	*	4.53	3.35	1.31	6.02
AAA	13483.3	4.49	3.81	1.41	5.64
MLB	7217.3	4.22	3.76	1.35	5.91

* The NLB Averages are based on 14643.3ip (R); 14605ip (K); 14581.3ip (H); 14307.7ip (BB); and 13206.7ip (ER).
Sources: Negro Leagues Researchers and Authors Group; Baseball-Reference.com; Seamheads.com Negro Leagues Database; *Center for Negro League Baseball Research*; Overmyer, *Black Ball and the Boardwalk*.

Negro League Clubs Were Markedly Better Than Minor League Teams

While Negro Leagues teams more than held their own while playing Major League squads, they absolutely dominated minor league competition. From the turn of the 20th century through 1948, league-affiliated and independent black ball clubs played well over 1,400 games against minor league teams and All-Star outfits, beating them nearly 60 percent of the time (Table 2.27).

Table 2.27 NLB vs. MILB 1900–1948

Leagues	W	L	T	Pct.	NLRPG	MLRPG
Low Minors	204	93	6	.687	6.34	4.20
Class A	125	111	8	.530	4.88	4.74
Class AA	168	156	7	.519	4.88	4.87
Class AAA	324	246	19	.569	4.98	4.32
Total	821	606	40	.575	5.22	4.45

Note: The minor leagues have been grouped according to their modern classifications. Prior to 1946, the leagues later considered Class AAA were called Double A; Class AA was A; Class A was B; and the remainder of circuits were either Class C or D.
Sources: Simkus, *Outsider Baseball*, 2014; NLB vs. MILB Database.

Black ball squads played most of their contests against major leaguers during the postseason, but many of their games with minor league clubs occurred before the regular season started. During the first decade of the 20th century, the Philadelphia Giants, Brooklyn Royal, Giants, and Cuban Stars annually made spring training tours against the teams of the New England, New York, and Tri-State Leagues, while the St. Paul Gophers played several pre-season contests against Minnesota and Wisconsin bush leaguers.[27]

However, as the losses began to mount, the attitude of the minor league magnates began to change. In early 1914, Pacific Coast League President Allan Baum encouraged his clubs to boycott Foster's American Giants, noting, "Why, organized baseball does not sanction it … and I am sure there is not another manager in the league who would consider playing with the Chicago Giants." Oakland Oaks owner J. Cal Ewing agreed, stating, "There are two classes I bar from playing in my ball park—colored tossers and bloomer girls." The *New York Age* retorted: "The cowardly practice of using the color prejudice subterfuge as a cloak to hide the white man's fear in open competition with the colored man in various avenues of endeavor will someday lose its effectiveness."[28]

After the Kansas City Monarchs took five out of six games from the Kansas City Blues of the American Association in October 1922, the mainstream *Kansas City Star* anointed them "city champions." In response, American Association president Thomas J. Hickey banned further competition between the two clubs. In October 1927, Judge Landis tried to shut down the integrated California Winter League by threatening permanent expulsion for all minor leaguers who played winter ball, but he ultimately couldn't make that ban stick. As several Negro Leagues squads played their home games in minor league parks, the beleaguered bush league owners were at least able to gain a financial edge by gouging the black squads on rental fees.[29]

When the batting records of the Negro Leagues and those of the three Double (later Triple A) Leagues are compared, the black ball circuits enjoyed a substantial statistical edge. Once African American clubs found their legs in the mid-teens, they posted lower batting averages (indicating a higher level of play) in almost every year until integration, faltering ever so slightly in but four seasons (Table 2.28).

Table 2.28 NLB and Class AAA Hitting Averages 1912–1948

| | NLB | | | | AAA | | | |
Year	BA	OBP	SLG	OPS	BA	OBP	SLG	OPS
1912	.269	.321	.351	.672	.268	.327	.352	.679
1913	.267	.323	.349	.672	.258	.316	.336	.653
1914	.269	.332	.360	.692	.264	.325	.342	.667
1915	.246	.312	.318	.630	.262	.324	.347	.671
1916	.256	.328	.328	.656	.262	.329	.341	.671
1917	.245	.317	.308	.625	.261	.327	.338	.666
1918	.266	.335	.335	.669	.252	.313	.319	.632
1919	.249	.324	.334	.658	.266	.326	.347	.673
1920	.251	.318	.323	.641	.277	.336	.377	.707
1921	.270	.333	.368	.702	.290	.351	.403	.755
1922	.275	.338	.381	.719	.284	.345	.392	.738
1923	.278	.337	.383	.720	.295	.354	.413	.767
1924	.272	.330	.370	.700	.293	.354	.418	.772
1925	.279	.344	.398	.742	.292	.353	.414	.767
1926	.273	.340	.384	.724	.288	.347	.401	.748
1927	.276	.337	.384	.721	.289	.345	.407	.752

Year	NLB BA	OBP	SLG	OPS	AAA BA	OBP	SLG	OPS
1928	.281	.338	.391	.729	.291	.348	.405	.753
1929	.289	.353	.411	.765	.294	.354	.422	.776
1930	.285	.340	.399	.740	.301	.361	.435	.796
1931	.265	.328	.363	.691	.291	.350	.411	.761
1932	.270	.325	.361	.685	.288	.348	.412	.760
1933	.274	.327	.385	.713	.290	.351	.413	.763
1934	.269	.328	.351	.679	.283	.348	.396	.744
1935	.285	.344	.414	.759	.288	.347	.408	.755
1936	.271	.334	.388	.722	.286	.344	.411	.755
1937	.268	.326	.376	.702	.280	.337	.396	.733
1938	.266	.332	.373	.705	.274	.340	.389	.729
1939	.267	.331	.367	.698	.278	.339	.396	.735
1940	.266	.333	.366	.701	.271	.335	.379	.714
1941	.253	.312	.346	.658	.268	.337	.372	.709
1942	.253	.316	.335	.651	.262	.330	.361	.691
1943	.267	.330	.357	.687	.266	.324	.344	.669
1944	.264	.310	.354	.664	.265	.341	.357	.698
1945	.264	.320	.354	.674	.274	.352	.369	.721
1946	.257	.321	.356	.676	.264	.345	.366	.711
1947	.277	.346	.383	.729	.270	.347	.391	.738
1948	.274	.339	.370	.709	.272	.352	.405	.757

Note: Higher averages are shown in Gray

Table 2.29 NLB and Class AAA Hitting Totals 1912–1948

	BA	OBP	SLG	OPS
NLB	.268	.330	.364	.694
AAA	.277	.341	.383	.724
% Difference	3.4	3.3	5.2	4.3

Sources for Tables 2.28, 2.29: Negro Leagues Researchers and Authors Group; Baseball-Reference.com; Seamheads.com Negro Leagues Database; *Center for Negro League Baseball Research*; Overmyer, *Black Ball and the Boardwalk*; Snelling, *The Pacific Coast League*; Wright, *The American Association*; Wright, *The International League*.

The Negro Leagues' WHIP and K/9 pitching numbers also compare favorably to those of the high minors. From 1912 through 1948, Negro Leagues pitchers allowed fewer base runners than Triple A hurlers in every season but five, and they failed to strike out more batters just once. By posting markedly better league statistics and making "mincemeat" of Triple A squads on the playing field, the Negro Leaguers laid waste to the notion that their circuits or players were of minor league quality.[30]

Table 2.30 NLB and Class AAA Pitching Metrics 1912–1948

Year	WHIP NLB	AAA	K/9 NLB	AAA
1912	1.307	1.420	4.893	3.897
1913	1.309	1.284	4.907	3.725

Year	WHIP		K/9	
	NLB	AAA	NLB	AAA
1914	1.372	1.312	4.696	3.782
1915	1.246	1.298	4.719	3.744
1916	1.343	1.403	4.529	3.990
1917	1.285	1.368	4.395	3.467
1918	1.374	1.268	3.748	3.318
1919	1.327	1.365	4.136	3.318
1920	1.277	1.382	4.345	3.192
1921	1.374	1.528	4.308	3.468
1922	1.363	1.490	4.557	3.447
1923	1.405	1.529	3.779	3.187
1924	1.382	1.542	4.061	3.374
1925	1.444	1.536	3.677	3.494
1926	1.393	1.498	3.466	3.288
1927	1.370	1.485	3.420	3.092
1928	1.397	1.487	3.879	3.155
1929	1.430	1.543	3.686	3.310
1930	1.364	1.599	3.184	3.693
1931	1.358	1.534	4.358	3.437
1932	1.330	1.536	4.172	3.683
1933	1.351	1.564	4.733	3.631
1934	1.341	1.532	4.702	3.730
1935	1.478	1.555	4.462	3.904
1936	1.509	1.509	4.597	4.057
1937	1.375	1.482	5.154	3.963
1938	1.404	1.478	4.956	3.905
1939	1.392	1.478	4.465	4.044
1940	1.431	1.425	4.769	3.862
1941	1.321	1.425	4.281	3.847
1942	1.327	1.375	4.549	3.753
1943	1.419	1.362	4.563	3.756
1944	1.312	1.444	4.369	3.794
1945	1.341	1.534	4.927	3.628
1946	1.328	1.425	4.767	4.297
1947	1.429	1.491	5.082	4.176
1948	1.438	1.517	5.466	4.437

Note: Higher Whip averages and lower K/9 totals are shown in Gray

Table 2.31 NLB and Class AAA Pitching Averages 1912–1948

	WHIP	K/9
NLB	1.369	4.251
AAA	1.464	3.662
% Difference	6.7	14.9

Sources for Tables 2.30, 2.31: Negro Leagues Researchers and Authors Group; Baseball-Reference.com; Seamheads.com Negro Leagues Database; *Center for Negro League Baseball Research*; Overmyer, *Black Ball and the Boardwalk*; Snelling, *The Pacific Coast League*; Wright, *The American Association*; Wright, *The International League*.

Negro League Players Flourished After Entering Organized Baseball

During the 15 years following Jackie Robinson's 1946 debut with the Montreal Royals, at least 332 former Negro Leaguers entered Organized Baseball. Seventy-six of these players eventually made it to the Major Leagues, while 125 competed in the three Triple A circuits. Not every player was successful, but on the whole, and despite incredible hardships, the former Negro Leaguers out-performed their white counterparts.[31]

The Negro Leaguers were not met with open arms when they crossed the line. Physical intimidation, death threats, and a steady stream of racial slurs issued from fans and fellow players alike, and tremendous difficulty in locating places to eat and sleep was the rule, not the exception. Monte Irvin ruefully recalled that pitchers threw "at us like we were something good to eat." Lorenzo "Piper" Davis later remembered that the patrons of the Pacific Coast League called him "more names than I thought we had," while 19-year-old Hank Aaron was said to have led the 1953 South Atlantic League "in everything but hotel accommodations."[32]

A total of five Negro Leaguers participated in Organized Baseball during the 1946 season. By 1951, their numbers had risen to 113. However, the majority of Major League teams preferred to hang on to their racist past. At the end of that 1951 season, five full years after Robinson signed with the Dodgers, only five of the 16 big league clubs had black players on their rosters. Perversely, the organizations that *did* integrate strictly adhered to the unwritten "fifty-fifty" rule, wherein no more than four black players could be in a team's lineup at any one time. The end result of this woefully slow integration process was that several qualified African Americans were left languishing in the minors until their opportunity to play in the Major Leagues had passed them by (see Appendix V).[33]

Most crucially, the majority of the black players who did get their chance prospered on the field, and the floodgates were finally forced open. During the 30 years after integration, former Negro Leaguers outhit their white competition in both Triple A and the Major Leagues by a substantial margin (Tables 2.32; 2.33). Hank Aaron famously averred that the only sure way to smash the color line was to "play so good that they can't remember what color you were before the season started."[34]

Table 2.32 Negro Leaguers Class AAA Batting Totals 1946–1976

	BA	OBP	SLG	OPS
NLAAA	.286	.357	.433	.790
AAA	.264	.337	.386	.723
% Difference	7.7	5.6	10.9	8.3

Table 2.33 Negro Leaguers MLB Batting Totals 1947–1976

	BA	OBP	SLG	OPS
NLMLB	.277	.361	.455	.815
MLB	.255	.324	.380	.704
% Difference	7.9	10.2	16.5	13.6

Sources for Tables 2.32, 2.33: Clark and Lester, *The Negro Leagues Book*; Baseball-Reference.com.

Negro Leagues pitchers also experienced more than their share of success in Organized Ball. Forty-four black ball hurlers made it as far as Triple A, while 21 of their number reached the Majors. However, despite allowing fewer runs and base runners, while striking out more batters at both levels over a period of 30 years, the black twirler became an endangered species due to what can only be termed racist beliefs by big league front offices. By 1968, fewer than one in ten Major League pitchers were black. When the 1986 season started, only 5.7 percent of Major League African Americans were pitchers. Their black battery-mates had it even worse; at the beginning of that 1986 campaign, there were no African American catchers in either big league.[35]

Table 2.34 Negro Leaguers Class
AAA Pitching Totals 1946–1975

	PCT	ERA	WHIP	K/9
NLAAA	.514	3.81	1.41	5.46
AAA	.500	3.92	1.45	5.29
% Difference	2.7	2.9	3.0	3.1

Table 2.35 Negro Leaguers
MLB Pitching Totals 1947–1969

	PCT	ERA	WHIP	K/9
NLMLB	.552	3.76	1.35	5.91
MLB	.500	3.91	1.35	4.89
% Difference	9.4	4.0	0	17.3

Sources for Tables 2.34, 2.35: Clark and Lester, The Negro Leagues Book; Baseball-Reference.com.

Despite being greatly outnumbered, the former Negro Leaguers captured several major and minor league batting and pitching titles while garnering numerous awards and honors. Nine of these players were eventually elected to the National Baseball Hall of Fame. Included in this group are Willie Mays and Hank Aaron, generally acknowledged as two of the five greatest players of all time. In the 40 years after Jackie Robinson's breakthrough, non-whites won 18 percent of the MLB Cy Young awards, 25 percent of the ERA titles, 39 percent of the home run crowns, and 48 percent of the batting championships, despite comprising less than 25 percent of the big league population during this period. After Robinson was named the Major League Rookie of the Year in 1947, black players received eight of the first 11 National League freshman awards. Nine of the 11 men voted the National League MVP between 1949 and 1959 were former Negro Leaguers.[36]

In 1952 alone, ex–Negro Leagues players topped the leader board in 46 minor league hitting and pitching categories (Tables 2.36, 2.37, 2.38). Beginning in 1955, former Negro Leaguers led the National League in total bases for nine consecutive seasons. More dubiously, in 12 of the 13 years between 1949 and 1961, the player hit by the most pitches in the American League had gotten his start in the Negro Leagues. Larry Doby insisted that black Major Leaguers were much more likely to be thrown at than white batters. Beanballs aside, the big league success the black ball players achieved lent a tremendous validity to the Negro Leagues. As Gene Benson sagely told Jackie Robinson, "Where you're going ain't half as tough as where you been."[37]

Table 2.36 Organized Baseball Batting Titles
Won by Negro Leaguers 1946–1971

Leagues	G	AB	R	H	D	T	HR	RBI	TB	BA	SLG	BB	HP	SB	Total
Low Minors	4	5	7	7	5	2	10	9	5	11	6	1	1	5	78
Class A	1	0	5	4	5	3	1	6	5	8	7	0	0	1	46
Class AA	2	2	5	8	4	3	4	6	0	7	3	0	0	0	44
Class AAA	3	7	10	12	7	11	7	8	3	11	2	1	1	10	93
American	2	0	2	1	1	5	2	1	1	0	2	0	12	3	32
National	8	1	6	4	4	6	10	8	12	4	10	2	2	8	85
Total	20	15	35	36	26	30	34	38	26	41	30	4	16	27	378

Table 2.37 Organized Baseball Pitching Titles
Won by Negro Leaguers 1946–1965

Leagues	G	GS	CG	IP	W	PCT	SH	SV	ERA	WHIP	K	K/9	Total
Low Minors	2	4	2	4	9	6	4	0	3	0	8	0	42
Class A	1	1	0	3	3	0	0	0	2	1	5	0	16
Class AA	0	1	0	1	4	0	0	0	4	0	1	0	11
Class AAA	0	0	0	2	3	2	1	0	1	2	3	3	17
American	1	0	0	0	0	0	0	0	0	1	0	0	2
National	0	0	0	0	2	2	2	0	1	2	4	3	16
Total	4	6	2	10	21	10	7	0	11	6	21	6	104

Table 2.38 Major League Awards Won by Negro Leaguers

	GG	AS	ROY	MVP	CY	HOF
American League Players	4	21	0	1	NA	2
American League Pitchers	0	3	0	0	0	1
National League Players	17	74	4	9	NA	6
National League Pitchers	0	6	2	1	1	0
Total	21	104	6	11	1	9

Sources for Tables 2.36, 2.37, 2:38: Clark and Lester, *The Negro Leagues Book*; Dixon with Hannigan, *The Negro Baseball Leagues: A Photographic History*, 1992; Baseball-Reference.com; *Center for Negro League Baseball Research.*

Black Players Have Dominated the Post-Segregation Era

As the former Negro Leaguers led the charge into Organized Baseball, a new generation of black players followed closely behind, bypassing the segregated circuits altogether. Sixty-eight members of this first wave got as far as Triple A during the first ten years of integration, while 54 graduated to the Major Leagues by the close of the 1959 season.[38]

Although hampered by a quota system that restricted their opportunities, this first generation of black players hit and pitched well above league average in both the major and high minor circuits (Tables 2.39, 2.40, 2.41, 2.42). Black players also provided more bang for the buck. They were generally paid less than their white counterparts, yet the clubs that employed the higher number of non-white players usually finished higher in the standings. The first three NL teams to integrate—the Dodgers, Giants, and Braves—won 12 out of the league's 13 pennants between 1947 and 1959.[39]

Table 2.39 First Generation Black Players Class
AAA Batting Totals 1949–1975

	BA	OBP	SLG	OPS
BAAA	.276	.350	.415	.764
AAA	.263	.335	.385	.720
% Difference	4.7	4.3	7.2	5.8

Table 2.40 First Generation Black Players
MLB Batting Totals 1953–1980

	BA	OBP	SLG	OPS
BMLB	.273	.343	.422	.764
MLB	.255	.322	.380	.702
% Difference	6.6	6.1	10.0	8.1

Table 2.41 First Generation Black Players Class
AAA Pitching Totals 1952–1975

	PCT	ERA	WHIP	K/9
BAAA	.556	3.35	1.30	6.17
AAA	.500	3.83	1.43	5.54
% Difference	10.1	14.3	10.2	10.2

Table 2.42 First Generation Black Players
MLB Pitching Totals 1953–1976

	PCT	ERA	WHIP	K/9
BMLB	.522	3.55	1.31	5.67
MLB	.500	3.79	1.32	5.27
% Difference	4.2	6.8	0.8	7.1

Note: The term "First Generation" refers to black players who did not participate in the Negro Leagues and entered Organized Baseball during the first ten years of integration.

Sources for Tables 2.39, 2.40, 2.41, 2.42: Moffi and Kronstadt, *Crossing the Line: Black Major Leaguers*, 1994; Baseball-Reference.com.

As they rose through the ranks, these players found success at every rung of the ladder. In 1955, the initial wave of black players won 23 Class B, C, or D minor league batting and pitching titles. During the 1959 season, this first generation led the three Triple A circuits in 14 different statistical categories. In 1962, black players led the National League in games played, at-bats, runs, hits, doubles, triples, home runs, runs batted in, stolen bases, total bases, batting average, slugging percentage, and, of course, being hit by pitches.[40]

Table 2.43 Organized Baseball Batting Titles Won by
First Generation Black Players 1949–1972

Leagues	G	AB	R	H	D	T	HR	RBI	TB	BA	SLG	BB	HP	SB	Total
Low Minors	6	4	13	7	3	12	8	8	7	9	10	0	1	19	107
Class A	0	2	3	2	0	1	2	0	2	2	1	0	0	3	18

Leagues	G	AB	R	H	D	T	HR	RBI	TB	BA	SLG	BB	HP	SB	Total
Class AA	0	0	0	0	0	0	0	0	0	0	0	0	0	0	0
Class AAA	4	6	4	6	3	3	1	0	4	5	3	1	1	8	49
American	1	0	1	0	0	1	1	1	1	1	1	0	1	0	9
National	8	9	6	9	5	6	4	5	4	6	7	1	9	9	88
Total	19	21	27	24	11	23	16	14	18	23	22	2	12	39	271

Table 2.44 Organized Baseball Pitching Titles Won by First Generation Black Players 1950–1974

Leagues	G	GS	CG	IP	W	PCT	SH	SV	ERA	WHIP	K	K/9	Total
Low Minors	1	0	0	1	2	2	0	0	2	1	1	1	11
Class A	0	1	0	2	2	1	0	0	4	2	1	0	13
Class AA	0	1	0	0	0	0	0	0	0	0	0	0	1
Class AAA	0	0	3	2	2	7	3	0	0	0	1	2	20
American	0	1	1	0	3	3	1	0	0	0	0	2	11
National	0	0	1	0	1	0	4	0	1	1	1	0	9
Total	1	3	5	5	10	13	8	0	7	4	4	5	65

Table 2.45 Major League Awards Won by First Generation Black Players

	GG	AS	ROY	MVP	CY	HOF
American League Players	10	18	0	1	NA	0
American League Pitchers	0	7	0	0	1	0
National League Players	32	61	4	5	NA	5
National League Pitchers	9	10	0	1	2	1
Total	51	96	4	7	3	6

Sources for Tables 2.43, 2.44, 2.45: Dixon and Hannigan, *The Negro Baseball Leagues*; Baseball-Reference.com; Center for Negro League Baseball Research.

In 1967, 40 black players (5.57 percent of a total 718 big leaguers) accounted for more than half of the base hits made in the Major League. Nine of the top ten National League batting averages belonged to African Americans or Latinos. Twelve of the top 15 National League batters in 1969 were black, along with five of the top six hitters in the junior circuit. An African American failed to lead led the National League in slugging only twice between 1954 and 1978. In the 39 seasons from 1959 through 1997, a black player won the National League batting crown 32 times. Since 1947, a non-black player has led the National League in stolen bases only *four* times. In the 52 seasons between 1965 and 2016, black players captured 45 American League stolen base crowns.[41]

In the entire history of Major League Baseball, only four batters have amassed 5,900 or more total bases, and three of them—Hank Aaron, Willie Mays, and Barry Bonds—are African Americans. Despite getting a 71-year late start, eight of the top ten all-time home run hitters are black. Only Aaron, Mays, Alex Rodriguez, and Albert Pujols have over 3,000 hits and 600 home runs. Not one of the four would have been allowed in the Majors before 1947.[42]

From 1947 through 2013, African American players won 47 Most Valuable Player awards and Latinos 21, more than half of the 134 total. From 1947 through 2014, 29 percent of all Major League players were black. However, non-white players have contributed at least one-third of the yearly WAR (Wins Above Replacement) in the big leagues since the early 1960s and have hovered around the 40 percent mark since 1990. As historian Mark Armour pointed out, Major League Baseball would be "immeasurably worse" without integration.[43]

From 1959 through 1985, the league with more black players on their squad (i.e., the National) won 27 out of 31 All-Star Games (with one tie). Between 1947 and 1973, big league black hitters produced more hits, doubles, triples, and home runs, and stole more bases on average than white batters. During that same time frame, black pitchers struck out more hitters and allowed fewer base runners per inning. According to black baller Bill Yancey, "Hell, [we] always had players of that caliber, only we never got any recognition." The legacy of the Negro Leagues is clear: Since integration, the best players in the major leagues have been black. Evidence would indicate that the best baseball players have *always* been black.[44]

Table 2.46 White, Black and Latin MLB Batting and Pitching Averages 1947–1973

Years	Demographic	% AB	BA	SLG	% IP	WHIP	K/9
1947–1960	White	88.0	.261	.393	93.8	1.40	4.29
	Black	7.5	.280	.455	2.6	1.33	5.38
	Latin	4.5	.267	.385	3.6	1.39	4.59
1961–1968	White	64.0	.251	.380	87.8	1.28	5.69
	Black	22.0	.269	.421	5.9	1.27	6.45
	Latin	14.0	.267	.380	6.3	1.23	6.34
1969–1973	White	58.0	.251	.371	87.7	1.32	5.49
	Black	26.0	.270	.422	7.5	1.26	6.50
	Latin	18.0	.265	.366	4.8	1.30	5.35

Source: Yee and Wright, *The Sports Book*, 1975.

The Black Population of the Major Leagues Has Surpassed That of the Negro Leagues

A common argument holds that because African Americans made up only about 10 percent of the United States population during the segregated era, the Negro Leagues had fewer qualified individuals to choose from than did Organized Baseball, and thus had players on their rosters that were of lesser quality.[45]

However, African Americans have demonstrated they can produce more upper echelon professional athletes than their overall numbers would suggest. Between 1989 and 2017 for example, blacks comprised only 12.4% of the United States demographic and yet during those twenty-nine years (the same duration as NLB's 1920–1948 peak period) 66.5% of the players in the National Football League and 76.5% of those in the National Basketball Association were African American.[46]

While it is impossible to know how many Negro Leaguers would have played in the Major Leagues if given the chance, the number of black big leaguers since integration has been well documented. When Elijah "Pumpsie" Green broke in with the Boston Red Sox in 1959, thus fully integrating the big leagues, there were 87 black Americans or Latinos in the Majors (15.2 percent). The black population in the big leagues climbed past the 20 percent level during the 1964 season.[47]

By the time Major League Baseball expanded to 24 teams in 1969, the implicit "fifty-fifty" rule was on the way out (although the outfield was fast becoming the only position available for most African Americans). In September 1971, the Pittsburgh Pirates fielded an all-black starting nine and at that time had more black than white players on their roster. The number of black players in the big leagues reached 30 percent by 1984, and has remained well above that mark ever since. In fact, from the beginning of divisional play in 1969 through the 2016 season, one-third of all major leaguers have been black.[48]

Due to expansion, there are now nearly twice as many major leaguers than there were during the segregated era (750 to 400). Perhaps not coincidentally, this player increase (350) is equal to the yearly average of black major leaguers since 1969. In fact, in every season since 1995, the number of Black and Latin major leaguers has been the same or larger than the number of *white* big leaguers during the segregated era (Table 2.47).[49]

Table 2.47 Black MLB Population 1969–2018

Year	BP	LP	B/L	BP%	LP%	B/L%
1969	123	94	217	14.5	11.1	25.56
1970	124	99	223	14.6	11.7	26.27
1971	128	88	216	15.5	10.6	26.09
1972	133	90	223	16.1	10.9	27.06
1973	143	90	233	17.4	11.0	28.38
1974	150	99	249	17.4	11.5	28.92
1975	156	86	242	18.5	10.2	28.67
1976	147	94	241	18.0	11.5	29.46
1977	161	103	264	17.9	11.4	29.33
1978	157	102	259	17.4	11.3	28.65
1979	161	96	257	17.9	10.7	28.59
1980	159	106	265	17.4	11.6	28.93
1981	170	101	271	18.7	11.1	29.88
1982	167	109	276	17.9	11.7	29.61
1983	172	111	283	18.0	11.6	29.70
1984	172	112	284	18.4	12.0	30.37
1985	173	107	280	18.3	11.3	29.69
1986	174	112	286	18.3	11.8	30.01
1987	173	120	293	17.7	12.3	30.05
1988	168	141	309	17.3	14.5	31.76
1989	163	130	293	16.5	13.2	29.66
1990	171	152	323	16.6	14.8	31.36
1991	176	166	342	17.0	16.1	33.08
1992	168	157	325	16.7	15.6	32.27
1993	185	187	372	16.8	16.9	33.70
1994	170	176	346	17.2	17.8	34.91
1995	182	218	400	16.1	19.2	35.30
1996	183	233	416	16.0	20.4	36.46
1997	169	264	433	15.0	23.5	38.56
1998	170	271	441	14.3	22.8	37.18
1999	165	284	449	13.6	23.5	37.14
2000	157	304	461	12.8	24.7	37.48
2001	148	317	465	12.1	26.0	38.11
2002	131	323	454	10.8	26.5	37.27

Year	BP	LP	B/L	BP%	LP%	B/L%
2003	128	330	458	10.4	26.8	37.24
2004	126	346	472	10.1	27.7	37.85
2005	112	344	456	9.1	27.8	36.86
2006	112	346	458	9.0	27.8	36.85
2007	109	334	443	8.5	26.1	34.66
2008	106	353	459	8.2	27.3	35.55
2009	90	361	451	7.1	28.5	35.62
2010	98	340	438	7.8	27.2	35.07
2011	102	349	451	7.9	26.9	34.83
2012	92	346	438	7.2	26.9	34.11
2013	88	361	449	6.7	27.7	34.43
2014	88	343	431	7.3	28.3	35.59
2015	62	220	282	8.3	29.3	37.60
2016	62	214	273	8.3	28.5	36.80
2017	58	239	297	7.7	31.9	39.60
2018	63	221	284	8.4	29.5	37.87
Average	141	213	354	13.5	19.9	33.38

Note: The 2015–2017 numbers are based on opening day rosters and not yearly totals.
Sources: Armour and Levitt, *Ethnicity Totals by Year, 1947–2014*; Lapchick, "The 2016 Racial and Gender Report Card: Major League Baseball," Tidesport.org, 2016; Lapchick, "The 2019 Racial and Gender Report Card: Major League Baseball," Tidesport.org, 2019.

Conversely, during the lifetime of the Negro Leagues, the rosters of black ball clubs ranged from 14 to 20 players, although team photographs of the period rarely reveal squads larger than 16. Given that there were on average 13 league or league-associated franchises from 1920 until 1948, the average population of big time black ball on any given day was about 207 players (Table 2.48).[50]

Table 2.48 NLB Population 1920–1948

Year	Teams	Player Limit	Player Total
1920	9	135	196
1921	14	196	298
1922	11	165	215
1923	17	272	340
1924	17	264	353
1925	16	320	327
1926	16	248	322
1927	15	226	286
1928	15	224	322
1929	14	208	296
1930	9	126	210
1931	9	162	207
1932	19	275	379
1933	12	168	207
1934	11	165	219
1935	8	120	175
1936	7	105	152
1937	14	222	321
1938	14	224	319

Year	Teams	Player Limit	Player Total
1939	13	201	282
1940	13	194	325
1941	12	186	283
1942	12	216	307
1943	13	213	332
1944	12	216	315
1945	12	204	330
1946	12	228	334
1947	12	228	297
1948	12	210	289
Average	13	207	284

Note: Only league and league associated clubs were included. The player limit column reflects the team roster sizes set by the leagues before each season. The player total is the overall number of participants for that year. *Sources*: Clark and Lester, *The Negro Leagues Book*; Dixon and Hannigan, *The Negro Baseball Leagues*; Seamheads. com Negro Leagues Database; Baseball-Reference.com; *Pittsburgh Courier*; *Chicago Defender*.

Due to a variety of external factors—the expense involved in youth baseball; the lack of urban baseball diamonds; scholarship opportunities offered by other sports; and institutional racism—fewer black Americans have played big league baseball during the new millennium. However, a recent influx of black Latino players has more than offset the lack of an African American presence. Since 2001, at least 25 percent of all major leaguers have been of Latin American descent.[51]

Even with the decline in African American participation, the number of black Major League players has been higher than the average population of the Negro Leagues (207) in every season since 1969, and the apex of organized black ball (about 377 players during the chaotic 1932 season) has been surpassed by black big leaguers every year since 1995. Because at least 425 African Americans and Latinos currently play big league baseball every year, there are now more black major leaguers annually than there ever were Negro League players. It is a safe assumption that the 20th-century black ball circuits with yearly populations that rarely exceeded 300 players were big league as well.[52]

Major League Baseball Has Colonized the History and Culture of the Negro Leagues

Perhaps the greatest tragedy of the segregation era was that the players and management of Organized Baseball *knew* how good the Negro Leagues were, yet refused to do anything about it. Former big league player and manager John "Cub" Stricker opined in the fall of 1906 that the Philadelphia Giants would beat either the American or National League champions in a series. In 1923, MLB's mouthpiece, *The Sporting News*, editorialized:

In Organized Baseball there has been no distinction raised except tacit understanding that a player of Ethiopian descent is ineligible—the wisdom of which we will not discuss except to say that by such a rule some of the greatest players the game has ever known have been denied their opportunity. No player of any other "race" has been barred.[53]

Philadelphia Athletics owner Connie Mack later intimated to Hall of Fame third baseman Judy Johnson that the real reason for the ban was loss of white jobs that would result from integration: "Well, Judy, if you want to know the truth, there were just too many of you to go in."[54]

In the summer of 1939, *Pittsburgh Courier* columnist Wendell Smith's interviews with more than 35 Major League players, managers, and coaches revealed that the majority of those polled supported integration. Most famously, Brooklyn Dodgers manager Leo Durocher gushed, "I've seen plenty of colored boys who could make the grade in the Majors. Hell—I've seen a million." Phillies skipper James "Doc" Prothro ventured that the majority of big league teams would sign black players if they could, while Cubs pilot Charles "Gabby" Hartnett predicted that if allowed, there "would be a mad scramble for Negro players."[55]

While they wouldn't permit African Americans on their teams, the big leaguers were not above seeking their counsel or appropriating their style of play. In the fall of 1930, St. Louis Cardinals great Leonard "Pepper" Martin was so impressed by the Kansas City Monarchs' aggressive base-running during an All-Star game that "I made up my mind right then that I would play that type of ball in the Majors. I did it all that next season and throughout the World Series against the Athletics." During the first decade of the 20th century, black ball catcher George "Chappie" Johnson was employed as a spring training coach by Boston Nationals manager Fred Tenney. Johnson also trained the Cincinnati Reds during the late 1930s and was said to have tutored Hall of Famers "Rube" Waddell and Roger Bresnahan at the outset of their careers.[56]

It was also not uncommon for a white player during the segregated era to earn his big league shot after performing well against a black team. Jesse Hubbard, claimed he could name at least "fifty big leaguers," among them Milt Gaston, Roger "Doc" Cramer, Stan "Lefty" Baumgartner, and George Earnshaw, "who got their start playing us. All they had to do was beat one of those colored teams, and they were gone" After driving in the winning run with an infield single during an interracial game in January 1936, a young Joe DiMaggio reportedly declared, "Now I can make it with the Yankees. I finally got a hit off Satchel Paige."[57]

It was Ted Williams, DiMaggio's great contemporary, who proved to be the catalyst for the long-overdue recognition of the Negro Leagues, lobbying during his 1966 Hall of Fame acceptance speech for the induction of Satchel Paige and Josh Gibson "as symbols of the great Negro players who are not here only because they weren't given the chance." Satchel Paige was selected for induction into the Hall of Fame in 1971, the first of 35 black ball players and executives to be so honored over the next 36 years. Organized Baseball couldn't resist one last stab at segregation, however. The original plan was to house the Negro Leagues plaques in a separate exhibit of the museum, until public outrage and media pressure forced their move to the central plaque gallery. During a subsequent trip to the Hall, Paige told a luncheon gathering that too many young black minor leaguers were unjustly being denied a shot at the Majors. The legendary twirler was brusquely told to sit down by MLB official Joe Reichler, and he never went back to Cooperstown.[58]

In September 1988, the Pittsburgh Pirates became the first Major League team to honor the Negro Leagues when they raised the championship pennant of the 1948 Homestead Grays over Three Rivers Stadium and gave bronze medallions to ten former players. Perhaps more importantly, Pirates president Carl Barger formally apologized to the players during a pre-game ceremony, lamenting, "we cannot make up the opportunities that were missed." In the summer of 1993, banners for the Grays' nine NNL championships, and for the three captured by the Pittsburgh Crawfords, were hung in Three Rivers upper deck alongside those of the Pirates.[59]

At a Hall of Fame reunion in 1991, Baseball Commissioner Faye Vincent thanked the

75 Negro Leaguers present for their "unselfish" contributions to the game, and told them, "with sorrow and regret, I apologize for the injustice you were subjected to." A year later, Vincent told a meeting of the National Urban League that he would like to "at the very least ... offer full-fledged health insurance to [the] former players." In May 1993, MLB announced the creation of the Negro League Medical Plan, which would provide medical coverage for surviving Negro Leaguers and their wives.[60]

In January 1997, after a series of unpleasant lawsuits, MLB granted partial pensions to Negro Leaguers with at least four years of experience prior to 1947 or who had played a combined four years in the Negro Leagues and the Major Leagues. National League president Leonard Coleman remarked, "Baseball cannot restore the careers of these former Negro League players, but they were victims of discrimination outright and were prevented from making a living in the Major Leagues. The very least baseball can do is provide a pension."[61]

However, the stipend the eligible Negro Leaguers ultimately received was $10,000 a year, which paled in comparison to the $113,000 annual Major League pension of the time. Excluded from the newly-found largesse were several Negro Leaguers denied big league opportunities because of the quota system or military service. Former Kansas City Monarch Bob "Peach-Head" Mitchell led a campaign to provide compensation to those players with four years or less of Negro League service. MLB executive vice president (and future commissioner) Rob Manfred complained that Organized Baseball was already doing more than their fair share for the former black ballers and said that "No other employer has created a pension program for people who did not even work for them." For his part, Commissioner Bud Selig let on that "I'd like to take care of [the former players]. We're responsible."[62]

In May 2004, MLB agreed to pay 27 former Negro Leaguers with at least four years of experience prior to 1958, either $833 a month for four years or $375 a month for life. Two years later, a United States Court of Appeals upheld a summary judgment against nearly 1,000 white players who had claimed that MLB was discriminatory in granting the former Negro Leaguers pensions and medical benefits. Circuit Judge Stephen Reinhardt's opinion stated that "MLB's absolute ban on African-American players before 1947" prevented the Negro Leaguers from accruing the service time necessary to qualify for the pension."[63]

But it was on the playing field that Major League Baseball's recognition of the Negro Leagues was fully realized. On August 3, 1994, at Kauffman Stadium in Kansas City, the hometown Royals defeated the Oakland Athletics, 9–5, while wearing replica uniforms of the 1924 Kansas City Monarchs. During the following 26 seasons, big league squads would put on the throwback uniforms of Negro Leagues teams, with the MLB emblem on their sleeves, more than 90 times (Appendix VI).[64]

On a few occasions, the homage extended past the wearing of the Negro Leagues colors. During a June 2002 game in Detroit, all public address announcements and player introductions referred to the Detroit Stars and Pittsburgh Crawfords, and not the MLB Tigers and Pirates. In May 2006, the scoreboards at Cleveland's Jacobs Field read "Cleveland Buckeyes" and "Homestead Grays" throughout the game between the Indians and Pittsburgh. Two years later in Washington, D.C., the Nationals and Pirates both wore Grays uniforms, the Nationals donning Homestead's 1942 home whites, while Pittsburgh modeled the club's 1935 road jerseys. Throughout the game, the Washington PA announcer called both clubs the Grays.[65]

In most cases, the proceeds from the sale of uniforms from the throwback games (but not the gate receipts or concession money) were donated to charity or institutions such as the Negro Leagues Museum in Kansas City. The big leaguers generally embraced the opportunity to honor the memory of the black ball players. Washington Nationals outfielder Willie Harris noted, "It just reminds me that they paved the way for guys like me and guys that are coming along behind me." However, as *New York Times* columnist Chuck Klosterman pointed out, "when Major League Baseball celebrates the Negro leagues, it's celebrating a past that technically doesn't belong to it and that exists only because of its past prejudice."[66]

The wearing of throwback uniforms was only one example of how the Major Leagues appropriated the ideas and culture of the black ball circuits. By including their greatest stars in the Hall of Fame, flying their championship banners in their ballparks, paying their players pensions, and apologizing for their exclusion, Major League Baseball legitimized the big league status of the Negro Leagues several times over.

Summation

In an essay on league quality, historian Rob Neyer postulated, "I think we can agree that we've got a Major League if (a) there are teams playing a set and lengthy schedule, and (b) these teams are populated largely by the sport's best players." Because black ball teams usually did not own their own ballparks, their schedules were more difficult to arrange and thus more haphazard than Organized Baseball's. However, as sportswriter Harold Winston observed, "It took real organization to make a league like that operate." Negro Leagues squads did play a lot of games; between 1920 and 1927, the Hilldale Club averaged 163 contests a season.[67]

Independent black teams operating without the constraints of a league were able to schedule even more contests. The Cuban Giants played 165 games as far back as 1887. In 1931, the Homestead Grays played 174 games in more than 65 cities, in towns spread over eight states and the District of Columbia. The 24 double-headers (and one triple-header) the Grays endured in 1931 exemplified the grueling nature of black baseball. On seven occasions, the squad played four games in two days in multiple cities. During the sweltering dog days of August, the Grays participated in 36 games, winning 30 of them.[68]

As for having the best players, African and Latin Americans have dominated the Major Leagues since 1947, and they now make up nearly 40 percent of MLB's yearly population. Negro Leaguers beat big league teams more than half the time in head-to-head contests, demonstrated better pitching in league play, and performed well above average when they were finally allowed in the Majors.

In other words, Negro Leagues = Major Leagues.

Notes

1. Dick Clark and Larry Lester, *The Negro Leagues Book* (Cleveland: Society for American Baseball Research, 1994), 159; *Omaha World Herald*, July 30, 1962.

2. Jules Tygiel, "Black Ball," in *Total Baseball*, John Thorn and Pete Palmer, with David Reuther, editors (New York: Warner, 1989), 548; William F. McNeil, *Baseball's Other All-Stars* (Jefferson, NC: McFarland, 2000), 43; Davids, "Chronological Registry of 19th Century Black Players in Organized Baseball," in White, *History of Colored Base Ball, With Other Documents on the Early Black Game 1886–1936*, Jerry Malloy, editor (Lincoln: University of Nebraska Press, 1996), 162–168; Thorn and Palmer, *Total Baseball*, 1524, 1540.

3. Historian James E. Brunson III lists the St. Louis Brown Stockings (1870) and Chicago Uniques (1871) as among the first salaried clubs. James E. Brunson III, "William Albert 'Abe' Jones: Colored Baseballist and Old Chicago Settler, 1857–1931," *Black Ball* 5, no. 1 (Spring 2012): 59–60; *Charleston News and Courier*, March 25, 1886; Bill Plott, "The Southern League of Colored Base Ballists," *Baseball Research Journal* 3 (1974), SABR. org, accessed August 12, 2015, http://research.sabr.org/journals/archives/online/36-brj-1974; White, *History of Colored Base Ball*, 12.

4. *Philadelphia Inquirer*, September 4, 1869; Anthony DiFiore, "Advancing African American Baseball: The Philadelphia Pythians and Interracial Competition in 1869," in *Black Ball* 1, no. 1 (2008): 60–61, 64; Scott

Simkus, *Outsider Baseball* (Chicago: Chicago Review Press, 2014), 266. From 1900–1948, black squads went 309–268–20 (.534) against MLB; 771–560–38 (.577) while facing minor league baseball clubs; 2279–1020–70 (.687) versus semi-pros; and 33–7 (.825) against college teams, for a grand total of 3392–1855–128 (.643).

5. *Chicago Tribune*, October 1, 1900; *Los Angeles Times*, October 8, 1948. Although designated as a minor league, the 1900 American League contained a higher percentage of Major League-caliber players than either the 1882 American Association or 1884 Union Association had in their inaugural Major League campaigns. Marshall D. Wright, *Nineteenth Century Baseball: Year-by-Year Statistics for the Major League Teams, 1871 through 1900* (Jefferson, NC: McFarland, 1996), 318. After integration, Negro League baseball declined precipitously in quality of play, leading to the demise of the NNL in 1948. By 1951, the surviving Negro American League was considered a Class C-equivalent circuit. Scott Simkus, "Superstar Integration Model," *Outsider Baseball Bulletin* 2, no. 57: 1–2, Outsiderbaseball.com, accessed August 25, 2015, http://www.i70baseball.com/wp-content/uploads/Outsider-Baseball-Bulletin-070611.pdf.

6. Thomas Barthel, *Baseball Barnstorming and Exhibition Games 1901–1962* (Jefferson, NC: McFarland, 2007), 75; *Baltimore Afro American*, October 27, 1917; *New York Tribune*, October 25, 1922.

7. *Sporting Life*, November 6, 1909; Barthel, *Baseball Barnstorming*, 56, 59.

8. *New York Sun*, November 5, 1916; Neil Lanctot, *Fair Dealing and Clean Playing: The Hilldale Club and the Development of Black Professional Baseball, 1910–1932* (Syracuse, NY: Syracuse University Press, 2007), 173–174; John Holway, *Voices from the Great Black Baseball Leagues* (Revised edition, New York: Da Capo Press, 1992), 4.

9. Barthel, *Baseball Barnstorming*, 94, 102; Tygiel, "Black Ball," in *Total Baseball*, 555; Donn Rogosin, *Invisible Men: Life in Baseball's Negro Leagues* (New York: Atheneum, 1983), 184.

10. *San Francisco Call*, March 20, 1913; John Holway, *Black Giants* (Springfield, VA: Lord Fairfax Press, 2010), 28; *New York Age*, October 23, 1920; *Chicago Defender*, July 27, 1918.

11. Clay Davenport, "Paper Giants," in *It Ain't Over 'Til It's Over: The Baseball Prospectus Pennant Race Book*, Steven Goldman, editor (New York: Basic Books, 2007), 122; *Washington Post*, April 13, 1889; Donald Honig, *Baseball When the Grass Was Real* (New York: Coward, McCann, and Geoghegan, 1975), 172.

12. *Chicago Defender*, October 12, 1918, October 14, 1933.

13. Robert Peterson, *Only the Ball Was White* (New York: Oxford University Press, 1992), 253; Simkus, *Outsider Baseball*, 265–266.

14. Rogosin, *Invisible Men*, 123–124.

15. James, *The Bill James Historical Baseball Abstract*, 81–82.

16. *Chicago Defender*, September 30, 1922; *New York Age*, October 17, 1925; Rob Ruck, *Raceball: How the Major Leagues Colonized the Black and Latin Game* (Boston: Beacon Press, 2011), 65; Barthel, 130.

17. *Chicago Defender*, September 24, 1932.

18. Seamheads.com Negro Leagues Database, "1913 Season,," accessed September 10, 2016, http://www.seamheads.com/NegroLgs/year.php?yearID=1913; Seamheads.com Negro Leagues Database, "1923 Season," accessed September 10, 2016, http://www.seamheads.com/NegroLgs/year.php?yearID=1923; Holway, *The Complete Book of Baseball's Negro Leagues*, 175, 179; James Overmyer, *Black Ball and The Boardwalk: The Bacharach Giants of Atlantic City, 1916–1929* (Jefferson, NC: McFarland, 2014), 210.

19. John Thorn and Pete Palmer, *The Hidden Game Of Baseball: A Revolutionary Approach to Baseball and its Statistics* (Garden City, NY: Doubleday, 1985), 177–178.

20. Rany Jazayerli, "The Break," in *It Ain't Over 'Til It's Over*, 304–307; Clark and Lester, *The Negro Leagues Book*, 159–164.

21. Ruck, *Raceball*, 58, 69, 71, 93–96; Neil Lanctot, *Negro League Baseball: The Rise and Ruin of a Black Institution* (Philadelphia: University of Pennsylvania Press, 2004), 144.

22. Rob Neyer, "Was the Federal League Really a Major League?" thenationalpastimemuseum.com. November 28, 2012, accessed August 26, 2015, http://www.thenationalpastimemuseum.com/article/was-federal-league-really-major-league; *New York Press*, October 5, 1914; October 4, 1915; Paul Debono, *The Chicago American Giants* (Jefferson, NC: McFarland, 2007), 226.

23. Clark and Lester, *The Negro Leagues Book*, 255; David S. Neft, Richard M. Cohen, and Michael L. Neft, *The Sports Encyclopedia: Baseball 2000* (New York: St. Martin's Griffin, 2000), 92, 94, 102, 237, 247, 250, 253; Baseball-Reference.com, "Jose Acosta," accessed June 27, 2017, http://www.baseball-reference.com/players/a/acostjo01.shtml; Baseball-Reference.com, "Pedro Dibut," accessed June 27, 2017, http://www.baseball-reference.com/players/d/dibutpe01.shtml; Baseball-Reference.com, "Oscar Estrada," accessed June 27, 2017, http://www.baseball-reference.com/players/e/estraos01.shtml; Seamheads.com Negro Leagues Database, "History, All Time, Batting," accessed June 26, 2017, http://www.seamheads.com/NegroLgs/history.php?tab=bat_basic_at; Seamheads.com Negro Leagues Database, "History, All Time, Pitching," accessed June 26, 2017; http://www.seamheads.com/NegroLgs/history.php?first=1896&last=1944&tab=pit_basic_at.

24. Larry Lester, E-mail message to author, December 21, 2017; Holway, *Voices from the Great Black Baseball Leagues*, 131.

25. Holway, Voices from the Great Black Baseball Leagues, 119, 120.

26. John Holway, *Black Diamonds: Life in the Negro Leagues from the Men Who Lived It* (New York: Stadium Books, 1991), 72.

27. *Harrisburg Patriot*, April 23, 1906; *Scranton Truth*, April 26, 1909; *Boston Herald*, April 18, 1911; *La Crosse Chronicle*, May 9, 1909; May 10, 1910; April 30, 1911.

28. *New York Age*, February 5, 1914; *Chicago Defender*, April 11, 1914.

29. Larry Lester and Sammy Miller, *Black Baseball In Kansas City* (San Francisco: Arcadia, 2000), 6–7; *Baltimore Afro American*, October 15, 1927; Danny Wild, "Minors, Negro Leagues Grew Together: Rickwood Field One of Several Ballparks with Storied Histories,"MILB.com, accessed November 17, 2016, http://www. milb.com/news/article.jsp?ymd=20100201&content_id=8004320&fext=.jsp&vkey=news_milb; Lanctot, *Negro League Baseball*, 200–201; Rogosin, *Invisible Men*, 185.

30. TerryB, comment on jalbright, "Two Sources of Negro League Stats Online," Baseball-Fever.com, accessed August 12, 2015; Peterson, *Only the Ball Was White*, 81; McNeil, *Baseball's Other All-Stars*, 189, 195–196; William F. McNeil, *The California Winter League: America's First Integrated Professional Baseball League* (Jefferson, NC: McFarland, 2002), 240, 306.

31. These totals do not include the 28 Negro Leaguers who entered Organized Baseball in the 1960s, or the handful of players who started out in Organized Baseball before ending up in NLB. The number of Negro Leaguers who reached Triple A or the Majors was 129. Four players (Hank Aaron, Ernie Banks, Willard Brown, and John Kennedy) did not participate in Triple A. Clark and Lester, *The Negro Leagues Book*, 255–256, 262–336; Negro Southern League Museum Research Center, "Negro League Player Register," accessed April 1, 2018, http://www.negrosouthernleaguemuseumresearchcenter.org/Portals/0/Birmingham%20Player%20 Profiles/A-B.pdf.

32. Tygiel, "Black Ball," in *Total Baseball*, 559; Larry Moffi and Jonathan Kronstadt, *Crossing the Line: Black Major Leaguers, 1947–1959* (Jefferson, NC: McFarland, 1994), 4, 105.

33. Clark and Lester, *The Negro Leagues Book*, 262–336; Lee Lowenfish, "The Rise of Baseball's Quota System in the 1950s," *NINE: A Journal Of Baseball History And Culture* 16, no. 2 (Spring 2008): 53.

34. Moffi and Kronstadt, *Crossing the Line: Black Major Leaguers, 1947–1959*, 105.

35. Clark and Lester, *The Negro Leagues Book*, 313–336; Tygiel, "Black Ball," in *Total Baseball*, 561; Joel Zoss and John Bowman, *Diamonds in the Rough: The Untold Story of Baseball* (Lincoln: University of Nebraska Press, 2004), 188.

36. Thorn and Palmer with Reuther, *Total Baseball*, "Total Baseball Ranking," 2041; ESPN.com, "ESPN's Hall of 100," accessed December 15, 2016, http://www.espn.com/mlb/feature/video/_/id/8652210/espn-hall-100-ranking-all-greatest-mlb-players; Baseball-Reference.com, "Baseball Hall of Fame Inductees," accessed December 15, 2016, http://www.baseball-reference.com/awards/hof.shtml; Larry Lester, E-mail message to author, June 25, 2018; Neft, Cohen, and Neft, *The Sports Encyclopedia: Baseball 2000*, 752.

37. Phil Dixon with Patrick J. Hannigan, "Major and Minor League Titles 1946–1955," in *The Negro Baseball Leagues: A Photographic History* (Mattituck, NY: Amereon House, 1992); Clark and Lester, *The Negro Leagues Book*, 262–336; Baseball-Reference.com, "Yearly League Leaders & Records for Total Bases," accessed December 22, 2016, http://www.baseball-reference.com/leaders/TB_leagues.shtml; Baseball-Reference.com, "Yearly League Leaders & Records for Hit By Pitch," accessed December 22, 2016, http://www.baseball-reference.com/leaders/HBP_leagues.shtml; Zoss and Bowman, *Diamonds in the Rough*, 171; Holway, *Black Diamonds*, 72–73.

38. The number of first-generation black players to reach Triple A or the Majors was 70. Frank Robinson and Tony Taylor never played in the three high minor league circuits, but had long careers in MLB. Clark and Lester, *The Negro Leagues Book*, 255–256; 262–236; Moffi and Kronstadt, *Crossing the Line: Black Major Leaguers*, 3, 10.

39. Tygiel, "Black Ball," in *Total Baseball*, 560–561; Zoss and Bowman, *Diamonds in the Rough*, 187; Michael J. Haupert, "Pay, Performance, And Race During The Integration Era," *Black Ball* 2, no. 1 (Spring 2009): 50; Lowenfish, "The Rise of Baseball's Quota System in the 1950s," 53. The Dodgers (1951, 1959); Giants (1951); and Braves (1959) also participated in the two league playoffs during this time frame. Neft, Cohen, and Neft, *The Sports Encyclopedia: Baseball 2000*, 720.

40. Dixon with Hannigan, "Major and Minor League Titles 1946–1955," in *The Negro Baseball Leagues: A Photographic History;* Baseball-Reference.com, "1959 American Association Batting Leaders," accessed December 22, 2016, http://www.baseball-reference.com/register/leader.cgi?type=bat&id=ecc4882f; Baseball-Reference. com, "1959 International League Batting Leaders," accessed December 22, 2016, http://www.baseball-reference. com/register/leader.cgi?type=bat&id=2dece84d; Baseball-Reference.com, 1959 Pacific Coast League Batting Leaders," accessed December 22, 2016,http://www.baseball-reference.com/register/leader.cgi?type=bat&id-=8363447e.

41. Holway, *Voices from the Great Black Baseball Leagues*, 1; Baseball-Reference.com, "Yearly League Leaders & Records for Slugging %," accessed December 22, 2016, http://www:baseball-reference.com/leaders/ slugging_perc_leagues.shtml: Baseball-Reference.com, "Yearly League Leaders & Records for Batting Average," accessed December 22, 2016, http;//www.baseball-reference.com/leaders/batting_avg_leagues.shtml; Baseball-Reference.com, "Yearly League Leaders & Records for Stolen Bases," accessed December 22, 2016, http://www.baseball-reference.com/leaders/SB_leagues.shtml.

42. Baseball-Reference.com, "Career Leaders & Records for Total Bases," accessed December 22, 2016, http://www.baseball-reference.com/leaders/TB_career.shtml; Baseball-Reference.com, "Career Leaders &

Records for Home Runs," accessed December 22, 2016, http://www.baseball-reference.com/leaders/HR_career. shtml; Scott Boeck, "Albert Pujols Earns 3,000 Hit, Joining A-Rod, Hank Aaron, Willie Mays in Exclusive Club," USA Today.com, accessed May 24, 2018, https://www.usatoday.com/story/sports/mlb/2018/05/04/angels-albert-pujols-3000-hits-600-home-runs/557984002/.

43. Mark L. Armour and Daniel R. Levitt, *In Pursuit of Pennants: Baseball Operations from Deadball to Moneyball* (Lincoln: University of Nebraska Press, 2015), 136–137; Mark Armour, "The Effects of Integration, 1947–1986," *The Baseball Research Journal* 36 (2007): 57.

44. Frederick Ivor-Campbell, "The All-Star Game," in *Total Baseball*, 250–257; Min S. Yee, editor and Donald K. Wright, designer, *The Sports Book: An Unabashed Assemblage of Heroes, Strategies, Records, and Events* (New York: Holt, Rinehart, and Winston, 1975), 39; Holway, *Voices from the Great Black Baseball Leagues*, 1.

45. John Holway, e-mail message to author, September 9, 2015; Jim Overmyer e-mail message to author, September 9, 2015; TerryB, September 28, 2013, comment on Jalbright, "Two Sources of Negro League Stats Online," Baseball-Fever.com, September 4, 2013, accessed August 12, 2015, http://www.baseball-fever.com/ showthread.php?39148-Negro-Leagues-vs-Major Leagues&s=6086b28ebc6e705636848c4fc10aa990.

46. Wikipedia.com, "Historical Racial and Ethnic Demographics of the United States," accessed December 8, 2016, https://en.wikipedia.org/wiki/Historical_racial_and_ethnic_demographics_of_the_United_States; Richard Lapchick with Craig Malveaux, Erin Davison and Caryn Grant, "The 2016 Racial and Gender Report Card: National Football League," Tidesport.org. September 28, 2016, accessed December 8, 2016,http://www. tidesport.org/nfl-rgrc.html; Richard Lapchick with Theren Bullock, Jr, "The 2016 Racial and Gender Report Card: National Basketball Association," Tidesport.org. July 14, 2016, accessed December 8, 2016,http://www. tidesport.org/racial-and-gender-report-cards.html.

47. Moffi and Kronstadt, *Crossing the Line: Black Major Leaguers*, 3; Mark Armour and Daniel R. Levitt, *Ethnicity Totals by Year, 1947–2014*, data file included in e-mail message to author, November 10, 2016.

48. Tygiel, "Black Ball," in *Total Baseball*, 561; Lowenfish, "The Rise of Baseball's Quota System in the 1950s," 52–54; Ryan Cortes, "On This Day in 1971, the Pittsburgh Pirates Fielded the First All-Black and Latino Lineup," The Undefeated.com, accessed January 7, 2017, http://theundefeated.com/features/on-this-day-in-1971-the-pittsburgh-pirates-fielded-the-first-all-black-lineup/; Mark Armour and Daniel R. Levitt, "Baseball Demographics, 1947–2012," SABR.org, accessed August 11,2015, http://sabr.org/bioproj/ topic/baseball-demogaphics-1947-2012.

49. Armour and Levitt, *Ethnicity Totals By Year, 1947–2014*; Richard Lapchick, "The 2016 Racial and Gender Report Card: Major League Baseball," Tidesport.org, 2016, accessed December 8, 2016, http://www. tidesport.org/mlb-rgrc.html; Richard Lapchick, "The 2019 Racial and Gender Report Card: Major League Baseball," Tidesport.org, 2019, accessed August 23, 2019, http://www.tidesport.org/mlb-rgrc.html.

50. Lanctot, *Negro League Baseball*, 72, 156, 429; Peterson, *Only the Ball Was White*, 91; Clark and Lester, *The Negro Leagues Book*, 78, 98, 102, 116, 118, 126, 136, 138; Michael E. Lomax, *Black Baseball Entrepreneurs 1902–1931: The Negro National and Eastern Colored Leagues* (Syracuse, NY: Syracuse University Press, 2014), 223, 224, 226, 228, 229, 234, 235, 237, 238.

51. Armour and Levitt, "Baseball Demographics, 1947–2012,"; Ray Glier, "MLB Takes Notice as Percentage of Black Players in Baseball Remains Low," Aljazeera.com, accessed August 24, 2016, http://america. aljazeera.com/articles/2014/3/28/mlb-takes-noticeaspercentageofblackplayersinbaseballremainslow.html; Ruck, *Raceball*, 180–181; McNeil, *Baseball's Other All-Stars*, 46, 61.

52. Armour and Levitt, "Baseball Demographics, 1947–2012."

53. Sporting Life, September 1, 1906; Sporting News, December 6, 1923.

54. Peterson, *Only the Ball Was White*, 173.

55. Brian Carroll, "A Tribute To Wendell Smith," *Black Ball* 2, no. 1 (Spring 2009): 6–7; *Pittsburgh Courier*, July 15, 22, 29, August 5, 12, 19, 26, September 2, 1939.

56. *Pittsburgh Courier*, August 19, 1939, March 8, 1941; Frank Leland, *Frank Leland's Baseball Club* (Chicago: Fraternal Printing, 1910), 12.

57. Holway, *Black Giants*, 30; *Oakland Tribune*, January 27, 1936; Donald Spivey, *"If You Were Only White": The Life of Leroy "Satchel" Paige* (Columbia, MO: University of Missouri Press, 2012), 119; Larry Tye, *Satchel: The Life and Times of an American Legend* (New York: Random House, 2009), 96–97.

58. Tom Singer, "Teddy Ballgame Makes Difference for Negro Leaguers to Enter Hall," MLB.com, accessed January 9, 2017, http://mlb.mlb.com/mlb/history/mlb_negro_leagues_story.jsp?story=williams_ted, 2001; Spivey, *"If You Were Only White,"*274–276; Tye, *Satchel*, 268–270; Holway, *Black Giants*, xi.

59. *New York Times*, September 12, 1988, August 30, 1993; *Wall Street Journal*, September 14, 1988; *Pittsburgh Post-Gazette*, August 30, 1993.

60. Claire Smith, "Belated Tribute to Baseball's Negro Leagues," *New York Times*, August 13, 1991; Claire Smith, "On Baseball: A Dream is Dead. A Deed Survives." *New York Times*, July 28, 1992; *Greenwood Index Journal*, August 10, 1993.

61. Murray Chass, "Pioneer Black Players to be Granted Pensions." *New York Times*, January 20, 1997.

62. Chass, *New York Times*, January 20, 1997; Michael O'keefe, "Righting Wrongs Denied Opportunity, Negro Leaguers Seek Pension, Respect," *New York Daily News*, September 8, 2005.

63. Dan Steinberg, "MLB Agrees to Make Payments to Negro League Players," *Washington Post*, May 15,

2004; Adrien Martin. "Pensions Paid to Former Negro League Players not Discriminatory." Plainsponsor.com, accessed February 2, 2016, http://www.plansponsor.com/Pensions-Paid-to-Former-Negro-League-Players-not-Discriminatory/.

64. Jeffrey Flanagan, "Just Like Old Times: Royals Win Wearing Uniforms of '24 Monarchs, Kansas City Beats A's, Extends its Streak to 12 Straight," *Kansas City Star*, August 4, 1994.

65. *Pittsburgh Post-Gazette*. June 30, 2002; Scott Priestle, "Throw Johnson Back? Pitcher Lousy in Loss," *Columbus Dispatch*, May 21, 2006; *Annapolis Capital*, May 4, 2008; Duane Harris, "Satchel Vs Josh, Charlie Hustle, The Nationals as the Grays, Big Klu, Jackie, Pee-Wee," Ninety Feet Of Perfection.com, accessed January 9, 2017, https://90feetofperfection.com/2011/02/09/satchel-vs-josh-charlie-hustle-the-nationals-as-the-grays-big-klu-jackie-pee-wee/.

66. *Annapolis Capital*, May 4, 2008; Chuck Klosterman, "The Case For Throwback Baseball Uniforms," *New York Times Magazine*, January 9, 2015; Royal Heritage, "Royals in Monarchs Duds: Interview with Curt Nelson," Kcbbh.blogspot.com, accessed January 17, 2017, http://kcbbh.blogspot.com/2010/07/royals-in-monarchs-duds-interview-with.html.

67. Rob Neyer, "Was the Federal League Really a Major League?"; Lanctot, *Negro League Baseball*, 185, 188; Lanctot, *Fair Dealing and Clean Playing*, 232.

68. *Trenton Times*, November 3, 1887; Phil Dixon, American Baseball Chronicles: Great Teams: The 1931 Homestead Grays Volume One. (Bloomington, IN: Xlibris, 2009), 33, 326–338.

Measuring Equality

A Statistical Comparison of the Negro Leagues to the Major Leagues Based on the 1925 Season

RICHARD J. PUERZER

Introduction

When comparing the quality of play in the Negro Leagues to the Major Leagues, it is impossible not to consider performance statistics. Statistics are an inextricable component of professional baseball. However, until recently statistics have also been a hindrance to evaluating the performance of players in the Negro Leagues. It can be argued that the lack of solid data has generally undermined the perception of the quality of play in the black ball circuits. And when statistics are available, they are reasonably called into question as sample sizes are usually quite small. However, in recent years more reliable statistical information on the Negro Leagues has come available. Several websites, such as the Seamheads Negro League Database, have brought this information online for study.

Methodology

The approach taken in this inquiry was to compare the Negro Leagues and the Major Leagues based on data from the 1925 season. In 1925, there were two separate circuits, the Eastern Colored League and the Negro National League, making up what we today call the Negro Leagues. Each of these leagues had eight teams, and all 16 clubs played quite a few games. They did not play as many contests as Major League squads, but 1925 is as comparable as any year in history. For this essay, the Seamheads Negro League Database was utilized for statistics concerning the Negro Leagues, while Baseball-Reference.com was consulted for Major League data. It is important to note that Seamheads' 1925 season information is virtually complete, a unique occurrence in Negro Leagues research.[1]

The approach taken was to compare the population of Negro League players to that of Major League players in terms of common batting and pitching performance measures. That is, a data set of all players from each league, based on a minimum number of plate appearances for batters and innings pitched for pitchers, was generated. Then the mean, standard deviation, and shape of the distributions of performance data were compared. These comparisons were done utilizing standard procedures for evaluating the similarity of these two data sets. This study is not just a study of average performance, but of both the average and variation.

Comparison of Batting Averages of the Two Leagues

In 1925, 213 players in the Negro National League and Eastern Colored League had more than 40 plate appearances. Two batters cracked the .400 mark, with the highest average belonging to Oscar Charleston, who hit .427 for the Harrisburg Giants, followed by John Beckwith, who mashed .408 for the Baltimore Black Sox.[2]

Likewise, 340 major league players had 40 or more plate appearances. These players, of course, also came from 16 teams making up the American and National Leagues. Only one batter, Rogers Hornsby of the St. Louis Cardinals, hit over .400 and qualified for the batting title. Hornsby hit .403. However, when looking at the data set of batters with more than 40 plate appearances, Walter Johnson, the Washington Senators' star pitcher, batted .433 in 107 plate appearances.[3]

A box and whiskers plot of the two data sets is presented in Figure 3.1, and a summary of the batting average data sets is listed in Table 3.1. A box and whiskers plot provides a box representing the middle two quartiles, or 50 percent, of the data set, and "whiskers" or lines emanating from the box which represent the minimum and maximum values of the data set. The average of the data set is also displayed. These plots are used to provide a graphical representation of the spread, or variation, found in a data set. The box and whiskers plot for batting averages of the two leagues shows how similar they are in both the average and variation of the data.

Figure 3.1 Box and Whiskers Plot of Player Batting Averages

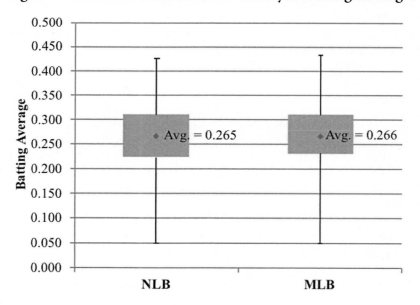

Table 3.1 Summary of 1925 Batting Average Data

League	Players	Mean BA	Standard Deviation of BA
NLB	213	.26556	.062697
MLB	340	.26688	.064431

Sources for Figure 3.1 and Table 3.1: Baseball-Reference.com; Seamheads.com Negro Leagues Database.

The difference between the average batting average of the two leagues was 0.00132. Likewise the spread of the data, as measured by the standard deviation of the batting averages of the two leagues, was also very similar, with a difference between the two values of only 0.001734.

In addition to simply comparing the means of the two leagues, a statistical test can be used to calculate if there is a statistically significant difference between the two values. An appropriate test in this case is a two-tailed Z-test, which is used to compare the equality of two proportions. This test showed that the batting averages of the two leagues were not significantly different (with a p-value of 0.97277). P-value is a measure of the probability of the equality. The closer the p-value is to zero, the less likely the two values are equal, while the closer the p-value is to one, the more likely the values are equal. In this test, the value is relatively close to one, indicating a high likelihood of equality.

Comparison of Slugging Percentages for the Two Leagues

Using the same data set of players, another measure of batting prowess, slugging percentage, was also analyzed. As with batting average, the two leading Negro Leagues hitters in terms of slugging percentage were Oscar Charleston and John Beckwith, who slugged .776 and .732 respectively. Likewise, Rogers Hornsby led the Majors by slugging .756, followed by St. Louis Browns outfielder Ken Williams, who slugged .613.[4]

A box and whiskers plot of the two data sets is presented in Figure 3.2 and a summary of the slugging percentage data sets is listed in Table 3.2.

**Figure 3.2 Box and Whiskers Plot of
Player Slugging Percentages**

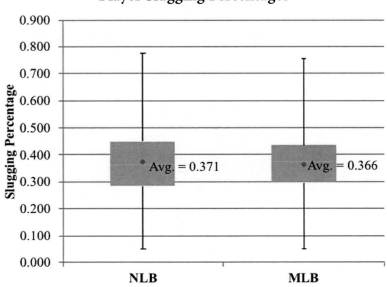

Table 3.2 Summary of 1925 Slugging Percentage Data

League	Players	Mean SLG	Standard Deviation of SLG
NLB	213	.370486	.015195
MLB	340	.366525	.012130

Sources for Figure 3.2 and Table 3.2: Baseball-Reference.com; Seamheads.com Negro Leagues Database.

The difference between the average slugging percentage of the two leagues was 0.003961. Likewise the spread of the data, as measured by the standard deviation of the batting averages of the two leagues, was also very similar, with a difference between the two values of only 0.003065. A two-tailed t-test, used to compare the equality of two means, showed that the slugging percentages of the two leagues were not significantly different (with a p-value of 0.695125, a value relatively close to one).

Comparison of Earned Run Average for the Two Leagues

An analysis of pitching data from 1925, as measured by Earned Run Average (ERA), does not show the same similarities between the two leagues. In 1925, 91 Negro Leaguers and 138 Major Leaguers pitched more than 30 innings. The two leading pitchers in the Negro Leagues, in terms of ERA, were Willie Foster, who split his time between the Chicago American Giants and the Birmingham Black Barons, with an ERA of 1.62 in 78 innings pitched, and Wilber "Bullet" Rogan of the Kansas City Monarchs, with an ERA of 1.99 in 181⅓ innings pitched. It is notable that there is a gap of nearly a full run between Rogan and his teammate Nelson Dean, the next-best pitcher in terms of ERA, who posted a mark of 2.87. In the Major Leagues, the best performance for a pitcher by Dolf Luque of the Cincinnati Reds, with an ERA of 2.63.[5]

A box and whiskers plot of the two data sets is presented in Figure 3.3, and a summary of the earned run average data sets is listed in Table 3.3.

Figure 3.3 Box and Whiskers Plot of Earned Run Average Data

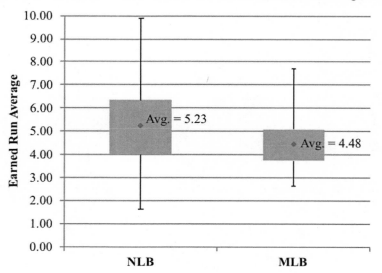

Table 3.3 Summary of 1925 Earned Run Average Data

League	Pitchers	Mean ERA	Standard Deviation of ERA
NLB	91	5.23154	1.69447
MLB	138	4.48299	1.01019

Sources for Figure 3.3 and Table 3.3: Baseball-Reference.com; Seamheads.com Negro Leagues Database.

The difference between the average ERAs of the two leagues was 0.749365 runs. Likewise the spread of the data, as measured by the standard deviation of the ERAs of the two leagues, was quite different, with a difference between the two values of 0.68793. A two-tailed t-test, used to compare the equality of two means, showed that the earned run averages of the two leagues were significantly different (with a p-value of less than 0.001, indicating a high likelihood of a significant difference in value), with the Major Leagues having the lower, and thus better value.

So while the hitting performance for the two leagues was very similar, the pitching performance, at least in terms of ERA, seems far different. In looking at the overall performance of the two leagues, the Negro Leagues had an overall ERA of 5.04, while the Majors had an overall ERA of 4.33. The Major Leagues were clearly more consistent, as reflected by the smaller variation in the data. This difference in ERA likely represents greater variance in the pitching talent in the Negro Leagues.[6]

However, this difference in the equality of pitching given the commonality in hitting performance is counterintuitive—how can there be a difference in one but not the other? One explanation was that there were considerably more unearned runs in the Major Leagues than in the Negro Leagues. In the Majors, 5.13 runs were scored per game, of which 16.61 percent were unearned (2,093 unearned runs out of a total of 12,595). On the other hand, in the Negro Leagues only 11.8 percent of the runs scored were unearned (614 unearned runs out of 5,217).[7]

This appears to be a systematic difference between the two leagues, most likely caused by dissimilar scorekeeping methods. The Major Leagues employed official scorekeepers, who assigned errors based on predetermined standards. On the other hand, the scorekeeping in the Negro Leagues, including the assignment of errors during the game, was a task handled on a more ad hoc basis by newspaper reporters, team officials, or even players. This would lead to a significantly different and usually less stringent approach to the assignment of errors.[8]

Comparison of Walks Plus Hits per Inning Pitched for the Two Leagues

Curiously, although the average ERA in the Negro Leagues was higher than the Majors, the average measure of the sum of walks and hits divided by innings pitched (WHIP) was lower. Bullet Rogan and Willie Foster both finished with a Negro Leagues–best WHIP of 1.00, although Rogan pitched over twice as many innings as Foster. Andy Cooper of the Detroit Stars was next with a WHIP of 1.08. In the Majors, Dolf Luque had a WHIP of 1.17, followed closely by "Dazzy" Vance of the Brooklyn Dodgers at 1.18.[9]

A box and whiskers plot of the two data sets is presented in Figure 3.4, and a summary of the data sets is listed in Table 3.4.

Figure 3.4 Box and Whiskers Plot of WHIP Data

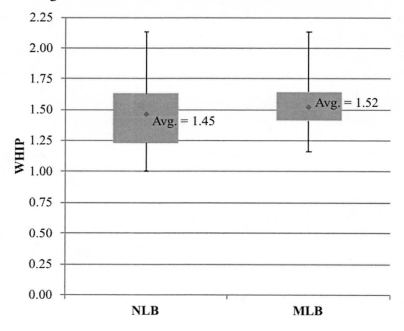

Table 3.4 Summary of 1925 WHIP Data

League	Pitchers	Average WHIP	Standard Deviation of WHIP
NLB	91	1.458352	0.253869
MLB	138	1.526572	0.187963

Sources for Figure 3.4 and Table 3.4: Baseball-Reference.com; Seamheads.com Negro Leagues Database.

The difference between the average WHIPs of the two leagues was 0.068221, a relatively small difference. Likewise the spread of the data, as measured by the standard deviation of the WHIPs of the two leagues, was quite similar, with a difference between the two values of only 0.029119. From the box and whiskers plot, it can be seen that the Negro Leagues had a larger variation in the data, but a lower average.

A two-tailed t-test, used to compare the equality of two means, showed that the WHIPs of the two leagues were significantly different (with a p-value of 0.0205, indicating a high probability of a difference), with the Negro Leagues having the smaller, or better value.

When evaluating the pitching in the two leagues, based on ERA, the Majors performed better. But when evaluating based on WHIP, the Negro Leagues performed better. Essentially this analysis shows the general equality and similarity in the balance of pitching and hitting in both leagues.

A Comparison of Offensive Statistics for the Two Leagues

Major League teams scored an average of 5.13 runs per game in 1925, while Negro Leagues squads tallied 5.63 runs per contest. While the amount of scoring was about the same, a close inspection of some basic offensive statistics reveals fundamental differences in the two circuits' style of play (Table 3.5).[10]

Table 3.5 Summary of 1925 Offensive Data

	H/G	D/G	T/G	HR/G	BB/G	SH/G	SB/G
NLB	9.46	1.42	0.49	0.54	3.06	1.29	0.94
MLB	10.14	1.77	0.48	0.48	3.15	1.04	0.57

Sources for Table 3.5: Baseball-Reference.com; Seamheads.com Negro Leagues Database.

Major League batters got on base more often during the 1925 season and smacked more doubles, while the Negro Leaguers stole more bases and placed greater emphasis on the sacrifice. Balls were hit out of the park more frequently in the Negro Leagues, but the home run was still not the primary means of scoring in either league. Rogers Hornsby led the Majors with 39 home runs in 138 games. However, Hornsby's 0.282 HR/game average was nearly identical to that of Oscar Charleston, who led the Negro Leagues with 20 home runs in 71 contests. The batters in both leagues racked up a similar number of three-base hits. In fact, in the Major Leagues there were more triples (1,171) than home runs (1,169).[11]

Results and Conclusions

The results of this data analysis indicate that the performance of players in the two leagues, based on both hitting and pitching rate-based statistics, was remarkably similar and balanced. While there was generally slightly more variation in the Negro Leagues data, indicating a greater range in the skills between the best and worst players, the variation was not considerably greater than in the Major Leagues. Overall, the comparison of the statistics of both leagues, with a focus on the distribution of ability, demonstrates that the pool of talent in both leagues was about equal. Therefore, this predicts that not only would the best players in each league do just as well in the other league, it also forecasts that the average players in each league would likewise be average in the other league. Given that the distribution of talent in both leagues in 1925 was similar to that in any other year, the conclusion that the Negro Leagues were equal to the Major Leagues is readily drawn.

Notes

1. All of the teams in the Major Leagues were scheduled to play 154 games. The Seamheads Negro Leagues Database has statistics for as many as 100 games for the Detroit Stars and 98 games for the Chicago American Giants in the Negro National League, as well as 74 games for the Atlantic City Bacharach Giants and 72 games for the Harrisburg Giants of the Eastern Colored League, Seamheads.com Negro Leagues Database, "1925 Season," https://www.seamheads.com/NegroLgs/year.php?yearID=1925&tab=1a; Baseball-Reference.com, "1925 MLB Team Statistics," http://www.baseball-reference.com/leagues/MLB/1925.shtml.

2. Seamheads.com Negro Leagues Database, "1925 Season, Batting, At Bats," accessed May 2017, http://www.seamheads.com/NegroLgs/year.php?yearID=1925&tab=bat_basic&lgID=All&bats=All&pos=All&qual=All&sort=PA_a; Seamheads.com Negro Leagues Database, "1925 Season, Batting, Batting Average," accessed May 2017, http://www.seamheads.com/NegroLgs/year.php?yearID=1925&tab=bat_basic&lgID+All&bats=All&pos=All&qual=All&sort=BA_a.

3. Baseball-Reference.com, "1925 MLB Player Standard Batting, Plate Appearances," accessed May 2017, http://www.baseball-reference.com/leagues/MLB/1925-standard-batting.shtml; Baseball-Reference.com, "1925 MLB Player Standard Batting, Hits/At Bats," accessed May 2017, http://www.baseball-reference.com/leagues/MLB/1925-standard-batting.shtml.

4. Seamheads.com Negro Leagues Database, "1925 Season, Batting, Slugging Percentage," accessed May

2017 http://www.seamheads.com/NegroLgs/year.php?yearID=1925&tab=bat_basic&lgID=All&bats=All&pos=All&qual=All&sort=SLG_a; Baseball-Reference.com, "1925 MLB Player Standard Batting, Total Bases/At Bats," accessed May 2017, http://www.baseball-reference.com/leagues/MLB/1925-standard-batting.shtml.

5. Seamheads.com Negro Leagues Database, "1925 Season, Pitching, Innings Pitched," accessed May 2017 http://www.seamheads.com/NegroLgs/year.php?yearID=1925&tab=pit_basic&lgID=All&qual=Y&role=All&sort=IP_a; Seamheads.com Negro Leagues Database, "1925 Season, Pitching, Earned Run Average," accessed May 2017 http://www.seamheads.com/NegroLgs/year.php?yearID=1925&tab=pit_basic&lgID=All&role=All&throws=All&qual=All&sort=ERA_a; Baseball-Reference.com, "1925 MLB Player Standard Pitching, Innings Pitched," accessed May 2017, http://www.baseball-reference.com/leagues/MLB/1925-standard-pitching.shtml; Baseball-Reference.com, "1925 MLB Player Standard Pitching, ERA," accessed May 2017, http://www.baseball-reference.com/leagues/MLB/1925-standard-pitching.shtml.

6. Seamheads.com Negro Leagues Database, "1925 Season, Pitching," accessed May 2017; http://www.seamheads.com/NegroLgs/year.php?yearID=1925&lgID=All&tab=pit_basic; Baseball-Reference.com, "1925 MLB Team Standard Pitching, ERA," accessed May 2017, http://www.baseball-reference.com/leagues/MLB/-1925-standard-pitching.shtml.

7. Seamheads.com Negro Leagues Database, "1925 Season, Pitching," accessed May 2017; http://www.seamheads.com/NegroLgs/year.php?yearID=1925&lgID=All&tab=pit_basic; Baseball-Reference.com, "1925 MLBTeam Standard Pitching," accessed May 2017, http://www.baseball-reference.com/leagues/MLB/1925-standard-pitching.shtml.

8. On the Homestead Grays a bench-player kept score, but as Buck Leonard noted, "maybe he didn't know how….or in the middle of the game, he'd have to go in…and some other player would have to finish the box score," Lanctot, *Negro League Baseball*, 142.

9. Seamheads.com Negro Leagues Database, "1925 Season, Pitching, Walks + Hits per Innings Pitched," accessed May 2017; http://www.seamheads.com/NegroLgs/year.php?yearID=1925&tab=pit_adv&IgID=All&Y&role=All&sort=WHIP_a; Baseball-Reference.com, "1925 MLB Player Standard Pitching, WHIP," accessed May2017, http://www.baseball-reference.com/leagues/MLB/1925-standard-pitching.shtml.

10. Seamheads.com Negro Leagues Database, "1925 Season, Batting," accessed May 2017, http://www.seamheads.com/NegroLgs/year.php?yearID=1925&lgID=All&tab=bat_basic; Baseball-Reference.com, "1925 MLB Team Standard Batting," accessed May 2017, http://www.baseball-reference.com/leagues/MLB/1925-standard-batting.shtml.

11. Baseball-Reference.com, "1925 MLB Player Standard Batting, Home Runs Hit/Allowed," accessed May 2017, http://www.baseball-reference.com/leagues/MLB/1925-standard-batting.shtml; Seamheads.com Negro Leagues Database , "1925 Season, Batting, Homeruns," http://www.seamheads.com/NegroLgs/year.php?yearID=1925&tab=bat_basic&lgID=All&bats=All&pos=All&qual=Y&sort=HR_a; Baseball-Reference.com, "1925 MLB Team Standard Batting," accessed May 2017, http://www.baseball-reference.com/leagues/MLB/1925-standard-batting.shtml.

Gray Area

Homestead vs. the Minor Leagues

Scott Simkus

On Monday, October 18, 1926, one week after the St. Louis Cardinals defeated Babe Ruth's New York Yankees in the World Series, Judge Kenesaw Mountain Landis made an announcement shocking the baseball world. Beginning the next season, one Negro team, managed and owned by a Negro businessman, would be permitted to enter the Class D Middle Atlantic League. This was a move intended to help "change our culture," explained Landis. "Not just baseball culture, but our national culture, our society." There was said to be an audible gasp at the press conference, inside Landis's cramped Chicago office.

Commissioner Landis explained that this process had secretly been in the works for more than two years and that beginning in 1927, the Homestead Grays of Pittsburgh, owned and operated by Mr. Cumberland Posey, would officially join an all-white Class D minor league. The Middle Atlantic League was selected because of its proximity to Pittsburgh, which would remain the Grays' home base. Most of the teams in the Middle Atlantic were located in Pennsylvania and West Virginia, with one in Maryland. All of them were either short train rides or bus trips from the Steel City, and after much deliberation, their owners had agreed to take part in this grand experiment.

This "process," as Landis repeatedly referred to it as, would include a mentoring program. All 16 Major League teams had agreed to provide modest financial support for the Grays, helping the club ramp up its operations to reflect the quality and professionalism expected in Organized Baseball, even at its lowest levels. Honus Wagner, the former Pittsburgh Pirates star, had been signed to help Cumberland Posey, serving as a bench coach for the Grays. Wagner, it was pointed out, had played minor league baseball with several Negro teammates back in the 1890s and was an admirer of nationally-known black stars such as John Henry Lloyd and Oscar Charleston.

Another Pittsburgh figure connected to the process was a young man named Art Rooney. Rooney was only 25 years old but had agreed to leave his capacity as player-manager of the Wheeling Stogies of the Middle Atlantic League to join the coaching staff of the Grays, serving as a sort of liaison, as he "knew the ropes," having played and managed in the league for a couple of seasons. Rooney would become nationally known later for founding the Pittsburgh Steelers professional football team in 1933. He was a Pittsburgher, he was ambitious, and he understood the sports business. Cumberland Posey, it would later be learned, was more excited about having Rooney as part of his team than Honus

Wagner, as Honus was known to spend a little bit too much time in local taverns, spinning yarns and sipping cold ones, instead of mentoring young players.[1]

The one thing never specified was the endgame. Landis never said specifically that he hoped the Homestead Grays would work their way up at some point, becoming a black-owned, all-black Major League club. Or was the goal to move them to Triple-A (using today's classification system), becoming a member of the International League or American Association, becoming a black-owned *feeder of talent* for an integrated Major Leagues? This was never really clarified.

I'll pause the narrative right here, because your jaw is probably lying on the floor. If you're somebody who *knows* your baseball history, knows the legend of Branch Rickey and Jackie Robinson, you're probably shocked that you've never heard this story before, right? Well, don't be. I made it up. All of it. This never happened. Commissioner Landis never held a press conference and never pursued such an initiative. Integrating professional baseball at any level never crossed his mind, at least not in an affirmative way. If he *had* been involved with something like this, had he been in favor of integrating the game 20 years before Jackie Robinson, it's probably an understatement to suggest that the world we live in would be a little bit different than it is today.

No, Cumberland Posey's Homestead Grays never entered the Middle Atlantic League, never crossed the line, and never disrupted the gentlemen's agreement. They stayed in the Negro Leagues, or sometimes operated as an independent traveling team, until a couple of years after Robinson made his mark in Brooklyn. But what if they had? What if Landis actually did this and the Grays had actually played in the white minor leagues?

An entire bookshelf could be filled with material speculating on how our society might have been altered had such an initiative been launched. But for the purposes of this project, we're going to focus on the easier questions: How would the Grays have fared had they entered the minor leagues? Would they have held their own, proving their capabilities as a ball club in the white minor league's lowest levels?

Although the Grays did NOT become an official member of the Middle Atlantic League in 1927, they DID begin playing those clubs in regular exhibition games during the spring. I'm not making this up. Spring games and late-season exhibition contests with MAL clubs would become an important part of the Grays' schedule, lasting a couple of decades, until the time of Jackie Robinson. The games were well-covered by the local papers in small-town Pennsylvania, as well as the larger dailies in Pittsburgh. To save everybody time, I've gone ahead and collected all the box scores on behalf of the group.

I was curious about how well the Grays performed. If modern writers can sometimes list these clubs among the greatest of all-time, black or white, then surely their performance against low-level minor league teams can serve as a "smell test" of sorts, to see if the evidence supports the assertion of their excellence. To get a large enough sample of games, I added some contests of the Pittsburgh Crawfords, another excellent Negro Leagues team, into the mix. The Crawfords' owner, Gus Greenlee, raided Cumberland Posey's roster beginning in 1932, and for about five years the Craws were as good, or better, than the Grays, using many of the same players. Josh Gibson, Oscar Charleston, Vic Harris, Jud Wilson, Cool Papa Bell, Judy Johnson, and many others played roles big and small with both the Grays and Crawfords in the 1930s. Like the Grays, the Crawfords played exhibition games against the Middle Atlantic League teams during the same era. In order to beef up the dataset, I also included about two dozen games against white minor league clubs who were *not* from the Middle Atlantic League. There are a few contests against outfits from the Western

League and American Association thrown into the mix, and as these were both higher classifications than the Class C Middle Atlantic League, tougher competition, they don't compromise the data in any way. They actually make it a little bit more meaningful.

Let us cut to the chase. In 99 games (most of them played during an 11-year span ranging from 1927 to 1937), the Grays-Craws conglomerate rolled up 76 victories versus only 20 defeats (plus three ties) against white minor league clubs. They dominated this mix of mostly Middle Atlantic teams. Their .792 winning percentage translates to a 122–32 record in a traditional 154-game season, and all but one of these games was played on the road, at the park of the host white minor league teams, with white umpires of their choosing handling the arbitration.

If Judge Landis had authorized their admission to the Middle Atlantic League, wondering if the Grays could prove themselves (maybe even hoping they *couldn't*), it would have become ridiculously obvious just a couple of weeks into the season that Homestead (or the Crawfords) were playing at the wrong level. Class D baseball was simply too easy for the manpower employed by the black teams from Pittsburgh. The Negro Leagues clubs averaged 7.8 runs per game, while allowing their opponents 3.7 per contest, making their 76–20 record right in line with Pythagorean expectations. The Negro Leagues teams rolled up a .812 team OPS, including 58 triples and 85 home runs, while limiting their white opponents to a .646 mark, as the minor leaguers managed only 31 three-baggers and 28 homers. Stolen bases? The Grays-Craws swiped 92, compared to 35 for their opposition. Their team fielding percentage was .965 for those 99 games, while their opponents committed 258 errors, resulting in a .938 marker. There really isn't a category, or any group of categories, where the Negro Leagues teams didn't dominate.

To the folks supporting the Scottdale Scotties, Charleroi Governors, or any of the other Middle Atlantic League franchises in the 1920s and 1930s, the domination by the black clubs wasn't a surprise. It was expected. In preview stories leading up the games, it was clearly understood that the matchup with the Homestead Grays or Pittsburgh Crawfords would serve as a litmus test, helping management gauge the caliber of their team. They knew they were going to lose most of the time. An impressive individual performance against the Grays or Craws could help a player secure a roster spot with the team, or even elevate them to a starting role, if their status was in limbo. Playing well against the black clubs from Pittsburgh was a big deal, for the team, its players, and fans.

Returning to the fictional integration scheme for a moment: *Had* it happened, there's no doubt that Art Rooney could have been a key ally for Cumberland Posey. In real life, Rooney and Posey were friends, with the Homestead Grays owner a regular guest at the lavish birthday parties hosted by Rooney over the years. When faced with financial difficulties during the 1930s, Rooney gave Posey money to help meet his financial obligations and never required repayment on these loans. The two men had met as competitors on Pittsburgh's integrated semiprofessional diamonds and had a genuine affection for one another. In 1933, during Rooney's first year as a franchise owner in the NFL, he had an African American named Ray Kemp on his roster. The Steelers would become known as one of the most progressive teams in professional football, in terms of providing opportunities for minorities, and the family's legacy as leaders in diversity was later acknowledged by the league. Today, there is the "Rooney Rule," requiring NFL franchises to interview minorities for all head coaching and Senior Football Operations jobs. Yes, Rooney and Posey would have been a match made in heaven, given a different set of circumstances.[2]

Back to the baseball diamond, it's interesting to dig a little bit deeper and look at the performances of the individual black players. History buffs may say, "Of course the Grays and Crawfords dominated, they had the likes of Josh Gibson, Smokey Joe Williams, Satchel Paige, John Beckwith, Buck Leonard, and Cool Papa Bell in their lineups!" Well yes, they did. They often had two or three men in their lineup who are now counted among the greats of the Negro Leagues, but not always. The roster was always changing a little bit from one year to the next. Sometimes they didn't have any future Hall of Famers on the field, although the remainder of the club always consisted of very good, if lesser-known ballplayers.

In my 99 game study, Josh Gibson appeared in only 21 contests. Oscar Charleston (who was in his mid–30s by this point and well past his prime), played in 30 games. Hall of Famer Buck Leonard played first base in just 23 games. Cool Papa Bell only shows up 13 times, but held his own (batting .310 with three stolen bases), while Hall of Famer Smokey Joe Williams was in his mid–40s when he pitched in these exhibitions against the Middle Atlantic League.[3]

For the record: Josh Gibson batted .417, with seven doubles, eight triples and four home runs. Oscar Charleston batted .369 with 41 hits in 111 at bats, hitting six home runs and stealing seven bases. Buck Leonard rolled up a .379 batting average with 11 doubles and two homers during the course of 23 games. John Beckwith, who should probably be in the Hall of Fame but isn't, clobbered Middle Atlantic League pitching to the tune of a .370 batting average with seven home runs in only 18 games. He added six doubles and four triples to his ledger, giving him a slugging percentage of .802 against white minor leaguers. Satchel Paige pitched seven times, going 2–1, with one game a seven inning no-hitter. In 33 innings pitched, he allowed only 14 hits, walked nine, and struck out 46 batters. His earned run average was 1.64. This was Paige, at his prime, pitching against white minor league teams. He was untouchable.

An outfielder named Vic Harris appeared in more games than any other man in this study. Harris was a protégé of Cumberland Posey's and later managed the Homestead Grays to several championships in the late 1930s and early 1940s. Vic Harris was a solid ballplayer, but not a superstar. In 80 contests, he collected 76 hits in 236 at-bats, good for a .322 batting average, with nine home runs and eight stolen bases.

This book wrestles with the idea of whether or not Negro Leagues teams were of Major League caliber. There will probably be some disagreement and counter-arguments from baseball's historians on this matter, but based on the evidence, I think we can all agree that the top black clubs were clearly superior to the white teams operating at Organized Baseball's lowest levels. And it's not even close.

Table 4.1 Grays/Crawfords vs. Organized Baseball 1924–1948

Leagues	W	L	T	PCT	RF	RA
MLB	21	15	1	.581	5.76	4.71
AAA	4	2	0	.667	5.67	4.17
AA	10	8	0	.555	5.67	3.78
A	7	3	1	.682	7.36	4.45
Low Minors	62	12	2	.829	8.26	3.50
Total	104	40	4	.716	7.18	3.92

Editor's Note: For point of reference, 30 contests the Grays and Crawfords played against Major League All-Star teams have been added to the 99-game study discussed in the text. There were 19 games (7 against MLB clubs) whose results were tallied for Table 4.1, for which box scores were unavailable. Included in all four tables are statistics from a handful of contests involving the 1934 and 1936 Negro National League All-Stars; the 1935 Negro Stars; and the 1937 Ciudad Trujillo squads, all of whom were predominantly comprised of Pittsburgh players. The Grays and Crawfords stars fared well against big leaguers: Not surprisingly, Josh Gibson led the way with 24 hits, including four homers, in 14 games against Major League all-star squads, good for a .369 batting average. Vic Harris batted .333 over the course of 17 games; and big John Beckwith hit .298 with four home runs and three triples in 12 contests. Hall of Famer Martin Dihigo rapped out a .340 average in 50 at-bats, along with three homers and five doubles, and James "Cool Papa" Bell put up a .348 mark along with two stolen bases in five games. Satchel Paige won two games against no losses in three appearances against the big leaguers, striking out 25 batters in 15 innings pitched, while posting a 2.40 ERA.

Table 4.2 Grays/Crawfords vs. Organized Baseball Hitting Statistics 1924–1948

	AB	H	D	T	HR	SB	SAC	HBP	BA	OBP	SA	OPS
HG/PC	1080	338	45	14	23	18	10	2	.313	.345	.444	.789
MLB	1085	297	48	15	19	14	7	5	.274	.323	.398	.721
HG/PC	149	41	11	2	3	4	1	1	.275	.335	.436	.772
AAA	146	38	9	2	0	2	1	0	.260	.333	.349	.683
HG/PC	605	161	26	5	9	17	9	4	.266	.322	.371	.694
AA	533	124	27	6	3	9	10	5	.233	.300	.322	.622
HG/PC	308	100	13	4	6	11	2	6	.325	.387	.447	.834
A	284	74	13	5	1	2	4	0	.261	.339	.356	.695
HG/PC	3648	1094	186	58	85	92	33	20	.300	.360	.452	.812
Low Minors	3210	772	160	31	28	35	36	21	.240	.311	.336	.646
HG/PC Total	4728	1432	231	72	108	110	43	22	.303	.360	.451	.811
OB Total	4292	1069	207	46	47	48	43	26	.249	.313	.352	.664

Table 4.3 Grays/Crawfords vs. Organized Baseball Pitching Statistics 1924–1948

	G	W	IP	H	R	BB	K	R/9	WHIP	K/9
HG/PC	30	18	270	297	156	74	153	5.18	1.37	5.10
MLB	30	11	260.7	338	173	50	156	5.97	1.49	5.39
HG/PC	4	3	37	38	17	16	26	4.13	1.46	6.32
AAA	4	1	37	41	23	12	26	5.59	1.43	6.32
HG/PC	16	10	141	124	63	44	116	4.02	1.19	7.38
AA	16	6	147	161	100	45	62	6.12	1.40	3.80
HG/PC	8	5	70.3	74	33	33	36	5.51	1.53	4.61
A	8	2	72	100	64	21	34	8.00	1.68	4.25
HG/PC	71	58	607	536	247	202	437	3.66	1.22	6.48
Low Minors	71	11	617	792	582	231	236	8.59	2.27	3.45
HG/PC Total	129	94	1125	1069	526	369	768	4.21	1.28	6.14
OB Total	129	31	1133.7	1432	959	402	514	7.61	1.62	4.08

Table 4.4 Grays/Crawfords vs. Organized Baseball Fielding Statistics 1924–1948

	PO	A	E	FA
HG/PC	810	345	43	.964
MLB	773	355	52	.956
HG/PC	108	37	7	.954

	PO	A	E	FA
AAA	111	58	9	.949
HG/PC	423	155	26	.957
AA	441	225	47	.934
HG/PC	212	94	12	.962
A	216	111	22	.937
HG/PC	1818	715	86	.967
Low Minors	1848	902	108	.939
HG/PC Total	3371	1346	174	.964
OB Total	3389	1651	310	.942

Sources for Tables 4.1., 4.2, 4.3, 4.4: Simkus Outsider Baseball Database.

Notes

1. Art J. Rooney Jr., and Roy McHugh, *Ruanaidh: The Story of Art Rooney and His Clan* (Pittsburgh: Geyer Printing, 2008), 14–16.

2. *Pittsburgh Courier*, February 7, 1942; Rooney Jr., and McHugh, *Ruanaidh*, 103–104.

3. The statistics for this study were compiled between 1927 and 1937 from the pages of the *Beckley Raleigh Register* (West Virginia); *Charleroi Mail* (Pennsylvania); *Cumberland Evening Times* (Maryland); *Daily Courier* (Connellsville, Pennsylvania); *Pittsburgh Courier*; *Pittsburgh Post-Gazette*; *Pittsburgh Press*; *Uniontown Herald* (Pennsylvania).

The Color of Money

*Salaries and Performance in
Pre- and Post-Integration Baseball*

Michael Haupert

The color barrier in MLB was finally pierced in 1947 when Jackie Robinson made his debut for the Brooklyn Dodgers. While he paved the way for the players who would come after him, for many stars of the Negro Leagues, the barrier fell too late. They were denied both the opportunity to play in MLB and the opportunity to reap the riches of MLB salaries. This essay examines the performance and remuneration earned by players in both leagues and estimates the cost to the Negro Leagues players of segregation.

> *Jackie's nimble*
> *Jackie's quick*
> *Jackie makes the turnstiles click*[1]

Introduction

Until April 15, 1947, it had been more than half a century since a man with black skin took an at-bat in an official Major League Baseball (MLB) game.[2] During that time, more than 25,000 player-seasons were logged, and more than $100 million was earned for doing so.[3] While excluded from the white man's pinnacle of baseball success, black players were not without their own hierarchical baseball employment ladder. Beginning in 1920, they created their own major leagues, segregated from the white leagues. These leagues produced games, championships, ticket sales, and jobs. They generated income for their league executives, players, ticket sellers, vendors, ushers, and umpires. In addition, the black baseball business contributed income to secondary industries, such as service stations, hotels, restaurants, sporting goods dealers, and printers (of tickets, programs, etc.).

But it wasn't the same. Segregation did not make the leagues "separate but equal." It merely made them separate. The financial heft of MLB dwarfed that of the various black leagues. They played shorter league seasons in smaller ballparks, often in smaller cities. The almost exclusively white national press paid scant attention to the leagues, further exacerbating their difficulty in drawing sufficient crowds and raising revenue. As a result, teams came and went, leagues folded and were reorganized, and records were lost or poorly kept.

Oddly enough, in one way these "Negro Leagues" (NLB) were way ahead of MLB.[4] While white players earned higher salaries, they were not free to choose their own place of employment due to the reserve clause, which would not be overturned until the 1970s. The NLB had no reserve clause. This worked to the benefit of the players, who could sell their services to the highest bidder, changing teams from season to season if they wished.

Just a quick look at Hall of Famers—who one would expect would be in the highest demand—exhibits the impact of the reserve clause. A sample of Hall of Famers who played between 1916 and 1976 includes 24 NLB players and 92 MLB players.[5] The average Negro Leaguer played for 4.8 teams in 16 years, changing teams every third year. The average major leaguer played 17.5 years with 2.5 teams, switching once every 9.6 years. Thirty-four percent of the MLB sample played their entire career with one team, while 24 percent of the NLB sample played their entire career with one team. However, every one of those players participated in only a single NLB season.

This essay will look at the salaries of black ballplayers relative to white ballplayers both before and after integration. I will focus only on hitters for the first part of this research, which focuses on the segregation era, because the available data for black pitchers is rather scarce, limiting the sample size to only a handful of pitchers over the years.

The Issues

Players in the Negro Leagues made less money than their MLB brethren—a lot less. This was a result of teams playing fewer games in smaller stadiums in front of smaller crowds. Of course, the reason was that MLB discriminated against black players, forcing them into a separate league. One reason that does not explain the difference in salaries is the level of output of the players. While a home run in the Eastern Colored League might not be worth as much as a home run in the National League, a power hitter in one league was a power hitter in the other, and both were rewarded for that power. When black players moved into MLB beginning in 1947, they were much better compensated for the same performance than they were when playing in segregated leagues.

Table 5.1 compares the average salaries of black and white players in segregated leagues with those of the average American manufacturing worker. The reason for this comparison is to give an example of what economists call "opportunity cost." In other words, what kind of salary were ballplayers giving up by playing baseball? The manufacturing wage is shown, as opposed to the overall average wage, in order to separate professional jobs (e.g., accountants, doctors, and teachers) from the jobs most ballplayers tended to have after they retired. During this period of time, few ballplayers had a college education, so they were qualified to work manufacturing jobs, but not higher-paying professional jobs.[6]

Table 5.1 Average Salaries 1917–1946

Year	Avg Manufacturing Wage	Avg MLB Salary	Avg NLB Salary	MLB/Avg Mfg Wage	NLB/Avg Mfg Wage	NLB/MLB Salary
1917	$883	$3227	$217	3.65	0.25	0.07
1918	$1107	$3431	$376	3.10	0.34	0.11
1919	$1293	$3423		2.65		
1920	$1532	$3877		2.53		
1921	$1346	$4300	$383	3.19	0.28	0.09
1922	$1283	$4957		3.86		

Year	Avg Manufacturing Wage	Avg MLB Salary	Avg NLB Salary	MLB/Avg Mfg Wage	NLB/Avg Mfg Wage	NLB/MLB Salary
1923	$1403	$5166		3.68		
1924	$1427	$5548		3.89		
1925	$1450	$6033		4.16		
1926	$1476	$6434	$374	4.36	0.25	0.06
1927	$1502	$6738	$493	4.49	0.33	0.07
1928	$1534	$6971	$600	4.54	0.39	0.09
1929	$1543	$6932	$448	4.49	0.29	0.06
1930	$1488	$7175	$559	4.82	0.38	0.08
1931	$1369	$7286	$896	5.32	0.65	0.12
1932	$1150	$6871	$128	5.97	0.11	0.02
1933	$1086	$6360		5.86		
1934	$1153	$5888		5.11		
1935	$1216	$6074		5.00		
1936	$1287	$6711		5.21		
1937	$1376	$7090		5.15		
1938	$1296	$7327		5.65		
1939	$1363	$6610	$154	4.85	0.11	0.02
1940	$1432	$7712	$885	5.39	0.62	0.11
1941	$1653	$8006	$1030	4.84	0.62	0.13
1942	$2023	$7276	$1350	3.60	0.67	0.19
1943	$2349	$6461	$1238	2.75	0.53	0.19
1944	$2517	$6674		2.65		
1945	$2517	$7516		2.99		
1946	$2517	$8944		3.55		

Sources: Haupert Professional Baseball Salary Database; Burton, "series D 739–764," *Historical Statistics of the United States*, 1989.

As can be seen from Table 5.1, white ballplayers compared quite favorably to their non–ballplayer neighbors, and baseball was only seasonal work. Many ballplayers worked in the off-season at jobs they would turn into careers after they retired.

Black player salaries were not nearly as generous. This applies both to comparisons with MLB players and manufacturing workers. But then, black workers in general did not fare as well as their white counterparts. They suffered from segregation in many lines of work besides baseball.[7] Prior to 1940, data on black and white wages in industries outside of baseball are very scarce. As a result, at this time we don't have a good wage series with which to compare black ballplayers to black manufacturing workers. The issue with seasonal work applies only in part to black ballplayers. Many of them played baseball all year long, moving south of the border to play in the Caribbean or Mexico during the winter. Those who did not searched out non-baseball jobs. Black ballplayers were even less likely than whites to have a college education. And in most cases, their off-season employment opportunities were less lucrative than what the average American manufacturing worker earned.

The point of the comparisons is illustrative. The first three columns in Table 5.1 list salaries, while the last three display ratios. Prior to integration, the average NLB player earned between 6 and 19 percent of the average MLB wage. The average MLB player, while underpaid relative to his production on the field, was paid handsomely relative to his friends on the assembly lines.[8] Between 1917 and 1946, white ballplayers earned on average anywhere between two and a half and six times the average manufacturing wage.

Clearly, and not surprisingly, white players were better paid. A few specific examples of salaries for black and white players in separate leagues will underscore the point. In 1928 Babe Ruth and Satchel Paige were widely recognized as among the best, if not the best, players in their respective leagues. Both frequently exploited their superstar stats by participating in profitable exhibition games. Ruth, in fact, ran afoul of Commissioner Landis one year for his post-season barnstorming. Paige often picked up exhibition game checks during the middle of the season, sometimes even abandoning his club's scheduled games to earn a more lucrative paycheck elsewhere for a one-off game. In 1928, Ruth earned $70,000. That same year, Paige earned $600 while pitching for the Birmingham Black Barons. While only 22 years old, he was 11–4 with a 2.32 ERA, 121 strikeouts, and only 25 walks in 132 innings pitched. Ruth didn't have a bad year either, hitting 54 home runs with a .323/.463/.709 slash line. And that was an off-year for the Babe. Paige, on the other hand, was on his way up, though his salaries didn't necessarily show it. We only have four observations of Paige's salary, from 1927 to 1930, when he played for Birmingham. Not counting winter ball or games pitched for other teams, he earned between $500–$1,422 during his tenure in Birmingham, for a four-year total of $3,368. That's how much Ruth earned in a week in 1928.

Let's take a look at another pair of Hall of Famers, this time contemporaries and catchers. In 1918 the 29-year-old veteran Louis Santop, playing in his seventh professional season, earned $730 playing for Hilldale. That same year, White Sox catcher Ray Schalk, age 25, also in his seventh season, earned $7,083, making him the highest-paid catcher in the league. Santop hit .412 in 17 games, and 68 at-bats. Schalk hit .219 in 108 games. For comparison, the average MLB player earned $3,431 in 1918, while MLB batting champ Ty Cobb was the highest-paid professional baseball player in the land that year at $20,000. He claimed his 11th batting title, hitting .382/.440/.515.

Determining Player Pay

It is neither difficult to establish nor surprising that in the segregated baseball industry, the black players were paid substantially less than the white players. But what determined their level of pay? For the past 50 years, economists have asked this question numerous times, and while their research has focused on a wide variety of potential causes, they all agree on the basics. Player pay is determined by experience, performance, and an intangible called the "superstar effect." Until recently, this research has focused only on MLB players due to the lack of available salary data and reliable performance data for Negro Leagues players.[9]

Most research on player salaries has occurred since free agency. This is primarily due to the greater availability of salary data since then. The first major study of baseball salaries was done by Gerald Scully (1974), who used data from the 1960s in his seminal analysis of what determined the salaries of MLB players. His research is relevant to this study because it was carried out using data from the reserve clause era of MLB. This is important because the nature of contracts has changed dramatically since the rise to power of the MLBPA under Marvin Miller in the mid–1960s, and free agency, which debuted a decade later. Prior to free agency, for example, multiyear contracts were rare. And until Miller came along, contracts were much more one-sided in favor of the owners.

Scully found that MLB players received a salary increase based on their performance and the number of years of MLB service. Pay increases based on experience are a function of improved performance. Players who stick around for another year of experience are, by definition, the better players.[10]

Of course, player salaries do not constantly increase as experience increases. Once past his prime, there is a tendency for a player's salary to begin a gradual decline. This makes sense because player skills do not increase constantly. They tend to increase up to a point and then begin to fall off, as age eventually takes its physical toll on even the most talented players.

Performance variables also affect player salaries. Quite understandably, the better the performer is, the bigger the paycheck. Of course, salaries actually reflect *expected* performance, not *actual* performance, since they are set in advance. Before the popularity of long-term guaranteed contracts, which have arisen with the power of the MLBPA, the performance impact on a player's salary tended to be short-run: a what-have-you-done-for-me-lately kind of approach. And contracts were rarely long-term or guaranteed. That is, in the days of the reserve clause, the owners based this year's salary on last year's performance, with perhaps a bit of emphasis on the past few years. But under the reserve clause, the previous season's performance had the biggest impact on the current year's salary. Even at that, contracts were a low-risk proposition for owners, since they could invoke the dreaded ten-day clause to release a player, ending their obligation to pay him any further salary. It goes without saying that the players did not have a similar right to break off their contract. In fact, quite the opposite, as the reserve clause gave the team the right to renew the contract at their discretion in perpetuity, which tied a player to his team for as long as the owner wished.

What performance variables are most important? It turns out that the answer to that question depends importantly on what period of baseball history you examine. But it also turns out that most of the major performance variables have explanatory power. For example, in his seminal 1974 study, Gerald Scully focused on slugging average (hitters) and strikeout/walk ratio (pitchers) as his performance variables of choice, but admitted that several other performance variables proved to be just as reliable at predicting salaries. Since that time, other research has focused on identifying other variables, including position, race, and a variety of performance variables.[11] Baseball fans know that there is no shortage of material on which to measure the performance of a ballplayer, and the sophistication and availability of such measures has only increased over time as sabermetrics, computing power, and the growth of websites like Baseball-reference.com and Seamheads.com has increased their availability.

The superstar effect is a slightly different issue and only applies to a small minority of ballplayers—the superstars, as the name suggests. The idea here is that some players become famous as much for who they are as for what they do. Most often, the superstar effect applies to the best performers, but sometimes it can, in the short run, apply to players who become famous for some other reason. For example, Mark Fidrych became a national sensation in 1976 for his eccentric behavior on the mound and his Rookie of the Year performance. His popularity went far beyond his performance, which was not statistically much different that year from Frank Tanana's. But Tanana, despite a much longer and more productive career, never graced the cover of *Sports Illustrated* (actually Fidrych didn't make it in his rookie year either, but he was on the cover June 6, 1977, and again on April 24, 1978). Babe Ruth, even as his skills eroded, was a draw with Boston fans, where his MLB career began, which is why the Braves purchased him from the Yankees in 1935. They didn't purchase him for his 40-year-old batting skills, but for his name, which helped sell tickets.

The linkage between performance and pay does seem to rely at least somewhat on the time period being used. Most of the literature focuses on the 1960s forward, due to the scarcity of salary data before then. However, my research on baseball salaries has allowed me to put together a far more substantial database than has previously been available. To my knowledge, my database of Negro League salaries is unique. This allows for a new look at performance and pay. In particular, this essay will focus on the period 1917–1946, a period for which I have black player salary data during the segregation era, and then separately will look at the period 1947–1959. The period was chosen as an "integration" period, defined simply by the time that it took for every team to integrate. The 1947 season, of course, was Jackie Robinson's debut; 1959 was the year the Red Sox finally became the last MLB team to employ a black player.[12]

Salaries and Performance in Segregated Baseball

There are two issues of interest here. First: how were black and white players compensated in their separate leagues? This is a straightforward look at segregated decision-making with an analysis of the differences, which are quite easy to explain. The second part is a bit more interesting. I will try to measure the cost of segregation by estimating the salary that the Negro Leagues players could have earned had they been compensated like MLB players. In other words, what if they had turned in their NLB performances in MLB?

Let's determine how salaries were set in the Negro Leagues, that is, what caused player salaries to vary over time and from player to player. There was no minimum or maximum wage or a reserve clause in the Negro Leagues, which is one reason players switched teams three times as often as big leaguers did, and why black ball teams had a difficult time preventing Major League squads from poaching their best players without compensation once the color barrier had been broken. The players who weren't good enough to be in MLB hung on for a few years after 1947 in a dwindling NLB, but eventually all lost their jobs.

So how were salaries set? Did players in the NLB get rewarded the same way MLB players did? Regression analysis, which allows us to solve the following equation by examining the data from hundreds of observations, can help give us the answers:

Salary Hitter X = β_1Performance Hitter X + β_2 Years' Experience Hitter X + γ.

Equations were tested using a variety of combinations of performance metrics, such as home runs, batting average, on-base percentage, slugging average, and stolen bases. Indeed, as Scully discovered, there are a large number of performance metrics that explain salary. In his sample set, which covered 1968 and 1969, he settled on slugging percentage as the best explanatory performance variable for hitters, and strikeout/walk ratios for pitchers. What this means is that the variation in player slugging averages over time and across players was a primary determinant of the difference in player salaries. In short, the higher a player's slugging average, the higher his salary. In the equation above, we can interpret these terms as follows. On the left-hand side of the equation, we have a player's salary.[13] On the right-hand side, we have the variables that determine that salary, each quite clear to a baseball fan, including years of experience. In the case of MLB players, the years of experience are measured as MLB experience, and for NLB players it is NLB experience.

The β in front of each variable is the coefficient, i.e., the multiplying factor of the variable, which in this case translates into the dollar value of an extra year of experience or a change in a performance variable, such as home runs or batting average. If β_2 in the above equation is 50, it means that each additional year of experience translates into a $50 salary increase for the following year.[14] As noted earlier, prior to the 1960s, multi-year contracts were extremely rare. Fewer than 3 percent of the contracts in my database for this period were for more than one year, and none of the NLB contracts in my sample were for more than one year. As a result, salaries were predominantly determined by last year's performance. Lou Gehrig, for example, saw his 1933 salary reduced by $2,000 to $23,000 after his performance in the 1932 season had tailed off from 1931, when he hit 46 home runs, drove in 185 runs, and batted .341 with a .662 slugging average. In 1932, he hit 34 home runs, drove in 151 runs, and raised his average to .349, but saw his slugging average dip to .621. It was the Great Depression, but Gehrig's 8 percent salary cut exceeded the league-wide average of 5 percent, and was more than three times the average decrease of the Yankees payroll.[15]

The economics literature is rich with research into what causes baseball salaries to vary, and as mentioned previously, a lot of different equations are used to explain this variation. Different eras saw salaries affected by different performance variables. In order to determine what impacted salaries during the segregation period of my study (1917–1946) and the integration period (1947–1959), I ran regressions of the form listed above for each of these periods, and in the former period, separately for NLB and MLB.

I have collected the salaries of 425 NLB players from a variety of sources over a period of time ranging from 1917 to 1955. I have built a much more substantial database consisting of more than 45,000 MLB salaries ranging from the 1870s through 2016.[16] Player performance data is taken from Baseball-Reference.com and Seamheads.com.

The Results of the Salary Regressions

Numerous salary equations were tested, and the one that worked the best, i.e., explained most of the variation in salary for NLB players, was of the form Salary = f(age, HR). That is, NLB hitter salaries were determined primarily by their age and the number of home runs they hit. For MLB hitters, salary was determined by age, batting average, home runs, and a "year effect." That is, there was something about the specific year that impacted salaries in some years. This was only the case for the sample that ran from 1917 to 1946. This is not surprising, given that this period covers both World War II and the Great Depression, years which were decidedly not normal ones in the U.S. economy.

You will notice that experience is not reflected in these equations, but instead is replaced by age, which is a related, but different variable. Age was used because it turned out to be better than experience at predicting player salaries. Obviously, age and experience are related, since both inexorably increase as a player continues to play. But they are also clearly different. A 30-year-old player has ten years of age on a 20-year-old player, but may have less experience. At age 20, Al Kaline was beginning his third season with the Tigers in 1955, while 32-year-old Mariners reliever Kazuhiro Sasaki was named the 2000 AL Rookie of the Year.

Estimating What a NLB Player Might Have Earned in MLB

Now that we have determined what explains salaries, let's take a look at how we can compare the compensation earned in NLB to MLB and measure the "cost" to the NLB player of discrimination. Let's take an example. In 1930, Judy Johnson was paid $1,170, a salary that was determined for the most part by the fact that he was 30 years old when he signed the contract, and the previous year he had hit five home runs. He batted .376 that year, which was not a determinant of his NLB salary, but would have affected his MLB salary had he played in that league. That kind of MLB performance would have earned him a paycheck of $7,682, approximately what 37-year-old George Sisler ($7,500) earned in his farewell season when he hit three home runs and batted .309 in 116 games. Lyn Lary, 24, also earned $7,500 in 1930, coming off his rookie year in which he hit .309 with five home runs.

Knowing what determined salaries in the NLB and MLB between 1917 and 1946 allows us to determine what black players would have been paid had they turned in their NLB performances in MLB. This is accomplished by taking the performance variables of the NLB player and plugging them into the MLB salary formula.

For example, assume a MLB player is rewarded with a $50 salary increase next year for each home run he hits this year.[17] So in 1921, when Babe Ruth crushed 59 home runs, that would translate into a $2,950 salary increase for 1922. If a NLB hitter is rewarded with a $10 salary increase for each home run, then when Oscar Charleston hit 15 homers in 1921, he could expect a $150 salary increase in 1922. Babe Ruth would get a bigger raise for two reasons: first, he hit more home runs. Second, he is rewarded more for each home run. The first reason is not discriminatory. Ruth hit more home runs than Charleston did, and players are rewarded for hitting home runs. He deserved more money for producing more. However, the second reason is discriminatory because Ruth received a bigger reward for each home run. We previously explained why MLB paid more for performance than NLB: bigger crowds, in bigger stadiums, in bigger cities, and played out over more games. But all of these factors become discriminatory because Oscar Charleston was prohibited from playing in those circumstances because of his race. In other words, this home run pay difference is entirely due to discrimination.

Table 5.2 shows the average production of MLB and NLB hitters. We can see that MLB hitters on average were nearly two years older than NLB hitters, had a slightly higher batting average, but batted three times as often as NLB hitters, primarily due to the greater number of league games that they played. One reason MLB hitters generated twice as many home runs as NLB batters was because they made more plate appearances. But note that NLB hitters had a lower AB/HR ratio (66.5) than did MLB hitters (100.3). I am not going to dwell on the comparison of performance statistics across leagues. That is an entirely different research project.

Table 5.2 Average Performance of NLB and MLB Hitters 1917–1946

	Age	*IP*	*K*	*BB*	*BA/ERA*	*AB*	*HR*
MLB Hitters	28.7				.289	351	3.5
NLB Hitters	26.9				.285	113	1.7
MLB Pitchers	28.4	171.5	57.7	9.8	3.88		
NLB Pitchers	27.9	67.2	33	4.6	3.91		

Table 5.3 Average Salaries Based on Similar Reward Coefficients

	Real Salary	*Black/White Salary*
MLB Hitters	$58,889	97.2%
What NLB hitters would have earned in MLB	$57,260	
NLB average salary/MLB average salary	$3,048/$58,889	5.2%

Note: Inflation adjusted for the base year 1982–84, the period most commonly used by the U.S. Bureau of Labor Statistics for calculating real values.

Table 5.3 shows salaries based on similar reward coefficients. The real salary column is the inflation-adjusted salary paid to MLB and NLB hitters. Note that NLB hitters were paid barely 5 percent of what MLB hitters earned. If the NLB hitters had played in MLB and maintained their offensive performance, their salaries would have increased by a factor of almost 20, from $3,048 to $57,260, about 97 percent of what the average MLB player earned. Note that these higher salaries would have been earned in far fewer at-bats. The point is clearly made here: NLB players were losing substantial amounts of money by being barred from playing in MLB—even if they had played only a fraction of the games played by white players.

Table 5.4 shows individual performance results to put some faces behind the numbers. These are the performances generated by players in the leagues they played in, and the salaries the NLB players would have earned had they put up those numbers in MLB. For comparison, I have listed average and maximum MLB salaries for each year.

Table 5.4 Examples of MLB Equivalent Salaries for NLB Players

NLB Player	Oscar Charleston	Josh Gibson	Turkey Stearnes	Pop Lloyd	Buck Leonard	Louis Santop
Year	1926	1944	1929	1929	1941	1918
Age	31	32	28	45	33	29
AB	255	123	241	131	158	68
HR	20	9	16	2	11	1
BA	.427	.358	.402	.374	.354	.412
MLB Equiv	$23,315	$21,080	$18,910	$18,364	$14,868	$7,653
MLB Avg	$6,434	$6,674	$6,932	$6,932	$8,006	$3,431
MLB Equiv/ MLB Avg	3.62	3.16	2.73	2.65	1.8	2.23
MLB Max	$52,000	$27,000	$70,000	$70,000	$55,000	$20,000
Max MLB Player	Babe Ruth	Joe Cronin*	Babe Ruth	Babe Ruth	Hank Greenberg	Ty Cobb
Age	31	37	34	34	30	31
AB	495	191	499	499	67	421
HR	47	5	46	46	2	3
BA	.372	.241	.345	.345	.269	.382

*Player-manager

The next step in this exercise is to estimate lost lifetime earnings. Again, I measure the lost earnings of similar NLB performances in MLB by calculating the MLB value of the NLB output. Once again, no attempt is made to convert NLB performance to MLB performance. This results in an upward bias of the lost income for NLB players, because it is unlikely that the performance would have translated perfectly. For example, in 1918 Louis Santop hit .412 while playing for two different teams. Even if Santop's Hilldale team faced MLB-quality opponents, it still stands to reason that his batting average would not stand up over an entire MLB season, since he batted only 78 times that year.

However, there has also been no effort made to adjust the NLB performance for the shorter season; i.e., Josh Gibson hit only nine home runs in 1944, but he only had 123 at-bats and teams played only about half as many games as did MLB squads. This downwardly biases the salary he could have expected in MLB because he undoubtedly would have hit more home runs had he batted more, and league executives of the time thought more in terms of power production than they did the ratio of HR/AB.

The row labeled MLB Equiv/MLB Avg shows the ratio of the estimated NLB converted MLB salary to the average MLB salary. The next row lists the highest MLB salary as a check on the reliability of these estimates—i.e., do these salaries look realistic, or are they out of proportion? The answer, as we can see, is that they look reasonable.

Let's take a look at one player as a case study of how much more valuable MLB performance is than NLB performance. Table 5.5 displays the salaries of Satchel Paige for four NLB years and five years of his MLB career. He earned a total of $3,368 during the prime of his career with Birmingham. In those four years he went 35–14, striking out 433 batters in 442 innings, while walking only 92. Now compare that to his first four years in MLB, recalling that he was a 41-year-old "rookie" in 1948 when he earned $15,000. Even when we adjust his 1927–30 salaries for inflation, he was paid considerably more in 1948, when he was 6–1 with a 2.48 ERA in 72.2 IP, striking out 43 and walking 22. Not bad, but not as productive as he was in 1930, when he went 10–3 and stuck out 95 batters and walked only 18 in 106 innings.

Table 5.5 The Salary Saga of Satchel Paige

NLB: Birmingham		MLB: Cleveland/ St. Louis	
1927	$688	1948	$15,000
1928	$600	1949	$15,000
1929	$1422	1951	$25,000
1930	$658	1952	$25,000
		1953	$25,000
Total	$3368	Total	$105,000

Table 5.6 Estimated Lost MLB Earnings and Actual MLB Earnings

NLB Player	Years	Lost Earnings	MLB Player	Years	MLB Earnings
Pop Lloyd	1906–1932	$223,098	Ty Cobb	1905–1928	$491,233
Oscar Charleston	1915–1941	$262,982	Jimmie Dykes	1919–1939	$184,100
Bullet Rogan	1920–1938	$176,914	Babe Ruth	1918–1934	$847,000
Cool Papa Bell	1922–1946	$168,415	Al Simmons	1925–1944	$287,000
Turkey Stearnes	1923–1940	$230,820	Charlie Gehringer	1925–1942	$209,400
Satchel Paige	1927–1947	$194,202	Luke Appling	1931–1948	$184,400
Josh Gibson	1930–1946	$160,949	Hank Greenberg	1934–1946	$275,000
Buck Leonard	1933–1948	$211,479	Frank Crosetti	1933–1947	$179,500

Table 5.6 shows the estimated lost lifetime earnings of several NLB stars, each paired with an MLB player who had a career of a similar time period and for whom we have complete salary data, just for comparison. These salaries certainly fall within reasonable ranges. Turkey Stearnes and his 18-year career in the NLB would have been worth $230,820

in MLB, just a bit more than the $209,400 Charlie Gehringer earned over the same length of career and almost the exact same years. Stearnes batted .344 with 176 home runs, 195 doubles, and 101 triples in 3,370 at-bats to Gehringer's lifetime .320 average, 184 homers, 574 doubles and 146 triples in 8,860 at-bats.

So what if we were to adjust for season length? What if, for example, Oscar Charleston had played 154 games in MLB in 1925 and maintained the same rate of productivity? That year, he hit .427 with 20 home runs in 71 games. That translates into a .427 average (assuming he averaged the same over more at-bats) and 43 home runs in 154 games. That performance would have generated an MLB salary of $51,985. That would have been a substantial salary in 1926 (remember performance in 1925 determines salary in 1926), but not as substantial as Babe Ruth, who earned $52,000 in the second year of a two-year contract.

The Integration Period

After integration, the salaries of black players who made it to the Majors increased dramatically, while those players left behind in the Negro Leagues saw their salaries stagnate. In fact, in the first few years after integration, the average black player earned nearly as much (more in 1951) as the average white player (Table 5.7). These results need to be tempered by a couple of observations. First, the samples are small. In the first years of an integrated MLB, there were only a few black players—and it should be noted that those blacks who did make it in the early years were anything but average. They were among the best the Negro Leagues had to offer. By 1952, a persistent wage gap had opened between white and black players, and it remained for the duration of the integration era.[18]

Table 5.7 Black and White Salaries after Integration

Year	Avg Mfg wage	Avg MLB Sal All Players	Avg Salary Black MLB	Avg Black MLB/Avg MLB	Avg NLB Salary	Max Black MLB Salary	Max MLB Salary
1947	$2793	$11,819	$5500	0.47		$6,000	$70,000
1948	$3038	$11,841	$10,250	0.87	$1971	$15,000	$65,000
1949	$3095	$13,672	$12,500	0.91		$25,000	$100,000
1950	$3302	$13,551	$12,000	0.89	$300	$36,000	$100,000
1951	$3608	$12,807	$18,000	1.41		$36,000	$90,000
1952	$3832	$13,668	$6000	0.44	$733	$39,750	$85,000
1953	$4053	$13,868	$6000	0.43	$720	$38,500	$85,000
1954	$4123	$14,381	$6000	0.42	$300	$39,500	$85,000
1955	$4356	$13,849	$7000	0.51	$298	$36,000	$67,500
1956	$4589	$15,005	$8000	0.53		$42,000	$58,000
1957	$4786	$16,358	$8000	0.49		$42,000	$65,000
1958	$4946	$16,521	$9500	0.58		$42,000	$65,000
1959	$5221	$16,516	$9500	0.58		$45,000	$75,000

Sources: Haupert "Pay, Performance, and Race during the Integration Era," *Black Ball*, Spring 2009; Burton, "series D 739–764," Historical Statistics of the United States, 1989.

The players who were left behind in the Negro Leagues were not only less talented on average, but they were left in a lower-quality league that had been decimated by the signing of the best players by MLB. This lower-quality league drew fewer fans, thus the falling salaries of Negro Leagues players after integration (see Table 5.7).

There are only two explanations for why white players ultimately began to earn substantially more than black players. One is that they may have been better players. The second is that whites were paid more than blacks for the same level of performance, that is, the black players were discriminated against. It is hard to tell if a pay gap is due to racism unless players have different pay, but by every other measure their performance is the same. We can better isolate these differences by once again using regression analysis.

Six different models of the salary regression were run, three each for pitchers and hitters (Tables 5.8 and 5.9). In each case, salary was regressed on performance variables and experience and age variables. The differences in the models come in the way race is treated. In the first case, all hitters (or pitchers, as the case may be) were observed in the same model with a variable included for race. This measure will pick up general differences in salary due to a player's skin color, if any exist. The results for this regression can be found in the first column of each table. In an effort to determine if black and white players were paid differently for similar performance or experience variables, separate regressions were run for white and black players. In this way, we can determine whether blacks and whites were rewarded for the same characteristics, and if so, whether they were rewarded at the same rate. These results are found in the last two columns of each table.

Table 5.8 Regression Coefficients on Hitters 1947–1959

$R^2 = .72$	Dependent Variable 1n Real Salary		
	All Hitters	White	Black
Intercept	9.342	9.020	9.738
Black	0.224*		
Age	0.006	0.024*	−0.000
NLB Experience	0.003		0.012
MLB Experience	0.079*	0.009	0.105*
Lag AB	0.001*	0.001*	0.001*
Lag HR	0.021*	0.023*	0.019*
Lag BA	1.379*	3.609*	0.944*
Lag SLG	−0.401	−0.470	−0.304

* = significant at .01

Table 5.9 Regression Coefficients on Pitchers 1947–1959

$R^2 = .57$	Dependent Variable 1n Real Salary		
	All Pitchers	White	Black
Intercept	9.880	10.183	10.234
Black	0.119*		
Age	−0.000	−0.007	−0.012
NLB Experience	0.015		0.033*
MLB Experience	0.055*	0.047*	0.078*
Lag G	0.003	0.004	−0.001
Lag ERA	−0.005*	0.009	−0.010

$R2 = .57$	Dependent Variable 1n Real Salary		
	All Pitchers	*White*	*Black*
Lag W	0.051*	0.057*	0.045*
Lag IP	0.000	-0.002	0.002
Lag SO	−0.001	0.002	-0.002

* = significant at .01

The model used is the standard semi-log form employed most frequently in the literature, which regresses the natural log of the dependent variable on the independent variables. The basic form of the model in each case is:

ln real salary = $\beta_1$race + $\beta_2$experience + $\beta_3$performance +ε.

A dummy variable is used for black players.[19] Use of the semi-log form means that the β values (coefficients on the variables) reported in the table can be read as percentages. In other words, they represent the percentage by which salary changes for a one-unit change in the dependent variable. For example, in Table 5.9, the value .051 in the first column of the lag W row indicates that each additional win by a pitcher results in a 5.1 percent salary increase the following year. Real salary is used to adjust for inflation, since the observations take place over the years 1947–1959.

Experience is measured separately for MLB and NLB. Playing in at least one game constituted a season for the experience measure. The player's age at midseason is also included. The correlation of these two variables is discussed below. The performance variables for hitters include lagged values of at-bats, home runs, batting average, and slugging average. For pitchers, the performance data include games, ERA, wins, innings pitched, and strikeouts, all lagged one year.

The R^2 value of .72 for hitter regressions means that 72 percent of the variation in salaries is explained by the variables in the table. The R^2 for pitchers is not as high, though 57 percent is still a strong result.[20]

Of interest is the race dummy, which takes on the value of 1 for black players, 0 otherwise. Note that for both pitchers and hitters, it is significant and positive, suggesting that being black was worth a 22.4 percent salary boost for hitters and nearly 12 percent for pitchers. This is almost certainly a result of the small number and high quality of the early black entrants into MLB, and not likely evidence of reverse discrimination on the part of white owners.[21]

NLB experience is insignificant for hitters but does exert a positive influence on pitcher salaries, though only about half the impact that MLB experience is worth. This suggests that MLB owners placed little value on NLB experience in salary determinations. MLB experience is significant and worth nearly 8 percent per year in additional salary for hitters and 5.5 percent for pitchers. When we consider the race-segregated models, these results hold, though their magnitude is slightly different. MLB experience was more important for black hitters than white hitters in determining salary. An additional year of experience was worth 10 percent for a black hitter, but age was more important for white hitters. For white pitchers, an additional year of experience was worth nearly 5 percent more in salary, while that year of experience was worth 7.75 percent for a black pitcher. In addition, NLB experience was also valued for black pitchers. Does this mean that black players were rewarded better for their years of experience or that they had to prove themselves over a longer period of time?

Looking at pitchers, the results suggest it may be the latter. When segregated by race, the only performance variable that is significant is lagged wins. The previous season's wins led to salary increases for pitchers, while a low ERA, high strikeout counts, and lots of innings pitched do not test significant in salary decisions. While wins were important for all pitchers, they paid better for white pitchers than black pitchers. White pitchers earned almost 30 percent more than black pitchers did for an additional win. The result of this difference is easily seen in Figure 5.1, which compares real salaries of white and black pitchers based on the lagged number of wins each had. The impact of the higher return to wins is clearly seen in this relationship, as the spread between black and white pitcher salaries increases with the number of wins.

Figure 5.1 Salary and Wins by Race 1947–1959

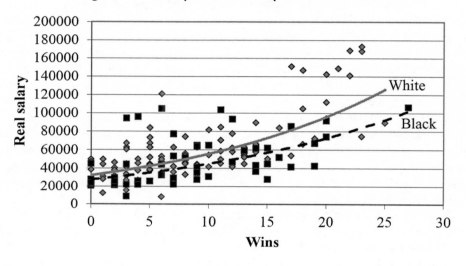

Figure 5.2 Real Salary by MLB Experience 1947–1959

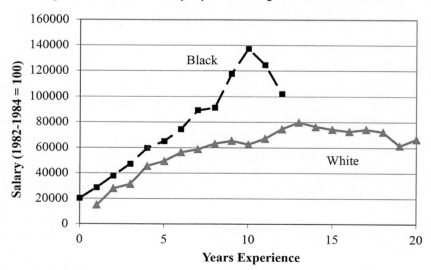

Figure 5.3 Real Salary by Race and Age 1947–1959

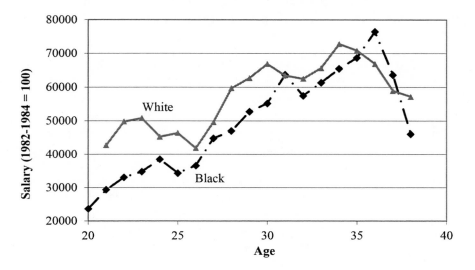

A similar analysis can be made for hitters. Black hitters were rewarded for years of experience—i.e., having proven themselves capable at the MLB level. White hitters, on the other hand, were rewarded merely for getting older, as can be seen by the significant coefficient on the age variable. While age is a proxy for experience, it is an imperfect one, and the results here lend support to the theory that black and white players were treated differently in regard to how they were compensated for their experience. MLB owners appeared willing to pay high salaries to black players, but only after they had proven themselves. Whites, on the other hand, were more likely to receive pro forma annual raises.

Player wages seldom decreased from one year to the next. This is not a phenomenon unique to baseball. Economist Truman Bewley explained this type of behavior as a rational response by firms to worker productivity. Rather than discipline unproductive workers with wage decreases, he hypothesized that firms would find it more useful to maintain steady wages and discipline workers by terminating them. Not decreasing wages also helps to maintain worker morale. If workers see that poor performance is punished with termination but that wages are allowed to increase over time, they are more likely to maintain higher morale. After all, they can control their own performance, but they have less control over their wage.[22]

This behavior appears to have had different effects on white and black players. If salaries tend to increase, or at least not decrease, from year to year, then the mere act of a player aging will correlate positively with his salary. But that can only happen if a player is still on the roster. Here is where the difference between white and black players lies. Because bench players were much more likely to be white than black, it was more likely that a white player stayed on the roster as he aged. Black players who were not clearly better than whites, i.e., good enough to win a starting job, were not likely to make the roster at all. In order for a black player to make a roster, he had to be good enough to win a starting job. Benchwarmers, role players, and marginal talents were white players. An aging slugger who was no longer able to handle a regular spot in the lineup, or a promising young left-handed pitcher who was not quite ready for regular duty, was a white player. Black players would have a place on the roster and add to their MLB experience as they aged only as long as they were starters. Before they were ready to hold a starting job and after their skills had eroded to the point that they were no longer able to contribute every day, they were unlikely to be on the roster at all.

Hitters were rewarded over a wider variety of performance variables than were pitchers. The coefficients on at-bats, home runs, and batting average are all significant for both black and white hitters. While black players were rewarded slightly better for accumulating more at-bats than were whites, this again may suggest that they had to prove themselves worthy of their salary. This result is also driven in part by the fact that black players were more likely to be starters than reserve players on MLB rosters. If a team was going to integrate, it was more likely to do so with a player good enough to play in the everyday lineup. While blacks were on rosters, they were few in number and rarely filled reserve rolls.

Blacks were rewarded at a higher rate for accumulating at-bats than were whites, but on the achievement performance variables, such as home runs and batting average, whites were paid better. The higher rate blacks earned for at-bats is not necessarily a positive result. This may reflect what appears to have been happening to MLB rosters at the time. They were integrated, but not all players had an equal chance at making a roster. A black player either had to prove he could excel in MLB, or he would not make the team. Average players were more likely to be white. In other words, the average black player had to be better than the average white player to make the team. As the results suggest, blacks were paid well for their performance, but even though integration took place, there was still discrimination.[23]

The other variables that affect salary are age and experience. They are closely related, yet they are not considered in the same way with regard to salary. This makes intuitive sense in that experience is indicative of future performance more so than age. However, they are obviously correlated, since a player who makes the MLB roster ages and gains experience at the same rate. When analyzing the role of age and experience, an apparent contradiction arises. Figure 5.2 illustrates what our model suggests, that black players were rewarded at a higher rate than white players for experience. But Figure 5.3 shows that white players were compensated better as they aged than were black players. So how is it possible that black players were rewarded at a higher rate for experience but less at every age? The answer lies in the details of this relationship.

The average white rookie was 22.2 years old, while the average black rookie was 26.3. Since black players were entering MLB at older ages, they were behind on the earning scale when measured by age. Looking at it another way, the average 27-year-old white player had five years of experience, while the average 27-year-old black player had less than one year. Because the black players were older on average when they entered the league, it meant that the experience level they achieved came at a later age than it did for white players. Therefore, a 27-year-old white player earned a salary increased by five years of experience, while a black 27-year-old had less than a full year of experience to help boost his salary.

Conclusion

It is no surprise that MLB hitters earned more than NLB hitters. They were compensated differently because they generated more income. This essay is a first attempt to measure what discrimination cost black players. But it underestimates the true cost because it only measures dollars, not emotional, social, or psychological costs.

So what does it all mean? The bottom line is that hitters were paid to hit home runs, and pitchers were paid to win games. And white players were better paid for each home run they hit and each game they won. After integration, black players who made it to the Majors were older than whites at every level of experience. As a result of this later career start, their career length and their total earnings lagged behind the average white player.

It appears that MLB owners, while they were ahead of the curve when it came to hiring black workers, still practiced discrimination in the workplace, albeit with more subtlety than an outright color barrier. While discriminatory practices are never to be condoned, it seems unreasonable to hold MLB owners to a higher standard of behavior than anyone else. They are to be lauded for their efforts at breaking down the color barrier and setting an example for other industries. At the same time, we need to recognize that like so many other white Americans at that time, they had a long way to go before they could be considered color blind.

Despite the pay differential and the shorter career, playing in the Majors was a far better deal financially than the Negro Leagues, and playing baseball for a career paid better than the average line of work most major leaguers could have hoped for. This is not a defense of discriminatory pay, merely an observation of the opportunity cost, and one possible explanation for why these players would put up with the discrimination they faced to play in the Majors. Not only were they pioneers, but they also recognized a good financial deal when they saw it.

Notes

1. A ditty circulating in the black press after Jackie Robinson was signed by the Dodgers. Lee Lowenfish, "When All Heaven Rejoiced: Branch Rickey and the Origins of the Breaking of the Color Line," *NINE: A Journal of Baseball History and Culture* 11, no. 1 (Fall 2002): 12.

2. Moses and Welday Walker played with Toledo of the AA in 1884 and were the last African Americans to openly appear in the Major Leagues until 1947. Merl F. Kleinknecht, "Blacks in 19th Century Organized Baseball," SABR Research Journals Archive, accessed January 2017, http://research.sabr.org/journals/blacks-in-19th-c-baseball.

3. Number of player-seasons calculated from Baseball-Reference.com. The salary data was taken from the Haupert Baseball Salary Database.

4. Throughout this essay, Negro Leagues will be used to refer to the several different leagues: Negro National League 1920–1931, Southern Negro League 1920, Eastern Colored League 1923–1928, Negro Southern League 1926, 1932, 1945, American Negro League 1929, East-West League 1932, Negro National League 1933–1948, Negro American League 1937–1960. Negro League Baseball Museum.com, accessed January 2017, https://www.nlbm.com/s/team.htm.

5. This time period avoids the Federal League and free agency, which both impacted the effect of the reserve clause.

6. Richard Topp, "Demographics," in *Total Baseball*, 408–409.

7. William Sundstrom, "The Color Line: Racial Norms and Discrimination in Urban Labor Markets, 1910–1950," *The Journal of Economic History* 54, no. 2 (1994): 382–396; Warren Whatley and Gavin Wright, "Race, Human Capital, and Labor Markets in U.S. History," in George Grantham and Mary MacKinnon, editors, *Labour Market Evolution* (London: Routledge, 1994).

8. Michael J. Haupert, "Player Pay and Productivity in the Reserve Clause and Collusion Eras," *Nine: A Journal of Baseball History and Social Policy Perspectives* 18, no. 1 (Fall 2009), 63–85.

9. Great strides have been made recently in collecting and disseminating NLB statistics. See Lawrence D. Hogan and Jules Tygiel, *Shades of Glory: The Negro League and the Story of African American Baseball* (Washington, DC: National Geographic Society, 2006), Seamheads.com Negro Leagues Database, and Dick Clark and Larry Lester, *The Negro Leagues Book* (Cleveland: Society for American Baseball Research, 1994).

10. Gerald W. Scully, "Pay and Performance in Major League Baseball," *The American Economic Review* 64, no. 6 (December 1974): 915–930.

11. Paul M. Sommers and Noel Quinton, "Pay and Performance in Major League Baseball: The Case of the First Family of Free Agents," *The Journal of Human Resources* 17, no. 3 (Summer 1982): 426–436; Yannis

M. Ioannides and Christopher A. Pissarides, "Monopsony and the Lifetime Relation between Wages and Productivity," *Journal of Labor Economics* 3, no. 1 (January 1985): 91–100; Andrew Zimbalist, "Salaries and Performance: Beyond the Scully Model, in *Diamonds Are Forever: The Business of Baseball*, Paul M. Sommers, editor (Washington, DC: Brookings Institution Press, 1992), 109–133; David C. Hoaglin and Paul F. Velleman, "A Critical Look at Some Analyses of Major League Baseball Salaries," *The American Statistician* 49, no. 3 (August 1995): 277–285; John Vrooman, "The Baseball Players Labor Market Reconsidered," *Southern Economic Journal* (October 1996): 339–360; Anthony Krautmann, "What's Wrong with Scully-Estimates of a Players Marginal Revenue Product?" *Economic Inquiry* 37, no. 2 (April 1999): 369–381; Anthony Krautmann, Elizabeth Gustafson and Lawrence Hadley, "A Note on the Structural Stability of Salary Equations: Major League Baseball Pitchers," *Journal of Sports Economics* 4, no. 1 (February 2003): 56–63; Jewell R. Todd, Michael McPherson, and David J. Molina, "Testing the Determinants of Income Distribution in Major League Baseball," *Economic Inquiry* 42, no. 3 (July 2004): 469–482; Michael Haupert and James Murray, "Regime Switching and Wages in Major League Baseball Under the Reserve Clause," *Cliometrica* 6, no. 2 (June 2012): 143–162; J. C. Bradbury, "What is Right With Scully Estimates of a Player's Marginal Revenue Product," *Journal of Sports Economics* 14, no. 1 (2013): 87–96.

12. The Red Sox became the last team to integrate when Pumpsie Green appeared in the Boston lineup on July 21, 1959.

13. All player salary data is from Haupert Professional Baseball Salary Database.

14. A player's salary is determined before a season starts, so this year's performance does not affect this year's salary. This year's salary was determined based on previous performance.

15. Several Yankees saw their salaries held constant, and three saw raises: Red Ruffing received a 25 percent salary increase to $10,000, George Pipgras got a 12.5 percent increase to $9,000, and Lefty Gomez got a whopping 60 percent raise to $12,000.

16. The NLB data come from Clark and Lester, *The Negro Leagues Book*, Hogan and Tygiel, *Shades of Glory*, Baseball Reference.com, and Seamheads.com. Negro Leagues Database. The MLB data comes from the contract card files at the National Baseball Library. The compilation of salaries has been built into the Haupert Baseball Salary Database.

17. The regression analysis determined that the value of a home run in MLB is worth five times as much as a home run in the NLB.

18. In earlier research, I found the first wave of black players were paid more than the average white player. That was with a limited sample of players, however, and after having increased the size of the sample significantly, that advantage of black player salaries over white disappears, Michael J. Haupert, "Pay, Performance, and Race during the Integration Era," *Black Ball* 2, no. 1 (Spring 2009): 37–51.

19. A dummy variable takes on the value of either 1 or 0, in this case 1 if a player was black, 0 if he was white. When multiplied by the coefficient, only those variables with a dummy value of 1 will have a value. So in this case, a positive coefficient on the black dummy variable indicates that black players got a pay bonus because they were black. The rationale for this is discussed in the text.

20. R^2 is a measure of the percentage of variation in the dependent variable, in this case salary that is explained by the independent variables included in the model.

21. Variables marked with an asterisk are "significant," that is, with 99 percent probability, they cause variation in the dependent variable. If a variable is "insignificant," it means that we cannot reject the hypothesis that the relationship between it and the dependent variable is simply coincidental.

22. Truman F. Bewley, "A Depressed Labor Market as Explained by Participants," *American Economic Review Papers and Proceedings* 85, no. 2 (May 1995): 250–54.

23. Armour, "The Effects of Integration, 1947–1986": 53–57.

Winning in the Crucible of White-Hot Competition

JEFFERY S. WILLIAMS

The day had finally come, and Joe Bostic was elated. On April 18, 1946, in Jersey City, New Jersey, Jackie Robinson became the first African American to play Organized Baseball in the 20th century, going 4-for-5 with a home run and two stolen bases for the Montreal Royals. Bostic and many other African American newspapermen such as Sam Lacy, Wendell Smith and Frank A. Young had advocated and agitated for a black player in the Major Leagues for years. When Robinson took his first step toward breaking baseball's color barrier, Bostic wrote:

> The most significant sports story of the century was written into the record books today as baseball took up the cudgel for democracy and an unassuming but superlative Negro boy ascended the heights of excellence to prove the rightness of the experiment. And prove it in the only correct crucible for such an experiment—the crucible of white-hot competition.[1]

Bostic understood the situation. Robinson's entry into competition with white ball players was not about whether black athletes could compete in Major League baseball; everyone in the game knew they could. Games between African American and white teams had been taking place for decades, and black teams had won enough to put the baseball world on notice—the Negro Leagues were overflowing with talented baseball players.

Rube Foster's formation of the Negro National League (NNL) in 1920 was the turning point in the history of black baseball. Before the NNL began operation, black teams had gone 90–121–9 (.427) against white big league clubs. Black teams especially struggled when more big league players were involved. Against Major League teams and all-star squads with eight or more Major Leaguers including the pitcher, black clubs were 37–76–6 (.327).[2]

The NNL and the other major black circuits that followed it greatly improved the performance of African American teams in interracial competition. From 1920 until Commissioner Kenesaw Mountain Landis stopped such games in 1924, Negro Leaguers were 29–30–2 (.492) against intact Major League clubs. From the inception of the NNL through 1948, Negro Leagues teams went 206–163–10 (.558) against big league all-star teams. The numbers clearly demonstrate that regular league play pushed the achievements of black clubs to new heights, and their success against white baseball's best were the first substantial steps toward integration of the Major Leagues.[3]

The results of interracial competition influenced executives Branch Rickey and Bill Veeck to desegregate Major League Baseball. However, the results of interracial games were downplayed by white players and the press, and the importance of these contests has been

75

largely ignored in narratives of baseball's integration. The creation of the NNL improved the talent and depth of African American baseball and eventually forced the integration of organized ball by demonstrating that some of the best players in the world were black.

Chasing Strands of Spaghetti

Robert Peterson, author of the seminal Negro Leagues history *Only the Ball Was White*, explained the pursuit of black baseball's story best. He wrote, "Tracing the course of the organized Negro Leagues is rather like trying to follow a single black strand through a ton of spaghetti. The footing is infirm, and the strand has a tendency to break off in one's hand and slither back into the amorphous mass." The difficulty of chasing strands of spaghetti has sentenced much of the saga of black baseball to obscurity. John Holway, another leading black ball writer, reflected, "what I had stumbled on by accident was a virtually unexplored continent. The world of black baseball history was not a mere footnote to baseball history—it was fully half of baseball history!"[4]

Interracial competition is where the black and white halves of baseball history meet. It is also a slippery strand of spaghetti, broken into a million pieces, and intentionally camouflaged by the men who took part in organizing and competing in games between black and white players. The unwritten rules of Jim Crow segregation said white men should not compete with black men. Perhaps seeking to uphold those rules and save his league from embarrassment, Commissioner Landis banned Major League teams from playing in off-season games. Landis later put limitations on playing barnstorming contests after October. The impetus behind the limitations on barnstorming was due, at least in part, to losses against Negro Leagues teams. The players responded by forming clubs made up of major and minor leaguers from various organizations, under such handles as the White Kings, Major League All-Stars, Pirrone's All-Stars, and Feller's All-Stars. Games went on every off-season, but major leaguers often played under assumed names or the contests were not publicized.[5]

Some of these games have disappeared in the mists of time. The most famous "lost" game reportedly took place at Los Angeles' Wrigley Field in the fall of 1934 between the Nashville Elite Giants and Dean All-Stars. Although there is no contemporaneous account of the contest, it provides an example of both the level of interracial competition and the difficulty in establishing an accurate historical record.

The Wrigley Field game pitted the talents of Dizzy Dean, that year's National League MVP and World Series hero, against the legendary Satchel Paige. Paige was an enormous box office draw in the 1930s and a pitcher who could match Dean's talents. According to legend, the contest lasted 13 innings before the black squad won, 1–0. Both teams were stocked with excellent players: Turkey Stearnes, Mule Suttles, Cool Papa Bell, and Willie Wells for Paige's crew, and Wally Berger, Dolph Camilli, Frank Demaree, and Gene Lillard for Dean's club.[6]

Berger was a standout player in the 1930s, hitting .298 with 34 home runs and 121 RBI in 1934. In 1935, he led the National League in home runs with 34 and RBI with 130. According to Berger, he had the only two hits for the major leaguers, including a smash off the center field fence that so angered Paige, he subsequently stuck out Camilli, Demaree, and Lillard on nine pitches. Cleveland Indians owner Bill Veeck claimed he was among a crowd of around 18,000 fans to witness the game. Veeck told *Collier's* magazine, in 1953, that both pitchers battled for the full 13 frames and Dean struck out 15 batters, only to be outdone by Paige, who fanned 17.[7]

In today's world of easy access to online newspaper archives, it is difficult to believe such a sensational game could have fallen in the baseball woods and made no sound. However, barnstorming contests of the time did occur without newspaper coverage. Baseball author Timothy Gay makes a strong case that the game did indeed take place. Gay points out that the showdown may not have been publicized because of Commissioner Landis' ban on barnstorming after October 31. Furthermore, promoters Ray Doan and Joe Pirrone had the ability to draw large crowds without advertising games in the newspapers, a strategy that allowed them to make a profit without Landis causing trouble for Dizzy Dean and the other Major League players. Finally, Gay wonders, "If the '34 L.A. game was just an urban myth, then why were Dean, Paige, Berger, Veeck and others not only adamant that the game was played, but in essential agreement over its details?" The Wrigley mystery game is the stuff of legend, and until a box score or a promotional poster is uncovered, that is where it will remain. Giving Paige credit for the win in what he called "the lost classic," Gay's records have Paige going 8–3 all-time in match-ups against Dean.[8]

Paige owed his talent to the baseball gods and his opportunity to Rube Foster. Paige's prowess on the mound and facility with a quip made him the most famous of all Negro Leagues players. His combination of ability and folksy philosophy was irresistible. Before Paige, there was Foster. Paige began in the Negro Leagues and hung on long enough to play in the Majors. Foster began playing for loosely constructed teams in ad hoc circuits, often held together with bubble gum and bailing wire. He built his own league for the expressed purpose of challenging the best white baseball had to offer. The result was the opportunity to play in the Negro Leagues, and later the Major Leagues, for hundreds of outstanding African American baseball players.

A Case of Greek Meeting Greek

Rube Foster first rose to prominence as one of the best pitchers in baseball—black or white. He achieved the same, if not greater, regard as a manager, general manager, and owner. He then founded and ran the first successful Negro League. Foster accomplished this extraordinary body of work in a short lifetime, before mental illness robbed the world of his abilities when he was only 47 years old. According to Robert Peterson, "Assessing Rube Foster's contribution to black baseball is easy. He was far and away the most important influence in raising the game to respectability, both artistic and financial." When Foster died in 1930, baseball integration was so far away many could not envision it, but Foster could. He knew he and other Negro Leagues players and executives had begun to blaze the trail Jackie Robinson would travel. The *Chicago Defender* stated, "Foster was not a 'Colored' baseball man—he was a person of consequence wherever baseball was discussed. He proved to a doubting public that white people have no monopoly on baseball."[9]

Andrew Foster was a man of consequence his entire adult life. Around 1898, the 19-year-old Texas native began pitching for squads such as the Waco Yellow Jackets and Fort Worth Colts, before leaving the state to pursue a big time baseball career, taking with him a fierce desire to compete with the best ballplayers in the world. When Frank C. Leland wrote Foster in 1902, inviting the already formidable hurler to join his Chicago Union Giants, the baseball magnate included the extra enticement that the Windy City squad would be competing with the top white teams. The 21-year-old Foster's reply was indicative of his competitive fire. He informed Leland, "If you play the best clubs in the land, white clubs, as you say, it will be a case of Greek meeting Greek. I fear nobody."[10]

Under the tutelage of black ball veteran and fellow southerner Dave Wyatt, Foster averaged nine strikeouts a game while posting a mark of 11–7 for the Union Giants and an integrated club in Otsego, Michigan. In 1903, the burly (230-pound) twirler headed east to pitch for the Cuban X-Giants and later the Philadelphia Giants, leading his clubs to four consecutive Eastern black ball titles. By 1908 the white press considered him on par with the best pitchers baseball had to offer and lamented, "if the color line didn't bar him he would be one of the stars of the big league."[11]

Over the course of a 21-year career (1898–1918), Foster rang up a combined record of 227–80 (.739) against stiff competition including black, Cuban, minor league, Major League, and strong semi-pro clubs. Along the way, he threw seven documented no-hitters while maintaining a 0.92 WHIP and a 1.87 ERA in over 2,700 innings pitched. The Texas native was at his peak in 1905, winning 35 games, including a no-hitter, against only five losses for the Philadelphia Giants, with an earned run average of 1.43. However, at this point, Foster later allowed, "I'd got as far as I could go [and] there was no hope of getting into the big league, so I kind of let myself go."[12]

Looking to improve his economic opportunities, Foster returned to Chicago in 1907 to pitch for and manage the Leland Giants, convincing six Philly players to go with him. In 1910, Foster helped attorney Beauregard Moseley wrest control of the Giants from Frank Leland. A year later, Foster and white saloon owner John Schorling (Charlie Comiskey's son-in-law) formed the Chicago American Giants out of the ashes of his old squad.[13]

Foster began his ascent as a manager by building an American Giants team that played baseball *his* way. According to Negro Leagues historian Larry Lester, "Foster exploited the game rules to every advantage known to the national pastime. He introduced the hit-and-run play, bunt-and-run, drag bunting, the double steals, the suicide squeeze play and tilting of the base lines for bunt control. Every Giant player was required to learn the art of bunting, including the sluggers. Each player eventually learned to become a switch hitter." Foster's strategy presaged today's sabermetrically driven defensive adjustments: "he moved his fielders for every batter. He moved the infield back and forth at will, brought them up on the grass like they were a set of mechanical players and sent them back at the proper time."[14]

By mastering the intricacies of the game, Foster's teams became tremendously successful. Under his leadership, the American Giants won seven Western black ball championships and three Negro National League crowns. Foster also knew a team of traveling black ballplayers had to go out of its way to avoid problems on the road, so he demanded that his squad always behave better than white teams. His mind seemed to always be on white baseball. In August 1907, Foster told the *Chicago Inter-Ocean*, "If only we had a chance that the white teams do, the opportunity to train and to go up against good teams all the time, I wouldn't be afraid to play any teams in the country."[15]

From his earliest days as a team owner, Foster advocated building a circuit modeled after the white major leagues. Writing in the December 16, 1911, *Indianapolis Freeman*, Foster articulated his case for a black league and opined that the best way to move black baseball forward was to institute a reserve clause similar to the one in the majors that prevented players from jumping from team to team. He wrote, "we will always be the underdog until we can successfully employ the methods that have brought success to the great powers that be in the present era—organization." Foster wanted to put teams in major cities from Louisville to Kansas City, creating a league that would help all owners to profit. He noted that the major black ball squads already made the same trips they would make under a league system.[16]

Foster argued, "we would receive better patronage, also a standing in baseball, and the winners in our league could force, by public sentiment, the same as Jack Johnson forced [Jim] Jeffries, the winners in the white league to meet us for the championship." Foster would continue to advocate the same sort of plan for the next nine years. His blueprint was simple: Organize a geographically logical circuit that would produce a champion who could then play the Major League winner. This true World Series would have made all parties money. In 1910, black heavyweight boxing titleholder Jack Johnson earned $65,000, which equates to around $1,670,000 today, for fighting Jeffries, the white former champion.[17]

Having faced and beaten the best the big leagues had to offer, Rube Foster could envision a world in which the segregated leagues came together to crown a true champion each fall. Foster was certain that with better organization, provided by a league structure, black baseball could compete with white baseball on and off the field. By the time of Foster's 1911 *Freeman* article, black clubs were 32–59–5 (.352) in all games dating back to 1885 against white major leaguers. However, since Foster's move to Chicago in 1902, black teams had gone 13–13–1 against white all-star conglomerations and 8–12–2 against intact big league clubs, for a much more competitive mark of 21–25–3 (.457).[18]

Big stars were beginning to emerge in African American baseball, and their exploits against white teams pushed the black game to greater heights. There was great pitching talent, including Rube Foster, who was an established star, and "Smokey" (or "Cyclone") Joe Williams, who was becoming one. Despite his enshrinement in Cooperstown in 1999, Williams is not well known today, but in 1952, when the *Pittsburgh Courier* polled "the top baseball men in the country" to create an all-time Negro Leagues team, the tall and rangy Texas fireballer edged Satchel Paige, 20 votes to 19, for the premier spot among pitchers. In fact, Williams' vote total tied with Oscar Charleston for the second-most on the entire list, behind only Josh Gibson.[19]

Among the best position players of the pre–Negro Leagues era was the spectacular John Henry "Pop" Lloyd, who was voted the top shortstop in the 1952 *Courier* poll, besting Willie Wells, Dick Lundy, and Dobie Moore. Pop Lloyd was one of many African American players known as "the black so and so." Josh Gibson was the black Babe Ruth; Oscar Charleston was the black Ty Cobb. Pop Lloyd was dubbed the black Honus Wagner, and the great Pirates shortstop was flattered by the comparison. In 1939, Wagner told the *Pittsburgh Courier*, "one day I had the opportunity to go see him (Lloyd) play. After I saw him play I felt honored that they should name such a great ball player after me."[20]

Foster was on hand in Cuba in the fall of 1910 when Pop Lloyd batted .314 for the Leland Giants as they captured seven out of 13 games (with one tie) against the top island squads, Habana and Almendares. A few weeks later, Lloyd outhit Ty Cobb, .500 to .368, during the Detroit Tigers' trip to Havana. Contemporary accounts indicate Cobb clowned a bit for the fans, juggling fly balls in the outfield. However, he also played to win—In Detroit's 4–0 victory over Almendares on November 27, Cobb finished off an inside-the-park home run with a head-first dive, and he was thrown out at the plate trying to score from first base on a single. The Tigers, led by Cobb and fellow future Hall of Famer Sam Crawford, went 7–4–1 against Cuban teams augmented by several Leland Giants, including 4–1 when the Georgia Peach participated. Cobb went hitless in the only loss he played in, as the Tigers "were outclassed at every angle" while being shut out by Habana's Luis "Chicho" Gonzalez.[21]

The World Series champion Philadelphia Athletics followed the Tigers to Cuba and lost six out of ten games against the Cuban and African American players. Future Hall of Fame pitchers Chief Bender and Eddie Plank started seven games for the Athletics and were beaten six times. Pop Lloyd hit a blistering .421 in 11 contests against the big league clubs, while fellow black ball legend Grant "Home Run" Johnson posted a .375 mark.[22]

Some of Organized Baseball's most powerful figures were beginning to see interracial competition as bad for business, both on the field and at the ticket window. That December, American League President Ban Johnson complained such games hurt his league: "I am opposed to barnstorming trips such as the Tigers and Athletics have made to Cuba. It doesn't help the game to have our star ball teams beaten in Cuba by negroes and half-breeds." Johnson announced that he would ask baseball's ruling body, the National Commission, to put a stop to such trips.[23]

The only recorded game pitting a black team against a major league outfit in 1911 saw the West Baden Sprudels beat the Pittsburgh Pirates, 2–1, in mid–September. In 1912, top black and white teams competed head-to-head more than ever before, with the African American clubs going 17–13–1, including a 3–1–1 mark against intact Major League squads. On October 27, the New York Lincoln Giants whitewashed the National League champion New York Giants, 6–0. A dominating Joe Williams allowed the Giants, supplemented by Yankees first baseman Hal Chase, only four hits, two of them by outfielder Red Murray, who had hit .270 and drove in 88 runs during the regular season before batting .323 in the 1912 World Series. The *Elmira Star-Gazette* remarked that the only thing keeping Williams out of the major leagues was his color. Smokey Joe proved the newspaper right nine days later when he stifled the Yankees, 6–0, again allowing only four hits.[24]

Rube Foster had seen with his own eyes that black players could compete with players from Organized Baseball. On the West Coast during the winter of 1912-1913, the American Giants captured the pennant of the integrated California Winter League. Rube Foster's outfit won 13 out of 24 games against teams with at least six current or former Major League players, although they managed only a 4–6 mark against squads with eight or nine big leaguers.[25]

In the December 20, 1913, *Indianapolis Freeman*, Foster reiterated his position that a league structure modeled after Organized Baseball would be better for black owners and players alike: "With the proper organization, patterned after the men who have made baseball a success, we will, in three years, be rated as other leagues are rated." To support his contention, Foster quoted the sporting editor of the *San Francisco Chronicle*, who had gushed, "the colored players here, representing the American Giants, would be stars in the big league. We hate to say how good this ball club really is.'"[26]

By the end of the First World War, black players had demonstrated their abilities to white players, coaches, scouts, and fans numerous times. However, 1919 was a disappointing year for African American clubs in head-to-head competition with the top white squads. On the heels of a 7–4 interracial record in 1917, black teams managed only a 6–9 mark in 1918 and went just 5–10–1 against white Major League outfits in 1919. Included in the tally was a 7–5 Atlantic City Bacharach Giants loss to the New York Giants in the only game involving an intact Major League team. Against such complete Major League squads, the black professionals' record now stood at 28–61–6 (.315) all time, although they had gone a respectable 10–15–2 during the teens.[27]

To go toe to toe with entire big league teams and win consistently, Rube Foster was convinced that black baseball needed structure. According to historian Leslie Heaphy, "Rube Foster believed the main goal of the Negro Leagues was preparing for integration; when that day arrived he wanted athletes to be ready to step forward."[28]

In his "Pitfalls of Baseball" series which appeared in the *Chicago Defender* in the winter of 1919-1920, Foster meticulously built the case for organization. The five "Pitfalls of Baseball" articles were Foster's black ball manifesto. The essays made a convincing argument for a well-structured league. Furthermore, they placed the league in a greater social context as part of the concentrated drive of major African American institutions towards integration. As always, Foster's focus did not stray far from competition against the white Major Leagues.

In "Pitfalls of Baseball, Part I," Foster painted black baseball as an enterprise in a sorry state. He called for what he referred to as a "reconstruction of the whole business." He pointed out that no team, save one, was making substantial money, and no player knew where he was going to play the next season nor where his paychecks would come from. The reader could easily infer that the lone team making money was Foster's American Giants. All of this doom and gloom was used to set up his argument that black baseball needed organization and leadership.[29]

"Pitfalls of Baseball, Part II" was Foster's clarion call for a strong black leader. He then claimed he would follow that strong leader, while making it clear he was that strong leader. Foster also took time to lambaste players for demanding more money while teams were suffering noting, "the smallest salary ... equals the salary of any post office carrier, clerk or city school teacher in the United States. [The ballplayers] have to put in about twenty hours per month for this, have all the time they need, sleep all day, yet they are underpaid."[30]

Part III got to the heart of Foster's desire for organization. The lack of structure in black baseball led to players jumping from team to team. This left ownership and fans without a stable product, and ownership competed for players by promising money they could not afford or did not intend to pay. The result was that players never had a steady paycheck. The answer to the problem, Foster again stressed, was organization: "what is needed is a foundation that we can build on, something that we can merit the wonderful attendance and pride our followers have in us."[31]

Part IV was a commentary on the owners involved with African American teams. Foster noted they had not made their money in baseball, but in other enterprises. Therefore, it was clear they were good businessmen, yet black baseball had exasperated them. He wrote of the many owners who left baseball behind, "They were honest and their dealings above suspicion. Still they realized that the way things were conducted, there was no future."[32]

Foster was always aware that baseball needed its fans, and he was never shy about appealing to them for help. In "Pitfalls of Baseball, Part IV," he both expressed his views of African American society and asked for the fans' assistance in making baseball a success:

> It is historic for years that Colored people will not stand for organizations outside the church and secret societies. They are so afraid to die, they support the church; so afraid when sick, they will suffer. They support such institutions. Outside of these they have proven they cannot agree, all of which is very regrettable; still it is true. There is no sane reason we could not as a people have things among us and pattern after the ways others have wrote success in history. It can be done, if we could only stop to consider what is best. Nothing is impossible if all parties are allowed to air their differences.[33]

By "all parties," Foster referred to the various owners of black ball clubs across the United States. He next called for a summit of these owners to organize a league. He proposed drawing up a league constitution, which would allow members to keep their current players and provide for a championship series between the winners of Eastern and Western divisions. Then Foster let his long-term intentions be known: After the African American playoff, "such champion team [will] eventually to play the winner among the whites."[34]

Foster's desire was to beat the men of white baseball at their own game both on the diamond and in the board room. In "Pitfalls of Baseball, Part V," he laid out his business plan. Foster again suggested emulating white baseball's league structure. He made clear this was the only way to stop the players from constantly moving from team to team. Player jumping led to battles amongst the owners and, eventually, more jumping. Foster insisted that preventing the seemingly endless player migrations was also a key to winning more games against white teams. Player jumping left black clubs in disarray and thinned their talent. A strong league would stabilize teams and aid in their development. This would allow the proposed league to crown a champion strong enough to win a true World Series against the best Major League team. Furthermore, Foster pointed out that Organized Baseball did not allow player tampering, and it led to greater revenues and, therefore, better player salaries. Finally, Foster warned that he was ready to leave black ball altogether if organization did not happen.[35]

No one in black baseball wanted Rube Foster to step away. Less than two months later, eight baseball magnates were meeting in Kansas City, Missouri, to hammer out the details of a new association, dubbed the "National Baseball League of the United States." Foster was more than prepared for the meeting. His fellow owners were "dumbfounded" to discover that he had already incorporated the proposed league in Illinois, Michigan, Ohio, Pennsylvania, New York, and Maryland. The inclusion of the last three states revealed Foster's intention to pursue his plan for an Eastern division, but only a representative from an as-yet-unformed Washington, D.C., team showed up in Kansas City. The eight owners present deposited $500 each to bind them to the fledgling organization, and a league constitution was drawn up by Topeka attorney Elisha Scott and some of the sportswriters present at the meeting, including Foster's former mentor, Dave Wyatt. The writers shifted a few players from one team to another, in the interest of making the league more competitive, and Foster was unanimously chosen as chairman.[36]

Rube Foster finally had his league. His American Giants snared the first three titles of the predominantly midwestern circuit, popularly known as the Negro National League, but the opposition to his juggernaut club became stiffer every year. The manager and owner Rube Foster must have hated losing games to the other NNL clubs, but the league chairman Rube Foster must have loved seeing the organization grow more and more competitive. He ran the league with vigor and kept it afloat despite the organizational and financial shortcomings of his fellow owners.[37]

The formation of the NNL was followed by the creation of the Eastern Colored League (ECL) in December 1922. The ECL would be led by owner Edward Bolden, whose Philadelphia Hilldale club had been an associate member of the NNL, and powerful booking agent Nat Strong. The ECL filled an important void in black baseball and furthered the immersion of Cuban and other Latin American players into the black game. Historian Adrian Burgos maintains that Cuban Stars owner and numbers man Alex Pompez "was the most significant force in the incorporation of Latino talent for much of the twentieth century."[38]

The ECL immediately upset Rube Foster by raiding the NNL for players. The war between the two leagues paradoxically led to a major advancement in black baseball—the first Colored World Series. Historian Michael E. Lomax noted that the East-West showdown was considered a "symbol of race pride and racial advancement," but was used by Foster to secure an agreement from the ECL to respect NNL player contracts. In the course of a thrilling series played in Philadelphia, Baltimore, Kansas City, and Chicago during the fall of 1924, the NNL's Kansas City Monarchs defeated Hilldale of the ECL, five games to four (with one tie).[39]

In 1924, the success of black ball clubs in integrated competition prompted baseball Commissioner Landis to forbid big league teams from playing any more interracial games under the MLB imprint. In other words, St. Louis Cardinals players could no longer take on the St. Louis Stars wearing their own uniforms or advertise themselves as the Cardinals. Black players were convinced that Landis instituted this rule to put an end to the defeats they were inflicting on MLB clubs. When Rube Foster complained to the commissioner about the limitation on games between black and white teams, Landis reportedly replied, "Mr. Foster, when you beat our teams, it gives us a black eye."[40]

However, Landis could never completely stop big leaguers from forming all-star squads to take on teams from the Negro Leagues. Landis' de facto ban did not slow the volume of competition or the increased success of the Negro Leaguers. The Judge had good reason to fear the prowess of the NNL and ECL. From the inception of Foster's league in 1920 through 1926, black teams dominated MLB all-star teams to the tune of a 53–31–4 record (.631). In 1925, big league teams went 8–3–2 (.727) against Major League outfits, and the following year black squads were a dominant 17–2–1 (.928) in interracial games played from Baltimore to Los Angeles. The Negro Leaguers' record would have been perfect if not for an extra-inning loss and another 1–0 defeat in which the only run was unearned. As far as the quality of their competition goes, it should be noted that black teams compiled a record of 15–4-1 in 1925 and 1926 when facing clubs made up of nine or more Major League players, including the pitcher.[41]

Unfortunately, Rube Foster's life took a tragic turn in 1925 when poison gas spewing from a broken line left him unconscious in an Indianapolis boarding house bathroom. He probably would have died had his players not come to look for him when he did not arrive at the ballpark. His behavior became increasingly erratic, and in September 1926 his wife Sarah was forced to summon the police after he became violent and reported hearing voices telling him "that he was going to be called on to pitch in organized baseball's world series." Soon after, he was institutionalized in the Kankakee, Illinois, State Hospital, where he spent the rest of his life before finally succumbing in December 1930. The cause of death was reported as "General Paralysis of the Insane."[42]

The *Chicago Defender* lamented Foster's passing as a "loss to mankind." Romeo Dougherty, the great *New York Amsterdam News* sports editor, later eulogized Foster by writing, "What Foster meant to Negro baseball was of such a nature his name will never die as long as Negroes play the game." In Los Angeles a couple of days before Foster died, the Philadelphia Royal Giants swept a doubleheader from a group of big leaguers playing for Shell Oil. The two victories gave black clubs a 15–5–1 advantage in 1930 and a record of 131–86–7 (.604) in all games played between major leaguers and Negro Leagues outfits since the formation of the NNL in 1920. From the first recorded interracial contest in 1885 through 1930, black teams were now 221–207–16 (.516) versus big league squads.[43]

Rube Foster had used his athletic talent and later his brilliant mind to forge a legacy that would not die, namely the creation and expansion of organized black baseball. Foster's legacy was carried forward by a legion of black players, who proved they could match the best Organized Baseball had to offer. To say the least, Foster left baseball in better condition than he found it.

Lincoln, Jefferson, Paige, Dean and Feller?

Ironically, after Rube Foster left the scene, it was the major leaguers Dizzy Dean and Bob Feller who did the most to popularize and legitimize off-season games between black and white teams. Dean, a simple man from a hardscrabble background in Arkansas, pushed baseball toward integration simply by recognizing and respecting the abilities of black baseball players. Feller followed Dean as a headliner in the unofficial interracial season. Feller's outstanding barnstorming teams gave black squads all they could handle and helped to legitimize the talents of Negro Leagues players in the process. The common denominator was Satchel Paige, who shared headlines with Dean and Feller for over a decade.

The Great Depression nearly destroyed black baseball. Without Foster's leadership, the Negro National League floundered and closed its doors following the 1931 season. The NNL was reformed in 1933 under the guidance of Pittsburgh numbers operator Gus Greenlee, but this new, predominantly Eastern-based circuit struggled to survive as well. Interracial baseball helped the game—black and white—ascend from the depths of the Depression.[44]

Large crowds gathered to watch interracial games throughout the 1930s. The players who put most of the fans in the seats during that period were, without question, Dizzy Dean and Satchel Paige. The pitchers shared a country charm fans could not resist, and it didn't hurt that both men could make batters—black, brown and white—curse their names. They were also shameless self-promoters who had risen from poverty to wealth and fame. According to the mores of Jim Crow America, the white man from Arkansas and the black man from Alabama should not have been friends, but baseball brought them together. According to Paige, the two "were about as alike as two tadpoles." Venues such as Yankee Stadium, Wrigley Field, Forbes Field, and League Park in Cleveland were happy to host their rivalry, and the turnstiles clicked with fans of both races hungry for a look at two of baseball's biggest characters and best pitchers.[45]

Dean deserves credit not only for competing against black teams during the Jim Crow era, but for heaping praise on his opponents. Dizzy, born, according to writer Joe Williams, "with a natural and profound contempt for the laws of grammar," went so far as to name Paige the greatest pitcher of all time. Dean said of his longtime rival, "I know the best pitcher I ever see and it's old Satchell Paige, that big lanky colored boy. Say, old Diz is pretty fast back in 1933 and 1934, and you know my fastball looks like a change of pace alongside that little pistol bullet old Satchell shoots up to the plate." In the mid–1930s, the two hurlers were at the height of their powers, and accounts of their head-to-head meetings indicate that Paige was better than Dean.[46]

In 1934, Dizzy Dean was on top of the baseball world. Not even a baseball smashing into his unique brain could keep him down. In Game Four of the World Series, Dean was attempting to break up a double play at second base when, according to sportswriting legend Grantland Rice, Tigers shortstop Bill Rogell's throw to first base "struck Dizzy Dean squarely on the head with such terrific force that it bounded twenty-five feet in the air and more than a hundred feet away into Hank Greenberg's glove in short right field ... the great Dizzy crumpled and fell like a Marionette whose string had snapped."[47]

The incident gave birth to the famous (although it never appeared in a newspaper) line, "X-Ray of Dean's Head Reveals Nothing." On October 9, Dean scattered six hits while shutting down the Tigers, 11–0, and clinching a world title for the Cardinals. Later that month, Dean was named the 1934 National League MVP. He had earned it, having won 30 games while saving seven more, and posting a 2.66 ERA. Instead of resting on his laurels, however, Dean went barnstorming with Satchel Paige.[48]

Two days after winning the World Series, Dizzy and his younger brother Paul were on the mound facing a black team. The elder Dean worked the first three frames, before Paul hurled the next two as the Dean All-Stars downed the Kansas City Monarchs, 8–3, in Wichita, Kansas. There were very few strikeouts for the Cardinals twirlers. The pair considered the Negro Leaguers "better hitters than the Detroit Tigers," with Dizzy declaring, "Don't expect me to strike out the Monarchs. They are really a major league ball club and I might say they are also gentlemen as well as players." The next night, the siblings pitched two innings apiece and were each nicked for one run, as the Monarchs blanked the Dean All-Stars, 7–0, in Kansas City. On October 22, the brothers each worked two innings and again allowed one run apiece, in a 5–3 loss to the Pittsburgh Crawfords in Columbus, Ohio.[49]

The next afternoon in Pittsburgh, Dean proved he did not take competition against black teams lightly. Facing an NNL All-Star squad consisting of mostly Crawfords players, Dean pitched two innings and then left the mound to play in the outfield. Satchel Paige also worked two innings before being relieved by Harry Kincannon. In the fifth inning, the Homestead Grays' Vic Harris tapped a pitch in front of the plate. Former Tigers catcher George Susce fielded the ball but threw wide of first base, and Harris hustled to second. Dean ran in all the way from left field to claim Harris had run inside the baseline and was guilty of interference. Local umpire James Ahearn apparently thought Dean's eyesight was stronger than his syntax. He called Vic Harris out. Harris, who had a history of run-ins with the arbiter, smashed Ahearn in the head with a catcher's mask and, according to the recap in the *Pittsburgh Post-Gazette*, "within a few seconds the rumpus was in full sway with fists flying, players gripping their bats in menacing fashion and everything in a turmoil…. Spectators leaped over the railing and into the melee."[50]

Crawfords manager Oscar Charleston, who had instigated a similar fracas in Indianapolis back in 1915, was in the middle again, "punching away enthusiastically." Josh Gibson had George Susce in a headlock and tossed both Dean and Crawfords left fielder Ted Page aside when they tried to make him relinquish his grip. A police squad ("maces in hand") eventually restored order, and the game continued sans the fiery Harris, whom Ahearn said he planned to sue. Ultimately, Grays owner Cum Posey had his friend, Pittsburgh Steelers owner Art Rooney, pull a few strings and get the case dismissed. Gibson later hit a home run for the NNL All-Stars as they came from behind to win, 4–3.[51]

The year 1936 was an outstanding one for baseball. In January, a 21-year-old Joe DiMaggio auditioned for a spot in the Majors by taking on a man who had never pitched an inning of big league ball. The last significant interracial contest of 1936 saw Satchel Paige and a teenage Bob Feller square off in the first of many barnstorming games. In between, Major League Baseball flourished. In February, Babe Ruth, Ty Cobb, Honus Wagner, Walter Johnson and Christy Mathewson were announced as the first players to be elected to the National Baseball Hall of Fame. In October, DiMaggio and Lou Gehrig led the Yankees to a World Series championship. Negro Leaguers finished 7–3 against white big league squads that included such stars as Feller, Vince DiMaggio, Johnny Mize, and Rogers Hornsby.[52]

Bob Feller would become a fixture in interracial baseball. Joe DiMaggio was not a common participant in integrated games, but his first meeting with Paige was the stuff of legend. On January 26, 1936, in Oakland, California, DiMaggio stepped in against the man he later said was "the toughest pitcher I ever faced." Paige opposed a Major League lineup. His ad hoc team was not of big league caliber. Negro Leagues veteran Ameal Brooks was hired to catch Paige, and the rest of the squad was filled out by local amateurs. Nevertheless, Paige dominated, fanning 15 batters. DiMaggio's performance foreshadowed a career that saw him strike out at an amazingly low rate, making contact against the fireballer in all four at-bats. In the tenth inning, with a man on third, DiMaggio hit a weak bouncer off Paige's glove for a single and the game-winning RBI. The big leaguers prevailed, 2–1. It was later reported that a Yankees scout exuberantly wired the big club, "DiMaggio All We Hoped He'd Be—Hit Satch One for Four." The telegram story has never been verified. However, it is plausible the Yankees would view DiMaggio holding his own against Paige as a sign he was ready to face big league pitching.[53]

Bob Feller got his first taste of integrated baseball when he was literally fresh off his father's Van Meter, Iowa, farm. Feller burst into Major League baseball like no player had before. In 1936, the 17-year-old Feller's fastball overwhelmed big league hitters. Feller equaled Dizzy Dean's MLB record with 17 strikeouts in one game. Following the season, promoter Ray Doan signed Feller up to pitch against a team of NNL All-Stars, the first of what would be many meetings with Paige. The *Des Moines Register* noted that the young Phenom "will be facing players who undoubtedly would be in the National or American league if they were white instead of black." In front of 5,000 fans in Des Moines, Feller struck out eight of the ten batters he faced. Paige and Feller each threw three shutout innings as the NNL All-Stars won, 4–2.[54]

Bob Feller was a fixture on the 1940s barnstorming circuit, and the presence of the wunderkind pitcher drew big crowds. Big crowds meant big money, and star players such as Vince DiMaggio, Johnny Mize, and Hal Trosky joined Feller for games against black and white teams. In 1937, the Kansas City Monarchs finished 2–4 against an excellent squad advertising themselves as the Major League All-Stars. The contests were well played and tightly contested. There were three one-run games, and the only blowout was a 10–0 win for the Monarchs in Oklahoma City. The *Daily Oklahoman* did its best to downplay the black club's victory, reporting that Feller struck out the side in his only inning of work, and afterward, "everyone might as well have gone home."[55]

Satchel Paige and several other black ball greats, including Josh Gibson and Cool Papa Bell, had spent the summer of 1937 in the Dominican Republic battling for a championship at the behest of dictator Rafael Trujillo. Paige later claimed that during the final game of the season, Trujillo surrounded the field with armed soldiers as a way to motivate his club to bring home the title. They did, and the black ball stars left for the States immediately. The story was slightly exaggerated, but it produced one of the lanky twirler's brilliant witticisms. When it was mentioned to him years later that baseball was a spiritual experience in the D.R., Paige replied, "Them guns wasn't spiritual. But they nearly made a spirit out of me."[56]

Bob Feller's arrival on the scene augured well for the white teams. From 1936 through 1948, various Major League all-star clubs went 81–54–3 (.600) against black squads, depleted by both the Second World War and defections of their best players to Latin American countries such as the D.R. and Mexico. In 1938, a black team failed to record a win against a big league team for the first time in 36 years, losing all three contests they participated in.[57]

Following World War II, Feller put together a team that dominated barnstorming competition. In games against African American teams from 1945 through 1947, Feller's All-Stars racked up a 27–9 (.750) record. Feller's presence and desire to win handed Negro Leagues teams more interracial losses than they had suffered since before the formation of the NNL. But Feller's participation in such contests was also a positive for black players.

The high-profile games between Paige and Feller always made headlines, and thousands of fans were reminded that only the color of their skin kept black men out of the big leagues.[58]

Bob Feller was complicated—more complicated than his simple Van Meter, Iowa, background would indicate. Of his frequent mound opponent, he once remarked, "The pre-war Paige was the best I ever saw, and I'm judging him on the way he overpowered and outwitted some of the best big-league hitters of the day." Feller also once said that if Jackie Robinson were white, "I doubt if they would consider him big league material."[59]

While recounting the contributions of Feller and Dizzy Dean to baseball's eventual integration, Pulitzer Prize–winning sports columnist Jim Murray once wrote, "Baseball in those days was as Jim Crow as an Alabama restroom. It had to preserve the fiction that lily-white baseball was the finest in the land. In baseball you didn't even get to the back of the bus. You walked." Murray understood that Dean and Feller were motivated by the mighty dollar when barnstorming with black teams. Nevertheless, he recognized that they deserved credit for risking the myth of white supremacy in fair competition. With just a hint of sarcasm, Murray noted, "When you talk about the giants of civil rights in the country you begin with Lincoln and Jefferson … and, of course, Dizzy Dean and Bob Feller."[60]

Dean and Feller will never be remembered as brave soldiers in the battle for racial justice, nor should they. However, as baseball moved toward integration, they helped reveal a secret: The National Pastime was not democratic. The best players in the country where all men were created equal did not all play in the Major Leagues.

A Perfect Coordination of Muscle and Brain

America's Jim Crow laws forbade every interracial interaction from sex to chess. Dating from the birth of the Cuban Giants in 1885 through 1946, the year Jackie Robinson smashed the color line, at least 637 interracial baseball games involving predominantly big league squads were played. During the same time, at least 3,278 African Americans were lynched.[61]

Famed sportswriter Fred Lieb claimed that big leaguers Rogers Hornsby, Tris Speaker, and Gabby Street were all members of the Ku Klux Klan. Although he often participated in games against black players, New York Yankees outfielder Jake Powell bragged in 1938 that during his off-season work as a policeman, he liked to crack "niggers on the head with my nightstick." Commissioner Landis immediately suspended Powell, but syndicated newspaper columnist Westbrook Pegler was unimpressed, reminding his readers that Major League Baseball "trades under the name of the national game, but has always treated Negroes as Adolph Hitler [*sic*] treats the Jews."[62]

Very often, though, it was the mainstream white press who were guilty of racism, subtly and overtly. In 1922, while discussing heavyweight contender Harry Wills' chances, a *Chicago Daily News* editorial perversely claimed that because Wills was black, he was more closely related to a gorilla and could therefore defeat the white champion, Jack Dempsey. The paper's ugly polemic both insulted the black populace and trivialized African Americans' victories in integrated competition.[63]

At that time, Jack Johnson's winning and holding of the heavyweight crown from 1908 to 1915 was the most significant black athletic achievement in American history. The *Daily News* comparison of black men to gorillas had a clear goal—render those victories meaningless. The best man did not win boxing matches; the most animalistic man did. In response, an African American newspaper, the *Topeka Plaindealer*, pointed out that the Detroit Stars, Indianapolis A.B.C.s, St. Louis Stars, and Kansas City Monarchs had all recently defeated Major League teams on the baseball diamond, a sport "requiring a perfect co-ordination of muscle and brain."[64]

Such interracial competition was against the law in many places in America, and it was against the rules of white supremacy everywhere. The two rules of white supremacy were: one, never admit a black person can do anything better than you; and two, never give a black person the opportunity to prove rule one wrong. When white major leaguers broke rule two by engaging in direct competition with Negro Leagues teams, they added a third rule: Advertise all games with black' squads as exhibitions.[65]

To this day, the legacy of the Negro Leagues suffers from a lack of recognition. Part of the problem stems from efforts by white players and press of the time to characterize losses to black teams as unimportant. Because baseball took "brains and brawn," any defeat had to be dismissed as an "exhibition" in order to uphold the myth of white supremacy. However, the reports of interracial games revealed players trying desperately to win. When black and white teams met on the diamond, no standings were kept, but everyone knew the score.

While comments about the strength of individual black players are easy to find, admissions by white players that black teams were up to big league standards are few and far between. With the help of the white press, Major League players were careful never to give black teams credit for their success in integrated competition. A 1903 meeting between two future Hall of Fame pitchers—one black and one white—is representative of the way African American victories were downplayed.

On August 3 of that year, Philadelphia Athletics southpaw Rube Waddell was hired by the Murray Hills, a New York City semipro team, to pitch against Andrew Foster and the Cuban X-Giants. Both men threw complete games, and the X-Giants captured the contest, 6–3, with Foster scattering seven hits to pick up the win.[66]

In an attempt to fool his Major League employers, Waddell pitched under the pseudonym "Wilson," but he was exposed by *Philadelphia North American* scribe Charles Dryden, who chastised Waddell for pitching without proper rest against the African American squad. The Athletics ace had pitched a complete game the day before and had logged 23 innings that week. According to Dryden, the black team did not win the game, the unpredictable Waddell and a band of amateurs lost it:

> We deem it worthwhile to announce that Mr. Waddell is still taking splendid care of himself and framing up a scheme to win the next game he pitches. The actor man has been unlucky of late, but he predicts that a change will soon come. Rather than have his wonderful arm go stale by resting on the Holy Sabbath, the strenuous Mr. Waddell pitched an exhibition game on that day and lost it. The Cuban X-Giants whacked the "Reuben" about a dozen times, and he struck out 12 of the Africans. Because his catcher had no life insurance, Mr. Waddell was obliged to cut out his curve ball. The catcher couldn't stand the pace, and the coons bumped the speedy straight ones.[67]

Dryden did all he could to protect white baseball supremacy. He reminded the reader that Waddell worked without proper rest, insinuated that the eccentric lefty was forced to pitch without one of his weapons, and only gave the X-Giants credit in disingenuous fashion while calling them "coons." In Jim Crow era newspapers, the backhanded compliment was almost as ubiquitous as the box score.

For Foster, the moniker "Rube," normally used to describe an unsophisticated, country bumpkin type, was a badge of honor won on the playing field. A few years later, he told a white newspaperman, "It was when we beat the Athletics [*sic*], with Rube Waddell pitching, that they gave me the name of the colored Rube Waddell." The derogatory descriptor fit the erratic Waddell much better than the erudite Foster, whose living quarters, the *Chicago Defender* once gushed, "could have easily been the home of one of our most pious ministers." A month before the Murray Hill contest, Ban Johnson had suspended Waddell for five days after he went into the stands to punch a fan in the nose. Later that season, Waddell's manager Connie Mack, suspended him indefinitely for his drunken behavior.[68]

Waddell has long been celebrated as one of baseball's colorful characters, while Foster was largely forgotten until historians such as Robert Peterson and John Holway resurrected his memory. While Waddell was a ticking time bomb on and off the field, his ability as a pitcher is unquestionable. During that 1903 season, Waddell led the Major Leagues in complete games and logged a record 302 strikeouts, an astonishing 115 more than the next pitcher. It was the second of six consecutive seasons in which Waddell led the American League in strikeouts. Indeed, 1903 was one of the best years in a career good enough to see Waddell enshrined in Cooperstown in 1946, 35 years ahead of Foster.[69]

George Waddell was given the nickname Rube for his simplicity and poor behavior, while Andrew Foster earned the nickname Rube for his prowess on the mound. Historian Sarah L. Trembanis later noted, "By employing the name 'Rube' Foster kept the name as a rhetorical trophy for a battle won. Therefore, the public use of the name 'Rube' for Foster was an attempt to point out the cracks in segregated baseball and the white supremacist theories that maintained that segregation." Trembanis asserted that Foster's use of the name made it difficult for white players to claim the color line was based on ability as opposed to race.[70]

An August 1907 article in the *Chicago Inter-Ocean* is another excellent example of the ability of the white press to give African Americans credit, while reminding the reader that African Americans were an inferior race. Columnist Frederic North Shorey began his two-page article heaping praise on Rube Foster, writing, "If you have never seen 'Rube' Foster … in action you are not qualified to discuss baseball." He immediately pulled back by noting that this was the opinion of "colored baseball fans." Describing a Leland Giants 1–0 victory over the Mike Donlin All-Stars, a semi-pro outfit led by current and former major leaguers Mike Donlin, Jake Stahl, Jimmy Callahan, and Jimmy Ryan. Shorey wrote, "so heavily have the colored population been realizing on their victory that it is said that there has been a veritable famine in chicken and watermelon on the South side." Foster was now so popular among Chicago's black population, Shorey claimed, that "Booker T. Washington would have to be content with second place."[71]

Shorey gushed that the big twirler possessed "all the speed of a Rusie, the tricks of a Radbourne, and the heady coolness and deliberation of a Cy Young," and owned that only his color kept him out of Major League Baseball. However, Foster was said to achieve his success with many "tricks," including throwing the ball to the plate when the batter was not ready and stalling until Mike Donlin was livid before pitching to him.[72]

Foster's appearance was described as "almost the typical stage darky—husky, black as coal … and without any ostensible neck." According to Shorey, most of the black fans in the stands were gambling, wore flashy clothes, and spoke in the insulting dialect commonly employed by the white writers of the time. A black man in a Panama hat informed Shorey, "If Rube don't win today Ah suah will walk home…. Ah've put mah last dollah on mah preference." Shorey ended his piece by heaping praise on Foster, describing his exclusion from Major League Baseball as "tragic." However, the overall tone of the article made clear that Rube Foster and other African Americans had no place in white baseball.[73]

In an era in which calling black people coons and darkies, displaying grotesque cartoons of their appearances, and making derogatory references to chicken and watermelon were accepted practices for the white mainstream press, American society was defined by the concentrated effort to keep African Americans in a subservient position—closer to slavery than true freedom. The view that black men were both dangerous and inferior was pervasive. The United States in which Foster and his brethren competed was a time in which segregation laws and, more often, community practices were used liberally to prevent African Americans from attaining the rights of true citizenship.

The epic October 1909 showdown between Foster's Leland Giants and the Chicago Cubs is a perfect illustration of just how hotly contested and socially significant interracial games were. In its pre-series write-ups, the *Chicago Tribune* reported that the Lelands had added St. Paul Gophers stars Bobby Marshall, a former football All-American at Minnesota, and infielder Felix "Dick" Wallace to their already formidable lineup. The *Tribune* was quick to point out the series' importance to the black community, noting, "the colored team's admirers say it is for the city title."[74]

The Cubs would be down a good man as future Hall of Fame second baseman Johnny Evers decided to forgo the series. Chicago manager and first baseman Frank Chance also declined to play, but the Cubs were not without talent. After capturing three National League pennants and two World Series in the three years previous, the North-siders had won 104 games in 1909, only to finish second to the Pirates, and they would re-take the pennant with 104 more victories in 1910. The Cubs pitching staff was anchored by future Hall of Famer Mordecai "Three Finger" Brown, who would start two games in the series. Brown was in his prime in 1909, finishing the season 27–9, with a 1.31 ERA and 0.873 WHIP. Orval Overall (20–11 with a 1.42 ERA in 1909) and Ed Reulbach (19–10, 1.78 ERA) would also pitch for the Cubs.[75]

Game One demonstrated how seriously the players were taking the series. Lelands centerfielder Charles "Joe" Green made a play that, had television cameras been around, would have been shown on ESPN until the end of time. In the eighth inning, Green broke his leg on a slide into third base, but the ball was thrown into the outfield by Cubs catcher Pat Moran. Green struggled to his feet and attempted to hop home, but he was tagged out when left fielder Jimmy Sheckard's peg to the plate beat him by three feet. Green collapsed in agony and had to be carried from the diamond. The Cubs won the game, 4–1, thanks in large part to six Giants errors, three of them by the imported St. Paul Gophers. Joe Green had captured the hearts of the fans and the deep regard of the *Chicago Inter-Ocean*, which reported, "The exhibition of Green was as game as anything seen on a ball field."[76]

Rube Foster would prove to be game in the second contest, and the Cubs acted as if they were playing for much more than money or a mere exhibition win. The Lelands put five runs across in the third inning to drive Ed Reulbach out of the game, but Orval Overall relieved him and shut down the Giants the rest of the way. Watching his club from the stands, Frank Chance, "the Peerless Leader," left the game in disgust during the sixth inning when two Cubs were caught on the hidden ball trick.[77]

Rube Foster, pitching for the first time since breaking his leg on July 12, was outstanding for seven innings, striking out three big league batters while scattering six safeties. The Giants led the Cubs, 5–1, in the bottom of the eighth, when Foster began to tire, allowing three hits and a run before center fielder Pete Hill bailed him out with a great throw to the plate. Foster was running on fumes in the ninth. He gave up three runs on four singles and a walk, and the game was tied at 5–5, with runners on first and third and two outs. *Chicago*

Tribune sportswriter Ring Lardner observed, "Rube, feeling that he was slipping, started to work about as fast as a hippopotamus would run on skis."[78]

Foster moved toward the Giants dugout to ask pitcher Charles "Pat" Dougherty to relieve him. According to Lardner, several Cubs emerged from their dugout to protest Foster's dilatory tactics, creating a crowd around umpire Mike Meyer near the first base line. The runner at third, Frank "Wildfire" Schulte, broke for home. Lardner wrote, "The ball was in the hands of Mr. Foster himself and there were a dozen or so of human beings between him and the plate. This was the situation when old Wildfire started down the home stretch. He wound up his spurt with a slide under the wire and the game was over."[79]

The Cubs immediately raced for their clubhouse, escorting the umpire away from an angry throng of Giants fans storming the field. The Cubs were also smart enough to lead Meyer away from the Leland Giants before a protest could be launched. According to Lardner, Foster was not stalling, but wanted Dougherty to relieve him. Furthermore, Foster "wanted to know how one Cub could be allowed to steal home when three or four others were standing on the diamond in conversation. There was no answer to this query since Meyer had made his ruling and the athletes had left the field."[80]

The Cubs had—literally—stolen the game from Foster and the Leland Giants. Winning by methods that would be considered unsportsmanlike today was common in baseball around the turn of the 20th century. Rube Foster had pulled his share of stunts, and he would continue to do whatever he could to win. Therefore, it is safe to assume Foster probably would have done the same thing if he were in Schulte's position, and the big man certainly would have argued his player was safe at home had the tables been turned. That both teams played as if their lives were at stake was almost obscured by the game's controversial finish.

Examining the game from a distance of more than 100 years, the fierce desire both teams had to win is apparent in Ring Lardner's animated description of the final inning. It is also worth noting that the *Chicago Tribune* treated the game as more than a mere exhibition. Lardner, who was not yet the celebrated author he would become but already a premier baseball writer, was dispatched to cover the contest. Furthermore, the game was the day's major sports story. The headline, "Cubs Rally Beats Leland Giants," was writ large at the top of the sports page.[81]

The Cubs did not act as if they were playing an exhibition; they competed hard to the last out, and they used two of their frontline pitchers. Finally, they celebrated as if they had won a big game, and they made certain the umpire would not make a call that would overturn their victory. In short, the Cubs played as if they agreed with the Giants fans—the series was for the Chicago City Championship.

The Cubs also took the third contest, as Three Finger Brown blanked the Giants, 1–0, on a cold and miserable day. The Lelands did not go down without a fight, however. Lefty Pat Dougherty tossed an immaculate inning, striking out the first three batters of the game, Heinie Zimmerman, Jimmy Sheckard, and Wildfire Schulte, on nine pitches. Cubs shortstop Joe Tinker tallied the only run of the day. After hitting a ground rule double to lead off the third frame, the future Hall of Famer was sacrificed over to third and registered on Brown's fly to left when his "neat slide" barely evaded catcher Pete Booker's sweeping tag.[82]

Foster never got another shot at the Cubs, but his Giants had won the respect if not the admiration of the mainstream sporting public. During the first two games of the series, the white fans in attendance had urged the umpires to treat the Giants fairly, or the teams should "quit playing." In an editorial a couple of days after the series, the *Chicago Tribune* warned about the evils of scheduling black clubs:

> Suppose the Cubs had lost their three games to the Leland Giants, and, by the way, none of the big leaguers victories was easy, does anyone think there would not be a large number of persons who would have been convinced firmly that the Lelands would be right up there fighting for the National League pennant if they were asked into that organization? It is all right to make money, but let us make it without losing our dignity.[83]

The Greatest Untapped Reservoir in the History of the Game

Brooklyn Dodgers General Manager Branch Rickey saw African American baseball players as his ticket to winning a world championship, informing his family, "The greatest untapped reservoir of raw material in the history of the game is the black race! The Negroes will make us winners for years to come." That simple statement does more to explain the integration of baseball than any other theory. The achievements and sacrifices made by U.S. black soldiers in World War II and the atrocities committed by the Nazis changed many Americans' views about race relations. Charles Houston and the NAACP had made strides in their legal campaign to end segregation. However, Rickey was motivated to bring a pennant to Brooklyn.[84]

Rickey had his own explanation. The "Mahatma" claimed he had witnessed first-hand the pain of racism as the baseball coach at Ohio Wesleyan in 1904. Rickey's first baseman was a black man named Charlie Thomas. During a trip to South Bend, Indiana, Thomas was refused lodging in a local hotel. Rickey convinced the staff to allow the young athlete to stay in his room. Years later, he recalled that a distraught Thomas wept openly and, looking at his hands, sobbed, "If I could only make them white." Historian Jules Tygiel described the retelling as "vintage Rickey," a biblical allegory in which Rickey himself was the hero. The story was at least partially true, and it is a good one. At the end of the day, however, baseball is not about social justice. Branch Rickey's goal as a baseball executive was to win games. He knew, from decades of reliable data, that black baseball players could help him do so.[85]

Branch Rickey's choice of Jackie Robinson to break the color barrier was based on the assumption that black players could excel at the Major League level. The Negro Leaguers' success in integrated competition led Rickey to believe he was getting a big league quality player. Jackie Robinson was chosen because of his strong character. Robinson had been a star athlete at UCLA and an army officer. More important to Rickey, Robinson was a devout Christian and had the backing of a strong partner in Rachel Robinson. Tygiel noted, "neither Rickey's scouts nor other black players considered Robinson the best player in the Negro leagues."[86]

Rickey did not need the best player in the Negro Leagues. This does not mean the Dodgers GM could have chosen anyone. Rickey reportedly considered integrating Organized Baseball with New York Cubans star Silvio Garcia, but when asked what his response to racial abuse from an opposing player would be, the great shortstop half-jokingly replied, "I kill him." Robinson would use his experience, faith, and the support of his family and friends to deal with the pressure that came with being a trailblazer. However, because Rickey was aware that many black players could compete with the best the majors had to offer, he was free to pick Robinson based upon more than just his attributes on the diamond. It was an inspired choice, but one made easier by the abundance of talent in the Negro Leagues.[87]

The Other Half of Baseball History

The integration of baseball can be viewed as a relay race. Rube Foster was not the first man to hold the baton, but he carried it fast and far by organizing a league and actively seeking competition with the best Organized Baseball had to offer. When Foster informed Frank Leland that he feared nobody, it may have merely been youthful bragging. However, Rube Foster lived up to his word by refusing to step aside for whites on or off the field. While they did not set out to be social engineers, Satchel Paige, Dizzy Dean, and Bob Feller took the baton from Foster and moved baseball closer to breaking the tape at the color line.

Branch Rickey and Jackie Robinson finished the race and got the glory. However, just as no one person can be credited with inventing the game; one or two people cannot be credited with integrating it. Robinson and Rickey's eventual success was due in large part to a long line of athletes who had previously demonstrated that black and white players could compete on equal footing. For many years, black sportswriters such as Frank Young, Sam Lacy, Wendell Smith, and Joe Bostic fought to integrate baseball as well.

The Negro Leagues were half of baseball history, and perhaps, as John Holway once mused, "the bigger half." The results of the interracial games following the emergence of the NNL imply that black baseball was becoming another major league. From 1885 to 1948, African American teams playing against Major League clubs and barnstorming squads containing five or more big leaguers, including the starting pitcher, amassed a 325–314–21 record, good for a .508 winning percentage. From 1885 through 1899, black teams went 10–32–1 (.238) against white big league outfits. Between 1900 and 1919, black clubs managed an 80–89–8 (.473) record against Major League teams and all-star aggregations. However, from Rube Foster's formation of the first Negro National League in 1920 through the demise of the second NNL in 1948, black ball squads improved to 235–193–12 (.549) against all-star and regular big league teams. In fact, from 1922 through 1924, teams from both the NNL and ECL went 19–11–2 (.633) against intact Major League squads before Commissioner Landis permanently banned such contests. In those 32 games, the Negro Leaguers defeated five different Major League clubs, including the 1922 World Series champion New York Giants on two separate occasions.[88]

The improved success of African American teams after the creation of the Negro National League is clearly demonstrated by the numbers. Understanding why the formation of the NNL coincided with an improvement in play is more difficult to pin down. The best answer might be that more consistent competition between black teams during the season and better training made their players more capable. In turn, stronger organization and increased opportunities to compete with major leaguers led to more consistent money. This made the Negro Leagues a more attractive option for young black athletes. There were certainly other reasons, and hopefully the work contained herein will foster future study. In the end, one conclusion is certain. Negro League teams could always compete with and often defeat white big league baseball clubs. The strength of black players was proven time and again—in the crucible of white-hot competition.

Table 6.1 NLB vs. MLB 1885–1948

	W	*L*	*T*	*PCT*	*RF*	*RA*
HH 1885–1889	9	24	1	.273	5.38	8.56
HH 1890–1894	1	4	0	.200	4.80	15.40
HH 1895–1899	0	4	0	.000	4.25	9.50

	W	L	T	PCT	RF	RA
HH 1900–1904	2	4	1	.333	5.28	6.43
AS 1900–1904	0	1	0	.000	3.00	5.00
HH 1905–1909	6	10	2	.375	3.89	3.72
AS 1905–1909	5	1	0	.833	5.00	4.17
HH 1910–1914	6	4	2	.600	4.25	3.25
AS 1910–1914	30	29	1	.508	3.67	3.25
HH 1915–1919	4	11	0	.267	2.33	4.73
AS 1915–1919	27	29	2	.483	3.22	3.93
HH 1920–1924	29	30	2	.492	4.44	4.62
AS 1920–1924	28	26	1	.519	4.60	4.78
AS 1925–1929	59	25	3	.702	5.40	3.93
AS 1930–1934	57	24	1	.704	5.55	3.91
AS 1935–1939	19	24	2	.442	4.27	3.70
AS 1940–1944	17	18	1	.486	3.42	3.80
AS 1944–1948	26	46	2	.361	3.71	5.00

Editor's Note: HH = Head to Head games. AS = All-Star contests. There is no evidence of interracial games with Major League teams in 1890, 1893, 1896, 1898, 1899, 1903, 1904, and 1940. The head-to-head era ended with Commissioner Landis' 1924 ban. The 1936 Cincinnati Reds and 1947 New York Yankees played black squads in spring training, but these were all-star aggregations and not league teams. The results of the games big league outfits played against integrated Cuban clubs have not been included in the totals.

Table 6.2 NLB vs. MLB Totals 1885–1948

	W	L	T	PCT	RF	RA
HH 1885–1899	10	32	1	.238	5.21	9.44
HH 1900–1924	47	59	7	.443	4.12	4.43
HH Total	57	91	8	.385	4.42	5.81
AS 1902–1919	62	60	3	.508	3.52	3.61
AS 1920–1948	206	163	10	.558	4.68	4.19
AS Total	268	223	13	.546	4.39	4.05
NLB vs. MLB 1885–1919	90	121	9	.427	3.90	4.91
NLB vs. MLB 1920–1948	235	193	12	.549	4.66	4.25
NLB vs. MLB Total	325	314	21	.508	4.40	4.47

Source for Tables 6.1, 6.2: Peterson NLB vs. MLB database.

Notes

1. Joe Bostic, *The People's Voice*, April 27, 1946.

2. Peterson NLB vs. MLB database. Although certainly indicative of NLB vs. MLB competition, these and following tallies are approximate due to the complexities of Negro Leagues research. The results of the individual games can be found in Appendices I and II.

3. *Ibid*. It should be noted that these "all-stars" were not always the best the majors had to offer. Nevertheless, they were good enough to have reached the top levels of the National Pastime.

4. Peterson, *Only the Ball was White*, 80; John Holway, *Voices from the Great Black Baseball Leagues* (New York: Dodd, Mead, 1975) xv.

5. The story of Landis' ban on barnstorming is long and complex. For an excellent explanation of the various rules applied by baseball's commissioner against barnstorming players, see: Thomas Barthel, *Baseball Barnstorming and Exhibitions Games,* 2007; Leslie Heaphy, *The Negro Leagues, 1869–1960* (Jefferson, NC: McFarland, 2003), 140.

6. .Mark Ribowsky, *Don't Look Back: Satchel Paige in the Shadows of Baseball* (New York: Simon & Schuster, 1994) 120–21.

7. Baseball-Reference.com, "Wally Berger," https://www.baseball-reference.com/players/b/bergewa01.

shtml; Ribowsky, *Don't Look Back*, 120–121; Richard Donovan, "Satch Beards the House of David (Continuing the Fabulous Satchel Paige)," *Collier's Weekly*, June 6, 1953: 23; Bill Veeck and Ed Linn. *Veeck—As In Wreck: The Autobiography of Bill Veeck.* (Chicago: University of Chicago Press, 2012), 183–84. In 1947, Veeck would become the second owner to ink a Negro Leagues player when he signed Larry Doby from the Newark Eagles. Unlike Branch Rickey, Veeck paid Eagles owner Effa Manley $10,000 for Doby's contract. Veeck would later add Satchel Paige to the Indians; at the time, Paige was rumored to be anywhere from 39 to 48 years old.

8. Timothy M. Gay, *Satch, Dizzy & Rapid Robert: The Wild Saga of Interracial Baseball Before Jackie Robinson* (New York: Simon & Schuster, 2010), 107, 291–294.

9. Peterson, *Only the Ball was White*, 115; "Rube Foster Passes," *Chicago Defender*, December 20, 1930.

10. Larry Lester, *Rube Foster in His Time: On the Field and in the Papers with Black Baseball's Greatest Visionary* (Jefferson, NC: McFarland, 2012), 6–7, 227–231; Peterson, *Only the Ball was White*, 104–105. Peterson did not include bibliographical information in his book. He was in contact with Foster's son, Earl, who was probably the owner of this letter.

11. Lester, *Rube Foster in His Time*, 9–10, 13; Phil S. Dixon, *Andrew "Rube" Foster: A Harvest on Freedom's Fields* (La Vergne, TN: Xlibris, 2010), 65, 73; *Washington Herald*, January 28, 1908.

12. Lester, *Rube Foster in His Time*, 193–195, 204–211, 223; Phil Dixon, *American Baseball Chronicles: Great Teams: The 1905 Philadelphia Giants Volume Three.* (Charleston, SC: Booksurge, 2006), 157–158; Dixon, *Andrew "Rube" Foster: A Harvest on Freedom's Field*, 73; Frederic North Shorey, "Well, Well, Man, Rube Foster Certainly Eats 'Em Alive," *Chicago Inter-Ocean*, August 11, 1907.

13. Lester, *Rube Foster in His Time*, 29–3 ; Lomax, *Black Baseball Entrepreneurs 1902–1931*, 118–119; Debono, *Chicago American Giants*, 32, 36.

14. Lester, *Rube Foster in His Time*, 103–104.

15. Debono, *Chicago American Giants*, 222–230; *Washington Post*, February 19, 1921; Frederic North Shorey, "Well, Well, Man, Rube Foster Certainly Eats 'Em Alive."

16. Rube was only interested in leagues that he could control. Foster declined to participate in Beauregard Moseley's attempt to form a black circuit following the 1910 season. See Lester, *Rube Foster in His Time*, 58–60. Andrew (Rube) Foster, "The Trouble in Colored Baseball," *Indianapolis Freeman*, December 16, 1911.

17. Foster, "Trouble in Colored Baseball." Prior to Jim Jeffries vacating the title in 1905, Johnson unsuccessfully attempted to goad the white champ into giving him a shot at the heavyweight crown. When the championship belt passed to Tommy Burns in 1906, Johnson was able to force a title fight by chasing the Canadian all over the globe. It was after Johnson won the title in 1908 that Jeffries, pressured by the white media and promotors, was coaxed out of retirement to fight the black champion on the Fourth of July in 1910. Johnson won by TKO in the 15th round, sparking race riots across the United States. The 1910 dollars to 2018 dollars calculation is from MeasuringWorth.com.

18. NLB vs. MLB database.

19. "Top Baseball Names Pick Greatest Team," *Pittsburgh Courier*, April 19, 1952.

20. *Pittsburgh Courier*, April 19, 1952; "Wagner Recalls Old-Time Stars Who Were Good Enough for Majors," *Pittsburgh Courier*, September 2, 1939.

21. Holway, *The Complete Book of Baseball's Negro Leagues*, 78–79; Jose Figueredo, *Cuban Baseball: A Statistical History, 1897–1961* (Jefferson, NC: McFarland, 2003), 88–89; "Tigers are Shutout by Habana Reds; Ty Cobb Fails to Hit," *Detroit Free Press,* November 29, 1910; Seamheads.com Negro Leagues Database, "1910–11 Winter Negro Leagues vs. Cuban Leagues, Batting," accessed May 31, 2018, http://www.seamheads.com/NegroLgs/year.php?yearID=1910.5&tab=bat_basic&pos=All&lgID=NvC&bats=All&qual=All&sort=OPS2_a.

22. Holway, *The Complete Book of Baseball's Negro Leagues*, 79–80; Figueredo, *Cuban Baseball: A Statistical History*, 90; Seamheads.com Negro Leagues Database, "1910–11 Winter Cuban Leagues vs. Major Leagues, Batting," accessed May 31, 2018, http://www.seamheads.com/NegroLgs/year.php?yearID=1910.5&tab=bat_basic&pos=All&lgID=CvM&bats=All&qual=All&sort=OPS2_a.

23. Holway, *The Complete Book of Baseball's Negro Leagues*, 79–80.

24. "Pirates beaten 2 to 1 by Colored Sprudels," *Pittsburgh Post-Gazette*, September 12, 1911; "Murray Stars in Exhibition," *Elmira Star-Gazette*, October 29, 1912; Baseball-Reference.com, "Red Murray," https://www.baseball-reference.com/players/m/murrare01.shtml#all_batting_postseason; "Lincolns Shutout Yankees," *New York Age*, November 7, 1912; NLB vs. MLB database.

25. "American Giants Win Flag," *Chicago Tribune*, December 30, 1912; NLB vs. MLB database.

26. Andrew (Rube) Foster, "What the Greatest Pitcher of His Time Thinks of the Baseball Situation," *Indianapolis Freeman*, December 20, 1913).

27. NLB vs. MLB database.

28. Heaphy, *The Negro Leagues*, 39.

29. Rube Foster, "The Pitfalls of Baseball, Part I," *Chicago Defender*, November 26, 1919.

30. Rube Foster, "The Pitfalls of Baseball, Part II," *Chicago Defender*, December 13, 1919.

31. Rube Foster, "Pitfalls of Baseball, Part III," *Chicago Defender*, December 20, 1919.

32. Rube Foster, "Pitfalls of Baseball, Part IV," *Chicago Defender*, December 27, 1919.

33. *Ibid.*

34. *Ibid.*

35. Rube Foster, "Pitfalls of Baseball, Part V," *Chicago Defender*, December 27, 1919.

36. "Baseball Magnates Hold Conference, Sporting Editor of Defender Elected Secretary" *Kansas City Call*, February 20, 1920; "Western Circuit organized: To Become Effective April 1, 1921" *Kansas City Call*, February 27, 1920.

37. Robert Cottrell, *The Best Pitcher in Baseball: The Life of Rube Foster, Negro League Giant* (New York: New York University Press, 2001), 158.

38. "Negro Base Ball," *Buffalo American*, December 14, 1922; Adrian Burgos, Jr., *Cuban Star: How One Negro-League Owner Changed the Face of Baseball* (New York: Hill and Wang, 2011) xiv.

39. Lomax, *Black Baseball Entrepreneurs 1902–1931*, 309.

40. Jules Tygiel, *Baseball's Great Experiment: Jackie Robinson and His Legacy* (New York: Vintage Books, 1983), 26; John Holway, *Blackball Stars: Negro League Pioneers* (Westport, CT: Meckler, 1988) 28.

41. NLB vs. MLB database; *Mount Carmel Daily News*, October 7, 1926.

42. "Gas Nearly Kills Andrew Rube Foster" *Chicago Defender*, June 6, 1925; "Rube Seeks Rest In Seclusion," *Pittsburgh Courier*, July 17, 1926; Cottrell, *The Best Pitcher in Baseball*, 171–73; Lester, *Rube Foster in His Time*, 226–227.

43. "Rube Foster Dead, Baseball's Most Colorful Figure is Called Out" *Chicago Defender*, December 13, 1930; Romeo L. Dougherty, "Baseball Season Not Definitely Closed Yet," *New York Amsterdam News*, October 6, 1934; NLB vs. MLB database.

44. Peterson, *Only the Ball was White*, 89, 92–93.

45. Leroy "Satchel" Paige with David Lipman, *Maybe I'll Pitch Forever* (Garden City, NY: Doubleday, 1962), 91.

46. Joe Williams, "Dizzy Dean's Radio Tongue is Literary Inspiration," *Pittsburgh Press*, April 24, 1950; "Satch Paige Greatest Pitcher, Dizzy Dean White Hurler Rates Moundsman Over Big Leaguers," *New York Amsterdam News*, September 24, 1938.

47. Grantland Rice, "Dizzy Dean Injured, as Tigers Tip Cards, 10–4," *Los Angeles Times*, October 7, 1934.

48. Alan Gould, "Near Riot by Fans Forces Removal of Medwick From Game in Sixth—Shutout Largest in Series History," *Minneapolis Tribune*, October 10, 1934; Baseball-Reference.com, "Dizzy Dean," https://www.baseball-reference.com/players/d/deandi01.shtml.

49. Bennie Williams, "All-Stars Defeat Monarchs 8–3," *Wichita Negro Star,* October 19, 1934; L. Herbert Henegan, "Monarchs Win from the Dean Brothers 7 to 0," *Kansas City Call*, October 19, 1934; "Monarchs Beat Deans," *Kansas City Times*, October 13, 1934; "What, Only Sixty!" *Cincinnati Enquirer*, October 23, 1934.

50. Edward F. Balinger, "Near Riot Mars Deans' Exhibition," *Pittsburgh Post-Gazette,* October 24, 1934.

51. Balinger, "Near Riot Mars Deans' Exhibition"; "Race Riot is Balked by Police," *Indianapolis Star*, October 25, 1915; Holway, *The Complete Book of Baseball's Negro Leagues*, 315.

52. NLB vs. MLB database.

53. Eddie Murphy, "Satchel Paige Makes Bow Here Against Major All-Stars," *Oakland Tribune*, January 26, 1936; Eddie Murphy, "Negro Hurler Sensation Loses 2–1," *Oakland Tribune*, January 26, 1936; Baseball-Reference.com, "Joe DiMaggio," https://www.baseball-reference.com/players/d/dimagjo01.shtml. DiMaggio struck out only 369 times in a 13-year career. Phil Pepe, "Everybody Talked Satch but Jackie was 1st," *New York Daily News*, February 12, 1971; Gay, *Satch, Dizzy & Rapid Robert*, 149.

54. "Negroes Oppose National Stars," *Des Moines Register*, October 7, 1936; "Feller On Mound For Nat'l League All-Stars' Outfit," *Iowa City Press-Citizen*, October 8, 1936.

55. NLB vs. MLB database; Bus Ham, "Negroes Win Farce," *Daily Oklahoman*, October 12, 1937.

56. Gay, *Satch, Dizzy & Rapid Robert*, 177.

57. NLB vs. MLB database.

58. *Ibid*.

59. Bob Feller, from *Holiday Magazine*, 1965, quoted in, Gay, *Satch, Dizzy & Rapid Robert*, 170; Jim Murray, "Feller's Best Pitch Was for Equality," *Los Angeles Times*, August 7, 1982.

60. Murray, "Feller's Best Pitch."

61. NLB vs. MLB database; Famous Trials.com, "Lynchings: By Year and Race," http://famous-trials.com/legacyf trials/shipp/lynchingyear.html.

62. Fred Lieb, *Baseball As I Have Known It* (New York: Coward, McCann & Geohegan, 1977), 57; John O'Donnell, *Quad City Times*, July 31, 1938; Westbrook Pegler, "Jake Powell's Blunder," *St. Louis Star-Times*, August 4, 1938.

63. *Topeka Plaindealer*, October 13, 1922.

64. *Ibid*.

65. Thom Rosenblum, "Unlocking the Schoolhouse Doors: Elisha Scott, 'Colored Lawyer, Topeka,'" *Kansas History* 36 (2013): 41.

66. Gary Ashwill, Agate Type, "Rube vs. Rube," accessed June 7, 2018, http://agatetype.typepad.com/agate_type/2012/03/rube-vs-rube.html; Lester, *Rube Foster in His Time,* 23.

67. Lester, Rube Foster in His Time, 23; Charles Dryden, "Rube Waddell Afraid to Give His Arm a Rest," Pittsburgh Press, August 5, 1903.

68. Frederic North Shorey, "Well, Well, Man, Rube Foster Certainly Eats Em Alive"; Lester, *Rube Foster in*

His Time, 22; George E. Mason, "Rube Foster Chats About His Career," *Chicago Defender*, February 20, 1915; *Franklin News-Herald*, July 21, 1903; *Harrisburg Daily Independent*, August 25, 1903.

69. Baseball-Reference.com, "1903 AL Pitching Leaders," http://www.baseball-reference.com/leagues/ AL/1903-pitching-leaders.shtml; Baseball-Reference.com, "Rube Waddell," http://www.baseball-reference.com/ players/w/wadderu01.shtml.

70. Sarah L. Trembanis, *The Set-Up Men: Race, Culture and Resistance in Black Baseball* (Jefferson, NC: McFarland, 2014), 153.

71. Frederic North Shorey, "Well, Well, Man, Rube Foster Certainly Eats 'Em Alive."

72. *Ibid.*

73. *Ibid.*

74. "Cubs and Lelands for Title? New City Champions Called Upon to Defend Honors Against Chicago League Pennant Winners," *Chicago Tribune*, October 18, 1909.

75. Baseball-Reference.com, "1909 Chicago Cubs Statistics," https://www.baseball-reference.com/teams/ CHC/1909.shtml.

76. "City Champs Win From Lelands, 4–1," *Chicago Tribune*, October 19, 1909; "Breaks Leg Sliding to Third Base; Hops Home on One Foot," *Chicago Inter-Ocean*, October 19, 1909.

77. R. W. Lardner, "Foster Argues; Schulte Scores," *Chicago Tribune*, October 22, 1909.

78. Lardner, "Foster Argues; Schulte Scores"; "Fluke Steal Home Gives Cubs Victory Over Leland Giants," *Chicago Inter-Ocean*, October 22, 1909.

79. Lardner, "Foster Argues; Schulte Scores."

80. *Ibid.*

81. *Chicago Tribune*, October 22, 1909.

82. R. W. Lardner, "Cubs Trim Giants in Final Game," *Chicago Tribune*, October 23, 1909; "Cubs Take Third Game From Giants," *Chicago Inter-Ocean*, October 23, 1909.

83. Cottrell, The Best Pitcher in Baseball, 48; "The Referee," Chicago Tribune, October 24, 1909.

84. Branch Rickey, "Branch Rickey to Arthur Mann, October 7, 1945," Arthur Mann Papers, Library of Congress, Washington D.C. Quoted in, Tygiel, *Baseball's Great Experiment*, 52.

85. Tygiel, *Baseball's Great Experiment*, 51–52.

86. *Ibid.*, 64.

87. Daniel A. Fernández, "Silvio Garcia, Jackie Robinson and the Racial Barrier in Major League Baseball," OnCuba.com, December 22, 2013, accessed June 29, 2018, https://oncubamagazine.com/sports/silvio-garcia-jackie-robinson-and-the-racial-barrier-in-major-league-baseball/.

88. Holway, *Voices from the Great Black Baseball Leagues*, xv; NLB vs. MLB database; *Chicago Defender*, October 14, 21, 1922.

The Top Ten Reasons Why the Negro Leagues Should Be Declared a Major League

TED KNORR

> **major league**, *n. A league at the highest level of organized or professional baseball; specifically, one of the two leagues (National League since 1876 and American League since 1901) that currently constitute the Major Leagues. Previous Major Leagues included the American Association (1882–1891), Union Association (1884), Players' League (1890) and Federal League (1914–1915)*
> —Dickson Baseball Dictionary[1]

These six leagues granted "official" Major League status owe their credential to the Special Baseball Records Committee (SBRC) appointed by Commissioner William Eckert in 1968. The committee consisted of representatives from both existing Major Leagues and three giants of historical baseball knowledge: Joe Reichler of the Office of the Commissioner, Jack Lang of the Baseball Writers' Association of America, and Lee Allen of the National Baseball Hall of Fame. It appears the SBRC considered only one other circuit—the National Association (1871–1875) which, although denied "major" status, was officially recognized as the first professional league.[2]

At the 2017 SABR convention in New York City, I asked David Neft, the editor of the 1969 Macmillan Baseball Encyclopedia, and John Thorn, the official historian of Major League Baseball, whether the SBRC had considered the Negro Leagues during their determinations. Both men said no. Neft expounded that the criteria for a major league depended on the size of the cities involved, the ability of the players, and the media coverage received. Thorn added that a major circuit had to complete a full season, and that their players joined other big leagues if they folded. According to Thorn:

> The question of the Negro Leagues is a philosophical question. It is not a statistical question. Major League Baseball will never incorporate the records of the Pittsburgh Crawfords because they never played any other team in what is determined to be Major League Baseball and the same criterion that MLB used to downgrade the National Association of 1871–75 would surely apply to the Negro Leagues in that more of their regular season contests were against non-league opponents than against league opponents.[3]

In point of fact, the Negro Leagues met all of the criteria set forth by Neft and Thorn: From 1920 through 1946, there were on average seven Negro League clubs operating out of the 12 Major League cities; the white mainstream press wrote on several occasions about black players big league quality; after integration, many Negro Leaguers matriculated into the Major Leagues; and only on a couple of occasions did a major black ball circuit fail to complete its full season. To pay the bills, Negro Leagues clubs were required to schedule a lot of minor league and semi-pro squads, but even then the majority of their games were against other top-flight black outfits. For example, between 1920 and 1929, the Bacharach Giants played nearly 60 percent of their games against league-level opponents (701 out of 1,205). While the Pittsburgh Crawfords never faced an intact major league team, the reverse is also true: the New York Yankees never took on the Crawfords, Homestead Grays, or Kansas City Monarchs.[4]

After researching the subject for over a quarter of a century, I have come to a conclusion that the most casual fan would assume to be true, while the staunchest baseball purist might think it heretical. I believe the Negro Leagues were indeed a Major League and should be designated as such. Advocating for the National Association, International Association, some 20th-century high minors, certain winter leagues, or select foreign circuits is left for someone else, and hopefully after the Negro Leagues have been properly and fittingly honored.

For the sake of clarity, I will use the term Major League Baseball (MLB) to mean the National and American Leagues and the phrase "other four defunct Major Leagues" to refer to the American Association, Union Association, Players' League, and Federal League. I also want to point out that modern baseball as we know it, with overhand pitching from a raised mound 60'6" away from home plate, where four balls constitute a walk, three strikes an out, and batters cannot dictate a high or low pitch, can be found only in the National League (since 1893), the American League, the Federal League, and the Negro Leagues. If you add a requirement that rosters be open to all who can make a team, you are left only with the Negro Leagues and Major League Baseball since April 15, 1947. In a manner of speaking, these are the only true Major Leagues.

I believe one more clarification is needed. While African Americans, Latinos, and other non-white folks have played baseball since the end of the Civil War and earlier, I define the "Major League" portion of black ball history as beginning with the founding of the Negro National League in 1920 and extending through Jackie Robinson's first season in Organized Ball in 1946. This period encompasses 27 years. This is consistent with the Hall of Fame's splitting of the Negro Leagues period into pre-league (prior to 1920) and Negro League (1920–1960). A more liberal definition could include the entire 1876–1946 period or 71 years.[5]

Without further delay, permit me to offer my top ten reasons why the Negro Leagues should be defined as a "Major" League.

Do the Right Thing!

Major League baseball began its 144th year in 2019, and for half that time blacks, many Latinos, and any player deemed non-white were prohibited from earning a living at the highest level their talents deserved. Despite serving their country in two world wars as well as every armed conflict before and since, and in spite of demonstrating their prowess on the diamond at every given opportunity, they were banned, both in writing and by so-called gentlemen's agreement, from participating in Organized Baseball. While I intend to demonstrate beyond any question that the quality of play in the black ball circuits was indeed the equal of all of the six big leagues, providing the Negro Leagues with Major League designation would be an appropriate gesture even if that weren't the case.

Table 7.1 MLB and NLB Lifespans

Professional League	Time Span	Years
MLB	1876–2019	144
Segregated MLB	1876–1946	71
Integrated MLB	1947–2019	73
NLB (Including Independent Era)	1876–1946	71
NLB (League Era)	1920–1946	27

Source: *The Baseball Encyclopedia*, 1969. According to the *Baseball Encyclopedia*, the first Major League was the National League which was founded in 1876, with 2019 being its 144th season. The duration of the Negro Leagues eras is the opinion of the author.

The Hall of Fame

The National Baseball Hall of Fame and Museum in Cooperstown, New York, was created to celebrate the greatest players in the game's history. Only two entities have players enshrined—the Major Leagues and the Negro Leagues. The Hall is a 501 (c) (3) not-for-profit educational institution dedicated, according to its mission statement, to preserving the history of the game, honoring its outstanding contributors, and connecting generations of fans. Preserve. Honor. Connect. In my opinion, to tell the story of baseball, especially prior to 1947, the Negro Leagues need a more prominent position. The Hall of Fame has done exemplary work in that regard with the induction of 35 Negro Leagues personages since 1971, and the beautiful traveling exhibition—*Pride & Passion*—which includes many black ball stories, exhibits, and artifacts. In addition, the Hall, through its Negro Leagues Researchers & Authors Group, has created a spectacular, if inaccessible, statistical database of the Negro Leagues period (1920–1946).

However, in telling the story of baseball during the pre-integration era, the Hall should more fully and seamlessly trumpet the story of the Negro Leagues. Instead of being banished to a separate section, Negro Leaguers could be incorporated into exhibits such as *Scribes and Mikemen* (broadcasters/writers), *Taking the Field* (19th century), *Sacred Ground* (old ballparks), *One for the Books* (great events), and *Autumn Glory* (World Series).

During a recent tour of the Hall, I observed that they recognized Joe Williams' 1930 27-strikeout game in *One for the Books*, but such inclusions are rare and trivialized by similar attention given to feats achieved in lesser circuits. Because they played fewer league games, seasonal and career black ball statistics are not comparable with MLB numbers, but accomplishments like hitting streaks and no-hitters could be recognized alongside similar big league achievements. I'd also like to see pennant winners, World Series champions, and East-West Classics displayed alongside corresponding MLB events. Such integration would be a much easier task if the baseball establishment declared the Negro Leagues as the seventh Major League.

Longevity

What makes a league major? Bill James offers the following litany in his *2001 Historical Baseball Abstract*: stability, structure, set schedules, inviolate rosters, competitiveness, quality of play, size of member cities, ballparks, attendance, media coverage, and contemporary designation. While all of these specifications are important, I find one additional factor, not considered by James or the Special Baseball Rules Committee, to be almost as determinant and necessary: longevity.[6]

Blacks and other non-whites played baseball at the highest level permitted to them for the entire 71 years of the Major Leagues' segregated era (1876–1946). Twenty-seven seasons elapsed between the formation of the Negro National League in 1920 through the end of Jackie Robinson's 1946 season with the Montreal Royals. The four defunct "Major Leagues" existed for a combined total of 14 years.

Table 7.2 Negro Leagues and Defunct Major Leagues Life-Spans

Professional League	Time Span	Years
NLB (Including Independent Era)	1876–1946	71
NLB (League Era)	1920–1946	27
American Association	1882–1891	10
Federal League	1914–1915	2
Players League	1890	1
Union Association	1884	1

Source: *The Baseball Encyclopedia*, 1969.

However, longevity cannot be the sole factor in determining the quality of a baseball league. For example, the International League has been in operation since 1884, but has always been considered a minor circuit.

Talent

There is no better repository of the greatest baseball talent than in Cooperstown. Table 7.3 illustrates the number of Negro Leagues Hall of Famers compared with the other four defunct Major Leagues.

Table 7.3 Negro Leagues and Defunct Major Leagues Hall of Fame Players

Professional League	HOF	Debuted In	Ten Years In	Only In
NLB	31	31	22	25
Players League	13	0	0	0
American Association	9	3	0	0
Federal League	5	0	0	0
Union Association	1	1	0	0
Defunct Leagues Total	28	4	0	0

Source: Baseball-Reference.com; tabulated by the author.

- The Negro Leagues have over twice as many Hall of Famers than the Players League; more than three times as many as the American Association, and three more than the other four defunct Major Leagues put together.
- All 31 Hall of Famers who appeared in the Negro Leagues started out in the Negro Leagues; only four Hall of Famers debuted in the other four defunct Major Leagues combined.

- Twenty-seven Hall of Famers played ten or more years in the Negro Leagues. Only two Hall of Fame players (Bid McPhee and Tommy McCarthy) lasted more than two years in any of the four defunct Major Leagues.
- Twenty-five of the 31 Negro League Hall of Famers played only in the Negro Leagues. No Hall of Famer played solely in any of the four defunct Major Leagues. In fact, all 334 Hall of Famers spent all or most of their careers in the National, American, or Negro Leagues. To me, this is a De facto admission by the Hall that the Negro Leagues were indeed a major league.

The sticky wicket is again the International League, which had about 100 Hall of Fame players grace its rosters over the years.[7]

Talent per Year

For those who might think that the only reason the Negro Leagues had more Hall of Famers than the defunct Major Leagues was because of their longer existence, I want to point out the following data (considering only the Negro Leagues 1920–46 period):

Table 7.4 Negro Leagues and Defunct Major Leagues Hall of Fame Players per Year

Professional League	Years	HOF	HOF/Year	Range HOF/Year
NLB	27	31	14.9	10–19
Players League	1	13	13.0	13
American Association	10	9	2.2	1–5
Federal League	2	5	4.0	3–5
Union Association	1	1	1.0	1
Defunct Leagues Total	14	28	3.0	1–13

Source: National Baseball Hall of Fame (baseballhall.org); Baseball-Reference.com.

In only one "major" league season among the 14 did the defunct circuits have more Hall of Famers (13) than there were in any of the 27 years of the formal Negro Leagues. In other words, 98 percent of the time, there were more Hall of Famers in the Negro Leagues than in the four former Major Leagues.

From this perspective, it also seems clear that the International League was just a way station for prospective major leaguers on the way up or former big leaguers on the way down, as the Triple A circuit contained no more than five future Hall of Famers in any season during the segregated era.[8]

Impact on Today's Game

The Negro Leagues had a greater impact on the modern game than any of the four defunct MajorLeagues. This can be shown by simply noting the last year that each circuit existed, with the Negro Leagues being the only organization among the five that operated in the last 100 years.

Table 7.5 Final Seasons of Defunct Major Leagues

League	Last Year
Union Association	1884
Players League	1890
American Association	1891
Federal League	1915
NLB	1946

Source: *The Baseball Encyclopedia*, 1969.

All four of the defunct Major Leagues were long gone when baseball's modern era began on April 15, 1947. By contrast, hundreds of former Negro League players entered Organized Baseball in the first decade of integration, with 54 of them making it to the Majors.[9]

During Ken Burns' film *Jackie Robinson*, black ball legend Buck O'Neil explained the Negro Leagues' impact on the modern game:

> Jackie took black baseball to the Major Leagues at the time baseball was a base to base thing … hit the ball, wait on first until somebody hits again. But in our baseball you got on base if you walked, you stole second … tried to bunt you over to third I actually scored runs without a base hit … this was our baseball.[10]

John Thorn offered to Burns that the Negro Leaguers brought speed and power to MLB, in addition to base stealing, sacrifices, and daring base running.daring base running.[11]

An examination of sacrifice bunt rates, stolen bases, and home runs in the last decade prior to integration and the first decade after all 16 franchises had promoted a black player to their Major League rosters indicates that Messrs. O'Neil and Thorn were correct with respect to speed and power but missed the boat with sacrifices. But why bunt when you can steal that base or waste an out when you have an opportunity to slam the ball over the fence?

Table 7.6 MLB Sacrifice, Stolen Base, and Home Run Rates 1937–1969

Period	SAC/100PA	SB/100PA	HR Rate
1930–1939	1.73	1.00	1.40
1960–1969	1.20	1.11	2.18
% change from 30–39	–31%	+11%	+56%

Source: Sinins, *Complete Baseball Encyclopedia*, 2016.

Another way to gauge the effect black players had on MLB is to look at the top ten leaders for sacrifices, steals, and home runs since Jackie Robinson's debut. Twenty-one (75 percent) of the players in these three categories would not have been allowed to play in the Majors prior to April 15, 1947. The game has changed, indeed.[12]

Table 7.7 MLB Sacrifice, Stolen Base, and Home Run Leaders 1947–2019

SAC	SB	HR
Omar Vizquel* 256	Rickey Henderson* 1406	Barry Bonds* 762
Tom Glavine 216	Lou Brock* 938	Hank Aaron* 755
Ozzie Smith* 214	Tim Raines* 808	Alex Rodriguez* 696

SAC	SB	HR
Nellie Fox 208	Vince Coleman* 752	Willie Mays* 660
Bert Campaneris* 199	Joe Morgan* 689	Albert Pujols* 656
Greg Maddux 180	Willie Wilson* 668	Ken Griffey, Jr.* 630
Phil Rizzuto 171	Bert Campaneris* 649	Jim Thome 612
Tim Foli 169	Kenny Lofton* 622	Sammy Sosa* 609
Juan Pierre* 167	Otis Nixon* 620	Frank Robinson* 586
Luis Aparicio* 161	Juan Pierre* 614	Mark McGwire 583

Note: Players marked with an * would not have been allowed in MLB prior to April 15, 1947. Bert Campaneris and Juan Pierre made the Top Ten in two categories.

Source: Baseball-Reference.com

All four of the defunct Major Leagues and the Negro Leagues have had an impact on the game of baseball over the years. For example, the American Association introduced the World Series, integration, Sunday baseball, and beer in the ballpark. The Union Association gave us a single-game strikeout record that stood for more than 100 years. The Players' League foreshadowed the MLB Players Association. The Federal League gave birth to Wrigley Field and an anti-trust settlement that protected the game's corporate interests. The Negro Leagues pushed for the integration of this country—prior to the desegregation of the U.S. military, ahead of the Montgomery bus boycott, in advance of Greensboro's lunch counter sit-ins, and before the University of Mississippi was forced to open its doors to black students—providing us with nothing less than our very soul, not to mention a better brand of baseball.

At the time of this writing, there have been 277 seasons of Major League Baseball throughout the course of 144 years. One hundred thirty of these seasons occurred during the segregated era. I certainly feel that it has been demonstrated that the Negro Leagues were indeed equivalent with the four defunct Major Leagues. However, those circuits participated in only 11 percent of all Major League seasons during the segregated era and only 5 percent of all Major League seasons through 2019 (Table 7.8).

Table 7.8 MLB Seasons 1876–2019

Leagues	Duration	Seg	Int	Total
National League	1876–2019	71	73	144
American Association	1882–1891	9	1	10
Union Association	1884	1	0	1
Players League	1890	1	0	1
American League	1901–2019	46	73	119
Federal League	1914–1915	2	0	2
MLB Total	1876–2019	130	147	277

Note: Both William White and Bumpus Jones played briefly in the National League during the 19th century, but they passed themselves off as white. Moses and Welday Walker played a total of 47 games for Toledo during the 1884 American Association campaign.

Sources: The Baseball Encyclopedia, 1969, Baseball-Reference.com.

To truly establish the Negro Leagues as equivalent, therefore, it is necessary to compare the play of the Negro Leagues with that of the American and National Leagues during the segregated era. I also think it would be instructional to consider the performance of African and Latin Americans during the 146 seasons since integration. The following two reasons make clear that black baseball players have certainly performed better than average once they were permitted to earn a living at a Major League level.

MVPs of the Integrated Era

Since 1947, 49 percent (70.5 of 144) of MLB's Most Valuable Player award winners would not have been permitted to participate in the Majors before that time.[13]

Hall of Famers of the Integrated Era

Of the 95 Hall of Famers who began their careers during the integrated era, 40 (42 percent) would not have been allowed in the Majors prior to 1947.[14]

Quality of Play in the Negro Leagues

How good was the quality of play in the Negro Leagues? Around the turn of the 21st century, historian William F. McNeil authored several innovative and mind-expanding volumes about outsider baseball. One of them, *Baseball's Other All-Stars,* provided a logical basis for assessing a league's quality of play within the book's statistical tables. The first table of *Baseball's Other All-Stars* purports to be a "Comparison of Professional Leagues" and is displayed in a slightly edited form below[15]:

Table 7.9 Professional Leagues Batting Averages

League	BA
MLB	.260
Class AAA	.287
Class AA	.306
NLB (1930–1950)	.308
Class C (1948–1954)	.321

Note: The circuits not under the Organized Baseball umbrella, with the exception of the Negro Leagues, have been removed from the original table.
Source: McNeil, *Baseball's Other All-Stars*, 2000.

In a note accompanying the chart, McNeil makes clear that he ranked the leagues in order of quality, with lower batting averages indicating a higher level of play. I strongly concur in theory but dispute his statistics. McNeil's implication is that the Negro Leagues, during the segregated era, were not Major League equivalent and were, in fact, roughly equal to Double A ball. Again, if his statistics were valid, I think he would have a point. I'm going to focus on the two organizations that we have the best data for—the Major Leagues and the Negro Leagues.

According to McNeil's table, the Major Leagues hit .260 during an unspecified period of time. Any baseball reference book or website will tell you that the Majors hit .266 during the segregated era and about 6–7 points less since 1947. Thus, per McNeil's thesis, the quality of Major League play has improved since the integration of black players. This data also reinforces the point that African American and Latino players have performed at a Major League equivalent level since 1947. During the Negro Leagues era (1920–1946), the Major League batting average was .276, which is not surprising since we know big league offensive numbers started increasing around 1920 before peaking in 1930.[16]

However, this number suggests a much better quality of play than the .308 average that McNeil attributes to the Negro Leagues between 1930 and 1950. When McNeil's book was published in 2000, there wasn't a lot of Negro Leagues data available. In my opinion, the best resource at the time was Macmillan's 1990 *Baseball Encyclopedia* which published career statistics for 131 of the best Negro Leagues players. I was not surprised, upon totaling these players' hits and at-bats, to come up with a cumulative batting average of .309. Thus, I assume McNeil's hitting totals—since he did provide endpoints for the period he measured—were taken from this source. He had calculated an average for the best Negro Leagues players, not the Negro Leagues in general. I now needed to find a better, more realistic, batting average for the Negro Leagues between 1920 and 1946.[17]

While it may be true that the statistics kept in the Negro Leagues were not as comprehensive as those compiled for MLB, thanks to the efforts of researchers such as Larry Lester, Wayne Stivers, Scott Simkus, Gary Ashwill, and Dick Clark, there is more box score-based data for the Negro Leagues available than ever before. Utilizing the statistics found on the Seamheads.com Negro League Database, it can be shown that the Negro Leagues—not just the best hitters—hit .270 during the period 1920–1946.[18]

NLB .270

MLB .276

Thus, according to William McNeil's thesis, the Negro Leagues and the Major Leagues were equivalent. I will not speculate as to which league might have actually been better.

Record of Negro League Teams vs. MLB and/or Partial MLB Teams

Shadowball, the fifth episode of Ken Burns' spectacular documentary, *Baseball*, touched on the competition between segregated black and white clubs:

> In cities and small towns all across the country there were other teams and other stars that may have been the greatest of the century but whose deeds would live only in the memory of those who saw them play. Over the years, black baseball stars played white Major League stars at least 438 times in off-season exhibition games. The Whites won 129 of those postseason games. Blacks won 309.[19]

Here is a compendium of Negro League vs. Major League games according to various author/researchers:

Table 7.10 NLB vs. MLB Totals

Researcher	NLB/MLB	PCT
Ken Burns	309–129	.705
William McNeil	614–266	.698
John Holway	89–67	.571
Bench5	132–110	.545
Scott Simkus	128–115	.527
Total	1292–667	.660
Average	258–133	.660

Sources: Ward, *Baseball*, 1994; McNeil, *The California Winter League*, 2002; Holway, Johnson, and Borst, *The Complete Book of Baseball's Negro Leagues*, 2001; Bench5, "Negro Leagues vs. Major Leagues," Baseball-Fever. com, 2006; Simkus, *Outsider Baseball*, 2014.

Now, while the results speak for themselves, I want to be clear. I do not think the typical Negro Leagues team, when pitted against a typical Major League team, would win 60–66 percent of the time. I do think the data suggests equivalency.

Using information gleaned from box scores, the internet researcher Bench5 further broke down his/her data set, into three separate groups as follows:

Table 7.11 NLB vs. MLB

Big Leaguers*	W	L	Pct.
1–3	36	12	.750
4–6	32	20	.615
+7	64	78	.451
Total	132	110	.545

* In addition to a MLB starting pitcher.
Source: Bench5, "Negro-Leagues vs. Major Leagues."

This brilliant piece of analysis shows what one would expect. Not all of the so-called Major League teams were equal or even big league at all. The Negro Leagues teams beat up on the squads with six or less MLB players but did not fare as well against clubs with more big league starters. Against teams with seven to nine major leaguers, they won only 45 percent of the time.

Where Bench5 erred, however, was in treating the Negro Leagues teams as a control group, as the black ball outfits were also of varying quality. I offer that if he had split the Negro Leagues squads into separate groupings based on talent, he would find that the games with relatively full Negro Leagues teams versus relatively full Major League clubs were more evenly divided and, QED, equivalency.

There are many other approaches, theories, and conjectures in this book, but if viewed by an open mind, the conclusion is unavoidable—the brand of ball, quality of play, and on-field talent within the Negro Leagues was equivalent to that of the Major Leagues. To think otherwise provides the impetus for a different question: Were the Major Leagues prior to the integration of the game truly major?

Notes

1. Paul Dickson, *The Dickson Baseball Dictionary*, 3d ed (New York: W. W. Norton, 2009), 527.

2. "Appendix B—Decisions of the Special Baseball Records Committee," in *The Baseball Encyclopedia*, David Neft, editor (New York: MacMillan, 1969), 2327.

3. SABR.org, "SABR 47: Baseball Records Committee," accessed August 17, 2017, https://sabr.org/convention/sabr47-committees, SABR47-David_Neft-John_Thorn-Baseball_Records_Cmte.mp3.

4. Peterson, *Only the Ball Was White*, 86, 175–179; 257–283; *Sporting News*, December 6, 1923; Overmyer, *Black Ball and The Boardwalk*, 250–258.

5. Lawrence D. Hogan, and Jules Tygiel, *Shades of Glory: The Negro League and the Story of African American Baseball* (Washington, DC: National Geographic Society, 2006), 161. The Negro National League was founded February 13–14, 1920, at the Paseo YMCA in Kansas City, MO. It can be argued that the Negro Leagues ended as early as August 1945, when Jackie Robinson signed with the Brooklyn Dodgers organization.

6. Bill James, *The New Bill James Historical Abstract* (New York: Free Press, 2001), 876–877.

7. Baseball-Reference.com, "Minor League Stats and History," http://www.baseball-reference.com/register/minor-league-stats.shtml. A year-by-year review of International League rosters is poetically bookended by Hall of Famers Frank Grant in 1886 and Jackie Robinson in 1946. In between, 47 other future Hall of Fame players appeared in International League games.

8. Baseball-Reference.com, "Minor League Stats and History."

9. Clark and Lester, *The Negro Leagues Book*, 255–256.

10. Jackie Robinson, directed by Ken Burns, Sarah Burns, and David McMahon (2016; Brighton, MA: PBS Distribution, 2016), DVD.

11. *Jackie Robinson*, DVD.

12. Lee Sinins, editor, *Complete Baseball Encyclopedia*, last modified November 3, 2016, http://www.-

baseball-encyclopedia.com/. I sorted the top ten sacrifice bunt, stolen base, and home run career leaders for the period 1947–2017.

13. Baseball-Reference.com, "MLB Most Valuable Player MVP Awards & Cy Young Awards Winners," http://www.baseball-reference.com/awards/mvp_cya.shtml. The data includes MVP winners through the 2017 season. The halved total derives from 1979, when Willie Stargell (who, as an African-American, would not have been allowed to play prior to 1947) and Keith Hernandez (who with a father of Spanish descent and a mother of Scots-Irish heritage would have been) shared the award. The author assumed all 54½ players (seven of whom were from the Dominican Republic, six from Puerto Rico, two from Cuba, two from Venezuela, one from Japan, one from Panama, and one of Dominican descent) would not have been permitted to play in MLB prior to April 15, 1947. This conclusion is supported by the fact that of the 7,931 MLB players prior to Jackie Robinson, fewer than 1 percent were of the aforementioned nationalities. In fact, only 42 players from those countries appeared in the majors between 1876 and 1946, with 36 of them being Cuban. The country of origin data is from Sinins, *Complete Baseball Encyclopedia*.

14. National Baseball Hall of Fame, "1960–1969," "1970–1979," "1980–1989," "1990–1999," "2000–2009," "2010-present," http://baseballhall.org/hall-of-famers/past-inductions/; Baseball-Reference.com, "MLB Baseball Hall of Fame Inductees," http://www.baseball-reference.com/awards/hof.shtml. The data includes Hall of Fame inductees through 2018.

15. McNeil, *Baseball's Other All-Stars*, 189.

16. McNeil, *Baseball's Other All-Stars*, 189. The cumulative batting average of MLB (1920–1946) was derived from Sinins, *Complete Baseball Encyclopedia*.

17. McNeil, *Baseball's Other All-Stars*, 189; "Negro Leagues Player Register," *The Baseball Encyclopedia*, 8th ed, edited by Rick Wolff (New York: Macmillan, 1990), 2581–2608.

18. E-mail message to editor, January 28, 2017

19. *Baseball, The Fifth Inning: Shadow Ball 1930–1940*, produced by Ken Burns and Lynn Novick (1994; Hollywood, CA: PBS Home Video, 2004), DVD.

PART TWO

Equity

I do not consider that I was born at the wrong time. I felt it was the right time, for I had a chance to prove the ability of our race in this sport, and because many of us did our very best to uphold the traditions of the game and of the world of sport, we have given the Negro a greater opportunity now to be accepted into the major leagues with other Americans.

—John Henry Lloyd

Hotel Resorts and the Emergence of the Black Baseball Professional

Riverine and Maritime Communities, 1867–1890

JAMES E. BRUNSON III

The colored dining-room waiters in both [Saratoga Springs] hotels discharge their duties with about equal promptitude. The large number of them who come from Philadelphia, it is well known, possess a pleasanter tone of voice and are more graceful in their deportment than those who hail from New York. That the Philadelphia colored waiters at present generally receive the preference in Saratoga is a clear reason why the New York colored waiters should study to discover their deficiencies.[1]

A base-ball game was played yesterday afternoon on the South Broadway Grounds, between the Unions, a Saratoga Club, and the Philadelphias, of the Grand Union [Hotel]. The result was a draw, each side scored 3. Frank Sanford made the best play of the Saratoga boys and B. Blanch did the same for the foreign club.[2]

At a meeting held July 19, 1876, the Union Base Ball Club (colored) of Saratoga, NY, was organized. The Unions have, it is said, has as fine an enclosed ground as there is in the State, and are ready to receive challenges from any colored club in the United States. They will share gate money liberally with visiting clubs, and give good accommodations. They are also prepared to receive propositions and make arrangements for games with all responsible clubs, as they oppose making an extended tour about the middle of September. All ball-tossers will please take notice, especially the Barbers, of Albany and Heavy Hitters of Johnston.[3]

Prologue: The Birth of Organized Black Baseball at Saratoga Springs, New York

In 1870, the Union Base Ball Club of Saratoga Springs, New York, reorganized. The Unions, composed of young hometown boys, were bankrolled by older black businessmen. At their team meeting, they elected the following officers: Alexander Brown, president/treasurer (owner of the Union Hall barbershop since 1858, from which the club derived its name), David Henry Granger, vice president (proprietor of the Granger barbershop), director John M. Van Dyke (barber), Frank Smith, team captain (hotel waiter), and Fred Sanford, secretary. Brown and Granger built the team an enclosed baseball grounds.[4] By 1876, the team's grander vision was national recognition.[5]

Saratoga Springs, New York, was, writes historian A.K. Sandoval-Strausz, a village resort "for prosperous city dwellers."[6] Between 1870 and 1890, it became a black ball mecca, a destination for the waiters of New York, Troy, Syracuse, Philadelphia, Pittsburgh, Baltimore, Richmond, Boston, New London, Providence, Washington, Chicago, St. Louis, St.

Croix, and Bermuda. In 1878, the number of black waiters at Saratoga Springs included Grand Union, 300; United States, 175; Congress Hall, 120; Windsor, 30; and Clarendon, 25.[7]

Saratoga Springs prized Philadelphia's waiters. They were not alone. In 1889, 4,500 black waiters of Philadelphia worked at the leading summer resorts.[8] Many found baseball fame. Between 1896 and 1899, the Bartram nine created a name at Sharon Springs, New York.[9] In 1897, the "Sharon Bartrams" defeated the Cuban X-Giants.[10]

Between 1873 and 1876, the Grand Union Philadelphias, Congress Hall Athletics, and Unions (Union Haymakers) contested for local bragging rights. Large crowds assembled to witness their games at the South Broadway grounds, an expansive, grassy knoll enclosed by a meandering rail-fence. It was an intense rivalry. The Union Haymakers soundly defeated the Athletics. The Union Haymaker-Grand Union Philadelphia match resulted in a draw.[11]

Congress Hall's black ball–waiters laid symbolic claim to the moniker Athletics. Black Philadelphians paid homage to a white hometown club that claimed professional status in 1876. While Philadelphia had no professional black club, the desire to form one—given the success of the Pythians (1866–1873) and Williams Club (1875–1876)—was surely felt.[12] For the transient Philadelphians of Saratoga, the name Athletics invoked civic pride. This commemorative act was no isolated gesture: in 1875, Philadelphia artist Thomas Eakins produced *Base Ball Players Practicing*, a painting that captures the prowess of three Athletics players. Between 1873 and 1885, black Philadelphians embraced the cognomen. Within the name nested a notion of entrepreneurship: Athletics, Keystone Athletics, and Ancient City Athletics left indelible tracks in the commercial and resort hotels of Philadelphia, Saratoga Springs, Babylon, Jacksonville, and St. Augustine. Philadelphia also birthed the Cuban Giants in 1885.

This essay links baseball's hotel-waiter subculture—Saratoga as the nexus to the black professional and the black cultural production of Eastern coastal communities.[13] It zeroes in on steamship culture and the resort/seaport communities of Rhode Island–Connecticut and South Carolina–Georgia–Florida between 1867 and 1890. While steamships had become a quaint form of transportation by the 1880s, maritime communities continued to nurture black ball and black cultural production (theater and music). Hotel waiters, barbers, and journalists played seminal roles in these developments.[14] From the Northern cities of New London, Providence, Saratoga Springs, and Philadelphia, to the Southern seaport towns of Baltimore, Beaufort, Savannah, San Marco, Jacksonville, and St. Augustine resort communities were a breeding ground for the black professional.[15]

For historian Thomas Graham, wealthy whites believed that blacks were particularly suited to play an entertainment role in the drama of resort life.[16] Whether through expectation, encouragement, or pecuniary ingenuity, they provided hotel amusements. From the antebellum era to the postbellum Gilded Age, commercial/luxury resorts, hotel attachés (barber shops), and steamship line companies employed black ball–waiters: in 1858, for example, Robert Henson, a waiter, organized Jamaica, New York's Unknown Base Ball Club.[17] By 1868, the waiters of Niagara Falls' Cataract and International hotels had ball clubs.[18] In the 1870s and 1880s, the *Saratogian* newspaper covered games of the Grand Union, Congress Hall, United States, and Clarendon nines. Black hotel staff also engaged in theatrical and musical performances.[19]

Black musical and theatrical talent penetrated the hotel entertainment industry.[20] It retained African idioms, mastered European styles, and invented uniquely American forms.[21]

In 1822, the Philadelphia bandmaster and composer, Francis Johnson, arrived at Saratoga Springs. Johnson's Brass and String Band performed at Congress Hall and the United States Hotel. His syncopated African rhythms impacted American music.[22] A contemporary noted his "remarkable taste in distorting a sentimental, simple and beautiful song into a reel, jig, or country-dance"[23] The antebellum South embraced such performances as well. Black waiters performed on luxury steamers. The New Orleans steamer *Magnolia*, captained by St. Clair Thomasson, hosted bridal parties in the 1850s. The *Times-Picayune* reported: "Among the Negro waiters there were always a half dozen musicians or more. During the concerts in the ladies' cabin, high-toned ladies sang sentimental songs, alternating with the plantation melodies of the darkey waiters."[24]

Saratoga Springs enticed tourists with its mineral waters—swampy in taste and smell—marketed as healing elixirs to improve their health.[25] Showman Phineas T. Barnum endorsed the brew as "superior to any water that I ever drank."[26] Tourists attached cultural meanings to the scenic landscapes. In 1843, a discerning critic noted that not all guests appreciated the natural environment: "The scenery in the neighborhood is of the wildest and most romantic character, but few of the *distingués* and the elegant visitors seem to be aware of it. Their time is spent mostly dressing, eating, drinking, intriguing, gossiping, lounging, and parading the piazzas and saloons of the hotels."[27] Social life overtook health and scenery as the main reason for the resort's popularity. "To occupy their guests' abundant available time," writes Sandoval-Strausz, "resort hotels sponsored concerts, lectures, nature walks, plays, recitals, masquerade balls, and countless other entertainments."[28] By the late 1850s, black employees provided not only musical and theatrical entertainment, but baseball exhibitions as well.

Saratoga Springs's black hotel employees were locals and transients. They shared complex social histories. Many had experienced enslavement; others represented the first generation removed from bondage. Many were related by blood. They created an independent society, a thriving community often removed from segregated social spaces. They became entrepreneurs, owning guest lodgings, barbershops, liveries, and boarding stables. They organized political, social, musical, theatrical, and baseball clubs.[29]

The hotel industry became a rite of passage for many black ball professionals. It brought together the best players, many thriving under peripatetic conditions. They moved throughout the country, from one hotel to another. They formed fraternal bonds. In search of baseball dreams, they migrated between summer and winter resorts. They honed athletic and theatrical/musical talent at Saratoga Springs, a crucial nexus for these migrations. Maritime and riverine communities became a destination, where they "spread the gospel of the national pastime across the United States."[30]

Since 1871, many black ball clubs had claimed professional status: The St. Louis Brown Stockings (1870–1871), Chicago Uniques (1871–1888), Richmond Black Swans (1883), St. Louis Black Stockings (1883–1885), Baltimore Atlantics (1884–1885), Chicago Gordons (1884–1887), Philadelphia Keystones (1885), Savannah Chathams (1883–1900), Jacksonville Athletics (1886), New Orleans Unions (1886–1888), Memphis Eclipse (1886–1889), Louisville Fall Citys (1886–1887), Boston Resolutes (1887–1888), Raleigh Nationals (1887–1889), Providence Colored Grays (1887–1888), Pittsburgh Keystones (1887–1889), New York Gorhams (1887–1892), Houston's Sunflowers (1888), and Galveston's Flyaways (1888) figured among them. Several of these teams had been part of proposed or organized professional leagues. Along the Eastern seaboard, many players worked in the hotel industry or on steamships as waiters, porters, drivers, and barbers.[31]

Saratoga Springs: A Mecca for Aspiring Black Ball Professionals

"There is less red tape at a Saratoga hotel than any other hostelry in America. But there are more [N]egroes. You will have no trouble with anybody if you make it right with the blacks."[32] Getting "the blacks" to the resort village was an orchestrated affair. Railway travel from Philadelphia to New York, passage on the steamer *Powell* or the steamer *Saratoga* (which originated at Troy) and omnibuses from the railway depot took them to the resort complex. This cost one month's pay which, in 1875, amounted to 25 dollars, five dollars less than that earned by white waiters. Fees/tips supplemented their incomes. They financed middle-class desires, including college tuition. They purchased wardrobes, objets d'art, souvenirs, and steamer trunks. Additional luggage was needed for the return trip home. In one fiasco, the steamer *Saratoga*—delayed for black waiters' baggage—left behind three truck-loads of trunks.[33]

By the late 1860s, black ball was regularly played at Northern summer resorts. Black hotel headwaiters played a crucial role in the formation of black clubs. John Murphy. Sr., who served as headwaiter of Niagara Falls Cataract Hotel, had a baseball club. His son played for the team in 1868.[34] Saratoga Springs likely organized hotel nines as well. Black headwaiters played a role in hotel management. White managers desired "a person of considerable consequence ... a man of steady and methodical habits, with a quick eye, to see that everything is done properly. He must be a rigid disciplinarian, and be always at his post."[35] In 1868, the Congress Hall headwaiter and assistant, Hans Shadd, and Robert P. Jackson—both mulattos—made Saratoga an objective point of pursuit for black workers.[36] Both men had been enslaved. In 1818, Shadd was born in Delaware; in 1822, Jackson was born in Philadelphia. Before landing at Saratoga in 1868, they had worked as Philadelphia waiters. The Congress Hall staff respected them, both men being presented a silver pitcher, ice tray, and two goblets. In 1869, Jackson became a headwaiter. Winfield Jackson, who worked alongside his father, became a headwaiter in 1869. After his retirement, Hans Shadd operated a catering business at Saratoga Springs and Philadelphia. Hotel headwaiters recruited staff with musical, theatrical, and baseball talents.[37]

The headwaiter, Robert Thompson, was a formerly enslaved Virginian. Thompson, "a small, well-made quadroon," resembled Stephen A. Douglas. He was the grandson of the Revolutionary War General Harry Lee, father of Confederate General Robert E. Lee. His grandmother, Jenny, was chambermaid to Lee's wife. General Harry Lee later sold Jenny and Robert to Colonel Samuel Stewart of Frederick County, Maryland, a wealthy planter who had a large number of enslaved blacks. Following Stewart's death, Thompson was freed by a clause in his will. He became a messenger in the U.S. Post Office. After falling in love with Jane Brandt, an enslaved Octoroon, he secured her freedom and they wedded. In 1867, he became headwaiter at Washington's National Hotel, where he supervised 100 waiters. In 1868, he became the Grand Union headwaiter. He interacted with former U.S. presidents, European royalty, poets/savants, statesmen, and historians. Following his death in 1875, Thompson's wife continued to operate a first-class laundry business at the Grand Union.[38]

David Henry Granger's biography is equally poignant and inspirational. Granger was born into enslavement in 1821, at Schoharie Court House, New York, about 64 miles southwest of Saratoga Springs. Granger's owner rented the youngster to a tavern public house (an early form of the hotel), where he worked for 15 years. After the business closed, Granger went to Utica and apprenticed as a barber. In 1841, he opened a barbershop in Saratoga's Grand Union Hotel. After the resort season ended, he returned to Utica. He moved to Saratoga permanently in 1843. Granger opened a barbershop in the St. Nicolas Building, head-quarters for the *Saratogian* newspaper, which later provided coverage of his Union Base Ball Club.[39]

For 20 years, Granger searched for his family. Fortuitous encounters led to happy re-unions. He located a sister and her husband; the latter was a local waiter. Granger found his mother and his father's sister, Hannah Dickson. Hannah, also enslaved, came to Saratoga in 1825. Following her freedom, she was a domestic in Saratoga and Troy. She married Henry Dickson, "a hard-working African, and an excellent cook [who] found employment every summer in some of the Saratoga hotels."[40] She was the wealthiest black woman in Troy. An employer convinced Hannah to deposit her savings in a bank. However, she kept possession of a "hoard of gold specie." The devout Presbyterian died at age 72; Hannah left her wealth to Granger.[41]

Granger's Union players labored as waiters.[42] They worked alongside Philadelphia men. A rivalry developed. The *Saratogian* reported: "The Union-Haymakers are composed exclu-sively of Saratogians, and the Athletic is a club made up of several Congress Hall waiters."[43] As if to distance themselves from Philadelphia teams, they called these clubs foreign.[44] Why? One answer is their monikers, which intensified an outsider status. Another answer is the recruitment of outside players. Recruiting black professionals to improve a team's chances was not unusual. The Philadelphias couldn't beat the Unions without help.[45] The Grand Union Philadelphias hired B. Blanch, a professional pitcher. In 1871, Blanch led the Troy Hannibals to a black tournament championship. In 1876, he held the Union-Haymakers to three runs. Later that year, the itinerant player hurled for Utica's Fearless Base Ball Club.[46]

The earliest black professional club that I have found was the St. Louis Brown Stock-ings. In 1870, St. Louis baseballist Dennis Smith wrote to the *Utica Observer*: "The St. Louis Base Ball Club, composed of men with money, has undertaken to pay the traveling expenses of a strong nine of colored baseballists to travel through the Eastern States early in 1871. They desire the addresses of the secretaries of colored clubs throughout the States North."[47] In 1871, Smith advertised in the *New York Clipper*. He sought "colored professionals," a "good catcher and good left hand pitcher. A good salary would be given for the season."[48]

In 1871, Chicago's Unique club—another team with money—toured Michigan, Upper Canada, Troy, Philadelphia, Pittsburgh, and Washington, D.C. Between 1872 and 1879, their fame grew while playing white and black clubs of Illinois, Indiana, Kentucky, Missouri, Kan-sas, Michigan, and Wisconsin. In 1875, Winona, Minnesota's Clippers (white) hired William Fisher, a pitcher of the Uniques. In 1876, Minneapolis's Blue Stars and St. Paul's Unions bat-tled for the black championship. The Blue Stars hired three Uniques players—James and Thomas Coombs, and William Berry—to defeat the Unions. In 1876, the Wilmington and Independent nines of Wilmington, Delaware battled for the championship. The Wilming-tons imported four members of Philadelphia's Williams club (Andrew Randolph, of Trenton Cuban Giants fame, likely played for this team). Whether Blanch was a Philadelphian is a moot point. He belongs among the earliest black professionals to play at Saratoga.[49]

Alexander Brown and David Henry Granger represent a link between barbers and Saratoga black ball. Granger opened his barbershop in 1843. Brown, a Baltimore native, had opened the Union Barbershop by 1858. They belonged to an artisan system that can be imagined as a guild. It "ensured decent work and decent prices for all practitioners through a system that took care of them from the moment they entered the trade until their death."[50] Black barbers invented the first-class tonsorial parlor, combining "upscale décor and mas-culine conviviality."[51]

Tonsorial artists—barbers and fashionable hair dressers—organized black ball clubs.[52] They belonged to a rich history: Henry Rosecranse Columbus, Jr., born into enslavement, learned the barbering trade at Kingston, New York. He played a form of baseball in the 1840s.[53] Baltimore's barber profession embraced baseball. Between 1842 and 1860, Baltimore's Colored Barber's Beneficial Society also had a strong organization.[54] In 1859, they hosted a picnic and more than 1,000 barbers attended.[55] This event coincided with the birth of the Hannibal Base Ball Club. The *Baltimore Bee* reported: "The Lord Hannibal Base Ball Club was formed in 1859, and expects to be admitted to the convention next fall."[56] The tonsorial arts changed black men *and* women into people of the world, establishing the basis for middle-class identity.[57]

Between 1869 and 1870, Saratoga, Albany, Johnston, Troy, Hudson, Canajoharie, Utica, Geneva, Rochester, Little Falls, and Schenectady formed a black ball circuit. Black tournaments received national attention, which explains why Dennis Smith advertised in the East.[58] In 1870, the Fearless club claimed black ball supremacy. The *Utica Observer* reported: "The Fearless Base Ball Club, the acknowledged colored champions of the State, are again in the field as fearless as ever and with a first-class muscular development."[59] Thomas and Samuel Freeman; John, Thomas and Reuben Lippen; William and Arlington Denike; Sarralt Logan, James H. Washington, Cesar Jackson, Charles Peterson, Robert Van Alstine, Peter Tonssant, and Joshua Atkins were tonsorial artists and members of the Fearless club.[60]

Troy's black tonsorial artists supported baseball. In the 1840s, Peter F. Baltimore routinely opened a summer resort barbershop at Saratoga (Baltimore's enslaved father had fought in the Revolutionary War). In 1867, he organized a team: "The Baltimore Base Ball Club (colored) will go to Hudson today."[61] In 1870, Troy participated in the black ball tournament.[62] In 1869, William Rich, a barber/caterer/gambler/real estate owner, organized the William Rich High School (which Rich provided financial resources and political clout to build) team.[63] The *Troy Press* jibed: "At a practice game of the William Rich Base Ball Club on the Putnam Grounds Monday, the Colored Knights of the willow seemed at one time more ambitious in the line of breaking shins, than attending strictly to the legitimate requisitions of the game."[64]

Black entrepreneurs created businesses in Saratoga Springs. In 1862, John C. Broughton, a Brooklyn saloonkeeper, opened the Broughton House, a three-story lodging that had 22 single and double rooms, dining facilities, and a cottage.[65] It boasted a garden with swings, outdoor stage, bowling alley, croquet grounds, billiard room, barbershop, bar, and billiard hall. (In 1870, Broughton and Alexander Brown of the Union nine received city liquor licenses.)[66] The *Saratogian* covered the resort's events: "The brilliantly illuminated parlors were rendered more brilliant by the dazzling gems and gay dresses of the fair participants, and the deep tints that prevailed in their toilettes contrasted most favorably with the somber garb of the gentlemen."[67] Regarding another affair, the *Saratogian* reported: "There was a fine hop at the Broughton House last evening, and the trippers of the light fantastic toe kept up the terpsichorean festivity until a late hour."[68] The Broughton House catered to black guests from across the country and hosted visitors from the Caribbean and England.[69]

Black baseballists supported this fashionable establishment. In 1883 and 1884, members of the Leonidas nine entertained guests; Julius Booker managed garden parties and musicales.[70] The Four Emperors, a quartette formed by Louis H. Buchanan, performed there.[71] Another Broughton House guest was "Frank Hart, the pedestrian who [was] identified with the Leonidas Base Ball Club."[72] Henry Bridgewater recruited Hart for the St. Louis Black Stockings. Isaac Judah resided at the Broughton House; Judah was manager of the Philadelphia Pythians. Andrew Jackson, another regular, played for the Grand Unions, Brooklyn's Remsens and Alpines, the Gorhams, and the Cuban Giants.[73] When the Cuban Giants scheduled games at Saratoga in 1890, they stayed at the Broughton.[74] When Broughton died in 1903, the resort was put up for sale.[75]

Between 1882 and 1883, the Clarendon Hotel waiters—managed by Stanislau K. Govern—dominated baseball in Saratoga County. The *Saratogian* reported: "The Clarendons defeated the Grand Unions in a well-contested game of baseball…. The playing of Strather, Barker, Boyd, Buchanan, and Wilson of the Clarendons was much enjoyed by the hundreds of spectators."[76] They were composed principally of Washingtonians—the Manhattan Base Ball Club—whom Govern also managed. Many of them had been playing since the 1870s: Benjamin Boyd, William Barker, Jacob C. Strather, William P. Hatton, William Brown, Robert Brown, James Washington, Samuel Alexander, and Benjamin Holmes. The Manhattans, organized in 1872 (if not earlier) claimed professional status in 1883.[77] Govern also organized Clarendon's Jolly Nine, black ball–waiters who performed musical and theatrical amusements.[78]

Between 1886 and 1890, black ball clubs flourished at Saratoga: "The baseball game yesterday between the Clarendon and Grand Union waiters was won by the former by a score of 17 to 8."[79] They also played independents: "The baseball game yesterday between the Grand Union waiters and the Flyaways was won by the former club. There was a large attendance."[80] In 1888, B. F. Palmer organized the Saratoga Giants, an independent semi-professional club. They played against black and white teams of Troy, Fort Edward, Albany, and Saratoga.[81]

By 1884, Saratoga Springs' black ball–waiters began migrating to other hotel resorts. In 1889, James H. Reed went to New London, Connecticut, a seaport community nicknamed "the Whaling City."[82] Reed was headwaiter of the Crocker House. For years, he had worked at Saratoga's United States Hotel, serving as secretary/treasurer of the Waiters' Club. He caught for the hotel nine. Reed became president of the New London Base Ball Association; the other officers were Calvin Wheeler, J. Burton, and M. Blue (of Philadelphia). Reed, a musician, accepted the position of chorister/organist for the Union Baptist Church. With declining interest in black ball, he returned to the United States Hotel in 1891.[83]

"Cracking Up a Chord": Black Ball Performance in New London, Connecticut

Before B.F. Palmer had organized the Saratoga Giants in 1888, the black ball–waiter had hurled for Buffalo's Genesee and Niagara Falls International hotel nines.[84] Palmer, a fine vocalist, sang with a quartette at the International House. In 1885, Palmer, Charles Gibbs, Charles Butler, and I.W. Butler—baseballists—organized the International Glee Club.[85] The *Niagara Falls Gazette* reported: "The International Glee Club has a fine selection of Southern melodies and old plantation songs…. In compliance to the request of many of the best citizens Mr. Joe Morris, the greatest colored ventriloquist, will give an exhibition of his remarkable talent."[86] Quartette singing was nothing less than "the black national pastime."[87]

For black quartettes, no song—sacred or secular—was immune to the spontaneous syncopated style of harmonizing. This unique black style, writes jazz archivist Lynn Abbott, is called "cracking up a chord."[88] The art of cracking up a chord derived from organic blended harmonies, described as weird or peculiar. The *New Haven Register* reported: "[The Norwalk Colored Glee Club] consists of a quartette of excellent voices and the singing possesses all of the peculiarities of the genuine Negro plantation melodies."[89] Mainstream antecedents (European or Euro-American inspired) were innocent, Abbott writes, of the rakish "minors" (fourth and fifth musical notes) "swipes," (pitch changes) and "snakes" (chords) that characterized black recreational male quartettes. They performed in school yards, lodge halls, barrooms, shoeshine stands, railroad stations, and private homes. This old sound was labeled "barbershop harmony."[90]

While tracing its origins to antebellum cultural practices—plantations, hotels, seaports, and whaling ships—this music penetrated the hotel industry. From New England to Florida, black ball–waiters cracked up a chord at summer and winter resorts. Its impact on black baseball's hotel-waiter subculture of Connecticut (Hartford, Middletown, Stonington, and New London), was extensive. The black community of New London County created a thriving seaport mecca, a cultural haven for aspiring entrepreneurs, musicians, thespians, and baseballists.[91]

In 1874, the Providence-Stonington Steamer Company offered first-class travel between Stonington, Providence, Newport, Boston, Philadelphia, Baltimore, and New York.[92] When the steamer *Rhode Island* landed at Stonington, New London County, Connecticut in 1875, baseball teams of black waiters—the Long Nines and Shorts—disembarked to play a championship match for a silver cup. George Garrison, team captain/pitcher, homered in the game. Following the match, a team secretary submitted an account to the *New York Clipper*: "The winners gave the cup to the Third Colored Baptist Church at Stonington, and went on their way rejoicing."[93]

Stonington's narrative of black ball also offers a story of racial prejudice and limited opportunities.[94] In 1867, an unnamed black player joined a white club of Stonington. When that nine challenged the Red Jackets of North Stonington, another white team, the latter club refused to play; a newspaper hyped the snub as a "cheerful exhibition of the war of the races."[95] Stonington's black ball–waiter teams regularly played black nines of Connecticut and Rhode Island.[96]

The resort town of Stonington was a major stop for the Fall River Line Company (Old Colony Steamer Company) of Massachusetts, which ran between New York and Boston. Black waiters had worked at the hotels since the 1840s.[97] Black stewards and head waiters, waiters, hairdressers/barbers, cooks and pantry men, and saloonkeepers were employed. They came from Bristol, Pilgrim, Providence, Middletown, Jersey City, and Macon, Georgia, where black ball emerged. New London County's social network was extensive. In 1887, the *City of Wooster* steamer joined the Fall River Line Company; two black ball–waiters worked for the steamer. The City of Wooster Association, black employees of the palace steamer, hosted annual social events. In the 1870s and 1880s, the Providence Apollo Club, composed principally black ballplayers, fraternized with Fall River Line employees.[98]

What was the relation of black ball to Stonington? One answer is family bonds. Since the 1850s, blacks of New London County struggled to build a middle-class society. They labored for Connecticut hotels and steamships. Henry L. Jordan, born in Stonington in 1850, was a Stonington Steamship Line steward for 30 years. Jordan married Lisato Henry, a Stonington woman. He likely played baseball in the 1860s.[99] His son, William Henry, married Stonington native Louise Freeman. He was a black ball–waiter. In 1886, he was player/manager for the Crocker House nine. When Henry left the Steamship Eureka for a New Orleans steamship company, William replaced him.[100] The *New York Freeman* identified the Jordan family as part of New London's elite, which historian Wilson Jeremiah Moses imagined as "racially responsible and worthy of respect."[101]

Between 1850 and 1870, New London's black population sought full citizenship. In 1848, Connecticut finally abolished black enslavement. The Third Colored Baptist Church, founded by Ely Dickenson of Philadelphia in 1846, felt the lingering effects of bondage. Some congregation members had been enslaved. In 1850, a federal census report identified 74 blacks and mulattoes over age 16 residing in Stonington; others lived in greater Stonington or on fishing ships in the harbor.[102]

In 1863, the Third Colored Baptist Church expressed concern about the dreadful strife imposed by the Civil War. Prior to the formation of black military units, they demanded to serve in the Union Army. They also resented non-citizenship while bearing the taxpayer's burden.[103] Suffrage mattered as well: "Whenever we are permitted to vote, we shall be sure not to vote for bondage or oppression in any form…. We have a destiny in common with all the sons and daughters of Africa which we are bound to fulfill."[104] In the Civil War's aftermath, the congregation laid bare its ongoing ill-treatment: "We are glad liberty has been proclaimed throughout the land and we are anxiously looking for the day when colored people of Connecticut shall enjoy equal privileges with the Freedman of the South; when Connecticut shall be as free as South Carolina."[105]

During this period, organized black ball became a prominent fixture in the community. In 1866, the *New London Weekly Chronicle* boasted of its "African" nine.[106] The *Washington National Republican* reported: "New London has a colored baseball club." The *Hartford Courant* snidely added: "They have a new base-ball club in New London, composed of colored gentlemen, called the Night Blooming Cereus Club. The club by any other name would smell sweet."[107] Baseball required capital, and the players duly noted an economic hardship: "The organization of the club was made with great difficulty for want of funds to purchase a ball and bat but a temporary loan of twenty-five cents—the amount of which they fell short was—obtained, and the club went immediately into active operations."[108]

The club garnered national attention. In 1867, the Phalon Night Blooming Cereus Perfume Company of New York City sent the city a framed picture of the Night Blooming Cereus flower. The white clothier and regatta rower, Charles N. Middleton, prominently displayed the photograph in his store window.[109] The moniker (derived from the delicate floral extracts used in a perfume) added to the club a patina of refined aesthetic sensibility; in 1869, the "Aromatics," a black ball club of New Orleans, perhaps paid homage to New London.[110] Between 1867 and 1869, the New London nine hosted several community socials. The Night Blooming Cereus Base Ball Club embodied self-improvement, self-determination, and social freedom.[111]

Why did the steamer *Rhode Island* nines present the Third Colored Baptist Church with a silver cup? While the gift seems unusual, black churches had historically supported baseball. In 1879, Raleigh, North Carolina's Black Methodist Church organized a team. The *Christian Advocate* reported: "It is called Methodist Heroes Base Ball Club, and is composed of colored boys, who wear a badge with the following description, Methodist Heroes B.B.C."[112] In 1883, New York's Abyssinian Baptist Church and Bethel Baptist Church nines played at Roton Park.[113] Following the demise of the National Colored Base Ball League in 1887, Reverend Harvey Johnson of Baltimore's North Street Baptist Church demanded an accounting from manager J.J. Callis of the Lord Baltimores.[114] The Third Colored Baptist Church's support of baseball was not surprising. Under the leadership of Reverend Solomon Gale, the church hosted festivals attended by locals and friends from other towns. By hosting the Long Nines and Shorts baseball match, the church sought to augment its operational funds.

Silver objects were presented not only to black headwaiters, but to black ball clubs as well. In 1868, Hartford's Oceanus defeated Middletown's Heroes for the black championship of Connecticut. The *Middletown Constitution* reported: "A silver pitcher was presented by L. S. Hall, and the ball used in the game given by C.E. Putnam were [sic] presented to the victors."[115] These men worked for the steamer *Oceanus* and steamer *Hero*.[116] The presentation of silver objects to churches suggests communion ware. Parishioners gifted silver objects as liturgical vessels. In 1864, Gilbert Tompkins gifted Hartford's Shiloh Baptist Church two silver goblets; Oliver Reed of Suffield's Second Baptist Church gave two silver plates. The Third Colored Baptist Church, a smaller house of worship, couldn't afford lavish communion ware, and the black ball–waiters gifted the parishioners a silver chalice.[117]

Social relationships and economics melded New London County to the black community. An unsuspected link was Jersey City. In the 1860s and 1870s, Henry DuBois Hallack, a tonsorial artist of Jersey City, belonged to the Oriental, Odd Leaf, and Keystone clubs. Between 1886 and 1889, Hallack was team president for New London's Crocker House nines. In 1873, John E. Jordan (William's brother) played for the Jersey City Keystones.[118] Freemasonry offers another clue. Black players belonged to Jersey City's Eureka Lodge, including Jordan. Blacks of Jersey City worked for the Providence-Stonington Steamer Company Line. Philadelphia's black ball waiters worked at New London. Frank Blue, who played for the Crocker House, later joined the Acme Colored Giants. John Dickenson, son of Reverend Dickenson, also played for the Crock House nine.[119] Guaranteed better wages, Hartford's black ball–waiters flocked to New London for summer employment, among them George Brown, of the Hartford Blues, in the 1880s.[120]

Black ball–waiters adopted Rhode Island and Connecticut as a second home. George and Jonas Fentriss, of the Norfolk Red Stockings, wintered in New London. They were black ball–waiters at Watch Hill, Rhode Island. William McNaughton and George Jennings embraced New London; they also played at Watch Hill.[121] George and William Johnson played for the Colored Providence Grays, Boston Resolutes, and Crocker House; George worked on New London's *City of Worcester* steamer; William was steward of the steamer *Providence*. James Cary, of Ansonia, worked for *City of Wooster* steamer. Cary hurled for the City of *Wooster* steamer and Crocker House nines, and the white Renfrew club of North Adams, Massachusetts. Oscar H. Smith of Brooklyn's Remsens pitched for the Crocker House nine.[122]

New London was a black mecca, a haven for entrepreneurs, musical/theatrical artists, and ballplayers. Both men and women owned resort lodgings. William L. Jordan opened the Jordan Hotel and Saloon. M.M. Barnswell, a New York widow, owned the Sound View Cottages. Black ball–waiters supported black talent. For Marie Selika Williams, the queen of staccato, the seaport was a retreat: Madame Selika resided with the Jordan family. She was the first black artist to perform at the White House. The concert singer Flora Batson, "The Double-Voiced Queen of Song," performed at Stonington.[123] The dramatist/elocutionist Ms. Henrietta Vinton Davis delighted New London audiences. She was a baseball fan; in 1883, Stanislau Govern, of Saratoga's Clarendon Hotel, feted the young tragedienne. When Davis attended an exhibition game, Stanislau K. Govern named a picked nine in her honor.[124] Georgia's Callender Minstrels, a black theatrical troupe that played baseball, performed at New London.[125]

Any serious history of black ball considers its relation to black performance. They are intimately connected. Antebellum musical innovation and mastery—juba banjo, mandolin, piano, pipe organ, fiddle, accordion, bones, and their physical bodies (gesticulations and vocalizations)—thrived among black laborers in seaport and riverine towns. Whaling ships and the music of black sea mariners crisscrossed the Mid-Atlantic, the coastal towns of Connecticut and Massachusetts, and New York Hudson River ports as far south as Albany.[126]

"Negro sea chanteys," an element of a whaling culture, were performed by enslaved labor. Descending from African work songs, they represent a form of modern American music. During his enslavement, abolitionist Frederick Douglass heard black sea chanteys while caulking whaling vessels in Baltimore shipyards. When Douglass escaped to freedom and arrived in New Bedford in 1838, he continued the occupation of ship caulker. He noted how the New Bedford shipyards were eerily devoid of the loud songs that he had heard in Baltimore. They contained subversive elements. Douglass reminisced how blacks moved in "unison, sang or chanted songs that simultaneously kept their work in rhythm. They shouted mocking defiance of those who owned them, and forced them to work."[127] "Blow, Boys, Blow," a black sea chantey, traveled by sea and became widely known. The chantey is also known as "Blow the Man Down," a packet-ship chantey heard on the Black Ball Line.[128]

It should not be surprising that the chantey penetrated black ball performances. In the mid–1870s, 25 black collegians of Hampton Institute served as waiters at Saratoga's United States Hotel.[129] William Speed, a dancer and baritone vocalist, was among them. Speed later came to Chicago and pitched for the Pytheus and Unique clubs. After a stint with the Georgia Minstrels, he organized the Tennessee Jubilee and Plantation Singers. From 1886 to 1890, Speed captained New York's Hicks-Sawyer Minstrel Base Ball Club. When the black troupe performed in Australia, audiences encored his virtuoso solos.[130]

Black ball–waiters of New London's Crocker and Pequot houses were thespians and musicians. Black ball–waiters John Bell and Albert Stewart, of the Crocker House, organized "The Big Four Minstrels" or "New London Colored Minstrels." Boasting 20 members, they performed under the name of the "Colored Base Ball Association," to raise funds for uniforms and the leasing of an enclosed grounds.[131] The Pequot House waiters, led by Julius Webster and Charles Lomax, formed a glee club. Former President Chester A. Arthur attended one of their concerts. The Pequot House Glee Club played for social events.[132] John H. Pitts formed a touring dramatic troupe. Originally from Waterbury, Pitts relocated to New London. He served as chorister and organist for the Union Baptist Church. He managed Norwich's black ball club.[133] James Reed (Crocker House nine) belonged to New London's Lyceum Theater Company.[134]

Savannah: Entrepreneurs, Black Ball–Waiters and Black Professionals

Between 1864 and 1880, the Reverend Ulysses L. Houston of Savannah, Georgia's First Bryan Baptist Church, spearheaded religious and social activities, mutual aid societies, and the financial means to sustain them. In 1865, Houston attended a meeting at General William Tecumseh Sherman's Savannah headquarters that resulted in Special Field Order No.15—the redistribution of confiscated coastal land in 40-acre tracts to formerly-enslaved blacks.[135] From 1868 to 1871, he served in the Georgia State Legislature. He helped to relocate thousands of black families to Skidway, one of Georgia's Sea Islands. He raised funds for yellow fever sufferers and the poor and destitute. The black waiters of the U.S. Revenue steamer *Boutwell* provided financial assistance to Houston's association.[136]

In 1879, the first interstate match for the black championship of the South, between the clubs of Georgia and Florida, was played at Brunswick, Georgia. Darien, Union Island, St. Marys, New Brunswick, Savannah, Fernandina, and Jacksonville competed. This "series of games was organized by the Our Boys Benevolent Association, colored, of Savannah."[137] Houston headed and financed this association.

Savannah's black newspapermen supported baseball. In 1875, Louis M. Pleasant, George A. Davison, and John H. Deveaux established the *Colored Tribune*. In 1879, Robert and Thomas T. Harden and D. Griffin created the *Weekly Echo*; Deveaux also worked for this paper. Between 1875 and 1888, Pleasant managed Savannah's Chathams and Broadways. Regarding an Augusta-Savannah match, the *Augusta Chronicle* reported: "A feature of the two clubs are the heavy-weight managers, Thompson of the Athletics, weighing 230 pounds, and Captain Louis M. Pleasant, of the Broadways, 300, making the combined weight of the two men 530 pounds."[138] In 1888, the *Atlanta Constitution* reported: "A series of colored excursions will occur this month. The first in order of importance will be from Savannah, under the management of L. M. Pleasant."[139] In 1892, Davison took charge of the Chathams. The *Colored Tribune* said: "Judge George Davison has been elected manager, and sent his acceptance to the last meeting of the club. The club has made a wise selection, for Judge Davison is an able manager."[140]

Black ball as a commercial enterprise, historian Michael Lomax notes, "exemplified the continuation and expansion of entrepreneurship, within the tradition of self-help activities that had distinguished black economic endeavors in antebellum America and the post–Civil War era."[141] Baseball, event planners, steamship companies, and towns collaborated. In 1877, Beaufort, South Carolina's Dauntless club, under the direction of the Reverend D.W. Bythewood of the Tabernacle Baptist Church, chartered the steamer *Cumberland* for an excursion, in which they played the Savannah Chathams. The steamship didn't show. Team captain Robert Barnes secured a smaller vessel, the steamer *O. M. Pettit*, the result being that fewer fans could attend the game.[142]

Black ball–waiters worked on Savannah steamships. William Grant had been enslaved on a Savannah steamer captained by Nick King of New Jersey. Between 1870 and 1871, Grant captained the Americas Base Ball Club.[143] The *Colored Tribune* reported: "The Gorrie and Ocean Steamship baseball clubs played their third game on Monday last."[144] In 1883, the *New York Globe* reported: "The grandest baseball contest ever inaugurated in the South comes off at Savannah, Georgia. The picked nines from the South will strike from the shoulder. A grand excursion will leave here for the Forest City."[145]

In 1875, Jacksonville's St. Johns ball club took a steamer to Savannah, where they played the Pacifics at Irish Park.[146] The club moniker—St. Johns—pays homage to Florida's longest river. "The St. Johns River provided the main transportation artery into the interior of East Florida," writes Graham, "with flotillas of steamboats taking travelers as far south as Sanford in Central Florida and as far inland as Silver Springs, where excursionists could behold one of the great wonders of the natural world."[147] Luxury steamships for pleasure seekers proliferated. In 1872, the Ocean Steamship Company of Savannah opened an Island Route for Florida. The steamer *Florida* stopped at Fernandina, Jacksonville, Palatka, and other landings on the St. Johns. It connected at Fernandina for Gainesville, Tampa, Key West, New Orleans, and Havana, Cuba. The *Morning News* reported: "This steamer was built expressly for this route, and is unequaled for speed, passenger accommodations and freight facilities." The Clyde Line operated steamers into Jacksonville from East Coast seaports, including New York City.

Southern resorts had been invaded by Northern black waiters since the early 1870s, before baseball became "a natural adjunct of resort life."[148] After summer employment in the

North, they worked winters at Jacksonville's Carlton, Nicholls, and St. James hotels.[149] Black musicians among them organized the "Southern Minstrels."[150]

The southern migration of black ball–waiters originated from New York, Washington, Harrisburg, Philadelphia, and Pittsburgh. Guy Day, William Shadney, James T. Hackett, George Parego, Alfred Sharp, George A. Smith, William Whitaker, Henry Johnson, and Robert Martin worked for Frank P. Thompson and Stanislau K. Govern at St. Augustine's San Marco.[151] Utica's John W. Anderson joined Jacksonville's St. James Hotel.[152] New England's George Jennings also worked at the St. James.[153] Between 1888 and 1890, Providence's Robert Jones worked at Jacksonville, St. Augustine, and Key West.[154] Between 1889 and 1891, Charles Booker (New York), Frank Miller (Pittsburgh), Clarence Williams (Harrisburg), Andrew Randolph (Philadelphia), W. R. Dorsey (Boston), John Frye (Reading), George A. Smith (New York), Arthur Thomas and Benjamin Smoot (Washington), Benjamin Price, Thomas and Samuel Gee, and Emmett Dabney (all from Richmond) worked at St. Augustine's Cordova, Ponce De Leon, and Alcazar.[155]

Not all of Florida's players were Northerners or waiters, for example, the Jacksonville Athletics. M.J. Christopher, center fielder/team secretary, operated a wholesale fruit business. He also owned a schooner. Christopher and R.A. Sanchez shipped West Indian curiosities to Atlantic City.[156] An 1880 census reveals that the team players worked in many professions and trades. William G. Garvin, a mulatto, was a school teacher; A.P. Brown and Francis Pierce were brick makers/building contractors[157]; Thomas Baxter, a mulatto, was a merchant; L. Hall, Andrew Jackson, and Lewis Coleman were barbers; John Hodges and James Green were laborers.[158]

Between 1884 and 1885, 60,000 tourists invaded Jacksonville, resulting in new hotel construction. Though railway travel eventually eclipsed steamers, the latter remained a romantic form of travel. In a column devoted to tourism, *Outing Magazine* proposed the following advice:

> The best means of reaching St. Augustine, Jacksonville, or Tampa is to take a steamer from Boston or New York or Savannah.... The line of steamers that run on this route are really first-class, the table is excellent, and the [black] employees of the company attentive, civil, and do all in their power to make passengers comfortable during the trip.[159]

Upon their arrival, deafening shouts of "Hotel Ponce de Leon, San Marco, and Magnolia Hotel" from "the throats of two or three dozen omnibus and carriage drivers greeted the visitors."[160] Hack drivers, almost all of them black, sporting brass-button coats and tall stovepipe hats—famous for their metallic cheek and unvarnished impertinence"—took them to hotels.[161] They were savvy enough to gauge what class of hotel their passengers might be able to afford.[162]

Hotel-driven settlement took place "in the sparsely populated coastal areas of southern Florida."[163] By 1889, St. Augustine was a premiere winter resort. Henry Flagler, the Standard Oil prince, built the Ponce De Leon, Alcazar, and Cordova. After the Hotel San Marco closed in 1889, head waiter Franklin P. Thompson coordinated transportation for the black waiters to St. Augustine. They organized black ball clubs. One tourist observed:

> Two nines of stalwart young colored men were engaged in the National Game as I passed through the city gates and the three bagger resulted immediately afterward, making intense excitement among the spectators on the stone wall nearby.[164]

Thompson, born in Charleston, West Virginia, in 1855, grew up in Carlisle, Pennsylvania. (Did he witness the match between the Carlisle Shaw and Harrisburg Monrovia clubs in 1866?) In 1878, he became headwaiter at the Ocean House, in Cape May, New Jersey. Between 1879 and 1883, he was headwaiter for Savannah's Pulaski House. Thompson played for Savannah's Chatham club. The Savannah-Jacksonville rivalry introduced him to a black ball town named for Andrew Jackson, the first military governor of the Florida Territory and seventh President of the United States.[165]

In 1883, Thompson accepted a headwaiter position in Philadelphia. Stanislau K. Govern befriended him.[166] Govern, a baseballist, was also a thespian. He performed in Washington's Ira Aldridge Dramatic Club. The *Washington Bee* reported: "Mr. S.K. Govern, the delineator of characters was received with storms of applause when he made his appearance on the stage, having been absent from the city for several months."[167] The dramatic club included ballplayers: William C. Chase, Fred C. Revels, Jr., J. Osborn, A.A. Syphax, Daniel H. Stewart, and Jacob Strather. Govern belonged to the Sparta Club, an organization comprised of baseballists and thespians. James D. Kennedy, of the New Orleans Pickwick nine, was a founding member.[168]

Govern's career shuttled between Washington, Philadelphia, Saratoga Springs, Jacksonville, St. Augustine, Cape May, and Clinton, New York.[169] In 1883, Govern organized the Philadelphia Brotherhood of Hotel Waiters of the United States. The Brotherhood sought to improve the lives of black waiters, cooks/caterers, and bellmen. It challenged job discrimination, collected dues, and hosted benefits for sickness, injury, and death, held classes for employees, and encouraged members "to preach the Brotherhood and its benefits."[170] Frank P. Thompson and Keystone Athletic players joined the organization, which spread to Cape May, Washington, and St. Louis. The Brotherhood marked the start of baseball business dealings between Thompson and Govern which impacted black players from New York to Florida.[171]

Thompson's history with Floridian black ball began with the Savannah Chathams. They won the Georgia-Florida championship tournament in 1879. The *Brunswick Advertiser* reported: "A match game of base-ball was played in this city on Thursday last by the Chathams, of Savannah and the Athletics, of Jacksonville, both colored, for the championship of Georgia and Florida, and a prize of a fine bat and ball. The Chathams were victorious."[172] In 1883, they claimed professional status. Captain Thomas A. Simmons was prepared to compete with any black club in the country for $500.[173]

Thompson's recruitment of black labor began at the Magnolia House; in 1883, he sent for Philadelphia waiters, who took the city steamer *Savannah* to Magnolia Springs.[174] He declared a commitment to the racial uplift in a letter to T. Thomas Fortune's *New York Globe*:

> In handling the many vexed questions of the problems of our race, affecting its past, present and future conditions—politically, socially, and intellectually—I feel that I re-echo the opinion of thousands to state that your paper may have a few equals, but no superiors. Just as *The Globe* continues the crusade against race injustice, and points our citizens to the higher, grander and nobler beacon lights in the arena of education and civilization—till you tire of this warfare, count me one of your staunch supporters.[175]

Thompson was a race man. As a civil rights activist, he engendered the respect of communities in the North and South. In 1890, he attended a game at St. Augustine, featuring Cap Anson's Chicago Colts. Thompson refused inferior black accommodations, choosing instead to sit among the white patrons. He was neither accosted nor humiliated by officials.[176]

In early 1885, Thompson scheduled a southern tour. The *Palatka News* reported: "The waiters of the Hotel San Marco, at St. Augustine, left for the North. They intend playing match games of base-ball in Southern cities. They call themselves the Ancient City Athletics, and headwaiter Frank P. Thompson will act as umpire."[177] Thompson alerted *Sporting Life* to his team's activities. They played black clubs of Jacksonville, Savannah, Charleston, Richmond, Washington, and Baltimore: "Monday last at Jacksonville, they defeated the local team by the close score of 26 to 18. Tuesday, they warmed the pets of Savannah 17 to 9."[178] The Baltimore Atlantics easily defeated them, 19 to 3.[179]

Because Thompson never claimed to have worked for Babylon's Argyle Hotel, Graham contends that he was never here; he never claimed to have worked at Savannah's Pulaski House either.[180] To the contrary, the evidence affirms his presence at both places. *Sporting Life* noted: "The Athletic Base Ball Club, organized last summer at Babylon, Long Island, and managed by Mr. Frank P. Thompson, of that city, has, during the winter, been continued at St. Augustine, Florida. The members were waiters at the San Marco Hotel, and nearly all belong in Philadelphia."[181]

In 1885, the Keystone Athletics claimed professional status: "The Athletic Base Ball Club, Mr. Thompson manager, has gone south on a professional trip. It is said to be a strong team."[182] In May and June, they played games in Philadelphia. In mid–June, they returned for their second season at Babylon's Argyle Hotel.[183] Thompson sent reports to *Sporting Life*.[184] In August, the Athletics returned to Philadelphia. John Lang, a white barber, assumed financial control. They became Lang's Colored Giants or Lang's Cuban Giants. In 1882, Lang had managed Philadelphia's Orions, which played New York's white professionals. He financed a tour through Pennsylvania and New York which included a game with the New York Mets.[185] Following dates at Mahanoy, the *Hazelton Sentinel* reported: "The Cuban Giants became financially wrecked at Mahanoy City, we learn. And have gone into winter quarters."[186]

Some historians still credit the Cuban Giants with being the first black professional team. They are also credited with inventing so-called baseball comedy, a spectacle of comic pantomime and monkeyshines. Neither claim is true. These cultural practices, which prefigured the so-called antics of the Cuban Giants, had been misrepresented for decades. In the 1860s and 1870s, blackface minstrelsy intensified the stereotyping of black cultural production.[187] The theatrical performances of the "Negro minstrel troupes" of Henry J. Wood and Richard M. Hooley—for example—derided black baseball. Newspapers mocked black players as foreigners, "Simon Pure Africans," "Sons of Ham," and "Ethiopians."[188] Graphic artists like Solomon Eytinge, Jr., and Thomas Worth ridiculed black participation in the national pastime.[189]

One of black ball's earliest cultural forms was the boss coacher/boss yeller. Teammates, opponents, and umpires received tongue lashings and gratuitous advice as to the performance of their duties, and the boss yeller took special care to ensure that the spectators heard him. This figure emerged during black enslavement; it belonged, in part, to the call and response experiences of communal labor. Corn-husking festivals of the plantation tradition invoked its visual imagery. "Cornfield ditties, cornfield singing or cornfield harmonizing" is the source of all distinctively black vocal harmony.[190] Men formed teams, and women encircled them. Team captains took center stage.[191] They encouraged the workers with humorous, catchy verses that they repeated or answered in harmony. Captains sang out rhymes that ridiculed opponents or rankled white owners, by name or implication. This vernacular became a modernist black baseball language.[192]

The earliest evidence for the boss yeller that I have uncovered surfaced in the Midwest. In 1871, the graphic vernacular of the black ball–waiters of Illinois—Springfield's Dexter Star and Jacksonville's Homeboys—entered the baseball lexicon: "You niggar!—git off dat fust base dar!"[193] Newspapers misrepresented this aspect of black aesthetic style as a comic novelty, but for black ball performers, this was not so. The *Scranton Republican* reported: "The coaching and the expressions employed to urge base runners about the bases and to rattle pitchers were such as only ingenious Negroes can originate."[194] These routines thrived throughout the country.

When the Cuban Giants visited Williamsport in 1885, Clarence Williams "managed to keep everyone in good humor and many and loud were the peals of laughter he provoked."[195] He engaged in similar vernacular displays against the big league St. Louis Browns:

> When George Tebeau came to bat one of the black players shouted: Heah comes dat great playah! Get back dar to the fence! Git back! And the smoke colored Giants moved out of sight. Tebeau struck out as he wildly fanned the air for the fourth time. The captain shouted: everybody come in. He's out.[196]

Here is another performance by Williams:

> Hit dat ball Mr. Johnsing. There's pretty uv room in de air. Now run wid de win. Rastus—dive—dive! Cum dis way Lemuel—don't embrace dat middle cushin' hyre, third base—lemme see you sprinter. Don't liner, don't linger.[197]

His routines so impressed white ball clubs that they often hired him as a coacher.[198]

This theatricality, often characterized in the press as peculiar, was astonishing. Somersaulting was, for example, an ancient practice. In 1870, the Chicago reporter Louis Meacham covered a match between the Blue Stockings and Pink Stockings. He noted the players' "irresistible propensity, for tumbling head over heels when in the act of running bases or going for fly catches. Somersaults, which would have permanently doubled up and disabled a White Stocking [player], were counted as nothing by they of the colored hose and resulted in much amusement among spectators."[199] In 1879, Peter Richmond of the Washington Mutuals homered against Washington's Nationals (white professionals). Richmond turned three complete somersaults as he rounded the bases.[200] In 1884, Jersey City's Orientals celebrated their victory by performing somersaults.[201] The Cuban Giants performed similar feats. In 1887, the *Topeka Capital* reported: "During a recent game the Cuban Giants were so tickled at something that they all turned somersaults simultaneously, while the crowd shrieked with laughter."[202]

Theatricality combined with musical talent. The Pittsburgh Keystones organized the Keystone Quartette in 1887, composed of Walter S. Brown, Henry Gant, J.W. Jenkins and John Armstrong.[203] Ambrose Davis, a founding member of New York's Gorhams—and St. Augustine waiter—was a champion cakewalker. A newspaper account describes him as "an ethereal looking colored dancing master" and "the best gent waltzer of Philadelphia."[204] Davis managed a Specialty Company which merged with the Tennessee Jubilee Company. In 1893, he performed for the Billy Jackson Octoroon Vaudeville Company. He later joined Benjamin M. Butler's—another baseballist—Plantation Vaudeville Company.[205] Baseballist William Selden, champion cakewalker and vocalist, performed in a vaudeville company.[206]

Frank P. Thompson's connections to Savannah and Jacksonville were significant. While living in Savannah, he befriended Thomas T. Harden. Between 1879 and 1885, Thomas T. Harden, Robert H. Harden and D. Griffin published the *Savannah Weekly Echo*.[207] The *Weekly Echo* devoted attention to black life in Georgia, South Carolina, and Florida. Harden zeroed in on civil rights and racial injustice. His broadsides received national attention: "Since we have launched out into the journalistic field, and have stemmed the billows of a tempestuous sun without sustaining any material injuries, it becomes for us to be men and to be frank and speak out boldly without fear, in order to be true to our trust."[208]

While Thompson walked quietly and carried a big stick, Harden's in-your-face style was threatening. National newspapers reprinted and mocked his editorial chanteys. After viewing his portrait cut in an issue of the *Echo*, Harden's friend, T. Thomas Fortune, jested:

> Editor Harden is a dangerous man. He prints a cut of himself on the editorial page with a dagger in his mouth, a Colt's revolver in each hand, two other daggers in his belt, and a sabre by his side. In addition he has an eye glass over his right eye and a puddle of blood on the shoulder. Brother Hardin, do you intend to attend the Colored Press Association in Detroit? If so, count us out. We quail before so much exhibition of earnest intention.[209]

Harden's swagger reaped criticism. The *Atlanta Constitution* snapped: "The *Savannah Echo* ought to change its name. It's not hot enough. The Blade, the Defiance, the Agitator, and the Scorcher call loudly for the Singer."[210] It was hot enough: prior to the name *Weekly Echo*, the newspaper was called the *Scorcher*.

The *Weekly Echo* supported baseball. In 1880, the Harden boys attended "The National Colored Base Ball Association" tournament; 11 teams from six cities participated.[211] Two thousand people watched the Chathams defeat Jacksonville's Athletics. The *Morning News* reported: "Robert H. Harden presented the prizes with an excellent address, which was received with loud applause... the championship medal and $10 in gold was presented to the Chathams who were pronounced champions of the South."[212] Following Robert's death in 1884, Thomas sold his newspaper to baseballist George A. Davison, but remained as editor. In 1885, he moved to Jacksonville and became an editor for the *Southern Courier*.

Harden joined a new black ball enterprise. He became manager of the Southern League of Colored Base Ballists, and in April of 1886, the baseballist announced its formation.[213] The *New Orleans Times-Democrat* reported: "The manager of the Southern League of Colored Base Ballists, T.T. Harden, at Jacksonville, has issued a notice to all first-class clubs that have a good record and desire to enter the league. All information that may be desired will be furnished by the manager at Jacksonville, Florida."[214]

In May, 25 delegates convened at Jacksonville, and "considerable business was transacted but not made available to the public."[215] League officials were John Jones, President; Thomas T. Harden, manager; L.H. Jones, treasurer; and M.J. Christopher, secretary. Harden read the report and recommendations of the League, which were promptly adopted. He helped to coordinate the League schedule. The league officials negotiated "to play a series of exhibition games with the Cuban Giants of Philadelphia."[216]

Hotel teams joined the league. George Welton managed St. Augustine Hotel's Tallapoosa and Swift Butterflies clubs; he also managed the Welton Orchestra. Lewis Pittman managed Palatka's Putnam House nines: the Mutuals, Water Lilies, and Happy Kids.[217] John W. Smith managed Jacksonville's St. James Hotel Athletics. Edward Labritere and John Strong managed Jacksonville's Clippers. Willie McKinney and Willie Lewis managed the Macedonias of Jacksonville. Samuel Edwards managed Fernandina's Florida House Inn Daisy Cutters. Richard Mitchell managed La Villa's Roman Cities. Eddie Jones managed Tallahassee's Callathumpian team. Joseph Magrass managed Pensacola's black nine.[218] Three Savannah clubs requested membership: The Broadways (managed by Louis M. Pleasant), Lafayettes (named for manager Albert S. Lafayette), and Jersey nines.[219]

Thompson didn't have direct involvement in the league. In 1886, he worked at Boston's Vendome Hotel. W.R. Dorsey, C.C. Randolph and Andrew Randolph—also black ball–waiters of Florida—worked for the Vendome.[220] Thompson and R.B. Pope opened Boston's Coddington House. It was a black ball headquarters. The *New York Freeman* announced: "The proprietors of the Coddington, Messrs. R.B. Pope and F.P. Thompson, cordially extended an invitation to the citizens to call and see these shining lights of the baseball profession."[221] His bond with the Cuban Giants remained strong: "Frank P. Thompson, the proprietor of the Coddington House, Boston, and who was formerly the manager of the Cuban Giants, offers a gold scarf pin to the member of the Giants making the best general average in to-day's game. The ornament is in the form of two bats crossed and a ball in the lower angle."[222]

Thompson impacted St. Augustine's community in other ways. In 1889, he helped to increase membership of black churches and engaged in charity work. He hosted concerts and fundraisers. He coordinated benefits for the 900 hotel workers in the city.[223] The Ponce de Leon Hotel waiters published *The Black Herald*. The newspaper announced daily activities. It had a society editor, managing editor, and sports editor. It sold for one dollar a copy.[224]

In 1890, Thompson managed the Hotel Kaaterskill Base Ball Club; he headed the hotel dining room department. Among his staffers was Gerald Tucker of Bermuda, who owned a tailoring business on the side.[225] When he returned to the Ponce De Leon that winter, Tucker followed. In 1892, Thompson managed Bluff Point's Hotel Champlain Base Ball Club. By 1900, he had become headwaiter-in-chief of the Florida East Coast Hotel Company." Thompson hired 70 headwaiters and employed 700 waiters for the company.[226]

The Black Ball Mecca of Providence, Rhode Island

Rhode Island black ball traces to 1870; along the Seekonk River, in East Providence, an enslaved community dated back to Mintus Northup, father of Solomon Northup (of the "Twelve Years a Slave" narrative). During Christmas holidays—the period between harvesting and planting—black ball was the most popular leisure activity. In December of 1870, a large crowd witnessing a game was ordered to disperse by a police officer. After the officer left, unfazed spectators returned to the spectacle, and the black players completed the winter classic.[227] Like the winter holidays, Emancipation Day was a festive occasion for bringing the black community together. In 1877, the Excelsior and Theological clubs of Providence engaged in a friendly game of black ball. The Excelsiors, captained by Abraham Hall, represented the Excelsior Beneficial Association. The Providence and Newport black freemasons also hosted an annual Emancipation Day picnic. The celebration featured games between the lodge teams. The *New York Freeman* reported that 5,000 people attended a holiday excursion to Rocky Point, where the Providence Colored Grays and Newport Puritans crossed bats.[228]

Between 1870 and 1872, Providence's Cambria club played local clubs (black and white) and Brooklyn's black hotel nines. The *Providence Evening Press* reported: "An interesting game of base-ball between Cambrias and Flying Boys, two club composed of colored members, took place in Dexter Training Ground yesterday afternoon, was witnessed by several hundred spectators."[229] They played Brooklyn's Ocean and Monitor clubs. The *Evening Press* reported: "The Cambria Base Ball Club, of this city played two matches in Brooklyn, NY, last week, one with the Monitors and the other with the Oceans."[230]

In 1882, black ball employees of Providence formed unions at the Narragansett, Continental, Dorrance, and City hotels for the mutual protection of the workers. The union addressed labor issues and financial support. It organized society events, and ball clubs. The Barber's Beneficial and Protective Association formed to address similar needs.[231] Its members traveled as far as Richfield Springs, New York, for business meetings, and they supported social activities (including baseball games) of fellow waiters.[232]

While hotels permitted sociability among white guests and black labor, they reinforced racial anxieties and class hierarchies. They misconstrued the meaning of black working-class cohesiveness. After a violent encounter with a black waiter, for example, the New London Pequot House's French chef, Clerget, fled, with 20 black waiters in hot pursuit.[233] The hotel manager acknowledged the offensive nature of his actions.[234] Managers responded to disruptive behavior by imposing an outrageous system of illegal fines and penalties.[235] Black employees reacted to the abusive behavior with sabotage. In 1886, the Pequot House staff protested poor treatment at the hands of a white headwaiter from Philadelphia. Many workers quit. The *New York Freeman* reported: "Dissatisfaction has caused many of the waiters of the Pequot House to leave for other places…. The Pequot House nine have disbanded, owing to some of their best men leaving."[236]

The Providence hotels—Narragansett and Dorrance—had the best nines.[237] Headwaiter George Brown, of Hartford, captained the Dorrance club. Headwaiter E. Richard Jones managed the Narragansetts. The Whackers, Old Reliables, Columbias, Magnolias, Colored Grays, and Hawthornes rounded out the city's black clubs. They played for pride, love of the game, and money. When the Whackers reorganized in 1884, they challenged Brown University to a friendly game. Following the nine's acceptance, the Whackers distributed handbills to promote the contest. When they arrived at the grounds, the Browns refused to play. The Magnolias were a formidable adversary. The *New York Freeman* reported: "[The Colored Grays] were the opponents of the Magnolia nine, George Johnson, captain, and were defeated."[238] They also played the Boston Resolutes. The Hawthornes boasted that they had won 16 out of 17 games played in 1887. Gambling occurred. When the Pawtuckets (white) avenged a previous loss to the Colored Grays, "several colored sports lost considerable money."[239]

In 1886, the Narragansett waiters—precursors of the Colored Grays—moved toward professional status. Manager E. Richard Jones purchased the rights to the white Providence Grays' moniker and their uniforms. Jones leased Messer Park, home of the Providence Grays. They played at the enclosed grounds. Admission was 15 cents. They scheduled home and road games with white and black teams. They played Rhode Island, Connecticut, and Massachusetts teams. The Whackers and Magnolias declared professional status in 1884.[240]

Despite claims to the contrary, many of the Colored Grays were native to, or called Providence, home.[241] Oran L. Skipworth was from Providence. From 1882 to 1884, Skipworth was a Washington clerk of the U.S. Pension Office. He left this post to become bookkeeper for the tonsorial parlors of H.E. Burgess and J.H. Shephard. This prosperous enterprise had 16 chairs and six bathrooms with cold, hot and electric baths. Skipworth, I believe, played for Washington's Whacker club.[242] The team name links the Washington and Providence nines. He remained committed to his hometown. Skipworth often returned home to participate in state elections (he became a state representative). In 1885, he left Washington for good. In 1886, Skipworth performed in a black production of Shakespeare's *Richard III*. The cast included the famed black thespian, J.A. Arneaux, and the black ball–waiters, Frank O. LaPene and George Jackson. Skipworth was described as "a refined gentleman."[243]

William L. Pierce and George Brown, black ball–waiters of the Narragansett, played for the Magnolias and Hawthornes. Brown also pitched for the Hartford Blue Stockings.[244] They were also musicians who headlined at Providence's Old Dime Museum. Pierce toured with the Lightfoot and Turner Star Concert Company. He starred as the "Wandering Minstrel." He gave "an excellent representation of the tyrant Dionysus" in *Damon and Pythias*.[245] Pierce organized benefits for Flora Batson and for the Burnside Cadets. The Burnside Cadets, organized in 1867 or 1868, included ballplayers. Baseballist George Vessels of the Colored Grays headed the Burnside Cadets.[246] Pierce, an all-around athlete, skated for the black Narragansett Polo Club and cycled with the black Rambler Club. The tenor vocalist would join Billy Kersands Minstrels. Pierce was dubbed the "Beau Brummel of the Afro-American Stage." Brown, the "oseto soloist," performed "wondrous feats with his bones."[247]

Black ball–waiters of New London and Providence attended Howard University. New London's R.C. Morse (player-manager for the Howard nine in 1884), T.A. Jenkins, W. Carter, and William Spilliard of the Pequot House and Crocker House attended Howard. Providence's Daniel Penno attended Howard, and he likely played ball there in the early 1880s. Daniel and Louis Penno were the sons of a black Portuguese father and black mother. Louis, like his father, worked on fishing vessels. In 1886, the brothers played for the East Greenwich Alerts, an otherwise all-white local club; Louis covered first base; Daniel pitched, played third base and shortstop. Dan joined the Colored Grays and continued to play for the Alerts. In 1887, the Boston Resolutes signed him; however, he chose to remain in Providence. He would play for the Boston Resolutes, New York Colored Giants, Cuban X-Giants, Gorhams, and Greater New York Colored Giants.[248]

The black men of Providence organized the Apollo Club; its membership had the best baseball, musical, and theatrical talent.[249] Benjamin Lightfoot, William Pierce, George Brown, and George Jackson comprised the Crescent Quartette. George Brown and George Jackson gave parlor entertainments at the homes of black society and at Newport and Narragansett Pier Hotels.[250] Baseballists Frank O. LaPene and James V. Beuzard, character artists, "amused the audience for a considerable length of time by their songs and jokes."[251] They belonged to the larger black community, which linked the populations of Connecticut and Rhode Island.[252]

This melding of black ball and black cultural production was also evident in riverine communities in Minnesota, Ohio, Kentucky, Tennessee, Illinois, Missouri, Mississippi, and Louisiana. Henry Bridgewater, for example, began his career as a cabin boy, waiter, and barber. He left the riverway to open a saloon. Failing in this endeavor, Bridgewater briefly returned to the steamboat river culture of the Mississippi. A federal census report lists his occupation as "river man." He worked as a porter on the steamer *Red Wing*, which ran between St. Louis and St. Paul, Minnesota. In the mid–1870s, St. Louis had several black ball clubs affiliated with riverboats. The steamer *Red Wing* had a competitive team. Bridgewater also dabbled in theater. "The Stage," Bridgewater argued, "is giving employment to a great many colored people, and the number will increase. There is much latent talent in the race and theatrical life is pleasing to the Negro."[253] The *St. Louis Post Dispatch* added: "Bridgewater was a minstrel himself a good many years ago, but he says he wasn't a success and he doesn't like to tell about it."[254] He ultimately made his impact on black ball, becoming a successful professional player, manager, and team owner.

Table 8.1 Black Teams vs. Organized Baseball 1869–1885

Date	NLB	OB	Result	League
1869				
Sep. 3	Philadelphia Pythian	Philadelphia Olympic	L 23–44	NABBP
Sep. 17	Philadelphia Pythian	Philadelphia City Items	W 27–17	NABBP
Sep. 20	Washington, D.C. Alert	Washington Olympic	L 4–56	NABBP
Oct. 12	Washington, D.C. Mutual	Washington Olympic	L 15–24	NABBP

Date	NLB	OB	Result	League
1874				
Aug. 29	Washington, D.C. Mutual	Lynn (MA) Live Oaks	L 0–17	NAABBP
Aug. 30	Washington, D.C. Mutual	Boston Stars	L 11–19	NAABBP
1875				
Sep. 11	Washington, D.C. Mutual	Lowells (MA)	L 6–17	NAABBP
Sep. 13	Washington, D.C. Mutual	Lowells (MA)	L 7–10	NAABBP
Sep. 15	Washington, D.C. Mutual	Lowells (MA)	L 1–8	NAABBP
1877				
Aug. 8	Washington, D.C. Mutual	Troy (NY) Haymakers	L 5–16	LA
Aug. 9	Washington, D.C. Mutual	Lowells (MA)	L 0–10	LA/NEA
Aug. 10	Washington, D.C. Mutual	Lowells (MA)	L 0–7	LA/NEA
Aug. 11	Washington, D.C. Mutual	Troy (NY) Haymakers	W 3–2	LA
Aug. 16	Washington, D.C. Mutual	Fall River (MA)	L 1–16	LA/NEA
Aug. 17	Washington, D.C. Mutual	Rhode Islands	L 0–6	NEA
Aug. 19	Washington, D.C. Mutual	Rhode Islands	L 2–10	NEA
1879				
Aug. 1	Washington, D.C. Mutual	Washington Nationals	L 6–19	NA
1882				
July 19	Philadelphia Orions	Philadelphia Phillies	L 1–17	LA
July 20	Philadelphia Orions	New York Metropolitans	L 5–19	LA
Sep. 6	Long Branch (NJ) Washingtons	New York Metropolitans	L 0–11	LA
1883				
Apr. 28	St. Louis Black Stockings	Saginaw (MI) Grays	L 6–20	NWL
Apr. 30	St. Louis Black Stockings	Saginaw (MI) Grays	L 2–8	NWL
1884				
Apr. 17	Chicago Gordons	Terre Haute (IN)	L 1–9	NWL
Apr. 18	Chicago Gordons	Terre Haute (IN)	L 2–14	NWL
Apr. 24	Chicago Gordons	Saginaw (MI) Grays	L 1–25	NWL
Apr. 25	Chicago Gordons	Saginaw (MI) Grays	L 7–12	NWL
Apr. 27	Chicago Gordons	Saginaw (MI) Grays	L 5–10	NWL
May 11	Chicago Gordons	Milwaukee Brewers	L 9–11	NWL
May 23	Chicago Gordons	Springfield (OH)	L 2–7	OA
May 29	Chicago Gordons	Springfield (OH)	L 7–15	OA
1885				
May 25	Boston Resolutes	Springfield (MA)	L 4–14	SNEL
May 27	Boston Resolutes	Newburyport (MA)	L 4–10	ENEL
Jun. 6	Boston Resolutes	Brockton (MA)	L 3–15	SNEL
Jun. 15	Boston Resolutes	Biddeford (ME)	L 4–26	ENEL
Jun. 16	Boston Resolutes	Portland (ME)	L 5–21	ENEL
Sep. 21	Boston Resolutes	Haverhill (MA)	L 15–22	ENEL

Editor's Note: The road to equality on the playing field was an arduous one. Although undeniably skilled, the very best early black teams fared so poorly against top-notch white competition that one wonders if the main obstacle wasn't psychological in nature. Indeed, long-time black ball player and manager Dave Malarcher painfully observed that "the propaganda of keeping the Negro out of the Major Leagues made even some of the Negroes think we didn't have the ability." From 1869 through 1885, African American squads went 2–34 against Organized Baseball outfits. Black clubs did beat many professional non-league squads, however, and the experience several of their players gathered would be put to good use with the Cuban Giants, the first great black team.

League Abbreviations: ENEL=Eastern New England League; IA=International Association; LA=League Alliance; NA=National Association; NAABBP=National Association of Amateur Base Ball Players; NABBP=National Association of Base Ball Players; NEA=New England Association; NWL= Northwestern League; OA=Ohio Association; SENL-Southern New England League.

Table 8.2 Cuban Giants with Playing Experience Against Organized Baseball Teams

Cuban Giants	*Former NLB/Integrated Teams*
Ben Boyd	Washington Mutuals
Julius Forbes	Philadelphia Orions
Jack Frye	Reading (PA) Actives (Interstate Association)
Abe Harrison	Philadelphia Orions
Ben Holmes	Washington Mutuals; Boston Resolutes
George Jackson	Philadelphia Orions
Harry Johnson	Boston Resolutes
Andrew Randolph	Boston Resolutes
Richmond Robinson	Washington Mutuals; St. Louis Black Stockings
William Selden	Boston Resolutes
Shep Trusty	Philadelphia Orions; Millville (NJ)
William Whyte	St. Louis Black Stockings; Boston Resolutes
George Williams	Philadelphia Orions

Sources for Tables 8.1 and 8.2: White with Malloy, *History of Colored Base Ball;* NLB vs. OB Database.

Notes

1. A. K. Sandoval-Strausz, *Hotel: An American History* (New Haven, CT: Yale University Press, 2007), 179; "Mid-Summer Retreats," *New York Herald,* December 6, 1872; "Our State Institutions," *New York Times,* May 28, 1870; "Watering Place Secret," *Hudson Daily Star,* July 2, 1870; "Our Business Houses," *Los Angeles Herald,* November 22, 1873.

2. "Shorts," *Saratoga Springs Daily Saratogian,* August 4, August 12, 1876.

3. "Short Stops," *New York Clipper,* July 29, 1876.

4. "Base Ball," *Saratoga Springs Daily Saratogian,* May 19, 1870.

5. "Short Stops," *New York Clipper,* July 29, 1876.

6. Sandoval-Strausz, *Hotel,* 112.

7. "The Colored Waiters' Fees," *Pittsburgh Commercial Gazette,* May 5, 1878.

8. "The Philadelphia Waiter," *Chicago Inter-Ocean,* July 30, 1889.

9. "Sharon Springs," *Albany Evening Journal,* August 12, 1897; "Fort Plain," *Utica Daily Press,* July 13, 1899.

10. "Sharon Springs," *Albany Evening Journal,* August 12, 1897.

11. "Shorts," *Saratoga Springs Daily Saratogian,* August 12, 1876.

12. "The Base Ball Field," *Wilmington Journal,* August 18, 1875; "The Base Ball and the Bat," *Philadelphia Times,* July 20, 1882.

13. "Saratoga Springs," *New York Freeman,* July 16, 1887; "Chapter on Base Ball," *Troy Daily Times,* July 17, 1888; "Chat From the Watering Place," *Troy Daily Times,* July 27, 1888; "Forged Orders," *Troy Daily Times,* September 7, 1888; "Saratoga Springs," *New York Age,* August 18, 1888.

14. Jerry Dickey, "African American Waiters and Cake Walk Contests in Florida East Coast Resorts in the Gilded Age," in *Working in the Wings: New Perspectives on Theatre History and Labor,* Elizabeth Osborne and Christine Woodruff, editors (Carbondale: Southern Illinois University Press, 2015), 135.

15. Michael Lomax. *Black Baseball Entrepreneurs, 1860–1901: Operating by Any Means Necessary* (Syracuse, NY: Syracuse University Press, 2003); Wilson Jeremiah Moses, "Lost World of the New Negro, 1895–1919: Black Literary and Intellectual Life Before the Renaissance," *Black American Literature Forum* 21, no. 1/2 (Spring-Summer. 1987): 61–84.

16. Thomas Graham, *Mr. Flagler's St. Augustine* (Gainesville: University of Florida, 2014), 18.

17. "Base Ball," *Jamaica Farmer and Advertiser,* December 28, 1858; "Base Ball," *New York Weekly Anglo-African,* December 3, 1859; "Special Notices," *New York Weekly Anglo-African,* March 24, 1860.

18. "Base Ball," *Niagara Falls Gazette,* July 1, 1868.

19. "The Twenty-Ninth Anniversary Celebration of the Colored People," *Lockport Daily Journal,* August 4, 1868.

20. Myra Beth Young Armstead. *Lord, Please Don't Take Me in August: African Americans in Newport and Saratoga Springs, 1870–1930* (Urbana: University of Illinois Press, 1999), 67–68; Sandoval-Strausz, *Hotel,* 180.

21. Christopher J. Smith, *The Creolization of American Culture: William Sidney Mount and the Roots of Blackface Minstrelsy* (Champaign: University of Illinois Press. 2013), 34–35, 83, 84–85.

22. Charles Kelley Jones, *Francis Johnson (1792–1844): Chronicle of a Black Musician in Early Nineteenth-century Philadelphia* (Bethlehem, PA: Lehigh University Press, 2006); *Philadelphia Public Ledger*, August 20, 1842; "Frank Johnson and Band Mobbed," *Philadelphia Inquirer*. May 22, 1843; *Philadelphia Inquirer,* June 27, 1843; "Reminiscences of Saratoga," *Saratoga Springs Daily Saratogian*, November 16, 1874.

23. ExplorePAhistory.com, "Francis Johnson Historical Marker," http://explorepahistory.com/hmarker. php?markerId=1-A-268.

24. Smith, *The Creolization of American Culture*, 35; "River News," *Louisville Daily Courier*, May 7, 1856; "Stories Told in a Hotel Rotunda," *New Orleans Times Picayune*), January 19, 1879.

25. "A Novel Thing in North America," *Elizabeth City Star*, May 15, 1824; "United States Hotel, Saratoga Springs," *New York Post*, July 16, 1824; "Saratoga Powders," *Brooklyn Long Island Star*, July 30, 1840; "An Interesting Journey," *New York Post*, August 9, 1844.

26. "Saratoga Water," *Brooklyn Eagle*, July 9, 1866.

27. "United States Hotel Saratoga Springs, Aug. 11th, 1845," *New York Herald*, August 13, 1845.

28. Sandoval-Strausz. *Hotel*, 88–89.

29. "Local," *Saratoga Springs Daily Saratogian*, October 10, 1868, August 30, 1871; "Shorts," *Saratoga Springs Daily Saratogian*, August 20, 1876; "Meeting of the Hayes and Wheeler Club," *Saratoga Springs Daily Saratogian*, August 24, 1876; "The G.U.H.W.P.C.," *Saratoga Springs Daily Saratogian*, August 4, 1877; "Shorts," *Saratoga Springs Daily Saratogian*, July 19, August 1, 1886.

30. Sandoval-Strausz. *Hotel*, 22; Douglas Walter Bristol, Jr. *Knights of the Razor: Black Barbers in Slavery and Freedom* (Baltimore, MD: Johns Hopkins University Press, 2009), 64.

31. "Gossip of the Game," *Chicago Tribune*, June 19, 1881; "Base Ball Notes," *Philadelphia Times*, March 18, 1883; "Sporting Sundries," *St. Louis Post Dispatch*, April 25, 1883; "Base Ball Notes," *Philadelphia Times*, January 20, 1884; "Colored Professionals to Play," *Chicago Tribune*, June 11, 1884; *Savannah Tribune*, November 3, 1894.

32. "Fees to Saratoga Waiters," *Titusville Herald*, August 8, 1870.

33. "The Saratoga Retrenchment," *New York Sun*, April 24, 1875; "City Notes," *Troy Daily Times*, September 6, 1876; "Home Matters," *Troy Daily Times*, September 27, 1883; "Local Gossip," *New York Freeman*, April 30, 1887.

34. "Base Ball," *Niagara Falls Gazette*, July 1, 1868; "The Twenty-Ninth Anniversary Celebration of the Colored People," *Lockport Daily Journal*, August 4, 1868.

35. "The Head Waiters at the Hotels," *Saratoga Springs Daily Saratogian*, September 5, 1868.

36. "Local," *Saratoga Springs Daily Saratogian*, May 14, 1872.

37. "Special Notices," *Philadelphia Inquirer*, January 2, 1864; "Presentation at Congress Hall," *Saratoga Springs Daily Saratogian*, August 19, 1868; "The Head Waiters at the Hotels," *Saratoga Springs Daily Saratogian*, September 5, 1868; "Colored Masons at Law," *Philadelphia Times*, May 8, 1883.

38. "The Head Waiters at the Hotels," *Saratoga Springs Daily Saratogian*, September 10, 1868; "The City," *Washington Critic*, August 4, 1869; "The Blood of Harry Lee," *Buffalo Courier*, September 16, 1871; "The Season at Saratoga," *New York Daily Graphic*, July 28, 1875; Eli Perkins, "Bond and Free," in *Frank Leslie's Popular Monthly*, Mrs. Frank Leslie, Ellery Sedgwick., editors, New York: Frank Leslie Publishing House, Volume 3 (January–June 1877), 745–750.

39. "Death of a Miser," *Saratoga Springs Daily Saratogian*, May 21, 1874.

40. *Ibid.*

41. *Ibid.*

42. "Shorts," *Saratoga Springs Daily Saratogian*, February 10, 1885.

43. "Shorts," *Saratoga Springs Daily Saratogian*, June 24, 1874.

44. "Shorts," *Saratoga Springs Daily Saratogian*, August 12, 1876.

45. "Local," *Saratoga Springs Daily Saratogian*, September 15, 1874.

46. "Base Ball," *Gloversville Intelligencer*, July 20, 1871; "Grand Base Ball Tournament," *Geneva Gazette,* September 10, 1876; "Colored Ballists," *Geneva Courier,* September 20, 1876.

47. "Base Ball," *Utica Daily Observer*, November 29, 1870.

48. "Base Ball," *New York Clipper*, April 8, 1871.

49. "The Mutuals and Clippers," *Winona Republican*, August 14, 1875; "Base Ball," *Winona Republican*, September 13, 1875; "Base Ball," *Winona Republican*, September 15, 1875; "The Clippers," *WinonaRepublican,* September 16, 1875; "The Ball and Bat," *Winona Republican*, September 20, 1875; "The Ball Field," *Wilmington Journal*, August 9, 1876; "Ball Playing," *Minneapolis Tribune*, September 21, 1876.

50. Bristol, Jr. *Knights of the Razor*, 48–49.

51. Bristol, Jr. *Knights of the Razor*, 59–66.

52. Bristol, Jr. *Knights of the Razor*, 59–66; "Barber Shop," *Utica Daily Observer*, May 14, 1867; *Harrisburg Independent*, June 10, 1867; "Base Ball," *Utica Morning Herald*, November 3, 1867; "Another Muffin Match," *Cleveland Plain Dealer*, August 15, 1868; "Fashionable Weddings," *Utica Morning Herald*, June 3, 1869; "Base Ball Items," *Altoona Evening Mirror*, May 29, 1876; "Base Ball," *Altoona Evening Mirror*, July 19, 1876; "Base

Ball Items," *Altoona Evening Mirror*, July 24, 1876; "Local Brevities," *Wilmington Journal*, September 10, 1885; "Home Clubs at Base Ball," *Wilmington News*, September 18, 1885.

53. "A Colored Resident," *Kingston Daily Freeman*, August 19, 1881; "Slavery Days in New York," *New York Evening Telegram*, May 31, 1888; "Born a Slave in Ulster County," *Johnston Fulton County Republican*, June 14, 1888.

54. "Notice," *Baltimore Sun*, July 25, 1842; "The Anniversary of the First Colored Barber's Beneficial Society," *Baltimore Sun*, July 16, 1846; "The Fifth Anniversary of the First Colored Barber's Beneficial Society," *Baltimore Sun*, July 15, 1847; "The Eighth Anniversary of the First Colored Barber's Beneficial Association," *Baltimore Sun*, July 13, 1850.

55. "Our Baltimore Letter," *New York Weekly Anglo-African*, August 20, 1859.

56. "Base Ball," *Baltimore Bee*, July 15, 1876.

57. "Philadelphia Barber Shops," *Brooklyn Union*, August 31, 1885.

58. "Notes and Comments," *Detroit Free Press*, September 30, 1871.

59. "The Fearless Base-Ball Club," *Utica Daily Observer*, May 4, 1870.

60. "Base Ball," *Utica Daily Observer*, October 24, 1866; "Base Ball," *Utica Morning Herald*, November 3, 1867; "Base Ball Extraordinary," *Utica Daily Observer*, October 29, 1868; "Base-Ball Matters," *Cincinnati Commercial Tribune*, August 18, 1869; "Events of the Week," *Utica Weekly Herald*, September 14, 1869; "Fearless and Heavy Hitters," *Utica Daily Observer*, September 21, 1869; "Grand Celebration of the Ratification of the Fifteenth Amendment," *Utica Daily Observer*, June 17, 1870.

61. "Base Ball," *Troy Daily Whig*, September 3, 1867.

62. "On the Half Shell," *New York Clipper*, August 20, 1870.

63. "Public Meeting," *Troy Daily Whig*, July 19, 1836; "Suffrage Meeting," *Troy Daily Whig*, March 11, 1846; "Meeting of Colored Citizens," *Troy Budget*, March 24, 1842; *Troy Daily Whig*, June 12, 1844; "Grand Concert," *Troy Daily Whig*, September, 1844; "To the Citizens of Troy," *Troy Budget*, November 4, 1849; "Statement of Votes," *Troy Daily Whig*, November 16, 1856; "Latest News Items," *Troy Daily Times*, August 3, 1858; "New Items," *Batavia Daily Herald*, November 12, 1859; "Base Ball," *Troy Daily Whig*, September 3, 1867; "Examination of the William Rich School," *Troy Daily Whig*, February 18, 1868; "Base Ball in a New Phase," *Troy Press*, August 25, 1869; "Proceedings of the Colored State Convention," *Utica Morning Herald*, January 25, 1869; "On the Half Shell," *New York Clipper*, August 20, 1870.

64. "Base Ball in a New Phase," *Troy Press*, August 25, 1869.

65. "Shorts," *Saratoga Springs Daily Saratogian*, May 22, 1874; "Mysterious Disappearance," *Saratoga Springs Daily Saratogian*, August 29, 1882; "Saratoga Locals," *New York Globe*, July 19, 1884.

66. "The Committee of Forty-Two," *Saratoga Springs Daily Saratogian*, February 22, 1872.

67. *Saratoga Springs Daily Saratogian*, August 24, 1870.

68. "Shorts," *Saratoga Springs Daily Saratogian*, August 29, 1882.

69. "Saratoga Springs," *New York Freeman*, July 2, 10, 17, 1886; "Bermuda Visitors," *New York Freeman*, September 3, 1887; "Saratoga Springs," *New York Freeman*, September 17, 1887.

70. "Saratoga Locals," *New York Globe*, July 19, 1884.

71. "Saratoga Locals," *New York Globe*, September 20, 1884.

72. "Saratoga," *Washington People's Advocate*, July 28, 1883; "Shorts," *Saratoga Springs Daily Saratogian*, August 4, 1883.

73. "Base Ball," *New York Herald*, September 16, 1884; "What the Club is Doing," *Trenton Times*, August 24, 1886; "Base Ball," *Long Island Star*, October 2, 1886.

74. "The Saratoga Season," *New York Age*, August 2, 1890.

75. "Funeral of J. C. Broughton," *Brooklyn Standard Union*, May 9, 1903

76. "Base Ball," *Saratoga Springs Daily Saratogian*, July 2, 1882.

77. "Saratoga," *Washington People's Advocate*, July 28, 1883.

78. "Saratoga Salmagundi," *Saratoga Springs Morning Express*, August 13, 1883.

79. "Shorts," *Saratoga Springs Daily Saratogian*, August 6, 1886.

80. "Shorts," *Saratoga Springs Daily Saratogian*, July 18, 1886; "Saratoga Chips," *Saratoga Springs Daily Saratogian*, August 28, 1886.

81. "A Saratoga Postscript," *Troy Daily Times*, July 18, 1888.

82. "Taking in the History of New London, a City Shaped by the Sea," *New York Times*, August 15, 2014.

83. "Saratoga Gossip," *New York Globe*, July 7, 1883; "Saratoga Notes," *New York Globe*, August 11, 1883; "Advertisement," *New York Globe*, August 18, 1883; "Saratoga Springs," *New York Freeman*, July 7, 1887; "New London News," *New York Age*, January 31, February 1, 1890; "New London, Conn., Items," *Indianapolis Freeman*, May 3, 1890; "New London News," *New York Age*, May 10, 1890; "New London Notes," *New York Age*, May 17, 31, 1890; "New London (Conn.) Flashes," *Indianapolis Freeman*, May 3, 1890; "New London Notes," *New York Age*, August 16, 1890; "Saratoga Springs," *New York Age*, July 11, 1891.

84. "Brief Mention," *Buffalo Express*, August 9, 1884; "Game Between Colored Amateurs," *Buffalo Courier*, August 15, 1884; "Brevities," *Niagara Falls Gazette*, August 21, 1885; "Saratoga Springs," *New York Freeman*, July 16, 1887; "Saratoga Springs," *New York Age*, August 18, 1888; "Chapter on Base Ball," *Troy Daily Times*,

July 17, 1888; "Local Jottings," *Albany Evening Times*, September 14, 1888; "Pith and Point," *Albany Morning Express*, September 21, 1888.

85. "Benefit Entertainment," *Niagara Falls Daily Gazette*, June 23, 1885; "The Concert Last Evening," *Niagara Falls Daily Gazette*, August 12, 1885; "Brevities," *Niagara Falls Daily Gazette*, August 21, 1885.

86. "Concert," *Niagara Falls Daily Gazette*, July 31, 1885; "The Glee Club," *Niagara Falls Daily Gazette*, August 3, 1885.

87. Lynn Abbott, "Play That Barber Shop: A Case for the African-American Origin of Barbershop Harmony," *American Music* 10, no. 3 (August 1992): 290.

88. Abbott, "Play That Barber Shop," 290.

89. "Selling for Hancock," *New Haven Register*, September 10, 1880.

90. Abbott, "Play That Barber Shop," 290.

91. "By the Thames," *New York Globe*, May 12, October 20, November 17, December 8, 1883; September 6, 20, 1884.

92. Thomas C. Buchanan, *Black Life on the Mississippi: Slaves, Free Blacks, and the Western Steamboat World* (Chapel Hill: University of North Carolina Press, 2004), 62.

93. "Short Stops," *New York Clipper*, June 19, 1875.

94. "New London Notes," *New York Freeman*, August 7, 1886.

95. "Almost a Base Ball Game," *Norwich Aurora*, September 18, 1867; "State Items," *New Haven Columbian Register*, October 5, 1867.

96. "New London Notes," *New York Freeman*, August 7, 1886.

97. "Robbery," *Norwich Courier*, January 6, 1841.

98. "By the Thames," *New York Globe*, February 23, 1884; "Steamboat News," *New York Freeman*, August 20, 27, September 27, October 27, 1887; "Mortuary Notice," *New York Age*, January 2, 1892.

99. "New London Notes," *New York Freeman*, July 31, 1886; "New London News," *New York Freeman*, August 21, 1886.

100. "New London News," *New York Freeman*, June 5, July 17, 1886; "New London Notes," *New York Freeman* February 26, 1887; "New London News," *New York Freeman*, July 2, 23, 1887; "New London News," *New York Age*, July 19, 1890; "New London, CONN," *New York Freeman*, August 9, 1890.

101. Moses, "Lost World of the New Negro," 61–84.

102. John V. Hinshaw, "Third Stonington: The Afro-American Baptist Church on Water Street," *Historical Footnotes* Volume 29, Number 2 (May 1992): 5.

103. *Ibid.*, 6.

104. *Ibid.*

105. *Ibid.*, 7.

106. *National Republican* (Washington, DC), October 12, 1866; *New London Weekly Chronicle*, October 20, 1866.

107. "State Items," *New Haven Columbian Register*, August 24, 1867; "The National Game," *New London Democrat*, July 13, 1867; "New London County," *Hartford Courant*, August 7, 1868; "Summary of the News," *New York Sabbath Recorder*, August 13, 1868.

108. "State Matters," *Hartford Courant*, October 13, 1866.

109. *New London Democrat*, July 20, 1867.

110. "Daily Items," *Hudson Daily Star*, September 22, 1869.

111. "New London and Vicinity," *New London Democrat*, Dec. 11, 1869.

112. "Editorial Breviary," *Raleigh Christian Advocate*, May 28, 1879.

113. "Ho! For Roton Point!" *New York Globe*, August 18, 1883.

114. "Baltimore Brevities," *New York Freeman*, June 11, 1887.

115. "Local News," *Middleton Constitution*, Aug. 5, 1868.

116. "State Items," *New Haven Columbian Register*, August 24, 1867; "The National Game," *New London Democrat*, July 13, 1867; "Local News," *Middletown Constitution*, October 2, 1867; "Brief Mention," *Hartford Courant*, July 24, 1868; *New Haven Columbian Register*, July 25, 1868; "Brief Mention," *Hartford Courant*, July 28, 1868; "Local News," *Middleton Constitution*, July 29, 1868; "Base Ball," *Hartford Courant*, July 31, 1868; "Local News," *Middleton Constitution*, Aug. 5, 1868; "New London County," *Hartford Courant*, August 7, 1868; "Brief Mention," *Hartford Courant*, Sept. 9, 1868; "New London County," *Hartford Courant*, July 24, 1869; "New London and Vicinity," *New London Democrat*, December 11, 1869.

117. Henry N. Jeter, *Pastor Henry N. Jeter's Twenty-five Years Experience with the Shiloh Baptist Church: And Her History. Corner School and Mary Streets, Newport, R.I.* (Newport, RI: Remington Printing Company, 1901), 32.

118. "New London Notes," *New York Freeman*, November 13, 1886.

119. "Base Ball," *Jersey City Journal*, July 10, 1868, July 19, 1870, March 20, 1871, June 27, 1873; "Good Samaritans," *Jersey City Journal*, June 26, 1873; "Odd Leaf Social Club," *Jersey City Journal*, March 28, 1878; "By the Thames," *New York Globe* May 3, 1884; "Jersey City Locals," *New York Freeman*, April 17, 1886; "New London News," *New York Freeman*, July 17, 1886, July 23, 1887; "Steamboat News," *New York Freeman*, August 20, 1886; "New London Notes," *New York Age*, August 16, 1890.

120. "Thirty-Five Waiters," *New Haven Register*, July 3, 1882.

121. "Colored Nine, 14; High School, 1," *Springfield Republican*, June 6, 1888; "Springfield News and Comment," *Springfield Republican*, June 24, 1888; "Notice," *Springfield Republican*, August 17, 1888.

122. "Norfolk News," *New York Globe*, June 9, September 15, 1883; "New London Letter," *New York Globe*, February 3, 1883; "By the Thames," *New York Globe*, August 9, 1884; "New London Notes," *New York Freeman*, June 26, July 10, 1886; "New London News," *New York Freeman*, July 2, 1887; "New London News," *New York Age*, February 1, March 29, 1890; "New London, CONN," *New York Age*, May 30, 1890; "New London News," *New York Age*, October 15, 1890; "News and Comment," *Sporting Life*, May 6, 1898.

123. "New London Notes," *New York Freeman*, January 26, 1886.

124. "New London News," *New York Freeman*, February 23, 1883; "Base Ball," *Saratoga Springs Daily Saratogian*, August 4, August 6, 1883; "Miss Davis Makes a Speech," *New York Globe*, August 23, 1884; "New London News," *New York Freeman*, February 13, June 5, 1886, February 19, April 23, 1887; "Advertisement," *New York Freeman*, June 25, 1887; "New London, CONN," *New York Age*, May 31, 1890; "New London News," *New York Age*, July 26, 1890; "New London Notes," *New York Age*, July 26, 1890.

125. "New London Letter," *New York Globe*, January 27, 1883; "By the Thames," *New York Globe*, March 15, 1884.

126. "Women to the Front," *Albany Times*, May 1, 1885.

127. William S. McFeely, *Frederick Douglass* (New York: W. W. Norton, 1995), 78–79.

128. Maud Cuney-Hare, *Negro Musicians and Their Music* (Washington, DC: Associated Publishers, 1936).

129. "The Hampton Students," *Saratoga Springs Daily Saratogian*, August 16, 1877.

130. "Amateur Base Ball," *Chicago Sunday Times*, April 25, 1875; "General Gathering," *Chicago Inter-Ocean*, June 19, 1879; "General Gathering," *Janesville Gazette*, September 23, 1880; "Hicks and Sawyer's Minstrels," *New York Freeman*, May 28, 1887; "The Diamond," *San Francisco Daily Alta*, July 28, 1888; "Amusements," *Sydney Morning Herald (Australia)*, September 3, 1888; "Sporting Echoes," *Brisbane Figaro and Punch (Australia)*, November 8, 1888.

131. "New London Notes," *New York Freeman*, March 19, 1887; "New London News," *New York Freeman*, April 9, 1887; "New London News," *New York Age*, April 19, 1890.

132. "New London Notes," *New York Freeman*, July 31, 1886; "New London News," *New York Freeman*, October 23, 1886; "New London Notes," *New York Freeman*, June 11, September 3, 1887.

133. "New London News," *New York Freeman*, July 30, 1887; "New London News," *New York Age*, December 7, 1889.

134. "London News," *New York Age*, March 29, 1890.

135. James Lee McDonough, *William Tecumseh Sherman; In the Service of My Country* (New York: W. W. Norton, 2016), 568–570.

136. "Matters and Things Laconically Noted," *Savannah Tribune*, September 14, 1876; *Savannah Tribune*, September 26, 1876.

137. "An Inter-State Match Between Colored Base Ballers," *Savannah Morning News*, August 22, 1879; "The Excursion to Brunswick," *Savannah Morning News*, August 29, 1879; "An Inter-State Match Between Colored Base Ballers," *Savannah Morning News*, August 22, 1879.

138. "No Title," *Augusta Chronicle*, April 23, 1885.

139. "A Month of Excursions," *Atlanta Constitution*, July 8, 1888.

140. "Base Ball League," *Savannah Tribune*, February 13, 1892.

141. Lomax, *Black Baseball Entrepreneurs, 1860–1901*, 35.

142. *Beaufort and Port Royal Tribune and Commercial*, August 23, 30, 1877.

143. "Fourth of July Celebration," *Savannah Morning News* July 4, 1870; "Base Ball," *Savannah Daily Advertiser*, June 7, 1871; "A Gang of Burglars," Savannah Daily Advertiser, August 17, 1871.

144. *Savannah Tribune*, August 31, 1889.

145. "Notes and Comment," *New York Globe*, May 5, 1883.

146. "Matters and Things Laconically Noted," *Savannah Morning News*, August 24, 1875.

147. Graham, *Mr. Flagler's St. Augustine*, 53.

148. *Ibid.*, 178–179.

149. "Letters from Jacksonville News Gossip," *Savannah News*, October 27, 1879.

150. "Jacksonville News Gossip," *Savannah News* March 10, 1877.

151. "Base Ball," *Saratoga Springs Daily Saratogian*, July 10, 1882; *New York Globe*, April 21, 1883; "Saratoga Gossip," *New York Globe*, July 7, 1883; "Local Base Ball Matters," *Hartford Courant*, September 13, 1883; "Howard's Letter," *Harrisburg State Journal*, May 3, 1884; "Colored Clubs at Union Park," *Baltimore American*, April 28, 1885; "Base Ball Notes," *Philadelphia Times*, May 19, 1885; "Camden 13; Gorham 8," *Philadelphia Record*, May 5, 1887; "Baseball at Brighton," *New York Evening Telegram*, July 21, 1887; *Elgin Morning Frank*, October 14, 1882; "Diamond Dust," *St. Louis Globe Democrat*, April 28, 1883; "Howard's Letter," *Harrisburg State Journal*, May 3, 1884; "Colored Clubs at Union Park," *Baltimore American*, April 28, 1885; "Base Ball Notes," *Philadelphia Times*, May 19, June 2, 1885; "Babylon," *Huntington Long Islander*, August 21, 1885.

152. "Syracuse," *Cleveland Gazette*, April 11, 1885; "Y.M.C.A.," *Watertown Daily Times*, May 25, 1889; "City and Vicinity," *Watertown Daily Times*, December 24, 1889; "Utica, NY," *Cleveland Gazette*, April 25, 1885.

153. "The Two States," *Augusta Chronicle*, April 18, 1879; "An Inter-State Match Between Colored Clubs," *Augusta Chronicle*, August 23, 1879; "Georgia Victorious," *Brunswick Advertiser*, August 30, 1879; "Base Ball Tournament," *Macon Telegraph*, August 27, 1880; "Things in Georgia," *New York Globe*, March 17, 1883; "New London Notes," *New York Freeman*, April 10, 1886.

154. "Saratoga Locals," *New York Globe*, July 5, 1884; "Base Ball Notes," *Pittsburgh Dispatch*, July 27, 1889; "Easy for the Keystones," *Pittsburgh Dispatch*, July 28, 1889; "Base Ball Matters," *Hudson Evening Gazette*, September 7, 1889; "Local Jottings," *Albany Times*, September 28, 1889; "Life at St. Augustine," *New York Age*, March 1, 1890; "The Richfielders Win," *Richfield Springs Mercury*, August 14, 1890; "Newburgh Notes," *New York Age*, January 1, 1891.

155. "Masks in an Ancient City," *New York Age*, March 2, 1889; "Incidents at St. Augustine," *New York Age*, March 6, 1889; "From St. Augustine," *New York Age*, February 8, 1890; "From St. Augustine," *Philadelphia Sporting Life*, February 7, 1891.

156. "An Inter-State Match Between Colored Clubs," *Augusta Chronicle*, August 23, 1879; "City Affairs," *Brunswick Advertiser*, August 23, 1879; "The Base Ball Tournament," *Savannah Morning News*, August 25, 1880; "Colored Business Men of Jacksonville," *New York Globe*, April 26, 1884; *New York Freeman*, July 30, 1887.

157. "Colored Business Men of Jacksonville," *New York Globe*, April 26, 1884.

158. "Florida Affairs," *Savannah Morning News*, November 18, 1879; "The Chatham Base Ball Club and the Late Contest," *Savannah Morning News*, August 27, 1880; "Sporting," *New Orleans Daily Picayune*, September 12, 1883; "Colored Base Ballists," *Jacksonville Florida Times Union*, May 23, 1886.

159. "Pleasure and Travel Resorts," *Outing 9*, no. 5 (February): 500.

160. Graham, *Mr. Flagler's St. Augustine*, 148–149.

161. *Ibid.*

162. *Ibid.*

163. Sandoval-Strauss, *Hotel*, 117–118.

164. "Utica, NY," *Cleveland Gazette*, April 25, 1885.

165. "A Head Waiter Caned," *Savannah Morning News*, April 16, 1879; "City Affairs," *Brunswick Advertiser*, August 23, 1879; "Georgia Victorious," *Brunswick Advertiser*, August 30, 1879; "Base Ball Tournament," *Macon Telegraph*, August 27, 1880; "Things in Georgia," *New York Globe*, March 17, 1883; *New York Globe*, April 21, 1883.

166. "Philadelphia Letter," *Washington Bee*, May 8, 1886.

167. *Ibid.*

168. "Pizarro at Ford's," *Washington People's Advocate*, April 26, 1879; "Local," *Washington People's Advocate*, December 6, 1879; "The Sparta Club," *Washington People's Advocate*, January 17, 1880; "Condensed Local," *National Republican*, April 21, 1880; "The Ira Aldridge Dramatic Club," *Washington People's Advocate*, April 24, 1880; "Musical and Dramatic," *National Republican*, April 28, 1883.

169. "Seashore Hotel Help," *Philadelphia Times*, May 27, 1885.

170. "Quaker City," *New York Globe* October 25, 1884; "Hotel Brotherhood," *Washington Bee*, April 3, 1886; "The Cateres' Fete," *Washington Bee*, June 19, 1886; "Philadelphia Letter," *Washington Bee*, August 7, 1886.

171. Lomax, *Black Baseball Entrepreneurs, 1860–1901*, 51.

172. "City Affairs," *Brunswick Advertiser*, August 23, 1879; "Georgia Victorious," *Brunswick Advertiser*, August 30, 1879.

173. "Things in Georgia," *New York Globe*, March 17, 1883; "Base Ball," *Sporting Life*, May 6, 1885; "Base Ball Notes," *Philadelphia Times*, May 19, June 2, 1885.

174. "Base Ball," *Saratoga Springs Daily Saratogian*, July 10, 1882; "Quaker City Gossip," *New York Globe*, December 22, 1883; "Quaker City Items," *New York Globe*, December 29, 1883.

175. "Mr. Frank P. Thompson; Magnolia," *New York Globe*, April 21, 1883.

176. "Life at St. Augustine," *New York Age*, February 22, 1890.

177. *Palatka Daily News*, April 28, 1885.

178. "Base Ball," *Baltimore Sun*, April 28, 1885; "Colored Clubs at Union Park," *Baltimore American and Commercial Advertiser*, April 28, 1885; *Sporting Life*, April 29, 1885.

179. "Colored Clubs at Union Park," *Baltimore American and Commercial Advertiser*, April 28, 1885.

180. Graham, *Mr. Flagler's St. Augustine*, 178–179; "A Head Waiter Caned," *Savannah Morning News*, April 16, 1879.

181. "Notes and Comments," *Sporting Life*, April 29, 1885.

182. "The Ugly Club at Dinner," *New York Freeman*, May 16, 1883.

183. "Base Ball Notes," *Philadelphia Times*, May 19, June 2, 1885.

184. "Notes and Comments," *Sporting Life*, July 1, 1885.

185. "Base Ball," *New York Herald*, September 7, 1882; "Howard's Letter," *Harrisburg State Journal*, May 3, 1884; "Base Ball," *Baltimore Sun*, April 28, 1885; "Colored Clubs at Union Park," *Baltimore American*, April 28, 1885; *Sporting Life*, April 29, 1885; "Babylon Village," *Babylon South Side Signal*, August 22, 1885; "Notes of

the Game," *New York Times*, August 30, 1885; "Among the Sports," *Trenton Times*, September 9, 1885; "Baseball Brevities," *Hazelton Sentinel*, October 5, 1885; "Around the Bases," *New York Herald*, October 6, 1885.

186. "Baseball Brevities," *Hazelton Sentinel*, October 5, 1885.

187. Jacqui Malone, *Steppin' on The Blues* (Urbana: University of Illinois Press, 1996), 135.

188. "Negro Minstrels," *Bloomington Pantagraph*, December 1, 1864; "The Sons of Ham," *Wilmington Journal*, July 24, 1873; "Ethiopian Minstrelsy," *Nashville Daily Patriot*, January 18, 1861.

189. "A Big Thing in Cork," *New York Times*, September 18, 1865; "Base Ball," *National Republican*, September 21, 1869.

190. Abbott, "Play That Barber Shop," 305.

191. Smith, *The Creolization of American Culture*, 82.

192. James E. Brunson, III, "Black Aesthetic Style; or Baseball Minstrelsy Reconsidered," *Black Ball* 8 (2015): 100–102.

193. Brunson III, "Black Aesthetic Style," 97.

194. "Colored Base Ball," *Scranton Republican*, July 23, 1889.

195. "Base Ball Yesterday," *Williamsport Daily Gazette and Bulletin*, August 20, 1885; "Those Giants," *Williamsport Daily Gazette and Bulletin*, September 23, 1885.

196. "Base Ball Brevities," *Niagara Falls Gazette*, June 22, 1887.

197. *Ibid.*; "Sportive Pressings," *Utica Daily Press*, October 14, 1887; "Base Ball in Town," *Syracuse Standard*, April 27, 1888.

198. "Those Giants," *Williamsport Daily Gazette and Bulletin*, September 23, 1885.

199. "Base Ball," *New York Herald*, July 21, 1882; "Base Ball From a Colored Point of View," *Chicago Tribune*, August 24, 1870.

200. "The Ball Grounds," *National Republican*, August 2, 1879.

201. "Base Ball," *Jersey City Journal*, October 1, 1884.

202. "Notes," *Topeka Daily Capital*, August 24, 1887.

203. "The Keystone B. B. Club," *Cleveland Gazette*, March 26, 1887; "An Enjoyable Banquet," *Pittsburgh Dispatch*, March 22, 1890; "An Enjoyable Banquet," *Pittsburgh Daily Post*, March 22, 1890.

204. "Walking for the Cake," *New York Herald*, January 11, 1883; "An Irishman Cut by a Negro," *New York Herald Tribune*, August 25, 1883; "A Serious Discussion," *New York Globe*, September 1, 1883.

205. "The Giants Triumphant," *Trenton True American*, August 14, 1886; "Variety and Minstrel Gossip," *New York Clipper*, October 24, 1886; "Variety and Minstrelsy," *New York Clipper*, October 14, 1893; "Theatrical Jottings," *New York Age*, August 5, 1909.

206. "Cake Walk Tonight," *Boston Post*, February 25, 1892; "Chased a Cake," *Boston Globe*, February 26, 1892; "Base Ball," *Trenton Times*, March 3, 1898.

207. George Presbury Rowell, editor, Rowell's *American Newspaper Directory* (New York: George P. Rowell, 1883), 644.

208. "Launched into Journalism," *Rochester Democrat and Chronicle*, September 3, 1882.

209. "Editor Harden; Savannah." *New York Globe*, April 12, 1884.

210. *Atlanta Constitution*, June 6, 1882.

211. "The Colored Base Ball Tournament," *Savannah Morning News*, August 24, 1880.

212. "Base Ball Tournament," *Savannah Morning News*, August 26, 1880.

213. "Gossip of the Game," *St. Louis Post Dispatch*, April 1, 1886; "Notes," *Cincinnati Enquirer*, April 25, 1886; "Diamond Gleams," *Rochester Democrat and Chronicle*, May 24, 1886; "Base Ball at St. Augustine," *Jacksonville Florida Times Union*, May 25, 1886.

214. "The Colored League," *New Orleans Times Democrat*, April 26, 1886.

215. "Colored Base Ballists," *Jacksonville Florida Times Union*, May 23, 1886.

216. "Diamond Dust," *Charleston News and Courier*, March 25, 1886; "Gossip of the Game," *St. Louis Post Dispatch*, April 1, 1886; "A Colored Base Ball League," *Charleston News and Courier*, April 8, 1886; "A Caught on the Fly," *Charleston Observer*, April 11, 1886; "Our Race's Doings," *Cleveland Gazette*, April 17, 1886; *New York Clipper*, April 24, 1886; "Preparing for Games," *Atlanta Constitution*, June 8, 1886; "The Colored League," *New York Clipper*, June 26, 1886.

217. "City Notes," *Palatka Daily News*, August 21, 1885.

218. "National Colored Base Ball Association," *Savannah Morning News*, August 9, 1880; "City Notes," *Palatka Daily News*, June 4, 1884, August 22, 1885; "Gossip of the Game," *St. Louis Post Dispatch*, April 1, 1886; "The Colored League," *New Orleans Times Picayune*, April 26, 1886; "Colored Base Ballists," *Jacksonville Florida Times Union*, May 23, 1886; "St. Augustine Excursion," *Palatka Daily News*, June 15, 1887.

219. "Colored Base Ballists," *Jacksonville Florida Times Union*, May 23, 1886.

220. "The Coddington House," *New York Freeman*, October 30, 1886; "New England Colored Men," *New York Freeman*, September 11, 1886; "Boston's Easter Program," *New York Freeman*, April 9, 1887; "Queen Victoria's Jubilee," *New York Freeman*, June 25, 1887.

221. "Gossip," *New York Freeman*, September 17, 1887.

222. "Philadelphia Letter," *Washington Bee*, May 8, 1886; "The Coddington House," *New York Freeman*, October 30, 1886.

223. Graham, *Mr. Flagler's St. Augustine*, 199.

224. "Multum in Parvo," *St. Paul Appeal*, March 1, 1890.

225. "The Winter in Florida," *New York Age*, May 15, 1890; "At Kaaterskill Peak," *New York Age*, July 12, 26, 1890.

226. "Cuban Giants Handicapped," *New York Age*, March 2, 1889; "Incidents at St. Augustine," *New York Age*, March 6, April 6, 1889; "Life at St. Augustine," *New York Age*, March 1, 1890; "From St. Augustine," *Sporting Life*, February 21, 1891; "Saratoga Springs," *New York Age*, June 13, 1891; "New York State Grange Day," *Watertown Daily Times*, August 12, 1895; "The Waiter," *Indianapolis Freeman*, November 17, December 8, 1900; "F.P. Thompson Dead," *Indianapolis Freeman*, December 30, 1905; "Negro Professional Baseball Got Start in 1885 in Babylon, LI," *California Eagle*, April 27, 1939; "Sol White Recalls Baseball's Greatest Days," *Pittsburgh Courier*, March 12, 1927.

227. Lomax, *Black Baseball Entrepreneurs, 1860–1901*, 10–11; "Local News," *Providence Evening Press*, December 5, 1870; Paul Finkelman, editor, *Encyclopedia of African American History, 1896 to the Present: From the Age of Segregation to the Twenty-First Century* (London: Oxford University Press, 2009), 205.

228. "Fifteenth Amendment Celebration," *Providence Evening Press* May 18, 1870; "Emancipation Day," *Providence Press*, August 4, 1877; "Emancipation Day," *Providence Evening Press*, August 2, 1884; "Rhode Island Celebration," *New York Freeman*, August 7, 1886.

229. "Local News," *Providence Evening Press*, September 12, 15, 1870.

230. "Local News," *Providence Evening Press*, October 13, 31, 1870.

231. "Providence Paragraphs," *New York Freeman*, April 5, 1884.

232. "A Providence Ball," *New York Globe*, March 8, 1884; "Providence Driftings," *New York Freeman*, January 23, 1886.

233. "Cook Clerget's Escape," *New Haven Register*, September 8, 1885.

234. Robin D. G. Kelly, *Race Rebels: Culture, Politics and the Black Working Class* (New York: Free Press, 1994), 21–23.

235. *St. Paul Appeal*, March 3, 1888.

236. "New London Notes," *New York Freeman*, August 7, 1886.

237. "Providence Driftings," *New York Globe*, September 27, 1884; "Some Fine Lady Skaters," *New York Freeman*, January 2, 1886; "Narragansett Waiters, 16; Dorrance Waiters," *Providence Sunday Telegram*, June 13, 1886.

238. "Rhode Island News," *New York Freeman*, July 10, 1886.

239. "Providence Driftings," *New York Freeman,* May 2, 1885; "Providence Briefs," *Cleveland Gazette*, August 15, 1885; "Rhode Island News," *New York Freeman*, July 10, 1886; "Providence People," *New York Age*, June 2, 1888.

240. "Providence Driftings," *New York Freeman*, February 27, 1886; "Horse Shoes, 3; Colored Grays, 2," *Providence Sunday Telegram*, July 4, 1886; "Notes From the Diamond," *Providence Sunday Telegram*, July 14, 1886; "Base Ball Notes," *Providence Sunday Telegram*, August 1, 1886; "Providence Letter," *New York Freeman*, April 2, 1887; "Easter in Providence" *New York Freeman*, April 16, 1887; "Providence People," *New York Freeman*, April 23, 1887; "Resolutes vs Providence Grays," *Boston Herald*, April 15, 1887; "Two Colored Nines," *Boston Globe*, April 15, 1887; "Rhode Island Matters," *New York Freeman*, June 4, 1887; "Providence Politeness," *New York Freeman*, July 23, 1887.

241. Lawrence D. Hogan and Jeffrey Statts, "Baseball in the Ocean State: Rhode Island Black Baseball, 1886–1948," in *The Cooperstown Symposium on Baseball and American Culture 2000*, William M. Simons and Alvin L. Hall., eds (Jefferson, NC: McFarland, 2001), 259–260.

242. "Alexandria Affairs," *Washington Critic*, July 7, 1882; "Base Ball," *Washington Sunday Herald*, July 16, 1882; "Pertinent Paragraphs," *Washington Critic*, July 17, 1882; "Laconic Locals," *Washington Critic*, June 19, 1883; "Notes About Town," *Washington Critic*, June 29, 1883.

243. "Locals," *Washington Bee*, April 7, 1883; *Washington Bee*, September 26, 1885; "Richard Himself Again," *New York Freeman*, November 7, 1885.

244. "Hartford News," *Hartford Courant*, April 17, 1885; "Diamond Gossip," *Boston Globe*, April 18, 1885; "Base Ball Notes," *Hartford Courant*, May 30, 1885.

245. "The Drama in Providence," *New York Freeman*, November 13, 1886.

246. "Providence Echoes," *New York Freeman*, February 13, 1886; "Providence Siftings," *New York Freeman*, March 27, 1886; "Providence Echoes," *New York Freeman*), July 3, 1886; "Providence Pencilings," *New York Freeman*, July 24, 1886; "Rhode Island Incidents," *New York Freeman*, August 14, 1886; "Norwich (Conn.) News," *New York Freeman*, May 14, 1887; Henry T. Sampson, *Blacks in Blackface: A Sourcebook on Early Black Musical Shows* (Lanham, MD: Scarecrow, 2014), 1137.

247. "Providence Letter," *New York Freeman*, May 22, 1886.

248. "Notes from the Diamond," *Providence Sunday Telegram*, July 25, 1886; "Two Colored Nines," *Boston Globe*, April 15, 1887; "Diamond Echoes," *Boston Herald*, May 20, 1888; "Cuban Giants Reorganized," *Philadelphia Inquirer,* February 1, 1892; "Senators Win on Wild Pitching," *New York Herald*, April 17, 1893; "Gorhams Lose to Reading," *Philadelphia Inquirer,* June 5, 1894; "X-Giants, 6; Chester, 1," *Philadelphia Inquirer*, May 24, 1896; "Amateur Base Ball" *Brooklyn Eagle*, September 6, 1897; "Games on the Diamond," *Jersey City Journal*, September 26, 1898.

249. "Shorts," *Saratoga Springs Daily Saratogian*, July 4, 1884; "Notes from the Diamond," *Providence Sunday Telegram*, July 25, 1886; "Two Colored Nines," *Boston Globe*, April 15, 1887; "Atlantics, 19: Colored Grays, 1," *Providence Sunday Telegram*, July 10, 1887; "Caught Napping," *Boston Globe*, May 22, 1888.

250. "The Apollo Ball," *New York Freeman*, January 16, 1886; "Providence People," *New York Freeman*, July 17, 1886; "Floating Trifles," *Providence Sunday Telegram*, August 31, 1886; "Apollo Club Entertainments," *New York Freeman*, November 13, 1886; "Providence People," *New York Freeman*, January 15, 1887; "Apollo Club Celebration," *New York Freeman*, May 30, 1891.

251. "Providence Letter," *New York Freeman*, May 22, 1886.

252. Ancestry.com, "1880 United States Federal Census," http://search.ancestry.com/search/db.aspx?dbid=6742html; "Alerts, 11; River Points, 7," *Providence Sunday Telegram*, May 2, 1886; "River Points, 6; Alerts, 4; 11 innings," *Providence Sunday Telegram*, May 16, 1886; "New London Notes," *New York Freeman*, June 5, 1886; "Horsehoes, 3; Colored Grays, 2," *Providence Sunday Telegram*, July 4, 1886; "Notes from the Diamond," *Providence Sunday Telegram*, July 25, 1886; "Two Colored Nines," *Boston Globe*, April 15, 1887; "Diamond Echoes," *Boston Herald*, May 20, 1888 "New London Notes," *New York Age*, September 20, 1890.

253. "Many Negroes on the Stage," *St. Louis Post Dispatch*, July 25, 1897.

254. *Ibid.*

Leading Off

The Cuban Giants

Tony Kissel

The Cuban Giants were one of the first success stories in black baseball history. They set out to become the best black ball club in America, and to play anyone, anywhere, and at any time. The team opened up the eyes of people of all colors to the skills possessed by African American ballplayers in the 19th century. The Cuban Giants were also the first black squad to play and defeat a Major League team.

Ten days before the 1885 Cuban Giants were scheduled to play their first game against a big league outfit, they were stranded in Mahanoy City, Pennsylvania, with no money. Manager John Lang left them and headed for Philadelphia to obtain funds so that the club could continue playing. But it was African American entrepreneur Frank P. Thompson who came to the team's rescue with enough cash to allow them to return to New York City.[1]

The New York Metropolitans of the American Association hosted the Giants at the Polo Grounds on October 5, and promptly scored nine runs in the first inning on the way to an 11–3 rout. New York newspapers used terms like "farce" and "minstrel performance" to describe the playing, and called the black squad "Lang's Colored Giants," "The Colored Giants," and "The Colored Cuban Giants."[2]

Five days later, the Giants were in Philadelphia to play the Philadelphia Athletics of the American Association. After four innings, the Athletics were clinging to a 7–6 lead, but scored five more runs in the fifth inning to put the Giants away. *Sporting Life* on October 14 noted that umpire Johnny Ryan's partial decisions contributed to the Giants' loss, along with lack of experience and poor base running. The *Philadelphia Record* referred to the team as the Orions since the four top hitters had played on that Philadelphia team earlier in the year. The Giants roster actually included players from several other black teams besides the Orions.[3]

Walter Cook became the new owner of the Cuban Giants in 1886, and he secured the Chambersburg Grounds near Trenton, New Jersey, for their home games. White spectators had no choice but to support a black team, and support them they did. On May 24, Chris Von Der Ahe's St. Louis Browns (AA) arrived to play an exhibition. Ben Boyd of the Giants scored the first run of the game, and the grandstands shook due to the crowd's excitement. But Giants pitcher Shep Trusty could not hold St. Louis, and the Major League team prevailed, 9–3. The *Trenton Daily True American* commented that Trusty was a sick man due to an accident two weeks earlier (Trusty would pass away in 1890). Catcher Art Thomas drew raves for his great success in batting, stylish catching in grand style, and throwing to bases with unerring skill. He caught several St. Louis base runners napping with his rapid pegs.[4]

In July of 1886, the Giants defeated both the Cincinnati Reds (AA) team and the Kansas City Cowboys (National League). On July 21, the Giants led Cincinnati, 6–0, on the way to a 9–4 win. A healthier Shep Trusty struck out seven Cincinnati batters and gave up no earned runs. Five days later, the Giants scored twice in the sixth inning to defeat the Kansas City Cowboys, 3–2. Clever base running led to two important runs.

Kansas City decided to stay in Trenton to play a rematch the following day. Shep Trusty chose to pitch again, but soon discovered he had nothing left, and the Giants quickly fell behind, 7–1, as Kansas City avenged their previous day's defeat with an easy 13–4 victory. The Cuban Giants had split their four games against Major League teams in 1886.

In 1887, the Cuban Giants played 165 games, and their win-loss record was 107–54–4.[5] Twenty-one of those losses were to professional baseball teams, and the Giants played 18 games against Major League teams. The Giants' first game against a Major League club in 1887 was with the New York Metropolitans (AA) on April 11. Shep Trusty was staked to an early 2–0 lead, but the Mets pounded out 17 hits for an easy 19–7 win before 2,500 Trenton spectators. On April 13 and 14, the Washington Nationals (NL) hosted the Giants and won both games, 7–5 and 14–2. Coverage of the first contest by *Sporting Life* noted, "the entire colored population turned out to see the Cuban Giants and the game was filled with laughable incidents."[6]

In game two, most of the 900 spectators hailed from the Afro-American side of Washington D.C. The two Williams players on the Giants, George and Clarence, each got four hits in the two games, and pitcher Billy Whyte replaced Shep Trusty.

Anyone who read the newspaper report of the May 3 game between the Giants and the Philadelphia Athletics (AA) was probably in a state of shock by the 16–0 drubbing inflicted by the Giants. While it boosted the confidence level of the Giants and sent a message to Major League teams, this game cannot be counted as a true matchup. The Athletics chose to divide their squad into two teams that day in order to play two games. They sent six pitchers and three catchers over to play the Giants. If the Giants felt insulted, they took their anger out on the field. The *Trenton Times* observed, "The Athletics were weak at every position except catcher." That had to be the best line of the day![7]

On the sixth of May, the Giants played a return engagement with the New York Metropolitans. New York had an early lead of 2–0, but the Giants scored nine runs by the fourth inning on the way to an easy 11–4 victory. On May 25, many prominent Trentonians were among the 2,800 spectators on hand at the East State Street Grounds to witness one of the best games of the year. The Detroit Wolverines were 21–7 on the season, on their way to a National League–best 79–45 record. The Giants had just scored 27 runs in two games against other Major League teams. What made this contest notable was Detroit's decision to use ace pitcher Charles Getzien instead of a lesser pitcher who could have used the work.

In the first inning, Clarence Williams scored the first run of the game, helped by a muffed Detroit throw. The entire grandstand again shook with the stamping of feet and the thumping of canes and umbrellas. These were mostly white spectators! Getzien settled down and retired nine Giants in a row. Meanwhile, Billy Whyte was not touched for any runs, so the score after three innings stood Giants 1, Detroit 0. With two outs in the fourth, Abe Harrison got a hit and Art Thomas hit a rocket over the left fielder's head. Thomas barely beat the throw home, and now the lead was 3–0 after four innings. A reporter wrote that the applause Thomas earned lasted more than two minutes.[8]

A leadoff error got Fred Dunlap to first base for Detroit in the fifth inning. Billy Whyte had a one-hitter up to this point, but the error opened the gates for Detroit. Three hits later, the score was tied, 3–3, and that is how the fifth inning ended. The Giants answered with another run when Jack Frye's double hit the right field fence, scoring George Williams. The Giants led, 4–3, after six innings. With only three innings left, both sides increased their intensity.

Getzien held the Giants scoreless in the top of the seventh inning. Jack Rowe led off for Detroit, and his grounder to shortstop Abe Harrison was booted for an error. Charlie Ganzel's single put two runners on with no outs. But Billy Whyte induced Sam Thompson to pop up. Whyte hustled to make the catch and also tagged Ganzel for a double play. The leadoff error became important now as it cost the Giants a third out. Hardy Richardson came up and drove a long two-run home run to the outfield fence, drawing applause. The seventh inning ended with Detroit ahead, 5–4.

Getzien put the side down in order in the home half of the eighth. Newspaper accounts differ over what happened in the bottom of the inning. Detroit tacked on three insurance runs thanks to four base hits, though the *Trenton Times* reported that both Ben Boyd and Ben Holmes dropped fly balls which "allowed several men to score." Yet the *Times* recorded no errors for the Giants, and the *Trenton Daily True American* recorded it as either one or two errors.[9]

It didn't really matter as the Giants went down in order again in the ninth—Getzien had completed the game by retiring the last nine batters in a row. Despite the 8–4 defeat, Trenton spectators seemed happy on their way out of the ballpark and made comments like "the Cuban Giants are good ballplayers you can bet!" and "one of the best clubs in the country." Yes indeed.[10]

The results were similar on June 2, when Philadelphia (AA) came from behind to beat the Giants, 14–9, in a slugfest. Ben Boyd and Abe Harrison each had four hits, and Clarence Williams led off the game with a home run to center field. Cincinnati (AA) arrived on the following day, and the Giants fell behind 6–0 early. They rallied to tie the game, 7–7, in the sixth inning, but Cincinnati prevailed, 9–7. On June 14, the Giants defeated Cincinnati, 8–5, with Ben Boyd getting four hits and Billy Whyte outdueling Billy Widner.

The June 21 headline in the *Trenton Times* read, "Giants Defeat Giants." It could have just as easily been "Sweltering Heat Defeats the Cuban Giants." The New York Giants (NL) easily beat them, 17–6, led by Mike Dorgan's four hits, Buck Ewing's and Danny Richardson's triples, Roger Connor's double, and Monte Ward's two hits. But it was the lack of defense that led to the Cuban Giants' shellacking. Art Thomas, Abe Harrison, and George Williams made a combined ten errors that led to 11 unearned runs.[11]

Through June of 1887, the Giants' record versus Major League squads was only 3–7. Their record would turn around three weeks later. Indianapolis (NL) visited Trenton and was defeated, 8–4, as the Giants collected ten more hits and made only one error. Their base stealing and wonderful sliding was noted in the press.

The *National Police Gazette* on August 6 observed, "The Clevelands were talking about what they were going to do with the Cuban Giants, but if they take our advice they will keep their hands off. The Cuban Giants are colored fellows but Caesar's Ghost, how they can play ball." Cleveland took the newspaper's advice and never stopped at Trenton.[12]

On September 11, the St. Louis Browns (AA) refused to play an exhibition game with the Giants, citing the color of their opponent's skin as the reason. It was one reason why, but the *New York Sun* on September 13 added, "Base Ball Men hereabouts think that the color of the players was only an excuse…. It is a well-known fact that the players of our local clubs have never had any objections to playing with colored players."[13]

The Giants suffered a loss to Philadelphia (AA) of 13–6 on September 25. A week or two later, Giants manager J.M. Bright took the team to watch a game between New York and Philadelphia on a day off. Here was another opportunity for an interview with the players to explore their feelings about watching a Major League game. Either nobody noticed or nobody cared. The Giants played two great games against major leaguers on October 9 and 10. First, they destroyed the Baltimore Orioles (AA), 12–2, in six innings, and then tied New York (NL), 2–2, in a game called by darkness. New York's Danny Richardson suffered a fractured cheekbone when Art Thomas applied a hard tag to his face at first base.[14]

In late October, the Cuban Giants journeyed out west to play Indianapolis (NL) and Cincinnati (AA). The Indianapolis Hoosiers defeated them, 17–11 and 2–0, with both teams combining for 14 errors in the sloppy first game. The Giants became so angry in the second game due to the umpire's decisions that they left the field after the sixth inning. The following day, the Giants defeated Cincinnati, 6–5, with George Parego pitching the victory. The major leaguers got some measure of revenge the next day, defeating the Cubans, 18–6, in a six-inning, rain-shortened game. The *Cincinnati Enquirer* on October 23 commented, "The visitors are ball-players from the word go…. They are great base-runners."[15]

Apparently the major leagues didn't need great base runners. In 1888, the color line was slowly being drawn, and black ballplayers in the International League had to find different uniforms. The Cuban Giants had proven to everyone including themselves that they could play at the Major League level. In the 18 games played in 1887 against Major League outfits (not counting the 16–0 whitewashing of the Athletics), the Giants either held a lead or were tied in 12 of the games. But over the next seven seasons, the Giants would play only five games against the Washington (NL) team and seven games against all the other Major League clubs.

In April of 1888, the Cuban Giants played a three-game series against the Washington Nationals (NL) in Washington, D.C. The big leaguers outscored them by 23 runs in the series. George Stovey was a losing pitcher in one game, running out of gas in the eighth inning. George Williams was compared to Frank Grant by the *National Republican*. Clarence Williams, known as the King of Coachers, expressed his displeasure at one umpire's calls this way, "You certainly is biased, Mister."[16]

The Detroit (NL) Wolverines visited Trenton on June 7. Mindful of the close contest in the previous season, Detroit took no chances, jumped on the Giants early, and never let up. The final score was 15–1, with the Giants contributing 13 errors and being held to only three hits. Dan Brouthers had five hits in the game.

On July 3, the Washington (NL) team visited Trenton to play a fourth game with the Giants. Trailing 5–4, Washington exploded for six runs in the fifth inning and defeated the Giants, 11–6. Dummy Hoy was singled out for two miscues in center field for Washington. Poor umpiring was also mentioned in one report. Billy Whyte pitched a 2–0 shutout against the Philadelphia Athletics (AA) on July 23 and gave up only four hits without issuing a base on balls.[17]

In the *New York Age* of January 9, 1889, Giants manager S. K. Govern wrote an article about a train ride from Jersey City, New Jersey, down to St. Augustine, Florida. The 576 black passengers on board the train were heading down to work at the three hotels owned by Henry Flagler in the St. Augustine area. Musicians, quartets, an entire band, housekeepers, waiters, and last but not least, the Cuban Giants were on board.

According to Govern, when the train pulled into the station in Washington D.C.,

"Manager William Burkett of the Washington (NL) team came down to the depot to pay his compliments and wish the Cuban Giants a successful winter." He urged the Cubans to return in time, if possible, to play two games in Washington April 12 and April 13, and save them two games in Trenton, on April 18 and 19.[18]

Manager Burkett ignored the color line, and his team did play the Giants on April 12 in Washington D.C. The local black population came out in force and witnessed Washington win a close contest, 3–2. Despite giving up only four hits, George Stovey earned the loss. Meanwhile, Frank Grant hit a double and a triple. The Boston Beaneaters (NL) visited Trenton on May 7 and took home a 5–2 victory. King Kelly received a huge ovation from the Trenton spectators who came out to see him play. The last game of 1889 between the Giants and big leaguers was played on May 31 before only 100 spectators. The Cincinnati Reds (AA) eked out a 1–0 victory in a five-inning game shortened by rain.

The Cuban Giants played only three games against Major League teams in the 1890s. The first game, on March 12, 1891, was played in St. Augustine. The Giants used a lineup composed of local hotel waiters and only a few year-round players. The Cleveland Spiders (NL) clobbered them, 15–1. On July 12, 1891, the Giants hosted the Cincinnati (AA) nine at the Long Island Grounds in Long Island City with 1,000 spectators watching. Cincinnati beat the Giants, 11–5.

Three more seasons passed before the Giants would get to play another Major League team. They finally got their shot on Sunday, September 2, 1894, at Koehler's Park in Newark, NJ, against the St. Louis Browns (NL). Newspaper coverage was limited to the *Newark Evening News*, as several St. Louis and Newark newspapers ignored the game completely. No box score exists, but the line score indicated that the Cuban Giants defeated St. Louis, 13–9. The Giants jumped on pitcher Dad Clarke for five quick runs as spectators hissed the pitcher for lobbing the ball up to Giants batters so they could hit it. St. Louis clawed back and took a 9–8 lead in the seventh inning. But it was the Giants' day as they scored five more runs to seal the victory.

After the game, a reporter from the *Newark Evening News* interviewed a spectator who supposedly was a friend of one of the St. Louis players. According to this spectator, the player complained, "I don't care if we get beat 100 to nothing. Is it any wonder the men are sulking? Look at the management we are under. We played an exhibition game Friday at Orange. Yesterday we had to play two games at Philadelphia. We have two more games on for tomorrow, and the management makes us jump out here and play these fellows today." Perhaps it was good that all of the St. Louis newspapers took the day off from covering the team. You can imagine what would have been written about giving up 13 runs to a black club.[19]

Nobody asked any members of the 1894 Cuban Giants if life on the road was difficult. They compiled a record of 124–22–3 while playing the entire season as a traveling club! Facing hostile spectators, biased umpires, and hotel owners who suddenly had no rooms for them, they had every right to sulk and complain. But they didn't, and managed to win 14 out of 20 games against minor league teams.

The 1894 Giants roster was loaded with major league-level talent. Frank Grant, Sol White, Grant "Home Run" Johnson (making his black ball debut), Clarence Williams, George Williams, George Stovey, John Nelson, William Selden, John Patterson, Andrew Jackson, and Oscar Jackson all should have been given a chance to perform at the highest level. Their play inspired the next generation of black ballplayers to carry on the tradition of excellence.

Table 9.1 Cuban Giants vs. Major League Baseball 1885–1894

Year	Record	PCT	RF	RA
1885	0–2	.000	5.00	12.00
1886	2–2	.500	4.75	7.00
1887	6–12–1	.333	6.89	9.00
1888	1–5	.167	3.17	9.83
1889	0–3	.000	1.33	3.00
1891	0–3	.000	3.33	10.67
1894	1–0	1.000	13.00	9.00
Total	10–27–1	.270	5.42	8.74

Editor's Note: Unlike the black clubs that preceded them, the Cuban Giants were competitive against Organized Baseball teams, from their inception in September 1885 right through the 1895 season, after which most of their players formed the pointedly named Cuban X-Giants. In the 19th century, minor league teams were categorized by the number of players they could protect from Major League squads. The Cuban Giants played outfits from A, B, and those National Agreement circuits that had no classification (NC), including the National Colored League of 1887, the only Negro League ever recognized by Organized Baseball. The team also competed against clubs from several strong independent leagues, as well as the reserve teams of the New York Giants and Philadelphia Athletics. In addition, the Giants were members of three minor leagues: the independent Middle States League (1889), the non-classified Eastern Interstate League (1890), and the independent Connecticut State League (1891). The results in the four tables also include games by the York Monarchs of 1890 and the 1891 Big Gorhams, both of whom were comprised almost exclusively of Cuban Giants players.

Table 9.2 Cuban Giants vs. Minor League Baseball 1886–1895

Year	A	B	NC	IND	Overall	PCT	RF	RA
1886	—	—	3–14	6–8–1	9–22–1	.290	4.37	6.87
1887	9–5	—	14–7	17–17	40–29	.580	7.93	6.67
1888	—	—	6–8	7–4	13–12	.520	5.31	4.85
1889	—	—	3–1	1–0	4–1	.800	6.00	3.60
1890	—	—	5–8–1	3–6	8–14–1	.364	7.13	9.96
1891	1–3	—	—	—	1–3	.250	7.50	12.25
1892	0–5	2–3	—	—	2–8	.200	5.10	13.80
1893	—	—	1–0	—	1–0	1.000	10.00	2.00
1894	3–2	—	6–3	5–1	14–6	.700	8.40	6.85
1895	—	5–10	—	4–0	9–10	.474	9.10	12.47
Total	13–15	7–13	38–41–1	43–36–1	101–105–2	.490	6.97	7.51

Table 9.3 Cuban Giants League Baseball Record 1889–1891

Leagues	Record	PCT	RF	RA
1889 MSL	55–17	.764	7.44	3.80
1889 MSL Exhibitions	7–3–1	.700	9.45	3.91
1890 EISL	40–16	.714	9.13	6.09
1889 EISL Exhibitions	5–4	.556	5.55	4.89
1891 CSL	8–10	.444	7.07	6.47
1889 CSL Exhibitions	5–0–1	1.000	13.02	5.80
Three Season Total	103–43	.705	8.06	4.98
Exhibition Total	17–7–2	.708	8.80	4.64
Total	120–50–2	.706	8.17	4.93

Table 9.4 Cuban Giants vs. MLB Reserve Teams 1887–1891

	Record	PCT	RF	RA
1887	4–1	.800	9.80	7.60
1888	2–1	.667	6.00	3.00
1891	2–0	1.000	9.00	4.50
Total	8–2	.800	8.50	5.60

Table 9.5 Cuban Giants vs. Organized Baseball 1885–1895

Classification	Record	PCT	RF	RA
MLB	10–27–1	.270	5.42	8.74
A	13–15	.464	6.71	9.36
B	7–13	.350	8.10	12.65
NC	38–41–1	.481	6.70	6.15
IND	43–36–1	.544	7.04	6.94
League Play	120–50–2	.706	8.17	4.93
Reserves	8–2	.800	8.50	5.60
Total	239–184–5	.565	7.34	6.56

Sources for Tables 9.1, 9.2, 9.3, 9.4, 9.5: Kissel Cuban Giants Database; Johnson, and Wolff, *Encyclopedia of Minor League Baseball*, 2007; Baseball-Reference.com; StatsCrew.com.

Notes

1. *City Item*, October 2, 1885; *New York Age*, October 15, 1887; White, *History of Colored Base Ball*, 8, 10.
2. *Trenton Times*, September 2, 1885; *Reading Eagle*, September 16, 1885.
3. *Philadelphia Record*, October 11, 1885; *New York Age*, October 15, 1887; White, *History of Colored Base Ball*, 8.
4. *Trenton True American*, May 25, 1886.
5. *Trenton Times*, November 3, 1887.
6. *Sporting Life*, April 20, 1887.
7. *Trenton Times*, May 4, 1887.
8. *Trenton Times*, May 26, 1887.
9. *Trenton Times*, May 26, 1887; *Trenton True American*, May 26, 1887.
10. *Trenton Times*, May 26, 1887.
11. *Trenton Times*, June 21, 1887.
12. *National Police Gazette*, August 6, 1887.
13. *New York Sun*, September 13, 1887.
14. *Sporting Life*, October 19, 1887.
15. *Cincinnati Enquirer*, October 23, 1887.
16. *National Republican*, April 18, 20, 1888.
17. *Trenton True American*, July 5, 1888.
18. *New York Age*, January 19, 1889.
19. *Newark Evening News*, September 3, 1894.

Rube Foster

Negro League Giant

ROBERT C. COTTRELL

He was inarguably the most important figure in black baseball. Without his steward-ship and vision, far fewer students of the game would know much about 34 others whose plaques join his at the National Baseball Hall of Fame in Cooperstown, New York. Thanks to his determined genius, Cool Papa Bell, Oscar Charleston, Martin Dihigo, Josh Gibson, Buck Leonard, Satchel Paige, and Cristobal Torriente achieved greatness on Negro Leagues playing diamonds. His founding of the Negro National League enriched fellow admin-istrators Effa Manley, Cum Posey, Ben Taylor, and J.L. Wilkinson. And the formation of Organized Black Baseball enabled even earlier stars, ranging from Sol White to Pop Lloyd, Jose Mendez, and Smokey Joe Williams, to achieve greater notoriety. Its considerable sta-tus in baseball circles resulted in the signing of black ball veterans who became household names because of their storied major league careers. Jackie Robinson led the way, soon followed by Roy Campanella, Larry Doby, Monte Irvin, Willie Mays, Hank Aaron, and Ernie Banks.

Andrew "Rube" Foster was the pathfinder, an almost mythical pitcher, manager, and administrator who helped to ensure that black players had a stage allowing them to partic-ipate, however inequitably, in the National Pastime. The obstacles proved considerable and the course of development uneven, but Foster persevered at eventual great cost to his own health and longevity. The founding of the Negro National League, nevertheless, provided an institutional framework that afforded black ballplayers a means to compete against other skilled performers, to acquire reputations that fostered barnstorming, and to establish im-perfectly calculated records that historians and fans still examine. The league lasted a bare year beyond Foster's passing, but its success over a 12-year time span led to other black circuits, which continued for the next three decades or so, admittedly in sometimes erratic fashion.

Foster's own story has been conveyed in a small but growing body of sports litera-ture, but it merits a retelling, particularly because his name still elicits little if any recogni-tion from the vast bulk of baseball fans. By contrast, starting with biographical treatments during the first decade of the 20th century, while Foster was still a young pitching sensation, he elicited contemporaneous accounts of his life and career, with comparisons drawn to the greatest players, managers, and administrators in Organized Baseball. Such accounts were hardly infrequent over more than two decades, with an array occurring in 1930, the year he died at the age of 51. From that point until his entry into the Baseball Hall of Fame in 1981,

Foster occasionally garnered analyses attesting to his singular importance on the playing field, but particularly as one of the game's greatest managers and the founder of the first long-lasting black baseball league. Baseball historians continue to attest to his historic role, but more casual students of the game still know too little about Rube Foster.[1]

He was born on September 17, 1879, in Winchester, Texas, a township located 54 miles southeast of Austin, the fifth child of the Reverend Andrew Foster and his wife, Evaline Foster. A regular attendee of his father's services at the Methodist Episcopal Church, little Andrew grew up with the promises of Reconstruction, as exemplified by the Thirteenth, the Fourteenth, and the Fifteenth Amendments to the U.S. Constitution that still engendered hopes in the black community. Those hopes would be dashed as black elected officials lost their posts and disenfranchisement became the norm, fueled, as slavery had been, by the threat or actuality of violence. Andrew came of age as Jim Crow took hold, leading to his attendance at an all-black school, which he refused to attend after the eighth grade.

A hulking young man, broad-shouldered and tall for the era—estimates range from 5'10" to 6'4"—Foster soon became renowned for his pitching prowess. After witnessing him pitch for the itinerant Waco Yellow Jackets, a white sportswriter from Austin enthusiastically related that "Foster had him intoxicated with his playing." In 1902, Frank C. Leland of the Chicago Union Giants, a team that competed against top white ball clubs, hired Foster, who was judged "a twirler of no mean ability" and struck out 13 batters in his debut. Leaving the Union Giants at midseason, in the fashion of the many ballplayers of the day who readily jumped from team to team, Foster began pitching for the heretofore white Otsego, Michigan, club. One teammate recalled, "Foster had a reputation as a gunman and was never seen without his Texas pistol."[2]

Next joining the Cuban X-Giants, the leading black ball team of the East, Foster publicized himself as "the best pitcher in the country." His manager insisted that Foster's fastball matched that of Amos Rusie, the major league fireballer, and he possessed a wicked curve. On the other hand, Foster had to learn how to keep runners on base, heading for Major League ballparks whenever he could to check out the action. By the 1903 campaign, Foster was a bona fide star as his team competed for the "colored world championship of the world" against the Philadelphia Giants. Foster achieved four complete-game victories, ensuring that his reputation continued to ascend. That season, Foster also went up against the Philadelphia Athletics' ace southpaw, Rube Waddell, besting him, 6–3. Reporters also began calling Foster "Rube."[3]

Along with catcher Chappie Johnson and second baseman Charlie Grant, whom New York Giants manager John McGraw futilely attempted to pass off as a Native American, Foster departed for the team he had just helped to defeat. The surging black population of Philadelphia was only surpassed by Baltimore, New Orleans, New York City, and Washington, D.C. But Jim Crow reigned in that Northern city too, as blacks of all classes congregated in the city's southern district. Still, as W.E.B. Du Bois noted, eligible black Philadelphians could vote, although he saw them as beholden to a political machine. The White House exemplified the era's racism, with President Theodore Roosevelt a progressive but one who viewed blacks as "backward," lazy, and shiftless, while favoring the maintenance of "race purity."

During his first year with the Philadelphia Giants in 1904, Foster tossed a pair of no-hitters, during one of which he delivered 17 strikeouts, and again helped lead his team to "the colored championship of the world." Facing his former employers, the Cuban X-Giants, Foster fanned 18 batters in winning the first game, 8–4, before allowing only two hits while leading the Phillies to a 4–2 victory in the decisive third contest.[4]

Before the beginning of the 1905 season, Foster and a number of his teammates played ball for the Royal Poinciana Hotel in Palm Beach, competing against leading white and black players. His second season with the Philadelphia Giants was still more successful, as the team compiled a 134–21–3 mark. Foster later claimed he won 51 games for what was perhaps one of the strongest black ball clubs ever. The Phillies lineup included future Hall of Fame first baseman Sol White, outfielder Pete Hill, and Foster, along with second baseman Charlie Grant, shortstop Home Run Johnson, third baseman Bill Monroe, and pitcher-right fielder Danny McClellan. The *Philadelphia Item* deemed the squad "the most remarkable batting aggregation of colored ball players ever gathered together." During the fall, Foster and three other Philadelphia Giants went to Cuba to join the Cuban X-Giants.[5]

Back in Philadelphia, the *Evening Telegraph* lauded Foster:

> If Andrew Foster had not been born with a dark skin, the great pitcher would wear an American or National League uniform. Rube Waddell, Cy Young, Mathewson, McGinnity and others are great twirlers in the big leagues and their praises have been sung from Maine to Texas. Foster has never been equalled [*sic*] in a pitcher's box.

Conveying agreement with that assessment, the *Indianapolis Freeman* exclaimed, "Andrew Foster deserves every word of praise ever said of him. He is undoubtedly among the very best pitchers that America affords."[6]

In 1906, the still potent Philadelphia Giants joined the short-lived International League of Independent Professional Ball Clubs, winning its third straight championship. H. Walter Schlichter, the white owner of the Giants, broached the idea of competing against a major league squad to decide "who can play base ball the best—the white or the black Americans." He also helped to organize the National Association of Colored Baseball Clubs of the United States and Cuba, which included leading black ball teams: his own, the Brooklyn Royal Giants, the Cuban Giants, and the Cuban Stars. One purpose was to prevent salaries from rising, but a number of ballplayers soon jumped ship, including black ball's greatest performer, Rube Foster. He again played winter ball in Cuba, leading the Fe ball club into a championship series against Almendares.

The next year Sol White, in his *History of Colored Base Ball*, called Foster "one of the best colored pitchers the game has produced." The book also spoke of Foster's performance in championship series and contained an essay by him, appropriately titled "How to Pitch." White offered a concluding analysis about black players who "possessed major league qualifications," naturally including Foster in the mix.[7]

Disgruntlement regarding attempts by Schlichter and other white owners to reduce expenses provided Foster with an opportunity to return to Chicago and induce various teammates to join in that venture. Calling for players to unite and "starve together," if need be, Foster led an exodus to the Leland Giants.[8] The black population in Chicago, concentrated on the city's South Side, was approaching 40,000 people and would soon experience explosive growth. Racism was not altogether absent in an era that experienced publication of Thomas Dixon's *The Clansman*, an ode to the Ku Klux Klan, and the creation of W.E.B. Du Bois' all-black civil rights organization, the Niagara Movement.

Having led his teams to four straight "colored world's championship" crowns, Foster retained his reputation as black ball's best pitcher. He became player-manager of the Leland Giants, having convinced star outfielder Pete Hill and several other Philadelphia Giants to move to Chicago. Prior to the start of the season, columnist John L. Footslug of the *Indianapolis Freeman* indicated that black Americans were more drawn now to "America's great game." But he bemoaned "the color line," the "barrier that is insurmountable," which kept top black players from competing in Organized Baseball. He suggested, "Today we have Foster … and a number of others who would be major-league stars if their color was not against them."[9]

The 1907 version of the Leland Giants performed brilliantly, with a 110–10 record that included 48 consecutive wins during one extended stretch, which involved competition against leading black teams and Chicago semipro units. In August, the Lelands took four out of six games from Mike Donlin's All-Stars, made up of several top major leaguers, with Foster starring. Several of the world champion White Sox came to watch Foster pitch and commented that while he possessed no style or motion, "his execution was fearful." The Leland Giants were proclaimed "the best organized semi-pro team in the world today."[10] Foster threw at least his fourth no-hitter, in defeating South Chicago to win the South Side championship. Large crowds often turned out to watch the Leland Giants and Foster, sometimes surpassing attendance at Chicago's Major League ballparks.

The off-season again witnessed efforts to form a National Colored Baseball League, with Foster among those supportive of such a design. The following summer led to his Leland Giants continuing to excel, winning 53 of 57 contests at one point. The sports editor of the *Detroit Free Press* insisted that several of the Leland Giants would be major leaguers but for racial discrimination, "notably among these … 'Rube' Foster … among the best pitchers in the world, barring nobody." That sportswriter also called Foster "the best known Colored man in the world today."[11] The *Indianapolis Freeman* termed Foster's club the Midwest's "biggest drawing card," which might well "break that strong barrier of race prejudice."[12]

In February 1909, Foster led the Leland Giants through the American South, seemingly the first such venture by a professional baseball team, whether black or white. The tour covered more than 4,000 miles, including crossing Texas, leading to games against the San Antonio Black Bronchos ace pitcher, Smokey Joe Williams. Large crowds frequently resulted, much of that attributed to Foster, said to be "without a doubt the most popular ball player in the country."[13]

The Giants topped off the 1909 season with series against the Cuban Stars and the St. Paul Gophers, before battling the powerful Chicago Cubs, who had just won 104 games in National League competition. The Cubs won all three games, albeit in hard-fought contests, with Foster, who was rebounding from a broken leg and an extended layoff, failing to hold a late 5–2 lead in the second game. Cubs manager Frank Chance deemed the black ace "the most finished product I've ever seen in the pitcher's box."[14]

An embittered power struggle resulted in Frank C. Leland's departure from the Leland Giants. While allowed to keep the title of the team Leland had founded, Foster scrambled to find another playing field because Leland's new team, the Chicago Giants, retained the lease at Auburn Park. Working with the attorney Beauregard Moseley, Foster acquired a lease to Normal Park and grabbed players from the Philadelphia Giants, including stars John Henry Lloyd and Home Run Johnson. Once again, Foster headed a team that was soon considered black ball's finest and its best-paid, pulling down collective $250 weekly salaries. With the 1910 season impending, Foster led another major barnstorming tour, this one covering almost 9,100 miles.

Foster also produced a long article, "Success of the Negro as a Ball Player," which appeared in the April 16 edition of the *Indianapolis Freeman*. The black ballplayer had experienced "great strides … in the past few years," Foster wrote. Yet the game's top African American pitcher-manager-administrator worried about black ball's disorganized nature and lack of business acumen. He was pleased that black players were performing fewer comedic antics as in days past and had become careful students of the sport. Consequently, "we have players who are classed with the best in the land." Even top white figures in Organized Baseball recognized this, repeatedly offering statements such as "too bad he is a colored man" and "if so and so was only a white man he would be in the big leagues." As for the players themselves, Foster sang their praises:

> Physically, mechanically or mentally speaking, the colored player has no superior. We have players at this time who can safely be classed with the highest types; and considering our resources for training and traveling in the business, I doubt if any of the big league stars could maintain the high playing standard and preserve their physical make-up to the extent that the colored player has, when you consider that he is compelled to ride in ill-ventilated cars and make long jumps, and is forced to put up with all sorts of inferior hotel accommodations, [and] usually [plays] exhibitions on diamond that are likened unto the proverbial corn fields.

Notwithstanding such difficulties, black ballplayers could compete against "the best in the land."[15]

After singling out black battery mates, those operating "in positions … considered the head and brains of all clubs," Foster insisted on the need for a "colored league," which he viewed as "absolutely necessary." Given the realities of baseball's segregated makeup, he urged "proper financial backing and encouragement" for black ball.[16] The accomplishments of black players, Foster and sportswriter David Wyatt both recognized, were being attested to by someone as noteworthy as former Representative Charles Phelps Taft, brother of President William Howard Taft. The owner of the Philadelphia Phillies, Charles Taft met with Foster, lauding his pitching prowess. Wyatt was hardly surprised, for black baseball demonstrated the participants' "moral and physical welfare" and appealed to "persons in all walks of life, who appreciate intelligence." Significantly, Wyatt continued, such individuals called into question "the time-worn color line and have openly declared the Negro baseball player the equal of the best and worthy of the same loyal consideration which has been shown the white players."[17]

The 1910 Leland Giants, a team Foster considered his finest, included the great player-manager, Pete Hill, John Henry Lloyd, Home Run Johnson, catcher Bruce Petway, and pitchers Frank Wickware, Pat Dougherty, and Bill Lindsay. Thomas I. Florence, "Sporting Editor" for the *Indianapolis Freeman*, termed Foster's squad "the greatest organization of Negro ball players that has ever been gathered together in this country." Going still further, he added, "They are the best all-around ball players in the world today, barring none."[18] Foster went 18–2–1, and Wickware 18–1, for a team that boasted a 123–6 record. Hill, Johnson, Lloyd, and Petway all batted around .400. John McGraw purportedly told Foster, "If I had a bucket of whitewash that wouldn't wash off, you wouldn't have five players left tomorrow."[19]

After the 1910 season, the Leland Giants traveled to Cuba, where they played top professional teams, before joining the locals for a series against the Detroit Tigers, who had won three consecutive American League titles from 1907 to 1909. The Tigers dominated but Petway twice threw Ty Cobb out at second base, and Lloyd, Johnson, and Petway outhit the AL batting champ.

During the winter, Foster joined with other black ball leaders in supporting the formation of a league of their own. Introduced as "the great Negro pitcher of international fame," Foster spoke at a gathering in Chicago, referring to black baseball's "ups and downs" while warning that "the time was ripe for organization without which the Negro would soon be regulated out of game entirely."[20] The call for a National League of Ball Players came to naught, but the latest endeavor helped to sustain Foster's determination to organize black baseball.

Notwithstanding Foster's fondness for his 1910 Leland Giants, his name became more associated with the team he now helped to found, the Chicago American Giants, one of black ball's legendary units. For over a decade, the American Giants would stand as the most important team in black baseball, and was frequently its very best. Foster employed "a race-horse brand of baseball" that came to be associated with the American Giants.[21] Sportswriters continued to extol his baseball genius, while depicting his team as equal to virtually any other, an analysis that appeared to be justified by the American Giants' performance against other black squads, top minor league teams, and major leaguers.

Joining with Foster in establishing his new team was John C. Schorling, a white bar owner who happened to be the son-in-law of Charles A. Comiskey, owner of the Chicago White Sox. The American Giants found a home at South Side Park, located at 39th and Wentworth Avenue, where the former grandstands and bleachers of the White Sox had been gutted. Schorling paid for a new playing field, able to accommodate 9,000 fans, with major league dimensions and majesty that led Foster to acclaim it "the finest semi-pro park in the world."[22] Although Comiskey sought to convince the Chicago American Giants magnates that they should avoid scheduling home games when the White Sox were in town, Foster refused to play heed. Fans paid 50 cents for admission and free ice water, and they flocked to watch black ball's most famous team, sometimes outnumbering crowds appearing at Chicago's Major League parks.

With its "fast-paced, thinking-man's brand of baseball," the Chicago American Giants became a dynasty, one that its manager and co-founder immodestly advertised as "The Greatest Aggregation of Colored Baseball Players in the World."[23] Like other top black ball teams, the American Giants toured extensively, heading across the South and then on to the Pacific Coast. Black newspapers heralded the American Giants' tour, as they captured the Palm Beach Hotel crown, won the Chicago city championship, and put together a 78–27 record in winning their first of four straight Western titles. Foster was unable to rehire Pete Booker, Home Run Johnson, or John Henry Lloyd, and another new team, the Lincoln Giants, proved formidable, with pitchers Cannonball Dick Redding and Smokey Joe Williams. But Bruce Petway and Pete Hill remained with Foster, whose American Giants also included left fielder Frank Duncan, right fielder Jap Payne, pitcher Frank Wickware, and second baseman Bill Monroe, Rube's old Philadelphia Giants teammate. The monthly payroll came to $1,500.

While his latest ball club proved an immediate success, Foster continued to worry about black ball's viability, perhaps because expenses continued to rise. Contributing another lengthy article to the *Indianapolis Freeman*, he worried about "the petty jealousy over prosperity ... that has sounded the death-knell of Negro baseball." Foster flung a number of accusations at Frank C. Leland and another former associate, Major R.R. Jackson. Although they had pilfered players from him, Foster continued, he had put together "the best colored club ever gotten together, the only club capable of measuring arms with big league clubs." But he emphasized again the need for *organization*, insisting that "enough good men" with sufficient capital could enable black baseball to flourish.[24]

In January 1912, Juli Jones, Jr., writing in the *Philadelphia Tribune*, bemoaned the continued presence of racial barriers facing black ballplayers. Winter ball in Cuba had long provided top black players from the United States, including Foster and many of his teammates, with the opportunity to compete against Cuban teams as well as minor and major leaguers. Now, after the drubbing the 1910 World Champion Philadelphia Athletics and other big league clubs had experienced on the Caribbean island, Organized Baseball magnates sought to prevent Foster and other black Americans from meeting up against white players. American League owners had already enacted such a ban in 1911. New York Giants skipper John McGraw went along with the prohibition, while expressing "the highest regard for the American colored player." McGraw indicated that "he would give anything in the world if Rube Foster was a white man."[25]

While pitching less frequently in 1912, when he put together an 8–4–1 record and remained a large drawing card, Foster led the American Giants, who won 112 of 132 games. He went head-to-head against the great Cuban pitcher, Jose Mendez, as the two lasted all 12 innings of a 2–2 tie. The American Giants later entered the four-team California Winter League, which included several major leaguers. Foster's team came out on top, then successfully barnstormed in the Midwest.

Writing in the February 15, 1913, edition of the *Indianapolis Freeman*, Billy Lewis again broached the idea of "a colored league." Noting the American Giants' recent triumphs in the California Winter League, Lewis indicated that sportswriters in California compared Foster's team favorably with the top major leaguers, including Ty Cobb and Christy Mathewson. The journalists contended "that those dusky knights of the diamond stood right in their class, and near about the head." Recognizing that Organized Baseball remained off-limits, Lewis argued for "the next best thing." New "colored leagues" would delight fans, both black and white.[26]

The American Giants continued barnstorming through the start of the new season in late April. During their lengthy excursion, plaudits poured forth. Following their defeat of the Portland Beavers, a sportswriter wrote, "Don't think for a moment that the American Giants, the colored ball players, do not understand the grand old game of baseball and, what is more to the point, understand how to play it." Another journalist offered, "Sakes alive, an, but them brunette gentlemen suttingly 'kin play baseball." Indeed, "if only they could be treated with a permanent whitewash" a white owner would sign them all, sweep to the Pacific Coast pennant, and then petition for entry into Organized Baseball.[27] Portus Baxter of the *Seattle Post-Intelligencer* discussed "Colored Giants a Wonderful Team," extolling Chicago's "colored wonders" who were unquestionably of major league quality.[28] The *Chicago Defender* particularly singled out Foster for praise, calling him "the greatest ball player and manager in the business and one of the greatest and headiest men in the business, white or black."[29]

The American Giants dropped a hard-fought series that summer against the New York Lincoln Giants, guided by player-manager John Henry Lloyd, center fielder Spot Poles, and pitchers Cannonball Dick Redding and Smokey Joe Williams. But the *Indianapolis Freeman* continued to laud Foster as "the best baseball manager in the country." It favored the holding of a banquet in his honor, for "no man in this baseball field has done more to uphold baseball sport among the colored people of this country than Mr. Foster."[30]

During the spring of 1914, the American Giants carried out another Western tour. Unhappy about the loss of the title of "the world's colored champions," Foster began raiding other top teams, including the Lincoln Giants. From that team alone, Foster snared John Henry Lloyd, Smokey Joe Williams, third sacker Billy Francis, left fielder Jude Gans, and pitcher Lee Wade. With returning veterans like Pete Hill and pitchers Pat Dougherty and Bill Lindsay, the American Giants, as the *Chicago Defender* saw matters, were "absolutely the best team of ball tossers that has ever been gathered together. They will be equal to any team in the big leagues."[31] The *Seattle Post-Intelligencer*'s Portus Baxter now called the American Giants "colored demons," and saluted Lloyd. "All that has been said and printed about Shortstop Lloyd … falls short of the truth. He is undoubtedly one of the greatest players ever seen on a ball field."[32]

In another article that appeared in the Seattle newspaper, Foster predicted that the Jim Crow barrier in Organized Baseball would soon come crashing down. The appearance of the new Federal League ensured that would occur, the new circuit having thinned the ranks of the Majors. That meant "the colored ranks" would quickly "be invaded … because there is no other way out of it." Cubans were now being admitted and "they'll let us in soon," Foster suggested. Then he predicted, "When they let the black men in, just watch how many present-day stars lose their positions." According to baseball experts, Foster indicated, five members of his own team were "as good as any big leaguer of the present day": Pat Dougherty, Pete Hill, John Henry Lloyd, Bruce Petway, and Smokey Joe Williams.[33]

The 1914 campaign proved to be another remarkably successful one for Rube Foster, with his American Giants powering their way to a 126–16 record. In September, the American Giants swept the Eastern champion Brooklyn Royal Giants to capture "the colored world's series." The *Indianapolis Freeman* saluted Foster yet again, terming him "the greatest baseball teacher-manager of the age. The race is proud of him and the sporting writers of all papers delight to write about his superior ability."[34] That winter, Foster led his squad to Havana and then readied for another tour out West. Before that excursion began, Foster agreed to an interview with the *Chicago Defender*'s George E. Mason. Calling the American Giants "the standard of colored baseball clubs," Mason praised Foster for paying the top salaries in black ball and for being the only manager to cover every payroll. Foster was also the first black ball administrator to guide his team through the South. And only his nattily attired ballplayers were transported in a private Pullman car.[35]

As the American Giants readied for the next season, the *Indianapolis Freeman*'s Billy Lewis reflected on Foster's teams. His players, Lewis insisted, "look to him as a child would to its parents." They enjoyed their uniforms, the best in "shadowball," and their private sleepers. They acted in the fashion Foster demanded, like gentlemen. His latest version of the American Giants stood as "the standard of colored base ball," while their boss had "brought more prominence to the race," in the arena of America's leading sport, than anyone else.[36] While Foster had lost John Henry Lloyd, he had added the slugging catcher Louis Santop, cleanup hitter Hurley McNair, pitcher Richard Whitworth, and three pitchers who were returning after some time away—Walter Ball, Big Bill Gatewood, and Frank Wickware.

In yet another Western loop, the American Giants battered the Portland Beavers' Stanley Coveleski, a future Hall of Famer. Roscoe Fawcett of the *Oregonian* labeled Foster "the black McGraw," as the American Giants continued their latest successful tour.[37] The 1915 season was marked by a controversial series with C.I. Taylor's Indianapolis ABCs and an explosive battle with the Cuban Stars. The American Giants later captured the California Winter League yet again, then failed to undertake a planned trip to Hawaii, but competed in the Cuban National League in the spring before playing games from Gulfport, Mississippi, to Seattle.

On April 10, 1916, Charles Crockett, writing in the *Indianapolis Freeman*, posed the issue Foster and other black ball luminaries had long grappled with: "Suppose We Had a Colored Baseball League?" Foster, Crockett conjectured, would unquestionably become president of such a circuit as "he will know more about who to select to look after these other cities than I do." Moreover, a black league would "make the game more popular with our boys, they would work harder, there would not be baseball going to waste." As Crockett saw matters, "many good 'Colored' boys" revered baseball but saw no means to make it a profession. But a league would allow people to "hear more about our stars," to "know more about them." And "there would be more money in the game for us." Everyone would benefit: players, administrators, and fans.[38]

Having put the previous, somewhat disappointing season behind him, Foster considered the 1916 American Giants to be stronger still. John Henry Lloyd and Jude Gans had returned to the team late during the previous campaign, joining catcher Bruce Petway, infielders Leroy Grant, Harry Bauchman, and Billy Francis, along with outfielders Pete Hill and Frank Duncan, with Jess Barber soon in the lineup too. The top pitchers were Tom Johnson, Richard Whitworth, Frank Wickware, and an aged but still effective Rube Foster. Writing for the *Chicago Defender*, Mr. Fan predicted that "the Giants would make the Chicago White Sox look like a bunch of bush leaguers."[39] The preseason travels of the American Giants spanned 20,000 miles and produced a 57–15 mark. Six thousand fans showed up for opening day, and other games garnered sizable crowds. In August, the American Giants regained "the colored world championship," having defeated the New York Lincoln Stars. They later also bested their nemesis, the Indianapolis ABCs, in another series that reputedly entitled them to be proclaimed black ball champs. The *Chicago Defender* offered a photograph of Rube Foster with the accompanying caption: "Brainiest Man in Baseball…. Who Did More to Put Chicago on the Baseball Map than the Big League Teams."[40] In early October, the American Giants whipped the multi-racial All Nations, who were based in Kansas City, Missouri, and boasted the stellar pitchers John Donaldson and Jose Mendez. At different points, White Sox stars Joe Jackson, Ray Schalk, Ed Walsh, and Buck Weaver sat in attendance, watching the American Giants in action.

The American Giants competed against the Indianapolis ABCs in yet another round of the series designed to decide "the colored championship of the world." Controversy swirled about the series, as often proved the case when the two teams met, and a forfeit victory was among the handful apparently enabling the ABCs to prevail in the nine-game series. Even that result was contested, with a leading sportswriter and Foster both challenging the notion that the American Giants' skein of Western titles had come to an end. After heralding the ABCs as "a wonderful ball club" with tremendous courage, Foster reflected on himself: "I have been the recipient of many honors in baseball the past twenty-two years; have received many demonstrations from fans of all races, have tasted the joy of wonderful achievements … but in my life never have I felt so happy as at the close of the last game, when the fans rushed on the diamond and asked to shake my hand. I felt even greater in defeat."[41] The *Indianapolis Freeman*, which had long praised Foster, now contained a cartoon displaying "The Rube," sporting a bandit mask and a pistol on which was etched "BLUFF," and was directed at the ABCs' manager, C.I. Taylor. Words coming out Foster's mouth read, "Hand me that grip," in reference to a suitcase tagged "World's Colored Championship." Taylor refused: "I will not, it's mine." The title of the cartoon was "AN ATTEMPTED HOLDUP."[42]

Putting behind the two most recent seasons, which effectively ended Foster's long run as an instrumental force on teams that could be considered the "world's colored champions," the great Chicago American Giant was about to begin another long run at the top of black ball. In the process, he cemented his reputation as the most important figure in black baseball, one who could be favorably compared with Connie Mack and John McGraw.

Meanwhile, David Wyatt of the *Indianapolis Freeman* provided information about plans to establish "a colored baseball league," headed by an unnamed "Moses" determined "to lead the baseball children out of the wilderness." The league was to be run by African Americans who would, at a minimum, have "complete control of their grounds." White entrepreneurs, Wyatt charged, had dismissed the possibility of such a league, intending to garner larger profits "through methods that degrade and make beggars and make bums of the athletes and then blind the public with the immoral aspect of the players." Wyatt did point to one area of great concern for fans of baseball, the most statistically conscious major sport. The dearth of reliable black ball statistics, Wyatt pointed out, denied players their "most valuable possession." It also ensured that "a verifiable, historical record" was absent, something that would "haunt veterans of black baseball."[43]

The American Giants spent the winter traveling through the South into Texas, again winning the Palm Beach championship in the process. Beginning their regular season on Chicago's South Side, the American Giants appeared still more potent, with Bruce Petway catching; an infield made up of Leroy Grant, Bingo DeMoss, Billy Francis, and John Henry Lloyd; and outfielders Frank Duncan, Pete Hill, and Jess Barber. Batting averages plummeted during that deadball season, perhaps as baseballs were wound differently due to wartime constraints, while Cannonball Dick Redding and Tom Williams shone on the pitching mound. David Wyatt reported that boisterous crowds as large as 15,000—many fans "howling" and "raving"—appeared at Schorling Park to watch the hometown American Giants.[44] This time, Chicago easily won the season series against the Indianapolis ABCs, and they also prevailed against a number of white semipro squads that featured ex–big leaguers.

Once again, Organized Baseball magnates sought to preclude their players from competing against black ball participants. David Wyatt warned against the too-ready praise heaped on black players, which he believed only kept "the Negro athlete down in the rut" and undoubtedly enraged American League president Ban Johnson and other major and minor league leaders. Foolish comparisons, Wyatt charged, had led the National Commission to prohibit major league teams from barnstorming. He now worried that black players and semipro teams might be excluded from big league stadiums.[45]

The 1917 season unfolded during the first months that the United States was an official combatant in World War I. But large crowds continued to show up to watch black ball's most famous team, including a shutout of the Central League Stars, an array of white ballplayers. After losing to the American Giants, Indianapolis ABCs manager C.I. Taylor acknowledged, "Rube Foster has the greatest Colored aggregation in the business, and every true sport ought to give him praise…. Foster's club is truly the World's Colored Champions for 1917….All honor to him and his magnificent ball club."[46] The American Giants had indeed beaten an array of the top black teams, while going 17–4-2 in head-to-head matches against the ABCs.

Foster predicted that the next year would prove "the greatest … in Colored baseball." But the First World War threatened black ball as it did the major and minor leagues.[47] Many players were draft-eligible, and a 10 percent surcharge would be tacked on to ticket prices at sporting venues. The American Giants captured the Palm Beach championship and beat a number of top Southern teams, but soon lost pitchers Tom Johnson and Cannonball Dick Redding to the draft, pitcher Tom Williams to a drunken spree, and peerless shortstop John Henry Lloyd because of his failure to show up for the Palm Beach games. The American Giants met the 86th Division team from Camp Grant, comprised of big leaguers, and the Fairbanks-Morse Beloits, a franchise also featuring major leaguers. More American Giants were drafted, including Jude Gans, Leroy Grant, and Frank Wickware, as the decimated team faced its usual complement of opponents but also leading semipro nines. Having dropped a doubleheader to the Beloit squad, the American Giants swept a rematch that included a game against right-hander Dickey Kerr, soon to shine with the Chicago White Sox. In a third doubleheader, which Foster's team lost, it had to face a roster that temporarily included White Sox star third baseman Buck Weaver. The American Giants proceeded to win a series against an all-star team with a number of ex-minor and major leaguers. The *Chicago Defender* did indicate that recent setbacks experienced by the American Giants underscored the paucity of top-flight pitchers outside Organized Baseball. On the other hand, Foster's team cobbled together a 77–27 record, compelling the *Defender* to proclaim him "a leader of great ability."

That leading black newspaper felt it necessary to favorably analyze Foster, whom it called "a genius," yet again:

> Those who meet Foster with that everyday pleasant smile do not know that he does more work in one season than all the Colored managers combined. First he has the White Sox within four blocks of him as a competitor, which in itself is some task to compete with, yet his following is so great we do not know the Sox are here so far as a handicap to him. He has to book all attractions for the Giants, arrange the dates for all the other big cities, often financing them; also arranging it so that they will be able to continue in the game; has to superintend the American Giants [*sic*] park, and many times when the Giants are in need of his advice he is sent for to straighten out some dissatisfied patron or to help keep the crowds back, yet manage and direct the Giants. Even with all this on his shoulders he is the most successful Colored man in baseball, the only one that has made it a business.[48]

The *Chicago Defender* also praised Foster's system, "Rube Ball," which he had total control of, from signing players to devising a schedule.[49] Indeed, despite losing a number of top players and releasing John Henry Lloyd, Foster still molded a powerhouse. He too credited his system, which had been perfected. It had enabled him to create his own dynasty that ran from the Leland Giants through the Chicago American Giants. His championship success went back still further, all the way to Foster's starring role with both the Cuban X-Giants and the Philadelphia Giants. He had won over 225 games as black ball's finest pitcher, had thrown a minimum of four no-hitters, and at one point triumphed in six straight "colored world championship" contests. He had done well in the Cuban winter leagues, compiling a stronger mark—18–11—than either Frank Wickware or Smokey Joe Williams. His 170 wins in black baseball and the Cuban League bettered the official victory total of both William Foster, the top left-hander who was his half-brother, and the legendary Satchel Paige.[50]

Still more remarkable was his leadership of both the Leland Giants and the Chicago American Giants, who competed for the "colored world championship" year after year. They also toured widely, from Cuba to the West Coast, often playing ball against top minor and major leaguers, while at least holding their own. Foster's American Giants did so in style as well, garnering the highest salaries in black ball, sporting the sharpest uniforms, riding in Pullmans, and residing, however temporarily, in first-rate hotels. All of these occurred under the partnership of Foster and owner John Schorling, the two having such faith in one another that no contract was ever signed. As David Malarcher, who later succeeded Foster as the Giants' skipper, indicated, the acclaim and stability of the Chicago franchise helped to sustain other black teams and independent squads too. "The American Giants were the greatest attraction on the road, and Chicago, the greatest drawing city when at home."[51] All the while, Foster honed his ball club, while trying to shield his players from Jim Crow practices.

More and more, even former competitors and players on other teams applauded that figure's baseball acumen, his reliance on "Rube Ball." Frank Forbes called him both "a mastermind" and "a thieving son of a bitch," who had his playing field doused so his American Giants could drop down bunt after bunt. He also employed frozen baseballs to diminish the potency of opposing sluggers like Louis Santop.[52] In the words of David Malarcher, Foster employed "scientific baseball."[53] Former Leland Giant Arthur Hardy called Foster "a natural psychologist" and "a strict disciplinarian."[54]

Notwithstanding the American Giants' marked success, black ball's commercial viability remained in question, leading F.C. Lane, editor of *Baseball Magazine*, to pose the question in an article devised prior to Armistice, "Where, or where, have the colored ball clubs gone?" Lane asked, "What has become of the dusky entertainers whose antics—and genuine playing skill—erstwhile sent thrills of joy through the breasts of both white and negro gatherings?" He worried particularly because black teams "played some of the best ball anyone could ask to see." The top ball clubs, Lane declared, "had attained eminent distinction." The finest of "the agile coons," he wrote, "have been as good as their white rivals."[55]

In fact, the leading black teams, including the Chicago American Giants, appeared to be in reasonably good shape as the war came to an end. Like their counterparts in Organized Baseball, the American Giants eagerly anticipated the return of players who had gone overseas. And baseball, both in the Major Leagues and in black ball, would thrive with attendance much enhanced during the 1919 season. Black and white players continued to compete against one another in barnstorming and semi-pro contests. The racial animus that tainted the era had hardly diminished, notwithstanding the service performed by black soldiers and workers alike during the period of U.S. engagement in World War I. Thus, cries of "Nigger!" "Coon!" and "Monkey!" rippled across baseball parks.[56]

After nearly two decades of competing at black ball's highest levels, Rube Foster remained relegated to a Jim Crow version of the sport he revered. Through first the Leland Giants and then the American Giants, he had helped to make Chicago the centerpiece of black ball. Since his arrival over a decade earlier, the city had undergone remarkable alterations, a number of which proved troubling to many. As part of an exodus out of a seemingly ever-more hostile South, blacks had migrated in large numbers to a number of Eastern and Midwestern cities, including Chicago. More opportunities beckoned in the form of jobs and schooling, but the reception was not altogether welcoming. While whites-only mandates were less frequently encountered, de facto segregation was plentiful. Still, blacks continued arriving in Chicago, with 110,000 calling the city their home by the end of the decade. Most resided in the city's South Side, including the Black Belt where jazz artistry and sporting houses could both be found, to the chagrin of the great black leader, Booker T. Washington. The *Chicago Whip*, a militant black newspaper, viewed the area differently, deemed it an urban "Bohemia of the Colored folks," a "Mecca for Pleasure."[57] Some came, spurred on by recruiters, who included Robert S. Abbott of the *Chicago Defender*, one of the nation's foremost African American newspapers. Abbott's paper was also a stalwart supporter and champion of both Rube Foster and black ball. Newspapermen like Abbott and baseball moguls such as Foster were part of Chicago's vibrant black middle class, which including politicians, ministers, and business operators. Leaders of the black community helped trigger a protest that led to the banning of D.W. Griffith's cinematic adaptation of the novel, *The Clansman*, by Thomas Dixon, *The Birth of a Nation*.

Notwithstanding contrasting images about the city they were migrating to, Southern blacks could well encounter a host of problems, with good jobs scarce, severe housing shortages, sharp rent increases, and pervasive racism and discrimination. Historian Thomas Philpott contends that segregation in Chicago was more severe than in the American South.

The *Chicago Tribune* spread tales about the "peril" of diseases like tuberculosis being transmitted by the new arrivals and insisted African Americans exhibited "almost no standard of morals."[58] During the summer of 1917, scores of bombs were hurled at houses where blacks resided, while white gangs and athletic clubs promised to keep blacks away from various parks or neighborhoods.

Amid all of this, Rube Foster continued to serve as an exemplar for black Americans, as the Chicago-based publication, *Half-Century Magazine*, underscored in a lengthy treatment in March 1919. Termed "the greatest Colored athlete of his day," Foster was deemed a brilliantly skillful pitcher, a similarly successful manager, and an administrator who had wholly transformed black baseball.[59] With such plaudits only recently delivered, Foster got together with his former star player Pete Hill, now manager of the Detroit Stars, to shape another strong black ball club that could provide a nucleus for the league he continued to envision. A number of American Giants moved over to the Stars, including Frank Duncan, Bruce Petway, Frank Wickware, and first baseman Edgar Wesley, soon joined by fireballer John Donaldson. "The Big Chief," as Foster was known, retained several veterans from his latest championship lineup but also added a number of new players.[60] Particularly noteworthy was the addition of outfielders Oscar Charleston and Cristobal Torriente, two of the greatest all-around black players of the era. Hill, who had been the Giants' captain for over a decade, was supplanted in that role by second baseman Bingo DeMoss.

Schorling Park was expanded to accommodate crowds as large as 20,000. Impressive attendance figures led the *Chicago Defender* to assert that "the drawing powers of the American Giants are greater than any other team in semi-pro baseball," and to proclaim Chicago "the best baseball city in the world."[61] Enthusiastic crowds cheered as the American Giants again shone on the baseball diamond during a month-long stay in Detroit, where Foster's team wrestled with the Stars in front of "the largest crowds that ever witnessed semi-pro games."[62] Despite the loss of their home field advantage, the Giants captured the western title by beating Detroit eight out of 14 times.

That occurred as racial unrest beset the city of Chicago, where tensions were exacerbated by a vying for space—occupational, residential, and recreational—only months after the end of U.S. involvement in World War I. During the summer of 1919, blacks were again assaulted in public venues, with white mobs hunting down and killing African Americans. A "bomb war," the *Chicago Whip* charged, was raining down on black residents.[63] In late July, a race riot erupted alongside Lake Michigan. Bloodletting went on for five days, culminating in 38 deaths, around 500 wounded, and hundreds of homeless. When Governor Frank Lowden proposed a multiracial committee to ascertain how "racial segregation" might be made more acceptable, the *Chicago Whip* responded with fury. It denounced "separation or segregation" altogether, refusing to accept treatment that stigmatized blacks as inferior or stymied their development and happiness. The *Chicago Whip* called for new black leaders, in the fashion of "the new Negro" recently extolled by A. Philip Randolph and Chandler Owen in their publication, *The Messenger*. W.E.B. Du Bois of the NAACP praised those who refused to cower in the face of white vigilantes, while the organization's Walter F. White warned that no American city was as beset by "political trickery, chicanery and exploitation." The *Chicago Whip* saluted the New Negro, who "wants to be treated as a man and consideration on the basis of merit and citizenship. The New Negro is disgusted with lynching and mob violence. He believes in defending his life and his home and all other sacred institutions."[64]

The sheer viciousness of the Chicago race riot no doubt appalled Rube Foster, who must have been saddened by the slow pace of change. He had confronted Jim Crow barriers his entire life, from his early years in southeast Texas to his extended stays in New Jersey, Philadelphia, and Chicago. Organized Baseball's segregated nature kept him and other stellar players, managers, and administrators, no matter their skill level, out of the minor and major leagues. This was perhaps saddest of all, for Foster was a genuine triple-threat. Having been black ball's greatest pitcher, he became its finest manager and then its most innovative administrator. He competed whenever possible against top white players and teams, personally performing at a high level and ensuring that his teams did as well.

The latest racial conflagration in Chicago must have cemented Foster's determination to establish a black baseball league, something he predicted just before the summer 1919 eruptions. "We will have the circuit at last," he prophesied on July 2, 1919.[65] *Chicago Defender* columnist Cary B. Lewis indicated that fall "a circuit of western clubs" loomed. That appeared inevitable given that the just wrapped up baseball season had been "so prosperous" with such loyal fans and substantial attendance that "a colored league" appeared to beckon. Foster was "the man responsible," having dreamed "for years to see men of his Race have a circuit of their own."[66]

Delivering his own missives, Foster insisted that prosperity would elude black owners and players "until they are organized." He wrote that black ball participants required "a very strong leader" with "able lieutenants" and the public's confidence. Now, Foster stated, it was necessary to turn to "tried" leadership and away from the disgraceful nature of present black ball.[67]

Foster also assailed the propensity of owners of black ball clubs to raid players from other teams and called for something akin to the reserve clause in Organized Baseball, with teams able to retain their own collection of ballplayers. He believed the practice was so egregious that "managers do not trust players, nor do the players trust the managers." Foster, of course, was delivering such warnings, notwithstanding his willingness to pirate players from other teams whenever the need or opportunity arose. In late December 1919, the American Giants leader proclaimed:

> This will be the last time I will ever try and interest Colored club owners to get together on some working basis. I have so often been refused the necessary capital, not desiring to give to others the chance of monopolizing Colored baseball, but they are not going to continue to wait on me with their money. They can do so and leave me where I am. I have made the effort; it's now up to the ones that expect to permanently figure in baseball to get together.[68]

Both the *Indianapolis Freeman's* Charles Marshall and Indianapolis ABCs manager C.I. Taylor backed the establishment of a black league. Marshall wrote, "Organized baseball is on and Andrew (Rube) Foster is at the helm. Or, we might say that this great captain of the national game has started the ball to roll…. I think the forming of a Colored baseball league may be the outcome." C.I. Taylor had fired off a letter to his arch-rival, acknowledging, "You are the man of the hour to strike the blow which will weld into one harmonious organization, the colored clubs of this country." Taylor praised Foster highly: "I say in view of your superior knowledge, executive ability and thorough knowledge of baseball, your national reputation as the greatest organizer the game has produced coupled with the confidence of the baseball public throughout the country would have in an organization headed by your self, you are particularly fitted to set this wheel in motion."

The *Chicago Defender*, in its February 7, 1920, edition, revealed that the long-hoped-for gathering of black ball leaders would soon take place in Kansas City, Missouri. No figure had been more desirous of such a meeting "than the Chicago 'chief.'" The initial session occurred on February 13, with Foster elected "temporary president," who the *Indianapolis Freeman* suggested had "more at stake than any fifty men in baseball that could be named." Foster now asserted, "Gentlemen, the assets of the baseball club which I represent is more than all the Negro baseball clubs in existence, still if it pleases you I am willing to throw all these assets upon the mercy of the decision of this body of newspaper men who are present." The plan called for league play to begin in April 1921. Careful thought was given to creating balance in the nascent circuit, soon to be called the Negro National League, but Foster made sure that his American Giants remained formidable.[69]

In a lengthy piece in the *Competitor* discussing the new league, Ira F. Lewis called particular attention to Foster's role:

> And to his undying credit let it be said that he has made the biggest sacrifice of anyone. For be it known that his position in the world of colored baseball was reasonably secure, inasmuch as he controlled the situation pretty much not only in Chicago, where baseball is the fourth meal of the day, but in the Middle West. With ideal park location, and supported by unlimited backing both in money and patronage, Mr. Foster could have defied organization for many years. But, happily, he has seen the light,—the light of wisdom and the spirit of service to the public. From now on he will begin to be the really big man in baseball, he should be, by virtue of his knowledge of the game from both the playing and business ends.

At the same time, Lewis pointed to the need to develop new talent, young players who could become "Petways, Grants, Hills, Reddings, Williams, Charlestons, Taylors."[70]

In the *Freeman*, Charles Marshall looked forward to salary caps, a playing schedule, regular admission prices, and "professional major league ball playing … not outlaw or semi-professional" baseball. Marshall was most pleased about Foster's selection as league president: "This wily old master of the great game is best suited for guiding the organization safely past all of the pitfalls and loopholes that it is certain to encounter in baseball."[71] The eight-team Negro National League actually began operations on May 1, 1920. Foster continued to lay the foundation for the NNL, whose motto was "We Are the Ship, All Else the Sea."[72]

In the league's inaugural season, the American Giants thoroughly outclassed the competition, purportedly smashing attendance marks in Detroit, Kansas City, Indianapolis, and St. Louis. Approximately 200,000 fans showed up at Schorling Park to watch Chicago and its top stars: pitchers Dave Brown and Tom Williams, Dave Malarcher, and Cristobal Torriente, the batting champion. The American Giants also conducted a Southern loop starting in late September.

Rube Foster's team would capture the first three Negro National League championships before experiencing something of a slide, perhaps induced by the slackening skills of several of the American Giants and the manager's surfeit of responsibilities. He had been instrumentally involved with 16 black ball title holders in the span of 21 years, the last 11 attained with the Leland Giants and the Chicago American Giants. Foster emphasized the need for black ball to be both "a profession" and "a business," which required rigorous training and planning.[73]

By 1923, Foster was attempting to ward off a perceived threat from the new Eastern Colored League, dominated by Nat Strong. His team came in third behind both the Kansas City Monarchs and the Detroit Stars, and they finished runner-up to the Monarchs the following season. That campaign was difficult in other ways, as mounting criticism came his way, along with calls for his departure from the league presidency. His sportsmanship was questioned, as was his supposed determination to manipulate umpires and enable "his gang of roughnecks" to operate at will. His drive to win no matter the costs, the *Kansas City Call* charged, was "killing the organization which he heads."[74] On the other hand, Foster got Edward Bolden of the Eastern Colored League to agree to a world championship match pitting the winners of the new circuits. David Malarcher noted how proud Foster was of that accomplishment, which "really put him in the category of Ban Johnson and Judge Landis."[75] The initial championship series saw the Monarchs nip the Hilldale Daisies. The two teams met again the following year, with the result reversed, much to Foster's chagrin.

That year proved trying for Foster, whose American Giants were playing good, but not spectacular ball, when in late May he was nearly asphyxiated in a rooming house in Indianapolis. Carbon monoxide poisoning possibly resulted, leading to brain damage. Mental deterioration clearly set in, and the 1926 season saw Foster depart as the Chicago manager and Negro National League president. After a psychotic episode, Foster was declared insane and committed to the Kankakee Asylum. Fifty-one-year-old Rube Foster died at the sanitarium on December 9, 1930.

From the period of his forced early retirement from the game he revered, Foster was included in discussions regarding the finest black ball performers. Black baseball competitors invariably selected Foster as among its greatest pitchers and its finest manager and administrator. Months before his death, the *Chicago Defender* offered a photo of Foster, titled "The Greatest," and captioned as follows:

> He was the greatest pitcher our Race has ever known. He ranked with Cy Young, Christy Mathewson, Joe McGinnity, and other greats. He was a master mind of baseball and was ranked by the daily newspapermen as one of the three greatest managers of the country. The other two were John McGraw of the New York Nationals and Connie Mack of the world champion Philadelphia American leaguers. Foster was also the brains and the founder of the Negro National Baseball League, and it was due to his long hours and hard work plus the worry of running the league that caused him to lose his health.[76]

A mere few weeks before Foster died, Frank A. Young of the *Chicago Defender* discussed "The Master Mind of Baseball." Young placed Foster alongside Connie Mack and John McGraw "in a class by themselves." As Young noted, "No other living human, unless perhaps … Babe Ruth, has been able to have devoted to him the amount of daily newspaper space that was once given Rube Foster."[77] On Foster's passing, the *Chicago Defender* asserted that "Andrew 'Rube' Foster, the master mind of baseball, perhaps the most colorful figure the game has ever known, was called out by Umpire Father Time."[78] Thousands paid homage as Foster's body lay in state.

Nevertheless, with the passage of time, Foster's legend faded, although occasionally analysts would recall his oversized impact on black baseball. By the 1960s, in keeping with Ted Williams' admonition during his induction ceremony to the National Baseball Hall of Fame, talk of Foster's inclusion could be heard. Robert Peterson's epochal *Only the Ball Was White*, published in 1970, offered a full chapter on "Rube from Texas." Peterson wrote, "If the talents of Christy Mathewson, John McGraw, Ban Johnson, and Judge Kenesaw Mountain Landis were combined in a single body, and that body were enveloped in a black skin, the result would have to be named Andrew (Rube) Foster."[79] But while Satchel Paige became the first longtime Negro Leaguer admitted into the Hall of Fame, it took another decade before Foster was selected, despite being, as Peterson called him, "the most impressive figure in Negro baseball history." At the time of his induction in the summer of 1981, baseball chronicler John B. Holway termed the black ball giant "The Father of Black Baseball."[80]

No single individual proved more instrumental in ensuring the viability of black ball, its maintenance, and eventual flourishing, essential before Organized Baseball opened its doors to a trickle of African American players. Rube Foster's vision, determination, and persistence enabled the black version of America's national pastime to continue during a good portion of the Jim Crow era. His successes and those of his compatriots on the playing field served as a rebuke to those who absurdly contended that blacks were unable to compete against white counterparts. The tragedy remains, nevertheless, that so many careers of some of the finest players, managers, and administrators to grace American baseball diamonds remain forgotten or little remembered. During the first decades of the 20th century, Foster battled against racial stereotypes and stigmas, doing so with considerable grace and courage, while serving as a model and mentor for other black ball giants.

Notes

1. To date, there are four book-length biographies of Andrew "Rube" Foster: Charles E. Whitehead's *A Man and His Diamonds* (New York: Vantage Press, 1980); my book, *The Best Pitcher in Baseball: The Life of Rube Foster, Negro League Giant* (New York: New York University Press, 2001); Phil S. Dixon's, *Andrew "Rube" Foster: A Harvest on Freedom's Fields* (La Vergne, TM: Xlibris, 2010); and Larry Lester's *Rube Foster in His Time: On the Field and in the Papers with Black Baseball's Greatest Visionary* (Jefferson, NC: McFarland, 2012). My *Blackball, the Black Sox and the Babe: Baseball's Crucial 1920 Season* (Jefferson, NC: McFarland, 2002) is a collective biography of four seminal figures, including Foster.

2. Howard A. Phelps, "Andrew 'Rube' Foster," *The Half-Century Magazine* (March 1, 1919): 8; Peterson, *Only the Ball Was White*, 105; *Chicago Tribune*, May 4, 1902; *St. Paul Appeal*, June 14, 1902.

3. Peterson, *Only the Ball Was White*, 105; Gary Ashwill, "Rube vs. Rube."

4. "Phila. Giants Victors," *Philadelphia Record*, September 2, 1904; "Colored Championship," *Philadelphia Record*, September 4, 1904.

5. "The most remarkable batting aggregation …" *Philadelphia Item*, May 26, 1905, 2.

6. "Base Ball," *Philadelphia Item*, October 28, 1905, 7; Cuban X-Giants-All Cubans' box score, *Philadelphia Item*, October 28, 1905, 7.

7. White, *History of Colored Base Ball*, 55–57; Andrew Foster, "How to Pitch," in White, *History of Colored Base Ball*, 96, 99.

8. George E. Mason, "Rube Foster Chats about His Career," *Chicago Defender*, February 20, 1915, 9.

9. John L. Footslug, "In the World of Sport," *Indianapolis Freeman*, April 27, 1907, 7; Footslug, "In the World of Sport," *Indianapolis Freeman*, August 31, 1907, 7.

10. Charles Dryden, "Leland Giants Drub All Stars," *Chicago Tribune*, August 28, 1907, 6.

11. Phelps, "Andrew 'Rube' Foster," 8.

12. "Champion Leland Giants to Go South for Spring Training," *Indianapolis Freeman*, February 20, 1909, 7.

13. "Leland Giants Complete a Successful Southern Trip," *Indianapolis Freeman*, May 15, 1909, 7.

14. "Former World's Champions Defeat Leland Giants," *Indianapolis Freeman*, October 16, 1909, 4; "Cubs Beat Leland Giants 4–1," *Chicago Tribune*, October 19, 1909, 8; "Cubs' Rally Beats Leland Giants," *Chicago Tribune*, October 22, 1908, 12.

15. Rube Foster, "Success of the Negro as a Ball Player," *Indianapolis Freeman*, April 16, 1910, supplement, 9.

16. *Ibid.*

17. David Wyatt, "Season 1910 To Be Banner," *Indianapolis Freeman*, April 16, 1910, supplement, 10.

18. Thomas I. Florence, "Who I Think Will Win the Championship," *Indianapolis Freeman*, April 16, 1910, supplement, 10.

19. Billy Lewis, "The American Giants!" *Indianapolis Freeman*, March 8, 1915, 7.

20. Rube Foster, "Pitfalls of Baseball," *Chicago Defender*, December 13, 1919, 11; Harold C. McGath, "In the Field of Sport," *Indianapolis Freeman*, January 14, 1911, 7.

21. Cottrell, *The Best Pitcher in Baseball*, 62.

22. Rube Foster, "Negro Base Ball," *Indianapolis Freeman*, December 23, 1911, 16.

23. Cottrell, *The Best Pitcher in Baseball*, 63; Clark and Lester, *The Negro Leagues Book*, 21.

24. Foster, "Negro Base Ball," 16.

25. Juli Jones, Jr., "Baseball in Cuba," *Philadelphia Tribune*, January 27, 1912, 7.

26. Billy Lewis, "Baseball Is now the Subject," *Indianapolis Freeman*, February 15, 1913, 7.

27. Billy Lewis, "The American Giants Getting Recognition," *Indianapolis Freeman*, April 12, 1913, 7.

28. Portus Baxter, "Colored Giants a Wonderful Team," *Seattle Post-Intelligencer*, April 3, 1913, 11; Baxter, "Colorful Phenoms Bat out Victory," *Seattle Post-Intelligencer*, April 6, 1913, part 4, 11.

29. Local Sports," *Chicago Defender*, April 26, 1913, 8.

30. "Americans Win," *Indianapolis Freeman*, August 30, 1913, 4; "The Foster Banquet," *Indianapolis Freeman*, August 30, 1913, 4.

31. "The Sporting World," *Chicago Defender*, March 21, 1914, 6.

32. Portus Baxter, "Colored Demons Play Here Today," *Seattle Post-Intelligencer*, April 3, 1914, 11; Baxter, "Seattle Loses a Great Game to a Great Team," *Seattle Post-Intelligencer*, April 4, 1914, 11; Baxter, "Two Giant Teams Will Battle this Afternoon," *Seattle Post-Intelligencer*, April 5, 1914, part 3, 1.

33. Royal Brougham, "'Rube' Thinks Black Men Will Play in Big Leagues," *Seattle Post-Intelligencer*, April 5, 1914, part 3, 1.

34. "'Rube' Foster Praised," *Indianapolis Freeman*, September 26, 1914, 1

35. George E. Mason, "Rube Foster Chats about His Career," *Chicago Defender*, February 20, 1915, 9.

36. Billy Lewis, "The American Giants!" 7.

37. Roscoe Fawcett, "Beavers Stronger, Says Rube Foster," *Oregonian*, April 2, 1915, 14.

38. Charles Crockett, "Suppose We Had a Colored Baseball League?" *Indianapolis Freeman*, April 22, 1916, 7.

39. Mr. Fan, "Rube Foster in Come Back Role," *Chicago Defender*, May 20, 1916, 7.

40. Andrew Rube Foster," *Chicago Defender*, September 6, 1916, 6.

41. Rube Foster, "Rube Wants Championship without Fighting for It," *Indianapolis* Freeman, November 11, 1916, 7.

42. *Ibid*.; J. R. Warren cartoon, "An Attempted Hold-Up," *Indianapolis Freeman*, December 2, 1916, 7.

43. David Wyatt, "The Annual 'Chestnut' Negro Base Ball League," *Indianapolis Freeman*, January 27, 1917, 7; David Wyatt, "Base Ball!" *Indianapolis Freeman*, March 3, 1917, 7.

44. David Wyatt, "Base Ball!" *Indianapolis Freeman*, June 16, 1917, 7.

45. *Ibid*.

46. C. I. Taylor to the Sporting Editor of the *Indianapolis Freeman*, September 29, 1917, 7.

47. Rube Foster, "The Season of 1917 Closes. Rube Foster Makes an Observation. The Status of the A.B.C.s of Indianapolis," *Indianapolis Freeman*, October 20, 1917, 7.

48. "Influenza Epidemic Closes Baseball Season for American Giants," *Chicago Defender*, November 2, 1918, 9.

49. "Rube Foster," *Chicago Defender*, November 2, 1918, 9.

50. Cottrell, *The Best Pitcher in Baseball*, 120–121. Larry Lester contends that Foster's record in black ball was 191–60, with a 1.82 E.R.A., including four no-hitters with the Philadelphia Giants and three with the Leland Giants.

51. David Malarcher to Robert Peterson, December 16, 1968, 1, Malarcher Ashland Collection File, National Baseball Library, Cooperstown, New York; Malarcher notes from tape, n.d., 8, Malarcher Ashland Collection File.

52. John Holway, *Blackball Stars: Negro League Players* (New York: Carroll & Graf, 1992), 18.

53. Robert Gardner and Dennis Shortelle, *The Forgotten Players: The Story of Black Baseball in America* (New York: Walker, 1993), 2.

54. Peterson, *Only the Ball Was White*, 109–110.

55. F. C. Lane, "The Colored Clubs," *Baseball Magazine* (December 1918): 117.

56. Cottrell, *The Best Pitcher in Baseball*, 128.

57. *Ibid*., 130.

58. *Ibid*., 131.

59. Phelps, "Andrew 'Rube' Foster," 8.

60. "Giants' Recruits Work Hard," *Chicago Defender*, April 5, 1919, 11.

61. "Foster Asks Patience," *Chicago Defender*, April 19, 1919, 11; "Giants' Seating Capacity Enlarged," *Chicago Defender*, June 7, 1919, 11.

62. "All Chicago to Welcome American Giants Sunday," *Chicago Defender*, August 23, 1919, 11; "25,000 See Am. Giants," *Chicago Defender*, August 30, 1919, 11.

63. "Breaking the Shell," *Chicago Whip*, June 24, 1919, 8.

64. "A Dangerous Experiment," *Chicago Whip*, August 9, 1919, 8; "The Passing of Uncle Tom," *Chicago Whip*, August 9, 1919, 8; Radicals and Raids," *Chicago Whip*, January 10, 1920, 8; "The Cause of the New Negro," *Chicago Whip*, January 17, 1920, 8.

65. Foster to W. T. Smith, July 2, 1919, Rube Foster Clippings File, National Baseball Library, Cooperstown, New York.

66. Cary Lewis, "Baseball Circuit for Next Season," *Chicago Defender*, October 4, 1919, 11.

67. Rube Foster produced a series of essays under the heading "Pitfalls of Baseball," which appeared in the *Chicago Defender*, on November 29, 1919; December 13, 1919; December 20, 1919; December 27, 1919; January 3, 1920; January 10, 1920; and January 17, 1920. See Cottrell, *The Best Pitcher in Baseball*, 143–147.

68. Andrew Foster, "Pitfalls of Baseball," *Chicago Defender*, January 3, 1920, 9.

69. Cary Lewis, "Baseball Circuit for Next Season," *Chicago Defender*, October 4, 1919, 3, 11; "Negro Base Ball League Assured," *Indianapolis Freeman*, February 21, 1920, 3; "Baseball Magnates Hold Conference,"

Chicago Defender, February 14, 1920, 11; "Baseball Men Write League Constitution," *Chicago Defender*, February 21, 1920, 9.

70. Ira F. Lewis, "National Baseball League Formed," *The Competitor* 1 (March 1920): 66.

71. Charles Marshall, "National Negro Baseball League Is Formed," *Indianapolis Freeman*, February 28, 1920, 7.

72. "'Rube' Assigns Players to Giants," *Chicago Defender*, March 20, 1920, 9.

73. "Rube Foster Tells What Baseball Needs to Succeed," (first article), *Chicago Defender*, December 10, 1920, 10.

74. "Rube Foster's 'Sportsmanship,'" *Kansas City Call,* July 11, 1924, 6.

75. David Malarcher to Robert Peterson, January 16, 1969, 3.

76. "The Greatest," Chicago Defender, May 3, 1930, 9.

77. Frank A. Young, "Rube Foster—The Master Mind of Baseball," *Abbot's Monthly* (November 1, 1930): 42–43, 49.

78. "Rube Foster Dead," *Chicago Defender*, December 13, 1930, 1, 4.

79. Peterson, *Only the Ball Was White*, 103–115.

80. John B. Holway, "Rube Foster: Father of Black Game," *Sporting News*, August 8, 1981, 19.

John Donaldson

Restoring the Legacy of
Segregated Baseball's Greatest Pitcher

Pete Gorton

"One player always stands out in our memory—that of graceful polished and classy John Donaldson. He was the poetry and rhythm of baseball."[1]

John Wesley Donaldson (February 20, 1891–April 12, 1970) was an African American baseball pitcher who played for several Negro Leagues and semi-professional teams, including the All Nations club and the Kansas City Monarchs. In a career that spanned more than 30 years, he recorded more than 400 wins and was among the greatest pitchers of his era, black or white.[2]

Paul Eiffert was a catcher in the St. Louis Cardinals organization in the early 1920s. He retired from pro ball to raise sheep on a farm near St. Cloud, Minnesota. He knew John Donaldson and caught for him many times. Paul had soft hands. The kind of hands it took to catch lightning. In 1949, Paul was tragically killed when struck by a car while trying to cross a street. He left behind a wife, Mabel and two small children. His son Herman was three, and his daughter Faith was five. Mabel put together a scrapbook for her children that included a letter from John Donaldson.

Herman never really knew his father or anything about his baseball career. With a tear in his eye, an aged Herman Eiffert once shared this letter with me. "If your son wants to play ball," the letter read, "I would do all I could to encourage him [as] he may be a Big Leaguer." The letter was filled with insights into Paul Eiffert, an amazing hand-written letter. Not because it relates stories of the ball fields and conquest, but because it provides us with a glimpse of John Donaldson the human being.

"Remember me to Faith and Herman," John Donaldson wrote on his Chicago White Sox stationery. "Good old ball players never die, they just fade away." That was exactly what happened to John Donaldson. He faded away.

Negro League Ballplayers Were Equal
to Major League Ballplayers

The color line was firmly drawn in Organized Baseball around 1887, systematically eliminating non-white players from the field, forcing them to play somewhere else, anywhere else. "I had a world of my own. They didn't want me. It didn't make no difference to me," Satchel Paige said in his 1971 Hall of Fame induction speech. John Donaldson experienced a similar world. This world was not what most people today think it was.

John Donaldson played in over 550 cities and towns across the breadth and width of North America. Donaldson brought big league quality to this "world." Places like Eldora, Iowa, Graceville, Minnesota, and Beach, North Dakota—remote outposts where grain elevators were prominent landmarks and you could practically see forever in the distance. The story of this world is the same—gather a crowd, play a game, and move on to do it again tomorrow.

People who witnessed John Donaldson on the mound marveled at his physical ability. His 21st-century throwing style had contemporary baseball dignitaries drooling. Negro Leagues managers C.I. Taylor of the Indianapolis ABCs, Tenny Blount of the Detroit Stars, and Dizzy Dismukes of the Chicago American Giants wanted him for their clubs. Major League managers Frank Chance of the Chicago Cubs, Joe Cantillion of the Washington Senators, and Hughie Jennings of the Detroit Tigers valued what Donaldson could have done for their teams. Owners Charles Comiskey of the Chicago White Sox and George Lennon of the St. Paul Saints wanted what they knew they couldn't have. Journalists Tweed Webb of the *St. Louis Argus* and A.S. "Doc" Young of the *Chicago Defender* witnessed Donaldson in action and later ranked him as one of the top three all-time Negro Leagues pitchers. Hall of Fame ballplayer John Henry Lloyd said Donaldson was the best he ever faced. Powerful East Coast booking agent Nat Strong wanted Donaldson pitching in New York. The father of Negro Leagues baseball, Rube Foster, dined in Donaldson's home. Donaldson is linked to Branch Rickey through All Nations center fielder Elmer Brandell, whom the barrier breaker managed at the University of Michigan. Booker T. Washington knew of Donaldson's play with the All Nations. Hall of Fame pitcher Grover Cleveland Alexander said he would have given $100,000 to sign John Donaldson. Donaldson reportedly once struck out Ty Cobb three straight times. Exiled Chicago Black Sox Swede Risberg and Happy Felsh knew that a game with Donaldson meant a special payday.[3]

Today, John Donaldson's career is judged far differently. Donaldson's player page on the website Baseball-Reference.com sums up his accomplishments thusly: "It is hard to judge his abilities as many of his statistics were compiled against weak white semipro teams" Determinations such as these are based on where and who he played, and not how he played. However, Donaldson's critics do not see the entire picture. They never saw him play.[4]

But we can—recently discovered film footage from the 1920s captured John Donaldson throwing and hitting the baseball in his own inimitable style. The film was shot on August 16, 1925, in Fergus Falls, Minnesota, by professional photographer W.T. Oxley, and was found more than 80 years later by his grandson Rich. The 39-second footage shows Donaldson tossing three pitches from a game in which he struck out 18 batters from Battle Lake, Minnesota. Three Major League scouts were shown the recovered film and were asked for their opinions of what made Donaldson's throwing style unique.[5]

The Major League scouts liked what they saw. One noted that Donaldson possessed a "tall, lean and loose body type, durable frame," which would allow him to have a very long career. In fact Big John pitched for at least 33 seasons. The scout's report continued, "able to generate power from lower-half torque." Donaldson's legs were very powerful, the source of his lightning fastball. He had a three-quarter-arm slot delivery and hid the ball well, which prevented the batter from seeing the ball until the last instant. Another scout remarked that Donaldson "was not a short-armer, thus reducing stress on the arm ... like Satchel Paige."

Contemporary batters often said that Donaldson's fastball looked like a pea when it reached the plate. More than two decades later, the same analogy would be used to describe Satchel Paige's hard one. "I would not hesitate to sign this pitcher because of his arm action," the scout concluded. "There have been others worse who have gone on to the Hall of Fame."

The Greatest Colored Pitcher in the World

John Donaldson was born in 1891 in Glasgow, Missouri. Glasgow's main claim to fame was construction of the first all-steel bridge to span the Missouri river in 1879. A month before John Donaldson was born, a black man named Olli Truxton was lynched in the streets of Glasgow.[6]

John Donaldson grew up watching games at Rheas Ball Park. In 1908, he joined Glasgow's Hannaca Blues an all-black team owned by the town's mayor, Will Hannaca. In his first documented game, he broke his catcher's finger with his fastball. It has been said that John Donaldson attended George R. Smith College in Sedalia, Missouri. The school is known for being the alma mater of American composer and ragtime pianist Scott Joplin.[7]

In 1911, John Donaldson signed on with W.A. Brown's Tennessee Rats of Holden, Missouri, and immediately began grabbing headlines. His record that season was 41–3. In 1912, J.L. Wilkinson, a semi-pro ballplayer from Algona, Iowa, formed a team called the World's All Nations. The All Nations consisted of "Chinese, Japanese, Cubans, Indians, Hawaiians … and the Great John Donaldson, the best colored pitcher in the United States." Attitudes on race at the time believed a team with multiple ethnicities could not coexist, much less excel at the national game. The All Nations did both.[8]

Soon John Donaldson would become the star of the All Nations. His $150 a month salary meant he made a very good living as a ballplayer. He struck out more than 500 batters per year from 1912 through 1914, and probably in 1915 as well. With the All Nations, Donaldson pitched seven of his known 14 no-hitters. In 1912, the All Nations brought a gasoline-powered lighting system along on their tour so they could play night games. It was developed in Des Moines, Iowa, the team's home base, by the Swaine Gasoline Lighting Company. The lights were said to make the night "Light as Day." The club not only showed how multiple races could live and play together, they also popularized night baseball.[9]

On November 7, 1917, John Donaldson wed Eleanor Watson in Kansas City. The *Kansas City Sun* announced, "The Race's Greatest Base Ball Pitcher and one of its most charming young women to be married." It was the start of a 53-year union that lasted until his death in 1970. A month later, the groom was pitching in the California Winter League for the Los Angeles White Sox. Donaldson faced an entire team of "big league players," in the league opener and beat them 5–3, allowing only six hits while striking out 16 batters.[10]

Severely impacted by the Railway Control Act of March 1918, which placed heavy restrictions on train travel, the All Nations disbanded, and Donaldson signed with the Indianapolis ABCs. After refusing a pay cut, Donaldson moved on to New York in mid-season to headline the Brooklyn Royal Giants.[11]

Donaldson spent the 1919 season with the Detroit Stars. The Negro National League was formed in 1920, and he became a founding member of the Kansas City Monarchs. In later years, it was noted that Donaldson suggested the name to owner J.L. Wilkinson. Donaldson was in line to become the team's player/manager until the post was given to his former All Nations teammate, Jose Mendez, just prior to Opening Day. Donaldson anchored the Monarchs' pitching staff, played center field, and occasionally batted cleanup.[12]

Sources indicate that in 1920, a revamped All Nations squad played games at the same time as the Monarchs. This club continued with Donaldson as player/manager in 1922 and 1923. The All Nations made money in the Midwest, and Wilkinson profited. This source of cash buoyed the Monarchs franchise. Donaldson was a known profit maker outside of the league, and this lessened his dependence on it.[13]

In 1924, wary of the prospect of spending another summer traveling through the Midwest by automobile, Donaldson left the Monarchs prior to their first league game and joined the semi-pro Bertha Fisherman of central Minnesota. The opportunity was too good. The local business leaders in Bertha had started a special bank account and began saving for Donaldson's contract three years earlier.[14]

John Donaldson played baseball in Minnesota with semi-pro teams from 1924 to 1930. His salary topped $450 per month in 1926, which included a house to live in and several free weekends to rent himself out to small-town clubs looking for a huge payday. Reports say he made $115 per single pitching performance.[15]

In 1949, Donaldson became the first fulltime black scout in Major League Baseball history when he was hired by the Chicago White Sox. He scouted some of the greatest players ever to grace the game—Willie Mays, Henry Aaron and Ernie Banks. His influence on the game continued. He is credited with signing future major leaguers Bob Boyd, Connie Johnson, and Sammy Hairston.[16]

Segregated Legacies

John Donaldson faded away because his legacy was segregated. Not only did the color line prohibit black ball players from the opportunity to compete in Organized Baseball, it also robbed them of their rightful place in history. By keeping Negro Leagues statistics out of the Major League record books and by restricting their presence in the National Baseball of Fame, black ball players continue to be marginalized long after their playing careers have ended.

In 2007, the website johndonaldson.bravehost.com was launched in order to restore the legacy of John Donaldson, and since that time over 500 authors, researchers, and baseball historians have joined the ranks of The Donaldson Network. To this date, more than 5,500 articles related to the career of John Donaldson have been collected from more than 25 states in the U.S. and from Canada. Visitors to the site can access box scores, line scores, and articles covering John Donaldson's 408 wins and 5,035 documented strikeouts. Dates and locations are included as well as all known references for each individual game.

On April 19, 1952, the *Pittsburgh Courier* published their list of the all-time greatest players in black ball history. The five pitchers selected were Smokey Joe Williams, Satchel Paige, Bullet Joe Rogan, William Foster, and John Donaldson. John Donaldson remains the only pitcher from this group *not* enshrined in the National Baseball Hall of Fame.[17]

In 2006, a panel of Negro Leagues historians chose 17 black ball players and contributors for election into the Hall of Fame. John Donaldson made a short list of 39, but ultimately fell short of the necessary votes needed for selection. In January 2016, Jeff Idelson, the Hall's President, told *The Sporting News* that the 2006 inductees would be the final Negro Leaguers enshrined in the Hall, *"unless new research came out that would warrant another look."*[18]

The historians who bypassed John Donaldson for election judged his worthiness on the information and statistics then available. At the time, he was known to have 148 wins. Today the total is 408. In 2006, Donaldson was known to have 2,245 strikeouts. At present, more than 5,000 have been found. The 2006 study designated him as worthy of the final ballot of 39. These factors should allow Donaldson another look at possible induction, but don't take my word for it. Listen to former Kansas City Monarchs manager Buck O'Neil: "John Donaldson … showed Satchel the way, and the fact is, there are many people who saw them both who say John Donaldson was just as good as Satchel."

The film footage uncovered in 2006 demonstrates for all to see that John Donaldson's unique power-pitching delivery was decades ahead of his time. Donaldson's physical ability was without question coveted by the Major Leagues. Big League magnates John McGraw, Charles Comiskey, and Frank Chance were said to have endorsed him. Hall of Fame entrepreneur J.L. Wilkinson called Donaldson "the greatest pitcher that ever threw a baseball."[19]

Negro Leagues ballplayers were major leaguers in all but name. It is the responsibility of current and future generations of baseball fans to prevent the achievements of the Negro Leaguers from being nullified by faulty memory and sheer oversight. John Donaldson summed it up best in his request to Mabel Eiffert after the loss of her husband, and his trusted backstop: "Remember me."

Table 11.1 John Donaldson Pitching Statistics 1908–1940

Year/Team	G	W	L	SH	IP	H	R	ER	BB	K	R/9	ERA	WH	K/9
1908 HG	1	1	0	0	9	3	1	0	-	17	1.00	0.00	0.33	17.00
1909 HB	3	3	0	1	27	6	2	0	-	30	0.67	0.00	0.22	15.00
1910 HB	1	1	0	0	9	6	4	2	-	15	4.00	2.00	0.66	15.00
1911 TR	22	15	4	4	197.3	64	34	17	19	257	1.55	0.77	0.52	18.75
1912 AN	29	20	4	13	226.7	91	31	19	30	378	1.23	0.75	0.60	17.03
1912 LH	5	4	1	1	45	22	18	10	1	52	3.60	2.00	1.49	17.33
1913 AN	39	27	3	18	295.7	107	36	18	36	460	1.09	0.55	0.59	18.02
1914 AN	46	29	12	16	366.7	155	54	27	41	508	1.32	0.66	0.62	14.84
1914 TT	1	1	0	1	9	4	0	0	2	17	0.00	0.00	0.66	17.00
1915 KCC	1	1	0	1	9	0	0	0	1	19	0.00	0.00	0.11	19.00
1915 AN	39	27	4	13	298.3	135	50	25	30	411	1.51	0.78	0.65	17.26
1916 RP	6	1	4	1	49.7	39	25	14	12	30	4.53	2.54	1.16	8.53
1916 AN	44	33	5	19	327.7	161	44	31	36	312	1.22	0.86	0.67	12.07
16/17 LWS	5	2	1	0	34.3	29	23	13	4	16	6.03	3.41	1.14	6.45
1917 AN	44	22	6	5	243.3	125	63	34	22	107	2.33	1.26	0.76	8.57
17/18 LWS	5	2	3	0	36.3	26	26	19	0	22	6.44	6.26	0.95	7.24
1918 ABC	9	6	1	1	61.7	49	23	16	15	23	3.36	2.33	1.08	3.93
1918 BRG	17	7	9	2	138.7	145	61	42	23	47	3.96	2.91	1.27	4.12
1919 DS	18	10	5	3	130	104	45	31	30	66	3.11	2.15	1.06	4.91
1919 CAG	1	1	0	0	6	5	6	6	2	3	9.00	9.00	1.17	4.50
1920 AN	1	0	1	0	6	5	2	2	-	-	3.00	3.00	0.83	-
1920 KCM	19	9	8	2	139.3	131	60	38	21	57	3.87	2.45	1.17	5.16
1921 AN	1	0	1	0	6	5	6	3	1	10	9.00	4.50	2.33	15.00
1921 KCM	9	2	2	0	48.3	45	27	19	12	25	5.03	3.54	1.18	4.65
1922 AN	21	13	5	5	161.7	101	40	24	13	115	2.23	1.34	0.78	10.25
1923 AN	31	18	3	3	195	111	44	24	12	148	2.03	1.11	0.69	11.10
1924 BRT	25	20	3	5	212	122	48	20	21	320	2.04	0.85	0.67	13.58

Year/Team	G	W	L	SH	IP	H	R	ER	BB	K	R/9	ERA	WH	K/9
1925 BRT	26	18	5	4	202.7	136	70	36	30	244	3.11	1.60	0.83	10.83
1925 TT	10	3	6	1	92	72	36	20	19	125	3.52	1.96	0.99	13.55
1926 LS	36	13	16	3	276.7	195	96	64	33	274	3.12	2.08	0.84	10.16
1926 TT	3	1	2	0	28	34	13	6	3	37	4.18	1.93	1.32	11.89
1927 BRT	27	21	4	8	217.3	149	54	29	29	219	2.24	1.20	0.83	9.89
1927 TT	3	3	0	0	25	14	7	6	4	25	2.52	2.16	0.72	9.00
1928 MLR	15	7	5	2	109	112	50	28	16	62	4.13	2.38	1.17	5.58
1928 TT	5	1	3	1	36	25	12	8	2	11	3.00	2.00	0.76	3.76
1929 CHD	19	13	4	0	132.7	134	78	54	16	77	5.29	3.66	1.34	5.94
1930 STC	21	14	6	0	169.3	145	59	34	51	129	3.13	1.81	1.16	6.86
1930 TT	1	1	0	0	6	1	1	1	2	6	1.50	1.50	0.50	9.00
1931 CHD	8	2	3	0	56.7	49	33	19	10	29	5.24	3.02	1.06	5.12
1931 KCM	1	0	0	0	2	1	0	0	1	4	0.00	0.00	1.00	18.00
1932 KCG	1	1	0	0	11	7	4	2	0	9	3.27	1.64	0.64	7.36
1932 DAS	23	9	6	0	152.3	155	72	43	26	95	4.25	2.54	1.26	8.04
1932 TT	1	0	1	0	8.3	11	8	6	3	4	8.67	6.48	1.68	4.34
1933 DAS	6	5	1	2	53	28	11	5	7	52	1.87	0.85	0.69	13.00
1934 COG	1	1	0	1	9	2	0	0	–	23	0.00	0.00	0.22	23.00
1934 KCM	9	5	0	1	47	50	15	9	3	13	2.87	1.72	1.24	6.88
1935 COG	10	3	4	0	58.7	57	31	21	13	31	4.76	3.22	1.23	11.79
1936 COG	7	3	3	0	44.7	48	23	13	13	24	4.63	2.62	1.43	8.42
1937 COG	7	3	3	0	61	59	25	18	5	31	3.69	2.65	1.07	5.81
1939 COG	3	0	2	0	15	21	13	9	3	17	7.80	5.40	1.60	10.20
1939 KCM	6	4	1	0	34.3	38	21	10	12	12	5.50	3.18	1.45	3.14
1940 COG	3	2	1	0	21	24	9	7	4	17	3.86	3.00	1.33	7.28
1940 CPH	1	0	0	0	0.7	1	0	0	—	—	0.00	0.00	1.51	—

Editor's Note: African American teams are shown in gray (The All Nations clubs of 1912–1917 and 1920–1921 were integrated. The 1922–1923 All Nations were black). Because Donaldson's strikeouts and walks sometimes went undocumented, the WHIP and K/9 averages do not necessarily reflect the overall innings pitched totals.

Team Abbreviations: HG = Higbee (MO) Tigers; HB = Hannaca Blues (Glasgow, MO); TR = Tennessee Rats; AN = All Nations; LH = Lehigh (IA); TT = Town Teams; KCC = Kansas City Colts; RP = Royal Poinciana Hotel (Palm Beach, FL); LWS = Los Angeles White Sox; ABC = Indianapolis ABCs; BRG = Brooklyn Royal Giants; DS = Detroit Stars; CAG = Chicago American Giants; KCM = Kansas City Monarchs; BRT = Bertha (MN) Fishermen; LS = Lismore (MN) Gophers; MLR = Melrose (MN); CHD = Colored House of David; STC = St. Cloud (MN) Saints; KCG = Kansas City Giants; DAS = John Donaldson's All-Stars; COG = Chicago Giants; CPH = Palmer House All-Stars.

Town Teams: In addition to his regular employers, Donaldson would occasionally pitch for various small town teams. Big John worked a single contest (unless otherwise noted) for the following squads: David City, NE (1914); Plentywood, MT (3 games, 1925); Radville, SK (2 games, 1925); Minneota, MN (2 games, 1925); Lismore, MN (2 games, 1925; 1927); Madison, MN (1925); Moose Jaw, SK (2 games, 1926; 2 games, 1927); Alexandria, MN (1926); Moose Jaw, SK (2 games, 1927); Lismore, MN (1927); Scobey, MT (2 games, 1928); Arlington, MN (2 games, 1928); Cambridge, MN (1928); Holdingford, MN (1930); Fremont, NE (1932).

Table 11.2 John Donaldson Pitching Totals 1908–1940

Class	G	W	L	SH	IP	H	R	ER	BB	K	R/9	ERA	WH	K/9
SP/TT	573	362	107	129	4281	2618	1109	653	537	4456	2.34	1.38	0.80	12.07
Milb	19	4	10	0	114.7	123	82	53	32	73	6.61	4.27	1.46	6.87
MLB	7	2	5	0	56.3	46	38	24	0	24	6.07	4.56	0.97	7.36
NLB	96	40	39	8	726	572	275	172	120	482	3.41	2.15	1.08	7.07
Total	695	408	161	137	5158	3359	1514	902	689	5035	2.64	1.58	0.84	11.16

Editor's Note: The results have been displayed according to the class of opponent faced. In light of Donaldson's less than overwhelming record against stiffer competition, it should be noted that his teammates were almost always semi-pro in nature. Only 14 percent of his total appearances (100 out of 695 games) were made with big time black teams. Donaldson's overall statistics are based on 5155ip (R); 5128ip (ER); 5135ip (H); 4059.3ip (K); and 3604ip (BB).

Class Abbreviations: SP/TT = Semi-Pro and Town Teams; Milb = Minor League and Minor League All-Star teams; MLB = Major League and Major League All-Star Teams; NLB = Black independent and league teams.

Sources for Tables 11.1, 11.2: johndonaldson.bravehost.com; Negro Leagues Researchers & Authors Group.

Notes

1. *Lake Wilson Pilot*, June 4, 1942.

2. "John W. Donaldson," Baseball-Reference.com, accessed March 1, 2015, http://www.baseball-reference.com/bullpen/John_W._Donaldson; "Documented Wins of Southpaw Pitcher John Donaldson," Bravehost.com, accessed January 20, 2017. http://www.johndonaldson.bravehost.com/eg.html.

3. James A. Riley, *The Biographical Encyclopedia of the Negro Baseball Leagues* (New York: Carroll & Graf, 2002), 242.

4. "John W. Donaldson," Baseball-Reference.com.

5. *Long Prairie Leader*, August 20, 1925, 9; *Fergus Falls Journal Daily*, August 17, 1925, 4; *St. Paul Pioneer Press*, July 27, 2011.

6. National Association for the Advancement of Colored People, *Thirty Years of Lynching in The United States, 1889–1918* (New York National Association for the Advancement of Colored People, 1919. Reprint, Clark, NJ: The Lawbook Exchange, 2012), 80.

7. *Chicago Defender*, May 22, 1926, 10; "A Glasgow negro who caught for the Tigers had his right hand badly split and a finger broken by a pitched ball..." *Higbee Weekly News*, September 18, 1908.

8. *Wells Forum Advocate,* September 10, 1914, 1; *Leeds News*, June 26, 1913, 4; *Chicago Defender*, October 7, 1916.

9. "John Donaldson (pitcher)," Wikipedia.org, Accessed January 21, 2017, https://en.wikipedia.org/wiki/John_Donaldson_(pitcher); *New Ulm Review*, July 29, 1914, Sports Section 1.

10. *Kansas City Sun* October 20, 1917, 1; *Los Angeles Times*, December 10, 1917; *Chicago Defender*, December 22, 1917, 3.

11. "U.S. Railway Control Act, March 21, 1918," First World War. Com, accessed March 1, 2015, http://www.firstworldwar.com/source/railwaycontrolact.htm; *Chicago Defender*, July 13, 1918, 9.

12. *Kansas City Call*, May 28, 1948; *Kansas City Times*, April 16, 1920, 8.

13. *Omaha World Herald,* May 8, 1920, 5.

14. *Kansas City Call*, May 1, 1924, 6; *Bertha Herald*, January 26, 1922.

15. *Verndale Sun*, April 1, 1926, 8; *Lake Wilson Pilot*, June 4, 1942.

16. *Chicago Defender*, July 9, 1949, 27.

17. *Pittsburgh Courier*, April 19, 1952, 14.

18. *Sporting News*, January 26, 2016.

19. *Kansas City Call*, May 28, 1948.

The Measure of Failure

*Atlanta Baseball and Community
Development in the 1930s and 1970s*

THOMAS AIELLO

A case can be made that the Negro Leagues of the early 20th century were equivalent to its Major League counterpart, especially after a close examination of the talent and quality of play in both organizations. However, such comparisons can also be problematic because they establish the Major Leagues as the signpost of greatness, the measure of what quality should be, ignoring that much of Major League talent, teams, and towns were defined by failure. A profound lack of success defined many black teams as well, and their failure looked similar to that of comparable Major League squads. In some instances, the failure of a city's Negro Leagues club served as a bellwether for its later Major League team, an omen of what would be.

Such was the case in Atlanta, Georgia. The city's most notable Negro Leagues team was the Atlanta Black Crackers, founded in 1919 and appearing intermittently from the 1920s to the 1940s. That intermittence was the result of a lack of victories and a resulting lack of community interest from a black population that was, relative to time and place, thriving. The team's eighth, ninth, and tenth seasons, from 1935 to 1937, would witness both success and failure for the club in the Negro Southern League, ultimately leading to its entry in 1938 into the Negro American League. Thirty-five years after that move, the city's only Major League team, the Atlanta Braves, began its eighth, then ninth, then tenth seasons in the city, from 1973 to 1975, which would witness both success and failure in the National League. Hank Aaron would break Babe Ruth's home run record during the period, but a lack of victories would result in a lack of community interest from a population that was, relative to time and place, thriving.

The eighth, ninth, and tenth seasons of each team's tenure in Atlanta would demonstrate remarkably similar results both in play and in the city's general apathy toward professional baseball. What demonstrated the functional equivalency between the Black Crackers and the Braves was not the quality of their play or the enthusiasm of their constituencies. Rather, it was the inconsistency of their play and the apathy of their constituencies that made them so similar. It was a likeness built on mediocrity, one first modeled by the Black Crackers decades before the Braves moved to the South. And thus, Negro Leagues teams could also demonstrate major league equivalency in lack of success, and they could also be the bar for that equivalency, rather than the ones having to demonstrate that they could reach it.

The development of black baseball in Atlanta was fundamentally independent of the cutthroat business practices of a black elite class who were able to build empires in the early 20th century that fueled rivalries throughout the Auburn Avenue business district, the core of the community's economic viability. Still, the social separation among Atlanta's black population did not create an alliance among white and black elites.

In fact, a political movement among white activists in the early century led to a push to disfranchise black men to ensure that black elites would not assume any kind of approximate equality with whites. The racial line had to be maintained at all costs. Such race-baiting came to a head during the Atlanta Race Riot of 1906, in which dozens of black Atlantans were killed and many more wounded. Despite the restrictions on black voting and other white retrenchments that followed, the fear of further violence led civic leaders of both races to establish a line of communication, aiding racial cooperation to some degree, but simultaneously deepening the divide between upper- and lower-class black residents of Atlanta. It was, for the city's black elite, an attempt to find the order of a system to replace the "order" maintained by racial violence.[1]

"There are also certain psychological and social factors that must not be overlooked," admitted journalist Frank Marshall Davis. Black-white contact within class or profession was possible in Northern cities. "In Chicago an artist may associate with whites of similar interests," for example. "A Harlem physician may mingle with white doctors; a Bostonian may be the only Negro in his class at Harvard." Such wasn't possible in the South. "In hostile Atlanta, Negroes must turn to other Negroes. 'Race consciousness' develops as a defense mechanism," Davis explained. "If a Negro institution can satisfy the needs of the people, then it is no longer necessary to patronize inimical whites."[2]

Race consciousness was also an undeniable part of the development of black baseball in Atlanta. As historian Tim Darnell has noted, for example, the Black Crackers were founded in the wake of the Red Summer of 1919 and the racial violence that it generated. "In many ways," explained oral historian Clifford M. Kuhn, "the Black Crackers mirrored life in a segregated society. Finances were often shaky, scheduling and transportation uncertain, pay low, accommodations poor, and equipment inferior to that of white professional teams."[3]

Still, black boosters in the city wanted to bring legitimate baseball to the city and the region. An ownership group that included Sol Rivers, Robert DeReef, L.R. Lautier, H.L. Johnson, and Edgar Buckner ran the Atlanta Cubs in 1918, and the following year they responded to the idea of Crackers general manager Frank Reynolds, who was hoping to use a black baseball team to allow Ponce de Leon Park to make money when the Crackers were idle or away. Rivers and his partners recruited players from local black colleges, including Morehouse, Morris Brown, and Clark, to field a new team. They were named the Cubs as well, but throughout the season many fans began calling them the Black Crackers.[4]

"Way back there in the early twenties, there was a ball club here called the Atlanta Deppens," remembered former player Gabby Kemp, of that original semi-pro team comprised largely of students. "From that, they organized into the Black Crackers because they wanted to be a team like the white Crackers had then." The squad spent most of its time barnstorming as a way to compensate for poor local attendance. "Most of the time we was on trains," said Arthur Idlett, a player for the team in the 1920s. "The Atlanta white Crackers would let us have their old uniforms. They would buy uniforms every year and they'd give the Black Crackers the old uniforms."[5]

There were, of course, still problems for many of the players. Segregation and low pay dominated life on the road. "In those days the hotels owned and operated by Negroes were few," explained Kemp. When the team was able to find one, it would "maybe ask the manager of the hotel for maybe two or three rooms. And the ballplayers would go in, as many as they could, and just lie across the bed and go to sleep. Sometimes in the big, larger cities, we stopped at the YMCA." That combination of racial and financial hardship conspired to make life and baseball play even more difficult for the players. When the Black Crackers played a team on the road, the host team would "take out for the baseballs, they take out for the umpires, they take out for the park. Deductions, and we nicknamed it 'de ducks.' All them ducks got the money. So if there were anything left over, then you would divide it equally among the players."[6]

The goal, however, was participation in a larger organization. Atlanta hosted the first meeting of the Negro Southern League in March 1920, and the Black Crackers were a constituent part of its genesis. They were also, however, a constituent part of its early demise, as the team's owner, Sol Rivers, proved a thorn in the side of his counterparts, arriving late to meetings and disagreeing with the decisions of other owners. Ultimately, they voted the Black Crackers out of the league, and the loss of the South's largest city would spell the league's first of several demises.[7]

But the Black Crackers struggled on in fits and starts throughout the 1920s and 1930s. According to historian Allen Edward Joyce, "A succession of owner-promoters tried to establish a Black Cracker team, and most of them through ill-luck or bad management lost in the process the small amount of money they had." "When one entrepreneur lost interest, however, there was usually another there to finance the team for another year." The talent was never part of the team's problem. "Black players of major league caliber," Joyce explained, "barred from the white major leagues not because they lacked ability but because they were black, played for and against the Black Crackers at Ponce de Leon Park." Earl Mann, president of the city's white Crackers, even encouraged Black Crackers first baseman Red Moore to join the white team. "Mr. Mann said I ought to go to Cuba and learn how to speak a little Spanish, you know." Moore could "change my nationality, you understand, from black to some other. I said, 'No, it wouldn't do for me to do nothing like that, people in Atlanta know me.'"[8]

Though no Black Cracker joined the city's white counterpart, the team did often play home games in the white Crackers' Ponce de Leon Park. "We didn't have a permanent place. When the white Crackers were out of town, we would play out at Ponce de Leon. But sometimes, because of the cost of the park, it was more economical to play at Morehouse or Morris Brown, to cut down expenses." Even when playing at Ponce de Leon, however, "we weren't allowed to use the dressing facilities or the showers, so we'd dress at home before the game and take a shower at home after the game," explained Norman Lumpkin. E.B. Baynes described the bleachers at Ponce de Leon Park as rife with gambling. "At that time they had some kind of law in Georgia that you couldn't convict a man for gambling unless he was in a gambling house, and the house had to have a roof. And those bleachers did not have a roof over them."[9]

As the 1934 season closed, it was clear that black baseball in Atlanta had not been a financial success, but there were signs that improvements could change those fortunes. Crackers management had become far more willing to grant access to the Black Crackers. Automobile travel was far cheaper and more convenient than train travel. And Ponce de Leon Park was by that time equipped with lights, allowing for night games, which consistently drew larger crowds. "Baseball is banging on the door ready to come back," touted a team press release. "Your 1935 Black Crackers are indeed fortunate," as the club was "assured of support of white magnates."[10]

The team had also been hurt by the city's blue laws, which did not allow ballclubs to play on Sunday. As Arthur Idlett later explained, road games, usually played in a weekend series, were always more profitable. "They could play Sunday baseball in Mississippi," he said, "but they couldn't play Sunday baseball in Georgia." But to help the Black Crackers, in 1935, Atlanta mayor James L. Key changed the law for Ponce de Leon Park to allow Sunday baseball, on the condition that attendance demonstrated popular interest and justified the change. The team's first Sunday game drew 4,700 fans, a strong crowd, but the team continued to struggle financially because of constant ownership changes and financial mismanagement. "You'd have to do what you could do," said Idlett, "you couldn't carry a big team. We didn't carry but twelve players because of the economics. Pitchers had to play outfield and the catchers had to alternate at first base."[11]

Prior to the 1935 season, Atlanta's interest in a new incarnation of the Negro Southern League was represented by W.B. Baker, a Booker T. Washington High School teacher and sports promoter who managed over the rest of the decade, according to historian Allen Edward Joyce, to lure "a succession of owners into investing their money in the risky enterprise."[12]

"Baker called us in and he was going to make a business of it," said player Leroy Idlett. "He was going to give each man a contract. Well, we wanted to know, where was the money coming from after we signed the contract? He said he was going to try to get it from the gate receipts. Well, we knew that wouldn't work."[13]

The *Atlanta Daily World*'s Ric Roberts was glad the Black Crackers had been reconstituted in 1935, but knew that Atlanta fans "must be dragged back to baseball by various and sundry mechanisms." He was confident that ownership "plan to get you out to Ponce de Leon Park opening day if they have to swoon you with stimulants." That was the idea. Mayor James Key declared the day of the Black Crackers' home opener a holiday and encouraged employers to give workers time off to go to the park. There were more than 3,000 fans in the stands for that opening day, but only 1,700 for the following game. "Two more successive losses here and Atlanta will turn her back on the Black Crackers," wrote Roberts. "This is a funny town. Either you look like a million bucks or you are no good." Or, as a frustrated letter-writer to the *World* complained, some black fans were sitting in segregated grandstands for white Cracker games at Ponce de Leon, but "when their own Black Crackers are playing they are permitted to sit anywhere in the Park, and yet they will not patronize the Black Crackers."[14]

The 1935 team was managed by second baseman Sammy "Runt" Thompson, an accomplished journeyman who was the Southern League's Most Valuable Player during the 1931 season, and featured players like George "Jew Baby" Bennett, "one of the south's best and most noted baseball geniuses," who also served as a manager for part of the season. "When I first started out back in 1935," Red Moore explained, "I believe I was making a hundred and twenty-five dollars a month." It was clear, according to Clifford Kuhn, that "black ballplayers made considerably more money than the average black Atlantan, though generally less than their white counterparts." Among the stars of that 1935 team was Felix "Chin" Evans, who would go on to a long and successful black baseball career. Donald Reeves would hit .571 in games with available box scores, and two of the team's pitchers averaged more than a strikeout per inning, with Norman Cross striking out 31 hitters in 24 innings and "Rider" Brown amassing 29 strikeouts in 28⅓ innings.[15]

The crowds coming to see those players held steady through May and early June. A June 2 crowd of roughly 3,500 led Earl Mann, general manager of the white Crackers, to proclaim, "You played to far more fans than Little Rock or Knoxville are able to draw when they play the white Crackers here. We pledge you these grounds any day you have games billed and hope you can come out on Sunday dates when our team is out of town."

By August, however, the crowds had dissipated. The fickle Atlanta fans were not attending games, with the average home attendance hovering around 300. Combined with white teams protesting black play in Ponce de Leon, the mayor threatened to eliminate the ability to play on Sunday if the team did not start drawing crowds. "It seems that some of the lesser white nines from some of the wards are rather disgusted with the idea of handing Ponce de Leon Park over to people of our race for Sunday games," explained the *Atlanta Daily World*'s Ric Roberts. "Numerous charity and borough baseball outfits are aching to play at Poncey when the Crackers are away. Especially is this true of Sunday dates." Their pitch to Crackers management was that poor attendance at Black Crackers games meant that those white charity teams had a built-in audience that could make the park more money. It was a real fear for the team, which used the park as a mark of legitimacy.

Local insurance companies responded to the ultimatum, however, and in early June a game with the Birmingham Black Barons drew close to 5,000, as the "fans respond nobly to gestures of civic pride" in the team. "It's stuff like this that causes revolution," Roberts proclaimed. The revolution, however, never really materialized, but the team's newfound success, however brief, in turn convinced Percy Williams, an Auburn Avenue café owner, to invest in the team.

It also kept the insurance business involved. In late July, for example, Atlanta Life Insurance, founded by Alonzo Herndon in the twilight of the 19th century, gave away more than 2,000 Black Crackers tickets to policyholders, with the goal of "increasing the attendance to the game and helping those who are not able to pay the general admission."[16]

Atlanta apathy, however, did not prevent the rest of the state from finding identity in the team. Gabby Kemp, who joined the Black Crackers in 1935, described a trip that season to Thomasville, in south Georgia. "They had a beautiful parade, and a big old beautiful park and barbeques, they would start running barbeques and parades, and oh, down in those small towns, they had good race relations down there and those folks just go in there and say, 'Hey, John,' 'Hey, there,' 'Hey, ballplayer.' Oh, the food, they would have tables spread out like a family reunion or something like that for our ball club." On an early August trip to Anniston, pitcher and outfielder Donald Reeves threw a no-hitter against the locals. "Owner Percy Williams made Donald Reeves a promise," went one report, "that he would give him a quart of the choicest wine that Percy keeps in stock at his new Luncheonette establishment on Auburn Avenue if he would beat Anniston." And he did.[17]

But attendance in Atlanta never matched the regional enthusiasm, and ultimately the team lost access to Ponce de Leon toward the season's end. "The Ponce de Leon Park owners and administrators have decided that we are fed up on Negro baseball festivals," wrote Roberts. "They have essayed being very cordial and gentle about the matter though and have offered an excuse for the sudden exclusion of you and you and you from the premises. In the first place, they are a bit peeved over the poor fan backing that we have given our Crackers." The team ended its regular season on September 3, never again reaching the kind of attendance it had managed in early June, and there were doubts that the team, which ran at a financial deficit all season, could field a roster the following season.[18]

It was a frustrating endeavor to sports boosters like Roberts. He relayed the story of one confused fan. "I have wondered why these Atlanta people always pull against each other. When the White and Black Crackers play Memphis or just any outsider, the stands are always full of Atlanta born fans who root and shout for the visitors," he said. "It is sickening." Roberts agreed.[19]

The Black Crackers, however, would return the following season nonetheless. W.B. Baker had convinced Cum Posey's Homestead Grays to have their spring training in Atlanta, and the day after the Pennsylvania team arrived, Williams, James Andrews, Baker, S.M. Humphreys, and Louis Means met to field a 1936 Black Crackers team.[20]

Williams had been the financial fuel that made the team go, but an illness kept him away and threatened the team's ability to start the season. "The recovery of Percy Williams has the keynote to baseball sealed in this city," Roberts explained. "If he recovers rapidly enough there may be a paying franchise in this town before July is here." He did not recover rapidly, however. He died before April had run its course, but his partners met at the Butler Street Y following Williams' passing and, in the words of Joyce, "decided not to let the Black Crackers die with him." Ultimately, however, it was Percy Williams' widow Marion whose financial backing saved the team. The Black Crackers paid their Negro Southern League dues and began their season in early May.[21]

The team's first home game of the season was a no-hitter thrown by Roy "Snook" Welmaker against Chattanooga. Welmaker struck out 11 batters and even hit a home run in front of 2,900 fans. But again, just as in 1935, attendance soon began to lag. After a well-attended series against the Black Barons at Birmingham's Rickwood Field brought a much-needed payday for the club, Roberts chastised the efforts of his city. "There are 20,000 more of us in Atlanta than there are in Birmingham, and yet our civic pride is so low that we turn out no more than 1,000 fans to see the same show that 5,000 Birmingham fans paid to see." Sportswriter I.P. Reynolds was more diplomatic. "The Atlanta populace owes the baseball team a great attendance as a tribute to their gameness," he argued. "Anytime that group of athletes will venture into a game where failure after failure they have met, they deserve some credit."[22]

Welmaker, for his part, would continue his dominance through May. In another game that month, he struck out 14 in a one-hit victory over the Birmingham Black Barons. He would move to the Homestead Grays after several weeks in Atlanta. In games with available box scores, Henry "Red" Hadley hit .500, and the team's catcher hit .400, but there are not enough full box scores from the season to extrapolate those numbers over the full run of a summer. The team barnstormed through much of the season, their last home game coming on June 23 against the Memphis Red Sox. Even though they won that game, 29–2, and had 39 hits in the process, they could make far more money playing road games in the Midwest, and so spent much of July traveling. "Baseball is gone," lamented Roberts. "What became of the Black Crackers? The last time I heard of them they were in Knoxville but since that time they have faded out of the picture completely."[23]

The failure of local interest made the prospect of a 1937 season precarious at best, but local theater owner Mike Schaine, a white man, took over the team and imbued it with new capital. "Atlanta in the past has been a Mecca for mediocre base ball in some instances and in others the game has suffered miserable," wrote the *World's* J.C. Chunn. "That is behind us now." Schaine purchased legal title to both the team and the Black Crackers name in early April. "There is a man in Atlanta called Schaine," wrote Roberts. "He has a few pennies to spend on a GOOD ball club that can play GOOD opposition."

One of Schaine's first and most important moves was the hiring of Harry "Squab"

Jones as manager. Despite his race, Jones worked in the University of Georgia athletics department and was a respected man in Georgia who could help convince players to take a chance on a venture that was sure to be financially unstable at best. "Didn't nobody want to go to Atlanta to play no ball," remembered Jones. "Atlanta had been so rotten, rotten with ballplayers. Didn't nobody want to go to Atlanta to play ball."[24]

Along with Schaine, however, John and Billie Harden, owners of a gas station on Auburn Avenue, also purchased an ownership stake in the club. "They wanted a real baseball team," said Billie Harden. "That's what we wanted to give them. We bought the uniforms, and of course we bought all the baseballs, bats and other headgear and all that stuff. My husband bought a bus" to replace the series of cars that the team had previously used. "Our bus was one of the best buses that money could buy," said Gabby Kemp. The Hardens "had a beautiful filling station in front of their home. Mr. and Mrs. Harden were two very nice people and their friendship with the ball club was astounding. Our ball club was more like a family, a close-knit family." The Hardens became sole owners of the team in 1938.[25]

"Mr. Harden would buy the best equipment, the best protectors. We bought the same things that the major league ballplayers [bought]." As the team developed in the second half of the 1930s, Billie Harden claimed that "Ponce de Leon ball park used to be just overflowing. The enthusiasm was great! They just would pour out there to see them play the other teams coming here, because they were winning. And everybody likes a winner."[26]

The team played incredibly well during the 1937 season. It was unaffiliated with a specific league and therefore barnstormed through the South. But the Black Crackers did feature talented, familiar Atlanta players like Henry "Red" Hadley, Jack Thornton, and Gabby Kemp, as well as foreign talents like Cuban shortstop Ormond Sampson. "Today the Atlanta Black Crackers have the best ball club they have had since the days of Bill Shaw a decade and a half ago," Roberts claimed.

When home, the team's play encouraged more people to attend. On May 30, a doubleheader with Jacksonville drew more than 5,500 fans, and a July game against Cincinnati drew almost 7,000. It was the high-water mark for attendance, but the team drew well throughout the summer. "At last," notes Joyce, "someone was making professional black baseball in Atlanta pay." An August swoon on a Midwest road trip, however, lost money, and an angry Schaine abandoned the organization, only to return in mid–September.[27]

It wasn't Schaine's only frustration. That crowded game in late July featured thundershowers, which led to "the intermingling of white and colored patrons during the crowded game." That, in turn, led to charges filed against Schaine. The Black Crackers' owner, however, fought the charge, arguing that "no statute book in Georgia had a law which called for segregation at a baseball game." In an unusual turn for the Jim Crow 1930s, the judge in City Recorder's Court ruled in favor of the team, ruling that "future patrons to colored games will not see ropes and signs telling which way to go; that the men's rest room at the main entrance, heretofore excluded to colored men, will be used exclusively by them; that white men will be ushered to the rest room further from the gate by a directing policeman; and that a section to the far right end of the stand will be reserved for white patrons." It was a signal victory for black fans, and the *Atlanta Daily World* celebrated the decision. "Colored patrons of future Black Cracker games have been assured of better accommodations at Ponce de Leon park and the removal of evidences of segregation." For the white leader of the team, however, it was another in a series of frustrations that defined the late season.[28]

Schaine's frustration combined with the strongest season in the club's history would ultimately create the opportunity for a 1938 season that saw the team join the Negro American

League and compete for championships, but it was the period of development in the three prior seasons that set the stage for the team's more studied success.[29]

The 1938 club "was one of the best baseball teams with the best talent, man for man, that I believe has been put together in Atlanta, Georgia, up until the present day," said Gabby Kemp. That team won 19 straight games at one point and ultimately played the Homestead Grays in the Negro World Series. The Black Crackers took two games in Pittsburgh, "but the owner of the ball club refused to come to Atlanta to play us," said Kemp. "Therefore, the Homestead Grays were disqualified, and the Atlanta Black Crackers won the Negro national championship."[30]

But the team was unable to parlay that success, as the cost of travel outside of the South prohibited the Black Crackers from continuing with the Negro American League. The team would continue in various forms throughout the 1940s in several different incarnations of the Negro Southern League.[31]

"The people lived in a marginal world. They had very little outlet," explained the *Atlanta Daily World*'s Ric Roberts. "They lived in a sharply defined area. Baseball was an outlet. To sit where the whites sat—it was a moment of escape. It gave them something to look forward to. Blacks have always loved baseball. And so that was an outlet. And it gave them a chance to look at their heroes. They thought their boys could play anybody. They were sure that the black ballplayer was as talented as any other."[32]

Atlanta had long struggled with race conflict. Gilded Age concentrations of black citizens created by black schools and churches early became segregated enclaves prior to the turn of the century. Such could be a help or a hindrance. In the 1920s, for example, Atlanta elected a Ku Klux Klan mayor and served as the headquarters for the newly-revived organization. In 1952, however, Rufus Clement, president of Atlanta University, was able to take advantage of that segregated voting bloc to win a seat on the Atlanta school board, becoming the first elected black official since the 19th century. His ability to win and the lack of overt, grandstanding racism by Atlanta public officials in the 1950s and 1960s was the result of a large black voting bloc that could prevent virulent racists from winning. That was good, but it provided Atlanta with an undeserved reputation for racial moderation that ignored the problems of employment discrimination, pay disparity, segregation, city services, and education.[33]

Bill Russell, Harry Edwards, and so many other athletes and activists of the 1960s and early 1970s each in their own way gave lie to the myth that sports was a cure to the ills of society. At the same time, however, sports was also marshaled as a check against such countercultural messages by the likes of Richard Nixon, Spiro Agnew, and Ronald Reagan. That check coincided with a rise of sports in the Sunbelt, as new cities like Atlanta in the expanding South and West sought to burnish their reputations with professional, major league teams. In turn, those teams would, at least in the popular mind, take on the conservative values of those cities.[34]

They would also, in cities like Atlanta, feel the apathy of audiences not used to having such teams or such reputations. "The glory years of the Crackers had faded by the mid–1960s, and the arrival of a major-league baseball team seemed to most Atlantans as probable as the landing of a troop from Mars," explained former Braves executive Bob Hope. "When it happened, it was exciting, important, and almost mystical, something that big cities had and we could only dream about."

The courting of the Braves was a project, like the later effort with the Hawks, of Sunbelt civic development. Atlanta mayor Ivan Allen invested a substantial amount of time in bringing major league professional sports to the city. In 1965, a years-long freeway construction project was finally complete, and athletics was a way to validate the infrastructure efforts intended to bring the city into competition with other national metropolitan areas outside of the South. Allen had first attempted to woo the Kansas City Athletics, but after the deal fell through and the A's moved to Oakland, the mayor turned to the Milwaukee Braves.

The Braves had moved to Milwaukee from Boston in 1952, then won the World Series in 1957 with former Atlanta Cracker Eddie Mathews leading the way. But this was a high-water mark that would not be reached again, with attendance dwindling in response. Milwaukee was a small market near Chicago, a city with two teams. When the Washington Senators moved to Minnesota and became the Minnesota Twins in 1961, the Braves' position became even more precarious and helped encourage them to sell. "Life suddenly became different for Atlanta and the South," wrote Hope. "The city instantly became the unchallenged heart of the Southeast, a thriving metropolitan area about to jump over the remarkable one-million population mark."[35]

Though baseball was not associated with blackness as was the NBA, the presence of black athletes in the sport had hindered any attempt at recruiting major league franchises for the Jim Crow South prior to the Civil Rights Act of 1964 and the Voting Rights Act of 1965. Race would most certainly play a role in the reception of the team, as the Braves did have on their roster one of the most famous black athletes in the country, Henry Aaron, himself a former Negro Leagues player with the Indianapolis Clowns.[36]

More than 50,000 fans attended the team's first home game in April 1966, with Allen throwing out the first pitch, and attendance was healthy throughout the first season. "There was a novelty about the whole thing," said Joe Torre, the team's catcher. "At a game against the Giants, there were 45,000 fans in the stands, and you could hear a pin drop. The fans didn't know what to do at a ball game." And they were largely unwilling to come back to the stadium. The team was doing well, culminating in a 1969 National League Western Division championship behind stars like Torre, Orlando Cepeda, Phil Niekro, and of course Hank Aaron, but the stands were mostly unfilled. After 1969, the team's fortunes waned, as did the already sparse attendance. In 1971, for example, Hank Aaron hit his 600th homerun at home, but he did so in front of only 16,000 fans.[37]

By 1973, the Braves had competed for seven seasons in Atlanta, as had the Black Crackers in 1935. Its tenure from 1973 through 1975 would be colored by basic mediocrity, tinged with bouts of legitimate success, as was that of the Black Crackers from 1935 through 1937. And the broader Atlanta community of the 1970s responded much as did the black community of the 1930s.

In 1973, Aaron was pursuing Babe Ruth's record, and the team became the first to have three players hit 40 home runs in one season, with Aaron joined by Davey Johnson and Darrell Evans. Late in the season, the *Atlanta Daily World*, which considered the slugger the premiere black Southern athlete and celebrated all of his milestones, noted that Aaron had set the record for most home runs in one league with 709, explaining that 708 of Ruth's had been hit in the American League, the last six in the National. The *World* begged fans to attend games for the team's final homestand. "A sell-out crowd for each game could push the Braves' 1973 attendance toward the respectable 1,000,000 mark and save taxpayers some possible grief in the future. How about it Atlanta?" Atlanta, however, chose not to attend, consistent with the behavior of its fans since the 1930s. The Braves' average attendance in 1973 was a paltry 9,885.[38]

In the thick of Aaron's chase, with two weeks to go in the season, one Atlanta home game saw only 1,362 fans come through the turnstiles. Aaron ended the 1973 campaign just one home run short of the hallowed 714 mark. On April 4, 1974, he tied the record in Cincinnati, and he broke it during the Braves' home opener four days later, with more than 53,000 fans, expecting to see history, in attendance. "A new edition of the baseball record book chapter dealing with home runs will be written and this time it will include a king," the *World* noted, "none other than King Henry Aaron, who owns the record for the most homers." It was the largest Atlanta crowd ever to see a Braves game, but it would be a substantial anomaly for the rest of the season.

Atlanta was "a city which has been the brunt of baseball jokes and sneered at by sports fans in major league cities as a city where the fans do not know how to watch a ball game." But on the occasion of Aaron's homer, "the fans rose to the occasion" and "gave the Hammer the respect which was overdue." Again, however, it was not to last. That 1974 season, pitcher Tom House led the league in ERA, Ralph Garr was the batting champion, and the team finished just out of the playoff running. Still, by September, another home game attracted only 1,562 fans, and again the team failed to reach the million-attendance threshold.

Aaron was traded to the Milwaukee Brewers during the winter, and the team regressed in 1975, but the one thing that remained consistent was the lack of fans in the stadium. "Recently the Atlanta Braves have been complaining about 'negative reporting,' so here's a positive report on the Braves," wrote the *Atlanta Daily World*'s James Heath in 1975. "The Braves lead the major league in the number of lost fans compared with a year ago." During that 1975 season, the team averaged an attendance of 6,683. Atlanta placed 11th of 12 in National League attendance every year from 1973 to 1975, just edging the San Diego Padres in 1973 and the San Francisco Giants in the succeeding seasons.[39]

"If failure in baseball were fatal," wrote Bob Hope in 1991, "the Atlanta Braves would have died a long time ago. Since moving to Atlanta from Milwaukee in 1966, the Braves have had the worst record in the major leagues." As Allen Edward Joyce noted in 1975, "The major league Braves in their ten year history have yet to capture the loyalties of the local fans the way the independent, locally owned Crackers did before them." Still, just as the Black Crackers' mixed success between 1935 and 1937 ultimately led to a 1938 Negro American League season and the team's most notable accomplishments, the Braves' mixed success between 1973 and 1975 ultimately led in 1976 to the purchase of the team by Ted Turner, who vowed to make the team winning and relevant.[40]

There are comparative models for play on the field, as well, though such is a more difficult task because available statistics for the Black Crackers are limited. Using the numbers that do exist, however, and comparing 1973 to 1935, each team's eighth season, the Crackers' individual play far outpaced that of the Braves. No one on the latter team came close to Donald Reeves' .571 batting average. Hank Aaron, in fact, was the only 1973 Atlanta player to hit over .300 for the season. The 1935 Black Crackers had two pitchers averaging more than a strikeout per inning, while no one playing for the 1973 Braves even came close to such numbers. Even the great Phil Niekro averaged only a strikeout every two innings. Niekro did, however, pitch a no-hitter that season versus the San Diego Padres, matching Roy Welmaker's 1936 opening day gem against the Chattanooga Black Lookouts.[41]

The Braves' eighth, ninth, and tenth seasons in Atlanta were remarkably similar to those of the Black Crackers in their own eighth, ninth, and tenth seasons, both in play and in the city's general apathy toward its teams. Atlanta was beset by race and class issues in the 1930s and the 1970s, its sports teams were mediocre in both decades, and the respective communities of supporters for each club thus used them as a mirror for their broader social concerns. The Black Crackers were not a great baseball team, but neither were the Braves, and Atlanta proved a largely disinterested baseball city in both instances.

Such was the nature of their functional equivalency. It was a likeness built on mediocrity, one first modeled by the Black Crackers decades before the Braves moved to the South. And while the teams themselves were not overwhelmingly successful, they played a game that was built on failure, where the best hitters recorded outs the majority of the time, where every team but one lost the annual championship. So their inability to fill stadiums or take pennants was itself at the heart of what made the game so fascinating to so many.

Despite the Sunbelt growth of Atlanta from the 1930s to the 1970s, there were many people in the city who also felt failure, whether from racial or economic wounds, but they did not turn to their baseball team in large numbers to salve them. Thus we are left with racial tension, structural economic inequality, mediocre play, and community apathy as a response. Nothing could be more major league than that.

Notes

1. For more on the postbellum divisions of black Atlanta by social and economic status, see Allison Dorsey, *To Build Our Lives Together: Community Formation in Black Atlanta, 1875–1906* (Athens: University of Georgia Press, 2004); and Edmund L. Drago, *Black Politicians and Reconstruction in Georgia: A Splendid Failure* (Baton Rouge: Louisiana State University Press, 1982). For more on the role of the Atlanta Race Riot of 1906 as an arbiter of exacerbating those divisions, see David F. Godshalk, *Veiled Visions: The 1906 Atlanta Race Riot and the Reshaping of American Race Relations* (Chapel Hill: University of North Carolina Press, 2005); and Gregory Mixon, *The Atlanta Riot: Race, Class, and Violence in a New South City* (Gainesville: University Press of Florida, 2005).

2. Frank Marshall Davis, "Negro America's First Daily," *Negro Digest* 5 (1946): 87.

3. Tim Darnell, *The Crackers: Early Days of Atlanta Baseball* (Athens, GA: Hill Street Press, 2003), 124–125; Clifford M. Kuhn, Harlon E. Joye, and E. Bernard West, *Living Atlanta: An Oral History of the City, 1914–1948* (Athens: University of Georgia Press, 1990), 266.

4. Allen Edward Joyce, "The Atlanta Black Crackers" (MA thesis, Emory University, 1975), 13–15.

5. Kuhn, Joye, and West, *Living Atlanta*, 266.

6. Darnell, *The Crackers*, 129–130.

7. Heaphy, *The Negro Leagues, 1869–1960*, 42.

8. Joyce, "The Atlanta Black Crackers," 2, 5–6; Kuhn, Joye, and West, *Living Atlanta*, 272.

9. Darnell, *The Crackers*, 136; Kuhn, Joye, and West, *Living Atlanta*, 184, 266–268.

10. *Atlanta Daily World*, March 31, 1935, 5; Joyce, "The Atlanta Black Crackers," 32.

11. Heaphy, *The Negro Leagues*, 145; Kuhn, Joye, and West, *Living Atlanta*, 161, 266.

12. One of those owners was William J. Shaw, who had moved to Atlanta from Brunswick. Shaw ran an insurance business in the city and owned a local restaurant known as the Roof Garden. Joyce, "The Atlanta Black Crackers," 17, 33; Heaphy, *The Negro Leagues*, 98; Darnell, *The Crackers*, 125; Leslie Heaphy, "The Atlanta Black Crackers," in *The National Pastime: Baseball in the Peach State*, no. 30, Ken Fenster and Wynn Montgomery, editors (Lincoln, NB: Society for American Baseball Research, 2010): 30–36.

13. Joyce, "The Atlanta Black Crackers," 34.

14. *Atlanta Daily World*, May 5, 1935, 1, May 19, 1935, 5; Joyce, "The Atlanta Black Crackers," 36.

15. Kuhn, Joye, and West, *Living Atlanta*, 273; William J. Plott, *The Negro Southern League: A Baseball History, 1920–1951* (Jefferson, NC: McFarland, 2015), 127, 133–134; *Atlanta Daily World* March 10, 1935, 4; *Pittsburgh Courier*, June 29, 1935, A6; Darnell, *The Crackers*, 133.

16. *Atlanta Daily World*, May 29, 1935, 5, June 3, 1935, July 26, 1935, 1; Joyce, "The Atlanta Black Crackers," 37–38; Plott, *The Negro Southern League*, 128–129.

17. Kemp describes the south Georgia town of Thomaston, but it seems likely that he meant the south Georgia town of Thomasville, as Thomaston, Georgia, is not in the south of the state. Darnell, *The Crackers*, 127; *Atlanta Daily World*, August 3, 1935, 5.

18. Despite the end of the Black Crackers' regular season, an all-star team selected by the *Atlanta Daily World*'s Ric Roberts and comprised of players from the Crackers and the Jacksonville Red Caps played an early October series with a Northern all-star team. Joyce, "The Atlanta Black Crackers," 40; *Atlanta Daily World*, August 28, 1935, 5; Plott, *The Negro Southern League*, 132–133.

19. *Atlanta Daily World*, November 21, 1935, 5.

20. Plott, *The Negro Southern League*, 136; *Atlanta Daily World*, January 6, 1935, 5, March 13, 1936, 5; Joyce, "The Atlanta Black Crackers," 41–42.

21. *Atlanta Daily World*, April 27, 1936, 4; Joyce, "The Atlanta Black Crackers," 43.

22. *Atlanta Daily World*, May 11, 1936, 5, May 26, 1936, 5, May 27, 1936, 6.

23. *Atlanta Daily World*, May 29, 1936, 5, August 28, 1936, 5; Plott, *The Negro Southern League*, 138–140; Joyce, "The Atlanta Black Crackers," 43–45.

24. "Financial backing for the Black Crackers of 1937 is at the highest peak since the fat post-war days," Roberts claimed. "Even the genial and baseball loving late Percy Williams, a man who spent a thousand bucks or so backing his team, is overshadowed by the sort of dough President Schaine is dishing up for a first class ball club." *Atlanta Daily World*, April 12, 1937, 5, April 13, 1937, 5, April 20, 1937, 5; Joyce, "The Atlanta Black Crackers," 46–48.

25. Kuhn, Joye, and West, *Living Atlanta*, 270; Darnell, *The Crackers*, 134.

26. Darnell, *The Crackers*, 135; Kuhn, Joye, and West, *Living Atlanta*, 272.

27. After Schaine returned to the team, he sent it to Houston to play in a $10,000 tournament sponsored by the *Houston Post*. *Atlanta Daily World*, May 5, 1937, 5; *Chicago Defender*, May 29, 1937, 14, July 31, 1937, 21, September 4, 1937, 20; *Pittsburgh Courier*, May 29, 1937, 17; Heaphy, *The Negro Leagues*, 145; Joyce, "The Atlanta Black Crackers," 48–53; Plott, *The Negro Southern League*, 143.

28. *Atlanta Daily World*, August 12, 1937, 1.

29. Joyce, "The Atlanta Black Crackers," 54–57; *Chicago Defender*, December 18, 1937, 8.

30. Kuhn, Joye, and West, *Living Atlanta*, 265–266, 272–273; Darnell, *The Crackers*, 141–151.

31. Kuhn, Joye, and West, *Living Atlanta*, 273; Heaphy, *The Negro Leagues*, 222.

32. Joyce, "The Atlanta Black Crackers," 5.

33. Ronald H. Bayor, *Race and the Shaping of Twentieth-Century Atlanta* (Chapel Hill: University of North Carolina Press, 2000), 6–7, 12, 27, 29; Larry Keating, *Atlanta: Race, Class, and Urban Expansion* (Philadelphia: Temple University Press, 2001), 41–44.

34. Benjamin G. Rader, *American Sports: From the Age of Folk Games to the Age of Televised Sports*, 6th ed (Upper Saddle River, NJ: Prentice Hall, 2009), 240–242; See also Bill Russell, *Go Up For Glory* (New York: Coward-McCann, 1966); Harry Edwards, *The Revolt of the Black Athlete* (New York: The Free Press, 1969); Dave Meggyesy, *Out of Their League* (Lincoln: University of Nebraska Press, 1970); Jim Bouton, *Ball Four: My Life and Hard Times Throwing the Knuckleball in the Big Leagues* (New York: World Publishing, 1970); and Jack Scott, *The Athletic Revolution* (New York: The Free Press, 1971).

35. Bob Hope, *We Could've Finished Last Without You: An Irreverent Look at the Atlanta Braves, the Losingest Team in Baseball for the Past 25 Years* (Atlanta: Longstreet Press, 1991), 6–8.

36. The best biographical treatment of Hank Aaron's life in and out of baseball is Howard Bryant, *The Last Hero: A Life of Henry Aaron* (New York: Pantheon, 2010).

37. Hope, *We Could've Finished Last Without You*, 8–9.

38. Baseball-Reference.com, "Atlanta Braves Attendance, Stadiums, and Park Factors," accessed August 28, 2016, http://www.baseball-reference.com/teams/ATL/attend.shtml; Baseball-Reference.com, "1973 Atlanta Braves Schedule and Results," accessed August 28, 2016, http://www.baseball-reference.com/teams/ATL/1973-schedule-scores.shtml; *Atlanta Daily World*, September 11, 1973, 2, September 21, 1973, 4; Hope, *We Could've Finished Last Without You*, 9; Michael E. Goodman, *The Story Of the Atlanta Braves* (Mankato, MN: Creative Education, 2008), 27–33.

39. *Atlanta Daily World*, April 11, 1974, 1, 4, October 6, 1974, 10, July 20, 1975, 6; Baseball-Reference. com, "1974 Atlanta Braves Schedule and Results," accessed August 28, 2016, http://www.baseball-reference.com/teams/ATL/1974-schedule-scores.shtml; Baseball-Reference.com, "1975 Atlanta Braves Schedule and Results," accessed August 28, 2016, http://www.baseball-reference.com/teams/ATL/1975-schedule-scores.shtml; Hope, *We Could've Finished Last Without You*, 9; Michael E. Goodman, *The Story of the Atlanta Braves*, 27–33.

40. Hope, *We Could've Finished Last Without You*, 1, 9; Joyce, "The Atlanta Black Crackers," 1.

41. Baseball-Reference.com, "1973 Atlanta Braves Batting, Pitching, and Fielding Statistics," accessed September 6, 2016, http://www.baseball-reference.com/teams/ATL/1973.shtml; Plott, *The Negro Southern League*, 133–134; ESPN.com, "MLB Team History—Atlanta Braves No-Hitters," accessed September 6, 2016, http://www.espn.com/mlb/history/teams/_/team/Atl/history/no-hitters.

Changing the Way They Do Business

Jackie Robinson, Integration and the Origins
of Organizational Culture in Organized Baseball

MICHAEL E. LOMAX

On April 18, 1946, Jack Roosevelt Robinson made his International League (IL) debut against the Jersey City Giants at Roosevelt Stadium. In his first at-bat, Robinson worked the pitcher to a full count before grounding out to the shortstop. In the third inning with two men on base, Robinson drilled left-hander Warren Sandall's fast ball over the left field fence for a three-run home run. In the fifth inning, the Royals second baseman laid down a bunt that stunned the Giants infield as he dashed across first base ahead of the throw. Robinson stole second base, then went to third unexpectedly on a ground out to third base. When Giants relief pitcher Phil Otis entered the game, Robinson aggressively taunted him with attempts to steal home. Confused by his antics, Otis balked and Robinson trotted home. Robinson's debut in Organized Baseball couldn't have been scripted better by a Hollywood director. In five at bats, he hit safely four times, including a home run, stole two bases, and scored four runs, two of them on balks.[1]

There have been several scholarly studies that examined Jackie Robinson's rookie season with the International League Montreal Royals. Their works can be briefly summarized as follows. Jackie Robinson's spring training season in Florida was marred by several cancellations. He rebounded nicely with an excellent opening day performance against the Jersey City Giants. Throughout the season, Robinson was subjected to racial abuse in several IL cities, like Syracuse and Baltimore. In spite of this unwanted attention, Robinson performed spectacularly and led the Montreal Royals to the International League pennant and Little World Series championship.[2]

These studies contributed immensely to our understanding of Jackie Robinson's rookie season with the Montreal Royals. They revealed Robinson's courage and intestinal fortitude in the midst of a complicated and often hostile environment. However, the overwhelming focus on integration, the Civil Rights movement, and Robinson being accepted by his white teammates makes our understanding of his rookie season incomplete. What is often overlooked was the way Robinson's presence on the Royals marked the start of the transformation of Organized Baseball's organizational culture. Organizational culture, as defined here, represents the pattern of basic assumptions that a given group has invented, discovered, or developed in learning to cope with its problems—or challenges—of external adaptation and internal integration. It is a pattern of assumptions that has worked well enough to be considered valid and, consequently, to be taught to new members as the correct way to perceive, think, and feel in relation to those challenges. This essay examines the way Jackie Robinson transformed that culture during his rookie season with the Montreal Royals.

Jackie Robinson's rookie season with the Montreal Royals was a combination of complexity and triumph. His presence disrupted the Royals' chemistry, while he personally experienced a sense of alienation. Player and fan reaction to his presence on the diamond was, for the most part, mixed. Robinson endured the trash-talking from Syracuse players, although he received a generous reception from Buffalo fans throughout the season. The Royals second baseman's reception from Baltimore fans could be perceived as a threat to his safety. Despite this mixed reaction from the players and fans, Robinson's performance on the field appeared to offset any reception he received. It marked the beginning of players of white Eurocentric origin co-existing with players of color in the pursuit of pennants and World Series championships.

The Rise of a Baseball Pioneer

Jack Roosevelt Robinson was born in Cairo, Georgia, on January 31, 1919. He was the youngest of four brothers and one sister. His mother, Mallie Robinson, moved the family to Pasadena, California, in the 1920s, where he spent his childhood. By today's standards, Robinson was an at-risk youngster, and by his own admission a "full-fledged delinquent." Throughout his early life, several mentors would come to have a positive influence on him.[3]

Robinson developed a love of sports at an early age, which undoubtedly helped him deal with the traps of racism. In Pasadena, he competed with and against athletes of diverse cultures without allowing race to produce conflicts or resentments among them. The younger Robinson earned a spot on the baseball team at Pasadena Junior College (PJC), and his excellent fielding and timely hitting made him one of the favorites of Bulldogs coach John Thurman. Football was the sport Robinson excelled in, dazzling PJC fans with his athletic prowess. Robinson's athletic achievements sparked interest among several colleges and universities to recruit him. He ultimately decided to attend UCLA, where he would earn All-American honors in football.

In the spring of 1942, Robinson was drafted into the U.S. Army. No other period in his life exemplified Robinson's defiance of racism and segregation as did his brief military career. In April 1944, a dozen African American officers received orders to proceed to Camp Hood, Texas, and report to the 761st Tank Battalion. On July 6, 1944, Robinson became involved in a controversy that almost ended his military career. He boarded a military bus that took him from McCloskey Hospital in Temple, Texas, to Camp Hood, and sat next to Virginia Jones, the light-complected African American wife of a fellow officer. Robinson was aware Texas law required Jim Crow seating on busses, but he also knew that the army now prohibited segregation on its military bases. After driving approximately six blocks, the driver, Milton N. Reneger, ordered Robinson to move to the back of the bus. The young lieutenant refused. The driver threatened to make trouble for him when the bus reached the station. The conversation between Robinson and Reneger grew more intense. The military police were eventually called and Robinson was placed in shackles. That night Robinson got into a heated argument over the incident with his commanding officer Captain Gerald M. Bear, who subsequently filed five charges, including insubordination, against Robinson, resulting in a general court martial.

On August 2, 1944, Jackie Robinson's case went to trial. The trial lasted more than four hours. An able defense lawyer and the weakness of the case against him led the army judges to rule that he had acted within his rights in his refusal to bow to Southern tradition.

Robinson secured the two-thirds necessary for his acquittal and was found not guilty of all charges.

On August 28, 1945, Brooklyn Dodgers President Branch Rickey invited Robinson to his office. After staring briefly with the Kansas City Monarchs shortstop of the Negro American League, Rickey broke the silence by asking Robinson if he had a girl. When Robinson answered in the affirmative, Rickey replied: "Well marry her! A man needs a wife and a good home." After inquiring about his religious affiliation and the state of the Negro Leagues, Rickey asked Robinson if he knew why the former had brought him there. Robinson replied hesitantly that it might have something to do with the Brooklyn Brown Dodgers, an African American club in the United States League. "No, that's not it," Rickey proclaimed. "I want you to play for the Brooklyn Dodgers organization. Perhaps Montreal to start with."[4]

The statement startled and simultaneously overwhelmed Robinson. To be sure, Rickey acknowledged Robinson's ability as an exceptional athlete, but questioned whether he had "the guts." Robinson declared he wasn't afraid of anybody or anything on the playing field. The Mahatma interrupted and explained that he wanted a ballplayer "with guts enough not to fight back." At this point, the Dodgers president dramatically acted out physically the threats Robinson might endure. Rickey stressed the key to success was that Robinson could not fight back against the indignities. He read Robinson the words of Jesus that Rapini underscored: "Ye have heard that it hath been said an eye for an eye and a tooth for a tooth: But I say unto you, that ye resist evil: But whosoever shall smite thee on the cheek, turn to him the other also." After listening to Rickey's dramatic oratory, Robinson replied: "I have two cheeks, Mr. Rickey. Is that it?" Rickey nodded in the affirmative. As their meeting came to a close, Rickey offered Robinson a standard minor league contract for a player assigned to the International League Montreal Royals. He would receive $600 a month plus a $3,500 signing bonus.[5]

Thus what became known as the "noble experiment" was born. It was grounded in the Christian ethic of turning the other cheek. For three years, Robinson played to the best of his ability and would not fight back against aggressive plays or incidents with possible racial overtones. He was to carry himself as a gentleman both on and off the field. In this way, theoretically, the culture of Organized Baseball would change, and Jackie Robinson would be accepted by both players and fans.

In addition to signing Robinson, Rickey signed Negro Leagues pitcher Johnny Wright. A right-handed hurler who began his Negro Leagues career in 1937 with the Newark Eagles, Wright possessed a blazing fastball and an assortment of sharp-breaking curveballs. He joined the Homestead Grays in 1941 and pitched in the World Series in 1942, 1943, and 1945. In 1944, Wright entered the military service during World War II, serving in the Navy and pitching for the Great Lakes Naval station and the Floyd Bennett Air Field teams. On November 24, 1945, the *New York Amsterdam News* reported that Rickey signed Wright to a contract, making him the second African American player in the Dodgers organization.[6]

A Rocky Spring Training

Organized Baseball's first encounter with the South's laws, customs, and traditions during spring training occurred when the Brooklyn Dodgers' farm club, the Montreal Royals, traveled to Florida. Branch Rickey and members of the Committee on Baseball in New York City made arrangements with city officials in Daytona Beach, Florida, to train there.

Recognizing the potential economic boom to the local economy, city officials agreed to ease segregation laws prohibiting African Americans and whites from using its ballpark at the same time. Simultaneously, Rickey arranged for African American sportswriters Wendell Smith, Sam Lacy, and Billy Rowe to meet Robinson and his new bride, Rachel, upon their arrival in Florida. These sportswriters had connections in the African American community that Rickey lacked and would make the necessary arrangements for the Robinsons to insure a smooth transition into their new environment. With the assistance of a local NAACP official, Mary McLeod Bethune, the journalists located a family who offered their house to the Robinsons.[7]

The initial plan to house the Robinsons called for providing accommodations in Daytona Beach and Sanford, Florida. In Daytona Beach, they stayed at Joe Harris' house, a pharmacist and influential African American leader. The Dodgers and Royals were scheduled to begin spring training on March 1, so the Robinsons moved 40 miles south to Sanford, the site of the Dodgers' baseball school, or "Rickey University" as sportswriters had labeled it. There the Robinsons stayed at Mr. and Mrs. David Brock's home, a prominent African American couple, while the white players stayed at the lakefront Mayfair Hotel, which excluded people of color. Rickey's plan for the Royals to train in Sanford, however, was thwarted when a delegation from the town told the Dodgers president they would not allow African Americans and whites on the same field. As a result, Robinson and Wright returned to Daytona Beach.[8]

Rickey's plan to house the Robinsons was based on what could best be described as a separate-and-unequal doctrine. He accommodated Southern law, custom, and tradition by finding the best housing arrangements in the African American community. Rickey had personally visited the Brock home and declared: "If we can't put them in the hotels, then they should stay in some place that represents something. This is the type of home." Rickey's focus on developing a plan to house the Robinsons was understandable because this was one venue he had control over. What he could not plan for was Robinson's reaction to these segregated living arrangements or what would occur when the Royals began playing exhibition games.[9]

Robinson's initial response to this imposed segregation was annoyance, due primarily to the harrowing experience he and his wife, Rachel, had endured just getting to spring training. Upon their return to Daytona Beach from Sanford, the Robinsons found themselves back in their small room at the Harris's. Separate accommodations were also found for Wright, while the rest of the players lodged in the Riviera Hotel on the oceanfront. Although the Riviera was in an unpleasant state after its wartime use, Robinson wanted to stay with the rest of the players.

Author Arnold Rampersad states that Robinson later wrote that he and Rachel disliked this distinction "almost as much as [he] resented being chased out of Sanford, but we knew that there could be no protest." Robinson added: "[Mr. Rickey] had said that I would have to be a man big enough to bear the cross of martyrdom." In other words, not only would Robinson have to tolerate this segregated living arrangement, he would also have to accommodate to what Aldon Morris described as a system of domination that protected the privileges of white society and generated tremendous human suffering for African Americans.[10]

The city of Daytona Beach honored its commitment to ease segregation laws to allow for interracial contests to take place. Yet when the Royals returned there, they found themselves practicing in the city's African American district while the Dodgers trained in the white district. Daytona Beach officials had eased segregation, but were not about to eliminate it completely. In any event, on March 17 Jackie Robinson became the first African

American in the 20th century to play alongside whites on the same field in an Organized Baseball game during an exhibition between the Royals and the Dodgers. He faced the game with some trepidation because of the uncertainty of how the public would receive him and, most important, how he would perform against major leaguers like Pee Wee Reese, Pete Reiser, or Dixie Walker. A crowd of 4,000 fans greeted Robinson with a resolute volley of cheers—and a scattering of boos—when his name was announced.

Robinson's and Wright's experience outside of Daytona Beach, however, told a different story. On March 21, George Robinson, executive secretary of the Playground and Recreation Commission in Jacksonville, forbade Robinson and Wright to play in an exhibition game at Durkee Field against the Jersey City Giants. He explained: "It is part of the rules and regulations of the Recreation Department that Negroes and whites cannot compete against each other on a city-owned playground." Rickey's initial response was not to make waves. He stated that the Dodgers "have no intention of attempting to counter any government's laws and regulations. If we are notified that Robinson cannot play at Jacksonville, of course he cannot play." The Giants requested that the Royals leave Robinson and Wright at Daytona Beach. Instead, Rickey requested that he be notified of the ruling on the "official stationary of the city of Jacksonville." In this way, he attempted to place the responsibility on the city officials' shoulders. The Jacksonville Parks Commission voted unanimously to cancel the game.[11]

Two exhibition games in Deland and Sanford illustrated the types of barriers local officials erected to prohibit interracial contests. On March 25, the Royals were scheduled to play in Deland, Florida. Upon their arrival, they learned that the game had been canceled due to a malfunction in the lighting system. The contest was scheduled for the afternoon. Responding to the cancellation, Robinson declared: "What this had to do with the fact that the game was played in the daytime, no one bothered to explain."

On April 7, the Royals were scheduled to play the St. Paul Saints at Sanford, where local townspeople had previously expelled Robinson and Wright. Rickey ignored a request by city officials to leave the two players of color at the Dodgers camp. Robinson did start the game, and in his first at-bat beat out an infield single and promptly stole second base. When the next batter singled, he scored the game's first run on a close play at the plate. As Robinson was about to step onto the field for the third inning, the local chief of police ordered Montreal manager Clay Hopper to remove his second baseman or risk prosecution. Hopper replaced him.[12]

Several other cancellations occurred. These disruptions were both costly and bad for team morale. Without question, Robinson and Wright recognized that this chaotic spring training season was a direct result of their presence, undoubtedly causing insurmountable pressure on both of them. The pressure was further exacerbated by the fact that they still had to make the ball club. Even when they made the club, both players still had to deal with the issue of being segregated from the other players, a distinction that frustrated Robinson from the outset. Despite these obstacles, Robinson and Wright persevered, keeping to themselves and speaking only when spoken to.

Branch Rickey stuck with the overall experiment. His willingness to cancel exhibition games sent a subtle message that he was committed to Robinson despite the barriers erected by officials in these Florida cities. According to Wendell Smith, he answered the offended cities with defiance: "Without Robinson and Wright there'll be no games!" These exhibition games occurred in the context of an era when Southern whites had an established, comprehensive system of domination over people of color. The "tripartite system of domination" kept people of color under control economically, politically, and socially in cities and rural areas of the South. This system of domination was sanctioned by legislation and enforced by Southern governments. Moreover, exhibition games by baseball clubs from the North in no way would change "their southern way of life." Nevertheless, Jackie Robinson and Johnny Wright continued their journey of baseball integration during the regular season.[13]

A Royals Rookie

Jackie Robinson's debut with the Montreal Royals marked the start in transitioning Organized Baseball's organizational culture. Organizational culture in Organized Baseball can be divided into two categories—intra and inter. Intra-organizational culture refers to the interaction among the players themselves. Arguably the clubhouse (or locker room), dugout, and the diamond represents the players' work or office environment. A ball club endeavors to maintain some semblance of cohesion or "chemistry" within this environment to maintain their competitiveness. There were indications that both Robinson and Johnny Wright disrupted the Royals' chemistry, due to the external forces that impacted on them. However, if both men kept to themselves during spring training, there could possibly be a sense of isolation and alienation among them.[14]

The player-manager relationship also symbolized a ball club's intra-organizational culture. It appears Robinson's relationship with Royals manager Clay Hopper was one of indifference. Hopper played in the minor leagues in the 1920s and 1930s. He joined the Dodgers organization in 1942, and three years later managed the Southern League Mobile Bears, leading them to the league championship. In 1946, Hopper was promoted to become manager of the Triple A Royals. The owner of a Mississippi plantation, Hopper opposed Rickey signing Robinson, whose presence placed Hopper in a dubious position with his friends and neighbors down home. Yet Rickey prevailed on the Royals' manager, and Hopper greeted Robinson with a handshake. As an organization man, Hopper was one who did not make waves.

Bench jockeying was an invented tradition among the players. No topic was out of bounds, as personal appearance, ethnicity, and race were all considered "fair game." Players attempted to get under the skin of opposing players to throw them off of their game. The Syracuse Chiefs players sought to get under Robinson's skin, so to speak. With Robinson in the on-deck circle, a Syracuse player pushed a black cat in his direction, shouting, "Hey Jackie, there's your cousin clowning on the field." The umpire stopped play and ordered the Syracuse manager to silence Robinson's tormentors. Robinson failed to hit safely in the first game, but rebounded the following night with two hits in five at-bats.[15]

Inter-organizational culture references the ways in which players adapt to the forces outside their work or office environment. This includes their reaction to the fans and sportswriters. The fans represent Organized Baseball's consumer market. Fans—short for fanatics—root for the home team's success while vilifying the opposing club. They can embrace the players, particularly when they're performing well, or boo them, especially when they are in a batting slump. The fans get ecstatic whenever a manager disputes the umpire's call and have a tendency to demonize the arbiters on close calls the fans perceive the latter as missing.

In addition to the bench jockeying incident in Syracuse, Robinson also experienced torment in Baltimore, the IL's southernmost city. IL President Frank Shaughnessy called Rickey, imploring him not to bring the black players to Baltimore. Shaughnessy predicted that a riot would occur and it would "wreck organized baseball in that city." Both Rickey and Shaughnessy met on opening day at Jersey City, and the IL president repeated his plea. Shaughnessy exploded when Rickey dismissed his fears with one of his customary sermons. He warned the Dodgers president that "this is not the time for philosophical mouthings and silly platitudes. The people are up in arms in Baltimore."[16]

On an April Saturday night, Robinson debuted in Baltimore. A little over 3,000 fans showed up, reinforcing the reports of a boycott. Sitting behind the Royals' dugout, Rachel Robinson perceived this experience as worse than their journey in Florida. When Robinson appeared on the field, a man sitting behind her shouted, "Here comes that nigger son of a bitch. Let's get him now." Baltimore fans unleashed an unending torrent of abuse. People engaged "in the worst kind of name calling and attacks on Jackie I had to sit through." It was one of the few times Rachel feared for Jackie's safety, and she contemplated whether her husband should withdraw from the experiment.[17]

Because the evidence is limited, it is difficult to determine how the intra- and inter-organizational cultural forces impacted on Johnny Wright. Like Robinson, Wright confronted the jeers from Baltimore fans. He entered in relief in the sixth inning with the bases loaded and a five-run deficit. He retired the side without allowing a run. Wright completed the game, giving up no hits in a losing cause. Although his performance against the Orioles invoked optimism, Wright quietly faded away. The right-hander was used sparingly in the following weeks, and he made no public protest. On May 14, the Royals reassigned him to Three Rivers in the Canadian-American League. To replace Wright, Rickey signed Philadelphia Stars left hander Roy Partlow.[18]

The players in Syracuse and the fans in Baltimore did not entirely define Robinson's experience with the Royals. Jules Tygiel pointed out that Buffalo ranked perhaps as the most hospitable of the International League cities. Between games of a June doubleheader, the president of the Buffalo City Council hosted a ceremony honoring Robinson and Roy Partlow. Both men received gifts including cash, wallets, wristwatches, and traveling bags. Robinson received a warm reception in Buffalo throughout the season.[19]

Nonetheless, Syracuse, the other New York city, told a different story. Circumstances arose from the fans and the players. Bench jockeying directed at Robinson was peppered with overt racial overtones that exceeded the bounds of propriety. Toward the end of the season, Montreal General Manager Mel Jones berated the Chiefs' treatment of Robinson. "You've got the worst bunch of jockeys in the league from your club," Jones exclaimed. "He [Robinson] had to take a worse ride from your club." Since bench jockeying was a part of baseball culture, it was apparent the trash talk directed at Robinson crossed the proverbial line.[20]

The Syracuse players' trash talk paled in comparison to the hostility that accompanied any trip to Baltimore. The ominous crowd reaction in Baltimore that frightened Rachel Robinson in the first series continued throughout the season. On their trip to Baltimore, Robinson appeared in only one game. On the final play of that game, a brawl erupted at home plate, and the fans poured out onto the field to support the home town Orioles. Robinson was already in the clubhouse when the fight began. However, the fans surrounded the clubhouse. "Those fans were there, I would say until one o'clock," recalled Robinson's teammate, Spider Jorgensen. He added: "and they'd say 'come out Robinson, you son of a bitch. We know you're up there. We're gonna get you.'" Jorgensen and two other players remained with Robinson until the crowd dispersed and then, unable to get a cab, they escorted the Royals second baseman to his hotel on a city bus.[21]

Robinson's final visit to Baltimore was marred by epithets and threats of fan violence. He became the target of "unfunny humor" of others, declared African American sportswriter Sam Lacy. A fan seated near Lacy cracked that Robinson "ought to be behind a pair of mules." A close play at the plate in the first game of the series served as the stimulus of another riot. Fans invaded the diamond in protest, and four policemen arrived to control the crowd. Umpire Gus Winters and not Robinson, who had hit a home run, two singles, and stole home during the contest, was the target of their rage. Nevertheless, the memories of the earlier confrontation and fears for Robinson's safety haunted him and his Royals teammates.[22]

Robinson's performance on the field appeared to offset the mixed reaction he received from the players and fans. His .349 batting average eclipsed the Royals' team record set in 1930. Robinson hit only three home runs, but he also drove in 66 runs. He led the International League in runs scored (113), and his 40 stolen bases was second only to his teammate Marvin Rackley (65). At second base, Robinson ended up with the highest fielding percentage in the IL, as Montreal won the pennant by 18½ games. The sheer emotion inspired by both the players and fans, not to mention Robinson's performance on the field, moreover, appeared to counteract any reaction the Royals second baseman underwent, regardless of race.

More important, Jackie Robinson's experience with the Montreal Royals reveals that fan reaction to his presence on the diamond was not a monolithic one. To be sure, Robinson confronted racial hostility in the Southern city of Baltimore, but he also withstood the trash talking of players in the Northern city of Syracuse, New York. Yet by the same token, the Royals second baseman received a warm reception in Buffalo and was embraced by the Montreal fans. It was a testament to Robinson's athletic ability that he performed so well in the midst of this mixed fan reaction.

Robinson's influence on attendance was also significant—especially among African American fans. In his first road trip, thousands of African Americans poured into Ruppert Stadium in Newark for a game between the Royals and the Bears. In Buffalo and Baltimore, people of color accounted for approximately 40 to 50 percent of the fans at the respective ballparks.

Robinson's influence on attendance, however, proved to be a double-edged sword. To be sure the Montreal Royals specifically and the International League in general benefited from the increase in attendance. Yet this came at the expense of the Negro Leagues. Baltimore and Newark, for example, also had Negro League franchises—the Newark Eagles and the Baltimore Elite Giants. African American fans now had the choice either to watch these Negro Leagues teams, or witness Robinson compete with the Royals. It appeared the fans voted with their wallets and witnessed the Royals' second baseman perform in the IL. Whereas Negro Leagues owners attempted to affiliate with Organized Baseball, without success, they apparently neglected this phenomenon occurring in Montreal. It led to Organized Baseball competing with the Negro Leagues, favoring the former with considerable advantage and leverage.[23]

Sportswriters and the way they interacted with players also personified Organized Baseball's inter-organizational culture. Robinson's life story was illustrated in April in *Picture News*, published by Comic Magazines. Due to African American fans expressing their pride and sense of achievement engendered by Robinson's performance, African American sportswriter Sam Lacy embarked on a crusade to treat Robinson "as another player." The fans, teammates, and the manager were not to grant Robinson any preferential treatment. When Robinson's errors contributed to an early-season loss in Baltimore, Lacy composed a "Letter to Clay Hopper" urging him to "bawl Jackie [out] for his mistakes." Two weeks later, Lacy defended the right of the fans to boo Robinson in the name of "freedom of expression."

He added: "No fan exercises like the baseball fans what he considers an inalienable right to cheer or jeer as he sees fit."[24]

Sam Lacy's aspiration that Jackie Robinson received no preferential treatment was understandable. Treating Robinson like any other player would emulate the American ideal that all men are created equal regardless of race, creed, or color. What Lacy failed to recognize was that Jackie Robinson was different from any other player. For decades, the white Eurocentric power structure had erected the color line that denied players of color the opportunity to compete in Organized Baseball. Whereas some players of color managed to slip through the cracks, these athletes did not play in Organized Baseball regardless of playing ability. It resulted in these players competing in the segregated Negro Leagues. However, as a change in racial attitudes in the U.S. occurred—a direct result of World War II—Branch Rickey endeavored to tap into a cheap labor pool previously untapped by MLB owners. This is not to suggest that Rickey's desires for social justice did not contribute to bringing players of color into Organized Baseball—it did. But making the case that it was in the Brooklyn Dodgers' best economic interests to bring players of color into Organized Baseball provided Rickey the ideological justification to bring his partners—Walter O'Malley and Jack Smith—on board to support his decision.

Rickey's decision proved beneficial. Jackie Robinson's performance was instrumental in the Montreal Royals winning the International League pennant and Little World Series championship against the American Association Louisville Colonels. Robinson's performance provided Rickey with the ammunition necessary to integrate the Brooklyn Dodgers.

Conclusion

Jackie Robinson's rookie season with the Montreal Royals was a culmination of complexity and triumph. Whereas disrupting the Royals' chemistry occurred because of his presence—along with Johnny Wright—during spring training and the regular season, he undoubtedly experienced a sense of alienation by keeping to himself and not making waves. Player interaction from opposing players appeared to be mixed, yet he was subjected to bench jockeying in Syracuse, which could be interpreted as crossing the proverbial line due to its racial overtones. Fan reaction to Robinson's presence on the field was not a monolithic one. On the one hand, the Royals second baseman received a generous reception from Buffalo fans throughout the season. On the other hand, any trip to Baltimore could be perceived as a threat to Robinson's safety. In spite of this mixed reaction from players and fans, Jackie Robinson's performance on the diamond appeared to offset any reception he may have received. It marked the start of players of white Eurocentric origin and players of color at least co-existing with each other in the pursuit of pennants and World Series championships.

Notes

1. Robinson debut in *Chicago Defender*, April 27, 1946.
2. Arnold Rampersad has written the most definitive Robinson biography in *Jackie Robinson: A Biography* (New York: Alfred A. Knopf, 1997). Additional scholarship on Jackie Robinson include: Jules Tygiel, *Baseball's Great Experiment: Jackie Robinson and His Legacy*, 1983. Early scholarship on Robinson was essentially research articles. See, for example, Ronald A. Smith, "The Paul Robeson—Jackie Robinson Saga and a Political Collision," *Journal of Sport History* 6 (Summer 1979): 5–27. William Simons, "Jackie Robinson and the American Mind: Journalistic Perceptions of the Reintegration of Baseball," *Journal of Sport History* 12 (Spring 1985): 39–64.

Scholars have also examined the press reports regarding Robinson. See Bill L. Weaver, "The Black Press and the Assault on Professional Baseball's 'Color Line,' October, 1945-April, 1947," *Phylon* 40 (Winter 1979): 303–17; E. Franklin Frazier, *Black Bourgeoisie* (Glencoe, IL: The Free Press, 1957). Additional scholarship by journalist scholars include: William G. Kelley, "Jackie Robinson and the Press," *Journalism Quarterly* 53 (Spring 1976): 137–39; Pat Washburn, "New York Newspapers and Robinson's First Season," *Journalism Quarterly* 58 (Winter 1981): 640–44; idem. "New York Newspaper Coverage of Jackie Robinson in His First Major League Season," *Western Journal of Black Studies* 4 (Fall 1980): 183–92. In the 1990s, scholars began to re-examine Jackie Robinson's plight to commemorate the 50th anniversary of the re-integrating Major League Baseball. See: Steven K. Wisensale, "The Political Wars Of Jackie Robinson," *Nine: Journal of Baseball History and Social Perspectives* 1 (1993): 18–28; Anthony R. Pratkanis and Marlene Turner, "The Year Cool Papa Bell Lost The Batting Title: Mr. Branch Rickey and Mr. Jackie Robinson's Plea For Affirmative Action," *Nine: Journal of Baseball History and Social Perspectives* 2 (1994): 260–76; idem., "Nine Principles Of Successful Affirmative Action: Mr. Branch Rickey, Mr. Jackie Robinson, And The Integration of Baseball," *Nine: Journal of Baseball History and Social Perspectives* 2 (Fall 1994): 36–65; John Vernon, "Beyond The Box Score: Jackie Robinson, Civil Rights Crusader," *Negro History Bulletin* 58 (0ctober-December 1995): 15- 22; Michael E. Lomax, "'I Never Had It Made' Revisited: The Political, Economic, and Social Ideology of Jackie Robinson," *Afro-Americans in New York Life and History* 23 (January 1999): 39–60; Jules Tygiel, *Jackie Robinson Reader: Perspective on a American Hero* (New York: Plume, 1997); idem., *Extra Bases: Reflections on Jackie Robinson, Race and Baseball History* (Lincoln: University of Nebraska Press, 2002); idem., "Jackie Robinson: 'A Lone Negro' in Major League Baseball," in Patrick B. Miller and David K. Wiggins, eds., *Sport And The Color Line: Black Athletes and Race Relations in Twentieth-Century America* (New York: Routledge, 2004), 167–90; Joseph Dorinson, "Paul Robeson and Jackie Robinson: Athletes and Activists at Armageddon," *Pennsylvania History* 66 (Winter 1999): 17–26; Michael Berenbaum, "Jackie and Campy: Ethnicity in the 1950s," *The Jewish Journal* (April 18–24, 1997): 29, 31, 47; Arthur Diamond, *The Importance of Jackie Robinson* (San Diego: Lucent Books, 1992); Joseph Dorinson and Joram Warmund, eds., *Jackie Robinson: Race, Sports and the American Dream* (Armonk, NY: M. E. Sharpe, 1998). Richard Ian Kimball analyzes Robinson's reception from the local press in Indianapolis in "Beyond the 'Great Experiment': Integrated Baseball Comes to Indianapolis," *Journal of Sport History* 26 (Spring 1999): 142–62. Chris Lamb has written the most significant scholarly study on Jackie Robinson's first spring training in *Blackout: The Untold Story of Jackie Robinson's First Spring Training* (Lincoln: University of Nebraska Press, 2004). See also idem., "'I Never Want to Take Another Trip Like This One': Jackie Robinson's Journey to Integrate Baseball," *Journal of Sport History* 24 (Summer 1997): 177–91; Chris Lamb and Glen Bleske, "Democracy on the Field: The Black Press Takes on White Baseball," *Journalism History* 24 (Summer 1998): 51–59. Although it has several drawbacks, David Falkner examines Robinson's life in *Great Time Coming: The Life of Jackie Robinson from Baseball to Birmingham* (New York: Simon & Schuster, 1995). William C. Kashatus chronicles Jackie Robinson's baseball career in *Jackie & Campy: The Untold Story of Their Rocky Relationship and the Breaking of Baseball's Color Line* (Lincoln: University of Nebraska Press, 2014).

3. My brief bio on Robinson was drawn from my work in "Jackie Robinson: Racial Pioneer and Athlete Extraordinaire in an Era of Change," in David K. Wiggins, ed. *Out of the Shadows: A Biographical History of African American Athletes* (Fayetteville: University of Arkansas Press, 2006), 163–79.

4. Arnold Rampersad theorized that Robinson was asked to move because the bus driver believed he was sitting with a white woman. The bus incident and court martial are described in Rampersad, *Jackie Robinson*, 99–100; Rickey inviting Robinson into his office cited in Lee Lowenfish, *Branch Rickey: Baseball's Ferocious Gentleman* (Lincoln: University of Nebraska Press, 2007), 373–74.

5. *Ibid.*, 375–76.

6. *Washington Post*, November 13, 1945. Wright's biography in Riley, *The Biographical Encyclopedia of the Negro Baseball Leagues*, 883–84. *New York Amsterdam News*, November 24, 1945.

7. Tygiel, *Baseball's Great Experiment*, 99–105; Falkner, *Great Time Coming*, 126–28; Rampersad, *Jackie Robinson*, 237–46.

8. Rampersad, *Jackie Robinson*, 245–46.

9. *Ibid.*, 247.

10. *Ibid.*, 251. Aldon Morris, *The Origins of the Civil Rights Movement: Black Communities Organizing for Change* (New York: Free Press, 1984), 1–4.

11. George Robinson's comments in *New York Times*, March 22, 23, 1946; *New York Herald Tribune*, March 23, 1946. Rickey's comments in Tygiel, *Baseball's Great Experiment*, 108; *Los Angeles Sentinel*, April 4, 1946.

12. Robinson quote in Rampersad, *Jackie Robinson*, 259.

13. *Pittsburgh Courier*, April 13, 1946. Morris, *The Origins of the Civil Rights Movement: Black Communities Organizing for Change*, 4.

14. To develop my methodology for Organizational Culture, I am drawing primarily from the work of Edgar H. Schein. See "The Role of the Founder in Creating Organizational Culture," *Organizational Dynamics* (Summer 1983): 13–28. Other secondary sources on organizational culture include: Joanne Martin, "Organizational Culture and Counterculture: An Uneasy Symbiosis," *Organizational Dynamics* (Autumn 1983): 52–64. Gary B. Cunningham & M. Sagas, "Access Discrimination in Intercollegiate Athletics," *Journal of Sport Issues* 29 (2005): 148–63. Idem., "Examining the Main and Interactive Effects of Deep- and Surface-level Diversity on Job

Satisfaction and Organizational Turnover," *Organizational Analysis* 12 (2004): 319–32. Janet S. Fink, "Diversity in Sport? Utilizing Business Literature to Devise a Comprehensive Framework of Diversity Initiatives," *Quest* 51 (1999): 310–27. Richard E. Lapchick, *Race and Gender Report Card University of Central Florida* (The Institute for Diversity and Ethics in Sport, 2004). Richard M. Southall, D. E. Wells and M. S. Nagel, "Organizational Culture Perceptions of Intercollegiate Athletic Department Members," *The Applied Research in Coaching and Athletics Annual* 20 (2005): 65–92.

    15. In Tygiel, *Baseball's Great Experiment*, 121.

    16. In Lowenfish, *Branch Rickey: Baseball's Ferocious Gentleman*, 397. See also Falkner, *Great Time Coming*, 136.

    17. Tygiel, *Baseball's Great Experiment*, 122.

    18. *Ibid.*, 122, 126.

    19. *Ibid.*, 128.

    20. *Ibid.*, 128–29.

    21. *Ibid.*, 129.

    22. *Ibid.*

    23. Early in the 1946 season, the Negro Leagues attempted to affiliate themselves with Organized Baseball. They revised their player contracts to include the reserve clause and adopted Major League Baseball's constitution. Commissioner Happy Chandler, however, placed obstacles in front of the Negro Leagues that were difficult to overcome. See Lanctot, *Negro League Baseball: The Rise and Ruin of a Black Institution*, 284–86.

    24. Tygiel, *Baseball's Great Experiment*, 131–32.

Separate but Unequal

PHILIP J. LOWRY

On May 17, 1954, in *Brown v. Board of Education of Topeka*, the United States Supreme Court handed down a crucial decision that has forever changed the relationship between Americans of African heritage and Americans of European heritage. The ruling stated that separate but equal treatment of African Americans and European Americans was unconstitutional and that henceforth racial relationships must be equal and integrated, because time has proven that relationships designed to be separate but equal in actuality have proven to be separate but unequal.[1]

For professional baseball, which had historically operated with the separate institutions of Negro Leagues Baseball for African American players, and Major League and minor league baseball for European American players, the path from racial segregation to full racial integration would turn into a very long and winding road. On April 18, 1946, Jackie Robinson became the first acknowledged African American of the 20th century to play in the minors when he manned second base for the Montreal Royals of the International League in Jersey City, New Jersey, against the Little Giants, and the first African American in the Majors in 63 years when he started at first base for the Brooklyn Dodgers of the National League in Brooklyn, New York against the Boston Braves on April 15, 1947.[2]

Integration of the other 15 Major League teams was torturously slow. The last Major League team to include an African American did so 12 years after Robinson's inaugural game, when on July 21, 1959, Elijah "Pumpsie" Green pinch-ran for the Boston Red Sox against the Chicago White Sox.[3]

Although all 16 Major League Baseball teams were now integrated, it did not mean that racial progress was swift. Fans, fellow players, and even managers continued to treat black players with racist remarks and behavior. The stellar on-field accomplishments of stars such as Roberto Clemente, Willie Mays, and Henry Aaron gradually made fans and teammates alike aware of the outstanding abilities of Latin and Black ballplayers. But life was still uncomfortable for the black athletes of the latter half of the 20th century. As a youngster growing up in Pittsburgh, I was aware of the racist taunts hurled at Roberto Clemente and of how Pirates broadcaster Bob Prince stood up to defend Clemente every chance he got.

I became involved with the civil rights struggle in two ways during the 1960s. First, as a teenager, I accompanied my father daily to his summer job as a Recreation Supervisor in Braddock, Pennsylvania, an all-black town on the edge of Pittsburgh, about five miles from where we lived in an all-white town. I was the only white player on the Braddock summer basketball team, and through my experience there I became aware of what Braddock's schools were like.

The textbooks were all written before World War II, and most had missing pages. There were holes in the ceilings, and water spots on the gym floor when it rained outside. There weren't enough seats in the classrooms, and many students had to sit on the floor. At the same time, students in my town had brand-new schools, brand-new textbooks, a huge new telescope, and much higher teacher salaries.

The civil rights movement also provided the inspiration for my senior thesis at Harvard College, which focused on school desegregation in Mecklenburg County, North Carolina (Charlotte), and in Allegheny County, Pennsylvania (Pittsburgh). These efforts were very different, but in the end had the same outcome.

After five years of legal arguments, Mecklenburg County's desegregation plan was approved. After well over a decade of legal arguments, Allegheny County was ordered to implement a desegregation plan, which resulted in the creation of a new Woodland Hills School District.

One example of Major League Baseball's "separate but unequal" heritage would be the Negro Leaguers' struggles to be elected into the National Baseball Hall of Fame in Cooperstown, New York. The Negro Leagues operated from 1920 through 1963. During this period, exhibition games were played regularly between black ball clubs and teams consisting of big league players, with the results showing that black squads won more than half the time. This would suggest that the Negro Leagues were roughly equal to the Major Leagues in player ability and talent.[4]

Jackie Robinson was inducted into the Hall of Fame in July 1962, but the election of other African American players to Cooperstown was nearly non-existent. In 1971, the Hall took a step in the right direction by organizing a Committee on Negro Baseball Leagues, with the charter to elect deserving black ball players to the Hall. The committee's efforts were numbingly slow, selecting but one Negro Leaguer in 1971; two in 1972; one each in 1973, 1974, 1975, and 1976; and two in 1977. Then inexplicably, the committee voted itself out of business, stating that these nine Negro Leaguers were all that were deserving of membership in the Hall.[5]

In the 1980s, I was Chair of the Negro Leagues Committee for the Society for American Baseball Research (SABR). We began an effort to convince the Hall that many more of the top Negro Leaguers, those who were never allowed to play in the Major Leagues, should be elected to the Hall of Fame.

Compared to the nine black players from the segregated era inducted into the Hall, over 120 Major Leaguers had been elected from the same time period. We argued that if Negro Leaguers were equal on the playing field to Major Leaguers, then their numbers elected to the Hall should also be roughly comparable.

We also tried to impress upon the Hall that time was of the essence. As each year went by, the Negro Leaguers who had played during the 1920s through the 1960s were aging and passing away. Our efforts were rejected by the directors of the Hall, who cited a lack of statistics as their reason for not allowing additional Negro Leaguers to be elected.

Thus began our two decades–long effort to comb through every single sports section box score and commentary for every newspaper in the 32 Negro Leagues cities. It took almost 20 years, but in the end we accomplished our goal of providing statistics upon which the Hall of Fame could base its selection process. Our effort could never be 100 percent thorough, though. Here are some reasons why:

More than half of all Negro Leagues games were played away from the home team's city. For example, the Kansas City Monarchs might barnstorm along with the Chicago

American Giants for two weeks through small towns in Iowa and Illinois after a series in Kansas City and before an upcoming series in Chicago. Newspaper coverage of these barnstorming games was often sketchy and incomplete.

Another reason was that African American newspapers were frequently published weekly instead of daily. Teams would often play two games in one day, so a weekly newspaper might state that the Monarchs won nine out of 12 games the previous week, but include only one or two or three of the 12 box scores.

Despite these difficulties, our SABR Negro Leagues Committee was able to turn over the fruits of our labor to the Hall. We waited for what seemed an eternity. When the Hall created the Special Committee on the Negro Leagues in 2005, we were elated. Although the number was not as high as we hoped, the Special Committee selected an additional 17 black ball owners and players, bringing the grand total to 35 (between 1981 and 2001, the Veterans Committee had elected nine more Negro Leaguers).[6]

Most importantly, the Hall of Fame has treated the Negro League Hall of Fame members with dignity and equality. Originally, the Hall was going to display the Negro Leaguers in a "separate but equal" room, apart from the Major Leaguers. Many people criticized this hokey plan. Satchel Paige announced that he would refuse to be enshrined in a segregated space.

The Hall of Fame changed its mind. Negro Leaguers have *NOT* been confined to a different wing of the Hall, under the premise of "separate but equal." They are enshrined in the same hall as all of the Major Leaguers, under the premise of "equality and dignity."[7]

In 1981, I was invited to a unique, once-in-a-lifetime gathering of all living Negro Leagues veteran ballplayers in Ashland, Kentucky. The three-day reunion was sponsored by Ashland Oil Company, which paid for all travel, lodging and meal expenses for the attendees. I interviewed each one of the 88 former Negro Leaguers who participated in the event for my forthcoming book *Green Cathedrals*, which paid equal attention to Negro Leagues and Major League ballparks—something that had never been done before.

It was very emotional to see these ballplayers, many of whose on-field performances had been of Hall of Fame quality, but most of whom would never be allowed into the Hall of Fame. Their stories were amazing, from the yarns about small-town ballparks where they were the highlight of the summer for local residents, to big league ballparks playing before packed houses, to the annual Negro Leagues All-Star game in Comiskey Park played before 50,000 fans.

Notes

1. Hogan, and Tygiel, *Shades of Glory*, 325, 326.
2. Peterson, *Only the Ball Was White*, 194, 198.
3. Lanctot, *Negro League Baseball*, 387–389.
4. Holway, *The Complete Book of Baseball's Negro Leagues*, 10–11.
5. Hogan, and Tygiel, *Shades of Glory*, xviii–xx; Holway, *The Complete Book of Baseball's Negro Leagues*, 463–464; Baseball-Reference.com, "MLB Baseball Hall of Fame Inductees," http://www.baseball-reference.com/awards/hof.shtml. Roy Campanella's 1969 induction made him the only other African-American besides Robinson enshrined in Cooperstown until 1971.
6. Hogan, and Tygiel, *Shades of Glory*, xviii–xxii; Baseball-Reference.com, "MLB Baseball Hall of Fame Inductees," http://www.baseball-reference.com/awards/hof.shtml.
7. Hogan, and Tygiel, *Shades of Glory*, xviii.

Monuments

The Shaping of Negro Leagues Public Memory

JOSH HOWARD

Modern professional baseball—meaning Major League Baseball (MLB), MLB franchises, and related organizations—has a complex relationship with the history, memory, and legacy of the Negro Leagues. Generally, modern professional baseball has given significant attention to the Negro Leagues starting in the 1970s through the present, although several recent developments threaten that attention.

Most commonly, professional baseball's presentation of the Negro leagues followed the same celebratory narrative of "overcoming," best represented by Jackie Robinson, with the occasional tragic narrative of "what if," generally represented by individuals like Satchel Paige or Josh Gibson. Further, by shaping a celebratory public memory of the Negro Leagues, modern professional baseball forwards the idea that MLB is the pinnacle of baseball achievement, an idea that is certainly true today but was not strictly true for the first half of the 20th century.

In forwarding MLB supremacy, modern professional baseball reduces the Negro Leagues to a lower status as a "lesser" or "minor" league in terms of importance, legacy, and player ability. Some may argue that these narratives are a net positive in that the Negro Leagues are being recognized at all, but modern professional baseball profits off this legacy, which is especially troubling given that the very institutions which perpetuated the segregated past are now those who are profiting. Finally, while some baseball organizations celebrate the Negro Leagues past, many others simply ignore it, effectively relegating the public memory of the Negro Leagues to the forgotten sidelines of public history.

Before exploring the details of professional baseball's activities in interpreting the past, it must be noted that the shaping of public memory is not necessarily a conscious act. Public memory, as the term is deployed here, refers to the shared understanding of the past generally understood (but not necessarily wholly agreed upon) by a population. Public memory is constantly in flux and is primarily visible through the character of a society or culture's traditions, monuments, public events, and so on. Often, those with the power to shape public memory do so subconsciously, without intent, or completely by accident, although there are many cases where the converse of each of these is true.

As will be seen, professional baseball organizations certainly had intent in shaping their individual brands, image, or history, but it is highly unlikely any (other than perhaps MLB itself) were concerned with the national public memory of the Negro Leagues. Generally, the public memory of the Negro Leagues came to prominence during the "culture wars" of the late 1980s and early 1990s.[1] Franchises, fans, and others debated and negotiated the place of the Negro Leagues in relation to MLB, but by the early 2000s, amnesia sank in as Americans sought reconciliation and solace in their national pastime during the post–9/11 environment.[2] Gone were the complex, contested stories of men who encountered segregation and racism; in its place were flattened tales of ballplayers overcoming, celebration, and individual willpower.[3]

A Brief History of Negro Leagues Commemoration

Statues commemorating specific individuals related to America's baseball past are a relatively recent phenomenon.[4] Only three statues depicting individuals are known to have been created between 1865 and 1955. Of those three, two are in cemeteries far removed from baseball fields, while the third was an art piece that went missing and was presumed stolen not long after its creation.

It was not until April 1955 that the first statue was installed at a baseball site as an object of commemoration. With the blessing of the city, the Pittsburgh Professional Baseball Association—a group of retired professional white ballplayers—raised money and ultimately commissioned sculptor Frank Vittor to create a statue of Honus Wagner in honor of his prolific playing career and importance to the Pittsburgh Pirates' on-field success. The statue was installed in Schenley Park, a site near to the Pirates home, Forbes Field, and its dedication attracted a wide range of baseball luminaries, including Cy Young, Pie Traynor, and Wagner himself.[5]

It should be noted that while the Pirates did not directly contribute to this statue's creation, the franchise has since adopted the statue as its own by relocating it to Three Rivers Stadium in 1972 and its current home of PNC Park in 2001. Despite the popularity of the Wagner statue, the majority of professional clubs, cities, and organizations did not follow suit. From this point to 1980, only four statues were unveiled, all by professional MLB franchises.[6]

Beginning in the mid–1980s, public commemoration of the baseball past came into vogue for baseball clubs and communities as these places realized the potential in connecting their institution to baseball heritage. Seven new statues were unveiled between 1985 and 1990, another 12 between 1991 and 1995, and a whopping 46 between 1996 and 2000, including a dozen installed at the Negro Leagues Baseball Museum, established in 1997.

The vast majority of installations were of nationally relevant baseball figures with unique local relevance, such as Bob Gibson at Busch Memorial Stadium in St. Louis, Joe DiMaggio at the National Italian American Sports Hall of Fame, and Harry Caray at Wrigley Field. A few installations were of lesser-known individuals who were local leaders, like Ben Cheney (a businessman who funded Cheney Stadium in Tacoma, Washington) or Carl Erskine (a former Brooklyn Dodger who later dedicated his life to community service).

The commonality between all these installations is the intent of funders and creators to shape public sport heritage by changing public space. All of these statues had a clear purpose, which may not have necessarily been explicit or intentional, but can most easily be seen with the multitude of Jackie Robinson statues. Several locations erected statues during the 1990s in an act of reconciliation, including the site of the first integrated spring training game (Daytona, Florida), the first integrated minor league game (Jersey City, New Jersey), the first integrated professional team (Montreal, Canada), the site of Robinson's collegiate career (Los Angeles, California), and another in Stamford, Connecticut, where Robinson lived after 1955. Each of these locations lay claim to a portion of Robinson's legacy, which has only grown in stature and importance since his death.

This sharp increase in memorializing baseball's past was relatively sudden and has no single explanation, but there are a few that offer some explanation.[7] First, this increase ran concurrent to a broader increase in interest for memory, nostalgia, and commemoration during the late 1980s and 1990s. This era also marked a time when baseball, as a sport and entertainment industry, experienced its greatest crisis since the Black Sox scandal–the 1994 strike and cancellation of the World Series. Attendance declined by as much as 20 percent after the strike. One strategy to lure fans back to the ballpark was to appeal to baseball history and nostalgia, both of which had been threatened by the supposed "greed" of MLB owners and players. MLB franchises also turned to nostalgia-based advertising and marketing, best exemplified by the Baltimore Orioles' celebrations of Cal Ripken, Jr.'s games-played record and installation of a Babe Ruth statue.[8]

In addition, during the late 1990s, baseball executives became concerned over declining attendance, especially among African American fans, not to mention public criticism of MLB's declining numbers of black players, lack of black managers and executives, and total absence of minorities among ownership groups. Beginning in 2004, the MLB established April 15 as Jackie Robinson Day as a day set aside as an "inspirational reminder" of Jackie Robinson, to honor black baseball history, and to reach out to African American communities.[9] The Baseball Hall of Fame also revived the dormant Special Committee on the Negro Leagues in early 2006 to provide depth to honorees from the Negro leagues. This committee chose to enshrine 17 players and executives for their contributions to pre-integration black baseball.

The Smithsonian National Museum of Natural History even got in on the act, creating the highly-popular "Baseball as America" exhibit. This exhibit aimed to connect a shaken post–9/11 museum-going public with a metaphor for the American past—baseball. The exhibit focused on the origins and growth of the game and included an impressive collection of artifacts, such as Norman Rockwell paintings, Andy Warhol portraits, a copy of "Casey at the Bat," and dozens of other iconic pieces. Stories of the Negro Leagues were present in several places, but were most visible in two key locations: in exhibits dedicated to triumph of ideals over injustices, and in the gift shop.

Exhibits largely celebrated the most famous African American ballplayers, primarily Jackie Robinson, while largely ignoring post–1947 problems and ongoing issues of race in the nation. If one was not aware, then baseball seemed strongly all-inclusive for the majority of the twentieth century.[10] The gift shop sold a wide range of materials, including replicas of Negro Leagues jerseys, shirts, and caps. As pointed out by cultural critic Michael Butterworth, this presence does not mark a concern for historical underrepresentation, but rather an attempt to exploit "the pleasures that (mostly) white audiences gain through the consumption of black culture."[11] This was, in so many words, the commoditization of segregation via baseball nostalgia. In many ways, "Baseball as America" was similar to the efforts of MLB franchises to shape public memory while commodifying and subjugating the Negro Leagues past.

As of this writing, statues are present at 26 of 30 MLB stadiums, and 20 of those 26 stadiums contain statues of ballplayers. Just three ball clubs maintain statues of Negro Leagues ballplayers at their respective stadiums: the St. Louis Cardinals and Cool Papa Bell (dedicated in 1991), the Washington Nationals and Josh Gibson (dedicated 2009), and the Cleveland Indians and Larry Doby (dedicated in 2015).

However, the vast majority of cities with MLB clubs today were home, at one point, to professional Negro Leagues teams, meaning that those respective franchises can lay claim to a local Negro Leagues heritage and could, if they so desired, commemorate the Negro Leagues. Thirteen of the 26 current MLB metropolitan areas were once the home to a major Negro League club: Atlanta, Baltimore, Chicago, Cincinnati, Cleveland, Detroit, Houston, Kansas City, New York, Philadelphia, Pittsburgh, St. Louis, and Washington, D.C. Another 11 cities hosted other professional or semi-professional black teams, including Boston, Dallas, Denver, Los Angeles, Miami, Milwaukee, Minneapolis–St. Paul, San Diego, San Francisco–Oakland, Seattle, and Tampa. Only two MLB cities—Phoenix and Toronto—do not possess a heritage of professional African American baseball, although each of these cities certainly possesses a history of amateur black baseball teams and leagues.

For the past two decades, MLB teams have invoked black ball history through statues, special celebrations, and Negro Leagues throwback days in order to tell a story of reconciliation, peaceful integration, and racial harmony. Primary examples of this would be the MLB creation of Jackie Robinson Day, the league-wide retirement of Robinson's number, and events like the special 2008 Negro Leagues Player Draft.[12] The Dodgers' continuing embrace of Jackie Robinson and the leadership role of Hank Aaron in the Atlanta Braves' annual Heritage Weekend are two ways in which individual franchises have also engaged this past.[13]

To further illustrate how the Negro Leagues are portrayed in modern baseball, it helps to look at a few examples. In the past decade, the Washington Nationals and Pittsburgh Pirates were leaders in how to interpret and share their respective African American pasts in a meaningful way. However, one of these two franchises—the Pirates—has not maintained this appreciation for the Negro Leagues past. In order to understand the legacy and memory of the Negro Leagues, we must understand how professional baseball is presenting that legacy.

The Washington Nationals

The Washington Nationals deserve some positive publicity for the statues at Nationals Park. When the Nationals arrived in D.C. from Montreal, the franchise embarked upon a campaign to connect the club's history to the District's rich baseball past, specifically the history of the Washington Senators (1901–1960, now the Minnesota Twins) and the Washington Senators (1961–1971, now the Texas Rangers). The Nationals also included the Homestead Grays, who primarily played in the Negro National League, in the District's baseball heritage. To illustrate this new baseball lineage, the Nationals commissioned three statues of players who made their careers (primarily) playing for these three predecessor clubs. Walter Johnson represented the first iteration of the Senators, Frank Howard the second, and Josh Gibson the Homestead Grays.

The Nationals statues present Josh Gibson—a man who never played outside of the Negro Leagues—on equal standing with Walter Johnson, an all-time great and part of the National Baseball Hall of Fame's inaugural class of five. The second iteration of the Senators lasted only a decade, but Frank Howard was that club's star player during the latter half of that decade as a four-time All-Star. By presenting the three statues together, the Nationals are presenting Gibson and the Grays on an even level as Johnson, Howard, and the Senators.

Further, the Nationals place Homestead Grays players on equal standing with Senators and Expos greats through the creation of a franchise "Ring of Honor" in 2010. The Ring of Honor consecrates both franchise and city greats, including ten individuals associated with the Senators, two Expos, and six Grays, all of whom are displayed equally within the stadium. In other words, through statues and the Ring of Honor, the Nationals franchise recognized the Grays as having just as much a role in Washington sporting history as either Senators franchise.

It is important to note that in their move to D.C., the Nationals had to confront the legacy of Washington Senators racism lingering in the city's public sporting memory. The Senators maintained a presence in the District from 1901 to 1960. After team president Clark Griffith died in 1955, his adopted son and nephew, Calvin, began exploring the possibility of moving the team west. In 1960, Calvin Griffith pulled the trigger, moving the club to Minnesota, with the Senators being replaced in 1961 by a new expansion club. Years later, Calvin Griffith stated that his primary motivation in moving the Senators to Minnesota was the lower African American population. In Griffith's mind, the Washington black population was poor and rowdy, creating a fan base that did not provide enough of a financial incentive for the club to stay.

Today, though, the Nationals respect and acknowledge the Negro Leagues past in the District. Griffith's actions made that past difficult and contradictory. However, the Nationals are a distinct franchise from the Senators, so creating a new public history from whole-cloth becomes easier while doing the same thing for an overall franchise rebranding.

The Pittsburgh Pirates

As Opening Day approached in 2014, the Pittsburgh Pirates rapidly dismantled their space dedicated to Negro Leagues memory. From 2006 to 2014, Legacy Square contained seven statues of Negro Leagues stars who plied their trade in Pittsburgh for the Crawfords or the Homestead Grays: Cool Papa Bell, Josh Gibson, Oscar Charleston, Judy Johnson, Buck Leonard, Satchel Paige, and Smokey Joe Williams. Speaking to MLB.com in 2006, Sean Gibson—the grandson of Josh Gibson and president of the Josh Gibson Foundation—expressed his amazement at the Pirates' construction of Legacy Square: "We never thought anything like this would be created, this is a great honor."

Further, Pirates owner and CEO Kevin McClatchy hoped Legacy Square would create a new spirit of historical engagement within the Pirates ballpark: "This exhibit inspires, educates and emotionally connects people of all ages to … the remarkable story of the Negro leagues. A lot of people say PNC Park is the best ballpark in America. Well, PNC Park just got a lot better." Generally, baseball fans, historians, and the Pittsburgh community applauded the Pirates again for taking a leadership role in interpreting Negro Leagues baseball.

Without contacting anyone in the Pittsburgh community or Pirates fandom, the Pirates front office decided to "renovate" Legacy Square. The explanation given was that Legacy Square and the popular left field concourse now attracted "too many" fans, so it would be prudent to spread fans more evenly throughout the ballpark. Note that this was an identical problem faced the next year by the Washington Nationals, who simply relocated statues to a different gate. Upon discovering the Pirates had outright discarded most of Legacy Square, spare for the statues, Sean Gibson contacted the club. The Pirates agreed to donate the statues to the Foundation, but demanded they be removed as soon as possible. Lacking storage facilities, Gibson was forced to turn to an auctioneer, who agreed to handle the sale with approximately 75 percent of the proceeds going to the Josh Gibson Foundation. The seven statues sold for more than five times the expected return, bringing $226,950.[14]

What's strange about the Pirates' decision is that the franchise has typically been a leader in acknowledging Major League Baseball's role in segregating America's sporting past. During the 1988 season, the Pirates—led by a young Barry Bonds and Bobby Bonilla—commemorated the 40th anniversary of the Homestead Grays' victory in the last Negro Leagues World Series. A pregame ceremony raised a banner for the Grays and honored living members of both the Grays and Pittsburgh Crawfords. The banner only remained for a week, but for that week the franchise effectively recognized the 1948 Grays as equals to the Pirates' own World Series championships. During the ceremony itself, the Pirates president apologized for the role the club played in segregation, and Commissioner of Major League Baseball A. Bartlett Giamatti went so far as to decry segregation, saying of professional baseball's role: "We must never lose sight of our history. Insofar as it is ugly, never to repeat it, and insofar as it is glorious, to cherish it."[15]

This 1988 ceremony was, at the time, a truly groundbreaking moment for professional sport in America. Throughout the 1990s and 2000s, the Pirates continued this new trend by hosting annual Negro Leagues nights and installing permanent Grays and Crawfords championship banners at Three Rivers Stadium in 1993. The Pittsburgh-area community embraced this past as well with the most notable event being when the city of Homestead changed the name of the Homestead High-Level Bridge to the Homestead Grays Bridge in 2002.

Although the Foundation's return of the statues was quite significant, Sean Gibson himself was none too happy with the outcome, succinctly stating: "No dollar amount is more important than our history."[16] Ironically, one week after the statues went to auction, the Pirates played an interleague series in Kansas City, where players visited the Negro Leagues Museum with media in tow. Players reported the experience to be enlightening and humbling, while at least a few others spoke of the "debt" they owed to Negro Leaguers. More recently, the Pirates blatantly profited off Pittsburgh's Negro Leagues clubs; the Free Shirt Friday promotion for September 9, 2016, was a Homestead Grays t-shirt. In advertising this promotion, the Pirates used the image of current player Josh Harrison, an African American man, further conflating black bodies today with the past of segregation and the Negro Leagues in a lazy attempt at pandering.

In a 2016 interview with the website, The Undefeated, Pirates vice president of communications and broadcasting Brian Warecki claimed the decision to destroy Legacy Square was "to refresh the way in which we pay tribute to Pittsburgh's great Negro League history and players, and to raise needed funds in support of a Negro League exhibit that will be seen by hundreds of thousands of visitors year-round and not just in the ballpark." Sean Gibson disagrees with Warecki's claims, clearly stating, "It's a shame that the Pirates are providing a scapegoat based off their sole decision to remove the statues from PNC Park. Their decision was not based on raising funds for Josh Gibson Heritage Park."[17]

Despite a few small promotions, the Pirates effectively proclaim that the Pittsburgh Crawfords and Homestead Grays have nothing to do with the Pirates brand any longer, and if a fan wants to know about the Crawfords or Grays—or black baseball history in general—then they should visit the Forbes Field landmark, the Western Pennsylvania Sports Museum, or the Negro Leagues Baseball Museum. In other words, PNC Park is for the Pirates and the Pirates only.

While the Pirates distance themselves from Pittsburgh's black history, other teams continue to emphasize their city's black history in permanent ways. Notably, the Cleveland Indians constructed a statue of Larry Doby during the same month as the Legacy Square auction, the Los Angeles Dodgers announced plans for a new Jackie Robinson statue, and the Kansas City Royals continue to develop strong partnerships with the Negro Leagues Baseball Museum.[18]

MLB's Official Statistics

Baseball statistics are critical to fans. The entire field of sabermetrics emerged from baseball statistics, and statistical analysis is more important to baseball than to the vast majority of other sports. The most popular database for baseball statistics, Baseball-Reference.com, does not include Negro Leagues statistics on a player's default page. Instead, Negro Leagues statistics are categorized separately and alongside minor league statistics.

For instance, as of this writing, the main page for Satchel Paige displays statistics for only 476 innings of Paige's career, all after the age of 40. For visitors to this page ignorant of Paige's significance, they may think of him as simply an outlier in the annals of baseball. Only by clicking the small link for "Negro, Mexican, & Minor League Stats" within the site header links will a visitor find details on Paige's 18-plus seasons in the Negro Leagues. The header link itself is further problematic as it equates the Negro Leagues with minor league baseball, a blatantly untrue equation.

The very nature of baseball statistics makes the game less accessible for those interested in the Negro Leagues. The white Major Leagues employed professionals who kept fairly rigorous statistics on every game. In contrast, the Negro Leagues usually could not afford such record keeping. Thus, many Negro leagues statistics are incomplete. However, the emergence of several online newspaper archives and websites such the Seamheads Negro League Database, has made more black ball statistics available than ever before. Though some data will be forever lost to time, real progress has been made in building up foundational knowledge.

Conclusion

Modern professional baseball has a diversity problem, as can be seen with its ownership, front office staffs, and coaching staffs. Of course, leadership is aware of this and has been for at least 30 years. Some important strides were taken to correct problems, such as the creation of the Reviving Baseball in Inner Cities (RBI) program, recognizing the ability of Negro Leagues players, and establishing the "Selig Rule," which mandated that at least one minority candidate interview for all front office and managerial openings, but the vast majority of observers recognize that not enough is being done.[19]

A potential avenue for professional baseball to explore is to engage the public history and memory of the Negro Leagues. In doing so, the Negro Leagues would not be seen as merely potential profit for MLB or its franchises. These organizations actively resisted integration, raided the Negro Leagues of their talent, and ultimately forced franchises—and significant black entrepreneurship—to fold. The idea that MLB franchises and their nearly 100 percent white ownership should profit off of this past is concerning and potentially unethical.

However, this does not mean that there are no ways forward for modern professional baseball. A cynical observer could easily decry professional baseball's commemoration of the Negro Leagues as profit-chasing, and those accusations would hold true if remembrances revolved around shallow attempts to sell tickets or merchandise, such as special one-night-only giveaways or "feel-good" events designed to cheer fans up and absolve a (still) primarily white-owned league of guilt. Most teams commemorate their franchise's past, and some celebrate the history of their city or region. Most franchises could—and should—incorporate the Negro Leagues into their heritage through monuments, memorials, and public observances.

In conjunction with such efforts, modern professional baseball must also reach out to individuals and groups with a stake in the presentation of the Negro Leagues past. Some have already provided examples, such as the Kansas City Royals' partnership with the Negro Leagues Baseball Museum or the NBHOF's somewhat flawed efforts with the Special Committee on the Negro Leagues in the 1970s and in 2006. The Negro Leagues Baseball Museum partnership has been especially fruitful in developing a better historical awareness of the Negro Leagues in Kansas City, which only makes sense given the preeminence of the Kansas City Monarchs. Efforts such as this could serve as models to improve on going forward in other locales. For instance, MLB teams already partner with local organizations, but more should actively seek out local organizations related to the Negro Leagues and black history. One example could be the Pittsburgh Pirates working with the Josh Gibson Foundation, the Western Pennsylvania Sports Museum at Heinz History Center, the Teenie Harris Archive, and others in developing future programming related to the Negro Leagues.

Another possibility could be the restoration of the NBHOF's Special Committee on the Negro Leagues as a regular elective body. Perhaps not surprisingly, none of the four current Hall of Fame veterans committees (Today's Game, Modern Baseball, Golden Days, or Early Baseball) allow for the selection of Negro League participants. As of this writing, there are 178 white players, managers, executives, and umpires from the segregated era enshrined in the HOF, and thirty-five (16.4%) negro leaguers. However, of the ninety-five post-integration players who have been inducted into the Hall, forty (42.1%) have been African Americans or Latin Americans, who would have almost certainly been banned prior to 1947—It is not a stretch to suggest, especially when one considers that at least 33% Major League players since 1969 have been Black or Latino, that a more equitable representation of HOF enshrinees from the pre-integration era is necessary. To correct the imbalance a new Negro League committee needs to be established to oversee the selection of an additional twenty-five blackball players, managers, owners, and umpires. In a related gesture, Negro League statistics need to be included on MLB.com, in all official MLB publications, and wherever MLB statistics appear.[20]

Efforts such as these could also help with professional baseball's declining minority attendance as well as repair in some part recent image problems, such as the Pirates destruction of Legacy Square or the Atlanta Braves move out of the city and into Cobb County. Orioles outfielder Adam Jones, famously called baseball, "a white man's sport" for a reason.[21] Modern professional baseball needs to alter its image by embracing broad public histories, lest MLB's market share be swept up by sports that attract far more diverse audiences such as the NFL, NBA, and professional soccer. A more honest engagement with the past could lead to better engagement with minorities throughout each franchise's locality, not to mention other fans who simply appreciate the Negro Leagues.

Aside from an increased presence in the Hall of Fame and the inclusion of black ball statistics into the official record, what should MLB be doing differently in presenting Negro

Leagues heritage? Perhaps a better way to commemorate the Negro Leagues past is to recognize it for all its complexities. For instance, the debut of Jackie Robinson was certainly a momentous event worthy of celebration, but it was also an event marked with sadness as Robinson's success meant the end for the Negro Leagues. By interpreting both sides of the coin, the Negro Leagues and black history both come more into focus.

The recognition of lesser-known African American ballplayers and pioneers, including (perhaps especially) those who were largely unsuccessful could be another way to present Negro Leagues history. For instance, the Dodgers could celebrate relatively forgotten pioneers like Roy Partlow and John Wright alongside luminaries like Jackie Robinson and Roy Campanella. Neither Partlow nor Wright achieved success in the white major leagues, but both were successful Negro Leagues players who played alongside Robinson in the minor leagues in 1946. Stories like Partlow's and Wright's can highlight the realities of breaking the color barrier, meaning the tale of the color line becomes much more real, Robinson's achievements become that much better, and the Negro Leagues can be properly represented in the public memory of baseball.

Notes

1. For more on the culture wars, see James Davison Hunter, *Culture Wars: The Struggle to Control the Family, Art, Education, Law, and Politics in America* (New York: Basic Books, 1991), and Andrew Hartman, *A War for the Soul of America: A History of the Culture Wars* (Chicago: University of Chicago Press, 2015).

2. Michael Butterworth, *Baseball and Rhetorics of Purity: The National Pastime and American Identity During the War on Terror* (Tuscaloosa: University of Alabama Press, 2010), 1–28.

3. For more on the characteristics of public memory, see Michael Kammen, *Mystic Chords of Memory* (New York: Vintage Books, 1991), 1–14, and Carol Blair, Greg Dickinson, and Brian L. Ott, eds, *Places of Public Memory: The Rhetoric of Museums and Memorials* (Tuscaloosa: University of Alabama Press, 2010), 5–11. For more on the relationship between the relationship between memory and trauma, see Susan Sontag, *Regarding the Pain of Others* (New York: Picador, 2004).

4. Note that this is in stark contrast to other memorialization campaigns, notably the movement to commemorate the American nation, the Civil War, and the Confederacy. From 1870 to 1910, a "Party of Memory" grew in power that sparked interest in and defined national public memory. Public organizations and governments installed dozens of Confederate memorials between 1890 and 1930, peaking around 1910, with a sharp increase during the 1950s and 1960s. For more, see Kammen, *Mystic Chords of Memory*, 101–131, 194–227, Martha Norkunas, *Monuments and Memory: History and Representation in Lowell, Massachusetts* (Washington, DC: Smithsonian Institution Press, 2002), and William Fitzhugh Brundage, *The Southern Past: A Clash of Race and Memory* (Cambridge, MA: Harvard University Press, 2009).

5. Nicholas P. Ciotola, "From Honus to Columbus: The Life and Works of Frank Vittor," in *Italian Americans: Bridges to Italy, Bonds to America*, Luciano J. Iorizzo and Ernest E. Rossi, eds (Youngstown, NY: Teneo Press, 2010), 148–149; William Hageman, *Honus: The Life and Times of a Baseball Hero* (Champagne, IL: Sagamore, 1996), 179–181. Marilyn Evert, *Discovering Pittsburgh's Sculpture* (Pittsburgh: University of Pittsburgh Press, 1983), 24–25.

6. The six statues include: Connie Mark at Shibe Park (Philadelphia), Dickey Kerr at the Houston Astrodome, Stan Musial at Busch Memorial Stadium (St. Louis), and Ty Cobb at Atlanta-Fulton County Stadium. C. B. Stride, F. E. Thomas, and J. P. Wilson, "From Pitch to Plinth: The Sporting Statues Project," accessed 2016, http://sportingstatues.com.

7. As Michael Kammen observed, "public interest in the past pulses; it comes and goes." Kammen, *Mystic Chords of Memory*, 10.

8. Howard Bryant, *Juicing the Game: Drugs, Powers, and the Fight for the Soul of Major League Baseball* (New York: Viking Penguin, 2005), 53–66. The Orioles have installed seven more statues at Camden Yards since 2011: two of Brooks Robinson, Frank Robinson, Earl Weaver, Jim Palmer, Eddie Murray, and Cal Ripken.

9. "MLB: Every April 15 to be Jackie Robinson Day," *USA Today*, March 3, 2004.

10. Butterworth, *Baseball and Rhetorics of Purity*, 166.

11. *Ibid.*, 76.

12. This draft, the brainchild of Hall of Famer Dave Winfield, was a ceremony held before the 2008 First-Year Players' Draft where each team "selected" a living Negro league ballplayer. Justice Hall, "MLB Honors Negro Leaguers in Draft," MLB.com, accessed 2016, http://m.mlb.com/news/article/2845552/.

13. "Atlanta Braves Heritage Weekend," Atlanta.Braves.MLB.com, accessed 2016, http://m.mlb.com/braves/tickets/info/heritage-weekend.

14. Hunt Auctions.com, accessed 2016, http://huntauctions.com/live/view_lots_items_list_closed.cfm?auction=50&start_number=201&last_number=300.

15. Rob Ruck, *Sandlot Seasons* (Urbana: University of Illinois Press, 1993), xvi.

16. Brian O'Neill, "Statues Honoring Negro Leagues Gone from PNC Park Entrance," *Pittsburgh Post-Gazette*, July 30, 2015, accessed 2016, http://www.post-gazette.com/opinion/brian-oneill/2015/07/30/-Brian-O-Neill-Statues-honoring-Negro-Leagues-gone-from-PNC-Park-entrance/stories/201507300007.

17. John Harris, "Is There No Place in Pittsburgh for Negro League All-Stars?," The Undefeated.com, accessed November 1, 2016, https://theundefeated.com/features/is-there-no-place-in-pittsburgh-for-negro-league-all-stars/.

18. "Larry Doby, AL's First African-American Player, Honored with Statue," ESPN.com, July 25, 2015, accessed 2016, http://espn.go.com/mlb/story/_/id/13318996/indians-honor-larry-doby-unveiling-bronze-statue-progressive-field; Dylan Hernandez, "Dodgers Plan Jackie Robinson Statue at Stadium," *Los Angeles Times*, April 15, 2015, http://www.latimes.com/sports/dodgers/dodgersnow/la-sp-dn-dodgers-jackie-robinson-statue-20150515-story.html; Dee Jackson, "Royals Honor Kansas City's Negro Leagues Heritage," kshb.com, May 15, 2016, accessed 2016, http://www.kshb.com/sports/royals-honor-kansas-citys-negro-leagues-past.

19. The "Selig Rule" (established in 2013) which is effectively a modification of the NFL's "Rooney Rule" has not been viewed as a success as of this writing. Richard Justice, "Selig Rule First of its Kind in Sports," MLB.com, August 26, 2013, accessed 2016, http://m.mlb.com/news/article/58500104/; Jack Moore, "How MLB Stays White," Vice Sports, May 7, 2015, accessed 2016, https://sports.vice.com/en_us/article/how-mlb-stays-white; Adrian Burgos, Jr., "MLB Teams Are Making a Farce of the Selig Rule," Sporting News.com, May 19, 2015, accessed 2016, http://www.sportingnews.com/mlb/news/selig-rule-diversity-dan-jennings-craig-counsellmanagers/181ixmen2bpnw1deeqm7ww8e9g.

20. National Baseball Hall of Fame.org, "Eras Committees," accessed June 20, 2019, https://baseballhall.org/hall-of-famers/rules/eras-committees; Wikipedia.com, "List of members of the Baseball Hall of Fame," accessed August 29, 2019, https://en.wikipedia.org/wiki/List_of_members_of_the_Baseball_Hall_of_Fame; demographics note; Armour and Levitt, *Ethnicity Totals By Year, 1947–2014*; Lapchick, "The 2016 Racial and Gender Report Card: Major League Baseball"; Lapchick, "The 2019 Racial and Gender Report Card: Major League Baseball."

21. Harold Craw, "Broadening Baseball's Audience," MILB.com, April 3, 2016, accessed 2016, http://m.milb.com/news/article/2012041128411590; Marc Fisher, "Baseball is Struggling to Hook Kids," *Washington Post*, April 5, 2015, accessed 2016, https://www.washingtonpost.com/sports/nationals/baseballs-trouble-with-the-youth-curve—and-what-that-means-for-the-game/2015/04/05/2da36dca-d7e8-11e4-8103-fa84725dbf9d_story.html; Keli Goff, "Have Black Americans Left Baseball?," The Root.com, April 19, 2013, accessed 2016, http://www.theroot.com/articles/culture/2013/04/why_blacks_are_leaving_baseball_dave_winfield_others_weigh_in/; Bob Nightengale, "Adam Jones on MLB's lack of Kaepernick protest: 'Baseball is a white man's sport,'" USA Today.com, September 13, 2016, accessed June 24, 2019, https://www.usatoday.com/story/sports/mlb/columnist/bob-nightengale/2016/09/12/adam-jones-orioles-colin-kaepernick-white-mans-sport/90260326/.

Appendix I

NLB vs. MLB, 1885–1924

Note: Only contests known to have been played between black ball clubs and organizations advertised and/or acknowledged to be intact Major League teams have been listed. Games for which box scores were unavailable are marked with an asterisk (*). Inn=Innings; FF=Forfeit.

Team Abbreviations: Br. Royal Giants = Brooklyn Royal Giants; Chi. Am. Giants = Chicago American Giants; Chi. Col. Giants = Chicago Columbia Giants; Chicago White Sox = Chicago White Stockings; Cincinnati Red Sox = Cincinnati Red Stockings; K. C. Cowboys = Kansas City Cowboys; K. C. Monarchs = Kansas City Monarchs; L. A. White Sox = Los Angeles White Sox; New York Mets = New York Metropolitans; N. Y. B. Giants = New York Bacharach Giants; Phi. Athletics = Philadelphia Athletics; Washington Nats = Washington Nationals; W. B. Sprudels = West Baden Sprudels.

Date	NLB	MLB	Result	Location
1885				
Oct. 5	Cuban Giants	New York Mets	L 3–11, 6 inn	New York, NY
Oct. 10	Cuban Giants	Phi. Athletics	L 7–13, 6 inn	Philadelphia, PA*
1886				
May 28	Cuban Giants	St. Louis Browns	L 3–9	Chambersburg, NJ
Jul. 21	Cuban Giants	Cincinnati Red Sox	W 9–4	Chambersburg, NJ
Jul. 26	Cuban Giants	K. C. Cowboys	W 3–2	Chambersburg, NJ
Jul. 27	Cuban Giants	K. C. Cowboys	L 4–13	Chambersburg, NJ
1887				
Apr. 11	Cuban Giants	New York Mets	L 7–19	Trenton, NJ
Apr. 13	Cuban Giants	Washington Nats	L 5–7	Washington, D.C.
Apr. 14	Cuban Giants	Washington Nats	L 2–14	Washington, D.C.
May 3	Cuban Giants	Phi. Athletics	W 16–0	Trenton, NJ
May 6	Cuban Giants	New York Mets	W 11–4	Trenton, NJ
May 24	Cuban Giants	Detroit Wolverines	L 4–8	Trenton, NJ
Jun. 2	Cuban Giants	Phi. Athletics	L 9–14	Trenton, NJ
Jun. 3	Cuban Giants	Cincinnati Red Sox	L 7–9	Trenton, NJ
Jun. 14	Cuban Giants	Cincinnati Red Sox	W 8–5	Trenton, NJ
Jun. 20	Cuban Giants	New York Giants	L 6–17	Trenton, NJ
Jul. 14	Cuban Giants	Indianapolis Hoosiers	W 8–4	Trenton, NJ
Sep. 25	Cuban Giants	Phi. Athletics	L 6–13	Weehawken, NJ
Oct. 9	Cuban Giants	Baltimore Orioles	W 12–2, 6 inn	New York, NY
Oct. 10	Cuban Giants	New York Giants	T 2–2, 8 inn	Trenton, NJ

Date	NLB	MLB	Result	Location
Oct. 16	Cuban Giants	New York Giants	L 5–11	New York, NY*
Oct. 20	Cuban Giants	Indianapolis Hoosiers	L 11–17, 7 inn	Indianapolis, IN
Oct. 21	Cuban Giants	Indianapolis Hoosiers	L 0–9, 6 inn, FF	Indianapolis, IN
Oct. 22	Cuban Giants	Cincinnati Red Sox	W 6–5	Cincinnati, OH
Oct. 23	Cuban Giants	Cincinnati Red Sox	L 6–18, 6 inn	Cincinnati, OH*
1888				
Apr. 17	Cuban Giants	Washington Nats	L 2–10	Washington, D.C.
Apr. 18	Cuban Giants	Washington Nats	L 3–14, 8 inn	Washington, D.C.
Apr. 19	Cuban Giants	Washington Nats	L 5–9, 7 inn	Washington, D.C.
Jun. 7	Cuban Giants	Detroit Wolverines	L 1–15	Trenton, NJ
Jul. 3	Cuban Giants	Washington Nats	L 6–11	Trenton, NJ
Jul. 23	Cuban Giants	Phi. Athletics	W 2–0	Trenton, NJ
1889				
Apr. 12	Cuban Giants	Washington Nats	L 2–3, 8 inn	Washington, D.C.
May 7	Cuban Giants	Boston Beaneaters	L 2–5	Trenton, NJ
May 31	Cuban Giants	Cincinnati Red Sox	L 0–1, 5 inn	Trenton, NJ
1891				
Mar. 20	Cuban Giants	Cleveland Spiders	L 1–15	St. Augustine, FL
Jul. 12	Cuban Giants	Cincinnati Reds	L 5–11	New York, NY
Oct. 10	New York Gorhams	New York Giants	L 4–6	New York, NY
1892				
Apr. 6	New York Gorhams	New York Giants	L 1–36, 8 inn	New York, NY
1894				
Sep. 2	Cuban Giants	St. Louis Browns	W 13–9	Newark, NJ*
1895				
Apr. 11	Page Fence Giants	Cincinnati Reds	L 7–11	Cincinnati, OH
Apr. 12	Page Fence Giants	Cincinnati Reds	L 2–16, 7 inn	Cincinnati, OH
1897				
Jun. 24	Cuban X-Giants	Cincinnati Reds	L 1–3, 7 inn	Cincinnati, OH
Jun. 25	Cuban X-Giants	Cincinnati Reds	L 7–8	Cincinnati, OH
1900				
Sep. 25	Chi. Col. Giants	Milwaukee Brewers	L 3–4, 11 inn	Joliet, IL*
Oct. 1	Chi. Col. Giants	Chicago White Sox	W 5–3	Chicago, IL
Oct. 7	Chi. Col. Giants	Chicago White Sox	L 4–8, 5 inn	Chicago, IL
1901				
Sep. 30	Cuban X-Giants	Phi. Athletics	T 4–4, 11 inn	Philadelphia, PA
1902				
Oct. 2	Philadelphia Giants	Phi. Athletics	L 3–8	Philadelphia, PA
Oct. 6	Philadelphia Giants	Phi. Athletics	L 9–13	Philadelphia, PA
circa Oct.	Chi. Col. Giants	Chicago White Sox	W 9–5	Chicago, IL*
1905				
Jun. 5	Cuban X-Giants	Brooklyn Superbas	W 7–2	Atlantic City, NJ
Jun. 6	Cuban X-Giants	Brooklyn Superbas	L 1–2	Atlantic City, NJ
1906				
Apr. 14	Philadelphia Giants	Phi. Athletics	T 13–13, 10 inn	Atlantic City, NJ
Sep. 18	Br. Royal Giants	Phi. Athletics	T 3–3	Atlantic City, NJ
Sep. 19	Br. Royal Giants	Phi. Athletics	W 5–1	Atlantic City, NJ
Sep. 20	Br. Royal Giants	Phi. Athletics	W 3–2	Atlantic City, NJ
Sep. 21	Br. Royal Giants	Phi. Athletics	L 1–3	Atlantic City, NJ

Date	NLB	MLB	Result	Location
Sep. 24	Br. Royal Giants	Phi. Athletics	L 0–2	Atlantic City, NJ
Sep. 25	Br. Royal Giants	Phi. Athletics	W 7–3	Atlantic City, NJ
Oct. 12	Philadelphia Giants	Phi. Athletics	L 4–5	Chester, PA
Oct. 13	Philadelphia Giants	Phi. Athletics	L 0–5	Camden, NJ
1907				
Oct. 19	Philadelphia Giants	Phi. Athletics	L 0–3	Camden, NJ
1908				
Nov. 20	Br. Royal Giants	Cincinnati Reds	W 9–1	Havana, CU
1909				
Oct. 8	Philadelphia Giants	Phi. Athletics	L 2–5	Camden, NJ
Oct. 8	Br. Royal Giants	New York Yankees	W 9–6	South Norwalk, CT*
Oct. 18	Leland Giants	Chicago Cubs	L 1–4	Chicago, IL
Oct. 21	Leland Giants	Chicago Cubs	L 5–6	Chicago, IL
Oct. 22	Leland Giants	Chicago Cubs	L 0–1, 7 inn	Chicago, IL
1911				
Sep. 11	W. B. Sprudels	Pittsburgh Pirates	W 2–1	West Baden, IN
1912				
May 26	Smart Set	New York Giants	T 3–3	Paterson, NJ
Jul. 14	Smart Set	St. Louis Browns	W 9–7	Paterson, NJ
Oct. 8	W. B. Sprudels	Cincinnati Reds	L 1–2	West Baden, IN
Oct. 27	Lincoln Giants	New York Giants	W 6–0	New York, NY
Nov. 5	Lincoln Giants	New York Yankees	W 6–0	New York, NY*
1913				
Oct. 5	Lincoln Giants	Philadelphia Phillies	W 9–2	New York, NY
Oct. 6	W. B. Sprudels	Cincinnati Reds	L 4–7, 8 inn	West Baden, IN
Oct. 7	W. B. Sprudels	Cincinnati Reds	L 0–9	West Baden, IN
1914				
Oct. 11	Lincoln Giants	Philadelphia Phillies	W 10–4, 8 inn	New York, NY
Oct. 18	Lincoln Giants	New York Giants	L 0–3	New York, NY
Oct. 25	Lincoln Giants	New York Giants	T 1–1	New York, NY
1915				
Oct. 3	Lincoln Giants	Buffalo Blues	W 3–0	New York, NY
Oct. 9	Lincoln Giants	New York Giants	L 0–5	Madison, NJ
Oct. 10	Lincoln Giants	New York Giants	L 2–4	New York, NY
Oct. 17	Lincoln Stars	New York Giants	L 2–9	New York, NY
Oct. 17	Lincoln Giants	Philadelphia Phillies	W 1–0	New York, NY
Oct. 24	Lincoln Giants	Philadelphia Phillies	L 2–4	New York, NY
1917				
Oct. 6	Hilldale	Phi. Athletics	W 6–2	Darby, PA
Oct. 13	Hilldale	Phi. Athletics	L 5–11	Darby, PA
Oct. 20	Hilldale	Phi. Athletics	L 4–10	Darby, PA
1918				
Sep. 14	Hilldale	Boston Red Sox	W 9–0, FF	Darby, PA
Sep. 22	Br. Royal Giants	New York Giants	L 0–7	Jersey City, NJ*
	Br. Royal Giants	New York Giants	L 0–1, 7 inn	2nd Game*
Oct. 27	Philadelphia Giants	New York Giants	L 1–3, 7 inn	New York, NY
Nov. 3	Philadelphia Giants	New York Giants	L 1–4	New York, NY
1919				
Oct. 7	Bacharach Giants	New York Giants	L 5–7	Philadelphia, PA*

Date	NLB	MLB	Result	Location
1920				
Oct. 4	Hilldale	Phi. Athletics	L 1–2	Philadelphia, PA
Oct. 4	St. Louis Giants	St. Louis Cardinals	W 5–4, 10 inn	St. Louis, MO
Oct. 5	Br. Royal Giants	Washington Senators	L 1–2	Washington, D.C.
Oct. 5	Hilldale	Philadelphia Phillies	L 2–5	Philadelphia, PA
Oct. 5	St. Louis Giants	St. Louis Cardinals	L 0–5	St. Louis, MO
Oct. 6	Br. Royal Giants	Washington Senators	L 2–3	Washington, D.C.
Oct. 6	Hilldale	Philadelphia Phillies	L 3–4	Philadelphia, PA
Oct. 7	Br. Royal Giants	Washington Senators	W 5–4	Washington, D.C.*
Oct. 8	Br. Royal Giants	Washington Senators	W 4–2, 8 inn	Washington, D.C.
Oct. 8	St. Louis Giants	Philadelphia Phillies	W 7–1	St. Louis, MO
Oct. 9	Lincoln Giants	New York Giants	W 4–1, 11 inn	New York, NY
Oct. 9	K. C. Monarchs	Philadelphia Phillies	L 3–5	Kansas City, MO
Oct. 10	St. Louis Giants	St. Louis Cardinals	L 0–6	St. Louis, MO
Oct. 10	K. C. Monarchs	Philadelphia Phillies	L 0–1	Kansas City, MO
Oct. 11	K. C. Monarchs	Philadelphia Phillies	L 0–3	Kansas City, MO*
Oct. 21	St. Louis Giants	St. Louis Cardinals	W 7–3	St. Louis, MO
Nov. 13	L. A. White Sox	Philadelphia Phillies	L 1–2, 10 inn	Los Angeles, CA*
Nov. 14	L. A. White Sox	Philadelphia Phillies	W 6–4	Los Angeles, CA
1921				
Oct. 3	St. Louis Giants	St. Louis Cardinals	L 4–5, 11 inn	St. Louis, MO
Oct. 4	Bacharach Giants	Phi. Athletics	L 1–3	Mount Holly, NJ
Oct. 4	St. Louis Giants	St. Louis Cardinals	W 6–2	St. Louis, MO
Oct. 5	Bacharach Giants	Phi. Athletics	L 7–8	Reading, PA
Oct. 6	Bacharach Giants	Phi. Athletics	W 12–9	Reading, PA
Oct. 7	Bacharach Giants	Phi. Athletics	L 3–6	Trenton, NJ
Oct. 9	St. Louis Giants	St. Louis Cardinals	L 3–12	St. Louis, MO
	St. Louis Giants	St. Louis Cardinals	L 6–9	2nd Game
Oct. 10	St. Louis Giants	St. Louis Cardinals	L 3–10	St. Louis, MO
Oct. 13	Bacharach Giants	Phi. Athletics	L 1–5	Elmer, NJ
Oct. 14	Bacharach Giants	Phi. Athletics	W 11–4	Bridgeton, NJ
1922				
Oct. 2	St. Louis Stars	Detroit Tigers	W 5–4	St. Louis, MO
Oct. 2	Cuban Stars	Philadelphia Phillies	W 9–1	Burlington, NJ*
Oct. 3	Br. Royal Giants	Phi. Athletics	T 6–6	Delanco, NJ
Oct. 3	St. Louis Stars	Detroit Tigers	W 11–7	St. Louis, MO
Oct. 4	Br. Royal Giants	Phi. Athletics	W 6–2	Woodbury, NJ
Oct. 4	St. Louis Stars	Detroit Tigers	L 3–10	St. Louis, MO
Oct. 5	Br. Royal Giants	Phi. Athletics	W 8–1	Salem, NJ
Oct. 6	Br. Royal Giants	Phi. Athletics	W 4–1	Bridgeton, NJ
Oct. 7	Cleveland Tate Stars	Cleveland Indians	L 7–9	Cleveland, OH
Oct. 8	Cleveland Tate Stars	Cleveland Indians	L 2–5	Cleveland, OH
Oct. 10	Br. Royal Giants	Phi. Athletics	L 1–5	Gloucester, NJ
Oct. 11	Br. Royal Giants	Phi. Athletics	L 5–12	West Chester, PA
Oct. 11	Cuban Stars	Philadelphia Phillies	W 5–3	Bridgeton, NJ
Oct. 11	Cuban Stars	Philadelphia Phillies	W 4–2	Lambertville, NJ
Oct. 12	Br. Royal Giants	Phi. Athletics	L 3–4	Millville, NJ
Oct. 14	N. Y. B. Giants	New York Giants	W 5–4	Dover, NJ*

Date	NLB	MLB	Result	Location
Oct. 14	Bacharach Giants	Phi. Athletics	L 3–4, 8 inn	Wilmington, DE
Oct. 15	N. Y. B. Giants	New York Giants	W 3–1	Harrison, NJ*
1923				
Oct. 8	Detroit Stars	St. Louis Browns	W 7–6	Detroit, MI
Oct. 9	Detroit Stars	St. Louis Browns	W 7–6	Detroit, MI
Oct. 9	Hilldale	Phi. Athletics	W 3–0, 8 inn	Philadelphia, PA
Oct. 10	Detroit Stars	St. Louis Browns	L 8–11	Detroit, MI
Oct. 10	Hilldale	Phi. Athletics	W 3–2	Chester, PA
Oct. 11	Hilldale	Phi. Athletics	W 3–2	Philadelphia, PA
Oct. 12	Hilldale	Phi. Athletics	L 6–11	Philadelphia, PA
Oct. 13	Hilldale	Phi. Athletics	W 3–1	Darby, PA
Oct. 20	Hilldale	Phi. Athletics	W 9–4	Darby, PA
Oct. 20	Chi. Am. Giants	Detroit Tigers	T 5–5	Chicago, IL
Oct. 21	Chi. Am. Giants	Detroit Tigers	L 1–7	Chicago, IL
Oct. 22	Chi. Am. Giants	Detroit Tigers	W 8–6	Chicago, IL
1924				
Oct. 12	Baltimore Black Sox	Phi. Athletics	L 2–4	Baltimore, MD
	Baltimore Black Sox	Phi. Athletics	W 8–7, 7 inn	2nd Game

NLB 1885–1899: 10–32–1 (.238)
NLB 1900–1924: 47–59–7 (.447)
NLB Total: 57–91–8 (.391)

Appendix II

NLB vs. MLB All-Stars, 1902–1948

Note: Only games known or considered to have been played against five or more Major Leaguers (including the starting pitcher) are listed. The number of known Major Leaguers is shown in parentheses. Games for which box scores were unavailable are marked with an asterisk (*). Inn = Innings; FF = Forfeit.

Abbreviations: A-L = All-Leaguers; A. L. All-Stars = American League All-Stars; A-P = All-Professionals; A-S = All-Stars; Bal. Colored Giants = Baltimore Colored Giants; Bal. Elite Giants = Baltimore Elite Giants; Birm. Black Barons = Birmingham Black Barons; Chi. Am. Giants = Chicago American Giants; Chi. Un. Giants = Chicago Union Giants; Clev. Rosenblums = Cleveland Rosenblums; D-M-L All-Stars = DiMaggio's Major League All-Stars; E. C. Giants = Eastern Colored Giants; Gil. Union Giants = Gilkerson's Union Giants; K. C. Monarchs = Kansas City Monarchs; L. A. White Sox = Los Angeles White Sox; M-A-S = Major All-Stars; M. L. All-Stars = Major League All-Stars; M&M Leaguers = Meyers and Marquard's Leaguers; N. A. L. All-Stars = Negro American League All-Stars; Nash. Elite Giants = Nashville Elite Giants; N. B. = Naval Base; N. L. All-Stars = National League All-Stars; N. N. L. All-Stars = Negro National League All-Stars; N. Y. Bac. Giants = New York Bacharach Giants; N. Y. B. Yankees = New York Black Yankees; Oak. Colored Giants = Oakland Colored Giants; Ok. City = Oklahoma City; Phi. Royal Giants = Philadelphia Royal Giants; Pitt. Crawfords = Pittsburgh Crawfords; S. L. C. Occidentals = Salt Lake City Occidentals; San Bern. = San Bernardino; San Fran. = San Francisco; Sch. Mohawk Giants = Schenectady Mohawk Giants; 25th Inf. Wreckers = 25th Infantry Wreckers; W. B. Sprudels = West Baden Sprudels; Western P. S. B. = Western Pipe & Steel Boilermakers.

Date	NLB	MLB	Result	Location
1902				
Oct. 26	Black Stars	All Professionals	L 3–5	Chicago, IL (7)
1907				
Jul. 10	Leland Giants	All Professionals	L 1–11	Chicago, IL (8)
Aug. 8	Leland Giants	Donlin's All-Stars	W 1–0	Chicago, IL (6)
Aug. 27	Leland Giants	Donlin's All-Stars	W 3–1	Chicago, IL (6)
Aug. 30	Leland Giants	Donlin's All-Stars	W 8–4	Chicago, IL (6)
1908				
Feb. 26	Royal Poinciana	Ormond Hotel	W 8–2	Palm Beach, FL (8)*
Feb. 27	Breakers Hotel	Ormond Hotel	W 9–7	Palm Beach, FL (8)*

Date	NLB	MLB	Result	Location
1910				
Jan. 9	S. L. C. Occidentals	Newton's All-Stars	T 0–0, 12 inn	Los Angeles, CA (5)
Jan. 22	S. L. C. Occidentals	San Diego Pickwicks	L 0–1, 10 inn	San Diego, CA (5)
Jan. 23	S. L. C. Occidentals	San Diego Pickwicks	L 2–6	San Diego, CA (5)
Nov. 19	Chicago Giants	Doyles	L 2–4	Vernon, CA (5)
Nov. 24	Chicago Giants	San Diego Bears	W 1–0	San Diego, CA (5)
Nov. 26	Chicago Giants	San Diego Bears	L 4–6	San Diego, CA (5)
Nov. 27	Chicago Giants	San Diego Bears	W 5–2	San Diego, CA*
Dec. 4	Chicago Giants	McCormicks	L 1–3	Vernon, CA (6)
	Chicago Giants	McCormicks	L 4–8	2nd Game (6)
Dec. 11	Chicago Giants	San Diego Bears	W 6–5, 10 inn	Vernon, CA (5)
Dec. 18	Chicago Giants	Doyles	W 1–0, 11 inn	Vernon, CA (5)
Dec. 25	Chicago Giants	San Diego Bears	W 1–0	San Diego, CA (6)
	Chicago Giants	San Diego Bears	W 2–0	2nd Game (5)
1911				
Feb. 5	Chicago Giants	San Diego Bears	L 4–6	San Diego, CA (5)
	Chicago Giants	San Diego Bears	L 2–4	2nd Game (5)
Feb. 22	Chicago Giants	San Diego Bears	L 0–1	San Diego, CA (6)
Feb. 23	Chicago Giants	San Diego Bears	L 5–6	San Diego, CA (6)
Feb. 25	Chicago Giants	San Diego Bears	W 11–4	San Diego, CA (7)
Feb. 26	Chicago Giants	San Diego Bears	W 5–4, 10 inn	San Diego, CA*
Oct. 15	Lincoln Giants	All-Leaguers	L 3–5	New York, NY (6)
1912				
Oct. 6	Lincoln Giants	All-Leaguers	W 4–3, 10 inn	New York, NY (5)
	Lincoln Giants	All-Stars	L 0–2, 8 inn	2nd Game (5)
Nov. 1	Chi. Am. Giants	McCormicks	L 5–8	Vernon, CA (6)
Nov. 2	Chi. Am. Giants	McCormicks	W 7–3	Vernon, CA (6)
Nov. 3	Chi. Am. Giants	McCormicks	W 10–4	Vernon, CA (7)
Nov. 8	Chi. Am. Giants	Tufts-Lyons	L 1–5	Vernon, CA (7)
Nov. 10	Chi. Am. Giants	Tufts-Lyons	W 6–0	Vernon, CA (6)
Nov. 15	Chi. Am. Giants	San Diego Bears	L 2–3	San Diego, CA (8)
Nov. 16	Chi. Am. Giants	San Diego Bears	W 11–5	San Diego, CA (8)
Nov. 17	Chi. Am. Giants	San Diego Bears	L 2–7	San Diego, CA (8)
Nov. 22	Chi. Am. Giants	McCormicks	W 3–1	Vernon, CA (7)
Nov. 23	Chi. Am. Giants	McCormicks	W 7–3	Vernon, CA (7)
Nov. 24	Chi. Am. Giants	McCormicks	L 6–9	Vernon, CA (6)
Nov. 29	Chi. Am. Giants	Tufts-Lyons	L 1–4	Vernon, CA (6)
Dec. 6	Chi. Am. Giants	San Diego Bears	W 3–0	San Diego, CA (8)
Dec. 7	Chi. Am. Giants	San Diego Bears	L 4–6	San Diego, CA (8)
Dec. 8	Chi. Am. Giants	San Diego Bears	L 3–5	San Diego, CA (8)
Dec. 20	Chi. Am. Giants	San Diego Bears	W 9–0, FF	Vernon, CA*
Dec. 21	Chi. Am. Giants	San Diego Bears	W 7–6	Vernon, CA*
Dec. 22	Chi. Am. Giants	San Diego Bears	W 4–1	Vernon, CA*
	Chi. Am. Giants	San Diego Bears	W 16–1	2nd Game*
Dec. 25	Chi. Am. Giants	San Diego Bears	L 6–7, 10 inn	San Diego, CA (7)
Dec. 26	Chi. Am. Giants	San Diego Bears	W 4–1	San Diego, CA (8)
Dec. 27	Chi. Am. Giants	San Diego Bears	W 3–2	San Diego, CA (9)

Date	NLB	MLB	Result	Location
Dec. 28	Chi. Am. Giants	San Diego Bears	L 2–4	San Diego, CA (8)
Dec. 29	Chi. Am. Giants	San Diego Bears	L 1–8	San Diego, CA (8)
1913				
Jan. 1	Chi. Am. Giants	San Diego Bears	L 1–2	San Diego, CA (8)
Jan. 11	Chi. Am. Giants	San Diego Bears	L 2–3, 11 inn	San Diego, CA (7)
Jan. 12	Chi. Am. Giants	San Diego Bears	L 2–4	San Diego, CA (7)
Feb. 8	Chi. Am. Giants	San Diego Bears	W 4–0	San Diego, CA (7)
Feb. 9	Chi. Am. Giants	San Diego Bears	W 5–3	San Diego, CA (7)
Sep. 28	Lincoln Giants	Donlin's Stars	W 9–1	New York, NY (8)
Oct. 5	Sch. Mohawk Giants	All Americans	W 1–0	Schenectady, NY (5)
Oct. 12	Lincoln Giants	Mack's All Stars	L 0–1	New York, NY (8)
Oct. 19	Lincoln Giants	Mack's All Stars	W 7–3	New York, NY (9)
Nov. 2	Lincoln Giants	Zimmerman's A-S	L 0–1	New York, NY*
Nov. 4	Lincoln Giants	Bender's All Stars	W 2–1	New York, NY*
1914				
Oct. 4	Lincoln Giants	All-Federals	W 2–0	New York, NY (5)
Oct. 11	Indianapolis ABCs	Ownie Bush's A-S	L 3–6	Indianapolis, IN (5)
Nov. 3	Lincoln Giants	Eschen's A-L	W 2–1, 8 inn	New York, NY*
1915				
Oct. 10	Indianapolis ABCs	Ownie Bush's A-S	L 2–5	Indianapolis, IN (8)
Oct. 17	Indianapolis ABCs	Ownie Bush's A-S	W 3–2, 11 inn	Indianapolis, IN (6)
Oct. 24	Indianapolis ABCs	Ownie Bush's A-S	L 1–5	Indianapolis, IN (7)
Oct. 24	St. Louis Giants	East St. Louis Giants	T 1–1	East St. Louis, IL*
Oct. 31	St. Louis Giants	East St. Louis Giants	L 2–6	East St. Louis, IL (7)
Nov. 6	Chi. Am. Giants	San Diego Pantages	L 4–7	San Diego, CA (7)
Nov. 7	Chi. Am. Giants	San Diego Pantages	L 2–6	San Diego, CA (7)
Nov. 13	Chi. Am. Giants	Cline-Cline	W 4–0	San Diego, CA (7)
Nov. 14	Chi. Am. Giants	Cline-Cline	L 0–6	San Diego, CA (7)
Nov. 20	Chi. Am. Giants	San Bernardino	W 6–3	Riverside, CA (5)
Nov. 21	Chi. Am. Giants	San Bernardino	L 1–6	San Bern., CA (5)
Nov. 25	Chi. Am. Giants	San Diego Pantages	W 4–0	San Diego, CA (7)
Nov. 28	Chi. Am. Giants	San Diego Pantages	L 2–3	San Diego, CA (6)
Dec. 5	Chi. Am. Giants	Cline-Cline	W 17–5, 6 inn	San Bern., CA (6)
Dec. 12	Chi. Am. Giants	San Bernardino	L 3–8	San Bern., CA (5)
Dec. 19	Chi. Am. Giants	San Diego Pantages	W 7–3	San Diego, CA (6)
Dec. 25	Chi. Am. Giants	San Diego Pantages	W 4–3	San Diego, CA (7)
Dec. 26	Chi. Am. Giants	San Diego Pantages	W 3–2	San Diego, CA (6)
1916				
Oct. 8	St. Louis Giants	East St. Louis Giants	W 3–2	St. Louis, MO (6)
Oct. 22	St. Louis Giants	East St. Louis Giants	W 1–0	St. Louis, MO*
Nov. 16	25th Inf. Wreckers	All-Americans	L 0–6	Honolulu, HI (9)
Nov. 21	25th Inf. Wreckers	All-Americans	L 0–3	Honolulu, HI (9)
Nov. 26	25th Inf. Wreckers	All-Americans	L 2–7	Honolulu, HI (9)
Nov. 30	25th Inf. Wreckers	All-Americans	W 4–3	Honolulu, HI (9)
Dec. 5	25th Inf. Wreckers	All-Americans	L 1–5	Honolulu, HI (9)*
1917				
Feb. 25	L. A. White Sox	San Pedro Merchants	L 0–7	Vernon, CA (5)*

Date	NLB	MLB	Result	Location
Oct. 7	Indianapolis ABCs	Dolan's A-P	L 1–4	Indianapolis, IN (7)
	Indianapolis ABCs	Dolan's A-P	W 2–0, 5 inn	2nd Game (7)
Oct. 14	Indianapolis ABCs	Ownie Bush's A-S	W 6–1	Indianapolis, IN*
Oct. 14	Lincoln Giants	M & M Leaguers	W 5–4, 10 inn	New York, NY (5)
Oct. 21	Indianapolis ABCs	Muncie Grays	W 2–1	Muncie, IN (6)
Oct. 21	Chi. Am. Giants	All-Stars	W 9–3	Chicago, IL (9)
Dec. 9	L. A. White Sox	San Pedro Merchants	W 5–3	San Pedro, CA (5)*
Dec. 16	L. A. White Sox	San Pedro Merchants	L 3–4	San Pedro, CA (6)*
1918				
Jan. 1	L. A. White Sox	San Pedro Merchants	W 7–5	Los Angeles, CA (6)*
Jan. 6	L. A. White Sox	San Pedro Merchants	L 1–9	San Pedro, CA (5)*
May 19	Chi. Un. Giants	86th Division	L 2–13	Camp Grant, IL (6)
Jul. 20	Chi. Am. Giants	86th Division	W 1–0	Chicago, IL*
Sep. 15	Chi. Am. Giants	Joliet Standards	W 2–1	Chicago, IL (5)
	Chi. Am. Giants	Joliet Standards	L 4–8	2nd Game (6)
Sep. 29	Chi. Am. Giants	All-Stars	L 2–3	Chicago, IL (7)
Oct. 6	Chi. Am. Giants	All-Stars	W 4–2	Chicago, IL (7)
Oct. 13	Chi. Am. Giants	All-Stars	W 7–0	Chicago, IL (7)
1919				
Sep. 28	Bacharach Giants	Treat 'Em Roughs	W 5–1, 14 inn	New York, NY (5)
	Bacharach Giants	Treat 'Em Roughs	L 0–2, 6 inn	2nd Game*
Oct. 4	Hilldale	All-Americans	L 1–6	Darby, PA (5)
Oct. 11	Hilldale	All-Americans	T 0–0, 11 inn	Darby, PA (7)
Oct. 11	Chi. Am. Giants	Kansas City All-Stars	L 1–4	Kansas City, MO (6)
Oct. 12	Chi. Am. Giants	Kansas City All-Stars	L 3–8	Kansas City, MO (7)
Oct. 26	Lincoln Giants	Treat 'Em Roughs	W 8–5	New York, NY (7)
Nov. 2	Lincoln Giants	Treat 'Em Roughs	W 10–4	New York, NY (5)
	Lincoln Giants	Treat 'Em Roughs	L 2–7, 5 inn	2nd Game (7)
Nov. 3–5	25th Inf. Wreckers	Stengel's All-Stars	W 2 L 1	Nogales, AZ*
Nov. 4	Lincoln Giants	Treat 'Em Roughs	L 2–3	New York, NY (7)
Nov. 9	Lincoln Giants	Treat 'Em Roughs	L 3–8	New York, NY (7)
	Lincoln Giants	Treat 'Em Roughs	L 2–3, 7 inn	2nd Game (6)
1920				
Oct. 4	Bacharach Giants	Babe Ruth All-Stars	W 9–4	Philadelphia, PA (6)
Oct. 7	Hilldale	Babe Ruth All-Stars	W 5–0	Philadelphia, PA (5)
Oct. 13	Pittsburgh Stars	Polish Nationals	L 0–10	Buffalo, NY (5)
Oct. 24	Pittsburgh Stars	Polish Nationals	L 4–5	Buffalo, NY (5)
Oct. 24	L. A. White Sox	Blue's All Stars	L 4–5	Los Angeles, CA (7)
Oct. 31	L. A. White Sox	All-Stars	W 5–4, 12 inn	Los Angeles, CA*
Nov. 11	Lincoln Giants	Fisher's All-Stars	W 4–1	Los Angeles, CA (9)
Nov. 21	L. A. White Sox	Pirrone's All-Stars	W 4–2	Los Angeles, CA (7)
Nov. 28	L. A. White Sox	Edington's All-Stars	L 1–6	Los Angeles, CA (8)
Dec. 4	Lincoln Giants	Dyas All-Stars	L 8–9	Los Angeles, CA (7)
Dec. 12	L. A. White Sox	Pirrone's All-Stars	W 4–1	Los Angeles, CA (8)
1921				
Jan. 15	Lincoln Giants	Fisher's All-Stars	W 2–1	Los Angeles, CA (8)
Jan. 16	Lincoln Giants	Fisher's All-Stars	W 6–0	Los Angeles, CA (9)

Date	NLB	MLB	Result	Location
Jan. 22	Lincoln Giants	Love's All-Stars	W 4–2	Los Angeles, CA (8)
Jan. 23	Lincoln Giants	Love's All-Stars	L 1–3	Los Angeles, CA*
Oct. 11	K. C. Monarchs	All Nationals	L 3–4	Bethany, MO (9)
Nov. 5	Colored All-Stars	Pirrone's Stars	W 9–6	Los Angeles, CA (6)
Nov. 6	Colored All-Stars	Pirrone's Stars	L 9–12	Los Angeles, CA (5)
Nov. 11	Colored All-Stars	Fisher's All-Stars	W 5–2	Los Angeles, CA (8)
Nov. 12	Colored All-Stars	Fisher's All-Stars	W 4–0	Los Angeles, CA (7)
Nov. 13	Colored All-Stars	Fisher's All-Stars	L 4–5	Los Angeles, CA (7)
1922				
Jan. 14	Colored All-Stars	Meusel's All-Stars	W 3–2	Los Angeles, CA (7)
Jan. 15	Colored All-Stars	Meusel's All-Stars	L 6–7	Los Angeles, CA (8)
Jan. 18	Colored All-Stars	Meusel's All-Stars	W 11–5	Los Angeles, CA (7)
Jan. 22	Colored All-Stars	Meusel's All-Stars	W 5–4	Los Angeles, CA (7)
Feb. 4	Colored All-Stars	Meusel's All-Stars	W 5–4	Los Angeles, CA (8)
Oct. 15	Baltimore Black Sox	American Stars	W 4–0	Baltimore, MD (9)
Oct. 29	N. Y. Bac. Giants	Bancroft's All Stars	W 10–3	New York, NY*
Nov. 11	L. A. White Sox	Pirrone's All-Stars	W 4–3	Los Angeles, CA*
Nov. 12	L. A. White Sox	Pirrone's All-Stars	T 3–3	Los Angeles, CA (7)
Nov. 18	L. A. White Sox	Pirrone's All-Stars	L 4–9	Los Angeles, CA (6)
Nov. 19	L. A. White Sox	Pirrone's All-Stars	L 3–7	Los Angeles, CA (7)
1923				
Oct. 20	St. Louis Stars	Holke's All-Stars	L 1–7, 8 inn	St. Louis, MO (6)
Oct. 21	Indianapolis ABCs	All-Stars	L 3–5	Indianapolis, IN (6)
Oct. 21	St. Louis Stars	Holke's All-Stars	W 9–5	St. Louis, MO (6)
	St. Louis Stars	Holke's All-Stars	W 5–1, 5 inn	2nd Game (6)
Oct. 21	K. C. Monarchs	Tierney's All-Stars	W 7–5	Kansas City, MO (9)
Nov. 10	St. Louis Stars	Pirrone's All-Stars	L 6–11	Los Angeles, CA (7)
1924				
Sep. 30	Gil. Union Giants	May's All Stars	L 2–11	Fort Dodge, IA*
Oct. 1	Gil. Union Giants	May's All Stars	L 1–8	Boone, IA*
Oct. 2	Gil. Union Giants	May's All Stars	W 8–1	Eldora, IA*
Oct. 3	Gil. Union Giants	May's All Stars	L 3–8	Perry, IA*
Oct. 4	St. Louis Stars	O'Neil's All-Stars	W 5–2	St. Louis, MO (5)
Oct. 5	Colored All-Stars	Telling All-Pros	L 2–6	Cleveland, OH (5)*
	Colored All-Stars	Telling All-Pros	W 3–2	2nd Game (5)*
Oct. 5	St. Louis Stars	O' Neil's All-Stars	L 1–6	St. Louis, MO (5)
Oct. 6	St. Louis Stars	O' Neil's All-Stars	W 11–3	St. Louis, MO*
Oct. 7	St. Louis Stars	O' Neil's All-Stars	L 5–6	St. Louis, MO*
Oct. 11	St. Louis Stars	O' Neil's All-Stars	L 5–9	St. Louis, MO (6)
Oct. 12	Colored All-Stars	Telling All-Pros	L 1–6	Cleveland, OH (6)
Oct. 12	St. Louis Stars	O' Neil's All-Stars	L 2–7	St. Louis, MO*
Oct. 19	Lincoln Giants	Bronx Giants	L 1–5	New York, NY*
Oct. 26	Lincoln Giants	Bronx Giants	W 12–1	New York, NY*
Oct. 26	Colored All-Stars	Telling All-Pros	L 2–16, 5 inn	Cleveland, OH (6)
	Colored All-Stars	Telling All-Pros	W 5–3	2nd Game (6)
1925				
Oct. 24	Phi. Royal Giants	Major League A-S	L 3–7	Los Angeles, CA (9)
Oct. 25	Phi. Royal Giants	Major League A-S	W 7–3	Los Angeles, CA (8)

Date	NLB	MLB	Result	Location
Oct. 31	Phi. Royal Giants	Major League A-S	L 5–9	Los Angeles, CA (9)
Nov. 1	Phi. Royal Giants	Major League A-S	T 7–7	Los Angeles, CA (7)
Nov. 14	Phi. Royal Giants	Major League A-S	W 8–5	Los Angeles, CA (7)
Nov. 15	Phi. Royal Giants	Major League A-S	W 7–4	Los Angeles, CA (8)
Nov. 28	Phi. Royal Giants	Pirrone's All-Stars	W 6–4	Los Angeles, CA (9)
Nov. 29	Phi. Royal Giants	Pirrone's All-Stars	L 3–4	Los Angeles, CA (7)
Dec. 12	Phi. Royal Giants	Pirrone's All-Stars	W 4–0	Los Angeles, CA (9)
Dec. 13	Phi. Royal Giants	Pirrone's All-Stars	W 4–1	Los Angeles, CA (9)
Dec. 25	Phi. Royal Giants	Pirrone's All-Stars	T 2–2, 11 inn	Los Angeles, CA (8)
Dec. 26	Phi. Royal Giants	Pirrone's All-Stars	W 4–3	Los Angeles, CA (9)
Dec. 27	Phi. Royal Giants	Pirrone's All-Stars	W 4–2	Los Angeles, CA (8)
1926				
Jan. 16	Phi. Royal Giants	Pirrone's All-Stars	W 5–2	Los Angeles, CA (8)
Jan. 17	Phi. Royal Giants	Pirrone's All-Stars	W 8–7, 12 inn	Los Angeles, CA (8)
Oct. 1	Hilldale	Earl Mack's A-S	W 3–2	Wilmington, DE (9)
Oct. 2	Hilldale	Earl Mack's A-S	W 6–1	Darby, PA (9)
Oct. 3	Homestead Grays	Earl Mack's A-S	L 6–11,10 inn	Youngstown, PA (9)
Oct. 4	Homestead Grays	Earl Mack's A-S	W 6–5	Pittsburgh, PA (9)
Oct. 6	Hilldale	Earl Mack's A S	L 0–1	Bloomsburg, PA (9)
Oct. 7	Hilldale	Earl Mack's A-S	W 3–0	Bloomsburg, PA (9)
Oct. 8	Hilldale	Earl Mack's A-S	W 4–1	Bloomsburg, PA (9)
Oct. 9	Hilldale	Earl Mack's A-S	W 4–3	Darby, PA (9)
Oct. 11	Homestead Grays	Earl Mack's A-S	W 2–1	Pittsburgh, PA (9)
Oct. 17	Baltimore Black Sox	Rommel's All-Stars	W 3–1	Baltimore, MD*
	Baltimore Black Sox	Rommel's All-Stars	W 4–1	2nd Game*
Oct. 23	Phi. Royal Giants	Pirrone's All-Stars	W 9–0	Los Angeles, CA*
Oct. 24	Phi. Royal Giants	Pirrone's All-Stars	W 9–1	Los Angeles, CA (9)
Nov. 13	Phi. Royal Giants	Pirrone's All-Stars	W 2–1	Los Angeles, CA (8)
Nov. 14	Phi. Royal Giants	Pirrone's All-Stars	W 14–9	Los Angeles, CA (9)
Dec. 19	Phi. Royal Giants	Pirrone's All-Stars	W 4–3, 11 inn	Los Angeles, CA (9)
Dec. 25	Phi. Royal Giants	Pirrone's All-Stars	T 6–6, 12 inn	Los Angeles, CA (9)
Dec. 26	Phi. Royal Giants	Pirrone's All-Stars	W 2–0	Los Angeles, CA (9)
1927				
Oct. 4	Homestead Grays	A. L. All-Stars	L 0–4	Philadelphia, PA (7)
Oct. 5	Homestead Grays	A. L. All-Stars	L 2–7	Johnstown, PA (9)
Oct. 6	Homestead Grays	A. L. All-Stars	L	Fairmont, WV (9)*
Oct. 7	Homestead Grays	A. L. All-Stars	L 2–8	Uniontown, PA (9)
Oct. 8	Homestead Grays	A. L. All-Stars	W 5–0	Pittsburgh, PA (9)
Oct. 9	Homestead Grays	A. L. All-Stars	W 5–1	Youngstown, PA (9)
Oct. 9	Baltimore Black Sox	Jacobson's All-Stars	W 5–4, 7 inn	Baltimore, MD (6)
Oct. 10	Homestead Grays	A. L. All-Stars	L 7–8	Jamestown, NY (9)
c. Oct. 16	Homestead Grays	A. L. All-Stars	W–0	Unknown Site (9)*
Oct. 16	Baltimore Black Sox	Jacobson's All-Stars	W 5–2	Baltimore, MD (6)
c. Oct. 17	Homestead Grays	A. L. All-Stars	L	Unknown Site (9)*
Oct. 21	Bacharach Giants	A. L. All-Stars	L 0–3	Atlantic City, NJ (9)
Oct. 23	Baltimore Black Sox	Jacobson's All-Stars	W 8–7	Baltimore, MD (6)
Oct. 23	Hilldale Giants	Pirrone's All-Stars	L 1–5	Los Angeles, CA (7)
Oct. 29	Hilldale Giants	Pirrone's All-Stars	W 5–0	Los Angeles, CA (8)

Date	NLB	MLB	Result	Location
Oct. 30	Baltimore Black Sox	Jacobson's All-Stars	W 7–6	Baltimore, MD (7)
Oct. 30	Hilldale Giants	Pirrone's All-Stars	W 8–2	Los Angeles, CA (9)
1928				
Oct. 6	Hilldale	M. L. All-Stars	W 5–3	Darby, PA (8)
Oct. 7	Baltimore Black Sox	Maisel's All-Stars	L 5–8	Baltimore, MD (7)
Oct. 7	Homestead Grays	A. L. All-Stars	W 8–4	Sharon, PA (9)
Oct. 7	Cleveland Giants	Pirrone's All-Stars	W 4–3	Los Angeles, CA (8)
Oct. 8	Hilldale	M. L. All-Stars	W 7–2	Mt. Holly, NJ (9)
Oct. 8	Homestead Grays	A. L. All-Stars	W 9–5	Fairmont, WV (9)
Oct. 9	Homestead Grays	A. L. All-Stars	L 5–6	Philipsburg, PA (9)
Oct. 10	Homestead Grays	A. L. All-Stars	W 5–1	Pittsburgh, PA (9)
Oct. 11	Homestead Grays	A. L. All Stars	W 12–10	Butler, PA (9)
Oct. 12	Homestead Grays	A. L. All-Stars	L 4–6	Pittsburgh, PA (9)
Oct. 13	Hilldale	M. L. All-Stars	W 10–6	Philadelphia, PA*
Oct. 13	Homestead Grays	A. L. All-Stars	L 2–6	Columbus, OH (9)*
Oct. 14	Baltimore Black Sox	Maisel's All-Stars	W 9–3	Baltimore, MD (7)
Oct. 14	Homestead Grays	A. L. All-Stars	L 2–6	Columbus, OH (9)*
Oct. 21	Baltimore Black Sox	Maisel's All-Stars	W 2–1	Baltimore, MD (7)
	Baltimore Black Sox	Maisel's All-Stars	L 1–9, 5 inn	2nd Game*
Oct. 28	Baltimore Black Sox	Maisel's All-Stars	L 3–4	Baltimore, MD (8)
1929				
Oct. 12	Chi. Am. Giants	A. L. All-Stars	W 12–11	Chicago, IL (9)
Oct. 13	Lincoln Giants	Gehrig's Stars	W 6–3	New York, NY (6)
	Lincoln Giants	Gehrig's Stars	L 2–3, 6 inn	2nd Game*
Oct. 13	Baltimore Black Sox	Maisel's All-Stars	W 8–3	Baltimore, MD (6)
	Baltimore Black Sox	Maisel's All-Stars	W 2–1, 6 inn	2nd Game (6)*
Oct. 13	Chi. Am. Giants	A. L. All-Stars	W 10–1	Chicago, IL (9)
Oct. 14	Chi. Am. Giants	A. L. All-Stars	L 0–1	Chicago, IL (9)
Oct. 15	Chi. Am. Giants	A. L. All-Stars	W 7–6	Aurora, IL (9)
Oct. 17	Chi. Am. Giants	A. L. All-Stars	W 5–3	Springfield, IL (9)
Oct. 18	Chi. Am. Giants	A. L. All-Stars	W 12–6	Danville, IL (9)*
Oct. 19	Phi. Royal Giants	Pirrone's All-Stars	W 12–8	Los Angeles, CA (9)
Oct. 20	Lincoln Giants	Conroy's Stars	L 4–9	New York, NY*
	Lincoln Giants	Conroy's Stars	W 9–0, 5 inn	2nd Game*
Oct. 20	Baltimore Black Sox	Maisel's All-Stars	W 5–2	Baltimore, MD (5)
	Baltimore Black Sox	Maisel's All-Stars	W 8–0, 5 inn	2nd Game (6)
Oct. 20	Chi. Am. Giants	A. L. All-Stars	L 0–2	Chicago, IL (9)*
Oct. 20	Phi. Royal Giants	Pirrone's All-Stars	W 8–7	Los Angeles, CA (9)
Oct. 27	Baltimore Black Sox	Maisel's All-Stars	W 14–7	Baltimore, MD (5)
Oct. 31	Phi. Royal Giants	Pirrone's All-Stars	W 10–3	Los Angeles, CA (9)
Nov. 2	Phi. Royal Giants	Pirrone's All-Stars	L 3–11	Los Angeles, CA (8)
1930				
Oct. 3	Chi. Am. Giants	A. L. All-Stars	W 6–5, 10 inn	Chicago, IL (7)*
Oct. 4	St. Louis Stars	Carey's All-Stars	W 3–2	St. Louis, MO (8)
Oct. 5	Baltimore Black Sox	All-Stars	W 8–5	Baltimore, MD (7)
Oct. 5	Chi. Am. Giants	A. L. All-Stars	W 6–1	Chicago, IL (7)
Oct. 5	St. Louis Stars	Carey's All-Stars	L 5–11	St. Louis, MO (7)
Oct. 6	Chi. Am. Giants	A. L. All-Stars	W 7–6	Chicago, IL (7)*

Date	NLB	MLB	Result	Location
Oct. 8	St. Louis Stars	Carey's All-Stars	W 2–0	St. Louis, MO*
Oct. 12	Baltimore Black Sox	All-Stars	W 10–0	Baltimore, MD
Oct. 12	W. B. Sprudels	All-Stars	W 6–3	West Baden, IN*
Oct. 12	Chi. Am. Giants	Big League All-Stars	L 2–3	Chicago, IL*
	Chi. Am. Giants	Big League All-Stars	T 3–3, 7 inn	2nd Game*
Oct. 13	Chi. Am. Giants	Big League All-Stars	L 5–7	Chicago, IL*
Oct. 19	Baltimore Black Sox	All-Stars	W 1–0	Baltimore, MD (6)
	Baltimore Black Sox	All-Stars	L 0–1, 5 inn	2nd Game (5)
Oct. 26	Baltimore Black Sox	All-Stars	W 5–3	Baltimore, MD (7)
Oct. 29	Phi. Royal Giants	Earl Mack's A-S	L 3–6	Los Angeles, CA (9)
Nov. 11	Phi. Royal Giants	Shell Oilers	W 6–5	Long Beach, CA*
Nov. 23	Phi. Royal Giants	Kelly Kars	W 5–2	Los Angeles, CA (9)
	Phi. Royal Giants	Kelly Kars	W 6–3	2nd Game (9)*
Dec. 7	Phi. Royal Giants	Shell Oilers	W 4–3	Los Angeles, CA*
	Phi. Royal Giants	Shell Oilers	W 6–0, 6 inn	2nd Game*
1931				
Oct. 1	St. Louis Stars	Carey's All-Stars	W 10–8	St. Louis, MO (9)
Oct. 2	St. Louis Stars	Carey's All-Stars	W 18–1	St. Louis, MO (9)
Oct. 3	Hilldale	M. L. All-Stars	W 6–5	Philadelphia, PA (7)
Oct. 4	Hilldale	M. L. All-Stars	W 7–0	Fairview, NJ (7)
Oct. 4	Baltimore Black Sox	All-Stars	W 5–0	Baltimore, MD (5)
Oct. 4	Homestead Grays	O'Neil's Stars	W 18–0	Cleveland, OH (5)
Oct. 4	K. C. Monarchs	All-Stars	W 4–3	Kansas City, MO (9)
Oct. 10	Hilldale	M. L. All-Stars	W 2–0	Darby, PA (7)
	Hilldale	M. L. All-Stars	W 5–2, 7 inn	2nd Game (5)
Oct. 11	Hilldale	M. L. All-Stars	L 3–6	Camden, NJ (8)
Oct. 11	Baltimore Black Sox	All-Stars	L 2–5	Baltimore, MD (6)
Oct. 15	Phi. Royal Giants	Pirrone's All-Stars	W 8–1	Los Angeles, CA (9)
Oct. 17	Phi. Royal Giants	Pirrone's All-Stars	W 5–0	Los Angeles, CA (8)
Oct. 18	Baltimore Black Sox	All-Stars	L 4–6	Baltimore, MD (6)
Oct. 25	Baltimore Black Sox	All-Stars	W 3–2	Baltimore, MD (6)
1932				
Sep. 27	Pitt. Crawfords	N. L. All-Stars	W 11–2	York, PA (9)
Sep. 28	Pitt, Crawfords	N. L. All-Stars	L 8–20	Pittsburgh, PA (9)
Sep. 30	Pitt. Crawfords	N. L. All-Stars	W 4–2	Altoona, PA (9)
Oct. 1	Pitt. Crawfords	N. L. All-Stars	W 10–2, 8 inn	Pittsburgh, PA (9)
	Pitt. Crawfords	N. L. All-Stars	L 8–9	2nd Game (9)
Oct. 2	Pitt. Crawfords	N. L. All-Stars	W 5–4, 10 inn	Cleveland, OH (9)
	Pitt. Crawfords	N. L. All-Stars	W 4–2, 7 inn	2nd Game (9)
Oct. 9	Baltimore Black Sox	All-Stars	L 2–8	Baltimore, MD (7)
Oct. 11	K. C. Monarchs	All-Majors	W 6–2	Wichita, KS (5)
Oct. 16	Baltimore Black Sox	All-Stars	W 3–2	Baltimore, MD (8)
Oct. 23	Baltimore Black Sox	All-Stars	W 5–2	Baltimore, MD (8)
1933				
Oct. 2	K. C. Monarchs	Dean-Martin A-S	W 5–4	Kansas City, MO (6)
Oct. 4	K. C. Monarchs	All-Stars	L 4–5	Oxford, NE (6)*
Oct. 5	K. C. Monarchs	N. L. All-Stars	L 7–8	St. Joseph, MO (6)
Oct. 5	Chi. Am. Giants	Shevlin's All-Pros	W 3–0	Cincinnati, OH (9)

Date	NLB	MLB	Result	Location
Oct. 6	K. C. Monarchs	N. L. All-Stars	W 7–1	Omaha, NE (7)
Oct. 8	K. C. Monarchs	N. L. All-Stars	W 6–4	Kansas City, MO (8)
Oct. 10	K. C. Monarchs	N. L. All-Stars	L 2–14	Joplin, MO (8)
Oct. 11	K. C. Monarchs	N. L. All-Stars	W 3–0	Okla. City, OK (7)
Oct. 12	K. C. Monarchs	N. L. All-Stars	L 6–11	Wichita, KS (5)
Oct. 15	K. C. Monarchs	M. L. All-Stars	W 3–2	Kansas City, MO (9)
Oct. 15	Phi. Royal Giants	Pirrone's All-Stars	W 11–0	Los Angeles, CA (8)
	Phi. Royal Giants	Pirrone's All-Stars	L 3–4, 7 inn	2nd Game (9)
Oct. 16	Phi. Royal Giants	Pirrone's All-Stars	L 1–2	Los Angeles, CA*
Oct. 29	Phi. Royal Giants	Pirrone's All-Stars	W 11–3	Los Angeles, CA (8)
	Phi. Royal Giants	Pirrone's All-Stars	L 0–10, 7 inn	2nd Game (8)
Nov. 11	Phi. Royal Giants	Pirrone's All-Stars	W 9–4	Los Angeles, CA*
Nov. 12	Phi. Royal Giants	Pirrone's All-Stars	W 5–0	Los Angeles, CA (8)
	Phi. Royal Giants	Pirrone's All-Stars	L 1–4, 6 inn	2nd Game (7)
1934				
Sep. 23	Baltimore Black Sox	All-Stars	W 2–1	Baltimore, MD (5)
	Baltimore Black Sox	All-Stars	W 7–5, 7 inn	2nd Game (5)
Oct. 7	Baltimore Black Sox	All-Stars	L 2–8	Baltimore, MD (5)
Oct. 12	K. C. Monarchs	Dean All-Stars	W 7–0	Kansas City, MO (6)
Oct. 13	Nash. Elite Giants	Pirrone's All-Stars	W 14–5	Los Angeles, CA (9)
Oct. 14	Baltimore Black Sox	All-Stars	L 9–10	Baltimore, MD (6)
Oct. 14	K. C. Monarchs	Chicago Mills	L 3–13	Chicago, IL (9)
Oct. 14	Nash. Elite Giants	Pirrone's All-Stars	W 7–2	Los Angeles, CA (9)
	Nash. Elite Giants	Pirrone's All-Stars	L 3–6, 5 inn	2nd Game*
Oct. 17	N. Y. B. Yankees	Brooklyn Bushwicks	W 6–0	New York, NY (9)
Oct. 21	Baltimore Black Sox	All-Stars	L 6–9	Baltimore, MD (8)
Oct. 21	Pitt. Crawfords	Clev. Rosenblums	W 4–1	Cleveland, OH*
Oct. 22	Pitt. Crawfords	Dean All-Stars	W 5–3	Columbus, OH (6)*
Oct. 23	N. N. L. All-Stars	Dean All-Stars	W 4–3	Pittsburgh, PA (6)
Oct. 27	Nash. Elite Giants	Pirrone's All-Stars	W 9–8	Los Angeles, CA (9)
Oct. 28	Nash. Elite Giants	Pirrone's All-Stars	W 6–4	Los Angeles, CA (7)
	Nash. Elite Giants	Pirrone's All-Stars	W 10–4, 5 inn	2nd Game*
1935				
Oct. 6	K. C. Monarchs	Dean All-Stars	L 0–1	Kansas City, MO (6)
Oct. 9	Pitt. Crawfords	Dayton Shroyers	W 5–2, 10 inn	Dayton, OH (5)
Oct. 12	Negro Stars	Major League Stars	W 7–1	Philadelphia, PA (9)
	Negro Stars	Major League Stars	T 0–0, 5 inn	2nd Game (8)
Oct. 12	Chi. Am. Giants	Chicago Mills	W 3–0	Chicago, IL (9)
Oct. 13	Negro Stars	Major League Stars	L 0–3	New York, NY (8)
	Negro Stars	Major League Stars	L 0–1, 5 inn	2nd Game (8)*
Oct. 13	K. C. Monarchs	All-Stars	W 6–0	Kansas City, MO (7)
Oct. 14	Negro Stars	Major League Stars	W 11–1	York, PA (7)
Oct. 14	K. C. Monarchs	Clink Clair All-Stars	W 8–2	Omaha, NE (5)
Oct. 19	Phi. Royal Giants	Pirrone's Café A-S	W 8–3	Los Angeles, CA (9)
Oct. 20	Phi. Royal Giants	Pirrone's Café A-S	W 5–4	Los Angeles, CA (9)
	Phi. Royal Giants	Pirrone's Café A-S	L 2–4, 5 inn	2nd Game (9)
Oct. 25	Pitt. Crawfords	A. L. All-Stars	T 6–6, 11 inn	Mexico City, MX (9)
Oct. 26	Pitt. Crawfords	A. L. All-Stars	L 1–11	Mexico City, MX (9)
Oct. 27	Pitt. Crawfords	A. L. All-Stars	L 2–7	Mexico City, MX (9)

Date	NLB	MLB	Result	Location
Oct. 31	Phi. Royal Giants	Dean All-Stars	L 4–5	Los Angeles, CA (9)
1936				
Jan. 26	Negro Stars	Major League Stars	L 1–2, 10 inn	Oakland, CA (9)
Mar. 1	Brooklyn Eagles	Cincinnati Reds	W 5–4	San Juan, PR (9)
	Brooklyn Eagles	Cincinnati Reds	L 2–3	2nd Game (9)*
Mar. 3	Brooklyn Eagles	Cincinnati Reds	W 9–2	San Juan, PR (9)*
Mar. 7	Brooklyn Eagles	Cincinnati Reds	W 10–4	San Juan, PR (9)*
Oct. 1	N. N. L. All-Stars	M. L. All-Stars	L 1–2	Davenport, IA (9)
Oct. 2	N. N. L. All-Stars	M. L. All-Stars	W 5–2	Des Moines, IA (9)
Oct. 5	N. N. L. All-Stars	M. L. All-Stars	W 6–3	Denver, CO (9)*
	N. N. L. All-Stars	M. L. All-Stars	W 6–4	2nd Game (9)*
Oct. 7	N. N. L. All-Stars	M. L. All-Stars	W 4–2	Des Moines, IA (9)
1937				
Oct. 5	K. C. Monarchs	M. L. All-Stars	L 3–5	Davenport, IA (9)
Oct. 7	K. C. Monarchs	M. L. All-Stars	L 5–6	Cedar Rapids, IA (9)
Oct. 9	K. C. Monarchs	M. L. All-Stars	L 3–6	Manhattan, KS (9)
Oct. 10	K. C. Monarchs	M. L. All-Stars	L 0–1	Kansas City, MO (5)
Oct. 10	K. C. Monarchs	M. L. All Stars	W 5–4	Wichita, KS (9)
Oct. 11	K. C. Monarchs	M. L. All-Stars	W 10–0	Ok. City, OK (9)
Nov. 7	Phi. Royal Giants	White Kings	L 5–7	Los Angeles, CA (8)
Nov. 21	Detroit Stars	White Kings	L 4–6	Los Angeles, CA*
Dec. 25	Phi. Royal Giants	White Kings	W 13–6	Los Angeles, CA*
1938				
Oct. 4	N. A. L. All-Stars	A. L. All-Stars	L 4–5	Chicago, IL (9)*
Oct. 5	Omaha Monarchs	M. L. All-Stars	L 3–15	Van Meter, IA (6)
Oct. 9	N. N. L. All-Stars	All-Stars	L	Baltimore, MD*
1939				
Oct. 8	Colored All Stars	M. L. All-Stars	L 1–3	Baltimore, MD (9)
	Colored All Stars	M. L. All-Stars	L 0–2	2nd Game (9)*
Oct. 8	Phi. Royal Giants	Pirrone's All Stars	L 3–5	Los Angeles, CA (8)
	Phi. Royal Giants	Pirrone's All Stars	L 2–3 7 inn	2nd Game (8)
Oct. 11	Phi. Royal Giants	Pirrone's All Stars	W 5–2	Los Angeles, CA (9)
Oct. 15	Phi. Royal Giants	White Kings	L 5–6, 10 inn	Los Angeles, CA (7)
1941				
Oct. 5	K. C. Monarchs	M. L. All-Stars	L 1–4	St. Louis, MO (9)
Oct. 9	E. C. Giants	M. L. All-Stars	L 6–9	Los Angeles, CA (9)
1942				
May 24	K. C. Monarchs	Dean All-Stars	W 3–1	Chicago, IL (9)
May 31	Homestead Grays	Dean All-Stars	W 8–1	Washington, D.C. (6)
Oct. 11	Phi. Royal Giants	Pirrone's All-Stars	L 1–6	Los Angeles, CA (9)
	Phi. Royal Giants	Pirrone's All-Stars	L 1–4, 5 inn	2nd Game (9)
Oct. 18	Phi. Royal Giants	Pirrone's All-Stars	L 1–4	Los Angeles, CA (9)
	Phi. Royal Giants	Pirrone's All-Stars	L 2–8, 6 inn	2nd Game (7)
Nov. 8	Phi. Royal Giants	Major-Minor A-S	L 5–11	Long Beach, CA*
Dec. 27	Phi. Royal Giants	Los Alamitos N. B.	L 3–5	Los Angeles, CA*
1943				
Aug. 7	Chi. Am. Giants	Great Lakes N. B.	W 7–3	Great Lakes, IL (9)
Oct. 10	Bal. Elite Giants	Cambria All-Stars	L 1–10	Baltimore, MD*

Date	NLB	MLB	Result	Location
	Bal. Elite Giants	Cambria All-Stars	L 1–4, 5 inn	2nd Game*
Oct. 17	Bal. Colored Giants	Feistner's M-A-S	W 2–0	Long Beach, CA*
Oct. 24	Bal. Colored Giants	Pirrone's All Stars	L 2–8	Los Angeles, CA (9)
	Bal. Colored Giants	Pirrone's All-Stars	W 4–3, 6 inn	2nd Game (8)
Oct. 24	Kansas City Royals	Parker's All-Stars	W 7–2	San Diego, CA (5)
Oct. 31	Bal. Colored Giants	Pirrone's All Stars	W 4–3	Los Angeles, CA (8)
	Bal. Colored Giants	Pirrone's All Stars	T 6–6, 6 inn	2nd Game (7)
Oct. 31	Kansas City Royals	Parker's All-Stars	W 2–1	San Diego, CA (5)
Nov. 5	Kansas City Royals	Major All-Stars	L 2–4	Los Angeles, CA (9)
Nov. 7	Bal. Colored Giants	Pirrone's All Stars	W 11–8	Los Angeles, CA (9)
	Bal. Colored Giants	Pirrone's All Stars	L 3–4, 5 inn	2nd Game (8)
Nov. 10	Negro All-Stars	Lane's M-A-S	L 0–6	Los Angeles, CA (9)
Nov. 11	Kansas City Royals	Western P. S. B.	W 4–1	Los Angeles, CA (8)
Nov. 14	Kansas City Royals	Feistner's M-A-S	L 2–6	Los Angeles, CA*
	Kansas City Royals	Feistner's M-A-S	L 0–1, 7 inn	2nd Game*
Nov. 21	Kansas City Royals	Parker's All-Stars	L 0–3	San Diego, CA (6)
Nov. 28	Bal. Colored Giants	Parker's All-Stars	W 5–1	San Diego, CA (5)
1944				
Sep. 10	Bal. Elite Giants	Major All-Stars	W 8–0	Baltimore, MD (5)
Sep. 24	N.N.L. All-Stars	Major All-Stars	W 2–0, 7 inn	Baltimore, MD (5)
Oct. 11	Kansas City Royals	M. L. All-Stars	L 4–5	Los Angeles, CA (8)
Oct. 15	Birm. Black Barons	Galan's All-Stars	W 7–4	San Francisco, CA (7)
Oct. 20	Kansas City Royals	Feistner's All-Stars	W 3–0	Los Angeles, CA*
Oct. 22	Kansas City Royals	Feistner's All-Stars	W 3–1	Los Angeles, CA*
	Kansas City Royals	Feistner's All-Stars	W 2–0, 6 inn	2nd Game*
1945				
Oct. 2	Paige's All-Stars	Feller's All-Stars	L 2–4	Los Angeles, CA*
Oct. 3	Kansas City Royals	Parker's All-Stars	W 5–0, 7 inn	San Diego, CA (5)
Oct. 5	Paige's All Stars	Feller's All-Stars	L 0–11	San Francisco, CA*
Oct. 7	N. N. L. All-Stars	Dressen's All-Stars	L 4–5	New York, NY (9)
	N. N. L. All-Stars	Dressen's All-Stars	L 1–2, 5 inn	2nd Game (9)
Oct. 7	Kansas City Royals	D-M-L All-Stars	W 1–0	Los Angeles, CA*
	Kansas City Royals	D-M-L All-Stars	L3–4, 7 inn	2nd Game*
Oct. 9	Kansas City Royals	D-M-L All-Stars	L 5–9	Los Angeles, CA (9)
Oct. 10	Kansas City Royals	D-M-L All-Stars	L 7–22	Los Angeles, CA*
Oct. 10	Paige's All-Stars	Feller's All-Stars	W 4–3	Oakland, CA (6)
Oct. 10	Oak. Colored Giants	Gray's All-Stars	L 2–10	Sacramento, CA (6)*
Oct. 12	N. N. L. All-Stars	Dressen's All-Stars	L 0–10	Newark, NJ (9)*
Oct. 14	N. N. L. All-Stars	Dressen's All-Stars	L 1–4	New York, NY (9)
	N. N. L. All-Stars	Dressen's All-Stars	T 0–0, 5 inn	2nd Game (9)
Oct. 21	Kansas City Royals	Parker's All-Stars	W 4–1	San Diego, CA (7)
Oct. 24	Kansas City Royals	Feller's All-Stars	W 3–2	San Diego, CA (7)
Oct. 26	Kansas City Royals	Feller's All-Stars	L 2–3, 10 inn	Los Angeles, CA*
1946				
Sep. 30	Paige's All-Stars	Feller's All-Stars	W 3–1	Pittsburgh, PA (9)
Oct. 1	Paige's All-Stars	Feller's All-Stars	L 2–11	Youngstown, OH (9)
Oct. 1	Paige's All-Stars	Feller's All-Stars	L 0–5	Cleveland, OH (9)
Oct. 2	Paige's All-Stars	Feller's All-Stars	L 5–6	Chicago, IL (9)*

Date	NLB	MLB	Result	Location
Oct. 3	Paige's All-Stars	Feller's All-Stars	L 0–3	Cincinnati, OH (9)*
Oct. 4	Paige's All-Stars	Feller's All-Stars	L 2–4, 10 inn	New York, NY (9)
Oct. 5	Paige's All-Stars	Feller's All-Stars	L 3–5	West Haven, CT (9)*
Oct. 5	Paige's All-Stars	Feller's All-Stars	L 10–13	Newark, NJ (9)*
Oct. 6	Paige's All-Stars	Feller's All-Stars	W 4–0	New York, NY (9)
Oct. 6	Bal. Elite Giants	All Stars	W 6–1	Baltimore, MD*
	Bal. Elite Giants	All Stars	W 3–2	2nd game*
Oct. 6	Paige's All-Stars	Feller's All-Stars	W 7–4	Baltimore, MD (9)
Oct. 6	Robinson's All-Stars	Wagner's All-Stars	L 4–10	Cincinnati, OH (9)*
Oct. 7	Paige's All-Stars	Feller's All-Stars	W 4–3	Columbus, OH (9)*
Oct. 7	Robinson's All-Stars	Wagner's All-Stars	L 5–6	Youngstown, OH (9)*
Oct. 8	Paige's All-Stars	Feller's All-Stars	L 6–7	Dayton, OH (9)
Oct. 8	Robinson's All-Stars	Wagner's All-Stars	W 6–4	Pittsburgh, PA (9)
Oct. 10	Paige's All-Stars	Feller's All-Stars	L 5–7	Richmond, IN (9)
Oct. 12	Paige's All-Stars	Feller's All-Stars	L 2–3	Council Bluffs, IA (9)
Oct. 12	Paige's All-Stars	Feller's All-Stars	L 3–5	Wichita, KS (9)
Oct. 13	Bal. Elite Giants	Robertson's A-S	W 11–2	Baltimore, MD*
	Bal. Elite Giants	Robertson's A-S	T 2–2, 5 inn	2nd Game*
Oct. 13	Robinson's All-Stars	Wagner's All-Stars	W 10–5	Chicago, IL (9)*
Oct. 13	Paige's All-Stars	Feller's All-Stars	W 3–2	Kansas City, MO (9)
Oct. 14	Robinson's All-Stars	Wagner's All-Stars	W 8–0	Cleveland, OH (9)*
Oct. 14	Paige's All-Stars	Feller's All-Stars	L 1–4	Kansas City, MO (9)
Oct. 16	Kansas City Royals	Feller's All-Stars	L 3–4	Los Angeles, CA (9)
Oct. 17	Kansas City Royals	Feller's All-Stars	L 0–2	San Diego, CA (9)
Oct. 18	Robinson's All-Stars	Feller's All-Stars	L 0–6	San Fran., CA (9)*
Oct. 23	Kansas City Royals	Feller's All-Stars	L 4–12	Bakersfield, CA (9)
Oct. 24	Robinson's All-Stars	Feller's All-Stars	L	El Centro, CA (9)*
Oct. 24	Robinson's All-Stars	Feller's All-Stars	L 2–4	San Diego, CA (9)
Oct. 25	Robinson's All-Stars	Feller's All-Stars	L 3–4	Los Angeles, CA (9)*
Oct. 27	Kansas City Royals	Lemon's All-Stars	L 0–5	Los Angeles, CA*
1947				
Feb. 22	San Juan	New York Yankees	L 3–16	San Juan, PR (9)*
Feb. 23	Caguas	New York Yankees	L 4–6	San Juan, PR (9)*
Feb. 24	Ponce	New York Yankees	W 12–8	San Juan, PR (9)*
Feb. 25	Puerto Rico A-S	New York Yankees	W 7–6, 12 inn	San Juan, PR (9)*
Feb. 26	San Juan All-Stars	New York Yankees	L 6–8	San Juan, PR (9)*
Mar. 1	Vargas	New York Yankees	W 4–3	Caracas, VE (9)
Mar. 2	Magallanes	New York Yankees	L 4–5	Caracas, VE (9)*
Oct. 12	Kansas City Royals	Parker's All-Stars	L 3–4, 12 inn	San Diego, CA (9)
Oct. 14	Kansas City Royals	Feller's All-Stars	L 3–11	San Diego, CA (9)
Oct. 15	Kansas City Royals	Feller's All-Stars	L 1–2	Los Angeles, CA (9)
Oct. 16	Kansas City Royals	Feller's All-Stars	L 1–6	Oakland, CA (9)*
Oct. 17	Feller's All-Stars	Kansas City Royals	L 2–7	San Fran., CA (9)*
Oct. 18	Kansas City Royals	Feller's All-Stars	W 5–4	San Diego, CA (9)*
Oct. 19	Kansas City Royals	Feller's All-Stars	L 1–2	Los Angeles, CA (9)
Oct. 23	Kansas City Royals	Blackwell's All-Stars	W 4–3, 13 inn	Los Angeles, CA (9)
Oct. 26	Kansas City Royals	Blackwell's All-Stars	W 3–2	Los Angeles, CA (9)
Nov. 2	Kansas City Royals	Feller's All-Stars	W 8–0	Los Angeles, CA (9)

Date	NLB	MLB	Result	Location
1948				
Oct. 17	Kansas City Royals	M. L. All-Stars	L 2–4	Los Angeles, CA (9)
Oct. 24	Kansas City Royals	M. L. All-Stars	W 4–3	Los Angeles, CA (9)
Oct. 25	Kansas City Royals	M. L. All-Stars	W 7–5	San Diego, CA (9)
Oct. 31	Kansas City Royals	M. L. All-Stars	L 4–8	Los Angeles, CA (9)
Nov. 7	Kansas City Royals	M. L. All-Stars	L 7–8	Los Angeles, CA (9)
	Kansas City Royals	M. L. All-Stars	W 5–2, 6 inn	2nd Game (8)

NLB Total: 268–222–13 (.545)

Appendix III

NLB vs. MLB Batting, Pitching and Fielding Statistics, 1886–1948

Note: The players are listed by their given names. When first names were unavailable, the player's team has been included. The statistics have been derived from contests listed in Appendices I and II, and from games played in Cuba against major leaguers incorporated into the Seamheads.com Negro Leagues Database.

Similarly Named Players: William Bell (I) played from 1900 to 1904. William Bell (II) played from 1923 to 1937. Frank Duncan (I) played from 1909 to 1928. Frank Duncan (II) played from 1920 to 1939. Bill Holland (I) played from 1894 to 1908. Bill Holland (II) played from 1920 to 1941. George Johnson, Jr., played from 1896 to 1919. George Johnson played from 1909 to 1931. William Selden (I) played from 1887 to 1899. William Selden (II) played from 1907 to 1933. Charlie "Chino" Smith played from 1924 to 1931. Charlie "Red" Smith played from 1915 to 1919. John "Steel Arm" Taylor played from 1903 to 1920. John "Big" Taylor played from 1920 to 1928.

Team Abbreviations: ABC=Indianapolis ABCs; BBS=Baltimore Black Sox; BS = Black Stars; CAS=Colored All-Stars; CCG=Chicago Columbia Giants; CHG=Chicago Giants; CLG=Cleveland Giants; CUG=Chicago Union Giants; CG=Cuban Giants; ECG=Eastern Colored Giants HC=Hilldale Club; HG=Homestead Grays; KCM=Kansas City Monarchs; KCR=Kansas City Royals; LAWS=Los Angeles White Sox; LS=Lincoln Stars; OM= Omaha Monarchs; NAS= Negro All-Stars; NS=Negro Stars; NYG=New York Gorhams; PAS=Paige's All Stars; PC=Pittsburgh Crawfords; PG=Philadelphia Giants; PRG=Philadelphia Royal Giants; PS= Pittsburgh Stars; RAS=Robinson's All-Stars; SLG=St. Louis Giants; SLS=St. Louis Stars; SLO=Salt Lake City Occidentals; WBS=West Baden Sprudels; WRK=25th Infantry Wreckers.

Batting Statistics

Note on Batting Statistics: Players who only pinch-hit are denoted by an *. Players who only pinch-ran are denoted by a #. Because bases on balls, runs batted in, and stolen bases were not always divulged in box scores, these totals are understated. As at-bats were not always reported either, a small percentage of those totals have been estimated. G=Games; AB=At Bats; R=Runs; H=Hits; D=Doubles; T=Triples; HR=Home Runs; RBI=Runs Batted In; BB=Bases on Balls; SB=Stolen Bases; HBP=Hit by Pitch; SAC=Sacrifice Hits and Flies; BA=Batting Average.

Player	G	AB	R	H	D	T	HR	RBI	BB	SB	HBP	SAC	BA
Abernathy, Robert	2	8	0	2	0	0	0	3	0	0	0	0	.250
Abreu, Eufemio	9	29	3	6	0	0	0	3	5	0	0	1	.207
Alexander, Charles	1	3	1	1	0	0	0	0	0	0	0	0	.333
Allen, Johnny	1	4	1	1	0	0	0	0	0	0	0	0	.250
Allen, Newt	40	163	20	48	4	3	1	12	5	10	2	5	.294
Allen, Todd	3	10	2	1	0	0	0	0	1	1	0	0	.100
Allen, Toussaint	9	27	3	5	1	0	0	0	2	0	0	1	.185
Almeida, Rafael	55	188	24	60	6	1	1	22	21	10	3	5	.319
Anderson, Bill	1	2	0	1	1	0	0	2	0	0	0	0	.500
Andrews, Herman	1	1	0	1	0	0	0	0	0	0	0	0	1.000
Andrews, Peter	2	4	0	1	0	0	0	0	2	0	0	0	.250
Archer, Luke	1	1	0	1	0	0	0	0	0	0	0	0	1.000
Arnett, 1902 BS	1	4	0	0	0	0	0	0	0	0	0	0	.000
Arthur, A., 1936 NS	1	4	0	0	0	0	0	0	0	0	0	0	.000
Arumis, Joaquin	2	5	0	0	0	0	0	0	0	0	0	0	.000
Atkins, Joe	1	4	0	1	0	0	0	0	0	0	0	0	.250
Aulston, Clyde	1	2	0	0	0	0	0	0	0	0	0	0	.000
Austin, Frank	4	14	1	3	0	0	0	0	0	0	0	0	.214
Avery, Bill	1	2	0	0	0	0	0	0	1	0	0	0	.000
Baker, 1920 LAWS	1	2	0	0	0	0	0	0	0	0	0	0	.000
Ball, Walter	9	30	4	7	0	1	0	0	1	2	0	0	.233
Bankhead, Dan	1	0	0	0	0	0	0	0	1	0	0	0	.000
Bankhead, Sam	13	48	7	18	3	2	1	6	3	3	0	1	.375
Baranda, Manuel	5	18	2	4	0	0	0	0	0	0	0	1	.222
Barber, Jesse	49	200	30	45	4	1	2	10	9	5	3	5	.225
Barnes, Ed	2	4	0	1	0	0	0	0	0	0	0	0	.250
Barnes, John	6	20	3	5	2	0	0	0	0	0	0	0	.250
Baro, Alfredo	1	4	2	1	0	0	0	0	1	0	0	0	.250
Baro, Bernardo	10	41	7	18	5	0	0	7	4	0	0	1	.439
Barton, George	2	8	0	2	0	0	0	0	0	0	0	0	.250
Barton, Sherman	1	4	0	2	0	0	0	0	0	0	0	0	.500
Bassett, Lloyd	5	18	0	3	0	0	0	1	0	0	0	0	.167
Bauchman, Harry	13	50	4	12	1	1	1	4	0	0	0	0	.240
Baugh, Johnny	3	8	1	1	1	0	0	0	0	0	0	0	.125
Baynard, Frank	1	0	0	0	0	0	0	0	0	0	0	0	—
Baynard, William	2	8	0	3	1	0	0	0	0	0	0	0	.375
Beckwith, John	41	152	30	53	9	4	12	29	6	0	0	3	.349
Bell, Frank	1	5	1	4	1	0	1	2	0	1	0	0	.800
Bell, Fred	1	3	0	0	0	0	0	0	0	0	0	0	.000
Bell, James	52	183	30	57	9	3	0	8	26	21	1	1	.311
Bell, Louie	1	1	0	0	0	0	0	0	0	0	0	0	.000
Bell, William (I)	2	9	1	2	0	0	0	0	0	0	0	0	.222
Bell, William (II)	6	6	1	2	0	0	0	1	0	0	0	0	.333
Benavides, Prudencio	1	5	1	0	0	0	0	0	0	0	0	0	.000
Benjamin, Jerry	3	11	2	2	0	0	0	0	1	1	1	1	.182
Bennett, Sam	6	15	2	7	0	2	0	4	1	1	2	0	.467
Benson, Gene	12	48	4	8	1	0	0	1	0	0	0	0	.167
Berry, 1938 OM	1	4	0	0	0	0	0	0	0	0	0	0	.000
Beverly, Charles	5	16	1	2	0	0	0	0	1	0	0	0	.125

Player	G	AB	R	H	D	T	HR	RBI	BB	SB	HBP	SAC	BA
Bibbs, Junius	1	2	0	0	0	0	0	0	1	0	0	0	.000
Binga, Bill	2	7	1	1	0	0	0	0	0	0	0	0	.143
Bingham, William	3	10	1	3	1	0	0	0	0	0	0	0	.300
Bissant, John	1	5	1	3	0	0	0	1	0	1	0	0	.600
Black, Frank	3	12	0	1	0	0	0	0	0	1	1	0	.083
Blackman, Henry	13	39	11	10	0	1	1	2	1	0	0	1	.256
Blackwell, Charles	16	64	14	18	3	4	1	3	1	3	1	0	.281
Blake, Frank	2	5	1	2	0	1	0	1	0	0	0	0	.400
Blueitt, Virgil	1	3	1	1	0	0	0	0	0	0	0	0	.333
Bobo, Willie	2	8	0	1	0	0	0	0	0	0	0	0	.125
Bolden, 1938 OM	1	3	0	0	0	0	0	1	0	0	0	1	.000
Bonner, Robert	4	15	1	2	0	0	0	0	1	0	0	0	.133
Booker, Pete	20	62	7	12	0	0	0	2	4	0	2	3	.194
Bost, CHG 1910	2	4	0	0	0	0	0	0	0	0	0	0	.000
Bowman, Emmett	4	16	3	3	1	0	0	0	0	0	0	0	.188
Boyd, Ben	30	117	20	34	4	1	0	2	4	8	0	1	.291
Boyd, Fred	2	7	0	4	1	0	0	0	0	0	0	0	.571
Bradford, Charlie	2	7	1	2	0	0	1	1	0	0	0	0	.286
Bradley, Phil	8	30	3	5	1	0	0	0	0	3	0	1	.167
Bradley, Provine*	1	1	0	1	1	0	0	0	0	0	0	0	1.000
Brady, Farmer	1	0	0	0	0	0	0	0	0	0	0	1	.000
Bragg, Jesse	6	19	2	2	0	0	0	1	3	0	0	2	.105
Branham, Finis	6	13	1	3	0	0	0	0	1	0	0	0	.231
Brazelton, Clarkson	6	11	2	4	1	0	0	0	1	1	0	0	.364
Brewer, Chet	16	35	1	5	1	0	0	1	2	0	0	1	.143
Brewer, Gene	7	22	0	6	0	1	0	1	0	0	0	0	.273
Briggs, Otto	20	77	11	22	3	0	0	1	0	0	2	0	.286
Britt, George	16	47	5	10	1	0	0	0	2	1	0	0	.213
Britton, John	1	4	1	2	0	0	0	0	0	0	0	0	.500
Brooks, Ameal	6	22	3	6	0	1	0	0	0	4	0	0	.273
Brooks, Gus	2	8	2	3	1	0	0	0	1	0	0	0	.375
Brooks, Irvin	16	50	12	11	1	0	0	0	6	1	0	1	.220
Brooks, Jesse	4	15	1	0	0	0	0	0	1	0	0	0	.000
Brooks, Sidney	5	17	2	4	0	0	0	0	1	0	0	0	.235
Brown, 1934 KCM	1	1	0	0	0	0	0	0	0	0	0	0	.000
Brown, Barney	6	14	0	3	0	0	0	0	1	0	0	1	.214
Brown, Ben	1	3	0	0	0	0	0	0	0	0	0	0	.000
Brown, Dave	3	3	0	0	0	0	0	0	0	0	0	0	.000
Brown, E., 1911 WBS/ 1918 CUG	2	7	1	2	1	0	0	2	0	0	0	0	.286
Brown, Elias	8	32	4	12	2	1	0	1	1	0	0	1	.375
Brown, George	5	17	0	4	2	1	0	0	2	1	0	1	.235
Brown, Jim	4	12	2	6	0	0	0	1	1	0	0	0	.500
Brown, Larry	14	42	3	10	2	0	0	0	2	1	1	1	.238
Brown, Malcom	8	25	0	0	0	0	0	0	0	1	0	0	.000
Brown, Mike	1	4	0	1	0	0	0	0	0	0	0	0	.250
Brown, Ray	2	5	1	2	0	1	0	3	1	0	0	0	.400
Brown, Tom	1	1	0	0	0	0	0	0	0	0	0	0	.000
Brown, Willard	15	63	8	20	3	2	3	10	1	2	0	2	.317

Player	G	AB	R	H	D	T	HR	RBI	BB	SB	HBP	SAC	BA
Buckner, Harry	11	38	6	18	5	3	3	5	1	1	1	0	.474
Buford, 1914 ABC	1	0	0	0	0	0	0	0	0	0	0	0	—
Burbage, Knowlington	6	20	5	5	0	0	2	4	3	0	0	1	.250
Burnett, Fred	3	7	2	2	0	0	0	0	2	2	0	0	.286
Burns, Claude	3	12	0	1	0	0	0	0	0	0	0	0	.083
Burns, Pete	3	11	1	5	0	0	0	2	0	0	0	0	.455
Bustamante, Luis	26	88	10	19	2	2	0	4	7	4	0	2	.216
Butcher, Spencer	3	6	0	2	0	0	0	0	0	0	0	0	.333
Butts, Thomas	1	5	1	1	0	0	0	0	0	0	0	0	.200
Byas, Richard	1	4	0	1	0	0	0	0	0	0	0	0	.250
Byrd, Bill	3	8	2	2	1	1	0	0	0	0	0	0	.250
Cabanas, Armando	35	114	14	22	1	2	0	9	8	6	0	6	.193
Cabrera, Alfredo	47	160	11	38	4	1	0	15	10	10	0	8	.238
Cade, Joe*	1	1	1	1	0	0	0	0	0	0	0	0	1.000
Calderon, Benito	1	2	0	0	0	0	0	0	1	0	0	0	.000
Campanella, Roy	7	24	1	5	1	0	1	1	0	0	0	0	.208
Campos, Tatica	12	36	3	7	1	0	0	3	3	1	0	0	.194
Cannady, Walter	16	60	12	26	7	1	2	5	2	0	0	0	.433
Carillo, Lazaro	1	4	0	0	0	0	0	0	1	0	0	0	.000
Carlisle, Matthew	1	3	0	0	0	0	0	0	0	0	0	0	.000
Carr, George	48	173	34	54	10	2	4	15	16	8	2	0	.312
Carr, Wayne	2	3	0	0	0	0	0	0	0	0	0	0	.000
Carter, Charles	4	8	1	2	1	0	0	0	0	0	0	0	.250
Carter, Cliff	1	4	1	2	0	0	0	0	0	0	0	0	.500
Carter, Ernest	3	10	1	3	0	0	1	1	0	0	0	0	.300
Carter, Marlin	4	17	1	3	0	0	0	0	1	0	0	0	.176
Carter, Paul	1	3	0	0	0	0	0	0	0	0	0	0	.000
Cary, Arthur	1	4	0	0	0	0	0	0	0	0	0	0	.000
Casey, William	4	10	1	2	0	0	0	0	0	0	0	0	.200
Cash, Bill	1	2	0	0	0	0	0	0	0	0	0	0	.000
Cason, John	7	22	4	9	1	0	0	1	1	0	0	0	.409
Castillo, Julian	34	121	12	30	6	2	0	12	14	2	1	3	.248
Catto, Harry	2	4	0	1	0	0	0	1	0	0	0	1	.250
Chacon, Pelayo	28	98	5	25	1	1	0	7	6	7	1	3	.255
Chamberlain, Ed	1	3	0	0	0	0	0	0	0	0	0	0	.000
Charleston, Oscar	64	237	45	79	23	8	11	34	18	15	1	3	.333
Charleston, Porter	1	1	0	0	0	0	0	0	0	0	0	0	.000
Clark, 1937 KCM	1	4	0	0	0	0	0	0	0	0	0	0	.000
Clark, Al	2	5	0	0	0	0	0	0	0	0	0	0	.000
Clark, Morten	14	45	2	6	0	0	0	0	4	2	0	1	.133
Clarke, Bob	18	53	5	15	4	0	1	6	3	1	1	1	.283
Clayton, Leroy	3	10	3	4	0	0	0	0	0	0	0	0	.400
Cobb, Lorenza	4	11	0	1	0	0	0	0	0	0	0	0	.091
Cockrell, Phil	21	59	11	13	1	1	0	1	3	4	0	0	.220
Cole, 1928 CLG	1	3	1	0	0	0	0	0	1	0	0	0	.000
Collins, 1936 NS	1	4	0	2	0	0	0	0	0	0	0	0	.500
Collins, 1942 PRG	4	3	0	1	0	0	0	1	1	0	0	0	.333
Collins, 1944 KCR	1	0	0	0	0	0	0	0	0	0	0	0	—
Combs, Jack	1	2	0	0	0	0	0	0	0	0	0	0	.000

Player	G	AB	R	H	D	T	HR	RBI	BB	SB	HBP	SAC	BA
Concepcion, Monchile	1	4	0	0	0	0	0	0	0	0	0	0	.000
Cooper, E. 1915 LS	1	4	0	0	0	0	0	0	0	0	0	0	.000
Cooper, 1924 SLS	1	2	0	0	0	0	0	0	0	0	0	0	.000
Cooper, Andy	10	20	2	5	1	0	0	1	1	0	0	1	.250
Cooper, Anthony	1	4	0	1	1	0	0	0	0	0	0	0	.250
Cooper, Darltie	2	3	0	0	0	0	0	0	0	0	0	0	.000
Cornelius, Willie	2	3	0	0	0	0	0	0	0	0	0	0	.000
Crafton, Allie	1	2	0	0	0	0	0	0	0	0	0	0	.000
Crawford, Sam	4	6	0	1	0	0	0	0	0	0	0	0	.167
Creacy, Albert	9	36	4	8	1	0	1	1	0	0	0	0	.222
Crockett, Frank	1	4	1	1	0	0	0	0	0	0	0	0	.250
Crump, James	6	21	3	7	0	0	0	0	0	0	0	0	.333
Crutchfield, Jimmie	11	46	3	10	0	0	0	0	0	1	0	1	.217
Cullens, William	4	12	1	0	0	0	0	0	2	0	0	0	.000
Cummings, Napoleon	1	3	0	1	0	0	0	0	0	0	0	0	.333
Curry, Rube	9	21	3	2	1	0	1	1	2	0	0	0	.095
Dabney, John	1	3	0	0	0	0	0	0	0	0	0	0	.000
Dallard, Maurice	9	35	7	10	0	0	0	2	2	1	0	0	.286
Danage, Lunie	4	14	1	2	0	0	0	0	1	0	0	0	.143
Dandridge, Ray	7	24	4	8	3	1	0	2	1	1	0	0	.333
Daniels, Leon	1	1	0	0	0	0	0	0	0	0	0	0	.000
Davenport, Lloyd	2	9	1	4	0	2	0	2	0	0	0	1	.444
Davis, 1934 KCM	2	7	0	2	0	0	0	1	0	0	0	1	.286
Davis, 1942 PRG	3	11	0	2	0	0	0	0	0	1	0	0	.182
Davis, Ambrose	1	3	0	0	0	0	0	0	0	0	0	0	.000
Davis, Jack	1	4	0	0	0	0	0	0	0	0	0	0	.000
Davis, John "Quack"*	1	0	0	0	0	0	0	0	1	0	0	0	.000
Davis, Johnny	11	41	3	12	3	0	1	7	0	0	0	1	.293
Davis, Lorenzo	8	34	4	10	2	0	2	5	0	0	0	1	.294
Davis, "Red"	1	4	0	0	0	0	0	0	0	0	0	0	.000
Davis, Rosey	8	18	3	5	1	0	0	1	1	0	0	0	.278
Davis, Tom	1	4	1	1	0	0	0	0	0	0	0	1	.250
Davis, Walter	4	11	1	4	1	0	0	0	1	1	0	0	.364
Davis, William	1	4	0	2	0	0	0	0	0	0	0	0	.500
Day, 1902 PG	2	8	1	2	1	0	0	0	1	0	0	0	.250
Day, Wilson	21	71	10	22	5	0	1	5	10	1	0	2	.310
Deas, James	5	18	2	8	2	0	0	1	1	1	0	0	.444
Demery, Art	1	0	0	0	0	0	0	0	0	0	0	0	—
DeMoss, Elwood	17	60	7	16	2	0	0	1	4	9	0	5	.267
Dennis, Wesley	1	4	1	2	0	0	0	0	0	0	0	0	.500
Dewitt, Sam	1	1	0	0	0	0	0	0	0	0	0	0	.000
Dials, Oland	6	11	0	3	0	0	0	0	2	0	0	0	.273
Dihigo, Martin	14	59	6	18	5	0	3	3	1	0	1	0	.305
Dismukes, William	8	17	2	1	0	0	0	1	3	0	0	1	.059
Dixon, George	9	29	2	10	1	0	0	3	2	0	1	0	.345
Dixon, Herbert	43	150	28	50	16	3	2	17	12	9	2	5	.333
Doby, Larry	1	3	1	1	0	1	0	2	0	0	0	0	.333
Donaldson, John	5	17	2	2	0	0	0	2	2	0	0	0	.118
Dougherty, Pat	15	32	3	6	1	1	1	2	1	0	0	1	.188

Player	G	AB	R	H	D	T	HR	RBI	BB	SB	HBP	SAC	BA
Douglas, Jesse	4	14	1	2	1	0	0	0	1	0	0	0	.143
Douglass, Eddie	10	37	5	10	0	1	0	0	2	1	0	1	.270
Douglass, George	1	3	1	1	0	0	0	0	1	0	0	0	.333
Downs, McKinley	12	41	5	12	2	0	0	0	1	2	1	2	.293
Drake, Bill	5	15	0	1	0	0	0	0	0	0	0	0	.067
Dudley, Charles	10	30	4	6	1	1	0	0	2	1	0	0	.200
Dukes, Tommy	4	14	1	3	0	0	1	1	1	0	0	0	.214
Dunbar, Ashby	3	11	0	2	0	1	0	0	0	0	0	0	.182
Duncan, Frank (I)	43	162	17	39	8	3	3	17	8	6	5	4	.241
Duncan, Frank (II)	21	64	7	10	2	0	0	0	4	1	0	0	.156
Dunn, Joseph	4	16	2	3	0	0	0	0	2	0	0	0	.188
Dwight, Eddie	17	61	10	21	1	0	0	2	6	4	0	1	.344
Earle, Charles	16	47	6	11	2	1	0	1	5	1	4	0	.234
Easterling, Howard	20	69	8	20	3	4	1	7	6	1	1	1	.290
Eggleston, Bill	1	4	0	2	0	0	0	0	0	0	0	0	.500
Eggleston, Mack	9	27	2	8	2	1	0	0	2	0	0	1	.296
Ellis, 1911 WBS	1	4	1	3	2	0	0	0	0	0	0	0	.750
Else, Harry	1	3	0	1	0	0	0	0	1	0	0	0	.333
Emory, John	1	4	0	0	0	0	0	0	0	0	0	0	.000
Epps, Simon	1	3	0	1	0	0	0	0	0	0	0	0	.333
Erwin, 1938 OM	1	0	0	0	0	0	0	0	0	0	0	0	—
Evans, Bill	1	6	1	2	0	0	0	0	0	0	0	0	.333
Ewing, William	6	19	5	6	1	1	1	1	1	1	0	0	.316
Fabre, Isidro	6	17	3	3	0	0	0	1	2	0	0	0	.176
Fagan, Bob	23	81	13	17	1	2	1	1	3	1	2	1	.210
Farrell, William	2	8	1	4	0	0	0	0	0	0	0	0	.500
Farrell, Luther	4	11	0	2	0	0	0	0	1	0	0	1	.182
Fernandez, Jose Maria	1	3	0	1	0	0	0	0	0	0	0	0	.333
Fiall, George	1	5	1	1	0	0	0	0	0	0	0	0	.200
Fiall, Tom	11	44	3	8	0	0	0	0	1	0	0	1	.182
Fields, Romey	1	3	0	0	0	0	0	0	0	0	0	0	.000
Figarola, Rafael	17	57	3	8	1	1	0	2	2	0	0	1	.140
Fillmore, Jim	1	2	0	1	0	0	0	1	0	0	0	0	.500
Finley, Tom	2	5	1	1	0	0	0	1	0	1	0	1	.200
Finner, John	3	7	0	0	0	0	0	0	0	0	0	0	.000
Fisher, 1937 KCM*	1	1	0	0	0	0	0	0	0	0	0	0	.000
Flonnoy, 1941 ECG	1	4	2	3	1	0	0	1	1	0	0	0	.750
Flournoy, Willis	5	11	0	3	1	0	0	0	0	0	0	0	.273
Foote, Bill	3	10	1	2	1	0	0	0	0	0	0	0	.200
Footes, Bob	4	14	0	2	1	0	0	0	0	0	0	0	.143
Forbes, Frank	6	18	1	3	0	0	0	0	2	0	0	0	.167
Force, Bill	3	4	1	1	0	0	1	2	0	0	0	0	.250
Foreman, Sylvester	2	7	1	1	0	0	0	0	0	0	0	0	.143
Forrest, James	6	20	4	6	0	0	0	0	1	0	0	2	.300
Ford, 1918 CUG	1	4	0	0	0	0	0	0	0	0	0	0	.000
Foster, Andrew	9	24	1	6	1	0	0	0	0	0	0	1	.250
Foster, Bill	7	18	0	2	1	0	0	0	1	0	0	0	.111
Fowler, Bud (Jackson, John)	2	8	0	1	0	0	0	0	0	0	0	0	.125

Player	G	AB	R	H	D	T	HR	RBI	BB	SB	HBP	SAC	BA
Fox, 1945 PAS	1	2	0	0	0	0	0	0	1	0	0	0	.000
Francis, Bill	24	85	6	18	2	0	0	2	4	2	3	1	.212
Frye, Jack	22	83	14	17	6	1	0	6	4	6	0	0	.205
Fuller, William	1	3	0	1	0	0	0	0	0	0	0	1	.333
Gans, Judy	26	92	9	23	3	4	0	0	10	6	1	5	.250
Garcia, Regino	22	66	7	18	1	1	0	5	5	2	1	1	.273
Gardner, Floyd	13	48	10	14	2	0	0	0	6	5	0	1	.292
Gardner, Ken	2	5	0	0	0	0	0	0	0	0	0	0	.000
Gaston, Robert	1	0	0	0	0	0	0	0	0	0	0	0	—
Gatewood, Bill	22	51	5	11	3	1	1	2	1	2	2	0	.216
Gatewood, Ernest	5	16	3	2	0	0	0	0	2	0	0	1	.125
Gee, Thomas	1	3	1	1	0	0	0	0	0	0	0	0	.333
Gerry, 1920 PS	1	4	0	2	0	0	0	0	0	1	0	0	.500
Gibson, Josh	17	72	21	28	2	1	4	13	4	1	0	0	.389
Giles, George	15	64	16	24	4	2	0	4	6	8	0	0	.375
Gillespie, Henry	2	6	0	1	0	0	0	0	0	0	0	0	.167
Gilyard, Luther	1	0	0	0	0	0	0	0	0	0	0	0	—
Gisentaner, Willie	2	0	0	0	0	0	0	0	0	0	0	0	—
Glover, Thomas	2	4	0	0	0	0	0	0	0	0	0	0	.000
Goliah, Fred	4	15	1	2	1	0	0	1	1	0	0	0	.133
Gonzalez, Gervasio	50	171	15	39	3	3	0	15	14	2	3	8	.228
Gonzalez, Luis	16	33	3	4	1	0	1	4	3	0	2	2	.121
Gonzalez, Ramon	2	6	0	1	0	0	0	0	0	0	0	0	.167
Gordon, Austin	1	3	0	0	0	0	0	0	0	0	0	0	.000
Gordon, Wallace	1	3	1	1	1	0	0	1	1	1	0	0	.333
Graham, Dennis	16	66	13	18	1	1	1	4	1	2	0	0	.273
Grant, 1945 PAS	1	4	0	2	0	0	0	0	0	0	0	0	.500
Grant, Charlie	6	25	3	6	1	0	0	0	0	0	0	0	.240
Grant, Frank	7	24	4	7	3	1	0	2	2	0	0	1	.292
Grant, Leroy	20	76	8	23	7	0	0	3	2	2	0	1	.303
Gray, Willie	10	29	7	7	1	1	0	2	1	1	0	2	.241
Green, William	1	7	0	1	0	0	0	0	2	0	0	0	.143
Green, Joe	11	39	4	12	3	0	0	0	0	4	0	1	.308
Greene, Joe	7	17	1	5	1	0	1	3	0	0	0	0	.294
Gregory, 1915 SLG	1	3	1	1	0	0	0	0	0	0	0	0	.333
Griffin, Emerson	1	2	2	0	0	0	0	0	2	0	0	0	.000
Griffith, Robert	3	7	1	1	0	0	0	0	0	0	0	0	.143
Hairston, Sam	9	25	1	9	3	0	0	0	1	0	0	0	.360
Haley, Granville	4	15	2	3	1	0	0	0	0	1	0	0	.200
Hall, 1938 OM	1	3	0	1	0	0	0	0	0	0	1	0	.333
Hall, Blainey	13	47	5	14	2	0	0	0	5	0	0	0	.298
Hampton, Lewis	2	4	0	0	0	0	0	0	0	0	0	0	.000
Handy, Bill	9	37	3	8	3	0	1	2	0	0	0	0	.216
Hardy, Paul	1	4	0	0	0	0	0	0	0	0	0	0	.000
Harney, George	6	16	1	6	1	0	0	4	1	0	0	1	.375
Harris, Curtis	10	35	2	10	2	0	0	2	0	0	0	0	.286
Harris, Nate	18	71	3	11	0	0	0	0	1	3	1	3	.155
Harris, Ray	6	17	2	2	0	0	0	0	0	1	0	0	.118
Harris, Vic	22	84	11	24	1	1	1	4	4	2	0	2	.286

Player	G	AB	R	H	D	T	HR	RBI	BB	SB	HBP	SAC	BA
Harrison, Abe	27	101	20	34	6	2	1	5	2	4	2	1	.337
Harrison, Bert	1	4	0	1	0	0	0	0	0	0	0	0	.250
Harvey, Bob	4	12	0	2	0	0	0	0	0	1	0	0	.167
Harvey, David	3	4	0	1	0	0	0	0	0	0	0	0	.250
Harvey, Richard	1	3	0	1	0	0	0	0	0	0	0	0	.333
Hawkins, Lem	20	73	13	19	2	1	0	1	5	2	2	4	.260
Hawkins, Sam	3	12	1	1	0	0	0	0	0	0	0	1	.083
Hayes, Burnalle	1	0	0	0	0	0	0	0	0	0	0	0	—
Hayman, Sy	1	4	1	1	0	0	0	0	0	0	0	0	.250
Haywood, Albert	14	26	1	4	1	0	0	2	1	0	0	3	.154
Hensley, Logan	3	5	1	2	0	0	0	0	0	0	0	0	.400
Hernandez, Cheo	3	4	1	2	0	0	0	1	0	0	0	1	.500
Hernandez, Ricardo	39	127	17	23	1	1	0	7	10	23	2	6	.181
Herrera, Paito	11	33	6	9	3	0	0	0	1	0	1	1	.273
Hewitt, Joe	17	61	11	20	1	0	0	2	6	3	2	2	.328
Hidalgo, Heliodoro	49	172	16	38	6	0	1	12	15	10	4	1	.221
Hill, John	4	15	0	2	0	0	0	0	0	2	0	0	.133
Hill, Johnson	11	41	5	9	1	0	0	0	1	0	0	0	.220
Holland, Bill (I)	7	22	0	3	1	0	0	0	0	0	0	0	.136
Holland, Bill (II)	3	9	1	2	1	0	0	0	1	0	0	0	.222
Holloway, Crush	38	149	28	42	6	2	1	3	17	7	0	1	.282
Holmes, Ben	23	84	11	20	1	0	1	3	3	6	1	0	.238
Holmes, Frank	1	1	0	1	0	0	0	0	0	0	0	0	1.000
Holsey, Robert	1	2	0	0	0	0	0	0	0	0	0	0	.000
Holtz, Eddie	7	19	2	4	0	0	0	2	2	0	0	0	.211
Hooker, Leniel	2	4	0	0	0	0	0	1	1	0	0	0	.000
Hopkins, 1920 PS	2	7	0	2	1	0	0	0	0	1	0	0	.286
Hopkins, George	3	11	1	2	0	0	0	0	0	0	0	0	.182
Hoskins, Bill	19	69	6	22	7	0	1	8	6	2	0	2	.319
Hubbard, Jess	20	64	15	18	4	1	2	3	4	1	1	1	.281
Hudspeth, Robert	11	40	4	10	1	0	1	4	3	0	0	1	.250
Hughes, Sammy	11	43	9	16	2	1	0	1	6	5	0	0	.372
Hunter, 1938 OM	1	4	0	1	0	0	0	1	0	0	0	0	.250
Hunter, Bert	3	3	0	0	0	0	0	0	0	0	0	0	.000
Hutchinson, Fred	18	62	5	10	1	0	0	0	5	2	1	0	.161
Hutt, Oscar	4	10	1	0	0	0	0	0	2	0	0	2	.000
Hyde, Cowan	10	38	1	11	3	1	0	5	2	4	0	0	.289
Irvin, Monte	5	11	2	4	1	0	0	1	2	0	0	1	.364
January 1936 NS	1	5	0	0	0	0	0	0	0	0	0	0	.000
Jackson, Andrew	4	14	1	3	0	0	0	0	1	0	0	1	.214
Jackson, Bob	2	7	0	0	0	0	0	0	0	0	0	0	.000
Jackson, George	2	5	0	0	0	0	0	0	0	0	0	0	.000
Jackson, Norman	1	4	1	2	0	0	0	0	0	1	0	0	.500
Jackson, Oscar	4	14	4	9	2	0	0	0	2	3	0	0	.643
Jackson, Stanford	5	11	6	3	0	1	0	0	3	0	0	0	.273
Jackson, William	6	22	4	2	0	0	0	0	2	0	2	0	.091
James, Gus	3	9	1	2	0	0	0	0	0	0	0	0	.222
James, William	14	47	3	6	1	0	0	1	0	0	0	1	.128
Jasper, George	1	0	0	0	0	0	0	0	0	0	0	0	—

Player	G	AB	R	H	D	T	HR	RBI	BB	SB	HBP	SAC	BA
Jefferson, Ralph	4	16	0	1	0	0	0	0	0	0	0	1	.063
Jeffries, Harry	11	37	8	9	2	0	0	2	1	0	0	0	.243
Jeffries, Jim	10	31	6	6	1	1	0	0	2	1	0	3	.194
Jenkins, Clarence	1	4	2	1	0	0	0	0	1	1	0	0	.250
Jenkins, Horace	7	22	4	8	0	1	0	2	0	0	0	0	.364
Jessup, Gentry	4	13	2	2	0	0	0	0	0	0	0	0	.154
Jethroe, Sam	12	41	0	8	2	0	0	3	3	1	0	0	.220
Jiminez, Eusebio	2	8	0	1	0	0	0	0	0	0	0	0	.125
Johnson, Pete	1	4	1	2	1	0	0	0	1	0	0	0	.500
Johnson, 1945 PAS	1	3	1	1	0	1	0	0	0	0	0	0	.333
Johnson, Bryon	3	11	1	4	0	0	1	1	0	0	0	0	.364
Johnson, Cecil	1	2	0	0	0	0	0	0	0	0	0	0	.000
Johnson, Claude	4	16	4	6	1	1	0	0	0	0	0	0	.375
Johnson, Dan	1	1	0	0	0	0	0	0	0	0	0	0	.000
Johnson, George	12	44	2	9	0	1	1	3	0	0	0	1	.205
Johnson, George Jr.	23	80	5	18	2	0	1	2	5	1	2	5	.225
Johnson, Grant	35	129	21	40	4	2	2	6	12	2	2	4	.310
Johnson, Harry	4	13	4	3	0	0	0	0	1	0	1	0	.231
Johnson, Judy	32	121	19	34	1	3	1	7	4	1	0	1	.281
Johnson, Louis	9	21	1	1	0	0	0	0	2	0	0	0	.048
Johnson, Nate	1	2	1	1	0	0	0	0	0	0	0	0	.500
Johnson, Oscar	10	39	5	13	1	2	0	7	0	0	0	1	.333
Johnson, Sam	1	3	0	0	0	0	0	0	1	0	0	0	.000
Johnson, Tom	1	0	0	0	0	0	0	0	1	1	0	0	.000
Johnson, William	1	4	0	1	0	0	0	0	1	0	0	0	.250
Johnston, Wade	5	20	4	5	2	0	0	1	1	2	0	0	.250
Jones, Al	1	2	0	2	0	0	0	1	0	1	0	0	1.000
Jones, Bert	1	3	1	0	0	0	0	0	1	1	0	0	.000
Jones, Willie	2	6	0	1	0	0	0	0	0	0	0	0	.167
Jones, Willis	1	3	0	0	0	0	0	0	0	0	1	0	.000
Jordan, Robert	6	26	1	3	1	0	0	0	1	0	1	1	.115
Joseph, Walter	21	84	15	25	4	1	2	7	2	3	0	2	.298
Junco, Jose	4	2	0	0	0	0	0	0	0	0	0	0	.000
Keating, 1920 PS	1	1	0	0	0	0	0	0	0	0	0	0	.000
Kelley, Palmer	1	3	0	0	0	0	0	0	0	0	0	0	.000
Kellman, Edric	5	16	2	3	0	0	1	1	2	0	0	0	.188
Kennard, Dan	14	49	6	17	2	1	0	2	2	3	0	0	.347
Kenyon, Harry	2	7	2	2	1	0	0	2	0	0	0	0	.286
Kimbro, Henry	2	8	2	3	0	0	0	0	2	0	0	0	.375
Kimbro, Ted	5	19	3	2	0	0	0	0	0	0	0	0	.105
Kincannon, Harry	3	5	0	1	1	0	0	0	0	0	0	0	.200
Kindle, Bill	1	6	0	1	0	0	0	0	0	0	0	0	.167
Kranson, Floyd	4	9	0	1	0	0	0	0	0	0	0	0	.111
Kyle, Andy	4	13	1	4	0	0	0	0	0	0	0	0	.308
Kyle, W., 1920 LAWS*	1	0	0	0	0	0	0	0	1	0	0	0	.000
Lackey, Obie	5	20	2	6	1	0	0	0	0	1	0	0	.300
LaMarque, James	5	4	0	1	1	0	0	0	0	0	0	0	.250
Land, Bill	3	13	3	3	1	0	0	0	0	0	0	0	.231
Lane, 1936 NS	1	4	0	0	0	0	0	0	0	0	0	0	.000

Player	G	AB	R	H	D	T	HR	RBI	BB	SB	HBP	SAC	BA
Lane, Bill	16	61	1	8	0	1	0	1	0	3	0	1	.131
Langley, "Serious"	3	13	0	2	0	0	0	0	0	0	0	0	.154
Lankford, Ad	3	7	1	1	0	0	0	0	0	0	0	0	.143
Lee, 1938 OM	1	2	0	0	0	0	0	0	1	0	1	0	.000
Lee, Dick	1	3	0	0	0	0	0	0	0	0	0	0	.000
Lee, Holsey	13	26	4	3	1	0	0	0	1	1	0	0	.115
Leftwich, Leroy	1	2	0	0	0	0	0	0	0	0	0	0	.000
Lewis, Joe	13	38	3	8	1	0	0	0	1	0	1	0	.211
Lewis, Milton	1	3	0	0	0	0	0	0	0	0	0	0	.000
Lewis, Rufus	1	2	0	1	0	0	0	0	0	0	0	0	.500
Lightner, Charley	3	8	0	0	0	0	0	0	0	0	0	1	.000
Lindsay, Bill	12	29	3	8	0	0	1	2	2	0	0	1	.276
Lindsay, Clarence	2	6	1	2	1	0	0	0	0	0	1	0	.333
Leonard, James	3	7	1	0	0	0	0	0	1	0	0	1	.000
Leonard, Walter	11	36	2	10	0	1	0	4	4	1	0	1	.278
Levis, Oscar	1	4	0	1	0	0	0	0	0	0	0	0	.250
Lewis, Jerome	3	11	0	1	1	0	0	0	0	0	0	0	.091
Livingston, Lee	4	13	5	6	1	0	2	4	2	0	1	1	.462
Lloyd, John	50	181	20	60	8	3	1	22	21	15	0	6	.331
Lopez, Jose	4	6	0	0	0	0	0	0	1	0	0	0	.000
Louden, Louis	1	3	0	0	0	0	0	0	0	0	0	1	.000
Lundy, Dick	35	121	15	35	4	4	0	14	3	5	1	2	.289
Lyons, Bennie	1	4	0	0	0	0	0	0	0	0	0	0	.000
Lyons, Jimmie	21	83	6	12	1	1	0	1	5	3	0	0	.145
Mackey, James	83	290	48	101	11	5	8	22	29	4	0	5	.348
Madison, Robert	1	1	0	1	0	0	0	0	0	0	0	0	1.000
Magrinat, Jose	3	7	0	0	0	0	0	0	0	0	0	0	.000
Malarcher, Dave	6	18	2	7	1	1	0	1	1	3	0	0	.389
Malette, Arthur	1	1	0	0	0	0	0	1	0	0	0	1	.000
Malloy, Charles	1	1	0	1	0	0	0	0	0	0	0	0	1.000
Malone, William	24	79	8	16	4	1	0	1	5	2	1	0	.203
Mann, 1918 CUG	1	3	0	0	0	0	0	0	0	0	0	0	.000
Manning, Max	4	7	0	0	0	0	0	0	0	0	0	0	.000
Marcell, Everett	1	1	0	0	0	0	0	0	0	0	0	0	.000
Marcell, Oliver	21	74	15	18	3	0	0	2	0	2	0	3	.243
Markham, John	4	7	0	0	0	0	0	0	0	0	0	0	.000
Marsans, Armando	45	170	25	37	5	1	0	7	19	17	1	4	.218
Marshall, Bobby	1	1	0	0	0	0	0	0	0	0	0	0	.000
Marshall, Jack	2	7	1	1	0	0	0	0	0	0	0	0	.143
Martin, 1943 NAS	1	1	0	0	0	0	0	0	0	0	0	0	.000
Martinez, Manuel	1	3	1	1	0	0	0	0	0	0	0	1	.333
Mason, Charlie	5	12	2	4	0	1	0	1	1	0	0	0	.333
Matchett, Jack	4	6	0	1	0	0	0	0	0	0	0	0	.167
Mathis, Verdell	2	1	0	0	0	0	0	0	0	0	0	0	.000
Matthews, Fran	1	5	1	1	0	0	0	0	0	0	0	0	.200
Matlock, Leroy	6	21	2	5	0	0	2	3	0	0	0	0	.238
Mayweather, Ed	4	16	2	3	0	0	0	0	0	0	0	0	.188
McAdoo, Tullie	24	88	3	20	1	1	0	2	5	4	3	1	.227
McClain, Edward	1	4	0	0	0	0	0	0	0	0	0	0	.000

Player	G	AB	R	H	D	T	HR	RBI	BB	SB	HBP	SAC	BA
McClellan, Dan	6	23	2	7	0	2	0	2	0	0	0	0	.304
McClure, Bob	3	7	0	1	1	0	0	0	0	0	0	0	.143
McDaniel, Booker	7	7	0	0	0	0	0	0	0	0	0	0	.000
McDonald, Webster	14	38	7	10	1	1	0	0	0	0	0	1	.263
McDuffie, Terris	8	14	0	1	0	0	0	0	0	0	0	0	.071
McKinnis, Gready	2	5	0	1	1	0	0	0	1	0	0	0	.200
McLaughlin, Henry	1	2	1	0	0	0	0	0	1	0	0	0	.000
McMurray, Willie	3	9	0	1	0	0	0	0	0	0	0	0	.111
McNair, Hurley	18	74	11	20	3	4	0	4	3	1	0	2	.270
Meade, Fred	4	17	1	3	0	0	0	0	0	0	0	0	.176
Means, Lemuel	1	4	0	1	0	0	0	0	0	1	0	0	.250
Mederos, Lico	12	23	2	3	0	0	0	1	1	0	0	0	.130
Melton, Elbert	1	4	1	1	0	0	1	3	1	0	0	0	.250
Mendez, Jose	46	139	7	26	3	1	0	5	7	0	0	3	.187
Merritt, Bill	6	18	0	1	1	0	0	0	0	0	0	0	.056
Mesa, Pablo	2	7	2	1	0	0	0	0	1	0	0	0	.143
Meyers, George	4	10	0	3	1	1	0	0	2	0	0	0	.300
Middleton, Ed	3	12	0	2	0	0	0	0	0	0	0	0	.167
Miles, Jack	1	4	0	0	0	0	0	0	0	0	0	0	.000
Miles, Willie	3	11	2	2	0	0	0	0	0	1	0	0	.182
Miller, Eddie	3	8	0	1	0	0	0	0	1	0	0	0	.125
Miller, Frank	3	13	0	2	0	0	0	0	0	0	0	0	.154
Miller, Henry	4	3	0	1	0	0	0	0	0	0	0	0	.333
Miller, Joe	2	5	0	3	0	0	0	1	0	0	0	0	.600
Miller, Louis	7	26	3	3	1	0	0	1	1	0	0	3	.115
Miller, Percy	7	18	5	6	1	1	0	0	4	1	1	0	.333
Miller, Pleas	3	6	0	0	0	0	0	0	0	0	0	0	.000
Milliner, Eugene	6	24	4	5	0	0	0	0	0	1	0	0	.208
Milton, Henry	8	34	5	9	2	1	1	2	3	1	0	0	.265
Mirabel, Juanelo	1	3	0	2	0	0	0	0	0	0	0	0	.667
Mitchell, 1938 OM	1	4	0	0	0	0	0	0	0	0	0	0	.000
Mitchell, George	1	4	1	1	0	0	0	0	0	0	0	0	.250
Molina, Tinti	4	12	1	1	0	1	0	0	1	0	0	0	.083
Mongin, Sam	11	35	3	9	0	0	0	0	1	0	1	0	.257
Monroe, Bill	31	125	20	36	5	2	5	9	3	2	1	1	.288
Moody, Lee	3	12	1	2	0	0	0	0	1	1	0	0	.167
Mooney, Tom	3	5	0	0	0	0	0	0	0	1	0	0	.000
Moore, Eugene	4	13	1	5	1	0	0	0	0	3	0	0	.385
Moore, Harry	24	80	10	14	2	1	1	2	16	4	0	2	.175
Moore, Walter	21	64	6	20	2	3	0	4	4	0	0	3	.313
Moran, Carlos	37	125	21	34	6	2	0	7	18	3	3	2	.272
Moran, Francisco	1	4	0	0	0	0	0	0	0	0	0	0	.000
Moreland, Nate	4	10	0	2	0	1	0	0	0	0	0	0	.200
Morrison, W. 1924 CAS	3	9	0	3	1	1	0	0	0	0	0	1	.333
Morton, Sy	1	2	0	0	0	0	0	0	0	0	0	0	.000
Moss, Porter	2	3	0	1	0	0	0	0	0	0	0	1	.333
Mothell, Carroll	24	92	10	23	4	0	1	3	8	1	1	1	.250
Munoz, Jose	12	31	2	7	1	0	0	3	1	2	0	4	.226
Murray, Mitch	8	22	4	7	1	0	0	0	3	0	1	1	.318

Player	G	AB	R	H	D	T	HR	RBI	BB	SB	HBP	SAC	BA
Neil, Ray	15	61	3	14	2	0	0	5	5	1	0	0	.230
Nelson, Clyde	7	23	1	3	0	0	0	0	2	0	0	1	.130
Nelson, John	6	26	4	3	0	0	0	1	0	0	0	0	.115
Newberry, Jimmie	3	7	0	0	0	0	0	0	0	0	0	0	.000
Newcombe, Don	1	1	0	0	0	0	0	0	0	0	0	0	.000
Norman, William	1	5	1	1	0	0	0	0	0	0	0	0	.200
Oldham, Jimmy	3	7	1	1	0	0	0	0	0	0	0	0	.143
Oliver, Huddy	1	5	0	0	0	0	0	0	0	0	0	0	.000
O'Neal, Luther	1	1	0	0	0	0	0	0	0	0	0	0	.000
O'Neil, John	14	47	6	15	1	2	0	5	6	1	0	0	.319
Owens, Oscar	5	12	2	3	0	0	1	2	0	0	0	0	.250
Padron, Juan	1	2	0	0	0	0	0	0	1	0	0	0	.000
Padron, Luis	46	153	16	42	1	3	3	14	11	8	2	1	.275
Page, Ted	18	67	14	27	3	3	1	7	4	1	0	1	.403
Paige, Leroy	45	88	3	17	1	0	0	5	0	0	0	3	.193
Paige, William	1	4	0	1	0	0	0	0	0	0	0	0	.250
Palm, Clarence*	1	1	1	1	0	0	1	2	0	0	0	0	1.000
Palomino, Emilio	23	69	3	10	0	1	0	1	6	9	1	2	.145
Pareda, Pastor	21	41	3	5	0	0	0	0	1	1	2	3	.122
Parego, George	16	52	4	9	0	0	0	3	3	1	0	0	.173
Parks, William	21	84	7	23	1	0	0	2	1	0	0	0	.274
Parpetti, Agustin	32	109	8	30	0	2	1	12	9	8	3	3	.275
Partlow, Roy	1	2	0	0	0	0	0	0	0	0	0	0	.000
Patterson, Andrew	9	36	3	8	1	0	1	1	1	0	0	0	.222
Patterson, Gabe	1	2	0	0	0	0	0	0	0	0	0	0	.000
Patterson, John	10	40	6	12	1	2	1	1	1	2	0	1	.300
Payne, Andrew	12	45	2	9	1	0	0	3	0	1	0	1	.200
Pearson, Lennie	4	11	1	6	0	1	0	2	0	0	0	0	.545
Pennington, Art	1	5	2	2	0	0	0	1	0	0	0	0	.400
Pedroso, Eustaquio	23	47	3	12	3	1	0	4	6	1	1	1	.255
Perez, Javier	6	24	3	6	0	1	0	0	0	4	0	0	.250
Perez, Jose	1	4	0	2	0	0	0	0	0	0	0	0	.500
Perez, Julian	2	6	0	0	0	0	0	0	0	0	0	0	.000
Perkins, Bill	13	47	4	17	4	1	0	4	1	0	0	0	.362
Perry, Don	1	3	0	0	0	0	0	0	0	0	0	0	.000
Perry, 1936 NS	1	4	0	0	0	0	0	0	0	0	0	0	.000
Perry, Carl	5	12	2	2	0	0	0	0	1	0	0	0	.167
Peters, Frank	1	4	0	0	0	0	0	0	0	0	0	0	.000
Pettus, William	35	132	20	43	10	1	2	2	9	8	1	1	.326
Petway, Bruce	57	183	15	35	2	0	0	8	10	3	1	9	.191
Pierce, Herbert	2	3	1	1	0	1	0	0	0	0	0	0	.333
Pierce, William	30	103	14	25	4	1	3	7	9	1	0	1	.243
Poles, Ed	1	4	0	3	0	0	0	2	0	0	0	0	.750
Poles, Spottswood	20	84	18	36	5	0	0	0	6	6	1	0	.429
Pope, Dave	1	2	0	0	0	0	0	0	0	0	0	0	.000
Pope, Willie	2	3	1	1	0	0	0	0	0	0	0	0	.333
Porter, Andy	11	16	1	1	0	0	0	0	1	0	0	0	.063
Portuondo, Bartolo	9	34	10	8	1	1	0	1	5	2	2	2	.235
Powell, Melvin	3	11	2	5	1	0	0	0	0	0	0	0	.455

Player	G	AB	R	H	D	T	HR	RBI	BB	SB	HBP	SAC	BA
Powell, Russell	4	14	0	2	1	0	0	1	0	0	0	0	.143
Pryor, Anderson	3	12	1	3	0	0	0	0	0	0	0	0	.250
Pugh, Johnny	4	12	2	3	0	0	0	0	0	0	0	0	.250
Pullen, O'Neal	32	108	9	21	2	1	2	4	5	0	0	0	.194
Radcliff, Alex	3	12	1	4	0	0	0	0	0	0	0	0	.333
Radcliffe, Ted	16	46	3	11	1	0	0	4	1	0	0	0	.239
Ramirez, Ramiro	2	6	1	1	0	0	0	0	3	0	0	0	.167
Randolph, Andrew	4	12	0	1	0	0	0	0	0	1	0	0	.083
Ransome, 1920 PS	2	8	0	1	0	0	0	0	0	0	0	0	.125
Ray, Otto	8	21	2	7	1	1	1	2	0	0	0	0	.333
Rector, Connie	6	16	1	3	0	0	1	2	0	0	0	0	.188
Redd, Gene	1	4	0	0	0	0	0	0	0	0	0	0	.000
Redding, Dick	9	29	1	6	1	0	0	0	0	0	0	0	.207
Redus, Wilson	7	25	6	8	1	0	1	2	4	0	0	1	.320
Reese, John	7	21	4	4	0	0	0	0	1	1	0	1	.190
Reid, 1945 PAS	1	3	0	0	0	0	0	0	1	0	0	0	.000
Reid, Ambrose	2	8	0	0	0	0	0	0	0	0	0	0	.000
Renfroe, Othello	21	60	1	10	2	0	0	4	6	0	1	3	.167
Renoy, Moses	1	0	0	0	0	0	0	0	0	0	0	0	—
Richardson, Gene	1	1	0	0	0	0	0	0	0	0	0	0	.000
Richardson, Talmadge	1	3	1	1	0	0	0	0	1	0	0	1	.333
Ridgley, Randolph	3	9	0	2	0	0	0	0	1	1	1	1	.222
Riggins, Arvelle	12	43	5	7	2	0	0	1	6	0	0	0	.163
Rile, Ed	4	9	1	2	0	0	0	0	0	0	0	0	.222
Roberts, Elihu	2	9	0	2	1	0	0	0	0	0	0	0	.222
Roberts, Harry	1	4	0	0	0	0	0	0	0	0	0	0	.000
Roberts, Roy	1	2	0	1	0	0	0	0	0	0	0	0	.500
Robinson, 1910 SLO	3	9	0	0	0	0	0	0	1	0	0	0	.000
Robinson, Al	2	9	1	2	0	0	0	0	0	0	0	0	.222
Robinson, Jackie	4	14	4	4	1	0	0	0	1	0	0	0	.286
Robinson, James	2	8	1	2	0	0	0	0	0	0	0	0	.250
Robinson, Neal	6	9	1	3	1	1	0	4	1	0	0	0	.333
Robinson, Norman	1	4	1	2	0	0	0	0	0	0	0	0	.500
Rodriguez, Vicente	2	7	0	0	0	0	0	0	0	0	0	0	.000
Rogan, Wilber	46	166	25	55	7	5	3	18	12	5	0	6	.331
Rogers, Nat	2	7	1	1	0	0	0	0	0	0	0	0	.143
Rojo, Julio	5	17	0	3	0	1	0	0	0	0	0	0	.176
Rose, Haywood	4	12	2	2	0	0	0	0	0	0	1	0	.167
Ross, Dick	2	4	1	2	0	0	0	0	0	0	0	0	.500
Rovira, Jaime	2	1	0	0	0	0	0	0	0	0	0	0	.000
Royer, Carlos	3	5	0	3	0	0	0	0	1	0	0	0	.600
Russell, Branch	9	31	4	7	0	0	1	3	4	0	0	0	.226
Russell, Frank	1	5	1	2	0	0	0	0	0	0	0	0	.400
Russell, John	10	43	6	16	2	1	1	2	1	1	0	0	.372
Ryan, Merven	6	8	0	0	0	0	0	0	1	0	0	0	.000
Sampson, Tommy	7	25	3	10	1	1	0	5	0	1	0	0	.400
Sanchez, Gonzalo	4	11	0	3	0	0	0	1	0	1	0	1	.273
Santop, Louis	26	93	13	28	5	0	1	2	4	6	0	2	.301
Scales, George	12	47	0	10	0	0	0	3	2	0	0	2	.213

Player	G	AB	R	H	D	T	HR	RBI	BB	SB	HBP	SAC	BA
Scotland, Joe	1	3	0	0	0	0	0	0	0	0	0	0	.000
Scott, 1938 OM	1	4	0	2	2	0	0	0	0	0	0	0	.500
Scott, Bob	15	52	4	10	0	0	0	0	2	1	1	0	.192
Scott, John	6	20	1	2	0	0	0	1	1	0	0	0	.100
Seay, Dick	8	26	6	9	1	0	0	1	4	1	1	0	.346
Selden, William (I)	19	65	5	10	1	1	1	3	1	0	0	1	.154
Selden, William (II)	3	10	0	2	0	0	0	2	0	0	0	0	.200
Sergio, 1943 NAS	1	4	0	0	0	0	0	0	0	0	0	0	.000
Serrell, William	7	27	1	1	0	0	0	0	0	0	0	0	.037
Sharkey, 1924 CAS	3	5	1	3	0	0	0	0	0	0	1	0	.600
Shaw, George	1	4	1	1	1	0	0	0	0	0	0	0	.250
Shively, George	10	42	9	12	0	0	0	0	2	3	0	0	.286
Shorrs, 1920 LAWS	1	0	0	0	0	0	0	0	0	0	0	0	—
Silverio, Patrocinio	1	4	0	0	0	0	0	0	0	0	0	0	.000
Simms, Willie	11	39	6	7	1	0	0	0	4	1	0	0	.179
Smith, 1910 SLO	1	3	1	1	0	0	0	0	0	0	0	0	.333
Smith, 1936 NS	1	2	0	0	0	0	0	0	0	0	0	0	.000
Smith, 1946 RAS*	1	1	0	0	0	0	0	0	0	0	0	0	.000
Smith, Charlie "Chino"	4	10	5	7	3	0	1	2	2	2	0	0	.700
Smith, Charlie "Red"	1	1	0	1	0	0	0	0	0	1	0	0	1.000
Smith, Clarence	4	13	1	3	0	1	0	0	0	1	0	0	.231
Smith, Cleo	2	9	1	3	0	0	0	0	0	1	0	0	.333
Smith, Gene	6	22	1	5	0	1	1	5	0	0	0	0	.227
Smith, Harry	3	12	1	1	1	0	0	0	1	0	0	1	.083
Smith, Hilton	11	24	1	5	2	0	0	2	0	0	0	1	.208
Smith, Jimmy	1	4	0	1	0	0	0	0	0	0	0	0	.250
Smith, John	5	21	1	6	1	0	0	2	2	0	0	0	.286
Smith, Saki	5	20	1	7	1	0	0	2	0	1	0	0	.350
Smith, Wyman	1	3	1	1	0	0	0	1	0	0	0	1	.333
Snow, Felton	18	67	3	20	1	0	0	0	2	2	0	1	.299
Souell, Herb	13	49	6	15	3	1	0	7	0	4	0	1	.306
Spearman, Charles	24	83	8	26	1	0	0	2	3	1	0	0	.313
Stanley, John	4	7	0	1	0	0	0	1	0	0	0	0	.143
Starks, James	1	2	0	0	0	0	0	0	1	0	0	0	.000
Starks, Leslie	4	15	2	4	1	0	1	3	0	1	0	2	.267
Starks Otis	4	12	1	2	0	0	0	0	0	0	0	0	.167
Stearnes, Norman	25	94	20	38	9	1	4	7	7	9	0	2	.404
Steele, Ed	14	30	3	7	3	1	0	3	12	0	0	0	.233
Stephens, Jake	15	50	9	14	1	0	0	3	2	1	1	2	.280
Stevens, Frank	2	6	0	1	0	0	0	0	0	0	0	0	.167
Stevenson, Willie	1	2	0	0	0	0	0	0	0	0	0	0	.000
Stockard, Ted	1	2	0	0	0	0	0	0	0	0	1	0	.000
Stone, Ed	8	30	3	7	0	0	0	1	1	0	0	0	.233
Stout, 1936 NS	1	2	0	0	0	0	0	0	0	1	0	0	.000
Stovey, George	5	15	1	2	0	0	0	0	0	0	0	1	.133
Streeter, Sam	5	16	2	3	0	0	0	0	1	0	0	0	.188
Strong, Joe	2	5	0	1	0	0	0	0	0	0	0	0	.200
Strong, Ted	7	28	7	10	0	1	0	2	2	0	0	1	.357
Strothers, Sam	4	9	1	1	0	0	0	0	0	0	0	0	.111

Player	G	AB	R	H	D	T	HR	RBI	BB	SB	HBP	SAC	BA
Summers, Lonnie	2	6	0	0	0	0	0	0	0	0	0	0	.000
Summers, Smith	3	10	1	1	0	0	0	0	0	0	0	0	.100
Suttles, George	36	138	28	46	5	5	10	14	6	2	0	0	.333
Swinton, Norman	4	15	1	2	0	0	0	0	0	0	0	1	.133
Sykes, Frank	2	4	0	1	1	0	0	1	0	0	0	0	.250
Taborn, Earl	1	3	1	1	0	0	1	1	1	0	0	0	.333
Talbert, Danger	6	23	3	3	0	0	0	0	0	0	0	0	.130
Tatum, Reese	5	20	0	3	0	0	0	1	0	2	0	0	.150
Taylor, 1900 CCG	2	5	1	1	0	0	0	0	0	0	0	1	.200
Taylor, Ben	20	67	7	17	1	1	1	3	5	1	1	1	.254
Taylor, Charles	4	4	0	0	0	0	0	0	0	0	0	0	.000
Taylor, George	2	8	1	3	1	0	0	1	1	0	0	0	.375
Taylor Jim	34	119	12	28	4	3	1	3	4	4	2	0	.235
Taylor, John "Steel Arm"	3	5	0	0	0	0	0	0	0	0	0	0	.000
Taylor, John "Big"	4	7	1	3	0	1	0	0	1	0	0	1	.429
Taylor, Johnny	1	2	0	1	0	0	0	0	0	0	0	0	.500
Taylor, Leroy	6	24	4	4	0	0	0	1	1	1	0	0	.167
Teran, Recurvan	4	14	2	4	1	0	0	0	1	0	0	0	.286
Terrill, George	3	8	0	0	0	0	0	0	2	1	0	0	.000
Thomas, 1920 PS	2	8	1	2	0	0	0	0	0	0	0	0	.250
Thomas, Arthur	30	112	21	29	4	2	1	12	5	6	2	1	.259
Thomas, Clint	15	57	4	11	3	1	1	5	0	3	1	0	.193
Thomas, Dave	20	62	3	13	0	1	0	3	2	2	2	1	.210
Thomas, Ewell	3	9	2	4	0	0	0	0	0	0	0	0	.444
Thomas, Jules	20	73	5	15	1	0	0	1	3	0	0	0	.205
Thompson, Hank	13	49	10	17	4	1	2	4	2	1	1	0	.347
Thompson, Sam	2	5	0	2	0	0	0	0	0	0	0	0	.400
Thompson, "Speedboy"	2	6	0	1	0	0	0	0	0	0	0	0	.167
Torriente, Cristobal	26	96	12	31	5	2	3	14	8	6	0	3	.323
Treadwell, Harold	2	5	2	2	1	0	0	0	0	0	0	0	.400
Trent, Ted	7	15	1	2	0	0	0	0	0	0	0	0	.133
Trimble, 1945 PAS	1	4	1	2	0	0	0	0	0	0	0	0	.500
Trouppe, Quincy	17	55	7	13	3	0	1	5	5	1	0	0	.236
Trusty, Shep	9	32	6	8	2	0	0	5	1	1	0	1	.250
Trusty, Job	1	4	0	0	0	0	0	0	0	0	0	0	.000
Turner, Elbert	1	4	0	0	0	0	0	0	0	0	0	0	.000
Turner, William*	1	1	0	0	0	0	0	0	0	0	0	0	.000
Valdes, Rogelio	39	128	17	31	8	2	0	7	15	11	0	2	.242
Valdes, Simon	1	4	0	0	0	0	0	0	0	0	0	0	.000
Van Dyke, Fred	1	1	0	1	0	0	0	0	0	0	0	0	1.000
Vargas, Tetelo	1	2	2	0	0	0	0	0	2	0	0	0	.000
Villa, Manuel	17	56	6	7	0	2	0	2	0	2	0	3	.125
Wade, 1942 PRG/ 1943 NAS	3	10	0	1	0	0	0	0	0	0	0	0	.100
Walker, 1936 NS	1	4	1	0	0	0	0	0	0	0	0	0	.000
Walker, Jess	14	47	4	12	0	1	1	4	3	1	0	0	.255
Wallace, Dick	14	47	4	10	1	0	0	0	5	0	0	2	.213
Ward, Henry	1	3	0	0	0	0	0	0	0	0	0	0	.000
Ward, Tom	10	36	4	8	1	0	0	0	4	1	0	1	.222

Player	G	AB	R	H	D	T	HR	RBI	BB	SB	HBP	SAC	BA
Ware, Archie	6	21	2	5	0	0	0	2	4	1	0	0	.238
Warfield, Frank	38	129	23	27	2	2	0	1	11	11	0	2	.209
Warren, 1916 WRK	1	2	0	0	0	0	0	0	0	0	0	0	.000
Washington, Jasper	16	66	8	23	3	1	1	2	0	0	0	0	.348
Washington, Kenny	5	17	1	7	1	1	1	1	1	2	0	0	.412
Washington, Namon	2	8	0	1	0	0	0	0	0	0	0	0	.125
Washington, Pete	18	57	7	16	1	1	2	7	3	2	2	1	.281
Watkins, Murray	4	15	1	4	0	0	0	0	0	0	0	0	.267
Watson, Johnie	1	4	0	4	0	0	0	0	0	0	0	0	.000
Watts, Eddie	3	12	1	2	0	0	1	1	0	0	0	0	.167
Watts, Jack	1	3	0	0	0	0	0	0	0	0	0	1	.000
Webster, Pearl	3	13	1	3	0	0	0	0	0	0	0	0	.231
Webster, William	1	2	0	0	0	0	0	0	0	0	0	0	.000
Wells, Willie	38	130	25	47	9	6	2	6	13	8	1	4	.362
Wesley, Edgar	7	25	3	5	0	0	2	2	0	0	0	0	.200
West, Jim	11	41	5	11	1	0	0	2	0	0	0	0	.268
Whatley, Dave	1	5	1	2	0	0	0	0	0	0	0	0	.400
White, Chaney	13	49	4	10	0	1	0	2	1	3	0	0	.204
White, Sol	8	34	6	9	2	1	0	1	1	0	1	1	.265
Whitworth, Dick	6	17	3	1	0	0	0	0	1	0	1	0	.059
Whyte, Bill	18	54	7	6	0	0	0	0	3	0	0	0	.111
Wickware, Frank	13	32	3	5	0	0	0	0	2	0	0	0	.156
Wiley, Wabishaw	15	64	6	20	4	0	0	0	0	2	0	0	.313
Williams, 1932 PC#	1	0	1	0	0	0	0	0	0	0	0	0	—
Williams, Andrew	11	26	3	4	0	1	0	0	1	0	0	0	.154
Williams, Bobby	10	31	1	3	0	0	0	1	3	2	0	2	.097
Williams, Charles	3	6	1	2	0	0	0	0	1	0	0	0	.333
Williams, Charlie	5	19	1	3	2	0	0	1	0	0	0	0	.158
Williams, Chester	14	52	8	17	4	1	1	3	5	2	0	1	.327
Williams, Clarence	38	142	29	45	6	1	1	7	7	8	4	2	.317
Williams, George	29	116	23	38	6	2	0	5	2	1	1	1	.328
Williams, Gerard	3	10	3	3	0	0	0	0	2	0	0	0	.300
Williams, Hank	1	2	0	0	0	0	0	0	0	0	0	0	.000
Williams, Harry	3	11	3	3	0	0	0	1	1	0	0	0	.273
Williams, Jesse	24	95	4	23	6	2	0	3	8	4	0	1	.242
Williams, Joe	35	108	16	29	3	1	2	4	2	1	1	0	.269
Williams, John	8	13	0	3	0	0	0	0	1	0	0	0	.231
Williams, Marvin	1	4	0	1	0	0	0	0	0	0	0	0	.250
Williams, Nat	1	4	1	1	0	0	0	0	0	0	0	0	.250
Williams, Roy	2	5	0	0	0	0	0	0	0	0	0	0	.000
Williams, Tom	4	6	0	0	0	0	0	1	0	0	0	1	.000
Willis, Jim	3	8	0	1	0	0	0	0	0	0	0	0	.125
Wilson, Artie	14	57	5	15	3	0	0	1	2	2	0	0	.263
Wilson, Ed	4	12	1	5	1	0	0	0	0	0	1	0	.417
Wilson, Jud	28	101	21	41	14	0	3	14	3	5	0	0	.406
Wilson, Ray	5	18	2	5	2	0	0	0	0	0	0	0	.278
Winters, James	6	17	2	4	1	0	0	1	1	0	0	0	.235
Winston, Bobby	18	72	11	21	3	3	1	1	2	6	0	2	.292
Woods, Parnell	1	1	0	1	0	0	0	0	0	0	0	0	1.000

Player	G	AB	R	H	D	T	HR	RBI	BB	SB	HBP	SAC	BA
Woods, William	3	13	0	2	0	0	0	0	0	0	0	0	.154
Wright, Bill	27	99	8	32	2	3	1	4	4	3	3	1	.323
Wright, George	28	98	11	27	7	0	0	2	2	2	1	6	.276
Wright, Jack	1	3	0	2	1	0	0	0	0	0	1	0	.667
Wright, Zollie	4	13	0	1	0	0	0	0	2	0	0	1	.077
Wyatt, Ralph	1	5	1	3	0	0	0	0	0	0	0	0	.600
Yancey, Bill	7	25	0	1	0	0	0	0	1	0	0	1	.040
Yokely, Laymon	13	29	3	6	3	0	2	3	4	0	1	1	.207
Young, Berdell	1	3	0	1	0	0	0	0	0	1	0	0	.333
Young, Bob	1	4	1	1	0	0	0	1	0	0	0	0	.250
Young, Ed	1	5	2	2	0	0	0	0	0	0	0	0	.400
Young, John	1	1	0	0	0	0	0	0	0	0	0	1	.000
Young, "Slowtime"	2	3	0	0	0	0	0	0	0	0	0	0	.000
Young, Tom	18	66	9	18	5	2	0	4	4	1	0	1	.273
Zomphier, Charles	2	7	3	3	0	0	0	0	2	0	0	0	.429

Pitching Statistics

Note on Pitching Statistics: As box scores sometimes did not contain separate data when two or more pitchers were used in a game, only statistics that can be solely attributed to a player have been included. Because totals such as walks and strikeouts were under-reported, statistical anomalies and results from games where the individual innings pitched cannot be determined are described in footnotes. G=Games; GS=Games Started; CG=Complete Games; IP=Innings Pitched; H=Hits; R=Runs; BB=Bases on Balls; K=Strikeouts; W=Wins; L=Losses; SH=Shutouts; R/9=Runs Per 9 Innings Pitched.

Pitcher	G	GS	CG	IP	H	R	BB	K	W	L	SH	R/9
Alexander, Charles	1	0	0	6	3	3	0	5	0	0	0	4.50
Anderson, Bill	1	1	1	7	4	0	1	1	1	0	1	0.00
Andrews, Peter	1	0	0	5.3	11	7	0	0	0	0	0	11.81
Archer, Luke	1	0	0	3	1	2	3	5	0	0	0	6.00
Aulston, Clyde	1	1	0	7.3	10	5	7	2	0	1	0	6.14
Ball, Walter	2	2	2	18	15	6	3	6	1	1	0	3.00
Barnes, Ed	2	1	1	11	8	2	4	15	0	2	0	1.64
Baugh, Johnny	3	2	1	21.7	22	5	9	18	2	1	0	2.08
Bell, Fred	1	0	0	6	3	5	5	5	0	0	0	7.50
Bell, James	1	1	0	3	6	6	3	1	0	1	0	18.00
Bell, Louie	1	1	0	4	6	4	4	4	0	1	0	9.00
Bell, William (I)	1	1	0	6	—	13	2	0	0	1	0	19.50
Bell, William (II)[1]	5	3	1	10.3	11	2	2	7	2	1	0	1.74
Beverly, Charles	5	4	4	42	27	7	6	55	5	0	1	1.50
Bowman, Emmett[2]	2	1	1	8	3	5	11	10	0	1	0	5.63
Blake, Frank	1	1	1	5	2	0	2	3	0	0	0	0.00
Bradford, Charlie	2	2	2	14	17	7	7	7	0	2	0	4.50
Brady, Farmer[3]	1	0	0	—	—	—	2	0	0	0	0	—
Branham, Finis[4]	5	2	2	23.7	24	16	18	18	1	1	0	6.08
Brewer, Chet[5]	13	8	5	69	73	47	30	56	4	6	0	6.16
Britt, George[6]	11	8	5	75.3	66	30	23	45	6	2	1	3.58

Pitcher	G	GS	CG	IP	H	R	BB	K	W	L	SH	R/9
Brooks, Irvin	2	0	0	1	1	0	0	1	0	0	0	0.00
Brown, Ben	1	0	0	—	—	—	0	1	0	0	0	—
Brown, 1934 KCM	1	0	0	1.3	2	0	0	1	0	0	0	0.00
Brown, Barney	3	2	1	22	24	11	6	10	1	2	0	4.50
Brown, Dave	3	1	0	11.7	18	10	5	12	0	0	0	7.71
Brown, Ray	1	0	0	4	3	0	1	0	0	0	0	0.00
Buckner, Harry	7	6	4	52.7	45	20	10	24	4	2	0	3.42
Buford, 1914 ABC	1	0	0	0	0	0	0	0	0	0	0	—
Byrd, Bill	2	1	1	11	8	1	1	7	1	1	1	0.82
Cabañas, Armando	1	0	0	1	2	1	0	0	0	0	0	9.00
Cain, Marion	1	1	0	1	4	3	1	1	0	1	0	27.00
Carillo, Lazaro	1	1	1	8	11	14	6	1	0	1	0	15.75
Carr, Wayne	2	2	0	10.7	16	11	5	4	0	2	0	9.29
Carter, Clarence	3	3	2	18	11	11	6	9	1	1	0	5.50
Carter, Cliff	1	1	1	9	6	2	7	5	1	0	0	2.00
Carter, Ernest	3	2	2	23	31	18	3	8	2	0	0	7.04
Carter, Paul	1	1	1	9	7	0	—	6	1	0	1	0.00
Charleston, Porter	1	1	0	8	—	2	—	—	1	0	0	2.25
Cockrell, Phil[7]	11	11	9	88.7	72	28	18	35	8	2	3	2.84
Combs, Jack	1	1	0	6.3	11	6	1	1	0	0	0	8.53
Cooper, Andy[8]	10	7	3	50.3	59	36	13	26	3	3	1	6.44
Cooper, Darltie[9]	1	0	0	4.7	4	1	4	—	0	0	0	1.93
Cornelius, Willie	2	2	0	3	2	2	1	5	0	1	0	6.00
Crawford, Sam[10]	3	2	2	19	14	6	4	13	1	1	1	2.84
Curry, Rube[11]	8	6	5	56.3	66	26	19	42	3	2	0	4.15
Davis, Rosey[12]	5	1	1	19.3	15	6	4	12	2	0	0	2.79
Demery, Art	1	0	0	1	0	0	1	2	0	0	0	0.00
Dismukes, William	8	7	7	54	50	31	14	15	2	5	0	5.17
Donaldson, John	1	1	1	8	10	4	0	6	0	1	0	4.50
Dougherty, Pat	10	6	3	60.3	52	24	17	41	2	3	1	3.58
Drake, Bill[13]	5	4	3	35.3	39	21	9	7	1	2	0	5.35
Earle, Charles	3	2	2	20	18	14	6	7	1	1	0	6.30
Emory, John	1	1	1	8.3	11	5	2	1	0	1	0	5.40
Erwin, 1938 OM	1	1	0	1	6	7	1	0	0	1	0	63.00
Fabre, Isidro	4	3	3	29	22	11	12	7	2	1	1	3.41
Farrell, Luther	4	3	3	31	23	15	13	30	1	3	0	4.35
Fields, Romey[14]	1	1	0	—	—	—	3	2	0	0	0	—
Fillmore, Jim	1	0	0	4	4	4	6	3	0	0	0	9.00
Finner, John[15]	3	2	1	16.3	16	4	5	5	2	1	0	2.20
Flournoy, Willis	5	3	3	27	21	3	2	13	2	1	1	1.00
Force, Bill	3	1	0	7	7	8	3	4	1	1	0	10.29
Foster, Andrew	7	7	6	54.3	52	25	16	19	3	4	1	4.14
Foster, Bill	7	5	4	46.3	36	7	14	36	6	0	0	1.36
Frye, Jack	1	0	0	5	7	5	—	1	0	0	0	9.00
Gardner, Ken	2	2	1	13.7	13	10	5	10	0	1	0	6.59
Gatewood, Bill	17	12	10	108.3	112	54	30	63	4	8	2	4.49
Gillespie, Henry	2	2	0	14	7	6	10	8	1	1	0	3.86
Gisentaner, Willie[16]	1	0	0	—	—	—	0	0	0	0	0	—
González, Luis	15	11	7	99.3	86	41	21	26	6	5	1	3.71

Pitcher	G	GS	CG	IP	H	R	BB	K	W	L	SH	R/9
Glover, Thomas	2	2	1	13.3	14	6	5	7	0	1	0	4.05
Gregory, 1915 SLG	1	1	1	8	5	6	8	7	0	1	0	6.75
Griffin, Emerson	1	0	0	2	—	0	1	0	0	0	0	0.00
Griffith, Robert	3	1	1	12.7	10	3	3	9	2	0	0	2.13
Hampton, Lewis	1	0	0	3	—	0	—	—	1	0	0	0.00
Harney, George[17]	6	3	2	33.3	25	11	10	23	4	0	0	2.97
Harrison, Bert	1	1	1	12	6	0	0	9	0	0	1	0.00
Harvey, David	1	1	0	7	4	2	4	0	0	0	0	2.57
Harvey, Richard	1	1	1	8	18	9	1	4	0	1	0	10.13
Hawkins, Lem	1	1	0	—	—	—	—	—	0	0	0	—
Hayes, Burnalle	1	0	0	1	0	0	0	0	1	0	0	0.00
Hayman, Sy	1	1	1	8	8	5	1	1	0	1	0	5.63
Hensley, Logan[18]	2	1	0	6.3	10	11	5	1	0	1	0	15.63
Hernández, Cheo	3	1	0	8.3	9	5	4	2	0	0	0	5.40
Holland, Bill (I)	4	3	2	19	15	5	4	12	0	2	0	2.37
Holland, Bill (II)	3	3	3	27	24	8	4	25	2	1	1	2.67
Holmes, Frank	1	0	0	—	—	—	—	—	0	0	0	—
Holsey, Robert[19]	1	1	0	—	—	—	2	3	0	0	0	—
Hooker, Leniel	2	2	2	13	11	6	4	5	0	2	0	4.15
Hubbard, Jess[20]	7	7	7	60	61	21	14	42	4	3	1	3.15
Hunter, Bert	3	1	1	10.3	9	7	10	8	1	1	0	6.10
Jackson, George	1	1	1	8	13	15	1	1	0	1	0	16.88
Jasper, George	1	0	0	1.7	2	2	3	0	0	0	0	10.84
Jeffries, Jim	5	4	4	37	25	16	16	19	3	1	0	3.89
Jessup, Gentry	4	2	2	29	34	15	19	9	3	1	0	4.66
Johnson, Dan	1	0	0	2	—	3	0	—	0	0	0	13.50
Johnson, Louis	9	8	5	67.7	48	23	24	27	5	2	0	3.06
Johnson, Nate	1	0	0	5	3	2	4	1	0	1	0	3.60
Johnson, Tom	1	1	0	3	2	1	2	2	0	0	0	3.00
Jones, Al	1	0	0	4	3	0	3	1	1	0	0	0.00
Jones, Bert	1	1	1	8	8	5	3	6	0	1	0	5.63
Junco, Jose	4	1	0	9	19	15	4	2	0	2	0	15.00
Keating, PS 1920	1	1	0	2.3	4	3	2	2	0	1	0	11.57
Kelley, Palmer	1	1	1	8	19	13	3	1	0	1	0	14.63
Kincannon, Harry[21]	2	1	0	8	8	13	11	3	0	1	0	7.88
Kranson, Floyd	4	2	1	23	21	14	15	17	2	0	0	5.48
LaMarque, James	5	1	0	13.7	16	8	6	11	0	3	0	5.27
Lankford, Ad[22]	3	1	1	13	17	7	6	3	0	1	0	4.85
Lee, Holsey[23]	8	7	4	44	35	22	21	20	2	4	1	3.48
Leftwich, Leroy	1	1	1	5	3	0	1	4	0	0	1	0.00
Levis, Oscar	1	1	1	9	8	2	—	9	1	0	0	2.00
Lewis, Rufus	1	0	0	6	4	3	1	7	0	0	0	4.50
Lightner, Charley	1	0	0	—	—	—	—	—	0	0	0	—
Lindsay, Bill	9	7	6	58	41	23	21	43	4	4	1	3.57
Mackey, James	2	1	1	9.3	9	6	1	8	1	0	0	5.79
Malloy, Charles	1	1	0	3	6	2	3	0	0	0	0	6.00
Malone, William	2	2	2	16	34	31	4	6	0	2	0	17.44
Manning, Max	2	1	1	11	12	11	5	12	0	1	0	9.00
Markham, John	4	2	2	16.3	24	11	2	8	1	1	0	6.06

Pitcher	G	GS	CG	IP	H	R	BB	K	W	L	SH	R/9
Mason, Charlie	1	0	0	0	1	0	0	0	0	0	0	—
Matchett, Jack[24]	4	2	1	19	13	10	6	12	2	2	0	4.74
Mathis, Verdell	1	0	0	0.7	5	6	2	0	0	0	0	81.82
Matlock, Leroy	5	5	3	41	32	20	10	29	2	1	0	4.39
McClellan, Dan[25]	5	3	2	25	28	13	7	15	0	2	0	4.68
McClure, Bob	3	2	1	17	10	9	16	9	1	1	0	4.76
McDaniel, Booker	5	1	0	15	11	7	8	10	1	1	0	4.20
McDonald, Webster[26]	14	11	8	79.3	65	22	17	74	7	2	3	2.50
McDuffie, Terris[27]	8	4	2	37.7	19	9	9	20	2	2	0	2.15
McNair, Hurley	2	1	1	18	19	10	6	10	1	0	0	5.00
Mederos, Lico	11	6	2	51.7	50	27	14	12	3	5	0	4.70
Mendez, Jose	26	21	18	211.7	159	79	55	125	9	11	3	3.36
Merritt, Bill	3	2	2	25	11	6	8	18	2	1	0	2.16
Meyers, George	4	2	1	29.3	33	20	6	12	1	1	0	6.14
Miller, Frank	2	2	2	17	33	29	8	4	0	2	0	15.35
Miller, Henry	4	0	0	9.7	5	1	1	12	1	0	0	0.93
Miller, Joe	2	2	0	—	—	—	4	2	0	1	0	—
Miller, Percy	4	3	3	23.7	30	22	14	14	1	2	0	8.37
Miller, Pleas	1	1	0	—	—	—	0	0	0	1	0	—
Mirabel, Juanelo	1	1	1	9	8	3	1	7	1	0	0	3.00
Mooney, Tom	3	2	2	17.7	17	3	4	13	0	2	0	1.53
Moreland, Nate	3	2	2	22	28	12	5	25	0	2	0	4.91
Moss, Porter	2	1	1	9.7	10	8	6	9	0	0	0	7.45
Muñoz, Jose	11	9	8	86.7	67	24	20	30	5	3	0	2.49
Nelson, John	2	2	2	19	27	15	2	7	0	1	0	7.11
Newberry, Jimmie[28]	3	0	0	20	11	5	3	5	2	0	0	2.37
Newcombe, Don	1	1	0	2.7	0	2	4	0	0	0	0	6.77
Oldham, Jimmy	3	2	1	15.7	22	8	1	13	2	1	0	4.60
Owens, Oscar[29]	5	3	1	26	26	20	12	13	0	2	0	6.92
Padron, Juan	1	1	1	8	4	2	0	1	1	0	0	2.25
Padron, Luis	6	5	4	45	38	26	23	22	1	4	0	5.20
Paige, Leroy	45	44	9	233.7	149	67	73	296	14	10	2	2.58
Pareda, Pastor	21	12	9	130.3	128	58	38	54	5	6	2	4.01
Parego, George	2	1	1	12	22	10	1	13	1	0	0	7.50
Partlow, Roy	1	0	0	4.3	1	2	2	4	0	0	0	4.16
Pedroso, Eustaquio	20	17	13	143.3	119	53	38	52	7	10	3	3.33
Pérez, Julian	2	2	1	13	14	11	4	6	0	2	0	7.62
Pope, Willie[30]	2	1	0	4	5	3	2	1	0	1	0	6.75
Porter, Andy	11	5	2	50.3	42	28	19	35	4	2	0	5.01
Powell, Melvin	1	1	1	9	5	0	5	3	1	0	1	0.00
Radcliffe, Ted[31]	6	3	1	7.7	11	2	12	8	1	0	0	2.35
Rector, Connie[32]	3	3	3	25	27	10	5	17	1	2	0	3.60
Redding, Dick[33]	9	8	7	72	68	32	14	61	4	4	1	4.00
Renoy, Moses	1	0	0	1	5	5	1	0	0	0	0	45.00
Richardson, Gene	1	1	0	2	—	4	3	3	0	1	0	18.00
Rile, Ed[34]	2	2	0	1.3	3	3	6	0	0	1	0	20.25
Roberts, Roy	1	1	1	8	5	2	2	12	0	1	0	2.25
Rogan, Wilber	21	19	18	173.7	137	68	46	129	13	6	0	3.52
Ross, Dick	1	1	1	9	5	2	4	—	1	0	0	2.00

Pitcher	G	GS	CG	IP	H	R	BB	K	W	L	SH	R/9
Royer, Carlos	3	2	1	13	32	25	9	2	0	2	0	17.31
Ryan, Merven[35]	5	5	2	22.3	27	17	1	11	1	3	0	6.85
Selden, William (I)[36]	7	6	6	45	72	55	18	28	1	5	0	11.00
Shaw, George	1	1	1	8.3	11	8	2	0	0	1	0	8.67
Smith, 1910 SLO	1	1	1	8	10	6	0	2	0	1	0	6.75
Smith, Gene	1	0	0	4	1	2	2	1	0	1	0	4.50
Smith, Hilton[37]	9	4	2	44	35	7	6	27	3	0	1	1.43
Stanley, John[38]	4	1	1	15	11	0	6	14	1	0	1	0.00
Starks, Otis[39]	4	4	3	31.3	33	17	8	7	1	3	0	4.88
Stevens, Frank[40]	1	1	0	—	—	—	2	2	0	1	0	—
Stovey, George[41]	4	4	3	24	27	22	16	8	0	4	0	8.25
Streeter, Sam[42]	5	2	2	19	29	13	7	12	3	1	1	6.16
Strong, Joe	2	2	1	15.7	14	8	2	8	0	2	0	4.60
Sykes, Frank[43]	2	2	1	13	8	4	1	6	1	1	1	2.77
Taylor, Ben	2	1	1	11.7	5	3	3	13	1	0	0	2.32
Taylor, John "Steel Arm"[44]	2	1	1	9	5	2	0	5	0	1	0	2.00
Taylor, John "Big"	4	4	2	20.3	21	12	4	13	2	2	1	5.31
Taylor, Johnny	1	1	0	7	—	3	3	8	0	1	0	3.86
Thompson, Sam[45]	2	1	0	8.3	10	4	5	11	0	0	0	4.32
Thompson, "Speedboy"	2	2	1	9	11	6	—	6	0	0	0	6.00
Torriente, Cristobal	1	0	0	5	6	5	3	3	0	0	0	9.00
Treadwell, Harold[46]	2	1	0	7	5	5	6	4	0	0	0	5.14
Trent, Ted	7	4	4	43	36	17	12	59	4	0	1	3.56
Trusty, Shep[47]	8	8	7	59	67	52	14	48	4	4	1	7.93
Van Dyke, Fred	1	0	0	—	—	—	—	—	0	0	0	—
Whitworth, Dick	6	5	4	46	47	25	18	23	2	4	0	4.89
Whyte, Bill	11	11	11	87	82	54	27	46	3	7	1	5.59
Wickware, Frank[48]	12	9	8	82.3	55	22	43	55	7	2	4	2.40
Williams, Andrew[49]	10	9	6	66.3	70	44	29	39	2	7	1	5.97
Williams, Charles[50]	3	3	1	13.7	20	11	3	2	1	2	0	7.25
Williams, Joe[51]	31	28	28	258.7	202	101	47	245	19	8	6	3.51
Williams, John	8	0	0	31.3	27	14	11	8	0	3	0	4.02
Williams, Roy	2	1	1	16.7	12	5	5	6	1	0	0	2.70
Williams, Tom	4	1	1	18.3	16	8	11	6	1	0	0	3.93
Willis, Jim	1	1	1	6	6	4	0	6	0	1	0	6.00
Wilson, Ed[52]	1	1	0	—	—	—	2	0	0	0	0	—
Winters, James[53]	5	3	3	37.7	30	14	7	15	3	0	0	3.35
Wright, Jack	1	0	0	7	10	8	5	4	0	0	0	10.29
Yokely, Laymon[54]	13	12	9	90.7	77	44	50	55	8	2	0	4.38
Young, John	1	1	1	5	3	1	0	6	1	0	0	1.80
Young, "Slowtime"	1	1	1	5	8	4	0	0	0	0	0	7.20

Fielding Statistics

Note on Fielding Statistics: Multiple defensive positions are listed in order of most games played to least, with the main position depicted in **bold**. During the 1920s, putouts and assists were combined into a category called chances (C) in some publications.

For this tabulation, these chances are displayed after the number of putouts. Unassisted double plays are shown in brackets. Triple plays are denoted by a @. POS=Positions played; G=Games; PO=Putouts; C=Chances; A=Assists; E=Errors; FA=Fielding Average; DP=Double Plays.

Player	POS	G	PO/C	A	E	FA	DP
Abernathy, Robert	cf	2	4	0	0	1.000	0
Abreu, Eufemio	**c**/rf	9	47	9	2	.966	1
Alexander, Charles	p	1	1	1	0	1.000	1
Allen, Johnny	ss	1	2	7	1	.900	0
Allen, Newt	**ss**/2b/3b	40	71	99	6	.966	10 [1]
Allen, Todd	3b	3	2	6	0	1.000	0
Allen, Toussaint	1b	9	76	6	1	.988	2
Almeida, Rafael	**3b**/1b/rf/2b/ss/c/lf	55	125	79	22	.903	12
Anderson, Bill	p	1	0	0	0	.000	0
Andrews, Herman	cf	1	0/1	0	0	1.000	0
Andrews, Peter	rf/p	2	2	1	2	.600	0
Archer, Luke	p	1	0	1	0	1.000	0
Arnett, 1902 BS	rf	1	0	0	0	.000	0
Arthur, A., 1936 NS	ss	1	1	1	1	.667	0
Arumis, Joaquin	2b	2	0	7	1	.875	0
Atkins, Joe	rf	1	1	0	0	1.000	0
Aulston, Clyde	p	1	0	4	0	1.000	1
Austin, Frank	ss	4	9	5	0	1.000	1
Avery, Bill	c	1	1	0	0	1.000	0
Baker, 1920 LAWS	c	1	6	1	0	1.000	0
Ball, Walter	**rf**/p	9	12	9	1	.955	2
Bankhead, Dan	rf	1	0	0	0	.000	0
Bankhead, Sam	**2b**/lf/ss	13	28	20	3	.941	0
Baranda, Manuel	2b	5	11	14	0	1.000	2
Barber, Jesse	**3b**/rf/ss/cf/2b/lf/1b	49	69	61	17	.884	7
Barnes, Ed	p	2	0	1	0	1.000	0
Barnes, John	**c**/1b	6	31	4	3	.921	0
Baro, Alfredo	lf	1	0	0	2	.000	0
Baro, Bernardo	rf	10	27	4	1	.969	1
Barton, George	2b/rf	2	0	5	1	.833	0
Barton, Sherman	cf	1	4	0	0	1.000	0
Bassett, Lloyd	c	5	16	4	0	1.000	0
Bauchman, Harry	2b	13	25	47	6	.923	8
Baugh, Johnny	p	3	0	6	2	.750	0
Baynard, Frank	rf	1	0	0	0	.000	0
Baynard, William	c	2	12	1	0	1.000	0
Beckwith, John	**ss**/3b/1b/1f/c/2b/rf	41	76/29	64	10	.944	4
Bell, Frank	2b	1	3	3	2	.750	0
Bell, Fred	p	1	0	1	0	1.000	0
Bell, James	**cf**/lf	50	62/4	2	0	1.000	1
Bell, Louie	p	1	0	1	2	.333	0
Bell, William (I)	**rf**/p	2	2	2	1	.800	0
Bell, William (II)	**p**/cf	6	0	7	0	1.000	1
Benjamin, Jerry	cf	3	7	1	1	.889	0

Player	POS	G	PO/C	A	E	FA	DP
Benavides, Prudencio	rf	1	2	0	0	1.000	0
Bennett, Sam	**c**/lf/rf	6	5	2	0	1.000	0
Benson, Gene	cf/rf	12	21	0	0	1.000	0
Berry, 1938 OM	rf	1	1	0	0	1.000	0
Beverly, Charles	p	5	0	8	0	1.000	2
Bibbs, Junius	2b	1	1	0	1	.500	0
Binga, Bill	3b	2	0	2	0	1.000	0
Bingham, William	**rf**/lf	3	1	0	0	1.000	0
Bissant, John	lf	1	2	0	0	1.000	0
Black, Frank	rf	3	6	0	1	.857	0
Blackman, Henry	**3b**/ss/2b	13	18	21	6	.867	1
Blackwell, Charles	**rf**/lf/cf/3b	16	32	8	3	.930	0
Blake, Frank	p/cf	2	1	0	0	1.000	0
Blueitt, Virgil	2b	1	0	0	0	.000	0
Bobo, Willie	1b	2	0	0	0	.000	0
Bolden, 1938 OM	ss	1	2	4	0	1.000	0
Bonner, Robert	**1b**/ss	4	27	8	1	.972	0
Booker, Pete	**c**/1b/rf	20	148	16	5	.970	7
Bost, CHG 1910	2b	2	0	4	0	1.000	0
Bowman, Emmett	**p**/1b/rf/cf	4	13	7	0	1.000	1
Boyd, Ben	**cf**/2b/ss/3b/rf	30	38	8	9	.836	1
Boyd, Fred	rf	2	3	0	0	1.000	0
Bradford, Charlie	p	2	0	1	1	.500	0
Bradley, Phil	**c**/1b/ss	8	39	7	1	.979	3
Brady, Farmer	p	1	0	1	1	.500	0
Bragg, Jesse	**3b**/cf	6	5	4	0	1.000	0
Branham, Finis	**p**/rf	6	1/3	9	0	1.000	0
Brazelton, Clarkson	c	6	9	5	0	1.000	0
Brewer, Chet	**p**/rf/1b	16	12	17	1	.967	0
Brewer, Gene	3b	7	4	9	0	1.000	2@
Briggs, Otto	**rf**/cf/lf	20	37	3	2	.952	0
Britt, George	**p**/ss/c/3b	15	17	17	3	.919	1
Britton, John	rf	1	1	0	0	1.000	0
Brooks, Ameal	**rf**/c	6	21	1	1	.957	0
Brooks, Gus	cf	2	5	0	0	1.000	0
Brooks, Irvin	**cf**/2b/rf/ss/p	16	35	15	1	.980	2
Brooks, Jesse	3b	4	2	4	1	.857	0
Brooks, Sidney	**lf**/rf/2b	5	7	0	0	1.000	0
Brown, 1934 KCM	p	1	0	0	0	.000	0
Brown, Barney	**p**/lf/rf	5	2	2	0	1.000	0
Brown, Ben	rf/p	1	1	0	0	1.000	0
Brown, Dave	p	3	0	0	0	.000	0
Brown, E., 1911 WBS/ 1918 CUG	3b	2	1	4	1	.833	0
Brown, Elias	**rf**/lf	8	14	1	3	.833	0
Brown, George	**rf**/cf	5	5	0	1	.833	0
Brown, Jim	c	3	0/18	0	2	.900	0
Brown, Larry	c	13	63/41	4	2	.982	1
Brown, Malcom	**2b**/ss	8	16	14	4	.882	3

Player	POS	G	PO/C	A	E	FA	DP
Brown, Mike	1b	1	9	1	0	1.000	0
Brown, Ray	p/cf	2	2	0	0	1.000	0
Brown, Tom	3b	1	0	0	0	.000	0
Brown, Willard	cf/ss/lf/3b	15	19	6	5	.833	1
Buckner, Harry	p/rf	11	8	25	1	.971	2
Buford, 1914 ABC	p	1	0	0	0	.000	0
Burbage, Knowlington	lf/cf/rf	5	4	1	1	.833	0
Burnett, Fred	c/1b	3	27	1	2	.933	1
Burns, Claude	cf	3	7	0	0	1.000	0
Burns, Pete	c	3	11	2	2	.867	0
Bustamante, Luis	ss/2b/3b	26	31	69	15	.870	7
Butcher, Spencer	c	3	11	0	0	1.000	0
Butts, Thomas	ss	1	0	0	1	.000	0
Byas, Richard	1b	1	12	0	0	1.000	1
Byrd, Bill	p/cf	3	0	1	0	1.000	0
Cabanas, Armando	2b/lf/rf/cf	35	80	62	9	.940	9
Cabrera, Alfredo	ss/1b/3b	47	159	138	25	.922	20
Calderon, Benito	c	1	5	0	0	1.000	0
Campanella, Roy	c	7	23	3	0	1.000	0
Campos, Tatica	2b/1b/p	12	28	20	4	.923	2
Cannady, Walter	2b/3b/1b/cf	15	37	44	0	1.000	4
Carillo, Lazaro	p	1	0	0	0	.000	0
Carlisle, Matthew	2b	1	3	4	0	1.000	0
Carr, George	1b/3b/rf/lf/cf/ss	47	219	39	6	.977	13
Carr, Wayne	p	2	2	1	0	1.000	0
Carter, Charles	p	3	0	11	1	.917	0
Carter, Cliff	p	1	0	1	0	1.000	0
Carter, Ernest	p	3	1	2	0	1.000	1
Carter, Marlin	2b/ss/lf	4	4	6	1	.909	0
Carter, Paul	p	1	0	5	0	1.000	0
Cary, Arthur	rf	1	0	0	0	.000	0
Casey, William	c	2	14	0	0	1.000	0
Cash, Bill	c	1	0	0	0	.000	0
Cason, John	2b/c	6	14	16	1	.968	0
Castillo, Julian	1b	34	342	14	13	.965	19
Catto, Harry	lf/rf	2	2	0	0	1.000	0
Chacon, Pelayo	ss	28	78	82	12	.930	9
Chamberlain, Ed	1b	1	13	1	0	1.000	0
Charleston, Oscar	cf/1b/lf/rf	64	210/28	5	6	.975	12
Charleston, Porter	p	1	0	3	0	1.000	0
Clark, 1937 KCM	rf	1	4	0	0	1.000	0
Clark, Al	2b/ss	2	3	4	1	.875	0
Clark, Morten	ss/rf/2b	14	21	18	7	.848	2
Clarke, Bob	c	18	99	8	2	.982	1
Clayton, Leroy	1b	3	26	0	1	.963	2
Cobb, Lorenza	c	4	19	3	0	1.000	0
Cockrell, Phil	p/rf/1b	18	17	29	2	.958	1
Cole, 1928 CLG	3b	1	0	0	0	.000	0
Collins, 1936 NS	lf	1	2	0	0	1.000	0

Player	POS	G	PO/C	A	E	FA	DP
Collins, 1942 PRG	**rf**/lf/cf	4	2	0	1	.667	0
Collins, 1944 KCR	3b	1	0	0	0	.000	0
Combs, Jack	p	1	0/2	0	1	.667	0
Concepcion, Monchile	rf	1	1	0	0	1.000	0
Cooper, E. 1915 LS	rf	1	0	0	0	.000	0
Cooper, 1924 SLS	cf	1	1	0	0	1.000	0
Cooper, Andy	p	10	1	17	0	1.000	0
Cooper, Anthony	ss	1	1	3	0	1.000	1
Cooper, Darltie	p	1	0	0	1	0.000	0
Cornelius, Willie	p	2	0	0	0	.000	0
Crafton, Allie	lf	1	0	0	0	.000	0
Crawford, Sam	**p**/cf	4	0	2	0	1.000	0
Creacy, Albert	**3b**/2b	9	5	11	2	.889	1
Crockett, Frank	cf	1	0	0	0	.000	0
Crump, James	ss	6	7	14	2	.913	0
Crutchfield, Jimmie	**cf**/rf/lf	11	19	0	0	1.000	0
Cullens, William	**cf**/rf	4	3	2	0	1.000	0
Cummings, Napoleon	1b	1	8	1	2	.818	0
Curry, Rube	**p**/1b/rf	9	8	17	0	1.000	1
Dabney, John	1b	1	9	0	0	1.000	0
Dallard, Maurice	**1b**/lf/rf	9	63	1	1	.985	3 [1]
Danage, Lunie	2b	4	14	14	3	.903	0
Dandridge, Ray	**ss**/3b	7	6	14	2	.909	4
Daniels, Leon	c	1	0/3	0	1	.750	0
Davenport, Lloyd	cf	2	4	0	0	1.000	0
Davis, 1934 KCM	rf	2	3	0	0	1.000	0
Davis, 1942 PRG	**ss**/3b	3	0	3	0	1.000	0
Davis, Ambrose	2b	1	2	4	0	1.000	0
Davis, Jack	3b	1	4	4	1	.889	0
Davis, Johnny	**lf**/cf	11	24	0	1	.960	0
Davis, Lorenzo	**3b**/1b/cf	8	38	3	0	1.000	1
Davis, "Red"	lf/1b	1	6	1	0	1.000	2@
Davis, Rosey	**p**/rf/1b/lf	8	8/3	5	1	.941	0
Davis, Tom	ss	1	2	2	1	.800	0
Davis, Walter	**rf**/lf	3	2/5	0	0	1.000	0
Davis, William	cf	1	0	1	1	.500	0
Day, 1902 PG	lf	2	2	0	1	.667	0
Day, Wilson	**2b**/3b	21	34	51	11	.885	6
Deas, James	**c**/1b	5	22	7	1	0.967	0
Demery, Art	p	1	0	0	0	.000	0
DeMoss, Elwood	2b	17	21/19	31	6	.922	2
Dennis, Wesley	3b	1	0	0	0	.000	0
Dewitt, Sam	3b	1	0	0	0	.000	0
Dials, Oland	**cf** /lf/rf	6	6	0	0	1.000	0
Dihigo, Martin	**ss**/2b/cf	14	33	44	5	.939	6
Dismukes, William	p	8	4	16	3	.870	1
Dixon, George	c	9	50	6	1	.982	0
Dixon, Herbert	**lf**/cf/rf/3b	42	71/3	3	3	.963	0
Doby, Larry	2b	1	5	2	0	1.000	0

Player	POS	G	PO/C	A	E	FA	DP
Donaldson, John	**lf**/cf/p	5	10	1	0	1.000	0
Dougherty, Pat	**p**/rf	11	3	15	1	.947	0
Douglas, Jesse	**2b**/ss	4	9	8	2	.895	4
Douglass, Eddie	1b	10	88	5	1	.989	1
Douglass, George	cf	1	1	0	1	.500	0
Downs, McKinley	**2b**/3b	12	35	24	4	.937	3
Drake, Bill	p	5	0	12	1	.923	0
Dudley, Charles	**lf**/cf	10	14	2	0	1.000	0
Dukes, Tommy	c	4	45	1	0	1.000	0
Dunbar, Ashby	**lf**/cf	3	1	0	0	1.000	0
Duncan, Frank (I)	**lf**/rf	43	73	11	7	.923	3
Duncan, Frank (II)	**c**/rf/1b	21	102	10	2	.982	1
Dunn, Joseph	2b/3b	4	9	3	1	.923	0
Dwight, Eddie	**cf**/rf	17	33	1	2	.944	0
Earle, Charles	**rf**/cf/p/lf	18	11	13	1	.962	0
Easterling, Howard	**3b**/ss/1b/rf	20	13	38	7	.879	2
Eggleston, Bill	ss	1	6	1	0	1.000	0
Eggleston, Mack	rf	9	28	2	3	.909	0
Ellis, 1911 WBS	ss	1	1	3	2	.667	0
Else, Harry	c	1	11	2	0	1.000	0
Emory, John	p	1	0	0	0	.000	0
Epps, Simon	rf	1	0	0	0	.000	0
Erwin, 1938 OM	p	1	0	0	0	.000	0
Evans, Bill	cf	1	1	0	0	1.000	0
Ewing, William	c	5	23	3	0	1.000	0
Fabre, Isidro	**p**/cf	6	5	2	0	1.000	0
Fagan, Bob	**2b**/1b	22	46	43	7	.927	6
Farrell, William	1b/c	2	10	1	2	.846	0
Farrell, Luther	p	4	4	11	2	.882	0
Fernandez, Jose Maria	c	1	7	1	0	1.000	0
Fiall, George	ss	1	4	1	1	.833	0
Fiall Tom	**cf**/rf/lf	11	21	4	0	1.000	0
Fields, Romey	rf/p	1	1	1	0	1.000	0
Figarola, Rafael	c	17	71	27	6	.942	1
Fillmore, Jim	p	1	0	0	0	.000	0
Finley, Tom	3b	2	4	2	0	1.000	0
Finner, John	p	3	0	1	0	1.000	0
Flonnoy, 1941 ECG	3b	1	0	0	2	.000	0
Flournoy, Willis	p	5	6	4	2	.833	0
Foote, Bill	ss/lf/rf	3	4	0	1	.800	0
Footes, Bob	c	4	18	3	1	.955	0
Forbes, Frank	**ss**/lf	6	9	7	2	.889	2 [1]
Force, Bill	p	3	0/1	0	0	1.000	0
Foreman, Sylvester	c	2	17	2	1	.950	0
Forrest, James	**rf**/2b	6	5	2	0	1.000	0
Ford, 1918 CUG	rf	1	0	0	0	.000	0
Foster, Andrew	**p**/rf	8	4	23	2	.931	0
Foster, Bill	p	7	1/6	7	3	.824	0
Fowler, Bud (Jackson, John)	2b	2	9	7	2	.889	0

Player	POS	G	PO/C	A	E	FA	DP
Fox, 1945 PAS	3b	1	0	1	0	1.000	0
Francis, Bill	3b	24	31	29	7	.896	2
Frye, Jack	**1b**/2b/ss/lf/p	22	169	18	5	.974	6
Fuller, William	2b	1	1	3	0	1.000	0
Gans, Judy	**lf**/cf	26	42	4	4	.920	2
Garcia, Regino	**1b**/rf/c	22	109	4	7	.942	5
Gardner, Floyd	**cf**/rf/lf	13	14/12	0	0	1.000	0
Gardner, Ken	p	2	4	2	2	.750	0
Gaston, Robert	c	1	0	0	0	.000	0
Gatewood, Bill	**p**/rf	20	4	35	1	.975	1
Gatewood, Ernest	**c**/3b	5	27	9	1	.973	1
Gee, Thomas	c	1	3	1	1	.800	0
Gerry, PS 1920	cf	1	2	0	0	1.000	0
Gibson, Josh	c/lf/3b	17	76	11	3	.967	1
Giles, George	**1b**/2b	15	104	8	5	.957	3
Gillespie, Henry	p	2	0	3	1	.750	1
Gisentaner, Willie	p	0	0	0	0	.000	0
Gilyard, Luther	rf	1	0	0	0	.000	0
Glover, Thomas	p	2	0	4	0	1.000	0
Goliah, Fred	**rf**/2b/3b	4	10	2	1	.923	2
Gonzalez, Gervasio	c	50	267	58	10	.970	7
Gonzalez, Luis	**p**/rf	16	2	30	2	.941	0
Gonzalez, Ramon	2b/1b	2	5	4	1	.900	1
Gordon, Austin	lf	1	1	0	2	.333	0
Gordon, Wallace	2b	1	2	2	1	.800	1
Graham, Dennis	**rf**/3b	16	21	0	1	.955	0
Grant, 1945 PAS	1b	1	7	0	0	1.000	0
Grant, Charlie	**2b**/3b	6	13	12	0	1.000	3
Grant, Frank	**2b**/1b/rf	7	30	10	1	.976	0
Grant, Leroy	**1b**/2b	20	151/8	17	8	.957	5
Gray, Willie	cf	10	16	0	0	1.000	0
Green, William	lf	2	4	1	0	1.000	0
Green, Joe	**rf**/cf	11	14	3	2	.895	0
Greene, Joe	c	7	41	1	0	1.000	0
Gregory, 1915 SLG	p	1	0	0	1	.000	0
Griffin, Emerson	rf/p	1	1	0	0	1.000	0
Griffith, Robert	p	3	0	1	0	1.000	0
Hairston, Sam	**c**/rf	9	41	4	2	.957	1
Haley, Granville	**rf**/ss	4	8	1	0	1.000	0
Hall, 1938 OM	cf	1	1	0	0	1.000	0
Hall, Blainey	**lf**/rf	13	13	0	0	1.000	0
Hampton, Lewis	**p**/lf	2	0	1	0	1.000	0
Handy, Bill	2b	9	15	27	2	.955	5
Hardy, Paul	c	1	7	2	0	1.000	0
Harney, George	p	6	0/5	6	0	1.000	0
Harris, Curtis	**2b/lf**/1b/rf	10	52	4	0	1.000	3
Harris, Nate	**2b**/ss	18	23	48	9	.888	3
Harris, Ray	2b	5	15	19	1	.971	2
Harris, Vic	**lf**/cf	22	44	6	4	.926	1

Player	POS	G	PO/C	A	E	FA	DP
Harrison, Abe	ss	27	33	80	16	.876	7
Harrison, Bert	p	1	0	2	0	1.000	0
Harvey, Bob	cf/rf	4	1	2	0	1.000	0
Harvey, David	p	1	0	0	0	.000	0
Harvey, Richard	p	1	0	2	1	.667	0
Hawkins, Lem	**1b**/2b/p/3b	20	166	15	2	.989	9
Hawkins, Sam	3b	3	5	4	1	.900	1
Hayes, Burnalle	p	1	0	0	0	.000	0
Hayman, Sy	p	1	0	1	0	1.000	0
Haywood, Albert	c	12	74	4	1	.987	0
Hensley, Logan	**p**/lf	3	0	1	0	1.000	0
Hernandez, Cheo	p	3	0	2	0	1.000	0
Hernandez, Ricardo	**cf**/lf/3b/rf/1b	39	73	12	9	.904	5
Herrera, Paito	**2b**/1b/3b/rf/lf/cf	11	25	12	4	.902	2
Hewitt, Joe	**ss**/lf/2b/cf	17	41	40	4	.953	6
Hidalgo, Heliodoro	**cf**/3b	49	87	2	4	.957	1
Hill, John	**ss**/3b	4	8	10	2	.900	4
Hill, Johnson	3b	11	17	27	0	1.000	6
Hill, Pete	**cf**/lf/rf	74	135	11	11	.930	0
Holland, Bill (I)	**p**/cf/3b	7	7	10	2	.895	1
Holland, Bill (II)	p	3	10	3	0	1.000	0
Holloway, Crush	**cf** /rf/lf	38	74	7	2	.976	1
Holmes, Ben	3b	23	33	41	21	.779	2
Holmes, Frank	p	1	0	0	0	.000	0
Holsey, Robert	p	1	0/1	0	0	1.000	0
Holtz, Eddie	**2b**/3b	6	8	16	4	.857	3
Hooker, Leniel	p	2	1	3	1	.800	0
Hopkins, PS 1920	lf	2	2	0	1	.667	0
Hopkins, George	rf/2b	3	2	1	2	.600	0
Hoskins, Bill	lf	19	31	0	1	.969	0
Hubbard, Jess	**rf**/p/1b	18	16	16	2	.941	0
Hudspeth, Robert	1b	11	107	4	3	.974	3
Hughes, Sammy	**2b**/1b	11	61	16	3	.963	6 [1]
Hunter, 1938 OM	lf	1	0	0	1	.000	0
Hunter, Bert	p	3	0	2	0	1.000	0
Hutchinson, Fred	**ss**/3b	18	28	35	8	.887	3
Hutt, Oscar	1b	4	31	3	1	.971	1
Hyde, Cowan	**cf**/lf/rf	10	16	0	1	.941	0
Irvin, Monte	**cf**/3b/rf	5	7	1	1	.889	0
January 1936 NS	cf	1	2	0	0	1.000	0
Jackson, Andrew	3b	4	5	8	4	.765	1
Jackson, Bob	c/cf	2	7	0	3	.700	0
Jackson, George	lf/p	2	1	4	1	.833	0
Jackson, Norman	ss	1	0	0	0	.000	0
Jackson, Oscar	lf/c	4	12	2	1	.933	0
Jackson, Stanford	**3b**/**rf**/ss	5	0/6	0	2	.750	1
Jackson, William	**cf**/2b/lf/rf	6	12	1	1	.929	0
James, Gus	**1b**/rf	3	19	2	0	1.000	3
James, William	**2b**/lf	14	23	35	4	.935	1

Player	POS	G	PO/C	A	E	FA	DP
Jasper, George	p	1	0	0	0	.000	0
Jefferson, Ralph	lf/cf	4	4	1	1	.833	0
Jeffries, Harry	**3b**/2b	11	11/2	13	4	.867	0
Jeffries, Jim	**p**/3b/lf/rf	10	7	13	0	1.000	1
Jenkins, Clarence	rf	1	2	0	0	1.000	0
Jenkins, Horace	**rf**/lf/cf	7	4	0	0	1.000	0
Jessup, Gentry	p	4	0	4	1	.800	0
Jethroe, Sam	**cf**/lf/c	11	29	1	4	.882	0
Jiminez, Eusebio	2b	2	4	5	1	.900	0
Johnson, Pete	rf	1	0	0	0	.000	0
Johnson, 1945 PAS	rf	1	2	0	0	1.000	0
Johnson, Bryon	**ss**/rf	3	3	6	0	1.000	1
Johnson, Cecil	2b	1	1	0	1	.500	0
Johnson, Claude	2b/ss	4	6	15	0	1.000	0
Johnson, Dan	p	1	0	0	0	.000	0
Johnson, George	**cf**/lf/rf	12	26	0	2	.929	0
Johnson, George, Jr.	c/1b	23	203	14	3	.986	3
Johnson, Grant	**2b**/ss/3b	35	64	59	5	.961	8
Johnson, Harry	**rf**/2b/1b	4	7	3	0	1.000	0
Johnson, Judy	**3b**/2b/ss	32	50	61	6	.949	4
Johnson, Louis	p	9	2/3	16	5	.808	0
Johnson, Nate	p	1	0	0	0	.000	0
Johnson, Oscar	**c**/lf/1b/rf	10	46	10	4	.933	1
Johnson, Sam	ss	1	7	3	0	1.000	0
Johnson, Tom	p	1	0	1	0	1.000	0
Johnson, William	lf	1	2	0	0	1.000	0
Johnston, Wade	**cf**/lf	5	12	0	0	1.000	0
Jones, Al	p	1	0	0	0	.000	0
Jones, Bert	P	1	1	4	0	1.000	0
Jones, Willie	c/2b/ss	2	14	2	1	.941	0
Jones, Willis	lf	1	4	0	0	1.000	0
Jordan, Robert	**1b**/**rf**/c/ss	6	36	4	1	.976	3
Joseph, Walter	**3b**/ss	21	11	26	4	.902	1
Junco, Jose	p	4	0	3	0	1.000	0
Keating, PS 1920	p	1	0	1	0	1.000	0
Kelley, Palmer	p	1	0	0	0	.000	0
Kellman, Edric	3b/rf	4	3	7	0	1.000	1
Kennard, Dan	**c**/rf	14	60	12	2	.973	2
Kenyon, Harry	cf/lf	2	0/4	0	0	1.000	0
Kimbro, Henry	cf	2	4	0	0	1.000	0
Kimbro, Ted	**3b**/2b	5	6	9	0	1.000	0
Kincannon, Harry	p	3	0	1	0	1.000	0
Kindle, Bill	2b	1	1	3	2	.667	0
Kranson, Floyd	p	4	1	1	1	.667	0
Kyle, Andy	**rf**/cf/2b	4	5	2	1	.875	0
Lackey, Obie	2b	5	11	5	2	.889	2
LaMarque, James	p	5	0	5	1	.833	1
Land, Bill	**cf**/rf	3	3	3	1	.857	0
Lane, 1936 NS	1b	1	9	0	0	1.000	1

Player	POS	G	PO/C	A	E	FA	DP
Lane, Bill	**3b**/ss	16	19	33	6	.897	3
Langley, "Serious"	c	3	15	7	1	.957	0
Lankford, Ad	p	2	0	7	1	.875	0
Lee, 1938 OM	3b	1	1	3	0	1.000	0
Lee, Dick	cf	1	0	0	0	.000	0
Lee, Holsey	**p**/rf	11	9	19	0	1.000	0
Leftwich, Leroy	p	1	1	0	0	1.000	0
Lewis, Joe	c	11	66	9	1	.987	1
Lewis, Milton	1b	1	9	0	1	.900	0
Lewis, Rufus	p	1	0	0	0	.000	0
Lightner, Charley	**rf**/p	3	2	2	0	1.000	0
Lindsay, Bill	**p**/rf	12	4	24	0	1.000	1
Lindsay, Clarence	ss/3b	2	1	2	1	.750	0
Leonard, James	**lf**/cf	3	2	0	0	1.000	0
Leonard, Walter	1b	11	84	2	4	.956	5
Levis, Oscar	p	1	0	3	0	1.000	0
Lewis, Jerome	**2b**/3b	3	6	3	1	.900	0
Livingston, Lee	rf	4	2	0	1	.667	0
Lloyd, John	**ss**/2b/1b	50	136	132	21	.927	17
Lopez, Jose	3b	1	1	1	0	1.000	0
Louden, Louis	c	1	4	1	0	1.000	0
Lundy, Dick	ss	34	80	88	13	.928	12
Lyons, Bennie	1b	1	12	1	0	1.000	1
Lyons, Jimmie	**lf**/cf/1b/rf/lf	21	53/2	2	1	.983	3
Mackey, James	c/3b/ss/1b/p/2b/lf/cf	82	387	99	19	.962	13 [1]
Madison, Robert	lf	1	0	0	0	.000	0
Magrinat, Jose	**cf**/3b	3	7	3	1	.909	1
Malarcher, Dave	3b	6	3/7	6	0	1.000	0
Malette, Arthur	ss	1	0	4	0	1.000	1
Malloy, Charles	p	1	0	0	0	.000	0
Malone, William	**3b**/ss/lf/p/rf/1b/c	24	34	36	15	.824	1
Mann, 1918 CUG	1b	1	0	0	0	.000	0
Manning, Max	**p**/rf	3	0	0	1	.000	0
Marcell, Everett	lf	1	0	0	0	.000	1
Marcell, Oliver	**3b**/ss	21	32	33	12	.844	2 [1]
Markham, John	p	4	0	1	0	1.000	0
Marsans, Armando	**rf**/lf/2b/1b	45	168	16	7	.963	9
Marshall, Bobby	1b	1	3	1	2	.667	0
Marshall, Jack	2b	2	6	6	0	1.000	2
Martin, 1943 NAS	rf	1	0	0	0	.000	0
Martinez, Manuel	cf	1	3	0	3	.500	0
Mason, Charlie	**rf**/lf/1b/p	5	11	2	1	.929	0
Matchett, Jack	p	4	0	5	2	.714	0
Mathis, Verdell	p	1	0	0	0	.000	0
Matthews, Fran	rf	1	3	0	0	1.000	0
Matlock, Leroy	**p**/1b	6	12	4	0	1.000	0
Mayweather, Ed	1b	4	34	1	2	.946	1
McAdoo, Tullie	1b	24	239	12	5	.980	19
McClain, Edward	ss	1	1	1	0	1.000	0

Player	POS	G	PO/C	A	E	FA	DP
McClellan, Dan	**p**/cf/rf	7	3	10	1	.929	1
McClure, Bob	p	3	0	2	1	.667	0
McDaniel, Booker	p	5	0	5	0	1.000	0
McDonald, Webster	p	14	5/3	34	1	.977	1
McDuffie, Terris	p	8	0	6	0	1.000	0
McKinnis, Gready	lf	1	0	0	2	.000	0
McLaughlin, Henry	rf	1	2	0	0	1.000	0
McMurray, Willie	c	3	12	0	0	1.000	0
McNair, Hurley	**lf**/p/cf/rf	18	27	4	1	.969	0
Meade, Fred	3b	4	7	13	0	1.000	0
Means, Lemuel	1b/c	1	7	1	0	1.000	0
Mederos, Lico	**p**/cf	12	7	17	2	.923	1
Melton, Elbert	cf	1	0	0	0	.000	0
Mendez, Jose	**p**/ss/3b/2b/rf	46	49	121	7	.960	13
Merritt, Bill	**p**/cf	6	7	6	0	1.000	1
Mesa, Pablo	lf	2	3	0	0	1.000	0
Meyers, George	p	4	1	2	0	1.000	0
Middleton, Ed	lf	3	5	0	0	1.000	0
Miles, Jack	rf	1	1	0	0	1.000	0
Miles, Willie	cf	3	10	2	0	1.000	0
Miller, Eddie	3b	3	0/7	0	0	1.000	0
Miller, Frank	**p**/rf	3	0	8	1	.889	0
Miller, Henry	p	4	1	0	0	1.000	0
Miller, Joe	**p**/rf	2	0	3	1	.750	0
Miller, Louis	**3b**/2b	7	7	11	2	.900	0
Miller, Percy	p/lf	7	7	5	1	.923	0
Miller, Pleas	lf/p	3	1	3	0	1.000	0
Milliner, Eugene	rf	6	6	1	0	1.000	0
Milton, Henry	**rf**/lf/2b	8	13	1	0	1.000	0
Mirabel, Juanelo	p	1	0	1	0	1.000	0
Mitchell, 1938 OM	2b	1	1	5	1	.857	0
Mitchell, George	c	1	8	1	2	.818	0
Molina, Tinti	c/1b	4	33	3	1	.973	1
Mongin, Sam	**2b**/3b	11	24	12	1	.973	0
Monroe, Bill	**2b**/3b	31	63	81	9	.941	8
Moody, Lee	1b	3	21	1	0	1.000	2
Mooney, Tom	p	3	1	7	0	1.000	0
Moore, Eugene	rf	3	2	3	0	1.000	0
Moore, Harry	**cf**/1b/c/3b/2b/ss	24	62	7	3	.958	0
Moore, Walter	**ss**/3b/1b/2b	21	63	38	12	.894	6
Moran, Carlos	**3b**/rf/ss	37	55	83	18	.885	8
Moran, Francisco	1b	1	7	0	1	.875	1
Moreland, Nate	**p**/rf	4	2	6	0	1.000	0
Morrison, W., 1924 CAS	3b	3	8	7	1	.938	0
Morton, Sy	2b	1	0	0	0	.000	0
Moss, Porter	p	2	0	2	0	1.000	0
Mothell, Carroll	**2b**/1b/ss/3b	24	107	34	8	.946	5
Munoz, Jose	p	12	8	31	0	1.000	2
Murray, Mitch	c	8	36/2	4	0	1.000	0

Player	POS	G	PO/C	A	E	FA	DP
Neil, Ray	3b	14	18	37	2	.965	7
Nelson, Clyde	**1b**/3b	7	36	6	1	.977	2
Nelson, John	p/3b/lf	6	8	10	2	.900	0
Newberry, Jimmie	p	3	0	3	1	.750	0
Newcombe, Don	p	1	0	1	0	1.000	0
Norman, William	rf	1	0	0	0	.000	0
Oldham, Jimmy	p	3	0	7	0	1.000	0
Oliver, Huddy	ss	1	2	2	0	1.000	1
O'Neal, Luther	c	1	2	1	1	.750	0
O'Neil, John	1b	14	97	1	1	.990	14
Owens, Oscar	p	5	1	4	1	.833	0
Padron, Juan	p	1	0	1	0	1.000	0
Padron, Luis	**rf**/lf/cf/p/3b	46	69	36	9	.921	4
Page, Ted	**rf**/lf/cf	18	21	4	1	.962	0
Paige, Leroy	p	45	7	36	4	.915	3
Paige, William	2b	1	4	3	1	.875	0
Palomino, Emilio	**rf**/cf	23	23	3	1	.963	0
Pareda, Pastor	p	21	10	52	2	.969	3
Parego, George	**rf**/lf/1b/cf/p	16	25	12	5	.881	1
Parks, William	**rf**/1b/ss	19	55	6	7	.897	0
Parpetti, Agustin	1b	32	329	14	16	.955	17
Partlow, Roy	p	1	0	1	0	1.000	0
Patterson, Andrew	**2b**/3b	9	13	24	2	.949	2
Patterson, Gabe	cf	1	2	0	0	1.000	0
Patterson, John	**lf**/1b	10	30	4	1	.971	4
Payne, Andrew	**cf**/lf	12	19	1	0	1.000	0
Pearson, Lennie	**1b**/lf/rf	4	11	0	0	1.000	0
Pennington, Art	2b	1	3	5	0	1.000	2
Pedroso, Eustaquio	p	23	10	37	1	.979	1
Perez, Javier	ss	6	8	14	3	.880	1
Perez, Jose	c	1	9	1	0	1.000	0
Perez, Julian	**p**/rf	2	0	5	2	.714	0
Perkins, Bill	c	13	106	3	1	.991	1
Perry, Don	lf	1	1	0	0	1.000	0
Perry, 1936 NS	3b	1	1	0	0	1.000	0
Perry, Carl	2b	5	11	11	0	1.000	1
Peters, Frank	ss	1	0	0	1	.000	0
Pettus, William	**1b**/2b/c	35	289	26	7	.978	11
Petway, Bruce	**c**/1b	57	268/4	73	5	.986	4
Pierce, Herbert	c	2	5	0	0	1.000	0
Pierce, William	**1b**/c/ss	30	266	11	3	.989	18 [3]
Poles, Ed	ss	1	1	4	1	.833	1
Poles, Spottswood	**cf**/lf/rf	20	36	6	3	.933	1
Pope, Dave	cf	1	1	0	0	1.000	0
Pope, Willie	p	2	0	0	0	.000	0
Porter, Andy	p	11	2	10	0	1.000	1
Portuondo, Bartolo	3b	9	19	18	2	.949	2
Powell, Melvin	**cf**/p	3	0	5	0	1.000	0
Powell, Russell	c	4	25	3	3	.903	0

Player	POS	G	PO/C	A	E	FA	DP
Pryor, Anderson	2b	3	2/5	1	0	1.000	0
Pugh, Johnny	**3b**/cf	4	4	1	4	.556	0
Pullen, O'Neal	c	30	180	32	4	.981	0
Radcliff, Alex	3b	3	2	2	0	1.000	1
Radcliffe, Ted	**c**/p	16	18	4	0	1.000	1
Ramirez, Ramiro	cf	2	3	2	0	1.000	0
Randolph, Andrew	lf/1b	4	12	2	2	.875	0
Ransome, 1920 PS	1b/rf	2	2	0	0	1.000	1
Ray, Otto	**c**/rf	7	44	1	2	.957	0
Rector, Connie	p/cf/rf	5	3	9	1	.923	0
Redd, Gene	3b	1	1	1	0	1.000	0
Redding, Dick	p	9	1	21	0	1.000	0
Redus, Wilson	**rf**/lf	7	6	0	0	1.000	0
Reese, John	lf/rf	6	8	2	1	.909	0
Reid, 1945 PAS	cf	1	2	0	0	1.000	0
Reid, Ambrose	2b/lf	2	3	4	0	1.000	0
Renfroe, Othello	**c**/3b/2b/rf/lf	21	50	12	2	.969	2
Renoy, Moses	p	1	0	0	0	.000	0
Richardson, Gene	p	1	0	0	1	.000	0
Richardson, Talmadge	rf	1	1	0	0	1.000	0
Ridgley, Randolph	2b	3	6	13	2	.905	1
Riggins, Arvelle	**ss**/3b/2b	12	15/23	29	9	.882	5
Rile, Ed	p/1b	4	0/19	0	0	1.000	1
Roberts, Elihu	rf	2	5	2	0	1.000	0
Roberts, Harry	cf	1	1	0	0	1.000	0
Roberts, Roy	p	1	0	0	0	.000	0
Robinson, 1910 SLO	2b	3	6	12	3	.857	2
Robinson, Al	1b	2	22	1	0	1.000	0
Robinson, Jackie	**ss**/2b	4	8	12	2	.909	0
Robinson, James	cf/rf	2	3	0	0	1.000	0
Robinson, Neal	**lf**/**rf**/cf	5	4	0	0	1.000	0
Robinson, Norman	rf	1	0	0	0	.000	0
Rodriguez, Vicente	c	2	19	1	0	1.000	1
Rogan, Wilber	**p**/lf/cf/rf/3b	45	41	54	2	.979	2
Rogers, Nat	rf	2	4	0	0	1.000	0
Rojo, Julio	**c**	5	38	2	0	1.000	0
Rose, Haywood	**1b**/rf/c	4	21	0	0	1.000	0
Ross, Dick	p	1	0	0	0	.000	0
Rovira, Jaime	3b	2	1	0	1	0.500	0
Royer, Carlos	p	3	4	7	3	.786	0
Russell, Branch	**ss**/3b/rf	9	3	5	1	.889	1
Russell, Frank	2b	1	0	0	0	.000	0
Russell, John	2b	10	25	33	5	.921	6
Ryan, Merven	p	5	3	4	0	1.000	0
Sampson, Tommy	2b	7	18	20	3	.927	2
Sanchez, Gonzalo	c	4	17	5	1	.957	1
Santop, Louis	**c**/rf/lf	25	105	12	4	.967	0
Scales, George	**3b**/2b/1b/ss	12	18/3	23	2	.957	3
Scotland, Joe	cf	1	2	1	0	1.000	0

Player	POS	G	PO/C	A	E	FA	DP
Scott, 1938 OM	c	1	6	3	1	.900	0
Scott, Bob	**lf**/rf/1b	15	25	0	0	1.000	0
Scott, John	**cf**/lf/rf	6	9	0	2	.818	0
Seay, Dick	2b/3b	8	8	10	2	.900	1
Selden, William (I)	**lf**/p/cf/rf/c	19	19	30	10	.831	0
Selden, William (II)	ss	3	8	5	2	.867	0
Sergio, 1943 NAS	ss	1	0	3	1	.750	1
Serrell, William	2b	7	19	17	2	.947	6
Sharkey, 1924 CAS	lf/rf	2	2	0	1	.667	0
Shaw, George	p	1	0	3	0	1.000	0
Shively, George	**lf**/cf	10	21	1	3	.880	1
Shorrs, 1920 LAWS	c	1	4	2	0	1.000	0
Silverio, Patrocinio	c	1	3	1	4	.500	0
Simms, Willie	**lf**/cf/1b	11	18	2	0	1.000	2
Smith, 1910 SLO	p	1	0	2	1	.667	0
Smith, 1936 NS	rf	1	0	0	0	.000	0
Smith, Charlie "Chino"	rf	4	6	0	0	1.000	0
Smith, Charlie "Red"	lf	1	0	0	0	.000	0
Smith, Clarence	rf	4	3/3	0	0	1.000	0
Smith, Cleo	2b/3b	2	5	6	1	0.917	2
Smith, Gene	**cf**/rf/p	6	6	3	0	1.000	0
Smith, Harry	**cf**/1b	3	14	5	2	.905	0
Smith, Hilton	**p**/rf	10	4	9	1	.929	0
Smith, Jimmy	3b	1	1	0	0	1.000	0
Smith, John	rf	5	11	0	1	.917	0
Smith, Saki	**ss**/if	5	11	10	4	.840	1
Smith, Wyman	lf	1	0	0	0	.000	0
Snow, Felton	3b	18	16	20	6	.857	2
Souell, Herb	3b	13	16	17	4	.892	1
Spearman, Charles	**rf**/c/3b/lf/1b	24	64	12	3	.962	0
Stanley, John	p	4	0	3	0	1.000	1
Starks, James	rf	1	0	0	0	.000	0
Starks, Leslie	1b/rf	4	22	1	1	.958	2
Starks, Otis	p	4	1	2	1	.750	0
Stearnes, Norman	**lf**/cf	25	37/6	2	2	.957	1
Steele, Ed	rf	13	27	0	2	.931	0
Stephens, Jake	**ss**/2b	14	27	48	1	.987	5
Stevens, Frank	p/1b	2	10	2	1	.923	0
Stevenson, Willie	rf	1	1	0	0	1.000	0
Stockard, Ted	2b	1	1	4	0	1.000	0
Stone, Ed	**lf**/rf/3b	8	12	2	2	.875	0
Stout, 1936 NS	rf	1	0	0	0	.000	0
Stovey, George	**p**/rf/c	5	2	17	9	.679	0
Streeter, Sam	p	5	4	4	0	1.000	0
Strong, Joe	p	2	0	2	0	1.000	0
Strong, Ted	**1b**/rf	7	39	0	0	1.000	1
Strothers, Sam	**1b**/c/cf	4	20	0	2	.909	0
Swinton, Norman	**lf**/cf/1b	4	4	1	1	.833	0
Summers, Lonnie	rf	2	1	1	0	1.000	0

Player	POS	G	PO/C	A	E	FA	DP
Summers, Smith	lf	3	4	1	0	1.000	0
Suttles, George	**1b**/rf/lf/2b/3b/cf	36	123/16	12	3	.981	4
Sykes, Frank	p	2	0	4	0	1.000	0
Taborn, Earl	c	1	6	1	1	.875	0
Talbert, Danger	3b	6	12	9	0	1.000	0
Tatum, Reese	1b	5	39	0	3	.929	4
Taylor, 1900 CCG	cf	2	2	0	0	1.000	0
Taylor, Ben	**1b**/p	20	187	17	5	.976	5
Taylor, Charles	2b	2	0	0	0	.000	0
Taylor, George	1b	2	18	1	2	.905	0
Taylor, Jim	**3b**/2b	33	44	58	7	.936	1
Taylor, John "Steel Arm"	**p**/2b	3	3	5	0	1.000	1
Taylor, John "Big"	**p**/rf	4	1	6	0	1.000	0
Taylor, Johnny	p	1	0	1	0	1.000	0
Taylor, Leroy	**rf**/lf/cf	6	5	0	0	1.000	0
Teran, Recurvan	**3b**/1b/2b	4	7	8	2	.882	0
Terrill, George	**ss**/2b	3	5	10	5	.750	2
Thomas, PS 1920	ss/cf	2	5	5	1	.909	1
Thomas, Arthur	**c**/rf/1b/lf	30	187	31	36	.858	4
Thomas, Clint	**lf/cf**/c	15	29	1	0	1.000	0
Thomas, Dave	1b	20	131	7	5	.965	12
Thomas, Ewell	2b	3	4	5	0	1.000	0
Thomas, Jules	**cf**/lf/1b	19	46	3	3	.942	1
Thompson, Hank	**2b**/rf/lf	12	24	17	6	.872	9
Thompson, Sam	p	2	0	0	0	.000	0
Thompson, "Speedboy"	p	2	0	0	0	.000	0
Torriente, Cristobal	**cf**/rf/lf/p	26	40/1	8	5	.907	0
Treadwell, Harold	p	2	0	3	0	1.000	0
Trent, Ted	p	7	1	9	0	1.000	2
Trimble, 1945 PAS	2b	1	5	3	1	.889	0
Trouppe, Quincy	**c**/rf/lf/c	16	84	6	1	.989	0
Trusty, Shep	**p**/lf/rf	9	5	29	7	.829	0
Trusty, Job	3b	1	1	1	2	.500	0
Turner, Elbert	3b	1	0/4	0	0	1.000	0
Valdes, Rogelio	**lf**/2b/3b/ss	39	81	15	13	.881	6
Valdes, Simon	2b/cf	1	0	2	5	.286	0
Van Dyke, Fred	p	1	0	1	0	1.000	0
Vargas, Tetelo	ss	1	4	0	1	.800	0
Villa, Manuel	**rf**/2b/lf/cf	17	17	10	5	.844	2
Wade, 1942 PRG/1943 NAS	cf	3	8	0	1	.889	0
Walker, 1936 NS	2b	1	0	2	3	.400	0
Walker, Jess	**ss**/2b/3b	14	23	25	3	.941	3
Wallace, Dick	**3b**/ss/2b/1b	14	38	22	7	.896	1
Ward, Henry	1b	1	11	1	0	1.000	2
Ward, Tom	**lf**/cf/rf	10	14	0	2	.875	0
Ware, Archie	1b	6	55	4	1	.983	1
Warfield, Frank	**2b**/ss/3b	38	84	114	9	.957	9
Warren, 1916 WRK	cf	1	1	1	0	1.000	0
Washington, Jasper	1b	16	154	5	2	.988	12 [1]

Player	POS	G	PO/C	A	E	FA	DP
Washington, Kenny	**lf**/2b/1b	5	2	4	2	.750	0
Washington, Namon	lf/rf	2	2	1	0	1.000	0
Washington, Pete	cf	18	37	0	0	1.000	0
Watkins, Murray	3b	4	2	2	1	.800	1
Watson, Johnie	lf	1	0/4	0	1	.800	0
Watts, Eddie	2b/ss	3	4	6	1	.909	1
Watts, Jack	c	1	8	0	0	1.000	0
Webster, Pearl	1b/lf/rf	3	8	0	1	.889	0
Webster, William	c	1	4	1	0	1.000	0
Wells, Willie	**ss**/2b	38	58/21	67	11	.930	5
Wesley, Edgar	1b	6	47/11	2	4	.938	2
West, Jim	1b	11	83	1	1	.988	3
Whatley, Dave	rf	1	1	0	0	1.000	0
White, Chaney	**lf**/cf/rf	13	17	2	1	.950	0
White, Sol	**ss**/2b/1b	8	23	33	2	.966	0
Whitworth, Dick	p	6	2	19	0	1.000	1
Whyte, Bill	**p**/lf/rf	18	14	68	3	.965	2 [1]
Wickware, Frank	**p**/rf	13	1	27	3	.903	1
Wiley, Wabishaw	**c**/rf	15	142	12	3	.981	1
Williams, Andrew	p	10	2	19	1	.955	0
Williams, Bobby	**ss**/3b	10	8/13	18	11	.780	3
Williams, Charles	p	3	2	4	0	1.000	1
Williams, Charlie	2b	5	5/12	3	0	1.000	1
Williams, Chester	**ss**/2b	14	28	42	2	.972	3
Williams, Clarence	c/rf/cf/1b/lf	37	113	33	19	.885	3
Williams, George	**2b**/c/1b/3b	29	92	65	30	.840	8
Williams, Gerard	ss	3	7	11	2	.900	1
Williams, Hank	3b	1	3	0	0	1.000	1
Williams, Harry	3b	2	1	4	0	1.000	0
Williams, Jesse	**ss**/2b/3b	24	63	59	9	.931	12
Williams, Joe	p	31	12	65	3	.963	4
Williams, John	p	8	1	6	1	.875	1
Williams, Marvin	2b	1	0	0	0	.000	0
Williams, Nat	3b	1	1	3	1	.800	0
Williams, Roy	p	2	1	7	0	1.000	0
Williams, Tom	p	4	0	4	1	.800	0
Willis, Jim	**rf**/p	3	5	0	0	1.000	0
Wilson, Artie	ss	14	27	43	3	.959	12
Wilson, Ed	**rf**/p/1b	4	2	1	2	.600	0
Wilson, Jud	**3b**/1b/2b/lf/cf/rf/c	28	58	32	3	.968	2
Wilson, Ray	1b	5	51	1	0	1.000	4 [1]
Winters, James	**p**/1b	6	8	9	1	.944	1
Winston, Bobby	lf	18	25	4	2	.935	1
Woods, Parnell	3b	1	0	0	0	.000	0
Woods, William	cf	3	6	0	0	1.000	0
Wright, Bill	**cf**/rf/lf	27	49	2	7	.879	0
Wright, George	**ss**/2b	28	39	68	18	.856	10
Wright, Jack	p/1b	1	3	1	0	1.000	0
Wright, Zollie	**ss**/lf	4	6	10	0	1.000	2

Player	POS	G	PO/C	A	E	FA	DP
Wyatt, Ralph	ss	1	1	6	1	.875	3
Yancey, Bill	ss/3b	7	10	20	1	.968	1
Yokely, Laymon	p	13	2	39	4	.911	0
Young, Berdell	rf	1	0	2	0	1.000	0
Young, Bob	lf	1	2	1	0	1.000	0
Young, Ed	1b	1	9	0	1	.900	3
Young, John	p	1	0	1	0	1.000	0
Young, "Slowtime"	p	1	0	0	0	.000	0
Young, Tom	c	17	154	16	2	.988	0
Zomphier, Charles	2b	2	2	2	2	.667	0

Notes

1. Bell's totals include 3 strikeouts from an undetermined part of 16ip.
2. Bowman's totals included 5 walks and 4 strikeouts from an undetermined part of 10ip.
3. Brady's totals are from an undetermined part of 5ip.
4. Branham's totals include 3 walks and 3 strikeouts from an undetermined part of 9ip; his hit totals are based on 18ip.
5. Brewer's hit and run totals are based on 68.7ip; his walk/strikeout totals are based on 65.3ip.
6. Britt's walk and strikeout totals are based on 69.3ip.
7. Cockrell's hit totals are based on 82.7ip; his walk totals are based on 71.7ip; and his run totals are incomplete.
8. Andy Cooper's totals include 2 walks and 1 strikeout from an undetermined part of 9ip; his hit; run; walk; and strikeout totals are based on 49.7ip.
9. Darltie Cooper's run totals are incomplete.
10. Crawford's walk and strikeout totals are based on 18ip.
11. Curry's walk and strikeout totals are based on 53.3ip.
12. Davis' totals include 1 walk and 2 strikeouts from an undetermined part of 9ip; his walk and strikeout totals are based on 15.7ip.
13. Drake's strikeout totals are based on 26.3ip.
14. Fields' totals are from an undetermined part of 9ip.
15. Finner's strikeout totals are based on 12.3ip.
16. Gisentaner's totals are from an undetermined part of 9ip.
17. Harney's totals include 7 strikeouts from an undetermined part of 9ip.
18. Hensley's walk and strikeout totals are based on 2ip.
19. Holsey's totals are from an undetermined part of 9ip.
20. Hubbard's walk totals are based on 51ip.
21. Kincannon's totals include 6 walks and 6 strikeouts from an undetermined part of 9ip.
22. Lankford's walk and strikeout totals are based on 8ip.
23. Lee's totals include 5 runs, 5 walks, and 3 strikeouts from an undetermined part of 8ip; his hit and strikeout totals are based on 38ip.
24. Matchett's hit totals are incomplete.
25. McClellan's totals include 1 walk and 2 strikeouts from an undetermined part of 10ip.
26. McDonald's totals include 2 walks and 9 strikeouts from an undetermined part of 18ip; his hit totals are based on 78.3ip; and his strikeout totals are based on 69.3ip.
27. McDuffie's hit totals are based on 28.7ip.
28. Newberry's run totals are based on 19ip; his hit totals are based on 14ip.
29. Owens' totals include 2 walks and 1 strikeout from an undetermined part of 9ip.
30. Pope's totals include 2 walks and 1 strikeout from an undetermined part of 9ip.
31. Radcliffe's totals include 5 walks and 1 strikeout from an undetermined part of 9ip.
32. Rector's walk totals are based on 17ip.
33. Redding's strikeout totals are based on 69ip and his walk totals are based on 60ip.
34. Rile's totals include 2 walks from an undetermined part of 9ip.
35. Ryan's walk totals are based on 13.3ip.
36. Selden's totals include 6 walks and 3 strikeouts from an undetermined part of 8ip.
37. Hilton Smith's walk and strikeout totals are based on 39ip.
38. Stanley's totals include 2 walks and 3 strikeouts from an undetermined part of 9ip.
39. Starks' walk totals are based on 22.3ip.

40. Stevens' totals are from an undetermined part of 5ip.
41. Stovey's totals include 6 walks and 2 strikeouts from an undetermined part of 8ip.
42. Streeter's totals include 5 walks and 5 strikeouts from an undetermined part of 19ip.
43. Sykes' hit totals are based on 9ip.
44. "Steel Arm" John Taylor's totals include 2 strikeouts from an undetermined part of 9ip.
45. Sam Thompson's totals include 1 walk and 4 strikeouts from an undetermined part of 9ip.
46. Treadwell's totals include 1 run, 2 walks, and 1strikeout from an undetermined part of 8ip.
47. Trusty's walk totals are based on 53ip.
48. Wickware's hit totals are based on 79.3ip.
49. Andrew Williams' hit totals are based on 62.3ip.
50. Charles Williams' totals include 1 walk and 2 strikeouts from an undetermined part of 9ip.
51. Joe Williams' totals include 3 strikeouts from an undetermined part of 9ip; his hit totals are based on 234.7ip.
52. Wilson's totals are from an undetermined part of 10ip.
53. Winters' hit totals are based on 34.7ip; his walk totals are based on 25.7ip.
54. Yokely's run totals are based on 90.3ip and are incomplete.

Appendix IV

Batting and Pitching Statistics of Negro Leaguers in MLB and Triple A

Note: The players are designated by their given names. Only those Negro Leaguers who entered Organized Baseball by 1960 are listed. While the Negro Leagues statistics that have been included are indicative of the players' abilities, a variety of factors should be considered when comparing them to the Organized Baseball numbers. First, many of the Negro Leaguers who reached Triple A or the Majors were past their prime by the time they did so. Over one-third (45 of 129, or 35 percent) of these players did not attain those advanced levels before their 30th birthday. Twenty-five of them were age 33 or older. On average, these players made their NLB debuts at age 21. In AAA, the mean starting age was 28, although it was a year younger than that for MLB. Secondly, the Negro Leagues were in decline by the mid–1940s, when the majority of these players matriculated through the circuits due to a loss of manpower to Latin America; the United States Military; and eventually, Organized Baseball. Lastly, and most significantly, the Negro Leaguers' performances in Organized Baseball occurred in integrated leagues that were by definition, superior to the all-white and black outfits that preceded them. The age the players debuted at in each classification (if known) follows the particular league designation.

Sources: The MLB and Triple A statistics have been derived from Baseball-Reference. com. The Negro Leagues data was assembled from a variety of sources including Baseball-Reference.com; the Seamheads.com Negro Leagues Database; the *Center for Negro League Baseball Research;* Dick Clark and Larry Lester's *Negro Leagues Book;* John Holway's *Black Diamonds* and *Black Giants;* Lawrence Hogan and Jules Tygiel's *Shades of Glory;* and Scott Simkus' *Outsider Baseball Bulletin.* The statistics for the nine Cuban-born Negro Leaguers (denoted by a *) who also played in Organized Baseball are derived from Baseball-Reference and Seamheads.

Batting Statistics

Note on Batting Statistics: Because Negro Leagues data on bases on balls, runs batted in, and stolen bases was often under-reported, some of the totals are understated in these categories. A small percentage of NLB games played have been estimated as well. G=Games; AB=At Bats; R=Runs; H=Hits; D=Doubles; T=Triples; HR=Home Runs; RBI=Runs Batted In; BB=Bases on Balls; SB=Stolen Bases; HBP=Hit by Pitch; BA=Batting Average; NLB=Negro Leagues Baseball; AAA=Triple A Baseball; MLB=Major League Baseball; DNP=Did Not Play; NA=Statistics Not Available.

Player/League	G	AB	R	H	D	T	HR	RBI	BB	SB	HBP	BA
Aaron, Hank												
NLB/18	26	112	29	41	7	1	5	39	—	9	—	.366
AAA	DNP											
MLB/20	3298	12364	2174	3771	624	98	755	2297	1695	240	32	.305
Acosta, Jose*												
NLB/24	12	27	0	2	0	0	0	0	1	0	1	.074
AAA/26	80	172	9	22	3	4	0	0	0	2	0	.128
MLB/29	55	60	4	9	1	0	0	1	11	1	0	.150
Almeida, Rafael*												
NLB/19	38	143	22	39	3	6	0	12	7	2	0	.273
AAA/31	30	116	22	26	6	1	0	0	19	3	0	.224
MLB/25	102	285	32	77	13	6	3	46	25	7	3	.270
Alston, Tom												
NLB/17	NA											
AAA/21	576	2093	329	602	96	24	59	308	189	23	20	.288
MLB/23	91	271	30	66	15	2	4	36	25	3	2	.244
Altman, George												
NLB/22	3	8	3	1	1	0	0	0	0	0	0	.375
AAA/34	108	378	65	106	17	6	15	70	50	16	3	.280
MLB/26	991	3091	409	832	132	34	101	403	306	52	20	.269
Amoros, Sandy												
NLB/20	34	136	28	46	8	6	4	17	22	4	0	.338
AAA/22	765	2681	550	827	166	39	108	427	491	76	32	.308
MLB/22	517	1311	215	334	55	23	43	180	227	18	11	.255
Atkins, Joseph												
NLB/24	77	287	61	88	4	6	13	26	12	0	1	.307
AAA/32	8	13	1	2	1	0	1	3	0	0	0	.154
Austin, Frank												
NLB/22	256	1058	197	350	56	15	3	136	96	26	2	.331
AAA/27	1296	4607	520	1236	186	14	30	391	348	43	11	.268
Baker, Gene												
NLB/22	157	617	103	161	34	15	9	52	30	22	1	.261
AAA/24	629	2393	350	647	96	23	48	252	234	53	7	.270
MLB/28	630	2230	265	590	109	21	39	227	193	21	9	.265
Bankhead, Dan												
NLB/20	33	72	9	16	1	1	0	9	6	1	0	.222
AAA/28	90	176	30	59	7	3	2	30	11	0	2	.335
MLB/27	62	45	7	10	1	0	1	3	1	0	2	.222
Banks, Ernie												
NLB/19	99	369	53	110	27	3	8	67	5	10	2	.298
AAA	DNP											
MLB/22	2528	9421	1305	2583	407	90	512	1636	961	53	70	.274
Barnes, Frank												
NLB/20	39	87	10	17	5	0	0	6	2	1	1	.195
AAA/22	261	374	33	66	6	0	1	16	25	1	0	.176
MLB/29	21	10	3	1	0	0	0	0	0	0	0	.100
Barnhill, Dave												
NLB/23	109	255	35	66	5	3	0	24	25	1	1	.259
AAA/34	104	154	17	33	6	0	3	28	12	1	2	.214

Player/League	G	AB	R	H	D	T	HR	RBI	BB	SB	HBP	BA
Bernard, Pablo												
NLB/22	61	169	16	39	3	4	1	10	0	2	0	.231
AAA/29	225	757	73	191	32	5	5	56	40	0	1	.252
Black, Joe												
NLB/19	117	254	22	51	9	1	0	18	6	0	2	.201
AAA/27	78	129	8	26	4	0	3	17	8	0	1	.202
MLB/28	175	96	5	13	0	0	0	9	1	0	0	.135
Bond, Walt												
NLB/18	35	130	21	40	—	—	—	—	—	—	—	.308
AAA/22	550	1862	298	556	84	79	76	318	165	16	22	.299
MLB/22	365	1199	149	307	40	11	41	179	125	10	17	.256
Boyd, Bob												
NLB/20	293	1145	219	413	70	21	24	169	48	25	7	.361
AAA/25	579	2113	307	672	103	52	20	238	145	88	6	.318
MLB/25	693	1936	253	567	81	23	19	175	175	9	7	.293
Brantley, Ollie												
NLB/18	NA											
AAA/28	3	0	0	0	0	0	0	0	0	0	0	—
Bridges, Marshall												
NLB/19	33	91	23	28	5	1	2	20	12	11	2	.308
AAA/25	204	271	24	54	7	2	4	25	10	1	0	.199
MLB/28	206	59	6	7	1	1	1	6	3	0	1	.119
Brown, Willard												
NLB/20	604	2262	457	819	126	54	100	503	121	105	2	.362
AAA	DNP											
MLB/32	21	67	4	12	3	0	1	6	0	2	0	.179
Cabrera, Alfredo*												
NLB/24	28	98	9	24	6	2	0	12	9	5	2	.245
AAA	DNP											
MLB/32	1	2	0	0	0	0	0	0	0	0	0	.000
Cabrera, Lorenzo												
NLB/27	124	491	107	173	33	10	6	82	27	13	4	.352
AAA/31	51	145	13	32	6	3	0	12	5	0	0	.221
Caffie, Joe												
NLB/19	18	69	4	14	2	1	0	1	0	1	0	.203
AAA/22	789	2782	400	791	141	26	51	254	271	88	16	.284
MLB/25	44	127	21	37	2	1	3	11	10	3	2	.291
Calvo, Jacinto*												
NLB/21	22	85	10	23	3	0	0	5	6	7	0	.271
AAA/23	148	498	59	131	18	6	1	0	0	36	0	.263
MLB/19	34	56	10	9	1	1	4	0	3	0	0	.161
Campanella, Roy												
NLB/15	231	795	154	262	50	14	19	170	78	15	0	.330
AAA/25	170	563	95	160	30	5	26	114	89	7	3	.284
MLB/26	1215	4205	627	1161	178	18	242	856	563	25	30	.276
Clarke, Vibert												
NLB/17	118	270	45	85	7	5	1	24	12	10	1	.315
AAA/28	51	81	4	17	2	0	0	3	2	0	0	.210
MLB/27	7	6	0	1	0	0	0	3	0	0	0	.167

Player/League	G	AB	R	H	D	T	HR	RBI	BB	SB	HBP	BA
Clarkson, Buster												
NLB/24	252	895	181	281	58	13	35	204	86	26	2	.314
AAA/37	338	1057	177	332	46	7	37	196	163	17	13	.314
MLB/39	14	25	3	5	0	0	0	1	3	0	0	.200
Coleman, Clarence												
NLB/21	NA											
AAA/24	529	1568	224	403	52	14	50	209	145	48	20	.257
MLB/25	201	462	51	91	8	2	9	30	42	7	7	.197
Coleman, Elliott												
NLB/17	20	33	5	0	0	0	0	3	3	0	0	.000
AAA/23	27	17	3	1	0	0	0	0	0	0	0	.059
Crowe, George												
NLB/26	62	202	33	65	8	4	5	30	14	1	0	.322
AAA/30	407	1384	232	453	93	11	67	295	182	10	6	.327
MLB/31	702	1727	215	467	70	12	81	299	178	3	10	.270
Curry, Lacey												
NLB/20	NA											
AAA/27	588	2163	293	579	99	23	17	183	187	51	5	.268
Dandridge, Ray												
NLB/19	274	1027	164	349	61	22	6	144	52	25	1	.340
AAA/36	588	2320	343	724	107	9	35	286	135	10	0	.312
Davis, Johnny												
NLB/23	412	1454	245	416	72	21	55	258	117	17	2	.286
AAA/35	61	167	26	44	9	1	6	36	24	1	4	.263
Davis, Lorenzo												
NLB/25	496	1970	371	569	89	35	28	273	88	32	6	.289
AAA/33	664	2524	304	714	136	21	49	332	114	19	14	.283
Davis, Robert												
NLB/28	160	595	112	211	17	12	3	53	15	28	4	.355
AAA/36	77	257	28	82	13	3	4	35	12	1	2	.319
Day, Leon												
NLB/17	289	862	141	255	47	14	8	124	46	9	1	.296
AAA/34	20	27	5	7	1	0	0	1	2	0	1	.259
Dees, Charlie												
NLB/19	NA											
AAA/25	246	797	114	228	50	2	14	100	82	18	17	.286
MLB/28	98	260	27	69	12	1	3	29	15	5	9	.265
Dibut, Pedro*												
NLB/30	18	46	3	11	0	1	0	6	3	0	1	.239
AAA	DNP											
MLB/31	8	11	2	3	0	1	0	3	2	0	0	.273
Doby, Larry												
NLB/17	158	605	122	215	42	18	27	129	81	19	1	.355
AAA/34	9	27	2	6	0	1	0	3	0	0	0	.222
MLB/22	1533	5348	960	1515	243	52	253	970	890	47	38	.283
Donoso, Lino												
NLB/24	48	100	13	30	3	1	1	17	5	0	0	.300
AAA/31	88	111	7	25	2	1	1	10	1	0	0	.225
MLB/32	28	27	2	5	0	0	0	1	0	0	0	.185

Player/League	G	AB	R	H	D	T	HR	RBI	BB	SB	HBP	BA
Durham, Joe												
NLB/21	50	183	44	57	—	—	7	31	—	9	—	.311
AAA/26	827	2699	368	735	130	40	77	388	238	18	16	.272
MLB/25	93	202	25	38	2	0	5	20	21	1	0	.188
Easter, Luke												
NLB/22	117	434	53	146	33	14	23	42	20	3	3	.336
AAA/24	1327	4150	677	1227	224	17	269	919	738	6	44	.296
MLB/25	491	1725	256	472	54	12	93	340	174	1	28	.274
Estrada, Oscar*												
NLB/22	33	112	17	24	1	0	1	12	10	0	0	.214
AAA/30	1	0	0	0	0	0	0	0	0	0	0	—
MLB/25	1	0	0	0	0	0	0	0	0	0	0	—
Fields, Wilmer												
NLB/18	101	265	30	76	7	5	2	37	6	1	1	.287
AAA/30	51	165	24	48	10	1	2	13	15	2	1	.291
Formenthal, Pedro												
NLB/34	114	389	79	127	20	11	14	79	28	14	0	.326
AAA/39	204	624	83	183	22	7	21	96	118	5	11	.293
Gilliam, Jim												
NLB/17	287	1038	219	292	52	27	7	146	90	45	4	.281
AAA/22	303	1126	228	331	61	18	16	185	217	33	8	.294
MLB/24	1956	7119	1163	1889	304	71	65	558	1066	203	33	.265
Gladstone, Granville												
NLB/25	64	192	40	46	6	13	4	23	33	9	3	.239
AAA/26	505	1486	214	367	65	12	34	200	97	13	7	.247
Gonzalez, Rene												
NLB/26	32	129	22	39	8	1	4	21	13	3	0	.302
AAA/33	91	173	14	45	6	0	0	20	19	1	0	.260
Greason, Will												
NLB/23	69	142	19	24	6	4	1	19	11	0	0	.169
AAA/29	156	209	17	34	7	4	6	27	25	0	0	.163
MLB/29	3	1	0	0	0	0	0	0	0	0	0	.000
Hairston, Sam												
NLB/24	438	1561	270	508	79	21	24	205	119	20	4	.325
AAA/31	313	966	91	254	49	15	2	119	89	8	22	.263
MLB/31	4	5	2	2	1	0	0	1	0	0	0	.400
Harmon, Chuck												
NLB/23	NA											
AAA/32	413	1463	210	431	63	27	25	205	70	28	7	.295
MLB/30	289	592	90	141	15	8	7	59	46	25	5	.238
Harrell, Billy												
NLB/22	NA											
AAA/25	1319	4768	689	1321	215	63	105	573	411	79	14	.277
MLB/26	173	342	54	79	7	1	8	26	25	17	2	.231
Hartman, J.C.												
NLB/21	8	20	4	8	0	0	0	3	1	2	0	.400
AAA/27	548	1990	240	557	60	14	14	179	105	34	15	.280
MLB/28	90	238	13	44	6	0	0	8	7	2	2	.185

Player/League	G	AB	R	H	D	T	HR	RBI	BB	SB	HBP	BA
Heard, Jay												
NLB/26	105	205	28	61	2	0	0	5	0	0	0	.298
AAA/32	141	165	24	29	3	0	0	10	12	0	1	.176
MLB/34	2	0	0	0	0	0	0	0	0	0	0	—
Herrera, Juan												
NLB/18	137	509	97	154	26	10	19	91	15	11	6	.302
AAA/21	1137	3933	590	1140	168	25	187	660	508	52	52	.290
MLB/23	300	975	122	264	46	8	31	128	123	8	10	.271
Herrera, Paito*												
NLB/22	190	759	119	200	30	7	1	67	54	21	8	.264
AAA	DNP											
MLB/27	84	276	22	76	14	1	0	27	17	1	1	.275
Herrera, Roberto												
NLB/16	NA											
AAA/21	234	668	69	167	21	7	14	78	73	3	13	.250
Hoskins, Dave												
NLB/17	145	522	82	152	22	9	6	76	15	19	0	.291
AAA/28	253	381	48	96	14	5	5	54	24	1	0	.252
MLB/27	53	66	12	15	2	0	1	9	4	0	1	.227
Howard, Elston												
NLB/19	158	594	99	171	42	11	9	107	16	4	2	.288
AAA/24	277	994	136	306	43	25	32	179	64	5	11	.308
MLB/26	1605	5363	619	1471	218	50	167	762	455	9	26	.274
Irvin, Monte												
NLB/18	309	1122	241	383	68	17	44	258	119	43	1	.341
AAA/30	160	515	141	193	43	7	34	139	135	18	8	.375
MLB/30	764	2449	366	731	97	31	99	443	356	28	23	.298
Jethroe, Sam												
NLB/16	371	1470	368	495	95	32	25	123	75	152	9	.337
AAA/26	1020	3750	752	1108	189	62	119	457	518	232	57	.295
MLB/28	442	1763	280	460	80	25	49	181	177	98	25	.261
Johnson, Connie												
NLB/17	66	139	23	31	4	2	0	12	6	1	0	.223
AAA/30	124	186	18	38	3	0	0	18	6	0	1	.204
MLB/30	126	237	20	40	4	0	0	17	10	2	0	.169
Johnson, Lou												
NLB/20	2	5	1	0	0	0	0	0	0	0	0	.200
AAA/25	642	2429	400	730	118	49	70	317	157	82	49	.301
MLB/25	677	2049	244	529	97	14	48	232	133	50	53	.258
Jones, Hal												
NLB/20	22	75	12	17	—	—	—	1	—	—	—	.227
AAA/25	409	1451	243	380	78	14	68	269	171	3	19	.262
MLB/25	17	51	4	11	1	0	2	5	2	0	1	.216
Jones, Sam												
NLB/20	25	54	7	15	1	0	0	9	3	0	0	.278
AAA/25	356	295	16	46	5	0	2	22	9	0	0	.156
MLB/25	322	522	16	78	7	0	1	27	17	0	1	.149
Kennedy, John												
NLB/22	107	405	91	118	13	5	6	38	30	16	2	.291

Player/League	G	AB	R	H	D	T	HR	RBI	BB	SB	HBP	BA
AAA	DNP											
MLB/30	5	2	1	0	0	0	0	0	0	0	0	.000
Locke, Edward												
NLB/19	46	99	7	23	4	0	0	3	4	0	0	.232
AAA/43	NA											
Lopez, Raul												
NLB/19	26	46	9	5	0	0	0	3	5	0	0	.109
AAA/22	47	40	3	4	0	0	0	2	10	0	0	.100
Maroto, Enrique												
NLB/17	37	92	11	19	2	1	2	18	4	1	1	.206
AAA/25	2	0	0	0	0	0	0	0	0	0	0	—
Marsans, Armando*												
NLB/19	24	82	7	20	1	2	0	5	4	7	0	.244
AAA	DNP											
MLB/23	655	2273	267	612	67	19	2	221	173	171	16	.269
Marquez, Luis												
NLB/19	144	551	115	194	30	4	11	58	44	48	7	.352
AAA/23	1536	5640	928	1724	312	72	134	767	474	199	0	.306
MLB/25	99	143	24	26	5	1	0	11	16	7	3	.182
Mason, Hank												
NLB/20	15	35	3	5	2	0	0	2	1	0	0	.143
AAA/24	189	121	11	22	1	0	1	7	10	0	3	.182
MLB/27	4	3	0	0	0	0	0	0	0	0	0	.000
Mays, Willie												
NLB/17	132	479	100	147	27	6	10	75	17	14	0	.307
AAA/20	35	149	38	71	18	3	8	30	14	5	1	.477
MLB/20	2992	10881	2062	3283	523	140	660	1903	1656	338	44	.302
McCord, Clint												
NLB/21	119	388	59	114	14	5	3	43	17	11	3	.294
AAA/29	443	1560	186	416	71	22	20	165	138	7	12	.267
McCoy, Walter												
NLB/22	33	75	4	5	2	0	0	1	0	5	0	.067
AAA/27	5	8	0	0	0	0	0	0	1	0	0	.000
McDaniels, Booker												
NLB/26	88	213	23	48	10	1	1	20	14	4	0	.225
AAA/35	55	62	6	14	0	0	1	7	0	0	1	.226
McNeal, Clyde												
NLB/16	282	984	147	242	51	17	15	110	51	39	4	.246
AAA/25	4	8	0	1	0	0	0	0	0	0	0	.125
Miller, Henry												
NLB/20	127	239	26	46	3	0	1	15	12	2	0	.192
AAA/34	6	1	0	0	0	0	0	0	0	0	0	.000
Minoso, Orestes												
NLB/22	121	511	101	150	31	17	9	67	39	13	3	.294
AAA/26	358	1309	251	408	70	17	46	216	121	49	0	.312
MLB/26	1835	6579	1136	1963	336	83	186	1023	814	205	192	.298
Neal, Charlie												
NLB/18	NA											
AAA/23	231	1143	212	312	54	27	34	141	104	33	15	.273

Player/League	G	AB	R	H	D	T	HR	RBI	BB	SB	HBP	BA
MLB/25	970	3316	461	858	113	38	87	391	356	48	20	.259
Newcombe, Don												
NLB/17	30	64	8	14	1	0	0	6	1	2	0	.219
AAA/21	88	139	11	34	5	0	2	19	18	0	1	.245
MLB/22	452	878	94	238	33	3	15	108	88	2	3	.271
Noble, Ray												
NLB/26	116	333	49	91	18	5	5	42	22	6	4	.273
AAA/30	1170	3593	480	986	160	13	130	585	556	10	38	.274
MLB/32	107	243	31	53	6	1	9	40	25	1	3	.218
Osorio, Fernando												
NLB/19	22	35	4	6	1	1	0	2	0	0	0	.171
AAA/23	20	5	0	0	0	0	0	0	0	0	0	.000
Paige, Leroy												
NLB/20	244	576	53	132	11	8	1	36	11	7	0	.229
AAA/52	110	109	2	11	2	0	0	9	3	0	0	.101
MLB/42	179	124	2	12	0	0	0	4	3	0	0	.097
Parris, Jonathan												
NLB/19	76	290	35	68	10	2	2	27	11	15	2	.234
AAA/28	679	2442	346	724	134	10	76	385	235	27	11	.296
Partlow, Roy												
NLB/25	161	395	51	101	10	5	3	35	15	0	0	.256
AAA/35	10	13	3	2	0	0	0	2	1	0	0	.154
Paula, Carlos												
NLB/22	NA											
AAA/28	412	1315	189	401	63	17	43	218	114	12	7	.305
MLB/26	157	457	44	124	23	8	9	60	30	2	2	.271
Pearson, Len												
NLB/19	664	2488	453	770	135	42	75	439	150	73	0	.309
AAA/32	68	232	29	69	10	2	4	24	13	0	0	.297
Peeples, Nat												
NLB/23	102	337	79	109	23	3	3	57	16	47	1	.323
AAA/33	12	20	5	7	1	0	2	7	3	0	0	.350
Peete, Charlie												
NLB/21	31	84	11	18	2	2	2	8	6	1	2	.214
AAA/26	246	801	149	265	52	11	26	136	99	11	9	.331
MLB/27	23	52	3	10	2	2	0	6	6	0	1	.192
Pendleton, James												
NLB/24	75	302	52	91	11	9	6	47	25	4	0	.301
AAA/25	1138	4292	691	1265	191	85	112	633	354	102	19	.295
MLB/29	117	941	120	240	30	8	19	97	48	11	6	.255
Pennington, Art												
NLB/17	282	984	190	311	48	20	24	157	98	49	2	.316
AAA/26	20	53	7	11	1	0	0	2	18	1	1	.208
Perry, Alonso												
NLB/23	187	572	117	177	27	8	21	109	27	20	3	.309
AAA/26	21	33	0	8	0	0	0	7	3	0	0	.242
Pope, Dave												
NLB/21	9	38	10	10	0	3	2	6	1	0	0	.263
AAA/27	945	3450	537	1041	197	51	129	558	343	44	14	.302

Player/League	G	AB	R	H	D	T	HR	RBI	BB	SB	HBP	BA
MLB/27	230	551	75	146	19	7	12	73	43	7	4	.265
Pope, Willie												
NLB/28	20	54	4	11	2	1	0	4	1	0	0	.204
AAA/36	31	40	1	6	1	0	0	0	0	0	0	.150
Powell, William												
NLB/27	94	205	28	45	7	3	1	24	14	0	1	.220
AAA/32	152	249	23	44	6	1	0	19	22	0	0	.177
Prescott, Bob												
NLB/20	NA											
AAA/24	831	2640	406	749	135	27	119	491	379	19	21	.284
MLB/30	10	12	0	1	0	0	0	0	2	0	0	.083
Proctor, Jim												
NLB/19	NA											
AAA/21	77	58	5	14	0	2	0	5	2	0	0	.241
MLB/23	2	0	0	0	0	0	0	0	0	0	0	—
Raines, Larry												
NLB/21	61	235	54	70	—	—	4	22	—	11	—	.298
AAA/25	683	2547	375	717	115	38	32	248	104	122	15	.282
MLB/27	103	253	40	64	14	0	2	16	20	5	1	.253
Ritchey, John												
NLB/24	58	176	42	67	2	1	0	8	4	3	1	.381
AAA/25	694	1900	234	535	67	18	20	232	297	40	10	.282
Roberts, Curt												
NLB/17	219	823	117	233	46	11	6	104	49	10	9	.283
AAA/25	992	3804	614	1130	206	27	62	419	345	71	15	.297
MLB/24	171	575	54	128	24	9	1	40	62	7	7	.223
Robinson, Jackie												
NLB/26	47	163	36	63	14	4	5	23	21	13	3	.386
AAA/27	124	444	113	155	25	8	3	66	92	40	7	.349
MLB/28	1382	4877	947	1518	273	54	137	734	747	197	72	.311
Rodriguez, Hector												
NLB/24	37	151	31	41	3	3	0	14	14	8	0	.271
AAA/33	1385	4899	712	1379	189	49	40	498	589	82	48	.281
MLB/31	124	407	55	108	14	0	1	40	47	7	3	.265
Rogers, Jesse												
NLB/19	NA											
AAA/25	13	49	2	11	0	0	0	7	1	0	0	.224
Santiago, Jose												
NLB/18	5	11	0	0	0	0	0	0	1	0	0	.000
AAA/22	89	89	8	12	1	0	0	5	9	0	0	.135
MLB/25	27	9	4	4	0	0	0	0	2	0	0	.444
Scantlebury, Pat												
NLB/26	146	283	40	92	9	7	6	49	15	1	0	.325
AAA/36	372	442	50	98	19	5	2	29	26	2	5	.222
MLB/28	8	3	0	0	0	0	0	0	0	0	0	.000
Serrell, William												
NLB/21	304	1147	188	351	44	26	15	152	57	31	2	.306
AAA/31	62	169	20	41	11	1	0	15	7	3	0	.243

Player/League	G	AB	R	H	D	T	HR	RBI	BB	SB	HBP	BA
Sierra, Pedro												
NLB/16	NA											
AAA/33	NA											
Simpson, Harry												
NLB/20	140	434	71	120	20	4	6	55	41	5	1	.276
AAA/24	662	2304	370	674	113	38	96	445	278	10	25	.293
MLB/25	888	2829	343	752	101	41	73	381	288	17	10	.266
Smith, Al												
NLB/18	134	454	87	132	14	12	6	56	28	13	4	.291
AAA/22	351	1183	241	341	64	25	51	204	158	31	0	.288
MLB/25	1517	5357	843	1458	258	46	164	676	704	67	63	.272
Smith, George												
NLB/20	NA											
AAA/24	437	1624	226	408	69	20	18	126	151	26	12	.251
MLB/25	217	634	64	130	27	6	9	57	66	9	5	.205
Smith, John Ford												
NLB/22	66	150	19	50	8	2	0	29	10	0	2	.333
AAA/30	81	127	16	25	2	0	2	14	25	0	1	.197
Smith, Milt												
NLB/20	70	255	37	57	3	6	0	20	16	10	1	.223
AAA/23	1058	3644	565	1011	194	67	59	418	438	71	12	.277
MLB/26	36	102	15	20	3	1	3	8	13	2	1	.196
Smith, Theolic												
NLB/23	80	162	29	40	6	2	0	17	21	3	0	.247
AAA/39	110	134	11	24	3	1	1	11	7	0	0	.179
Smith, Willie												
NLB/19	25	49	10	19	1	2	0	9	1	0	2	.388
AAA/24	248	754	121	244	48	9	27	113	75	3	1	.324
MLB/24	691	1654	171	410	63	21	46	211	127	20	9	.248
Spearman, Al												
NLB/15	NA											
AAA/27	18	27	4	2	1	0	0	1	3	0	0	.074
Steele, Ed												
NLB/25	573	1904	461	604	82	28	28	270	171	67	23	.317
AAA/35	22	61	11	13	3	0	2	10	9	1	1	.213
Summers, Lonnie												
NLB/22	150	539	102	164	22	5	10	59	4	0	1	.304
AAA/36	168	425	37	96	23	2	8	64	43	2	4	.226
Taborn, Earl												
NLB/23	202	706	98	200	44	3	11	108	42	6	5	.283
AAA/26	33	97	66	24	5	1	0	6	10	0	0	.247
Taylor, Joe												
NLB/23	NA											
AAA/27	1133	3926	650	1124	213	29	200	694	499	43	44	.286
MLB/28	119	297	34	74	16	1	9	31	29	0	0	.249
Thompson, Hank												
NLB/17	192	707	166	241	30	15	20	107	72	30	5	.341
AAA/23	1093	3752	643	1024	139	42	159	588	645	62	25	.273
MLB/21	933	3003	492	801	104	34	129	482	499	33	22	.267

Player/League	G	AB	R	H	D	T	HR	RBI	BB	SB	HBP	BA
Thurman, Bob												
NLB/29	192	655	124	227	33	13	18	111	20	24	2	.347
AAA/32	664	2194	313	602	100	30	65	319	240	32	6	.274
MLB/38	334	663	106	163	18	11	35	106	67	1	5	.246
Torres, Ricardo*												
NLB/24	29	98	10	20	0	0	0	8	4	2	1	.204
AAA	DNP											
MLB/29	22	37	9	11	1	0	0	3	2	0	0	.297
Trice, Bob												
NLB/22	4	8	1	1	0	0	0	2	0	0	0	.125
AAA/27	108	191	34	48	8	1	9	32	14	0	2	.251
MLB/27	27	52	8	15	4	0	1	6	3	0	2	.288
Trouppe, Quincy												
NLB/17	287	915	189	282	34	16	19	126	112	15	14	.308
AAA/39	84	205	39	53	7	2	8	40	57	0	0	.259
MLB/39	6	10	1	1	0	0	0	0	1	0	0	.100
Tugerson, Jim												
NLB/28	24	63	15	22	—	—	5	18	—	—	—	.349
AAA/36	37	33	3	0	0	0	0	1	8	1	0	.000
Vargas, Roberto												
NLB/19	18	36	6	11	2	1	0	2	1	1	1	.305
AAA/27	94	71	8	21	3	2	0	9	2	0	0	.296
MLB/26	25	2	0	1	0	0	0	0	0	0	0	.500
Welmaker, Roy												
NLB/19	98	213	25	53	6	2	0	16	10	0	0	.249
AAA/36	146	148	14	27	2	1	1	10	4	0	0	.182
White, Charlie												
NLB/22	38	129	16	33	4	0	0	13	17	5	0	.256
AAA/23	792	2203	259	584	111	12	29	267	352	17	11	.265
MLB/26	62	123	17	29	5	0	1	12	14	0	1	.236
Williams, Jeff												
NLB/23	86	327	59	85	8	5	3	40	9	25	4	.260
AAA/25	17	59	9	12	1	1	0	7	6	0	1	.203
Williams, Marvin												
NLB/23	143	582	115	197	43	14	13	123	34	12	0	.338
AAA/30	73	237	38	57	10	3	8	43	32	4	0	.241
Williams, Willie												
NLB/22	378	1369	262	381	66	11	36	197	117	30	9	.278
AAA/27	36	128	16	30	3	2	2	14	8	0	1	.234
Wilson, Artie												
NLB/23	264	1097	229	408	37	17	5	81	70	48	9	.372
AAA/28	1317	5110	773	1600	157	79	8	372	342	159	10	.313
MLB/30	19	22	2	4	0	0	0	1	2	2	0	.182
Wilson, Bob												
NLB/22	190	770	123	248	37	7	14	115	33	13	4	.322
AAA/27	1162	4333	603	1381	271	35	88	648	185	59	47	.319
MLB/33	3	5	1	0	0	0	0	0	0	1	0	.000
Witherspoon, Les												
NLB/21	NA											

Player/League	G	AB	R	H	D	T	HR	RBI	BB	SB	HBP	BA
AAA/26	7	13	1	2	0	0	0	2	0	0	0	.154
Woods, Parnell												
NLB/24	349	1264	202	382	63	22	13	145	59	69	6	.302
AAA/37	40	91	14	25	3	2	2	15	6	4	2	.275
Wright, Johnny												
NLB/20	108	244	23	35	7	0	0	11	12	2	0	.143
AAA/29	2	0	0	0	0	0	0	0	0	0	0	—
Wyatt, John												
NLB/18	NA											
AAA/25	11	9	0	0	0	0	0	0	0	0	0	.000
MLB/26	435	83	2	4	0	0	0	1	3	0	1	.048

Pitching Statistics

Note on Pitching Statistics: Because Negro League totals such as walks, runs, and earned runs were often under-reported, the resulting statistical anomalies are described in footnotes. A small percentage of NLB games played and innings pitched have been estimated as well. G=Games; IP=Innings Pitched; H=Hits; R=Runs; ER=Earned Runs; BB=Bases on Balls; K=Strikeouts; W=Wins; L=Losses; HB=Hit Batters; SH=Shutouts; R/9=Runs Per 9 Innings Pitched; ERA=Earned Runs Per Game Average; NLB=Negro Leagues Baseball; AAA=Triple A Baseball; MLB=Major League Baseball; DNP=Did Not Pitch; NA=Statistics Not Available.

Pitcher/League	G	IP	H	R	ER	BB	K	W	L	HB	SH	R/9	ERA
Acosta, Jose*[1]													
NLB/24	9	56.3	66	25	23	9	18	5	1	0	2	3.99	3.67
AAA/26	78	512	632	251	196	84	150	29	25	0	0	4.54	3.54
MLB/29	55	213.3	265	119	107	68	45	10	10	4	1	5.02	4.51
Bankhead, Dan[2]													
NLB/20	51	293	227	116	52	63	246	20	10	11	4	3.56	2.93
AAA/28	59	343	290	170	148	228	221	26	13	7	3	4.46	3.88
MLB/27	52	153.3	161	116	111	110	111	9	5	3	1	6.81	6.52
Barnes, Frank													
NLB/20	50	315	291	151	123	154	237	22	12	4	2	4.31	3.51
AAA/22	247	1114	1017	507	425	567	848	75	67	44	20	4.10	3.43
MLB/29	15	36.7	40	26	24	35	30	1	3	3	0	6.38	5.89
Barnhill, Dave[3]													
NLB/23	96	657	579	259	180	178	404	52	37	20	9	3.84	2.78
AAA/34	88	389	374	224	200	177	278	24	18	9	4	5.18	4.63
Black, Joe[4]													
NLB/19	119	724.7	727.7	331	259	235	406	47	39	7	5	4.11	3.57
AAA/27	76	378.7	364	171	149	128	192	24	23	4	6	4.06	3.54
MLB/28	172	414	391	200	180	136	222	30	12	2	0	4.35	3.91
Brantley, Ollie													
NLB/18	NA												
AAA/28	3	5	4	1	1	0	0	0	0	0	0	1.80	1.80
Bridges, Marshall[5]													
NLB/19	23	150	143	87	32	64	126	9	11	3	0	5.22	4.23
AAA/25	170	724.7	659	350	304	353	554	43	43	17	5	4.35	3.78

Pitcher/League	G	IP	H	R	ER	BB	K	W	L	HB	SH	R/9	ERA
MLB/28	206	345.3	315	171	144	214	302	23	15	3	0	4.46	3.75
Clarke, Vibert[6]													
NLB/17	99	612	642	361	224	240	344	43	38	7	5	5.31	3.74
AAA/28	37	183	201	112	95	87	66	7	15	2	0	5.51	4.67
MLB/27	7	21.3	17	11	11	14	9	0	0	0	0	4.64	4.64
Coleman, Elliott[7]													
NLB/17	28	142	135	106	55	49	97	6	10	1	0	6.72	4.81
AAA/23	20	61	66	46	39	34	24	3	4	2	0	6.79	5.75
Davis, Johnny[8]													
NLB/23	24	116	127	63	48	61	73	9	7	4	2	7.24	5.51
AAA/35	DNP												
Day, Leon[9]													
NLB/17	114	766.3	668	358	276	261	462	67	31	15	7	4.20	3.45
AAA/34	14	40	33	10	7	23	20	1	1	1	0	2.25	1.58
Dibut, Pedro*													
NLB/30	18	109	116	61	49	32	31	7	8	3	1	5.04	4.05
AAA	DNP												
MLB/31	8	36.7	27	11	11	12	15	3	0	0	0	2.70	2.70
Donoso, Lino[10]													
NLB/24	47	250	221	102	69	104	202	19	9	10	2	3.67	2.71
AAA/31	31	347.7	328	138	121	95	220	26	15	5	4	3.57	3.13
MLB/32	28	96.7	108	58	56	39	39	4	6	1	0	5.40	5.21
Estrada, Oscar*													
NLB/22	8	58	63	41	30	19	25	0	5	1	0	6.36	4.66
AAA/30	1	0	0	0	0	0	0	0	0	0	0	—	—
MLB/25	1	1	1	0	0	1	0	0	0	0	0	0.00	0.00
Fields, Wilmer[11]													
NLB/18	73	251.7	220	94	69	65	114	49	16	2	4	3.36	3.05
AAA/30	DNP												
Greason, Will[12]													
NLB/23	76	517	495	280	217	245	372	31	30	8	3	4.87	3.78
AAA/29	136	537	501	282	243	311	376	26	31	7	1	4.73	4.07
MLB/29	3	4	8	8	6	4	2	0	1	0	0	18.00	13.50
Heard, Jay[13]													
NLB/26	118	644.7	642	305	175	137	425	52	31	13	10	4.26	2.96
AAA/32	131	509.7	490	251	215	211	248	28	30	11	2	4.43	3.80
MLB/34	2	3.3	6	5	5	3	2	0	0	0	0	13.51	13.51
Hoskins, Dave													
NLB/17	21	116.7	141	80	61	33	67	7	7	4	2	6.17	4.71
AAA/28	174	725.3	798	437	370	238	315	34	48	12	2	5.82	4.59
MLB/27	40	139.3	131	67	59	48	64	9	4	4	0	4.33	3.81
Johnson, Connie[14]													
NLB/17	65	400.7	370	216	106	132	270	36	15	12	5	4.71	3.42
AAA/30	65	536	501	240	207	211	378	43	21	10	6	4.03	3.48
MLB/30	123	716	654	302	274	264	497	40	39	7	8	3.80	3.44
Jones, Sam[15]													
NLB/20	33	219	211	153	115	105	160	14	10	2	2	6.29	4.86
AAA/25	356	1061	814	435	362	607	932	87	58	40	12	3.69	3.07
MLB/25	322	1643.3	1403	752	655	859	1376	102	101	60	17	4.12	3.59

Pitcher/League	G	IP	H	R	ER	BB	K	W	L	HB	SH	R/9	ERA
Locke, Edward[16]													
NLB/19	47	236	255	141	66	69	134	12	18	5	0	5.38	4.50
AAA/43	36	185	221	95	73	51	72	10	13	0	0	4.62	3.55
Lopez, Raul[17]													
NLB/19	27	149	152	84	33	62	118	7	9	4	1	5.07	4.50
AAA/22	39	147	172	123	104	128	97	4	17	6	0	7.53	6.37
Maroto, Enrique[18]													
NLB/19	34	191.7	141	110	43	58	109	23	5	5	1	5.19	3.36
AAA/25	2	2.7	0	0	0	0	0	0	0	0	0	0.00	0.00
Mason, Hank													
NLB/20	14	97	85	57	45	50	69	5	7	2	2	5.29	4.17
AAA/24	184	499	501	263	236	215	295	26	25	11	4	4.74	4.26
MLB/27	4	10.7	16	13	12	8	6	0	0	1	0	10.98	10.13
McCoy, Walter[19]													
NLB/22	46	297.3	262	184	74	101	222	16	22	7	1	5.57	3.39
AAA/27	5	26	26	23	18	18	9	0	4	0	0	7.96	6.23
McDaniel, Booker[20]													
NLB/26	79	449	411	181	117	116	304	38	18	3	8	3.63	2.79
AAA/35	55	181.3	195	112	102	103	103	11	13	1	1	5.56	5.06
Miller, Henry[21]													
NLB/20	103	587.3	607	366	283	230	337	41	30	8	6	5.81	4.49
AAA/34	6	9	16	15	14	7	3	0	0	0	0	15.00	14.00
Newcombe, Don[22]													
NLB/17	29	163	155	50	36	59	105	9	7	4	0	2.76	2.96
AAA/21	67	370	376	185	157	138	247	28	16	9	7	4.50	3.82
MLB/22	344	2154.7	2102	956	852	511	1129	149	90	30	24	3.99	3.56
Osorio, Fernando													
NLB/19	22	94	118	66	45	28	30	3	7	3	0	6.32	4.31
AAA/23	20	38.3	49	23	17	7	20	1	0	0	0	5.40	3.99
Paige, Leroy[23]													
NLB/20	326	1805.7	1354	678	387	346	1519	136	89	19	31	3.51	2.14
AAA/52	110	365	321	120	99	64	195	31	22	3	4	2.96	2.44
MLB/42	179	476	429	191	174	180	288	28	31	7	4	3.61	3.29
Partlow, Roy[24]													
NLB/25	102	634.3	588	275	198	186	378	41	27	8	6	3.92	2.90
AAA/35	10	29	26	18	18	16	19	2	0	1	0	5.59	5.59
Perry, Alonso[25]													
NLB/23	65	383.3	410	227	146	106	172	31	14	7	1	5.33	4.29
AAA/26	8	33	34	20	18	20	20	0	1	0	0	5.45	4.91
Pope, Willie[26]													
NLB/28	30	207.3	158	88	36	45	89	16	10	3	1	4.14	3.01
AAA/36	31	128	154	85	75	40	71	4	11	1	0	5.98	5.27
Powell, William[27]													
NLB/27	98	611	617	291	207	197	413	46	23	15	7	4.29	3.31
AAA/32	139	727	750	435	352	374	367	35	47	8	4	5.39	4.36
Proctor, Jim													
NLB/19	NA												
AAA/21	71	219	232	125	103	97	113	10	17	4	0	5.14	4.23
MLB/23	2	2.7	8	5	5	3	0	0	1	0	0	16.92	16.92

Pitcher/League	G	IP	H	R	ER	BB	K	W	L	HB	SH	R/9	ERA
Santiago, Jose													
NLB/18	7	47	34	26	12	14	33	4	3	1	0	4.98	3.37
AAA/22	89	312	341	190	164	161	200	15	27	0	6	5.48	4.73
MLB/25	27	56	67	38	29	34	29	3	2	10	0	6.11	4.66
Scantlebury, Pat[28]													
NLB/26	88	546	571	260	198	133	229	47	32	7	2	4.29	3.34
AAA/36	301	1079	971	439	370	360	632	72	54	7	13	3.66	3.09
MLB/38	6	19	24	14	14	5	10	0	1	0	0	6.63	6.63
Sierra, Pedro[29]													
NLB/16	26	61	63	48	—	—	—	7	6	—	—	7.08	—
AAA/33	NA												
Smith, John Ford[30]													
NLB/22	39	282.3	262	127	75	88	178	24	12	5	3	4.05	2.57
AAA/30	43	199	183	106	88	146	98	12	11	1	2	4.79	3.98
Smith, Theolic													
NLB/23	78	431.7	444	241	192	141	216	31	29	7	5	5.02	4.00
AAA/39	105	428	413	220	190	178	196	27	29	2	3	4.63	4.00
Smith, Willie[31]													
NLB/19	17	91	72	32	16	33	91	9	5	2	0	3.16	2.67
AAA/24	26	165	146	43	38	51	111	16	3	2	4	2.35	2.07
MLB/24	29	61	60	26	21	27	39	0	0	1	0	3.84	3.10
Spearman, Al													
NLB/15	5	23	24	25	17	11	10	0	3	0	0	9.78	6.65
AAA/27	16	94	90	48	38	27	34	3	9	0	1	4.60	3.64
Thurman, Bob[32]													
NLB/29	29	141.7	145	89	67	60	61	8	9	4	1	5.65	5.32
AAA/32	5	6	3	1	1	3	0	0	0	0	0	1.50	1.50
Trice, Bob													
NLB/22	1	2.7	3	5	4	2	2	0	0	0	0	16.92	13.53
AAA/27	66	404	386	183	151	137	91	27	22	4	4	4.08	3.36
MLB/27	26	152	185	113	98	60	28	9	9	0	1	6.69	5.80
Tugerson, Jim[33]													
NLB/28	35	211	128	69	61	71	147	18	7	0	0	4.85	4.29
AAA/36	35	136	129	68	53	61	69	5	12	1	2	4.50	3.51
Vargas, Roberto													
NLB/19	18	99	90	50	34	29	70	6	8	8	1	4.55	3.09
AAA/27	92	196	208	116	97	90	106	11	14	7	1	5.33	4.45
MLB/26	25	24.7	39	25	24	16	13	0	0	0	0	9.12	8.76
Welmaker, Roy[34]													
NLB/19	86	536.3	537	284	200	155	281	40	22	3	3	4.87	3.50
AAA/36	145	506	540	277	231	227	314	27	24	2	2	4.93	4.11
Wright, Johnny[35]													
NLB/20	95	672.7	613	264	220	181	374	51	26	14	10	3.53	3.00
AAA/29	2	6	5	0	0	5	3	0	0	0	0	0.00	0.00
Wyatt, John													
NLB/18	NA												
AAA/25	10	38	39	26	22	28	29	1	2	0	0	6.16	5.21
MLB/26	435	687.3	600	290	265	385	540	42	44	23	0	3.80	3.47

Notes

1. Acosta's AAA run and earned run totals are based on 498ip.
2. Bankhead's NLB totals are based on 188.3ip (walks); and 159.7ip (earned runs).
3. Barnhill's NLB totals are based on 581ip (runs); and 496.7ip (earned runs).
4. Black's NLB totals are based on 697.7ip (walks); 543.7ip (runs); and 522.3ip (earned runs).
5. Bridges' NLB earned run totals are based on 68ip.
6. Clarke's NLB earned run and walk totals are based on 538.3ip.
7. Coleman's NLB totals are based on 134ip (hits); 121ip (walks and strikeouts); and 103ip (earned runs).
8. Davis' NLB totals are based on 101ip (walks); and 78.3ip (runs and earned runs).
9. Day's NLB totals are based on 739.3ip (walks and strikeouts); and 719.3ip (runs and earned runs).
10. Donoso's NLB earned run and walk totals are based on 229ip.
11. Fields' NLB totals are based on 235.7ip (walks); 204.7ip (runs); and 147.7ip (earned runs).
12. Greason's NLB run totals are based on 390ip.
13. Heard's NLB totals are based on 564.7ip (walks); and 531.7ip (earned runs).
14. Johnson's NLB earned run totals are based on 278.7ip.
15. Jones' NLB earned run totals are based on 213ip.
16. Locke's NLB totals are based on 211ip (runs); 165ip (walks); and 132ip (earned runs).
17. Lopez's NLB earned run totals are based on 10ip.
18. Maroto's NLB totals are based on 191.7 (games); 190.7ip (runs); 187.7ip (hits); 126.7ip (strikeouts); 117.7ip (walks); and 115ip (earned runs).
19. McCoy's NLB earned run and walk totals are based on 196.7ip.
20. McDaniel's NLB earned run totals are based on 377.3ip.
21. Miller's NLB totals are based on 518.6ip (runs and walks); and 456.7ip (earned runs).
22. Newcombe's NLB run and earned run totals are based on 109.3ip.
23. Paige's NLB totals are based on 1783.7ip (strikeouts); 1738.3ip (hits and runs); 1732.3ip (walks); and 1626ip (earned runs).
24. Partlow's NLB totals are based on 582ip (runs); 562.7 (walks); and 549ip (earned runs).
25. Perry's NLB earned run totals are based on 306.3ip.
26. Pope's NLB totals are based on 191.3ip (runs); 162.3ip (hits); 148.7ip (strikeouts); 132.7ip (walks); and 107.7ip (earned runs).
27. Powell's NLB earned run and walk totals are based on 562ip.
28. Scantlebury's NLB earned run totals are based on 441.3ip.
29. Sierra's NLB innings pitched are based on 10 games.
30. John Ford Smith's NLB earned run totals are based on 262.7ip.
31. Willie Smith's NLB earned run totals are based on 54ip.
32. Thurman's NLB totals are based on 73.3ip (runs); and 60.7ip (earned runs).
33. Tugerson's NLB hit; run; earned run; and walk totals are based on 128ip.
34. Welmaker's NLB totals are based on 525ip (runs); and 514ip (earned runs).
35. Wright's NLB run; earned run; and walk totals are based on 660.7.

Appendix V

Black Minor League Batting
and Pitching Leaders, 1946–1975

Note: Only players who appeared in NLB and/or MLB prior to 1960 or in Triple A by 1955 have been listed. Statistics from two independent circuits—the Mexican League (1946–1954) and Provincial League (1946–1949)—have also been included.

Sources: The data has been derived from Baseball-Reference.com; the *Center for Negro League Baseball Research*; and Dick Clark and Larry Lester's *Negro Leagues Book*.

Batting Leaders

Note on Batting Statistics: All black batters from the immediate post-segregation era with at least 450 minor league plate appearances, who hit .300 or better, and/or accrued 150 home runs or 150 stolen bases, are listed. Many minor leagues did not publish run, runs batted in, or stolen base data prior to 1956, affecting some player totals. Players who appeared in the Major Leagues are highlighted in **bold**. Despite posting impressive numbers, 45 of these 97 players (46 percent) never got a shot at the big leagues. The players are designated by their given names. G=Games; AB=At Bats; R=Runs; H=Hits; D=Doubles; T=Triples; HR=Home Runs; RBI=Runs Batted In; SB=Stolen Bases; BA=Batting Average.

Player	G	AB	R	H	D	T	HR	RBI	SB	BA
Willie Mays	116	455	88	179	38	11	12	86	12	.393
Monte Irvin	160	515	141	193	43	7	34	139	18	.375
Ike Jackson	518	2072	443	736	150	34	87	483	23	.355
Hank Aaron	224	919	194	324	55	18	31	186	38	.353
Al Pinkston	1827	6729	1193	2368	461	75	250	1135	82	.352
Luis Villodas	160	590	107	206	51	5	10	103	3	.349
Jackie Robinson	124	444	113	155	25	8	3	66	40	.349
Alonso Perry	1021	3782	776	1320	238	65	179	888	89	.349
Orlando Cepeda	394	1529	174	521	93	15	73	199	6	.341
Vada Pinson	334	1321	92	449	79	33	33	77	37	.340
George Crowe	669	2374	443	803	165	29	103	524	33	.338
Tommy Davis	460	1774	282	594	81	27	49	255	103	.335
Felipe Alou	309	1086	68	362	47	11	46	45	11	.333
Walter Leonard	299	1009	204	336	70	7	40	237	22	.333
Fernando Pedrozo	564	2252	385	742	106	31	48	389	36	.329

Player	G	AB	R	H	D	T	HR	RBI	SB	BA
Vic Power	523	2024	272	666	121	42	52	258	30	.329
Rene Gonzalez	777	2912	551	956	170	28	131	619	52	.328
Lester Witherspoon	415	1491	303	481	88	36	40	299	46	.323
Ray Dandridge	896	3622	577	1166	177	21	46	454	67	.322
Silvio Garcia	511	2005	325	645	128	6	40	346	68	.322
George Handy	763	2816	525	905	134	22	72	467	64	.321
Chuck Harmon	1017	3911	555	1253	228	68	82	669	144	.320
Curt Flood	321	1180	108	378	52	17	44	88	9	.320
Leonard Hunt	403	1449	293	464	84	39	26	204	40	.320
Frank Robinson	292	1034	—	331	67	22	54	—	—	.320
Bob Boyd	933	3125	479	1000	169	57	48	417	109	.320
Horace Garner	997	3436	683	1094	179	38	156	752	97	.318
Lorenzo Cabrera	360	1365	202	434	67	24	20	196	33	.318
Nap Gulley	692	2488	440	790	170	23	75	521	47	.318
Harry Simpson	1030	3383	648	1074	174	60	162	705	16	.317
Edward Locke	661	1843	291	585	98	35	51	328	5	.317
Orestes Minoso	896	4041	697	1280	233	44	114	675	101	.317
Ray Mitchell	280	1038	—	328	53	13	27	—	—	.316
Art Pennington	917	3223	662	1016	142	50	74	527	102	.315
Willie McCovey	632	2263	252	713	147	41	105	262	16	.315
Len Tucker	1090	4046	924	1274	208	53	236	902	257	.315
Marvin Williams	1377	4858	952	1522	272	69	234	1020	65	.314
Billy Williams	446	1627	185	510	103	15	66	213	12	.313
Artie Wilson	1331	5152	780	1609	157	79	8	374	160	.312
Wes Covington	319	1233	13	385	54	27	50	27	1	.312
William Serrell	997	4066	664	1269	209	73	63	589	101	.312
Richard Newberry	461	1849	388	577	90	41	21	268	93	.312
Johnny Davis	397	1311	287`	409	62	5	81	335	10	.312
Bill Wright	543	2015	330	628	91	27	30	306	67	.312
Archie Braithwaite	229	883	147	275	40	6	10	136	24	.311
Dan Bankhead	832	2021	370	629	103	27	38	318	40	.311
Charles Peete	511	1808	309	562	98	29	47	271	25	.311
Ken Rodgers	654	2195	235	680	136	19	96	225	13	.310
Bob Wilson	1358	4665	658	1444	282	41	83	675	74	.309
Jeff Williams	429	1467	201	454	109	17	65	194	33	.309
Luis Marquez	1799	6555	1099	2028	360	80	176	937	217	.309
Robert Davis	152	553	71	171	31	8	12	74	2	.309
Lee Maye	892	3231	309	998	179	62	128	363	44	.309
Leon Kellman	566	1886	371	582	94	20	48	326	25	.309
Sandy Amoros	765	2681	550	827	166	39	108	427	76	.308
Pedro Formenthal	239	749	118	231	37	10	24	116	16	.308
Jim Zapp	354	1320	266	407	74	11	90	351	16	.308
Alphonso Gerrard	365	1311	187	404	44	16	4	154	57	.308
Mario Ariosa	1725	6013	975	1851	273	49	113	840	135	.308
Valmy Thomas	441	1316	38	405	57	8	33	42	0	.308
Leon Wagner	758	2415	256	743	114	31	154	303	30	.308
Nate Clifton	217	771	116	237	48	13	23	149	5	.307
Willard Brown	595	1303	199	400	81	7	46	345	9	.307
Clint McCord	1312	4682	757	1435	279	64	89	701	68	.306

Player	G	AB	R	H	D	T	HR	RBI	SB	BA
Bill Bruton	415	1713	130	525	80	47	12	62	30	.306
Carlos Paula	786	2463	137	754	125	54	56	163	7	.306
Claro Duany	527	1837	321	561	108	8	99	433	12	.305
Quincy Smith	653	2584	576	788	165	55	45	418	174	.305
Buster Clarkson	989	2388	534	728	122	17	101	545	75	.305
Sam Hairston	1147	3994	562	1215	248	35	53	607	18	.304
Bill White	450	1680	106	511	78	16	75	107	24	.304
Elston Howard	331	1178	158	358	49	27	41	221	5	.304
Willie Smith	431	1107	159	336	59	11	30	158	4	.304
Charlie Dees	1087	3826	549	1161	249	36	84	489	65	.303
Alejandro Crespo	455	2149	318	652	94	21	19	367	35	.303
Willie Kirkland	716	2633	210	796	110	58	176	118	19	.302
Rene Friol	1598	5323	699	1600	241	44	161	866	61	.301
Luke Easter	1327	3672	609	1102	192	15	247	843	6	.300
Dave Pope	1203	4669	724	1400	237	82	171	873	59	.300
John Ritchey	987	2848	427	853	119	31	29	413	87	.300
Joe Taylor	1478	4727	818	1411	264	38	239	880	74	.298
Carlos Bernier	2200	7680	1082	2291	303	123	200	827	331	.298
Juan Herrera	1676	5921	900	1761	268	39	306	1037	52	.297
Leonard Williams	789	3015	551	896	130	33	156	581	37	.297
Bob Prescott	1324	4312	421	1279	241	48	184	510	20	.297
Lou Johnson	1244	4158	734	1230	199	83	110	599	199	.296
Sam Jethroe	1020	3750	752	1108	189	62	119	457	232	.295
Nat Peeples	978	3229	623	939	135	25	122	592	218	.291
Willie Tasby	994	3438	269	995	188	35	156	296	45	.289
Fleming Reedy	1480	5209	897	1502	260	103	47	696	181	.288
Hector Rodriguez	2251	8206	1219	2341	300	105	58	866	181	.285
Hal Jones	919	3359	605	954	186	33	178	665	23	.284
David Mann	1524	5669	426	1597	197	119	83	252	217	.282
Ellis Burton	1213	4210	528	1155	217	41	169	388	60	.274
Roberto Sanchez	1579	5702	694	1553	255	80	153	597	141	.272
R. C. Stevens	1229	4241	544	1140	183	21	191	607	27	.269
Chuck Weatherspoon	1553	4973	713	1316	221	47	230	764	61	.265

Pitching Leaders

Notes on Pitching Statistics: All black players from the immediate post-segregation era who pitched at least 200 minor league innings, and maintained an ERA under 4.00 and/ or won over 75 games or struck out at least 500 batters, are listed. Many minor leagues did not publish strikeout data prior to 1956, affecting some player totals. Pitchers who appeared in the Majors are highlighted in **bold**. Despite posting impressive numbers, 33 of these 67 players (49 percent) never got a shot at the big leagues. The pitchers are designated by their given names. G=Games; IP=Innings Pitched; W=Wins; L=Losses; PCT=Winning Percentage; H=Hits; ER=Earned Runs; BB=Bases on Balls; K=Strikeouts; ERA= Earned Runs Per Game Average.

Pitcher	*G*	*IP*	*W*	*L*	*PCT*	*H*	*ER*	*BB*	*K*	*ERA*
Leroy Paige	111	367	31	22	.585	326	101	64	214	2.48
Diomedes Olivo[1]	187	512	36	26	.581	439	89	133	272	2.54
Orlando Pena[2]	451	1659	129	77	.626	1487	482	460	902	2.61
Al Jackson[3]	146	912	63	42	.600	781	269	342	561	2.65
Juan Pizarro[4]	108	839	66	26	.717	654	258	365	508	2.77
Al Spearman[5]	112	770	60	34	.638	714	243	201	184	2.84
Johnny Williams[6]	98	486	25	32	.438	320	154	407	318	2.85
Mike Cuellar[7]	236	1090	59	50	.541	954	347	374	636	2.86
Willie Smith	101	636	49	27	.645	516	207	315	501	2.93
Frank Barnes	448	2170	149	106	.584	1890	716	946	1714	2.97
Lino Donoso	385	2047	136	100	.576	1951	686	693	1471	3.02
Sam Jones	385	1196	95	62	.605	916	404	691	1001	3.04
Humberto Robinson[8]	249	1445	110	60	.647	1273	492	557	437	3.06
Federico Olivo[9]	457	1656	119	85	.583	1549	570	528	1073	3.10
Bob Gibson	81	451	25	25	.500	410	157	256	305	3.13
James Grant[10]	180	895.7	75	33	.694	822	313	426	231	3.15
Stan Jones	318	1193	91	55	.623	1089	419	363	970	3.16
Jose Santiago[11]	298	1404	108	76	.587	1264	493	552	1044	3.16
Roberto Vargas[12]	332	1470	102	82	.554	1371	521	657	857	3.19
Don Newcombe	122	748	61	26	.701	665	267	333	537	3.21
Barney Brown	74	526.7	30	28	.517	537	189	230	295	3.23
Lenial Hooker	49	329	21	15	.583	331	119	106	126	3.25
Pat Scantlebury[13]	381	1623	114	78	.594	1540	595	531	977	3.30
Raymond Brown[14]	149	957	63	46	.578	915	352	405	417	3.31
Brooks Lawrence[15]	252	1212	76	72	.514	1028	446	632	485	3.31
Johnny Wright	107	612	39	36	.520	545	227	339	366	3.34
Jim Proctor[16]	224	969	62	48	.564	857	349	371	511	3.38
Connie Johnson[17]	182	1034	77	44	.636	941	390	426	783	3.39
Elliott Coleman[18]	121	537	33	38	.465	476	205	254	221	3.43
Wilfredo Salas	244	1271	74	75	.497	3731	486	687	793	3.44
Roy Partlow[19]	60	358.7	28	9	.757	362	138	139	100	3.46
Hank Mason	266	937	60	46	.566	820	363	378	675	3.49
Dave Barnhill[20]	120	570	38	27	.585	499	224	248	278	3.54
Joe Black[21]	80	378.7	24	23	.511	366	149	128	192	3.54
Bennie Griggs	124	583.3	34	31	.523	535	230	251	447	3.55
Willie Pope	177	1093	65	60	.520	1100	431	401	699	3.55
Roy Welmaker[22]	180	760	49	36	.576	769	300	345	314	3.55
Jay Heard[23]	215	969.7	61	54	.530	910	384	409	569	3.56
Rene Valdes[24]	493	2095.3	152	111	.578	2033	837	736	1022	3.60
Pedro Naranjo[25]	63	335	18	24	.428	336	134	140	234	3.60
Ollie Brantley[26]	640	2082.3	155	99	.610	2104	836	692	954	3.61
Alex Newkirk	37	245	10	14	.417	224	99	103	75	3.64
Jim Tugerson[27]	235	1352	86	71	.585	1266	550	495	1038	3.66
Ramon Bragana	226	1557	82	85	.491	1642	637	657	537	3.68
Theolic Smith	204	1052.7	69	60	.535	1069	431	421	459	3.68
Fernando Osorio[28]	727	3558	227	170	.572	3731	1460	798	1730	3.69
Dick Ricketts[29]	301	1597	99	91	.521	1547	657	693	805	3.70
Edward Locke[30]	430	2349	170	132	.563	2399	977	685	1422	3.74
Bennie Daniels[31]	197	1283.7	83	69	.546	1191	535	658	449	3.75

Pitcher	G	IP	W	L	PCT	H	ER	BB	K	ERA
Charlie Beamon[32]	226	1219.3	81	69	.540	1100	509	726	439	3.76
Dave Hoskins	255	1204.3	71	60	.542	1217	505	384	575	3.77
Luis Cabrera	57	338	23	18	.561	326	142	147	227	3.78
Willie Hutchinson	46	232.3	10	13	.435	209	99	123	140	3.83
Pedro Sierra[33]	262	819	52	57	.477	844	349	362	528	3.83
Ruben Gomez[34]	184	826	62	30	.674	785	353	417	280	3.85
Raul Galata[35]	276	1438	81	88	.479	1452	623	873	886	3.90
Leon Day	133	605.3	37	35	.514	600	264	341	279	3.92
Dan Bankhead[36]	294	942	76	38	.667	837	393	574	591	3.94
Robert Griffith	53	278	17	16	.515	285	122	135	131	3.95
Marshall Bridges	243	1139	75	57	.568	1033	502	630	581	3.97
Nate Moreland	370	2191.7	154	110	.583	2273	970	732	1176	3.98
John Ford Smith	143	825	61	40	.549	818	370	421	501	4.04
Will Greason	252	1288.3	79	66	.545	1161	578	743	889	4.04
Booker McDaniels	185	880	52	60	.464	871	396	577	503	4.05
Earl Wilson[37]	186	919	57	48	.543	749	416	722	529	4.07
William Powell[38]	325	1385	71	86	.452	1383	651	732	739	4.23
Sam Williams[39]	246	1298	87	76	.534	1365	629	434	611	4.36

Notes

1. Diomedes Olivo's statistics (except record) are based on 152 games. His earned run and strikeout totals are based on 315ip.
2. Pena's strikeout totals are based on 1120ip.
3. Jackson's statistics are based on 141 games. His strikeout totals are based on 588ip.
4. Pizarro's strikeout totals are based on 565ip.
5. Spearman's statistics (except record) are based on 99 games. His strikeout totals are based on 340ip.
6. Johnny Williams' statistics (except record) are based on 94 games. His strikeout totals are based on 366ip.
7. Cuellar's statistics are based on 199 games.
8. Robinson's statistics are based on 237 games. His strikeout totals are based on 708ip.
9. Federico Olivo's statistics (except record) are based on 439 games. His strikeout totals are based on 1565ip.
10. Grant's strikeout totals are based on 285.7ip.
11. Santiago's statistics (except record) are based on 287 games.
12. Vargas' statistics (except record) are based on 314 games.
13. Scantlebury's statistics (except record) are based on 278 games.
14. Ray Brown's statistics (except record) are based on 147 games.
15. Lawrence's strikeouts are based on 711ip.
16. Proctor's statistics are based on 219 games. His walk and strikeout totals are based on 962ip; and his earned run and hit totals are based on 923ip.
17. Johnson's statistics (except record) are based on 179 games.
18. Coleman's strikeout totals are based on 344ip.
19. Partlow's strikeout totals are based on 155.7ip.
20. Barnhill's statistics (except record) are based on 116 games.
21. Black's statistics are based on 76 games.
22. Welmaker's strikeout totals are based on 254ip.
23. Heard's statistics are based on 196 games.
24. Valdes' statistics are based on 410 games. His strikeout totals are based on 1565.3ip.
25. Naranjo's statistics (except record) are based on 56 games.
26. Brantley's statistics (except record) are based on 637 games. His strikeout totals are based on 1401.3ip.
27. Tugerson's statistics (except record) are based on 226 games.
28. Osorio's statistics (except record) are based on 724 games.
29. Rickett's strikeout totals are based on 1326ip.
30. Locke's statistics (except record) are based on 421 games.
31. Daniels' strikeout totals are based on 776.7ip.
32. Beamon's statistics (except record) are based on 220 games. His strikeout totals are based on 773.3ip.

33. Sierra's statistics (except record) are based on 260 games.
34. Gomez's statistics are based on 153 games. His strikeout totals are based on 327ip.
35. Galata's statistics (except record) are based on 272 games.
36. Bankhead's earned run and strikeout totals are based on 897ip.
37. Wilson's strikeout totals are based on 536.7ip.
38. Powell's statistics (except record) are based on 321 games.
39. Sam Williams' statistics (except record) are based on 235 games.

Appendix VI

MLB/NLB Throwback Games, 1994–2019

Note: Only contests involving Major League teams have been listed, with the NLB squad represented shown in parentheses. Inn = Innings.

Date	MLB (NLB)	Location
1994		
Aug. 3	Kansas City Royals (Kansas City Monarchs) 9	
	Oakland Athletics 5	Kansas City, MO
1995		
Jul. 8	Kansas City Royals (Kansas City Monarchs) 4	
	Detroit Tigers (Detroit Stars) 1	Detroit, MI
Sep. 9	Seattle Mariners (Seattle Steelheads) 6	
	Kansas City Royals (Kansas City Monarchs) 2	Seattle, WA
1996		
Jun. 9	Detroit Tigers (Detroit Stars) 9	
	New York Yankees (New York Black Yankees) 7	Detroit, MI
Aug. 24	Kansas City Royals (Kansas City Monarchs) 9	
	Detroit Tigers (Detroit Stars) 2	Kansas City, MO
1997		
Jun. 28	Atlanta Braves (Atlanta Black Crackers) 9	
	Philadelphia Phillies (Philadelphia Stars) 1	Atlanta, GA
Jul. 4	Pittsburgh Pirates (Homestead Grays) 7	
	St. Louis Cardinals (St. Louis Stars) 5, 10 inn	St. Louis, MO
Jul. 5	Detroit Tigers (Detroit Stars) 11	
	Baltimore Orioles (Baltimore Elite Giants) 8	Detroit, MI
Jul. 13	Cleveland Indians (Cleveland Buckeyes) 12	
	Minnesota Twins (St. Paul Gophers) 5	Minneapolis, MN
1998		
Jun. 27	Cincinnati Reds (Cincinnati Buckeyes) 6	
	Detroit Tigers (Detroit Stars) 5, 13 inn	Detroit, MI
Aug. 1	Atlanta Braves (Atlanta Black Crackers) 3	
	St. Louis Cardinals (St. Louis Stars) 1	Atlanta, GA
Aug. 2	Atlanta Braves (Atlanta Black Crackers) 4	
	St. Louis Cardinals (St. Louis Stars) 3	Atlanta, GA
1999		
May 29	Chicago White Sox (Chicago American Giants) 7	
	Detroit Tigers (Detroit Stars) 1	Detroit, MI

Appendix VI

Date	MLB (NLB)	Location
2000		
Jul. 22	Kansas City Royals (Kansas City Monarchs) 8	
	Detroit Tigers (Detroit Stars) 5	Detroit, MI
	Detroit Tigers (Detroit Stars) 10	
	Kansas City Royals (Kansas City Monarchs) 6	2nd game
2001		
Jun. 23	Kansas City Royals (Kansas City Monarchs) 3	
	Cleveland Indians (Cleveland Buckeyes) 2	Kansas City, MO
Jul. 14	Kansas City Royals (Kansas City Monarchs) 7	
	Pittsburgh Pirates (Homestead Grays) 4	Pittsburgh, PA
Jul. 15	New York Mets (New York Cubans) 6	
	Toronto Blue Jays (Chatham All-Stars) 2	New York, NY
2002		
Jun. 29	Detroit Tigers (Detroit Stars) 2	
	Pittsburgh Pirates (Pittsburgh Crawfords) 1	Detroit, MI
Jul. 13	Toronto Blue Jays (Chatham All-Stars) 4	
	Boston Red Sox (Boston Royal Giants) 1	Toronto, ON
2003		
Jun. 29	St. Louis Cardinals (St. Louis Stars) 13	
	Kansas City Royals (Kansas City Monarchs) 6	Kansas City, MO
Jul. 26	Detroit Tigers (Detroit Stars) 5	
	Kansas City Royals (Kansas City Monarchs) 1	Detroit, MI
2004		
Jun. 13	New York Mets (New York Cubans) 5	
	Kansas City Royals (Kansas City Monarchs) 2	Kansas City, MO
Jul. 31	Detroit Tigers (Detroit Stars) 3	
	Chicago White Sox (Chicago American Giants) 2	Detroit, MI
2005		
Jul. 9	Pittsburgh Pirates (Pittsburgh Crawfords) 11	
	New York Mets (New York Cubans) 4	Pittsburgh, PA
Jul. 10	Minnesota Twins (St. Paul Gophers) 3	
	Kansas City Royals (Kansas City Monarchs) 2, 12 inn	Kansas City, MO
Aug. 6	Cleveland Indians (Cleveland Buckeyes) 4	
	Detroit Tigers (Detroit Stars) 2	Detroit, MI
2006		
May 20	Pittsburgh Pirates (Homestead Grays) 9	
	Cleveland Indians (Cleveland Buckeyes) 6	Cleveland, OH
Jun. 2	Washington Nationals (Homestead Grays) 10	
	Milwaukee Brewers (Milwaukee Bears) 4	Milwaukee, WI
Jun. 25	Kansas City Royals (Kansas City Monarchs) 6	
	Milwaukee Brewers (Milwaukee Bears) 0	Kansas City, MO
Jul. 15	Detroit Tigers (Detroit Stars) 6	
	Kansas City Royals (Kansas City Monarchs) 0	Detroit, MI
Aug. 11	Washington Nationals (Homestead Grays) 2	
	New York Mets (New York Cubans) 1	Washington, D.C.
Aug. 12	Pittsburgh Pirates (Homestead Grays) 3	
	St. Louis Cardinals (St. Louis Stars) 2	Pittsburgh, PA

Date	MLB (NLB)	Location
2007		
Jun. 23	Milwaukee Brewers (Milwaukee Bears) 7	
	Kansas City Royals (Kansas City Monarchs) 1	Milwaukee, WI
Jul. 1	Chicago White Sox (Chicago American Giants) 3	
	Kansas City Royals (Kansas City Monarchs) 1	Kansas City, MO
Jul. 21	Detroit Tigers (Detroit Stars) 10	
	Kansas City Royals (Kansas City Monarchs) 8, 11 inn	Detroit, MI
Aug. 3	Washington Nationals (Homestead Grays) 3	
	St. Louis Cardinals (St. Louis Stars) 2	Washington, D.C.
Sep. 6	Boston Red Sox 7	
	Baltimore Orioles (Baltimore Black Sox) 6	Baltimore, MD
2008		
May 3	Washington Nationals (Homestead Grays) 9	
	Pittsburgh Pirates (Homestead Grays) 8	Washington, D.C.
Jun. 22	Kansas City Royals (Kansas City Monarchs) 11	
	San Francisco Giants (San Francisco Sea Lions) 10	Kansas City, MO
Jun. 28	Pittsburgh Pirates (Pittsburgh Crawfords) 4	
	Tampa Bay Rays (Jacksonville Red Caps) 3, 13 inn	Pittsburgh, PA
Jul. 5	Milwaukee Brewers (Milwaukee Bears) 2	
	Pittsburgh Pirates (Pittsburgh Crawfords) 1	Milwaukee, WI
Jul. 26	Chicago White Sox (Chicago American Giants) 7	
	Detroit Tigers (Detroit Stars) 6	Detroit, MI
2009		
May 30	Chicago White Sox (Chicago American Giants) 5	
	Kansas City Royals (Kansas City Monarchs) 3	Kansas City, MO
Jun. 26	Pittsburgh Pirates (Homestead Grays) 5	
	Kansas City Royals (Kansas City Monarchs) 3	Pittsburgh, PA
Jun. 27	Pittsburgh Pirates (Homestead Grays) 6	
	Kansas City Royals (Kansas City Monarchs) 2	Pittsburgh, PA
Jul. 11	Cleveland Indians (Cleveland Buckeyes) 5	
	Detroit Tigers (Detroit Stars) 4	Detroit, MI
Jul. 25	Milwaukee Brewers (Milwaukee Bears) 4	
	Atlanta Braves (Atlanta Black Crackers) 0	Milwaukee, WI
Aug. 1	Detroit Tigers (Detroit Stars) 4	
	Cleveland Indians (Cleveland Buckeyes) 3, 12 inn	Cleveland, OH
Sep. 5	Baltimore Orioles (Baltimore Elite Giants) 5	
	Texas Rangers 4	Baltimore, MD
2010		
May 30	New York Mets (New York Cubans) 10	
	Milwaukee Brewers (Milwaukee Bears) 4	Milwaukee, WI
Jun. 12	Detroit Tigers (Detroit Stars) 4	
	Pittsburgh Pirates (Pittsburgh Crawfords) 3, 10 inn	Detroit, MI
Jul. 31	Kansas City Royals (Kansas City Monarchs) 4	
	Baltimore Orioles (Baltimore Elite Giants) 3	Kansas City, MO
Aug. 7	Minnesota Twins (St. Paul Gophers) 7	
	Cleveland Indians (Cleveland Buckeyes) 2	Cleveland, OH
Aug. 21	New York Mets (New York Cubans) 5	
	Pittsburgh Pirates (Pittsburgh Crawfords) 1, 6 inn	Pittsburgh, PA

Date	*MLB (NLB)*	*Location*
2011		
May 14	Atlanta Braves (Atlanta Black Crackers) 5	
	Philadelphia Phillies (Philadelphia Stars) 3	Atlanta, GA
Jul. 9	Cincinnati Reds (Cincinnati Tigers) 8	
	Milwaukee Brewers (Milwaukee Bears) 4, 10 inn	Milwaukee, WI
Jul. 16	Chicago White Sox (Chicago American Giants) 5	
	Detroit Tigers (Detroit Stars) 0	Detroit, MI
Jul. 23	St. Louis Cardinals (St. Louis Stars) 9	
	Pittsburgh Pirates (Homestead Grays) 1	Pittsburgh, PA
2012		
May 19	Pittsburgh Pirates (Pittsburgh Crawfords) 4	
	Detroit Tigers (Detroit Stars) 3	Detroit, MI
Jun. 9	Pittsburgh Pirates (Homestead Grays) 5	
	Kansas City Royals (Kansas City Monarchs) 3	Pittsburgh, PA
Jul. 21	Kansas City Royals (Kansas City Monarchs) 7	
	Minnesota Twins (St. Paul Gophers) 3	Kansas City, MO
Jul. 28	Washington Nationals (Homestead Grays) 4	
	Milwaukee Brewers (Milwaukee Bears) 1	Milwaukee, WI
2013		
Apr. 27	Detroit Tigers (Detroit Stars) 7	
	Atlanta Braves (Atlanta Black Crackers) 4	Detroit, MI
Jun. 1	Cincinnati Reds (Cincinnati Tigers) 2	
	Pittsburgh Pirates (Homestead Grays) 0	Pittsburgh, PA
Jun. 1	Atlanta Braves (Atlanta Black Crackers) 2	
	Washington Nationals (Homestead Grays) 1, 10 inn	Atlanta, GA
Jul. 20	Milwaukee Brewers (Milwaukee Bears) 6	
	Miami Marlins (Miami Marlins IL) 0	Milwaukee, WI
Aug. 24	Washington Nationals (Homestead Grays) 7	
	Kansas City Royals (Kansas City Monarchs) 2	Kansas City, MO
2014		
May 3	San Francisco Giants (San Francisco Sea Lions) 3	
	Atlanta Braves (Atlanta Black Crackers) 1	Atlanta, GA
May 18	Kansas City Royals (Kansas City Monarchs) 8	
	Baltimore Orioles (Baltimore Black Sox) 6	Kansas City, MO
May 24	Texas Rangers (Fort Worth Black Panthers) 12	
	Detroit Tigers (Detroit Stars) 2	Detroit, MI
May 30	Houston Astros (Houston Eagles) 2	
	Baltimore Orioles (Baltimore Elite Giants) 1	Houston, TX
Jun. 28	New York Mets (Brooklyn Royal Giants) 5	
	Pittsburgh Pirates (Pittsburgh Crawfords) 3	Pittsburgh, PA
2015		
Apr. 25	Detroit Tigers (Detroit Stars) 4	
	Cleveland Indians (Cleveland Buckeyes) 1	Detroit, MI
May 16	Boston Red Sox (Boston Royal Giants) 4	
	Seattle Mariners (Seattle Steelheads) 2	Seattle, WA
May 17	Kansas City Royals (Kansas City Monarchs) 6	
	New York Yankees 0	Kansas City, MO
Jun. 20	Atlanta Braves (Atlanta Black Crackers) 6	
	New York Mets (Brooklyn Royal Giants) 4	Atlanta, GA

Date	MLB (NLB)	Location
Jul. 18	Milwaukee Brewers (Milwaukee Bears) 8	
	Pittsburgh Pirates (Pittsburgh Crawfords) 5	Milwaukee, WI
2016		
May 15	Kansas City Royals (Kansas City Monarchs) 4	
	Atlanta Braves (Atlanta Black Crackers) 2, 13 inn	Kansas City, MO
Jun. 4	Detroit Tigers (Detroit Stars) 7	
	Chicago White Sox (Chicago American Giants) 4	Detroit, MI
Jun. 25	Milwaukee Brewers (Milwaukee Bears) 6	
	Washington Nationals (Homestead Grays) 5	Milwaukee, MI
Jun. 25	New York Mets (Brooklyn Royal Giants) 1	
	Atlanta Braves (Atlanta Black Crackers) 0, 11 inn	Atlanta, GA
Sep. 9	Cincinnati Reds (Cincinnati Tigers) 4	
	Pittsburgh Pirates (Homestead Grays) 3	Pittsburgh, PA
2017		
May 7	Cleveland Indians (Cleveland Buckeyes) 1	
	Kansas City Royals (Kansas City Monarchs) 0	Kansas City, MO
Jun. 16	Chicago Cubs (Leland Giants) 9	
	Pittsburgh Pirates (Homestead Grays) 5	Pittsburgh, PA
Jul. 1	Cleveland Indians (Cleveland Buckeyes) 4	
	Detroit Tigers (Detroit Stars) 1	Detroit, MI
Aug. 12	Milwaukee Brewers (Milwaukee Bears) 6	
	Cincinnati Reds (Cincinnati Tigers) 5, 10 inn	Milwaukee, WI
2018		
May 6	Kansas City Royals (Kansas City Monarchs) 4	
	Detroit Tigers (Detroit Stars) 2	Kansas City, MO
Jun. 9	Detroit Tigers (Detroit Stars) 4	
	Cleveland Indians (Cleveland Buckeyes) 2, 12 inn	Detroit, MI
Jul. 13	Pittsburgh Pirates (Pittsburgh Crawfords) 7	
	Milwaukee Brewers (Milwaukee Bears) 3	Pittsburgh, PA
Aug. 3	Milwaukee Brewers (Milwaukee Bears) 5	
	Colorado Rockies 3	Milwaukee, WI
2019		
Jun. 1	Milwaukee Brewers (Milwaukee Bears) 12	
	Pittsburgh Pirates (Pittsburgh Crawfords) 10, 13 inn	Pittsburgh, PA
Jun. 7	Milwaukee Brewers (Milwaukee Bears) 10	
	Pittsburgh Pirates (Pittsburgh Crawfords) 4	Milwaukee, WI
Jun. 23	Kansas City Royals (Kansas City Monarchs) 6	
	Minnesota Twins (St. Paul Gophers) 1	Kansas City, MO
Aug. 10	Kansas City Royals (Kansas City Monarchs) 7	
	Detroit Tigers (Detroit Stars) 0	Detroit, MI

Bibliography

Newspapers

Adrian Telegram (Michigan)
Akron Beacon Journal (Ohio)
Albany Evening Journal (New York)
Albany Evening Times (New York)
Albany Morning Express (New York)
Albany Times (New York)
Algona Advance (Iowa)
Altoona Evening Mirror (Pennsylvania)
Altoona Mirror (Pennsylvania)
Annapolis Capital (Maryland)
Asbury Park Press (New Jersey)
Atchison Daily Globe (Kansas)
Atlanta Constitution (Georgia)
Atlanta Daily World (Georgia)
Atlantic City Press (New Jersey)
Augusta Chronicle (Georgia)
Babylon South Side Signal (New York)
Bakersfield Californian (California)
Baltimore Afro American (Maryland)
Baltimore American (Maryland)
Baltimore American and Commercial Advertiser (Maryland)
Baltimore Bee (Maryland)
Baltimore Sun (Maryland)
Batavia Daily Herald (New York)
Beaufort and Port Royal Tribune and Commercial (South Carolina)
Beckley Raleigh Register (West Virginia)
Berkeley Daily Gazette (California)
Bertha Herald (Minnesota)
Bisbee Daily Review (Arizona)
Bloomington Pantagraph (Illinois)
Boston Globe (Massachusetts)
Boston Herald (Massachusetts)
Boston Post (Massachusetts)
Boyden Reporter (Iowa)
Bridgeton News (New Jersey)
Brisbane Figaro and Punch (Queensland, Australia)
Bristol Herald (Connecticut)
Brooklyn Eagle (New York)
Brooklyn Long Island Star (New York)
Brooklyn Standard Union (New York)
Brooklyn Union (New York)
Brunswick Advertiser (Georgia)
Buffalo American (New York)
Buffalo Courier (New York)
Buffalo Courier Express (New York)
Buffalo Express (New York)
Buffalo News (New York)
California Eagle (Los Angeles)
Canton Repository (Ohio)
Cedar Rapids Gazette (Iowa)
Charleston News and Courier (South Carolina)
Charleston Observer (South Carolina)
Charleroi Mail (Pennsylvania)
Chatham Press (New Jersey)
Chester Times (Pennsylvania)
Chicago Defender (Illinois)
Chicago Examiner (Illinois)
Chicago Inter Ocean (Illinois)
Chicago Sunday Times (Illinois)
Chicago Tribune (Illinois)
Chicago Whip (Illinois)
Cincinnati Commercial Tribune (Ohio)
Cincinnati Enquirer (Ohio)
Cincinnati Post (Ohio)
City Item (Allentown, Pennsylvania)
Cleveland Gazette (Ohio)
Cleveland Plain Dealer (Ohio)
Columbus Dispatch (Ohio)
Concordia Blade (Kansas)
Council Bluffs Daily Nonpareil (Iowa)
Council Bluffs News (Iowa)
Cumberland Evening Times (Maryland)
Daily Courier (Connellsville, Pennsylvania)
Daily Oklahoman (Oklahoma City)
Davenport Democrat (Iowa)
Davenport Democrat and Leader (Iowa)
Dayton Herald (Ohio)
Dayton News (Ohio)
Daytona Gazette News (Florida)
Decatur Daily Review (Illinois)
Des Moines Register (Iowa)
Detroit Free Press (Michigan)
El Paso Herald (Texas)
El Paso Times (Texas)
Elgin Morning Frank (Illinois)
Elizabeth City Star (North Carolina)
Elmira Star Gazette (New York)
Fergus Falls Journal Daily (Minnesota)
Franklin News Herald (Pennsylvania)
Geneva Courier (New York)
Geneva Gazette (New York)
Gloversville Intelligencer (New York)
Greeley Tribune (Colorado)
Green Bay Gazette (Wisconsin)

293

Greene Recorder (Iowa)
Greenwood Index Journal (South Carolina)
Harrisburg Independent (Pennsylvania)
Harrisburg Patriot (Pennsylvania)
Harrisburg State Journal (Pennsylvania)
Harrisburg Telegraph (Pennsylvania)
Hartford Courant (Connecticut)
Hazelton Sentinel (Pennsylvania)
Higbee Weekly News (Missouri)
Honolulu Advertiser (Hawaii)
Honolulu Star Bulletin (Hawaii)
Hudson Daily Star (New York)
Hudson Evening Gazette (New York)
Huntington Long Islander (New York)
Illinois State Journal (Springfield, Illinois)
Indiana Gazette (Pennsylvania)
Indianapolis Freeman (Indiana)
Indianapolis News (Indiana)
Indianapolis Star (Indiana)
Jacksonville Florida Times Union (Florida)
Jamaica Farmer and Advertiser (New York)
Jamestown Journal (New York)
Janesville Gazette (Wisconsin)
Jersey Journal (Jersey City, New Jersey)
Johnston Fulton County Republican (New York)
Joplin Globe (Missouri)
Joplin News Herald (Missouri)
Kansas City Call (Missouri)
Kansas City Journal (Missouri)
Kansas City Plain Dealer (Kansas)
Kansas City Star (Missouri)
Kansas City Sun (Missouri)
Kansas City Times (Missouri)
Kingston Daily Freeman (New York)
Kokomo Tribune (Indiana)
La Crosse Chronicle (Wisconsin)
Lake Wilson Pilot (Minnesota)
Leeds News (North Dakota)
Lockport Daily Journal (New York)
Long Beach Independent (California)
Long Island Star (New York)
Long Prairie Leader (Minnesota)
Los Angeles Herald (California)
Los Angeles Sentinel (California)
Los Angeles Times (California)
Louisville Daily Courier (Kentucky)
Lowell Daily Citizen and News (Massachusetts)
Macon Telegraph (Georgia)
Manhattan Chronicle (Kansas)
Manhattan Mercury and Nationalist (Kansas)
Marysville Tribune (Ohio)
Massillon Independent (Ohio)
Miami Daily News Record (Oklahoma)
Middleton Constitution (Connecticut)
Minneapolis Tribune (Minnesota)
Mount Carmel Daily News (Pennsylvania)
Mount Carmel Item (Pennsylvania)
Nashville Daily Patriot (Tennessee)
National Police Gazette (New York)
National Republican (Washington, D.C.)
New Haven Register (Connecticut)
New London Democrat (Connecticut)
New London Morning News (Connecticut)
New Orleans Daily Picayune (Louisiana)

New Orleans Times Democrat (Louisiana)
New Orleans Times Picayune (Louisiana)
New Philadelphia Times (Ohio)
New Ulm Review (Minnesota)
New York Age (New York)
New York Amsterdam News (New York)
New York Clipper (New York)
New York Daily Graphic (New York)
New York Daily News (New York)
New York Evening Telegram (New York)
New York Freeman (New York)
New York Globe (New York)
New York Herald (New York)
New York Herald Tribune (New York)
New York Post (New York)
New York Press (New York)
New York Sabbath Recorder (New York)
New York Sun (New York)
New York Times (New York)
New York Tribune (New York)
New York Weekly Anglo-African (New York)
New York World (New York)
Newark Evening News (New Jersey)
Newark Sentinel of Freedom (New Jersey)
New Haven Columbian Register (Connecticut)
Niagara Falls Daily Gazette (New York)
Niagara Falls Gazette (New York)
North Adams County Transcript (Massachusetts)
Norwich Aurora (Connecticut)
Norwich Courier (Connecticut)
Oakland Tribune (California)
Omaha World Herald (Nebraska)
Oregonian (Portland, Oregon)
Palatka Daily News (Florida)
Palm Beach Life (Florida)
Paterson Call (New Jersey)
People's Voice (New York)
Philadelphia Inquirer (Pennsylvania)
Philadelphia Item (Pennsylvania)
Philadelphia North American (Pennsylvania)
Philadelphia Public Ledger (Pennsylvania)
Philadelphia Record (Pennsylvania)
Philadelphia Times (Pennsylvania)
Philadelphia Tribune (Pennsylvania)
Pittsburgh Commercial Gazette (Pennsylvania)
Pittsburgh Courier (Pennsylvania)
Pittsburgh Daily Post (Pennsylvania)
Pittsburgh Dispatch (Pennsylvania)
Pittsburgh Post-Gazette (Pennsylvania)
Pittsburgh Press (Pennsylvania)
Postville Review (Iowa)
Providence Evening Press (Rhode Island)
Providence Press (Rhode Island)
Providence Morning Star (Rhode Island)
Providence Sunday Telegram (Rhode Island)
Reading Eagle (Pennsylvania)
Reading Times (Pennsylvania)
Richfield Springs Mercury (New York)
Riverside Independent Enterprise (California)
Rochester Democrat and Chronicle (New York)
St. Joseph Gazette (Missouri)
St. Joseph New Press (Missouri)
St. Louis Argus (Missouri)
St. Louis Globe Democrat (Missouri)

St. Louis Post Dispatch (Missouri)
St. Paul Appeal (Minnesota)
St. Paul Pioneer Press (Minnesota)
Sacramento Bee (California)
San Antonio Express (Texas)
San Bernardino News (California)
San Bernardino Sun (California)
San Diego Tribune (California)
San Diego Union (California)
San Francisco Call (California)
San Francisco Chronicle (California)
San Francisco Daily Alta (California)
San Jose Mercury News (California)
San Pedro News (California)
San Pedro Pilot (California)
Santa Ana Register (California)
Santa Barbara Morning Press (California)
Santa Cruz News (California)
Saratoga Springs Daily Saratogian (New York)
Saratoga Springs Morning Express (New York)
Savannah Daily Advertiser (Georgia)
Savannah Morning News (Georgia)
Savannah News (Georgia)
Savannah Tribune (Georgia)
Schenectady Gazette (New York)
Scranton Republican (Pennsylvania)
Scranton Truth (Pennsylvania)
Seattle Post-Intelligencer (Washington)
Seattle Times (Washington)
Sioux Falls Argus Leader (South Dakota)
Sporting Life (Philadelphia, Pennsylvania)
Sporting News (St. Louis, Missouri)
Springfield Republican (Massachusetts)
Springs Valley Herald (French Lick, Indiana)
Sydney Morning Herald (New South Wales, Australia)
Syracuse Standard (New York)
Titusville Herald (Pennsylvania)
Topeka Daily Capital (Kansas)
Trenton Times (New Jersey)
Trenton True American (New Jersey)
Troy Budget (New York)
Troy Daily Times (New York)
Troy Daily Whig (New York)
Troy Press (New York)
Uniontown Herald (Pennsylvania)
USA Today (McLean, Virginia)
Utica Daily Observer (New York)
Utica Daily Press (New York)
Utica Morning Herald (New York)
Utica Weekly Herald (New York)
Verndale Sun (Minnesota)
Wall Street Journal (New York)
Warren Tribune (Ohio)
Washington Bee (District of Columbia)
Washington Critic (District of Columbia)
Washington People's Advocate (District of Columbia)
Washington Post (District of Columbia)
Washington Star (District of Columbia)
Washington Sunday Herald (District of Columbia)
Watertown Daily Times (New York)
Wells Forum Advocate (Minnesota)
Wichita Eagle (Kansas)
Wichita Negro Star (Kansas)

Williamsport Daily Gazette and Bulletin (Pennsylvania)
Wilmington Journal (Delaware)
Wilmington Journal (Ohio)
Wilmington News (Delaware)
Wilmington News Journal (Delaware)
Winona Republican (Minnesota)
York Gazette and Daily (Pennsylvania)
Youngstown Vindicator (Ohio)
Zanesville Times Recorder (Ohio)

Books, Journals, Periodicals

Abbott, Lynn. "Play That Barber Shop: A Case for the African-American Origin of Barbershop Harmony." *American Music* 10, no. 3 (August 1992): 290.

Adelson, Bruce. *Brushing Back Jim Crow: The Integration of Minor League Baseball in the South.* Charlottesville: University Press of Virginia, 1999.

Armour, Mark. "The Effects of Integration, 1947–1986." *Baseball Research Journal* 36 (2007): 53–57.

Armour, Mark L., and Daniel R. Levitt. *In Pursuit of Pennants: Baseball Operations from Deadball to Moneyball.* Lincoln: University of Nebraska Press, 2015.

Armstead, Myra Beth Young. *Lord, Please Don't Take Me in August: African Americans in Newport and Saratoga Springs, 1870–1930.* Urbana: University of Illinois Press, 1999.

Barthel, Thomas. *Baseball Barnstorming and Exhibition Games.* Jefferson, NC: McFarland, 2007.

Bayor, Ronald H. *Race and the Shaping of Twentieth-Century Atlanta.* Chapel Hill: The University of North Carolina Press, 2000.

Bewley, Truman F. "A Depressed Labor Market as Explained by Participants." *American Economic Review Papers and Proceedings* 85, no. 2 (May 1995): 250–54.

Bjarkman, Peter C. *A History of Cuban Baseball 1864–2006.* Jefferson, NC: McFarland, 2007.

Bradbury, J. C. "What is Right with Scully Estimates of a Player's Marginal Revenue Product." *Journal of Sports Economics* 14, no. 1 (2013): 87–96.

Briley, Ron, ed. *The Politics of Baseball: Essays on the Pastime and Power at Home and Abroad.* Jefferson, NC: McFarland, 2010.

Bristol, Douglas Walter, Jr. *Knights of the Razor: Black Barbers in Slavery and Freedom.* Baltimore, MD: Johns Hopkins University Press, 2009.

Browne, Paul. *The Coal Barons Played Cuban Giants: A History of Early Professional Baseball in Pennsylvania, 1886–1896.* Jefferson, NC: McFarland, 2013.

Bruce, Janet. *The Kansas City Monarchs: Champions of Black Baseball.* Lawrence: University Press of Kansas, 1985.

Brunson III, James E. "Black Aesthetic Style; or Baseball Minstrelsy Reconsidered." *Black Ball* 8 (2015): 96–116.

_____. "William Albert 'Abe' Jones: Colored Baseballist and Old Chicago Settler, 1857–1931." *Black Ball* 5, no. 1 (Spring 2012): 52–75.

Bryant, Howard. *Juicing the Game: Drugs, Powers,*

and the Fight for the Soul of Major League Baseball. New York: Viking Penguin, 2005.

Buchanan, Thomas C. *Black Life on the Mississippi: Slaves, Free Blacks, and the Western Steamboat World.* Chapel Hill: University of North Carolina Press, 2004.

Burgos, Adrian, Jr. *Cuban Star: How One Negro League Owner Changed the Face of Baseball.* New York: Hill and Wang, 2011.

Burton, Donna, ed. *Historical Statistics of the United States: Colonial times to 1970 Bicentennial Edition* (2 volumes), United States Department of Commerce, Bureau of the Census: White Plains, NY: Kraus International Publications, 1989.

Butterworth, Michael. *Baseball and Rhetorics of Purity: The National Pastime and American Identity During the War on Terror.* Tuscaloosa: University of Alabama Press, 2010.

Carroll, Brian. "A Tribute to Wendell Smith." *Black Ball* 2, no. 1 (Spring 2009): 4–11.

Chadwick, Henry, ed. *Spalding's Base Ball Guide and Official League Book for 1890.* 1890. Reprint, St. Louis, MO: Horton Publishing, 1989.

Clark, Dick, and Larry Lester, eds. *The Negro Leagues Book.* Cleveland, OH: Society for American Baseball Research, 1994.

Cottrell, Robert Charles. *The Best Pitcher in Baseball: The Life of Rube Foster, Negro League Giant.* New York: New York University Press, 2001.

_____. *Blackball, the Black Sox and the Babe: Baseball's Crucial 1920 Season.* Jefferson, NC: McFarland, 2002.

Cuney-Hare, Maud. *Negro Musicians and Their Music.* Washington, D.C.: The Associated Publishers, 1936.

Darnell, Tim. *The Crackers: Early Days of Atlanta Baseball.* Athens, GA: Hill Street Press, 2003.

Davis, Frank Marshall. "Negro America's First Daily." *Negro Digest* 5 (1946) .

Debono, Paul. *The Chicago American Giants.* Jefferson, NC: McFarland, 2007.

_____. *The Indianapolis ABC's.* Jefferson, NC: McFarland, 1997.

Dickson, Paul. *The Dickson Baseball Dictionary.* New York: W. W. Norton, 2009.

DiFiore, Anthony. "Advancing African American Baseball: The Philadelphia Pythians and Interracial Competition in 1869." *Black Ball* 1, no. 1 (2008): 57–65.

Dixon, Phil. *American Baseball Chronicles: Great Teams: The 1905 Philadelphia Giants Volume Three.* Charleston, SC: Booksurge, 2006.

_____. *American Baseball Chronicles: Great Teams: The 1931 Homestead Grays Volume One.* Bloomington, IN: Xlibris, 2009.

_____. *Andrew "Rube" Foster: A Harvest on Freedom's Fields.* La Vergne, TN: Xlibris, 2010.

_____. *The Monarchs 1920–1938, featuring Wilbur "Bullet" Rogan.* Sioux Falls, SD: Mariah Press, 2002.

Dixon, Phil, with Patrick J. Hannigan. *The Negro Baseball Leagues: A Photographic History.* Mattituck, NY: Amereon House, 1992.

Donovan, Richard. "Satch Beards the House of David (Continuing the Fabulous Satchel Paige)" *Collier's Weekly,* June 6, 1953: 20–25.

Evert, Marilyn. *Discovering Pittsburgh's Sculpture.* Pittsburgh, PA: University of Pittsburgh Press, 1983.

Falkner, David. *Great Time Coming: The Life of Jackie Robinson From Baseball to Birmingham.* New York: Simon & Schuster, 1995.

Figueredo, Jose. *Cuban Baseball: A Statistical History, 1897–1961.* Jefferson, NC: McFarland, 2003.

Finkelman, Paul, ed. *Encyclopedia of African American History, 1896 to the Present: From the Age of Segregation to the Twenty-first Century.* London: Oxford University Press, 2009.

Gardner, Robert, and Dennis Shortelle. *The Forgotten Players: The Story of Black Baseball in America.* New York: Walker, 1993.

Gay, Timothy M. *Satch, Dizzy & Rapid Robert: The Wild Saga of Interracial Baseball Before Jackie Robinson.* New York: Simon & Schuster, 2010.

Goldman, Steven. *It Ain't Over 'Til It's Over: The Baseball Prospectus Pennant Race Book.* New York: Basic Books, 2007.

Goodman, Michael E. *The Story of the Atlanta Braves.* Mankato, MN: Creative Education, 2008.

Graham, Thomas. *Mr. Flagler's St. Augustine.* Gainesville: University of Florida. 2014.

Grantham, George, and Mary MacKinnon, eds. *Labour Market Evolution.* London: Routledge, 1994.

Hageman, William. *Honus: The Life and Times of a Baseball Hero.* Champagne, IL: Sagamore, 1996.

Haupert, Michael, and Kenneth Winter. "The Old Fellows and the Colonels: Innovation and Survival in Integrated Baseball." *Black Ball* 1, no. 1 (Spring 2008): 79–92.

Haupert, Michael J. "Pay, Performance, and Race During the Integration Era." *Black Ball* 2, no. 1 (Spring 2009): 37–51.

_____. "Player Pay and Productivity in the Reserve Clause and Collusion Eras." *NINE: A Journal of Baseball History and Culture* 18, no. 1 (Fall 2009): 63–85.

Haupert, Michael J., and James Murray. "Regime Switching and Wages in Major League Baseball Under the Reserve Clause." *Cliometrica* 6, no. 2 (June 2012): 143–162.

Heaphy, Leslie A. "The Atlanta Black Crackers." *The National Pastime: Baseball in the Peach State* 30 (2010): 30–36.

_____. *The Negro Leagues, 1869–1960.* Jefferson, NC: McFarland, 2003.

Herodotus, *The History,* David Grene, translator. Chicago: University of Chicago Press, 1987.

Hinshaw, John V. "Third Stonington: The Afro-American Baptist Church on Water Street." *Historical Footnotes* Volume 29, Number 2 (May 1992): 1–10.

Hoaglin, David C., and Paul F. Velleman. "A Critical Look at Some Analyses of Major League Baseball Salaries." *The American Statistician* 49, no. 3 (August 1995): 277–85.

Hogan, Lawrence D., and Jules Tygiel. *Shades of Glory: The Negro League and the Story of African American Baseball.* Washington, D.C.: National Geographic Society, 2006.

Holway, John. *Black Diamonds: Life in the Negro*

Leagues from the Men Who Lived It. New York: Stadium Books, 1991.

_____. *Black Giants.* Springfield, VA: Lord Fairfax Press: 2010.

_____. *Blackball Stars: Negro League Pioneers.* Westport, CT: Meckler, 1988.

_____. *Voices from the Great Black Baseball Leagues.* New York: Dodd, Mead, 1975. Revised edition, New York: Da Capo Press, 1992.

Holway, John, with Lloyd Johnson and Rachel Borst, eds. *The Complete Book of Baseball's Negro Leagues: The Other Half of Baseball History.* Fern Park, FL: Hastings House, 2001.

Honig, Donald. *Baseball When the Grass Was Real.* New York, New York: Coward, McCann, and Geoghegan, 1975.

Hope, Bob. *We Could've Finished Last Without You: An Irreverent Look at The Atlanta Braves, the Losingest Team in Baseball for the Past 25 Years.* Atlanta: Longstreet Press, 1991.

Ioannides, Yannis M., and Christopher A. Pissarides. "Monopsony and the Lifetime Relation between Wages and Productivity." *Journal of Labor Economics* 3, no. 1 (January 1985): 91–100.

Iorizzo, Luciano J., and Ernest E. Rossi, eds. *Italian Americans: Bridges to Italy, Bonds to America.* Youngstown, NY: Teneo Press, 2010.

James, Bill. *The Bill James Historical Baseball Abstract.* New York: Villard, 1986.

Jeter, Henry N. *Pastor Henry N. Jeter's Twenty-five Years Experience with the Shiloh Baptist Church: And Her History. Corner School and Mary Streets, Newport, R. I.* Newport, RI: Remington Printing Company, 1901.

Johnson, Lloyd, and Miles Wolff, eds. *Encyclopedia of Minor League Baseball,* 3d ed. Durham, NC: Baseball America, 2007.

Jones, Charles Kelley. *Francis Johnson (1792–1844): Chronicle of a Black Musician in Early Nineteenth-century Philadelphia.* Bethlehem, PA: Lehigh University Press, 2006.

Joyce, Allen Edward. "The Atlanta Black Crackers." MA thesis, Emory University, 1975.

Kammen, Michael. *Mystic Chords of Memory.* New York: Vintage Books, 1991.

Keating, Larry. *Atlanta: Race, Class, and Urban Expansion.* Philadelphia: Temple University Press, 2001.

Kelley, Brent. *Voices from the Negro Leagues: Conversations with 52 Baseball Standouts.* Jefferson, NC: McFarland, 1998.

Kelly, Robin D. G. *Race Rebels: Culture, Politics and the Black Working Class.* New York: The Free Press, 1994.

Kleinknecht, Merl F. "Blacks in 19th Century Organized Baseball." *Baseball Research Journal* 6 (1977)

Klosterman, Chuck. "The Case For Throwback Baseball Uniforms." *New York Times Magazine,* January 9, 2015.

Krautmann, Anthony. "What's Wrong with Scully-Estimates of a Players Marginal Revenue Product?" *Economic Inquiry* 37, no. 2 (April 1999): 369–381.

Krautmann, Anthony, Elizabeth Gustafson, and Lawrence Hadley. "A Note on the Structural Stability of Salary Equations: Major League Baseball Pitchers." *Journal of Sports Economics* 4, no. 1 (February 2003): 56–63.

Kuhn, Clifford M., Harlon E. Joye, and Bernard E. West. *Living Atlanta: An Oral History of the City, 1914–1948.* Athens: University of Georgia Press, 1990.

Lanctot, Neil. *Fair Dealing and Clean Playing: The Hilldale Club and the Development of Black Professional Baseball, 1910–1932.* Syracuse, NY: Syracuse University Press, 2007.

_____. *Negro League Baseball: The Rise and Ruin of a Black Institution.* Philadelphia: University of Pennsylvania Press, 2004.

Lane, F. C. "The Colored Clubs." *Baseball Magazine* (December 1918): 117.

Leland, Frank. *Frank Leland's Baseball Club.* Chicago: Fraternal Printing, 1910.

Leslie, Mrs. Frank, and Ellery Sedgwick, eds. *Frank Leslie's Popular Monthly* (New York: Frank Leslie Publishing House, vol. 3, January-June 1877.

Lester, Larry. *Rube Foster in His Time: On the Field and in the Papers with Black Baseball's Greatest Visionary.* Jefferson, NC: McFarland, 2012.

Lester, Larry, and Sammy J. Miller. *Black Baseball In Kansas City.* Charleston, NC: Arcadia, 2000.

Lewis, Ira F. "National Baseball League Formed." *The Competitor* 1 (March 1920): 66.

Lieb, Fred. *Baseball As I Have Known It.* New York: Coward, McCann & Geohegan, 1977.

Lomax, Michael E. *Black Baseball Entrepreneurs 1902–1931: The Negro National and Eastern Colored Leagues.* Syracuse, NY: Syracuse University Press, 2014.

_____. *Black Baseball Entrepreneurs, 1860–1901: Operating by Any Means Necessary.* Syracuse, NY: Syracuse University Press, 2003.

Lowenfish, Lee. *Branch Rickey: Baseball's Ferocious Gentleman.* Lincoln: University of Nebraska Press, 2007.

_____. "The Rise of Baseball's Quota System in the 1950s." *NINE: A Journal of Baseball History and Culture* 16, no. 2 (Spring 2008): 52–61.

_____. "When All Heaven Rejoiced: Branch Rickey and the Origins of the Breaking of the Color Line." *NINE: A Journal of Baseball History and Culture* 11, no. 1 (Fall 2002): 1–15.

Lowry, Philip J. *Green Cathedrals: The Ultimate Celebration of Major League and Negro League Ballparks.* New York: Walker, 2006.

Malone, Jacqui. *Steppin' on The Blues.* Urbana: University of Illinois Press, 1996.

McDonough, James Lee. *William Tecumseh Sherman; In the Service of My Country.* New York: W. W. Norton, 2016.

McFeely, William S. *Frederick Douglass.* New York: W. W. Norton, 1995.

McNeil, William F. *Baseball's Other All-Stars.* Jefferson, NC: McFarland, 2000.

_____. *Black Baseball Out of Season.* Jefferson, NC: McFarland, 2007.

_____. *The California Winter League: America's First Integrated Professional Baseball League.* Jefferson, NC: McFarland, 2002.

Moffi, Larry and Jonathan Kronstadt. *Crossing the Line: Black Major Leaguers, 1947–1959*. Jefferson, NC: McFarland, 1994.

Morris, Aldon. *The Origins of the Civil Rights Movement: Black Communities Organizing for Change*. New York: Free Press, 1984.

Moses, Wilson Jeremiah. "Lost World of the New Negro, 1895–1919: Black Literary and Intellectual Life Before the Renaissance." *Black American Literature Forum* 21, no. ½ (Spring-Summer. 1987): 61–84.

National Association for the Advancement of Colored People, *Thirty Years of Lynching in the United States, 1889–1918*. New York: National Association for the Advancement of Colored People, 1919. Reprint, Clark, New Jersey: The Lawbook Exchange, 2012.

Neft, David S., ed. *The Baseball Encyclopedia*. New York: Macmillan, 1969.

Neft, David S., Richard M. Cohen, and Michael L. Neft, *The Sports Encyclopedia: Baseball 2000*. New York: St. Martin's Griffin, 2000.

Nieto, Sevro. *Early U.S. Blackball Teams in Cuba*. Jefferson, NC: McFarland, 2008.

Osborne, Elizabeth, and Christine Woodruff, eds. *Working in the Wings: New Perspectives on Theatre History and Labor*. Carbondale: Southern Illinois University Press, 2015.

Overmyer, James. *Black Ball and the Boardwalk: The Bacharach Giants of Atlantic City, 1916–1929*. Jefferson, NC: McFarland, 2014.

Paige, Leroy "Satchel." with David Lipman, *Maybe I'll Pitch Forever*. Garden City, NY: Doubleday, 1962.

Peterson, Robert. *Only the Ball Was White: A History of Legendary Black Players and All-Black Professional Teams*. Reprint, New York: Oxford University Press, 1992.

Phelps, Howard A. "Andrew 'Rube' Foster." *The Half-Century Magazine* (March 1, 1919): 8.

"Pleasure and Travel Resorts." *Outing* 9, no. 5 (February): 500.

Plott, Bill. *The Negro Southern League: A Baseball History, 1920–1951*. Jefferson, NC: McFarland, 2015.

_____. "The Southern League of Colored Base Ballists." *Baseball Research Journal* 3 (1974)

Pollock, Alan J. *Barnstorming to Heaven: Syd Pollock and His Great Black Teams*. Edited by James A. Riley. Tuscaloosa: University of Alabama Press, 2006.

Pratkanis, Anthony R., and Marlene E. Turner. "Nine Principles of Successful Affirmative Action: Mr. Branch Rickey, Mr. Jackie Robinson, and the Integration of Baseball." *NINE: A Journal of Baseball History and Culture* 3, no. 1 (Fall 1994): 36–65.

Rader, Benjamin G. *American Sports: From the Age of Folk Games to the Age of Televised Sports*, 6th ed. Upper Saddle River, NJ: Prentice Hall, 2009.

Rampersad, Arnold. *Jackie Robinson: A Biography*. New York: Alfred A. Knopf, 1997.

Reach's Official American Association Base Ball Guide 1891. 1891. Reprint, St. Louis, MO: Horton, 1989.

Reichler, Joseph L., ed. *The Baseball Encyclopedia*. New York: Macmillan, 1979.

Reisler, Jim. *Black Writers/Black Baseball: An Anthology of Articles from Black Sportswriters Who Covered the Negro Leagues*. Jefferson, NC: McFarland, 1994.

Ribowsky, Mark. *A Complete History of the Negro Leagues 1884–1955*. New York: Carol Publishing, 1995.

_____. *Don't Look Back: Satchel Paige in the Shadows of Baseball*. New York: Simon & Schuster, 1994.

Riley, James A. *The Biographical Encyclopedia of the Negro Baseball Leagues*. New York: Carroll & Graf, 2002.

Rogosin, Donn. *Invisible Men: Life in Baseball's Negro Leagues*. New York: Atheneum, 1983.

Rooney, Art, Jr., and Roy McHugh. *Ruanaidh: The Story of Art Rooney and His Clan*. Pittsburgh: Geyer Printing Company, 2008.

Rosenblum, Thom. "Unlocking the Schoolhouse Doors: Elisha Scott, 'Colored Lawyer, Topeka.'" *Kansas History* 36 (2013): 41.

Rowell, George Presbury, ed. *Rowell's American Newspaper Directory*. New York: George P. Rowell, 1883.

Ruck, Rob. *Raceball: How the Major Leagues Colonized the Black and Latin Game*. Boston: Beacon, 2011.

_____. *Sandlot Seasons*. Urbana: University of Illinois Press, 1993.

Sampson, Henry T. *Blacks in Blackface: A Sourcebook on Early Black Musical Shows*. Lanham, MD: Scarecrow, 2014.

Sandoval-Strausz, A. K. *Hotel: An American History*. New Haven, CT: Yale University Press, 2007.

Schein, Edgar H. "The Role of the Founder in Creating Organizational Culture." *Organizational Dynamics* (Summer 1983): 13–28.

Schmidt, Martin B., and David J. Berri. "Research Note: What Takes Them Out to the Ball Game?" *Journal of Sports Economics* 7, no. 2 (May 2006): 222–233.

Schofield, John A. "Performance and Attendance at Professional Team Sports." *Journal of Sport Behavior* 6, no. 4 (1983): 196–206.

Scully, Gerald W. "Pay and Performance in Major League Baseball." *The American Economic Review* 64, no. 6 (December 1974): 915–930.

Simkus, Scott. *Outsider Baseball*. Chicago: Chicago Review Press, 2014.

Simons, William M., and Alvin L. Hall, eds. *The Cooperstown Symposium on Baseball and American Culture 2000*. Jefferson, NC: McFarland, 2001.

Smith, Christopher J. *The Creolization of American Culture: William Sidney Mount and the Roots of Blackface Minstrelsy*. Champaign: University of Illinois Press. 2013.

Snelling, Dennis. *The Pacific Coast League: A Statistical History, 1903–1957*. Jefferson, NC: McFarland, 1995.

Sommers, Paul M., ed. *Diamonds Are Forever: The Business of Baseball*. Washington, D.C.: Brookings Institute Press, 1992.

Sommers, Paul M., and Noel Quinton. "Pay and Performance in Major League Baseball: The Case of the First Family of Free Agents." *The Journal of Human Resources* 17, no. 3 (Summer 1982): 426–436.

Spivey, Donald. *"If You Were Only White": The Life*

of Leroy "Satchel" Paige. Columbia: University of Missouri Press, 2012.

Sundstrom, William. "The Color Line: Racial Norms and Discrimination in Urban Labor Markets, 1910–1950." *The Journal of Economic History* 54, no. 2 (1994): 382–396.

Swanton, Barry. *The ManDak League: Haven for Former Negro League Ballplayers, 1950- 1957*. Jefferson, NC: McFarland, 2006.

Thorn, John, and Pete Palmer. *The Hidden Game of Baseball: A Revolutionary Approach to Baseball and its Statistics*. Garden City, NY: Doubleday, 1985.

Thorn, John, and Pete Palmer, with David Reuther, eds. *Total Baseball*. New York: Warner Books, 1989.

Thorndike, E. L. *Thorndike Barnhart Advanced Dictionary*. Glenview, IL: Scott Foresman, 1974.

Todd, Jewell R., Michael McPherson, and David J. Molina. "Testing the Determinants of Income Distribution in Major League Baseball." *Economic Inquiry* 42, no. 3 (July 2004): 469–482.

Trembanis, Sarah L. *The Set-Up Men: Race, Culture and Resistance in Black Baseball* Jefferson, NC: McFarland, 2014.

Tye, Larry. *Satchel: The Life and Times of an American Legend*. New York: Random House, 2009.

Tygiel, Jules. *Baseball's Great Experiment: Jackie Robinson and His Legacy*. New York: Vintage Press, 1983.

Veeck, Bill, and Ed Linn. *Veeck—As In Wreck: The Autobiography of Bill Veeck*. Reprint, Chicago: University of Chicago Press, 2012.

Vrooman, John. "The Baseball Players Labor Market Reconsidered." *Southern Economic Journal* (October 1996): 339–360.

Ward, Geoffrey C. *Baseball: An Illustrated History*. New York: Knopf, 1994.

White, Sol. *History of Colored Base Ball, With Other Documents on the Early Black Game 1886–1936*. Compiled and introduced by Jerry Malloy. Lincoln: University of Nebraska Press, 1996.

Whitehead, Charles E. *A Man and His Diamonds*. New York: Vantage Press, 1980.

Wiggins, David K., ed. *Out of the Shadows: A Biographical History of African American Athletes*. Fayetteville: University of Arkansas Press, 2006.

Wolff, Rick, ed. *The Baseball Encyclopedia*, 8th ed. New York: Macmillan, 1990.

Wright, Marshall D. *The American Association Year-by-Year Statistics, 1902–1952*. Jefferson, NC: McFarland, 1997.

_____. *The International League Year-by-Year Statistics, 1884–1953*. Jefferson, NC: McFarland, 1998.

_____. *The National Association of Base Ball Players, 1857–1870*. Jefferson, NC: McFarland, 2000.

_____. *Nineteenth Century Baseball: Year-by-Year Statistics for the Major League Teams, 1871 through 1900*. Jefferson, NC: McFarland, 1996.

Yee, Min S., ed. *The Sports Book: An Unabashed Assemblage of Heroes, Strategies, Records, and Events*. New York: Holt, Rinehart, and Winston, 1975.

Young, Frank A. "Rube Foster—The Master Mind of Baseball." *Abbot's Monthly* (November 1, 1930): 42–49.

Young, William A. *J. L. Wilkinson and the Kansas City Monarchs*. Jefferson, NC: McFarland, 2016.

Zoss, Joel and John Bowman. *Diamonds in the Rough: The Untold Story of Baseball*. Lincoln: University of Nebraska Press, 2004.

Electronic Websites and Articles

Ancestry.com (https://www.ancestry.com/)

Baseball-Fever.com (https://www.baseball-fever.com/)

Baseball-Reference.com (https://baseball-reference.com/)

Bravehost.com (http://johndonaldson.bravehost.com/)

California Digital Newspaper Collection (https://cdnc.ucr.edu/)

Center for Negro League Baseball Research (http://www.cnlbr.org/)

ChicagoManualofStyle.org (https://www.chicagomanualofstyle.org/home.html)

Chronicling America (https://chroniclingamerica.loc.gov)

ESPN.com (https://www.espn.com/)

ExplorePAhistory.com (http://explorepahistory.com/)

FamousTrials.com (https://www.famous-trials.com)

FirstWorldWar.com (https://www.firstworldwar.com/)

GenealogyBank.com (https://www.genealogybank.com/)

Hunt Auctions, LLC (https://www.huntauctions.com/)

Library of Congress (https://www.loc.gov/)

Lincoln University of Pennsylvania's Early Records Online (https://hbcudigitallibrary.auctr.edu/digital/collection/lupa)

MeasuringWorth.com (https://www.measuringworth.com/)

Mid-Continent Public Library (https://www.mymcpl.org/)

National Baseball Hall of Fame (https://baseballhall.org)

NegroLeagueBaseballMuseum.com (https://nlbm.com/)

NegroSouthernLeagueMuseumResearchCenter.org (http://negrosouthernleaguemuseumresearchcenter.org/)

NewspaperArchive.com (https://newspaperarchive.com/)

Newspapers.com (https://www.newspapers.com/)

Old Fulton Postcards (www.fultonhistory.com/Fulton.html)

PercentageCalculator.net (https://percentagecalculator.net/)

Royal Heritage (http://kcbbh.blogspot.com/)

Seamheads.com Negro Leagues Database (http://www.seamheads.com/NegroLgs/)

The Sporting Statues Project (http://offbeat.group.shef.ac.uk/statues/)

StatsCrew.com (https://www.statscrew.com/)

Stonington History Society (https://www.stoningtonhistory.org/)

Thesaurus.com (https://www.thesaurus.com/)

Wikipedia.org (https://www.wikipedia.org/)

Armour, Mark and Daniel R Levitt. "Baseball Demographics, 1947–2012." SABR.org, 2015.

Ashwill, Gary. "Rube vs. Rube." Agate Type (agate-type.typepad.com), 2012.

Bench5. "Negro Leagues vs Major Leagues." Baseball-Fever.com, 2006.

Boeck, Scott. "Albert Pujols Earns 3,000 Hit, Joining A-Rod, Hank Aaron, Willie Mays in Exclusive Club." USAToday.com, 2018.

Burgos, Adrian, Jr. "MLB Teams Are Making a Farce of the Selig Rule." SportingNews.com, 2015.

Cortes, Ryan. "On This Day in 1971, The Pittsburgh Pirates Fielded the First All-Black and Latino Lineup." TheUndefeated.com, 2016.

Craw, Harold. "Broadening Baseball's Audience." MILB.com, 2016.

Eric. "Negro Leaguers and Standard Deviation, Part I." The Hall of Miller and Eric, 2017.

_____. "Negro Leagues: Measuring the Quality of Competition." The Hall of Miller and Eric, 2017.

Fernández, Daniel A. "Silvio Garcia, Jackie Robinson and the Racial Barrier in Major League Baseball." OnCuba.com, 2013.

Glier, Ray. "MLB Takes Notice as Percentage of Black Players in Baseball Remains Low." Aljazeera.com, 2014.

Goff, Keli. "Have Black Americans Left Baseball?" TheRoot.com, 2013.

Hall, Justice. "MLB Honors Negro Leaguers in Draft." MLB.com, 2008.

Harris, Duane. "Satchel Vs. Josh, Charlie Hustle, The Nationals as the Grays, Big Klu, Jackie, Pee-Wee." NinetyFeetofPerfection.com, 2011.

Harris, John. "Is There No Place in Pittsburgh for Negro League All-Stars?" TheUndefeated.com, 2016.

Jackson, Dee. "Royals Honor Kansas City's Negro Leagues Heritage." kshb.com, 2016.

Justice, Richard. "Selig Rule' First of its Kind in Sports." MLB.com, 2013.

Lapchick, Richard. "The 2019 Racial and Gender Report Card: Major League Baseball." Tidesport.org, 2019.

_____. "The 2016 Racial and Gender Report Card: Major League Baseball." Tidesport.org, 2016.

Lapchick, Richard, with Craig Malveaux, Erin Davison, and Caryn Grant. "The 2016 Racial and Gender Report Card: National Football League." Tidesport.org, 2016.

Lapchick, Richard, with Theren Bullock, Jr. "The 2016 Racial and Gender Report Card: National Basketball Association." Tidesport.org, 2016.

Martin, Adrien. "Pensions Paid to Former Negro League Players not Discriminatory." Plainsponsor.com, 2004.

Moore, Jack. "How MLB Stays White." Vice Sports (sports.vice.com), 2015.

Neyer, Rob. "Was the Federal League Really a Major League?" TheNationalPastimeMuseum.com, 2012.

Nightengale, Bob. "Adam Jones on MLB's lack of Kaepernick protest: 'Baseball is a white man's Sport,'" USAToday.com, 2016.

Simkus, Scott. "Piper in Chicago." Outsider Baseball Bulletin, vol. 2, issue 23 (Number 53) (June 8, 2011): 1–6. Outsiderbaseball.com.

_____. "Superstar Integration Model." Outsider Baseball Bulletin, vol. 2, issue 27 (Number 57): 1–4. Outsiderbaseball.com.

Singer, Tom. "Teddy Ballgame Makes Difference for Negro Leaguers to Enter Hall." MLB.com, 2001.

Sinins, Lee, ed. Complete Baseball Encyclopedia.

Wild, Danny. "Minors, Negro Leagues Grew Together: Rickwood Field One of Several Ballparks with Storied Histories." MLB.com, 2010.

Film and Video

Baseball, The Fifth Inning: Shadow Ball 1930–1940. Produced by Ken Burns and Lynn Novick. 1994. Hollywood, California: PBS Home Video, 2004. DVD.

Jackie Robinson. Directed by Ken Burns, Sarah Burns, and David McMahon. 2016. Brighton, Massachusetts: PBS Distribution, 2016. DVD.

Interviews and Correspondence

Ashwill, Gary. E-mail message with ed, January 16, 2018.

Brunson, James E. III. E-mail correspondence with ed, June 6, 2017.

Holway, John. E-mail message with ed, September 9, 2015.

Knorr, Ted. E-mail message with ed, January 28, 2017.

Lester, Larry. E-mail messages with ed, December 21, 2017, June 25, 2018.

Nathan, Daniel A. E-mail message with ed, August 26, 2015.

Shieber, Tom. Conversation with Larry Lester and editor, San Diego, CA, June 29, 2019.

Overmyer, Jim. E-mail message with ed, September 9, 2015.

Public Records

Contract Card Files, National Baseball Library, Cooperstown, New York.

Malarcher Ashland Collection File, National Baseball Library, Cooperstown, New York.

Rube Foster Official File, National Baseball Library, Cooperstown, New York.

About the Contributors

Thomas **Aiello** is an associate professor of history and African American studies at Valdosta State University in Georgia. He is the author of several books, including *The Kings of Casino Park: Race and Baseball in the Lost Season of 1932* (2011) and *Jim Crow's Last Stand: Nonunanimous Criminal Jury Verdicts In Louisiana* (2015). He has also written several articles and essays on Negro Leagues baseball and is the book review editor for *Black Ball*.

James E. **Brunson** III has published in *NINE*, *Black Ball*, and *Base Ball*. He has presented papers at NASSH, NINE, Frederick Ivor-Campbell 19th Century Base Ball, and Jerry Malloy Negro League conferences. He has also written two books, *The Early Image of Black Baseball* (2009) and the three-volume *Black Base Ball, 1858–1900* (2018).

Robert C. **Cottrell** has authored numerous books, including *The Best Pitcher in Baseball: The Life of Rube Foster, Negro League Giant*; *Blackball, the Black Sox, and the Babe: Baseball's Crucial 1920 Season*; and *Two Pioneers: How Hank Greenberg and Jackie Robinson Transformed Baseball—and America*. He is a professor of history and American studies at California State University, Chico.

Pete **Gorton** is a documentarian from Minneapolis. He runs The Donaldson Network, dedicated to the rediscovery of John Wesley Donaldson (johndonaldson.bravehost.com). He is a recipient of the SABR Negro Leagues Committee Tweed Webb Lifetime Achievement Award, and has contributed to many publications, including *Swinging for the Fences* (2005).

Michael **Haupert** is a professor of economics at the University of Wisconsin–La Crosse, executive director of the Economic History Association, and co-chair of the SABR Business of Baseball Committee. He is an avid baseball fan and appreciates the ability to combine his hobby with his work. He has published on the economics of baseball in several books and journals, including *NINE*, *Cliometrica*, *Black Ball*, *Base Ball*, and the *Baseball Research Journal*.

Josh **Howard** is a public historian with Passel Historical Consultants based in the Blue Ridge Mountains of Virginia. His research interests include the public history of sport and games, Appalachia, and government. He earned his doctorate in public history from Middle Tennessee State University.

Tony **Kissel** is a retired teacher and sales representative who researches minor league baseball in New York State. A mention of the Cuban Giants in an 1897 box score first captured his interest in the club and began a journey covering the last two decades. He is also the author of *Young John McGraw of Truxton* (2018), a book about the Hall of Famer's teenage years.

Ted **Knorr** is a retired government official from Harrisburg, Pennsylvania. He founded the SABR Negro Leagues Research Conference in 1998 and has hosted the event four times. He was one of the first historians to propose that the Negro Leagues were, indeed, a major league, and is the leading campaigner for Herbert "Rap" Dixon's election into the National Baseball Hall of Fame.

Larry **Lester** is the chairman of SABR's Negro Leagues Committee and a former co-chair of the National Baseball Hall of Fame's Negro Leagues Researchers and Authors Group. In 2016, he received SABR's prestigious Henry Chadwick Award, and the following year he was awarded the society's highest honor, the Bob Davids Award. He is listed as a writer, editor, or contributing researcher to more than 180 publications on African American history, including *The Negro Leagues Book* (1994), and *Black Baseball's National Showcase* (2001).

Michael E. **Lomax** is a retired professor of sport history from the University of Iowa. He has published two books and one anthology, along with several articles on the history of black baseball. His second book, *Black Baseball Entrepreneurs: The Negro National and Eastern Colored Leagues* (2014) won a SABR Baseball Research Award.

Philip J. **Lowry** is a retired philosophy professor and 14-year veteran of the United States Army, where he was an Infantry Captain and Airborne Pathfinder. He is the author of *Green Cathedrals, Baseball's Longest Games, Green Gridirons*, and the forthcoming *Country vs. Country International Baseball Encyclopedia*.

Todd **Peterson** is a Kansas City–based visual artist, historian, and educator. He was awarded Yoseloff-SABR Baseball Research Grants in 2006 and 2010, and has twice received the Normal "Tweed" Webb Lifetime Achievement Award for outstanding research. He is the author of *Early Black Baseball in Minnesota* (2010) and has made several presentations and published many articles on the Negro Leagues.

Richard J. **Puerzer** is an associate professor and chairperson of the Department of Engineering at Hofstra University in Hempstead, New York. His writings on baseball have appeared in: *Bittersweet Goodbye: The Black Barons, The Grays, and the 1948 Negro League World Series* (2017) and *Moments of Joy and Heartbreak: 66 Significant Episodes in the History of the Pittsburgh Pirates* (2018), as well as the journals: *Black Ball, Nine, The National Pastime, Zisk*, and *Spitball*.

Scott **Simkus** is the author of *Outsider Baseball: The Weird World of Hardball on the Fringe* (2014) and the lead consultant on the Strat-O-Matic Company's ground-breaking Negro Leagues board and computer games in 2009. His research has been profiled in *Sports Illustrated*, the *New York Times, Chicago Tribune*, and on NPR.

Jeffery S. **Williams** is a Ph.D. candidate in history at the University of South Carolina. His dissertation will address the interactions between the national office of the NAACP and local lawyers throughout the country. He is a native of Colorado and hopes to live to see the Rockies win the World Series.